Plate C

Plate D

Fundamentals of Interactive Computer Graphics

Fundamentals of Interactive Computer Graphics

JAMES D. FOLEY
The George Washington University
ANDRIES VAN DAM
Brown University

Addison-Wesley Publishing Company
Reading, Massachusetts • Menlo Park, California
London • Amsterdam • Don Mills, Ontario • Sydney

Sponsoring Editor: William B. Gruener
Production Editor: Rima Zolina
Designer: Herb Caswell
Illustration: ANCO/Boston
Cover Design: Richard Hannus
Art coordinator: Dick Morton

This book is in the
Addison-Wesley Systems Programming Series
Consulting editors: IBM Editorial Board

Library of Congress Cataloging in Publication Data

Foley, James D 1942–
Fundamentals of interactive computer graphics.

(The Systems programming series)
Bibliography: p.
Includes index.
1. Computer graphics. 2. Interactive computer systems. I. Van Dam, Andries, 1938– joint author. II. Title.
T385.F63 001.64′43 80-24311
ISBN 0-201-14468-9

Reprinted with corrections, July 1984

ISBN: 0-201-14468-9
IJKLMNOP-HA-8987654

To Our Families and Students

THE SYSTEMS PROGRAMMING SERIES

*The Program Development Process Part I—The Individual Programmer	Joel D. Aron
The Program Development Process Part II—The Programming Team	Joel D. Aron
*Mathematical Foundations of Programming	Frank Beckman
*An Introduction to Operating Systems	Harvey M. Deitel
*Structured Programming: Theory and Practice	Richard C. Linger Harlan D. Mills Bernard I. Witt
*Coded Character Sets: History and Development	Charles E. Mackenzie
*The Structure and Design of Programming Languages	John E. Nicholls
*The Environment for Systems Programs	Frederic G. Withington
*Communications Architecture for Distributed Systems	R. J. Cypser

*An Introduction to Database Systems, Third Edition	C. J. Date
*An Introduction to Database Systems: Volume II	C. J. Date
*Database Security and Integrity	Eduardo B. Fernandez R. C. Summers C. Wood
*Fundamentals of Interactive Computer Graphics	James Foley Andries van Dam
*Compiler Design Theory	Philip M. Lewis II Daniel J. Rosenkrantz Richard E. Stearns
*Sorting and Sort Systems	Harold Lorin
*Operating Systems	Harold Lorin Harvey M. Deitel

*Recursive Programming Techniques	William Burge
*Modeling and Analysis: An Introduction to System Performance Evaluation Methodology	Hisashi Kobayashi
Conceptual Structures: Information Processing in Mind and Machines	John F. Sowa

*Published

Foreword

The field of systems programming primarily grew out of the efforts of many programmers and managers whose creative energy went into producing practical, utilitarian systems programs needed by the rapidly growing computer industry. Programming was practiced as an art where each programmer invented his own solutions to problems with little guidance beyond that provided by his immediate associates. In 1968, the late Ascher Opler, then at IBM, recognized that it was necessary to bring programming knowledge together in a form that would be accessible to all systems programmers. Surveying the state of the art, he decided that enough useful material existed to justify a significant codification effort. On his recommendation, IBM decided to sponsor The Systems Programming Series as a long term project to collect, organize, and publish those principles and techniques that would have lasting value throughout the industry.

The Series consists of an open-ended collection of text-reference books. The contents of each book represent the individual author's view of the subject area and do not necessarily reflect the views of the IBM Corporation. Each is organized for course use but is detailed enough for reference. Further, the Series is organized in three levels: broad introductory material in the foundation volumes, more specialized material in the software volumes, and very specialized theory in the computer science volumes. As such, the Series meets the needs of the novice, the experienced programmer, and the computer scientist.

Taken together, the Series is a record of the state of the art in systems programming that can form the technological base for the systems programming discipline.

The Editorial Board

Preface

Interactive computer graphics is a field whose time has come. Until recently it was an esoteric specialty involving expensive display hardware, substantial computer resources, and idiosyncratic software. In the last few years, however, it has benefited from the steady and sometimes even spectacular reduction in the hardware price/performance ratio (e.g., personal computers for home or office with their standard graphics terminals), and from the development of high-level, device-independent graphics packages which help make graphics programming rational and straightforward. Interactive graphics is now finally ready to fulfill its promise to provide us with pictorial communication and thus to become a major facilitator of man/machine interaction. Pictorial communication is a medium that is both natural and efficient to human beings and yet is sufficiently precise for computer manipulation. Most people enjoy interacting graphically more than they do the more traditional and more limited alphanumeric communication techniques. Interactive graphics can be used to understand complex phenomena, to design technological artifacts, and to amuse—it is an extremely versatile, aesthetically pleasing and instructive medium.

The purpose of this book is to provide both a tutorial and a reference source for readers interested in the many aspects of modern interactive graphics: hardware, software, data structures, mathematical manipulation of graphical objects, the user interface, and the fundamental implementation algorithms. No prior background in graphics is needed, although a basic background in programming and data structures and some familiarity with computer architecture are assumed. The book is designed so that the reader can progress through a carefully designed sequence of presentation shells, starting with simple, generally applicable fundamentals and ending with the more complex and more specialized subjects.

Shell One: Basics.

In the field of graphics, as in most others in computer science, one learns best by doing. Therefore, after a general introduction in Chapter 1, we start immediately with graphics application programming in Chapter 2. This will prepare students at the earliest possible moment to write their own programs and thus deepen their understanding of the material and the issues presented. Since interaction is such a vital part of interactive graphics, we stress good program structures for user-friendly interactive dialogue design, and show, through a sequence of progressive examples, how picture plotting and input handling can be naturally integrated to achieve such a design. For our programming environment, we use Pascal and a subset of the "Core" Graphics subroutine package proposed as a standard by ACM SIGGRAPH [GSPC 79]. Chapters 3 and 4 treat fundamental hardware and software concepts to show how the simple graphics package of Chapter 2 can be easily implemented. Windowing, clipping, segmentation, and logical interaction handling are described. Chapter 5 treats specific techniques for using input devices, while Chapter 6 discusses design principles for the user-computer interface.

Shell Two: Mathematics, data structures, and display architecture.

We deepen our exploration of fundamentals by starting with the basic mathematics of two-dimensional and three-dimensional geometric and viewing transformations in Chapters 7 and 8. Chapter 9 provides a more detailed treatment of the geometric transformations and data structures useful for modeling objects to be displayed, especially those which can be represented in a hierarchical form. Chapter 10 shows how display processor architecture is evolving, especially with respect to functional distribution.

Shell Three: Modern raster technology.

Chapter 11 extends the basic raster techniques discussed in Chapter 2 to cover relevant device-independent algorithms in use today and gives a picture of raster graphics software. Chapter 12 provides an overview of current raster hardware technology.

Shell Four: Making realistic synthetic photographs.

This is the most advanced shell and covers the part of computer graphics that is both the newest and, to many people, the most exciting. Chapter 13 treats fundamental techniques for representing three-dimensional surfaces, and Chapter 14 introduces general strategies for making realistic pictures of three-dimensional objects. The classic problem of removing surfaces of solid objects hidden by other surfaces is addressed in Chapter 15. Chapter 16 discusses shading and texturing algorithms and various lighting models, and Chapter 17 treats models for representing and specifying color.

The layered structure of the book will, we hope, make it useful in a variety of settings. An introductory one-semester undergraduate course can use much of the material in the first three shells, with a sprinkling of introductory material from the fourth. A graduate course can progress more rapidly through the first three shells and concentrate more on the advanced material of shell four. Application programmers or students who have had a first course in graphics and are familiar with classical vector graphics can use the early shells to review basic notions and techniques before studying the newer material on raster graphics and the production of realistic-looking shaded and colored pictures.

We are grateful to the many people who have helped make this book possible, after we spent too many years seeing our less than full-time writing effort constantly outdated by rapidly moving developments in the field. Our colleagues on the original ACM SIGGRAPH Graphics Standards Planning Committee, Peter Bono, Dan Bergeron, Ingrid Carlbom, Jim Michener, and Elaine Sonderegger, helped us put many ideas into perspective as we pursued our common goal of producing a workable draft "Core" standard. We are especially indebted to Jim Michener for giving us the benefit of a superb, painstakingly detailed, red-pencil review which had a major impact on the content, style, and organization of this book. We thank Dan Bergeron, Jack Bresenham, Dick Bulterman, Ingrid Carlbom, John Dill, Steve Feiner, Alan Frieden, Bob Heilman, Graeme Hirst, Janet Incerpi, Abid Kamran, Jeff Lane, Lee Metrick, Norm Meyrowitz, Aragam Nagesh, Joe Pato, Jean Schweitzer, John Sibert, Alvy Ray Smith, Jagan Sud, Jim Templeman, Barry Trent, Victor Wallace, Gerry Weil, Turner Whitted, and Patricia Wenner, all of whom critically reviewed one or more of the chapters. Barry Trent implemented SGP and he and Gerry Weil checked out the Pascal programs; Adam Seidman implemented *LAYOUT* in Chapter 2 to check it out. Katrina Avery did her usual fine editorial work on the manuscript, while typing and editing were skillfully done by herself, Mary Agren, Karen Doell, Sandy Ballentine, Marilyn Henry, and Virginia Edwards. Earlier drafts were typed by Jacquelene Bowman, Betty Kirschbaum, Hilda Wagstaff, and Patricia Cisneros. We thank the Addison-Wesley staff, especially Dick Morton and Rima Zolina, for their patience and professional help, and the many individuals and organizations who provided us with photographs and illustrations. In particular, Lee Metrick, Dave Shuey, and Rick Thorne prepared illustrations especially for the book. As is customary in such endeavors, students in our graphics courses suffered the early drafts of our chapters, and we are grateful for their comments and perseverance. Finally, we are grateful to our former students and colleagues for keeping pressure on us, and especially to our families for keeping the faith and putting up with our many prolonged absences and excuses. (And a final thanks to the Thai Orchid Room for its "crispy spicy fish" which nourished us during our many writing marathons!)

Washington, D.C. — J.D.F.
Providence, R.I. — A.v.D.

August 1981

Contents

CHAPTER 7
GEOMETRICAL TRANSFORMATIONS

CHAPTER 8
VIEWING IN THREE DIMENSIONS

CHAPTER 9
MODELING AND OBJECT HIERARCHY

CHAPTER 10
ADVANCED DISPLAY ARCHITECTURE

CHAPTER 11
RASTER ALGORITHMS AND SOFTWARE

CHAPTER 12
DISPLAY ARCHITECTURE

CHAPTER 13
REPRESENTATION OF 3D SHAPES

CHAPTER 14
THE QUEST FOR VISUAL REALISM

CHAPTER 15
ALGORITHMS FOR REMOVING HIDDEN EDGES AND SURFACES

CHAPTER 16
SHADING MODELS

CHAPTER 17
INTENSITY AND COLOR

1 What is Interactive Graphics?

1.1 INTRODUCTION

We introduce the subject of computer graphics with several examples which will be familiar to most of our readers:

- High-speed *impact printers* used to produce pictures of cartoon characters or people (Fig. 1.1), often by overprinting;
- Drum or flatbed *plotters* used for generating line drawings such as 2D (two-dimensional) and 3D (three-dimensional) graphs (Fig. 1.2), pie charts, histograms, flowcharts, architectural diagrams, and circuit layouts;
- Film or video *recorders* for producing high-quality realistic-looking color pictures of real or imaginary objects for slides, movies, or TV. Examples are business graphs (Color Plate 1), logotypes for the TV networks (Color Plate 2), and scenes from science fiction epics (color Plate 13);
- *Storage tube display terminals* with keyboards and a screen cursor controlled by thumbwheels, used as alphanumeric time-sharing terminals as well as for interactive plotting of text and line drawings (Fig. 1.3). Whenever a new picture is to be drawn, the screen is erased with a flash and a new picture is generated, often a character or line at a time. Very detailed pictures with thousands of lines and characters may take minutes to generate on terminals connected over low-speed phone lines, but can look as precise as if a draftsman had drawn them;
- *Hobby (home) computers* with either a black and white or color TV set as a display, used for both text and plots, for playing games, etc. (see Color Plate 3). The pictures typically have low resolution: the individual dots which make up the characters, lines, and solid areas can easily be seen. The ideas behind the pictures are communicated clearly, however, despite the "graininess";

Fig. 1.1 Line-printer image simulating gray scale by overprinting (courtesy S. P. Harbison and Mad Magazine).

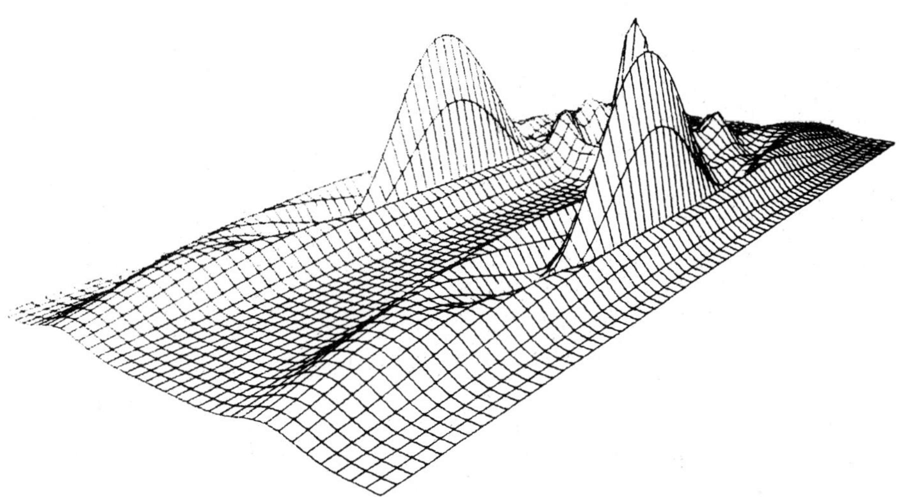

Fig. 1.2 A three-dimensional "ruled surface" (courtesy Calcomp Corporation).

- Microprocessor-based *video game processors*. With the simple type, one attaches to a home TV a black box that can generate crude text and drawings and sample the levers or paddles used as interaction devices. More elaborate arcade games, such as Asteroids, Space Invaders, Pac-Man, and Missile Command, test such skills as piloting and target-shooting, through nontrivial animation and changes of shape and color effects (Color Plate 4).

While there is great diversity among these forms of computer graphics in the type and quality of image and in the degree to which a user* can control the image dynamically, they all share one property: a picture of some object or objects is created and manipulated by a digital processor. Thus we say that *computer graphics* is the creation, storage, and manipulation of models of objects and their pictures via computer. *Interactive computer graphics* is the important case in which a user dynamically controls the pictures' content, format, size, or colors on a display surface by means of interaction devices such as a keyboard, lever, or joystick. The first three instances in the list above are therefore examples of "passive" offline computer graphics, and the last three are of interactive computer graphics (called *interactive graphics* for short). Our study of interactive graphics naturally subsumes the subject of passive computer graphics.

1.2 IMAGE PROCESSING AS PICTURE ANALYSIS

While computer graphics is concerned with the *synthesis* of pictures of real or imaginary objects, the related field of *image processing* (also called picture processing) treats the converse process: the *analysis of scenes* or *reconstruction* of two- or three-

*The term *user* in this book is synonymous with *viewer* or *(console) operator.*

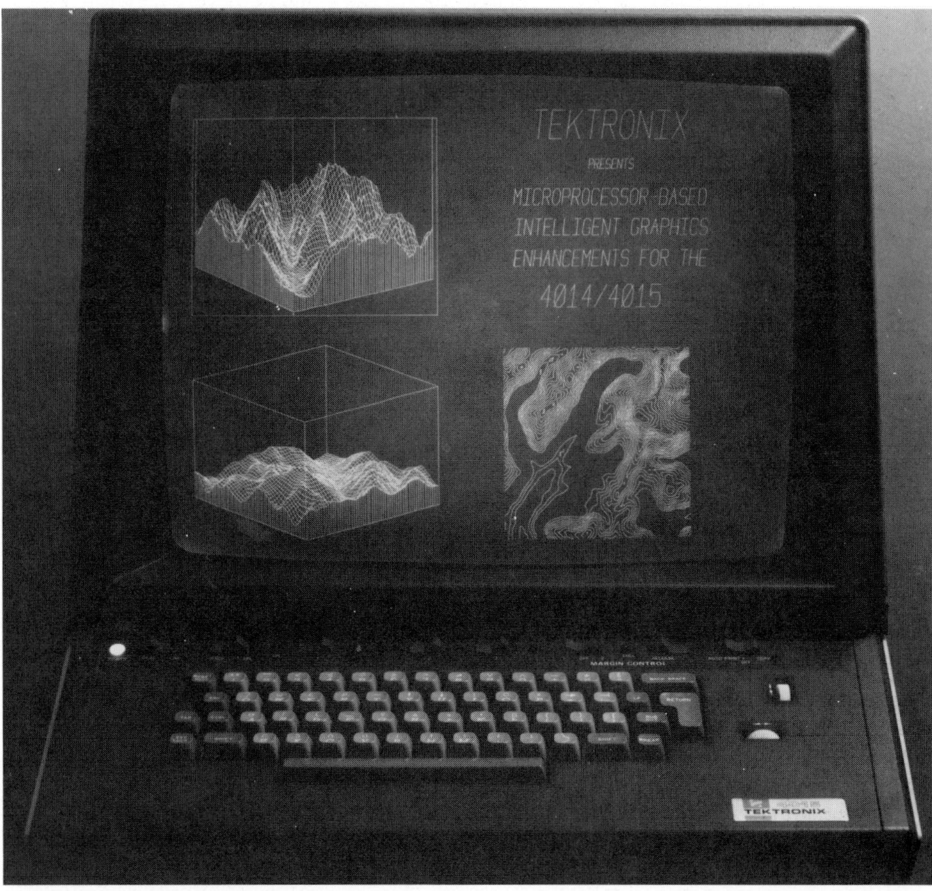

Fig. 1.3 Tektronix 4015–1 computer display terminal with keyboard and thumbwheel cursor controls (far right) (courtesy Tektronix, Inc.).

dimensional objects from their pictures. Picture analysis is important in the study of aerial surveillance photographs, slow-scan TV images of the Moon or Mars sent back to Earth by space probes, TV images from an industrial robot's "eye," chromosome scans and Pap smears, X-rays and CAT scans, and fingerprints. Subareas of image processing are called *image enhancement, pattern detection and recognition,* or *scene analysis and computer vision,* depending on the major objectives. These include improving the image by eliminating "noise" (noninformational detail such as "snow" on a TV screen), enhancing contrast, detecting and clarifying standard patterns, finding deviations (distortions) from standard patterns, or even recognizing (reconstructing) a three-dimensional model of objects in a scene from several two-dimensional images. An example of such a reconstruction is given in Color Plate 5; it is a 3D model of the upper thoracic region derived from a CAT scanner which is subsequently viewable in arbitrary sections. Another example is the representation, as seen by an industrial robot, of the relative sizes, shapes, positions, and colors of parts on a conveyor belt.

Despite the fact that both computer graphics and image processing deal with computer processing of pictures, they have until recently been quite separate disciplines. Now that high-resolution raster (TV) displays are becoming more common, however, the area of intersection between the two areas is growing. This is particularly evident in interactive image processing, in which human input helps guide or control the various subprocesses as the transformations of continuous-tone images are shown on the TV screen in real time.

1.3 ADVANTAGES OF INTERACTIVE GRAPHICS

We concentrate in this book on picture synthesis by means of interactive graphics because it is one of the most natural means of communicating with a computer. Our well-developed two- and three-dimensionally oriented eye–brain pattern recognition mechanism allows us to perceive and process many types of data very rapidly and efficiently if the data are presented pictorially. In fact, in many design, implementation, and construction processes, pictures are virtually indispensable for visualizing and communicating.

However, creating and reproducing a meaningful picture present problems that have stood in the way of widespread use of pictures. Thus the ancient Chinese proverb "a picture is worth a thousand words" was able to become a cliché in our society only after the introduction of technological means (the printing press and later photography) of producing and reproducing pictures easily and cheaply. It then became fast and easy to capture the essence of an idea or situation with an illustrative drawing or photograph—no longer was it necessary to painstakingly draw, carve, or paint individual copies of the scene.

Interactive computer graphics is the most important mechanized means of producing and reproducing pictures since the invention of photography and television; it also has the added advantage that with the computer we can make pictures of abstract, synthetic objects. Interactive graphics is a form of man–machine interaction which combines the best features of the *interactiveness* of textual (alphanumeric) communication via online keyboard terminals with the *graphical communication* of two-dimensional plotting. With interactive graphics, we are largely liberated from the tedium and frustration of looking for patterns and trends by scanning many pages of linear text on line printer listings or alphanumeric terminals.

While static pictures are often a good means of communicating information, dynamically varying pictures are frequently even better. This is especially true when one needs to visualize time-varying phenomena, both *real* (e.g., deflection of an aircraft wing in supersonic flight, or the evolution of a human face from childhood through old age) and *abstract* (e.g., growth trends such as the use of nuclear energy in the USA or the population movement from cities to suburbs and back to the cities, as functions of time). Thus a movie is often much more expressive in showing changes over time than, say, a sequence of slides. Similarly, a dynamic sequence of frames on a display console can often convey smooth motion or changing form better than a slowly changing sequence of individual frames, especially when the user can control the animation by adjusting its speed, the portion of the total scene and the amount of detail shown, and other effects. Much of interactive graphics technology therefore deals with hardware and software techniques for user-controlled motion dynamics and update dynamics.

With *motion dynamics,* objects can be moved and tumbled with respect to a stationary observer. Equivalently, the objects can remain stationary and the viewer can move around them, pan to select the portion in view and zoom in or out for more or less detail, as if looking through the viewfinder of a rapidly moving camera. Flight simulators (Color Plates B and C on the front endpapers) are used to train aircraft or ship pilots by letting them maneuver their simulated craft over a simulated 3D landscape (including other vehicles) portrayed on one or more cockpit windows which are actually large TV screens. Similarly, motion dynamics is used to let a user fly around and through buildings, molecules, two-, three-, or four-dimensional mathematical functions or "clouds" (scatter diagrams) of data points in two- or three-dimensional space. In another form of motion dynamics, the "camera" is held fixed but the objects in the scene are moved relative to the camera. For example, a complex mechanical linkage such as a gear train may be animated on the screen by rotating all the individual gears appropriately.

Update dynamics refers to the actual change of the shape, color, or other properties of the objects being viewed. For instance, one can display the deformation of a metal frame by user-applied loads (Color Plate 6), or the state changes in a block diagram of a computer in response to data and control flows (Fig. 1.4). The smoother the change, the more realistic and meaningful the result. Dynamic interactive graphics offers us a large number of user-controllable modes with which to encode and communicate information: the two- or three-dimensional shape of objects in a picture, their gray scale (grayness value between white and black) or color, and the time variations of these properties. This already large set is increasingly being extended by digitally encoded sound, so that objects and feedback from the program or the operating system can be heard as well as seen.

In summary, interactive computer graphics allows us to achieve much higher-bandwidth man-machine communication using a judicious combination of text with static and dynamic pictures than is possible with text alone. This higher bandwidth makes a significant difference in our ability to understand data, perceive trends, and visualize real or imaginary objects. By making communication more efficient, graphics makes possible greater productivity, higher-quality and more precise results or products, and lower analysis and design costs.

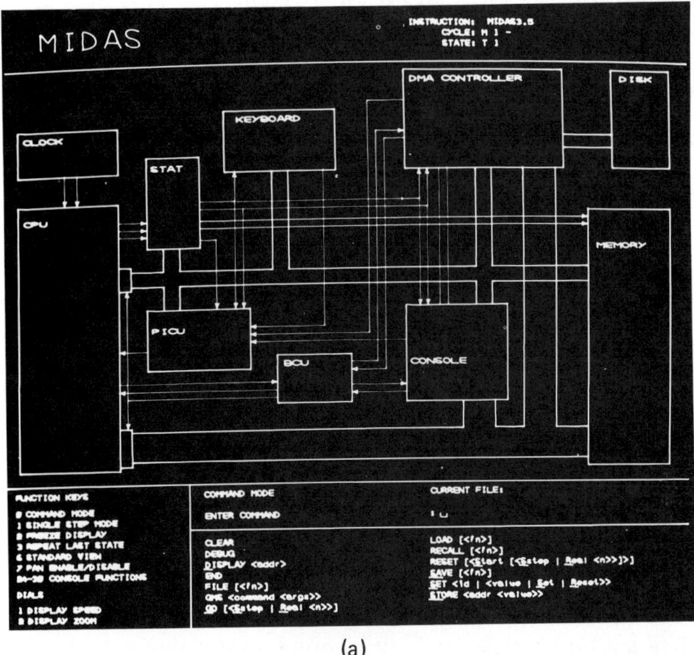

(a)

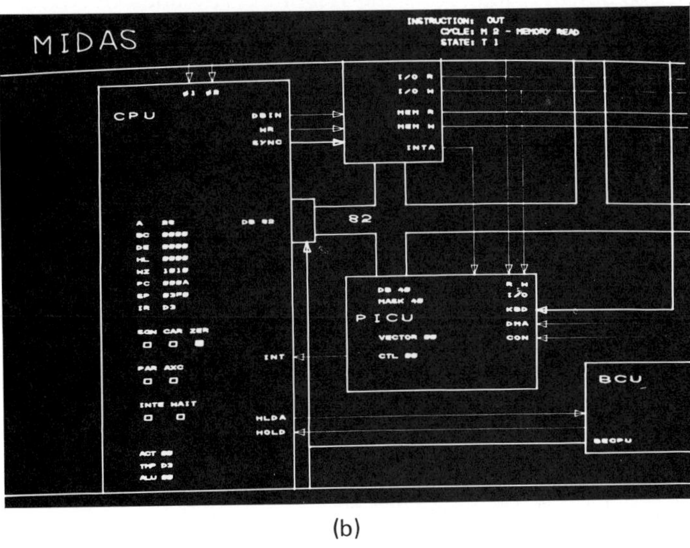

(b)

Fig. 1.4 Simulation and user-controlled animation of a microprocessor system: (a) overview of entire system; (b) detailed view of CPU chip, control chip, and priority interrupt-control chip. At this level of detail, internal registers are shown and active control lines are brightened (e.g., the SYNC line)[GURW 81].

1.4 SOME REPRESENTATIVE USES OF COMPUTER GRAPHICS

Computer graphics is used today in many different areas of industry, business, government, education, entertainment, and, most recently, in the home. The list of applications is enormous and growing rapidly as simple display devices become routinely affordable. Below we list a representative sample of such areas; we shall return to some of these later in this book.

(Interactive) plotting in business, science, and technology. Graphics today is probably still most frequently used to draw 2D or 3D graphs of mathematical, physical and economic functions, histograms, bar and pie charts, task scheduling charts, inventory and production charts, and a profusion of other plots. All are used to present trends and patterns in data in a meaningful and concise fashion in order to increase understanding of complex phenomena and to facilitate informed decision making.

Cartography. Computer graphics is used for the production of highly accurate representations on paper or film of geographical and other natural phenomena. Examples [HARV80] include geographic maps, relief maps, exploration maps for drilling and mining, oceanographic charts, weather maps, contour maps, oil exploration maps, and population density maps (Fig. 1.5).

Computer-aided drafting and design. In computer-aided design (CAD), interactive graphics is used to design components and systems of mechanical, electrical, electromechanical and electronic devices [PRIN71]. These systems include structures (such as buildings, chemical and power plants, automobile bodies, airplane and ship hulls and their contents), optical systems, and telephone and computer networks. The emphasis is sometimes only on producing precise drawings of components and (sub)assemblies, as in online drafting or architectural rendering. More frequently, however, the emphasis is on interacting with a computer-based model of the component or system being designed in order to test, for example, its mechanical, electrical or thermal properties. Often the model is interpreted by a simulator which feeds back the behavior of the system to the display console operator for further interactive design and test cycles. After objects have been designed, utility programs can *postprocess* the design data base to make parts lists, process bills of materials, define numerical control tapes for cutting or drilling parts, etc. The distinction between drawing and designing/postprocessing is briefly explored in Section 1.5.

Simulation and animation. Computer-produced animated movies of the time-varying behavior of real or simulated objects are becoming increasingly popular. We

Fig. 1.5 Four examples of mapping techniques: (a) a SYMAP conformant map; (b) a CALFORM map; (c) an ODYSSEY System PRISM map; (d) an ASPEX map (reproduced by permission of the Laboratory for Computer Graphics and Spatial Analysis, Harvard Graduate School of Design, Cambridge, Massachusetts). ►

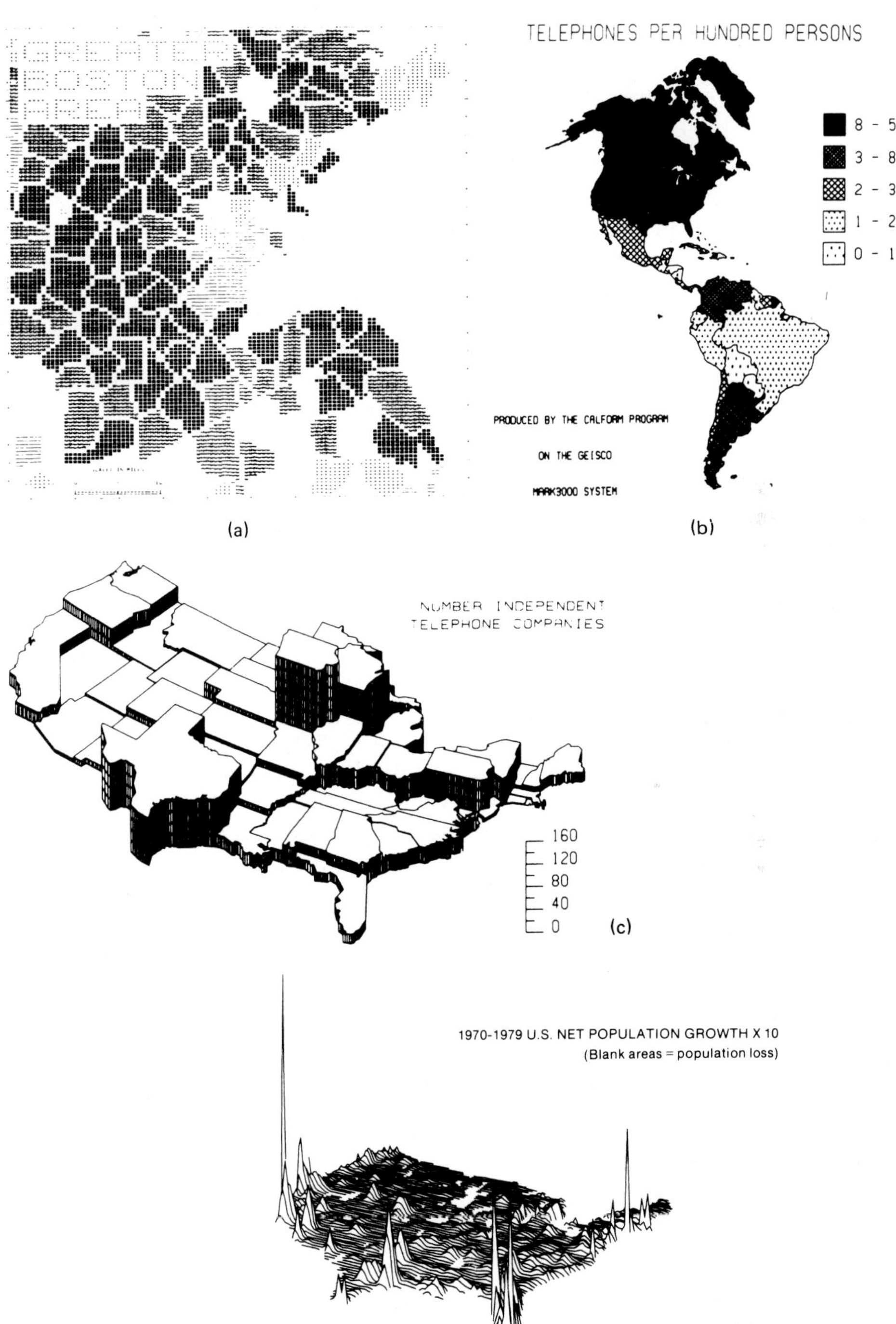
GREATER
BOSTON
AREA
TELEPHONES PER HUNDRED PERSONS
8 - 58
3 - 8
2 - 3
1 - 2
0 - 1
PRODUCED BY THE CALFORM PROGRAM
ON THE GEISCO
MARK3000 SYSTEM
NUMBER INDEPENDENT
TELEPHONE COMPANIES
160
120
80
40
0
1970-1979 U.S. NET POPULATION GROWTH X 10
(Blank areas = population loss)
Produced by Aspex Program
Harvard Laboratory for Computer Graphics & Spatial Analysis

(a) (b) (c) (d)

can study not only mathematical figures (Color Plates 7(a) and (b)) but also mathematical models for such scientific phenomena as hydraulic flow, relativity, nuclear and chemical reactions, physiological systems and organs, and deformation of structures under load, by seeing the effects of the transformations pictorially. A relatively new and also high-technology area is interactive cartooning (Color Plate 8); such cartoons have a very high visual quality and the simpler kinds are becoming cost-effective with the use of sophisticated computer graphics technology to eliminate routine steps [CATM78c]. Other sophisticated applications of animation are the flight simulators mentioned in Section 1.3. Simulators generate views not only of the fixed world in which the vehicle is moving, but also of special effects such as clouds, fog, smog, night-time lights, and other craft of various sizes and shapes, each on its own course. For the moon landings, astronauts piloting the lunar lander and its mother ship practiced docking maneuvers in a simulator. Similarly, the space shuttle pilots practiced maneuvers in a simulator for years before their maiden voyage.

As mentioned in the previous section, the execution and operation of hardware or software computer systems can also be nicely simulated and displayed graphically to show how components interact and change values (Figs. 1.4 and 1.6). And finally, at the other end of the price-performance spectrum, arcade games simulate a primitive, artificial 2D or 3D world in real time, with limited animation.

Process control. While a flight simulator or arcade game lets the user interact with a *simulation* of either a real or artificial world, many other applications enable the user to interact with some aspect of the real world itself. Status displays for refineries, power plants, and computer networks display data values from sensors attached to critical components in the system; the operator then responds to exceptional conditions (Fig. 1.7). Military commanders view field data (number and position of vehicles, weapons launched, troop movements, casualties) on *command and control* displays and revise their tactics as needed (Color Plate 9). Flight controllers at airports see computer-generated identification and status information along with the aircraft blips on their radar scopes and can thus control traffic more quickly and accurately than with the unannotated radar data alone. Spacecraft controllers monitor telemetry data and initiate corrective procedures as needed.

Office automation and electronic publication. As described in Section 1.5 below, the use of alphanumeric and graphic terminals to create and disseminate information in the office and even the home is increasing rapidly. Both traditional printed documents (hard copy) and electronic documents (soft copy) can be produced which contain not just text but also tables, graphs, and other 2D information [FEIN81].

Art and commerce. Computer art and advertising have the common goal of expressing a "message" and attracting the attention of the public with aesthetically pleasing pictures (Color Plate 2). Very sophisticated mechanisms are available to the creator of the picture for modeling the objects and for the representation of light and shadows (see Chapters 14 through 16). Teletext and Videotex (discussed briefly

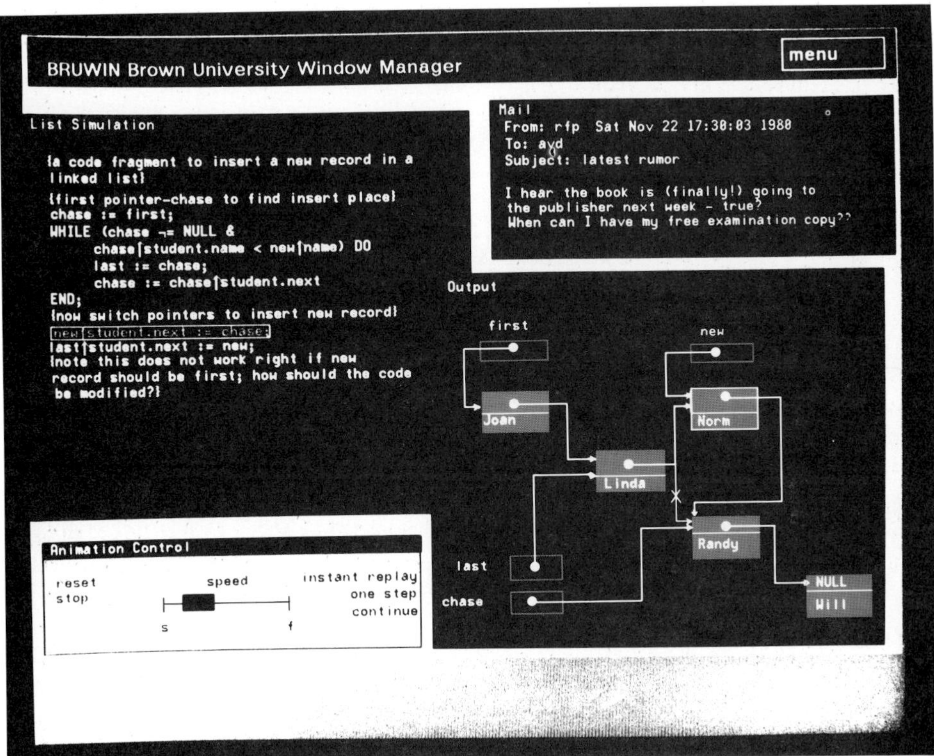

Fig. 1.6 Simulation and user-controlled animation of a simple linked-list insertion program. Separate areas of the screen show the program, the graphic representation, the animation controls, and some incoming mail.

in Section 1.6) offer much simpler but still informative pictures. Finally, the production of slides for commercial, scientific or educational presentations also has become a very cost-effective use of graphics, given the steeply rising labor costs associated with traditional means of creating and processing such material.

1.5 CLASSIFICATION OF APPLICATIONS

The diverse uses of computer graphics listed above differ considerably in a variety of ways. A number of criteria may be used to categorize applications. The first criterion is the *type of object and picture to be produced*; the range includes line drawings of two-dimensional objects (Fig. 1.4), line drawings of three-dimensional objects—often called *wire-frame pictures* (Color Plate A on the front endpapers, Fig. 1.8(a)), line drawings of three-dimensional objects with hidden edges removed (Figs. 1.8(b) and 1.8(c)), two-dimensional continuous-tone images with gray scale

Fig. 1.7 FOX 1/A System showing control display for chemical plant (courtesy Foxboro Company).

(Fig. 1.9), two-dimensional color images (Color Plate 1), and three-dimensional representations of shaded solid objects with hidden surfaces removed (Color Plates 14). Some of these objects are clearly abstract, some very real; similarly, the pictures can be purely symbolic (a simple 2D graph) or very realistic (a rendition of a still life). The same object can, of course, be represented in a variety of ways. For example, a circuit board can be portrayed by many different 2D symbolic representations as well as by 3D *synthetic photographs* of the actual board with hidden surfaces removed.

A second area of difference is *the type of interaction* and degree of control over the object or its image available to the user. The range here includes *offline plotting* with a predefined data base produced by other application programs or digitized from physical models; *interactive plotting* (cycles of "supply parameters, plot, alter parameters, replot"); predefining the object and *flying* around it in real time under

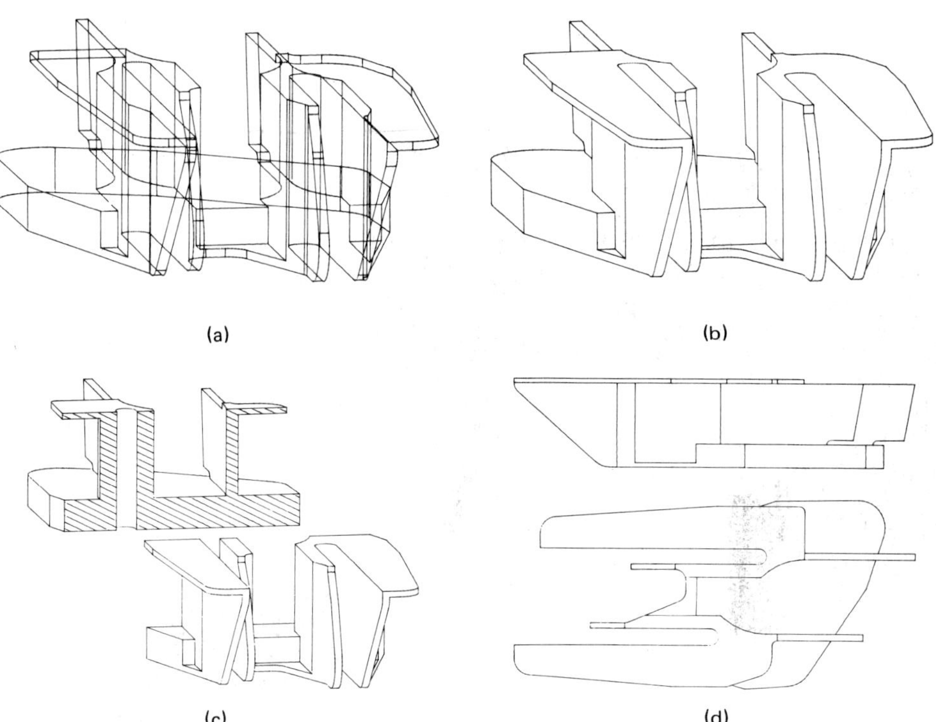

Fig. 1.8 ROMULUS three-dimensional solid geometric-modeling software. This sequence of pictures illustrates a model of a mechanical part which was generated by using the ROMULUS solid geometric-modeling software: (a) the object drawn in wire-frame mode without hidden lines removed; (b) a picture of the part with hidden lines removed; (c) the part sectioned and drawn with hidden lines removed; (d) an orthographic top and side view of the part. ROMULUS is a product of Shape Data Ltd. of Cambridge, England (courtesy Evans & Sutherland Computer Corporation).

user control, as is typical in flight simulators; and *interactive design,* in which the user, starting from a blank screen, defines an object, typically from predefined components, and then alters it at will, panning and zooming to get the desired view.

A third variation is in the *role of the picture,* or the degree to which the picture itself is the means to an end or the end in itself. In cartography, drafting and raster painting applications, the drawing is the primary product, while in many computer-aided design applications the drawing is merely a visualization of the geometric properties of the object analyzed (such as a circuit, bridge, piping system, aircraft wing or automobile fender). In these applications, the drawing phase is an important but small part of a larger process whose object is the construction and postprocessing of a common data base by an integrated suite of application programs. The database contains many other pieces of applications-oriented information about the components; this data is used to drive other applications programs, including those for computer-aided manufacturing. In the case of printed wiring board design programs, for example, this suite may include logic simulation, component placement, user-assisted conductor path routing, auditing for electrical shorts, discontinuities and clearances, artwork generation for photomasks and document production of assembly drawings, stock lists and drill tables [ASKG79].

A final difference lies in the logical and temporal *relationship between objects and their pictures.* The user may deal, for example, with only one picture at a time (typical in plotting), with a time-varying sequence of related pictures (as in motion or update dynamics), or with a structured collection of objects (as in many computer-aided design applications that contain hierarchies of assembly and subassembly drawings).

1.6 INTERACTIVE GRAPHICS IN THE FUTURE: THE NORMAL MODE OF INTERACTION

Computer graphics has been too often considered a special form of communication requiring special input–output hardware and software and therefore to be used only where essential. Many of the applications cited above seem somewhat exotic to most people, and many require considerable hardware resources (both processing power and storage) and high-quality output devices. Pilot-controlled flight simulation, an extreme example, involves several million dollars' worth of special-purpose computer display equipment per installation.

Fortunately, primarily because of the rapidly decreasing cost of hardware (especially memory and microprocessors), interactive graphics is now feasible and practical for the vast majority of applications that require only modest processor and display resources. Some of these applications are mentioned below to illustrate that graphics is coming of age as the normal means of user–computer communication (and even user–user communication).

As a first example, many introductory courses in computer science and other quantitative physical and social sciences now use interactive plotting and modeling or simulation on low-cost (TV-based) graphics terminals attached to time-sharing systems or personal computers. Simultaneously, a whole new generation of future college students is growing up with home computers that cost less than a thousand dollars and are given as presents or as a replacement for the traditional encyclopedia as "an investment in your child's future." Most of these home computers use low- to medium-resolution graphics terminals, increasingly with color, and their users are coming to view graphics as a natural, expected mode of communication rather than a unique mode requiring a special display device not easily available. The high cost of a convenient hard-copy output device on most home computers fortunately makes the old-fashioned habit of printing thick listings of output impossible and forces users to think in terms of simple and more compact graphical representations that typically fit on a single screen.

Another revolutionary development, now being imported to the US from Europe and Canada, will vastly increase interactive graphics literacy. It involves the use of broadcast television and/or the telephone system, plus a simple keyboard, to let TV viewers select items from customized "electronic newspapers," browse through online encyclopedias and yellow pages, and get stock quotations, entertainment listings, etc. [IEEE79].* Much of the information is transmitted in graphical form. These diagrams are still crude but are nonetheless effective in attracting the viewer's attention and communicating the necessary information (Color Plate 10) [BROW79]. Once this medium becomes sufficiently reliable and cheap, using a computer-connected TV as an information resource for text and graphics will become as natural and commonplace as using the telephone.

On yet another front, the burgeoning fields of *word processing* and *office automation* are introducing large numbers of office workers and other producers and manipulators of documents to computer-based work stations for document preparation and electronic messaging and mail. More and more of these work stations will be based on high-quality display screens suitable for interactive graphics. While the emphasis until recently was on strictly alphanumeric interaction, the demand for tables, charts, forms and figures is sufficiently strong that most systems can be expected to display them, along with surrounding high-quality "graphic arts" text, directly on the screen as they would appear on a hard-copy output device. This "what you see is what you get" design philosophy, in which the screen mirrors the printed page as much as possible, eliminates bothersome and unnatural formatting or typesetting codes whose effects are not seen on line. Indeed, if one can see a page just as it will look when printed, much of the need to print will disappear, especially for documents without lasting value. Instead, most transient documents will be created, distributed, and responded to by electronic mail/publishing.

In the area of high-technology research and development in computer science, one of the most exciting and promising recent developments is a new systems philosophy that has been developed to aid in most of the daily work done by "knowledge workers." This term (coined by P. F. Drucker [DRUC68]) describes professionals whose jobs involve to a significant extent the creation and manipulation of and interaction with written and spoken information. As early as the mid-sixties, D. Engelbart and his coworkers at Stanford Research Institute [ENGE68] developed time-shared systems which allow hierarchies of text and graphics to be manipulated in a powerful fashion on computer-driven television displays. With this system, all documents suitable for publication, whether programs, memos or manuscripts, are neatly handled by the same tool.

More recently, a new system with this philosophy was developed and has been used in production since the mid-seventies at Xerox Palo Alto Research Center [LAMP78]. It is based on several key principles. One is that most of one's daily

*In Videotex (also called Viewdata), pictures and text are communicated via a telephone line to the user's TV set, typically at 1200 baud, with user interaction at 75 baud. Teletext, which is far less interactive, broadcasts a repeated cycle of pictures to all viewers during the unused portions of a standard TV signal when no video information is being transmitted. A single picture at a time can then be selected for local storage and display by the viewer.

work—programming, communicating, writing and filing—can be done on a powerful personal (nonshared) minicomputer that is essentially self-sufficient. The personal work stations commonly available in 1981, called ALTOs, are connected in a cable network (the "Ethernet" [METC76]) to each other and to dedicated-purpose processors ("servers") that handle the communal file system and special peripherals (large disks, typesetters, plotters/recorders). The second principle is that interactive graphics should be the standard means of user interaction with all the subsystems and processes running on the personal computer. A black-and-white 808 × 608-point TV screen shows high-quality text and graphics essentially as it will be printed out on a high-resolution printer (Fig. 1.9). As of this writing, many commercial offerings by Xerox and its competitors are based on the "PARC model."

Many system and user programs on the ALTO employ a *window manager* to control multiple, typically overlapping windows, i.e., areas on the screen in which a page or piece of a page may be displayed. Each window is in essence a variable-size virtual screen that reflects the progress of some activity. The general effect is one of looking at a small desk with papers of varying sizes lying partially on top of one another (see also Fig. 1.6). With a pointing device one can instantaneously put a piece of paper on top of the others for reading or writing, move it around, or change its dimensions, all by manipulating the window in which it appears. When multiple activities are in progress simultaneously, their results can be displayed in their respective windows on the screen: one can edit a current program and scan a second for a module specification, run a third that may include some on-line animation effects, and in the background watch for incoming electronic mail and messages and display a real-time clock [MEYR81]. Thus the contents of pages on the desk, corresponding to multiple files and processes, change dynamically and independently, creating a powerful new paradigm for man–machine interaction [KAY77a,b; TEIT77].

It should be added that the power of this paradigm, and the ease and speed with which the user manipulates the parallel executing processes and their windows, yield a major increase in user productivity over more traditional time-sharing techniques. In fact, researchers who have used the system over a period of time claim that it provides a qualitative and quantitative improvement over conventional time-sharing on, say, 9600-baud cursor-driven alphanumeric terminals, which is as great as the improvement of that type of high-bandwidth time-sharing over batch processing with cards!

There appear to be two reasons for this favorable response, over and above the system's raw speed and ease of use. Most important, the inherent two-dimensionality and multiple-process orientation of the paradigm free the user from the restrictions of linear, sequential textual communication inherited from batch processing and its languages and tools and thereby increase the information transfer bandwidth enormously. Secondly, the total *environment* of tools plus their user interfaces is presented as an integrated whole, built top-down to fit into a consistent, coherent conceptual framework. All daily work, from computation to office automation tasks (such as electronic mail), is done with the same fundamental tools and with consistent conventions. (Most traditional time-sharing systems, in contrast, present

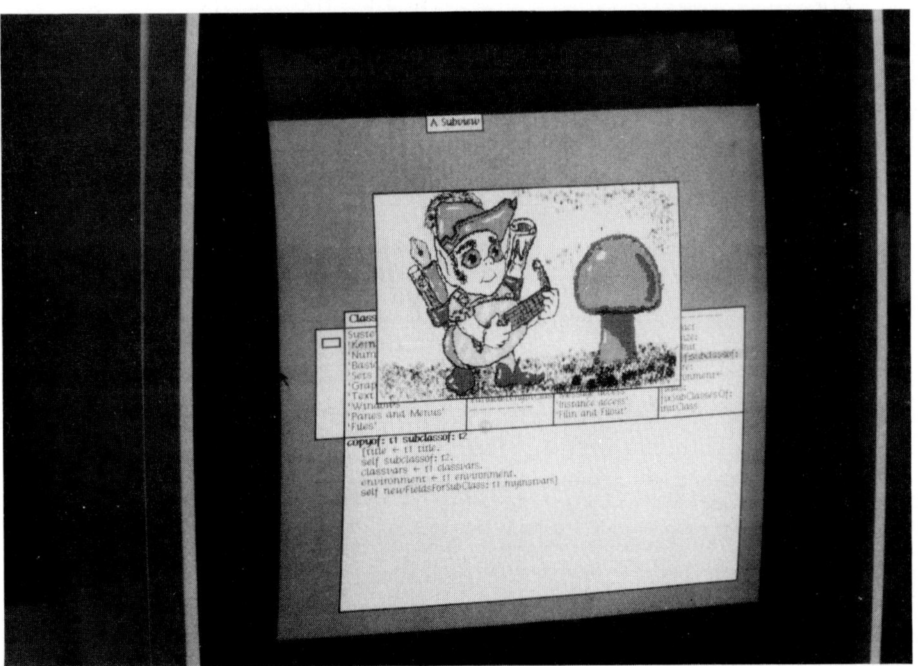

Fig. 1.9 Xerox Alto raster display with "Smalltalk" program; two windows are shown, one displaying graphics and a second displaying text (courtesy Xerox Palo Alto Research Center).

the user with a collection of unintegrated, often special-purpose tools gathered together in a bottom-up way with inconsistent usage conventions and a frustrating lack of uniformity of style.)

As a final pointer to the future use of sophisticated graphics in man–machine interaction, we note another pioneering research project by MIT's Architecture Machine Group [DONE 78]. With this system the users browse through a 2D "Dataland" world in real time, that is, at their own speed and with essentially instantaneous response. The data base consists of integrated text, photographs, sound cues, and television frames (the latter supplied via a laser-scanned optical videodisk). Material may be read or annotated with overlaid text or graphics. The user sits in a *media room* containing two personal displays with touch-sensitive screens, a wall-sized TV display, a specially instrumented chair with panning and zooming controls on the armrests, and octophonic sound. The system allows panning and zooming on a two-dimensional data base shown on the personal monitor; detail previously not displayed appears on the large screen as one moves closer to objects in the scene (Color Plate 11). Sound cues indicate the direction from which one is approaching an object and its distance. (A prototype commercial implementation of this MIT "Spatial Data Management System" is described in [HERO80].) In another system used for illustrating simple maintenance and repair tasks, sequences of frames from the videodisk may be arranged on the fly to form customized "movies." Research is being done on additional "personalization" based on user expertise, ratio of pictures to text, etc. This multimedia presentation gives us a preview of the exciting future modes of highly dynamic, high-bandwidth, personalized man–machine interaction.

1.7 BRIEF HISTORY OF COMPUTER GRAPHICS

While the future of interactive graphics as the standard means of user-computer interaction is rosy indeed, it is useful to understand where the field is today and how it arrived at its present state. Thus, this book is concerned with fundamental principles and techniques that were derived in the past and are still applicable today—and generally will be in the future as well. As usual, it is easier to chronicle the evolution of hardware than software, since hardware has had more influence on the way the field developed. Thus it is with hardware that we will begin.

Crude plotting on hard-copy devices such as teletypes and line printers dates from the early days of computing. MIT's 1950 Whirlwind Computer had computer-driven CRT displays for output (both for operators and for cameras to produce hard copy), while the SAGE Air Defense System in the middle 1950s was the first to use *command and control* CRT display consoles on which operators identified targets by pointing at them with light pens.* The beginnings of modern interactive graphics are found in Ivan Sutherland's seminal Ph.D. work on the Sketchpad drawing system [SUTH63]. He introduced data structures for storing symbol hierarchies which are built up via easy replication of standard components (a technique akin to the use of plastic templates for drawing flowchart or circuit symbols). He also developed interaction techniques for using the keyboard and light pen for choice-making, pointing, and drawing, and formulated, in addition, many other fundamental ideas and techniques still in use today. At the same time, the enormous potential for partially automating drafting and other drawing-intensive activities in computer-aided design (CAD) and computer-aided manufacturing (CAM) activities was also clear to manufacturers in the computer, automobile, and aerospace industries, and by the mid-sixties a number of research projects and commercial products began to appear. Prominent among these were General Motors' ambitious project for multiple time-shared graphics consoles for many phases of car design, the Digigraphic design system (first developed by Itek for lens design and later bought and marketed by CDC), and the IBM 2250 display system based on the General Motors prototype.

Much propaganda was made for a breakthrough in man–machine interaction: *the window on the computer* would form an integral part of vastly speeded-up inter-

*The CRT (cathode ray tube) is the display device which also forms the basis of home TV sets. The CRT and light-pen pointing devices are discussed in Chapter 3.

active design cycles. The results were not nearly so dramatic, however, since interactive graphics remained beyond the resources of all but the most technology-intensive organizations. Among the many reasons for this were:

- The *cost* of the graphics hardware (when produced without benefit of economies of scale);
- Significant *computing resources* required to support large databases, interactive picture manipulation, and the typically large suite of postprocessing applications programs whose input came from the graphics design phase;
- The *difficulty of writing large, interactive programs* for a time-sharing environment at a stage when both graphics and interaction were new to predominantly batch- (FORTRAN-)oriented programmers;
- *One-of-a-kind, nonportable software,* typically locked into a particular manufacturer's display device and produced without the benefit of modern software engineering principles for building modular, structured systems. When software is *nonportable,* moving to new display devices necessitates very expensive and time-consuming rewriting of working programs.

1.7.1 Output Technology

The display devices developed in the mid-sixties and still in use today are called *vector, stroke,* or *calligraphic displays.* They consist of a display processor, a display buffer memory, and a CRT with its associated electronics. The buffer stores the computer-produced *display list* or *display program;* this contains point and line plotting commands (with coordinate endpoint data) and character plotting commands (Fig. 1.10). These commands for plotting points, lines, and characters are interpreted by the display processor; it converts digital values to analog voltages which displace an electron beam writing on the phosphor coating of the CRT (the details will be described in Chapter 3). Since the light output of the phosphor decays in tens or at most hundreds of microseconds, the display processor must cycle through this list to *refresh* the phosphor at least 30 times per second to avoid flicker; hence the buffer holding the display list is usually called a *refresh buffer.* Note that in Fig. 1.10 the jump instruction loops back to the top of the display list to provide the cyclic refresh.

Both the buffer memory required for typical line drawings (8 to 32 kilobytes) and a processor fast enough to refresh at (at least) 30 Hz were very expensive in the sixties. Thus the advent in the late sixties of the direct-view storage tube (DVST), which obviated both the buffer and the refresh process, was the vital step forward in making interactive graphics affordable (Figs. 1.3 and 1.11). In a DVST, the image is stored (until erased) by writing it once with a relatively slow-moving electron beam on a storage mesh in which the phosphor is embedded. This small, self-sufficient terminal-sized device was ideal for an inexpensive, low-speed (300–1200 baud) telephone interface to a time-sharing system. It formed a most cost-effective alternative

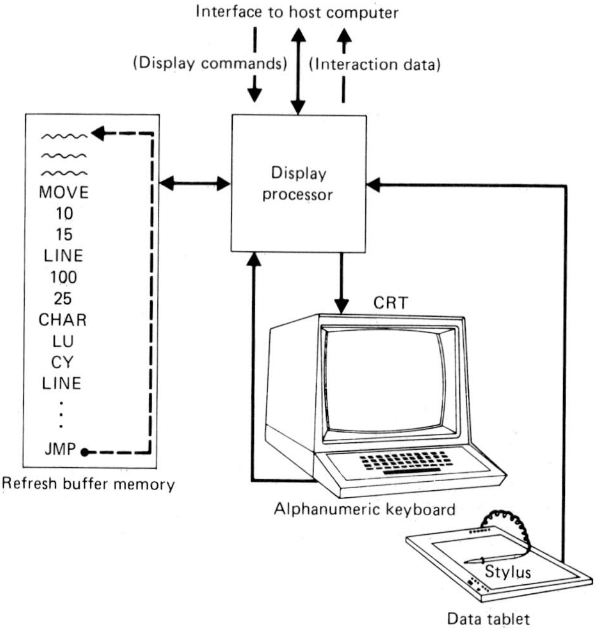

Interface to host computer
(Display commands)
(Interaction data)
MOVE
10
15
LINE
100
25
CHAR
LU
CY
LINE
JMP
Refresh buffer memory
Display processor
CRT
Alphanumeric keyboard
Stylus
Data tablet

Fig. 1.10 Typical refresh display device. Display list in memory shows symbolic representation of plotting commands followed by values (e.g., *x*, *y* coordinates or characters).

Interface to host computer
(Display commands)
(Interaction data)
Display processor
CRT
Vertical and horizontal cursor thumbwheels
Keyboard

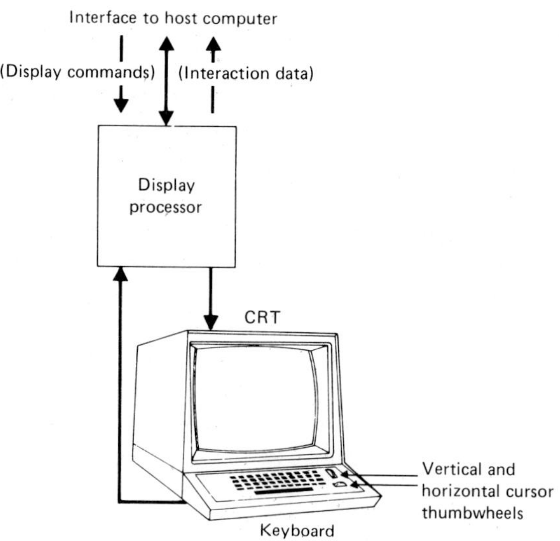

Fig. 1.11 Typical storage tube device.

to the bulky, complex refresh systems attached via expensive, high-speed interfaces to input–output channels or peripheral controllers. DVSTs allowed interactive plotting for many simple applications at costs often an order of magnitude smaller than those of refresh displays. Thus they helped introduce many users and programmers not interested in complex CAD applications to interactive graphics. Storage tubes are still popular today for applications that demand large numbers (tens of thousands) of high-precision lines and characters but do not need dynamic picture manipulation.

The next major hardware advance was to relieve the central computer of the heavy demands of the refreshed display device (especially user-interaction handling and picture updating) by attaching the display to a minicomputer. The minicomputer typically functions as a dedicated, stand-alone computer for running applications programs as well as servicing the display and user interaction devices. Often it can also run as an *intelligent satellite* to the main computer, handling user interaction but leaving large computation or large-database jobs to the mainframe. At the same time, the hardware of the display processor itself was becoming more sophisticated, taking over many routine but time-consuming jobs of the graphics software.

The mid-seventies achievement likely to contribute most to the development of the field was that of cheap raster graphics based on television technology. In *raster displays* the display primitives such as lines, characters, and solid areas (typically polygons) are stored in a refresh buffer in terms of their component points, called *pixels* or *pels* (short for *picture elements*). The image is formed from the *raster,* a set of horizontal *raster lines* each made up of individual pixels: the raster is thus simply a matrix of pixels covering the entire screen area. The entire image is scanned out sequentially, 30 times per second, one raster line at a time top to bottom, by varying only the intensity of the electron beam for each pixel on a line (Fig. 1.12). The storage needed is thus greatly increased in that the entire image of, say, 512 lines of 512 pixels, must be stored explicitly in a *bit map* containing only points that map one-for-one to points on the screen.* On the other hand, the actual display of the simple image can now be handled by very cheap, absolutely standard television technology.

The development that made raster graphics possible was that of inexpensive solid-state memory that can now provide refresh buffers considerably larger than those of a decade ago at a fraction of the price. Standard raster graphics systems do not (yet) have the resolution of a vector system (1280×1024 points versus 4096×4096), nor do they have hardware fast enough to provide general motion dynamics for high-resolution displays. This is because all pixels of a primitive such as a line or rectangle must be transformed in the buffer to their new coordinates, rather than just the endpoints of lines, as in the vector case. For a smooth, dynamic update of the entire 1280×1024 screen, more than a million pixels would have to be

*Other display organizations which avoid the explicit storage of all pixels, at the expense of increased logic and processing, are discussed in Chapters 10 and 11.

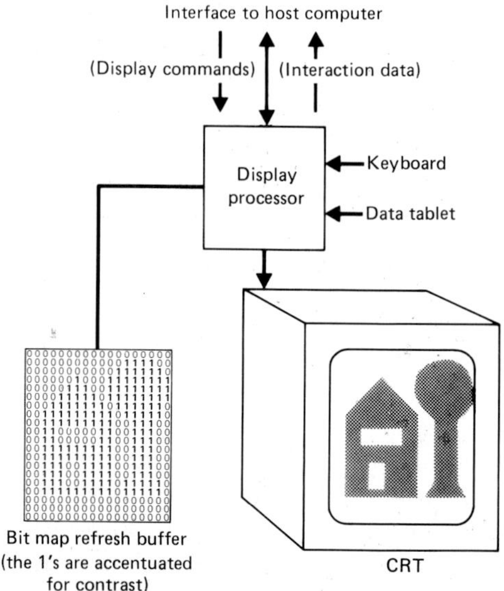

Fig. 1.12 Typical raster graphics display showing house and tree.

altered in less than a tenth of a second, a demand on computational resources not yet affordable in most systems.* Raster graphics does, however, make possible the display of solid areas, typically in color, which is an especially rich means for communicating information. Furthermore, the refresh process is independent of the complexity (number of lines, etc.) of the image, because the hardware is fast enough for each pixel in the buffer to be read out on each refresh cycle, regardless of whether it represents information or background. Thus there is no flicker. In contrast, vector displays often flicker when the number of primitives in the buffer grows so large that they cannot be read out and processed in a thirtieth of a second and the image is therefore not refreshed sufficiently often.

1.7.2 Input Technology

In a development parallel to that of better output technology, an improvement in input technology has also taken place. The clumsy, fragile light pen has largely been replaced by a thin stylus moved on a data tablet or by a transparent, touch-sensitive panel mounted on the screen. Also, audio communication holds much exciting potential for the future, since it allows hands-free input and natural output of simple instructions, feedback, etc. (Chapter 5 contains more details on input devices.) With these interaction devices the user can either type or draw new information, or point

---

*Increasingly, modern personal computers with integral bit-map raster displays do allow considerable dynamics. Also, Megatek's 7255 display system [MEGA81], costing about $60,000 in 1981, can display a dynamic 1024 × 1024 image in real time (see Chapter 10).

to existing information on the screen in order to specify operations or picture components to be operated upon. These interactions require no knowledge of programming: the user simply makes choices, answers questions, places predefined symbols on the screen, and draws or paints (by indicating consecutive endpoints to be connected by lines, or polygonal areas bounded by line segments to be filled in with a specified shade of gray or color).

1.7.3 Software and Portability

Steady advances in hardware technology have thus made possible the evolution of graphics displays from a one-of-a-kind special output device to a replacement for the ubiquitous alphanumeric display terminal as the standard human interface to the computer. One may well wonder whether software has kept pace. For example, how have the early difficulties experienced with graphics systems and application software been resolved? Many of them lay in the primitive graphic software available to application programmers. By and large, there has been a long, slow process of maturation. We have moved from low-level, *device-dependent* subroutine packages supplied by manufacturers for their unique display devices to higher-level, *device-independent* packages. These packages, typically supplied by independent developers, can drive a wide variety of display devices—plotters to high-performance vector and raster displays. The main purpose of a device-independent package used in conjunction with a high-level programming language is to induce *application program (and programmer) portability*. This portability is provided in much the same way that a ''high-level'' machine-independent language (such as FORTRAN) provides a large measure of portability: by isolating the programmer from most machine peculiarities and providing language features readily implemented on a wide spectrum of processors.

A significant development that started in the mid-seventies was a general awareness of the need for standards in such device-independent graphics packages. This culminated in a widely known specification for a *Core Graphics System* (called the *Core* for short) produced by an ACM SIGGRAPH Committee in 1977 [GSPC77] and refined in 1979 [GSPC79]. This proposed standard is based on some six to eight years' experience with several device-independent graphics packages and in essence embodies common concepts and practices in graphics programming (see Section 1.8). While it is still the subject of considerable debate in national (ANSI) and international (ISO) graphics standardization efforts, it has become quite clear that the 1979 Core will serve as an important baseline definition for an evolving and maturing series of standards, much as FORTRAN has served in the field of programming languages.* It seems clear that our notions of how to think about graphics program-

*We feel, however, that FORTRAN has lived considerably beyond its time in that it is far too restrictive in its flow-of-control constructs and data types. We have therefore adopted the more modern, structured Pascal for our programming language in this text.

ming are bound to change, perhaps fundamentally, as we move into the age of interactive graphics on powerful personal computers. Nonetheless we feel that Core terminology and Core implementations are rapidly becoming *de facto* (though interim) standards. We will therefore introduce graphics application programming in the next chapter by using a subset of the Core. (Note that the GKS package [ENCA80, ISO81] proposed as a 2D standard by ISO can be viewed as an adaptation of the Core.)

1.8 OVERVIEW OF THE PROGRAMMER'S MODEL OF INTERACTIVE GRAPHICS

The conceptual framework on which the Core is based is shown schematically in Fig. 1.13. We will describe it briefly here and return to it in later chapters for a more detailed treatment. The hardware component is a host computer that drives a *display device,* also called the *display unit, display,* or *graphics terminal* (such as in Figs. 1.10 through 1.12). The display itself consists of an *output* component (the *display screen,* or *view surface,* on which pictures are displayed) and an *input,* or *interaction component* (Fig. 1.14). This input component typically consists of a set of *logical devices,* including *keyboard devices* such as an alphanumeric keyboard for entering text, a function *button device* for invoking predefined options or functions, a *picking device* such as a light pen or data tablet stylus for indicating picture components on the screen, *valuators* such as control dials and levers for entering scalar values, and an *xy position indicator* or *locator,* such as a cross-hair thumbwheel, lever, or joystick (see Chapters 3 through 5 for details on all these devices). Note that one physical device may be used to implement one or more of these logical input functions.

The software consists of three components. The first is the *application program;* it stores into and retrieves from the second component, the *application data structure/data base,* and sends graphics commands to the third component—the *graphics system.*

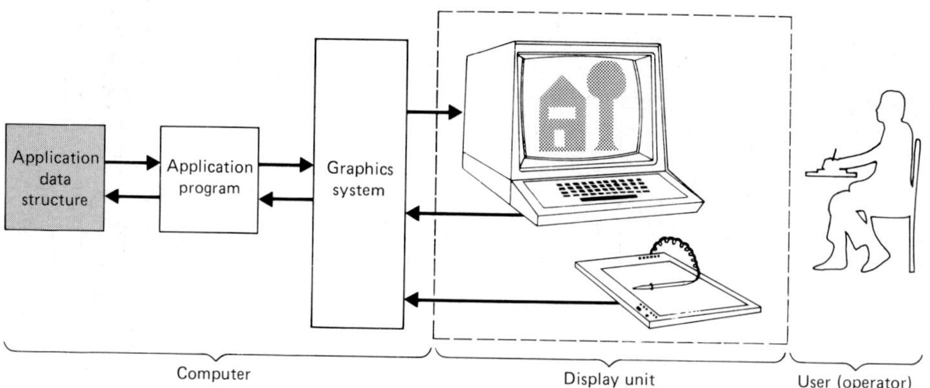

Fig. 1.13 The programmer's model of interactive graphics.

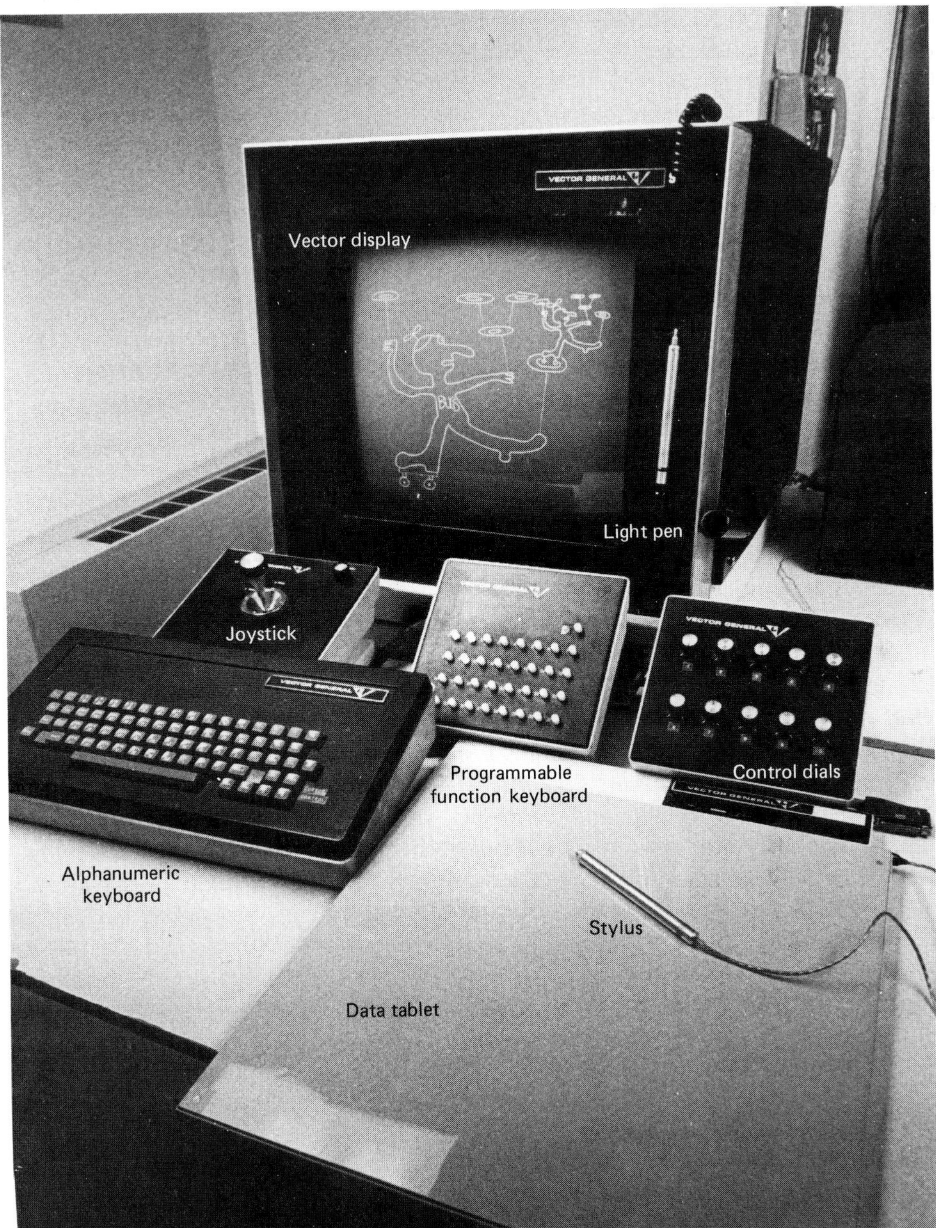

Fig. 1.14 Display console with common input devices (courtesy Dick Bulterman, Brown University).

The data structure holds descriptions of real or abstract objects whose pictures are to appear on the screen. The data structure thus stores all of the pertinent information for such "objects" as circuits, flowcharts, buildings, mathematical or statistical functions, airplane fuselages, molecules, nuclear-reactor models, and 3D landscapes and vehicles used for flight simulators.

The object's description typically contains *geometric* coordinate data that define the shape of components of the object, object *attributes* such as line style, color, or even surface texture, and *connectivity* relationships and positioning data that define how the components fit together. Often there is also nongeometric textual or numeric "property" information useful to a post-processing program and/or the interactive user. Examples of such data for computer-aided design applications include price and supplier data, thermal, mechanical, or electrical properties, and mechanical or electrical tolerances. Note that general-purpose database management systems are increasingly being used for the data structure function.

The application program describes the 2D or 3D geometry of the object whose picture is to be viewed on the view surface to the *graphics system,* which typically contains a collection of *output* plotting subroutines compatible with a high-level language such as FORTRAN or Pascal. This subroutine package drives the specific output device(s) and causes the device to display the picture, usually from the picture's display list representation in the refresh buffer that the package has just created.

The application program uses the graphics system much as it uses the input–output subsystem of the operating system to read and write records in files. The input–output subsystem maintains a file directory, organizes records on disks and tapes, and shields the application programmer from having to know the many device-dependent parameters and conditions. Similarly, the graphics system shields the application programmer from needing to know the specific low-level architecture of the display processor and the *xy* coordinate system of the physical screen.

While picture plotting is handled by the graphic system's output routines, input handling is controlled by its *input* routines that pass user-supplied input data to the application program as part of an interaction sequence. Thus the application program can also ask the graphic system to read values from (i.e., to *sample*) the control dials or locator input devices. Alternatively, the application program can put itself to sleep after having asked an input routine to wake it up when an *interrupt-generating* input device, such as a keyboard or stylus pick, is activated by the user.

With these input values, the application program can change its operating mode or state. For example, it can enter the procedure that corresponds to one of a number of possible commands listed in a "menu" on the screen, in response to the user's menu selection. In addition to executing such a change in flow of control, the program can simply alter a data value which then modifies the appearance of an object or changes an associated property.

The *output transformation* from object to picture and the *input transformation* from user action to object are treated in considerably more detail in Chapter 2 (from the application programmer's point of view) and in Chapter 4 (from the package implementer's point of view). With this preliminary understanding, however, we can now show how graphics application programs differ from "conventional" programs.

First of all, the two- and three-dimensional geometry of graphical objects represents a different type of data, one with its own rapidly evolving body of mathematics and algorithms. This is especially true in the exciting area of making realistic-looking pictures of three-dimensional objects (see Chapters 14–17). Second, interactive graphics programs are different from batch programs in that they tend to be *event-driven*; that is, they wait for the user to do something, react appropriately, and wait again. Essentially, the dialogue consists of a simple loop:

repeat
  provide a choice/pose a question;
  wait for the user to respond with one of n allowed values;
  case—branch on the answer to the appropriate procedure for that answer;
until stop {user responds with STOP}

Third, the use of a high-level device-independent graphics package makes interactive plotting and manipulation of simple graphs, charts, and drawings very straightforward, as will be shown in Chapter 2. For more complex applications, however, good graphics programming practice requires some understanding of a number of areas not always properly mastered by application programmers:

1. Construction of dialogue and interaction "languages," with proper attention to expressive power, consistency, good "human factors" of the human interface for ease and speed of interaction, and graceful and informative error handling (Chapter 6);
2. For three-dimensional graphics, the proper use of the mathematics of geometric transformation (Chapter 7) and of shape and surface description (Chapter 13);
3. For realistic pictures, hidden surface removal and the use of color, lighting, and shading models (Chapters 14–17);
4. Manipulation and display of a hierarchy of objects composed of subobjects (Chapter 9);
5. Good software engineering principles for creating a robust, extensible, and maintainable graphics program.

In general it is difficult to graft an interactive graphics interface onto an existing batch program: the style and structure of an interactive graphics application program are usually quite different from those of a batch program, and good program design therefore requires a before-the-fact, top-down analysis of all the required interaction sequences to lead to a properly structured design and implementation. In the next chapter, therefore, we skip the implementation details of graphics hardware and support software and start with graphics programming in order to teach both techniques and good (interactive) programming style by example.

EXERCISES

1.1 Make a list of applications of graphics in your organization and try to classify them in terms of the categories of Section 1.5. Can you group the applications into *equivalence classes* of applications that are essentially similar in structure?

1.2 Make a high-level user model of a typical interactive graphics application program with which you are somewhat familiar. Identify the major subsystems/modules. How vital is the graphics part; that is, could the application run almost as well if alphanumeric interaction were used? Conversely, how vital is the interactive part—would batch be almost as good?

1.3 Take a noninteractive graphics application that you are familiar with and discuss how one might improve its utility, ease of use or cost of use by making it an interactive graphics application. What would be easy to change, what would be hard, and why?

1.4 Describe applications that don't need or wouldn't be better with graphical interaction, and state why not. Try to characterize what it is about an application that makes it a good candidate for using interactive graphics.

1.5 Take your favorite application area, and try to determine to what extent interactive graphics has been used successfully in it. Use sources such as recent literature in the field, SIGGRAPH conference proceedings, and other graphics publications, as well as talks with experts in the field.

1.6 Assume that a picture containing a sequence of 500 connected 10-inch vectors is to be displayed on a refresh display. How many bytes of storage are required to store this picture for a 10×10-inch vector display that draws continuous lines between two endpoints on a 1024×1024 square grid? Assume a 12-bit "vector draw" opcode and 10 bits for each of the x and y data coordinates, i.e., 4 bytes for the opcode and (x, y) pair. Approximately how many bytes are required to store the same picture in raster bit map with the same 1024×1024 resolution? Which picture would look better and why? Which could be modified faster?

1.7 What is a reasonable resolution, in terms of the number of horizontal and vertical resolution units, for a black-and-white bit map raster display refreshed from the memory of a home microcomputer with 64 kbytes of RAM?

2 Basic Interactive Graphics Programming

2.1 MODELS, PICTURE DESCRIPTION, AND INTERACTION

The fundamental task of the designer of an interactive graphics program is to specify what classes of entities or objects are to be created and represented pictorially and how the user and the graphics program are to interact in order to create and modify objects and their pictures. In Section 1.8 we introduced the *programmer's model* of interactive graphics and its principal components, which symbolizes the output transformation from a representation of an object to its picture. In this chapter we will make the steps of these transformations more explicit by using program structures that are typical of interactive graphics applications.

As a conceptual framework, the programmer's model (Fig. 2.1) is useful in understanding how to partition the total job of transforming an abstract description of a two- or three-dimensional "world" consisting of one or more objects into a view or picture of that world. The individual steps in the transformation must be both intellectually manageable and easy to implement. In a similar vein, the interaction handling provided by the input transformation is also divided into steps in which the logical handling of the user inputs and their effects on the objects and/or pictures are distinguished.

This programmer's model is appropriate in the large majority of applications which involve some form of data structure, however rudimentary, for describing a picture. For some applications, however, the model must be modified somewhat. First, most display devices with advanced architectures of the type discussed in Chapter 10 can interpret the application data structure of Fig. 2.1 directly. Second, in certain raster graphics applications, the user operates directly on the lowest-level digital representation of an image stored in the display system as if working on ("painting") the image directly. In such a system an object and its image are identical—"what you see is what you get." Painting applications can be modeled by a re-

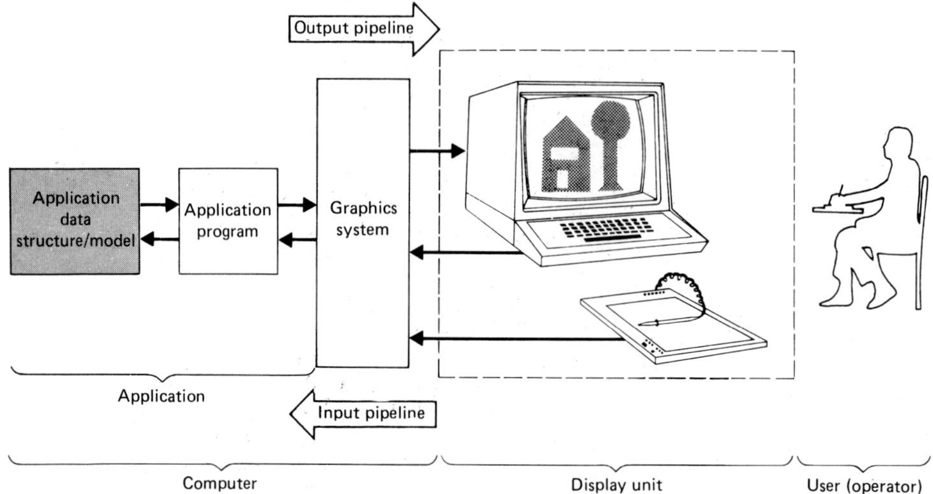

Fig. 2.1 The programmer's conceptual model of interactive graphics.

stricted version of the more general programmer's model in which the data structure component is absent or is equated to the *bit map* (discussed in Chapters 3 and 12).

We now describe the programmer's model with respect to the three major activities that take place in interactive graphics. These activities, described in more detail in Sections 2.1.1–2.1.3, are:

- *Application model construction.* The application programmer first constructs an *application model* of the objects that the user will manipulate and view. The term "application model" is not to be confused with our *conceptual* programmer's model of graphics, of which it is a part. An application model (or *model,* for short) denotes a collection of data representing objects and relationships in that data, typically stored in an application data structure. Thus the model represents the important properties of the objects relevant to a given application or set of applications. These objects can be concrete or abstract and can be visualized in a two- or three-dimensional world—for example, a mathematical function, an integrated circuit, a floor plan, a gear train, or a molecule;

- *Describing objects to the graphics system.* Having constructed an application model of the world as a set of one or more objects in an application data structure, the application programmer describes the model to the graphics system so that it can calculate and then display the particular view desired. The word *view* is used here both in the sense of a visual rendering of some geometric properties of the objects being modeled, as well as in the data-base sense of generating a two-dimensional presentation of some properties of the objects. These properties need not be *intrinsically* geometric in nature, as long as they can be visualized pictorially;

- *Interaction handling.* The application programmer makes possible an interactive user–computer dialogue via the input devices to allow the user to specify how to construct and modify objects and to indicate which views are to be displayed.

2.1.1 Application Modeling

As an example of application modeling, let's look at a simple interactive application program for designing office layouts. This program could be used by an industrial interior designer to make an application model of the inside of a typical office building for the purpose of designating what furniture is to be placed where in each office on each floor. A possible application model of this schematic two-dimensional world consists of the object "Office building" which is composed of subobjects "Floor 1" through "Floor 10" (as diagramed in Fig. 2.2). Each floor itself has a number of subobjects, typically "Offices." Each of these in turn has furniture subobjects, such as desks, chairs, bookcases, low room dividers, floor-to-ceiling partitions, and plants. This particular breakdown is, of course, arbitrary—many others would do as well.

A particular view of an office (sub)object in this hierarchical two-dimensional world is the conventional floor plan representation that uses two-dimensional furniture *symbols*, also known as icons or glyphs (Fig. 2.3). For our purposes, we will consider that the outline of each office, including windows and doors, is contained in a data structure predetermined by the architect. The decorator starts with this data structure and adds to it the furniture subobjects. Another, even simpler view of the model/world might consist of an entire office floor with each office shown to scale but with the furniture contents listed merely as character strings and not as graphical symbols. Note that neither of these types of high-level symbolic views resembles the detailed and realistic three-dimensional views of the building that architects and contractors would use in addition to floor plans.

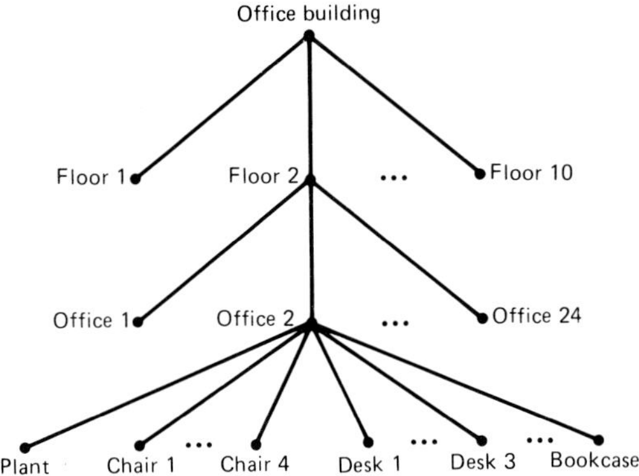

Fig. 2.2 The office building as a 3-level object.

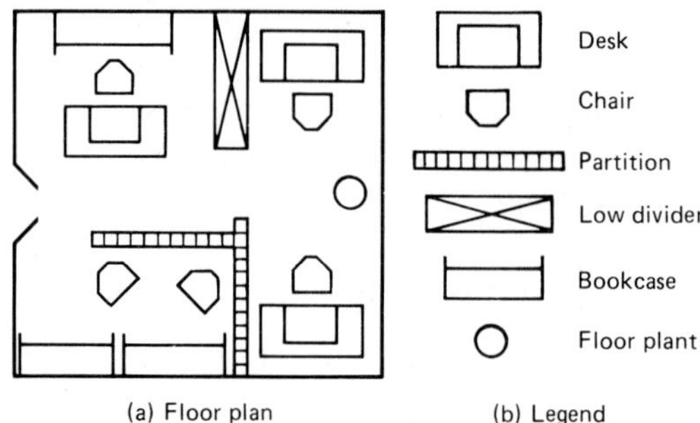

Fig. 2.3 A view of an office (its floor plan).

What specifically would be stored in the data structure for this application? The decorator must have available the geometry, i.e., the exact dimensions of each office and each piece of furniture and the exact layout of the two-dimensional symbolic shapes on the floor plans. Note that for this particular application the detailed three-dimensional description of the real furniture is not needed. In addition, the model might contain the manufacturer of each piece of furniture, the corresponding catalog data (catalog number, cost and other accounting information, materials and colors, delivery time, and the like), special requirements of future occupants of each office, etc. The point is that the data structure contains many nongeometric properties of objects that have no direct bearing on the visual representation of these objects. This nongeometric data is used by postprocessing application programs to do such tasks as cost estimation, producing order forms and inventory listings, and billing. It can also be used to guide the decorator in making room layout decisions under such expected constraints as color coordination, cost and delivery date. Some of this textual material, such as a color code or price, could be superposed on the symbolic layout to aid in quick visualization of alternatives. Thus the graphics visualization that produces floor plans is one of many processes that may operate on the shared data structure.

Having to store these various types of application-dependent data often results in a rather complex, interlinked data base. This data may be encoded, for example, in FORTRAN arrays, in a Pascal tree structure of records, or in a relational data base. We are not concerned here with methods of storing, retrieving, or manipulating these data structures, since these subjects are not strictly part of computer graphics, but we note in passing that general-purpose data-base management systems are increasingly being used for storing and retrieving graphics application data.

Models may be built by the application programmer in three ways: in batch mode, as output from a previous computation (graph plotting; cf. Section 2.6), or, of most interest to us, as a result of a step-by-step construction process guided by a user interacting with the application program to specify choices of components and geometric and nongeometric data (see Section 2.16 below). Particularly in this last case, the application program may make use of a special *modeling system* to construct and manipulate the model before describing it to the graphics system. Such modeling systems are treated in Chapter 9, where modeling is discussed in detail, including the important case of modeling object–subobject hierarchies such as those illustrated by the office building example briefly discussed here.

2.1.2 Describing Objects to the Graphics System

Whether a model is constructed interactively or as the output of another (batch) program, the user typically wishes to see a visual presentation or picture of some aspect(s) of the model. The application program must describe to the graphics system in geometric terms that portion of the world of which the user wishes a picture. The term *picture* is used here loosely and interchangeably with *view* and *image* to denote both traditional two- and three-dimensional geometric representations on the one hand and textual representations on the other. Regardless of whether or not the contents of the data structure are intrinsically geometric, they must be described to the graphics system as *graphic output primitives* such as points, lines, polygons, or character strings geometrically oriented in a two- or three-dimensional world. The application program must also specify to the graphics system what part of the object, seen from what vantage point, is to be displayed, and on what part of the *view surface* (i.e., the display medium, such as plotter paper or CRT screen) the image should appear.

Why are objects described to the graphics system in terms of low-level graphic output primitives? Rather than forcing the use of a "standard" data structure which could be inefficient or too confining for a given application, we prefer to be free to construct models of objects in a way appropriate to the application. Therefore, our general-purpose graphics system cannot be based on any particular "standard" data structure organization and we must describe the application-dependent model to it in terms of application-independent *universal* graphic primitives. These low-level primitives will typically be extracted or derived by the application program from the higher-level (possibly hierarchical) application-dependent model.

A useful paradigm that is especially natural for three-dimensional graphics representations is to consider the graphics system as a "synthetic camera." The application program provides the synthetic camera with a description of a scene consisting of one or more objects in a synthetic or imaginary world, either two- or three-dimensional. The synthetic camera then produces a view of the object(s) in that world; the exact view depends, of course, on how the camera has been set up and where it is located relative to the object(s) and the world. As with a Polaroid camera, the resulting snapshot is developed and is available nearly instantaneously for display on the view surface. The view surface may be thought of as a bulletin board and, as we will see, the snapshot (the image that is a particular view of one or more objects) may be of variable size, to cover the entire bulletin board or only some piece of it. The synthetic camera has a distinct advantage over normal cameras in that it can have the entire three-dimensional world in focus and can be directed to produce not only perspective but also orthographic and other projections of the same object (see Chapter 8).

The lack of modeling and structuring information in the graphics package means that the synthetic camera acts like a real camera: it can take a snapshot of the scene only in terms of its lowest-level visual elements and knows nothing about its organization or structure. The high-performance displays discussed in Chapter 10 are an exception to this rule: they have a facility for accessing a particular form of object hierarchy directly during the refresh cycle. In this special case, the synthetic camera/graphics package deals with object hierarchies as well as with primitives.

2.1.3 Interaction Handling

In the process of modifying or extending one or more partially completed objects on the screen* and altering their appearance, an interactive user is typically presented with a view of these objects. In a simple case, the user may merely specify how to reposition the synthetic camera to take a different view of the same object or how to change some nonviewable attributes of the object. Regardless of the user's intentions, input devices must be used to communicate these intentions to the application program. The application program decodes this user-supplied input and uses it either to direct the graphics system to change the viewing specification ("changing the settings on the synthetic camera") or to alter the model in the data structure.

Once the application program has modified the data structure, it directs the graphics system to produce an updated picture of the object on the screen (unless only a nonviewable attribute was changed). The user may also cause the image on the screen to be moved (analogous to moving the snapshot on the bulletin board).† Again, he can do this only by having the application program handle the input request and then signal the graphics system to execute the associated action. It is the interactive dialogue of output→input→output . . . between the user and the application program that lies at the heart of interactive graphics and forms the focus of this book. This sequential "ping-pong" model of user–computer interaction is in principle not difficult to implement. Furthermore, some modern graphics systems allow the use of a variety of input tools (sometimes even sound input and output) in parallel as well as simultaneous input and output, to approach more closely the multiple simultaneous communication modalities of human–human interaction. Formalisms (not to mention programming languages) for such "free-form conversation" are still the subject of research, and we will not concern ourselves with them in this text.

In summary, it is the application program's job to model and to interpret user input. The graphics system has no responsibility for building or modifying the model either initially or in response to user interaction; as a synthetic camera, it only

*We use the term *screen* as a shorthand for the more general term *view surface* that includes display screens, plotter or printer paper, microfilm, etc.

†In Chapter 8 we will see that the snapshot can also be rotated and even enlarged or shrunk.

makes pictures. Next we examine the facilities of the graphics system software that implements the synthetic camera.

2.2 INTRODUCTION TO THE SIMPLE GRAPHICS PACKAGE*

We now introduce the principal concepts of interactive graphics programming with examples using a simple, general-purpose graphics subroutine package. We have chosen to describe graphics programming in a high-level, machine- and display-device-independent language rather than at the level of the instruction set of the particular display unit. This allows us to present generally applicable concepts without getting bogged down in the idiosyncrasies of particular display processors. The *Simple Graphics Package* (SGP) we describe is similar to many existing subroutine packages (for example, [GSPC79]); it provides the application program with basic facilities such as line-drawing plotters and interactive displays for driving graphics hardware. Because SGP makes the application program independent of the specific hardware devices available, it can be used with different graphic configurations with minimal changes. Such a device-independent subroutine package thus provides program *portability* as well as a convenient, high-level interface to a given display device. The rationale for using such a graphics package parallels that for using high-level languages as opposed to assembly-level languages—in most situations today, programmer efficiency is more important than program efficiency. A device-dependent package that takes advantage of all the power of a special-purpose display system need be used only for applications (such as flight simulation) emphasizing the maximum run-time dynamics. We therefore use SGP in this text because it is representative of packages (including such adaptations of the Core as the proposed ISO standard GKS [ENCA80]) that support the type of medium-performance displays we expect to be prevalent in the near future.

SGP consists of a small but functionally complete set of application-independent facilities for creating arbitrary views of two-dimensional objects and for supporting interaction between the application program and its user. Higher-level graphic utility subroutine packages that use SGP subroutines are easily developed for specific application areas such as data plotting, computer-aided design, and cartography.

In this chapter we shall progress in small conceptual stages from the simple to the more complex, illustrating SGP features and graphics programming techniques by using them in a series of graduated examples. Each stage has a section that begins with a brief description of the problem to be solved by the program example(s) in that section. The accompanying figures illustrate the graphic result of the programming example. The expository progression begins in Section 2.3 with an explanation of the basic functions required for defining two-dimensional graphs of points and lines. Sections 2.4 through 2.7 cover techniques for producing drawings, while Sec-

*The remainder of this chapter is derived from [BERG78].

tion 2.8 covers character strings and Section 2.9 is a brief summary of output-only plotting. Section 2.10 then introduces basic interaction techniques and facilities (discussed further in the remaining sections) in the context of a simple but relatively complete application program. We restrict ourselves in this chapter to two-dimensional line drawing and interaction handling because they illustrate most of the problems and techniques of interactive graphics without the extra complication of three-dimensional viewing, hidden-surface removal, raster bit-map manipulations, etc. In fact, a large portion of graphic applications can be handled rather nicely with the set of facilities provided by SGP.

The programming examples, written in the Pascal programming language, are meant to encourage good programming style as well as to show typical interactive graphics program structures. Pascal was chosen as the base language because its rich set of control structures allows convenient, straightforward representation of the programming examples [JENS74]. Transforming these control structures to equivalent code in languages such as FORTRAN or BASIC is not difficult. Reserved words in the language are shown in boldface, procedure names are shown in upper-case italics, and other programmer-defined identifiers appear in lower-case italics. To make programs appear as simple as possible, some liberties have been taken with standard Pascal: global variables, symbolic constants and housekeeping routines are not declared, arrays are passed as parameters, not as types, and some pseudocode is used.

2.3 GRAPH PLOTTING

2.3.1 World Coordinates

Computer graphics is often used to display a simple relationship among variables as a two-dimensional graph. Such a graph typically has two axes and various character *markers,* such as dots or **x**'s, connected by lines. The markers are located at points relative to the origin of the graph specified by the values of the data that they represent. Figure 2.4 shows such a graph with a descriptive title included as part of the picture.* Using our prior terminology, we can say that there are two distinct entities to consider: the object and its picture. The object here is the graph, that is, the abstract relationship between the two variables; the picture is the geometric representation of the relationship produced by SGP as a *specific* view of that object. (Multiple views of the same object data are shown as separate graphs in Fig. 2.10.) We describe objects to SGP; it draws views of them according to our viewing specification.

To produce the graph shown in Fig. 2.4, the application program must describe the various *output primitives* such as points, lines, and character strings to SGP in

*The square border in Fig. 2.4 represents the boundary of the view surface on which the picture is displayed; it is *not* part of the picture itself. This border is present only on those figures that show visual output as it might appear on a screen.

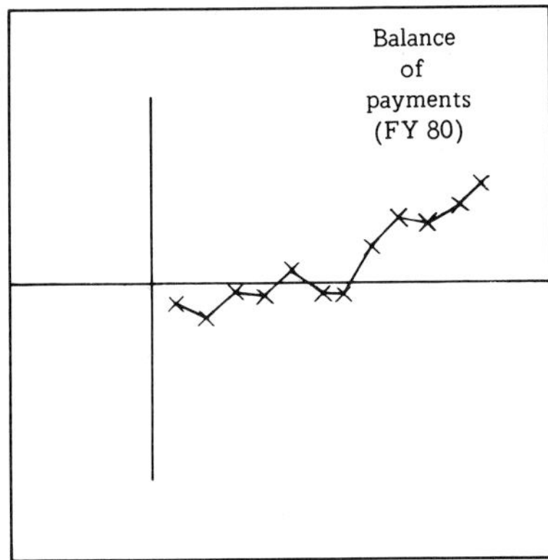

Fig. 2.4 Typical graph values represented by **x**'s connected by lines.

terms of positions and measurements in a cartesian coordinate system. These coordinates are inherently dimensionless, and thus the application program can define objects in terms of units that are natural to the application and to the user. For example, an acoustical engineer might want a plot of sound level in decibels against time in seconds, while a businessman might be interested in net profit in dollars plotted against thousands of widgets produced. These application- or user-oriented coordinates are naturally called *user coordinates.* Alternatively, since they help define objects in the user's 2D or 3D world, we refer to them as *world coordinates.* Objects must therefore be defined in the *world coordinate system* (or *world coordinate space*) both to store them in the application model and to describe them to SGP. For maximum flexibility we will use floating-point representation for world coordinates.

After objects have been described to SGP in terms of their component output primitives, SGP creates an image of objects on a screen by mapping the device-independent world coordinates to the device-dependent coordinates used by the hardware of the display device. In the rest of Section 2.3, we show how objects can be described to SGP in world coordinate output primitives which SGP then maps to the screen using the *WINDOW* specification discussed in Section 2.4.

2.3.2 Lines and Points

Many graphic devices construct a visible picture by moving a drawing mechanism or stylus (a CRT beam or plotter pen, for example) on the surface of the display device (the screen). After each graphic element is drawn, the so-called *current pen position* is updated—it corresponds to the current location of the drawing mechanism on the view surface, in *device coordinate space.* SGP has an analogous construct called the *current position* (CP); it takes on values corresponding to the current location of an imaginary stylus in *world coordinate space.* Each output primitive affects the value of the CP in a well-defined way. In other words, the application program takes geometric data from the data structure and traces the outline of the resulting object by specifying the location of each point and character and the beginning and end of each line, in terms of the world coordinate CP.

As an analogy to this definition process, think of digitizing an imaginary wire-frame object in world coordinate space by moving a stylus over each line and pushing a *digitize* button for each line's endpoint, as the CP is moved from endpoint to endpoint. The primary purpose of specifying primitives implicitly in terms of the CP is to reduce the number of arguments required for each of the output primitive procedure calls; one need not specify explicitly the starting point on each call to a line or character string primitive since it is determined by the result of the previous call.

To set the CP in world coordinate space without defining an output primitive, a procedure invocation such as the following can be used:

MOVE_ABS_2(10.0, 10.0)

The modifier *ABS* designates an absolute move of the CP, in contrast to the *REL*ative move considered below. The modifier 2 designates that this is a 2D primitive. To define a line from the CP (the *from* endpoint) to the *to* endpoint with cartesian (*x, y*) coordinates (12.0, 3.5), the application program would use the following procedure call:

LINE_ABS_2(12.0, 3.5)

If this *LINE** call were specified after the previous *MOVE,* a line would be defined from (10.0, 10.0) to (12.0, 3.5). Following a *LINE* invocation, the CP is set to the *to* endpoint of the line just drawn. Consequently, a *MOVE* followed by a series of *LINE* calls produces a sequence of connected lines. A series of disconnected lines is defined by interspersing *MOVE*s with successive invocations of *LINE.* The axes shown in Fig. 2.5 could be defined by the following primitive commands:

```
MOVE_ABS_2(-15.0, 0.0);
LINE_ABS_2(15.0, 0.0);          {defines x-axis}
MOVE_ABS_2(0.0, -6.0);
LINE_ABS_2(0.0, 6.0)            {defines y-axis}
```

The axes are shown here without conventional marker characters such as "•" or "**x**" for simplicity, although good practice usually demands such aids; character plotting is discussed in Section 2.8. Note also that we have shown world coordinate (*x, y*) values near endpoints of lines for expository purposes only; no text or annotation for the axis lines is defined by the above SGP invocations. Finally, Fig. 2.5 is

*As will be seen later, there are four specific procedures used to create lines. When we wish to refer to the general class of these line procedures, we write *LINE*, rather than *LINE_ABS_2*, etc. This convention is also used for *MOVE* and *POINT*.

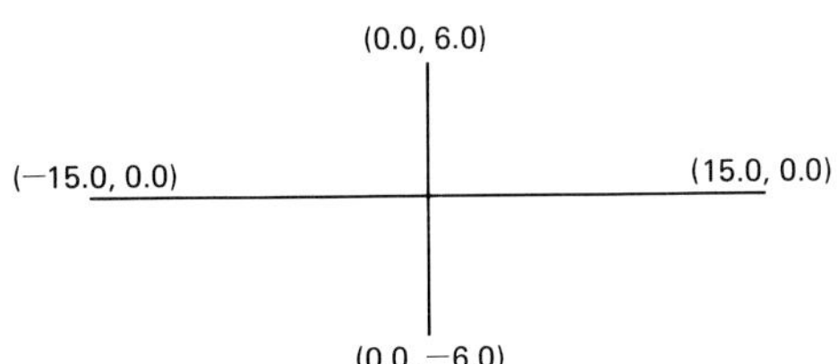

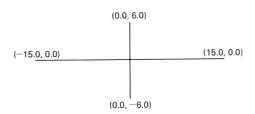

Fig. 2.5 Simple axes drawn by *MOVEs* and *LINEs*.

the symbolic representation of a simple abstract object in a 2D world coordinate system, not (yet) a drawing produced as a specific view of that object by SGP!

To move the CP and then define a distinct point (symbolized, say, by the predefined special marker ".") at the new CP, an invocation such as the following can be used:

```
POINT_ABS_2(12.0, 3.5)
```

The coordinates shown so far are called *absolute coordinates* because they specify absolute positions in world coordinate space. Points or the two endpoints of lines may also be specified in terms of a displacement in world coordinates from the current position. These displacement values are called *relative coordinates* and can be specified by invoking the SGP procedures *MOVE_REL_2*, *LINE_REL_2*, and *POINT_REL_2*. Relative coordinates are convenient, for example, for such objects as bar graphs or histograms in which one or both coordinates vary by a constant amount. The procedure below uses relative coordinates to define axes of specified size, centered at the point (*x0*, *y0*).

```
procedure AXES(x0, y0, delta_x, delta_y);
  {define lines from x0 - delta_x to x0 + delta_x and from y0 - delta_y to y0 + delta_y.
    Resultant object is a pair of axes centered about world coordinates (x0, y0).}
begin
  MOVE_ABS_2(x0 - delta_x, y0);            {leftmost part of x axis}
  LINE_REL_2(2 * delta_x, 0.0);            {define x axis}
  MOVE_REL_2(-delta_x, -delta_y);          {bottommost part of y axis}
  LINE_REL_2(0.0, 2 * delta_y);            {define y axis}
end
```

Figure 2.5 could then be specified by the procedure invocation shown below which specifies the axes' origin to be the world coordinate origin (0.0, 0.0):

```
AXES(0.0, 0.0, 15.0, 6.0)
```

The procedure invocation

```
AXES(5.0, 10.0, 15.0, 6.0)
```

would position the axes' origin at (5.0, 10.0).

2.4 WINDOWS AND CLIPPING

Graph plotting is an example of how SGP procedures may be used to define and plot objects illustrating mathematical or abstract relationships between variables. The objects, i.e., the graphs, are specified in the programmer's world coordinate system, and SGP must then convert world coordinates into the appropriate coordinates of the physical display device. To make this conversion, SGP must know what portion of the essentially unbounded (floating-point) world coordinate space contains the information the programmer wants to be displayed at this time. This rectangular region in the world coordinate system is called a *window.** The application program defines a window by invoking the SGP procedure *WINDOW,* whose arguments define the low and high limits of the window along each world coordinate axis. The generic format of a window specification is

WINDOW(min_x, max_x, min_y, max_y)

SGP uses this window specification to construct a mapping that causes the image of the window boundaries to coincide with the edges of the screen.† Furthermore, the programmer can make SGP display only that portion of an object which is "in view" by surrounding the desired part with an appropriate window. Any part of the object not in view inside the window is made invisible by SGP through a process known as *clipping*: any primitive lying wholly outside the window boundary is not mapped to the screen, and any primitive lying partially inside and partially outside is cut off (*scissored*) at the window edge before being mapped. If coordinates outside the specified window were not clipped, the results would not be well-defined. Indeed, the image displayed would vary from device to device because different physical devices behave differently when provided with coordinates outside their normal range—most systems will produce pictures with incorrectly drawn primitives due to overflow of internal coordinate registers. This effect is known as *wraparound*, an example of which is shown in Fig. 2.6.

Each output primitive defined by the application program is tested to see whether it is entirely inside the window (and thus should be displayed), intersects the window (and thus should be clipped so that only its visible parts are displayed), or lies entirely outside the window (and thus should not be displayed). The pieces that remain after testing and clipping are mapped to the screen. By adjusting the size of

*This standard graphics definition of *window* unfortunately conflicts with another use of the term found in the documentation of several screen-oriented text editors and raster graphics systems. There it designates an area on the screen (as in Section 1.6 on the Alto "window manager"). We will use the standard graphics term *viewport* for screen areas, as discussed in Section 2.7.

†As we shall see in Section 2.7, the window need not actually map to the entire screen; it may instead map to a viewport that covers only a subset of the screen. Because the default viewport for a square view surface is the entire view surface, the discussion and examples that follow apply to this common default.

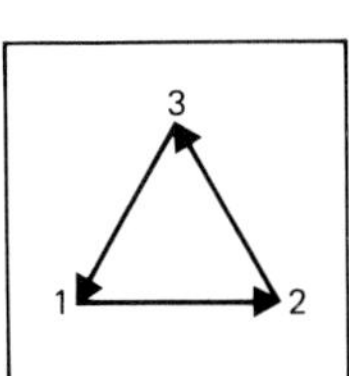

(a) Triangle in center of screen. Arrows show drawing order of relative lines: endpoint sequence is 1 → 2 → 3 → 1.

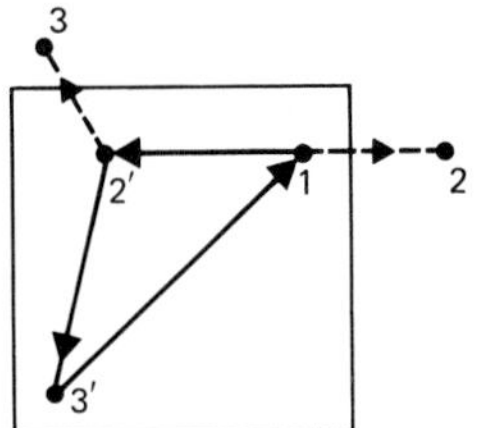

(b) Another sequence, with overflow in x and then y causing wraparound: 1 → 2, overflows to 2', 2' → 3, overflows to 3', 3' → 1.

Fig. 2.6 Effect of wraparound with analog vector generator.

the window relative to the size of the objects being displayed, arbitrary scaling effects can be produced, as shown in Fig. 2.7.

The application program can generate the largest possible picture of an entire scene by defining a window that just surrounds the set of all objects in the scene (Fig. 2.7(a)). A window larger than the scene also produces a picture of the entire scene, but the picture is smaller and has more blank space on the sides of the screen (Fig. 2.7(b)). Specifying a window smaller than the scene forces clipping and allows the application program to display a part of the entire scene to a scale larger than that of the previous cases (Fig. 2.7(c)). Thus by moving the window and selecting smaller or larger window sizes we can create the cinematic effects of *panning* and *zooming* in or out. In principle one can zoom in on a single primitive until it touches the boundaries, or zoom out until the entire scene blurs together as a single spot.

Note that in Fig. 2.7, as with the graphing example, we chose a normal two-dimensional illustration to show an easily visualized representation of both the objects and the window in the model's world coordinate system. In reality, object descriptions are stored in a structured collection of coordinate data in the model data structure, in some as-yet-unspecified way, and they have no visible representation until the application program describes them to SGP so that it can draw a view of the world. The remainder of this chapter discusses how the data structure is accessed and modified. Also, in Fig. 2.7 arbitrary scales were used for both world and screen coordinate systems, and thus at this point we can reach only qualitative conclusions about the effects of window size on the relative sizes of the resulting pictures. Clearly, the magnification is inversely proportional to the window size. The simple ratios for determining the degree of magnification are given in Section 4.2.2.

In summary, in order to obtain a picture that contains images of only those pieces of objects within a rectangular region in application-dependent world coordinate space, the application program first specifies a window to SGP to define the re-

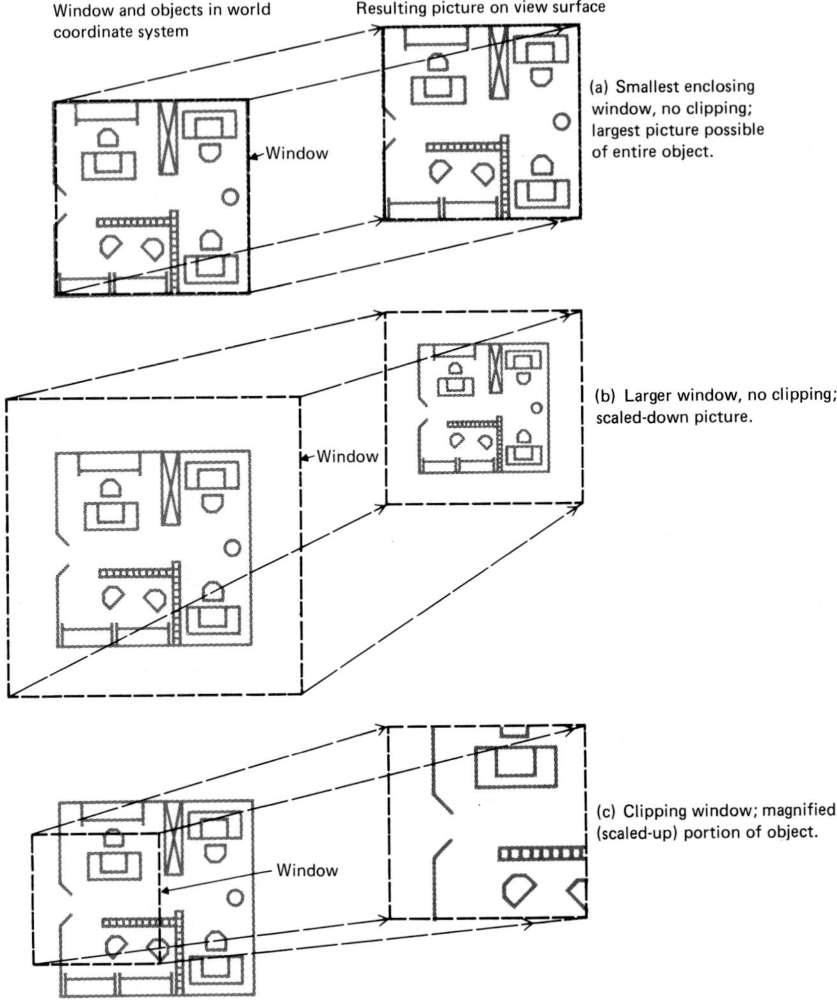
Window and objects in world coordinate system
Resulting picture on view surface
Window
(a) Smallest enclosing window, no clipping; largest picture possible of entire object.
Window
(b) Larger window, no clipping; scaled-down picture.
Window
(c) Clipping window; magnified (scaled-up) portion of object.

Fig. 2.7 Mapping window contents to view surface; clipping as needed. Dashed lines map corresponding corners of window and view surface.

gion for clipping and mapping to the view surface. Then the application program describes the objects in the world coordinate space to SGP in terms of graphic primitive function invocations such as *MOVE, POINT,* and *LINE.* Even if no clipping is intended, the programmer should use *WINDOW* to define the extent of his world coordinate system, so that SGP can perform the appropriate mapping from world coordinate to screen coordinates. A default window of 0.0 to 1.0 in x and y is otherwise assumed.

2.5 SEGMENTATION

After a picture of an object has been drawn, the user can interact with the object to modify the data structure (as described in Section 2.10). After making such changes the operator typically wishes to see an updated view of the modified object(s). For example, the operator who has deleted a data point in a function or a chair in an office layout probably wants to see the corresponding revised graph or floor plan. One approach to providing this new view could be to have the application program simply redescribe the entire altered object to SGP, even though only a part had changed. This brute-force approach would be very wasteful, however, because of the expense of the computations involved in clipping and mapping world coordinates to device-dependent coordinates (see Chapter 4). Naturally, we prefer to have the user's selective modification of the data structure result in only a correspondingly selective modification of the picture.

The concept of selective modification arises, of course, in nongraphics programs and data structures as well. For example, the standard way to avoid recompiling an entire program when a small piece is changed is to partition the program into separately compiled modules. These may be individually recompiled and linked in and out of the executable code sequence at load time (or even run time) for easy and fast selective updating of the program.

We can apply the same fundamental principle to our problem of selective data structure updating by partitioning the object description into segments that are individually displayed. These output *segments* are logically related collections of output primitives that are to be replaced as a whole. SGP can be told to delete an entire segment selectively or to add a segment containing a new piece of an object to the current display—when doing such operations, SGP need not reprocess the unchanged part of the scene. Segments are especially useful and efficient for dynamic graphics on refresh vector displays, as will be shown in Chapter 4.

What are the rules for applying segmentation? It is up to the application programmer to design the application program so that it can create segments that are natural for the user. For example, segments could contain single data points of a graph of points if the points are to be individually alterable, or the lowest-level subobjects (such as furniture in the office building model) if they are to be movable. Typically, each lowest-level "atomic" object of an object hierarchy is defined in its own segment.

The application program thus describes an object to SGP by creating one or more uniquely named segments. For each successive segment SGP generates the output primitives described, and then closes the segment when the application programmer specifies *CLOSE_SEGMENT*. That is, for each segment, the application program performs the sequence:

CREATE_SEGMENT(*segment_name*);

. . .

<calls to *MOVE*, *LINE*, etc.>

. . .

CLOSE_SEGMENT

The logic used here is loosely comparable to that of opening, writing to, and closing disk files. After the *CREATE_SEGMENT* call is executed, the current segment is considered the *open* segment and must be closed before *CREATE_SEGMENT* can be invoked again. (Unlike the case of disk files, only a single open segment may exist at any given time.) The first call to *CREATE_SEGMENT* after initialization sets the CP to the origin of the world coordinate space. Since the CP is a global SGP system variable, it is affected consecutively by each primitive in each segment.

Deletion of segments and the use of multiple segments are illustrated in later sections. For example, again unlike the case of disk files, previously created SGP segments may not be reopened and modified. As we shall see later in this chapter, the programmer must instead delete and recreate the segment. (The reasons for not allowing segment editing are based on difficulty and expense of providing device-independent means for segment editing, as discussed briefly in Chapter 9.) Accordingly, the call is named *CREATE_SEGMENT,* not *OPEN_SEGMENT.* At this point, it is sufficient to remember that all output primitives are placed in the current, open segment.

Segment names are chosen to be integers in SGP for several reasons. First, they are normally used only by the application program and are not assigned or manipulated by the user. Therefore they don't need to have the more general form of (external) character strings which, since they must be converted to internal form, are inefficient in both space and time. Second, as we shall see in Section 2.11, integer names are often convenient in that they allow mapping between data structure addresses of (sub)objects and their corresponding segments.

2.6 A SIMPLE GRAPH

Example 2.1 Suppose that for each of the months between October 1980 and September 1981 (i.e., fiscal year 1980), we have available the U.S. balance of payments figures (in billions of dollars) and that we want to plot balance of payments versus time (measured in months). We will define a procedure *PLOT_DATA* that will take three parameters: two arrays (x and y) and their dimension (n). We will pass the x coordinates in the array *months*[1..12] beginning with October 1980.* Thus, October is represented as *months*[1] := 1.0, November as *months*[2] := 2.0, etc. Suppose further that we will store each monthly balance of payment surplus/loss for the fiscal year in the array *bop_1980*[1..12]. The array's values are known to be floating-point numbers, say, in the range −5.0 to +5.0. A simple graphical representation,

*Although this explicit storage of values of the months seems unnecessary, it allows us to use *PLOT_DATA* as a somewhat general-purpose plotting routine which takes two data arrays (of size 100 in this case) as input parameters. In standard Pascal the array types passed would also have to be of size 100, requiring copying of the actual arrays. The parameter n is used to loop through the part of the array containing valid data.

such as Fig. 2.8, of these (fictional!) data could be produced by the following program segment:

```
begin
  WINDOW(-5.0, 15.0, -10.0, 10.0);          {window is 20 by 20}
  CREATE_SEGMENT(1);
    PLOT_DATA(months, bop_1980, 12);        {generate plot}
  CLOSE_SEGMENT
end
```

where *PLOT_DATA* is a plotting procedure defined as follows:

```
procedure PLOT_DATA(x,y: array[1..100] of real,     {maximum array}
                    n: integer);                    {actual number of values}
{this procedure defines a plot of the n data points whose coordinates are contained in
  the arrays x and y}
var
    i: integer;
begin
  {define axes using procedure from page 39, then lines}
  AXES(0.0, 0.0, 15.0, 6.0);
  MOVE_ABS_2(x[1], y[1]);
  for i := 2 to n do
    LINE_ABS_2(x[i], y[i])
end;     {procedure PLOT_DATA}
```

Note that with this particular window specification the *x* axis has been clipped but not the data.

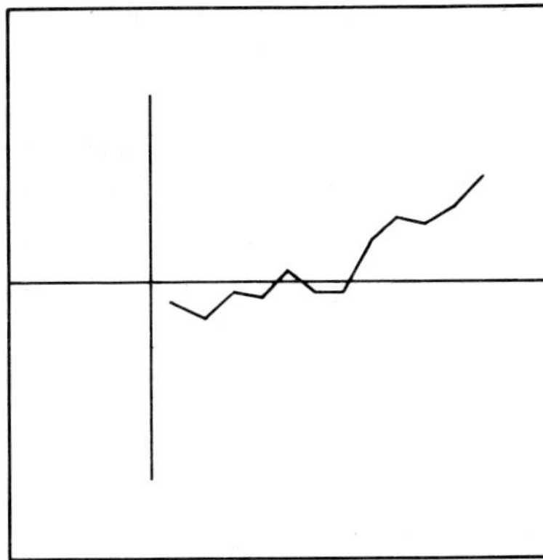

Fig. 2.8 Simple data plot of balance of payments versus month.

2.7 VIEWPORTS

A *viewport* is a rectangular portion of the screen onto which the window and therefore the window contents are mapped. In previous examples, the viewport had the default value of a square on the screen. It is often desirable, however, to map a window onto some portion of the screen that does not correspond to the default viewport. Figure 2.9 shows the general case of window-to-viewport mapping, including clipping. The clipping and window-to-viewport mapping processes are called the *viewing operation,* and their implementation is discussed in Chapter 4.

The application program can specify the viewport by means of the SGP *VIEWPORT_2* procedure. As with the *WINDOW* specification, exactly one current viewport can be in effect. The *VIEWPORT_2* call has the format:

VIEWPORT_2(min_x, max_x, min_y, max_y)

Because the viewport specification should be independent of the particular device used to display the picture, it is necessary to define a logical coordinate system that represents the screen in a device-independent manner. We can think of such a coordinate system as describing the view surface of a logical output device whose *normalized device coordinates* (NDCs) are real numbers in the range from 0 to 1 in both x and y, with the origin in the bottom left corner of the view surface. Thus in SGP all devices contain a unit square screen area, which is normally the largest square area they can contain. For nonsquare physical view surfaces this means that not all of the view surface is accessible to the SGP programmer; the inaccessible portion may be used by SGP for system and error messages, input device simulation, etc., as discussed in Chapter 4.* Since window corners map to their corresponding

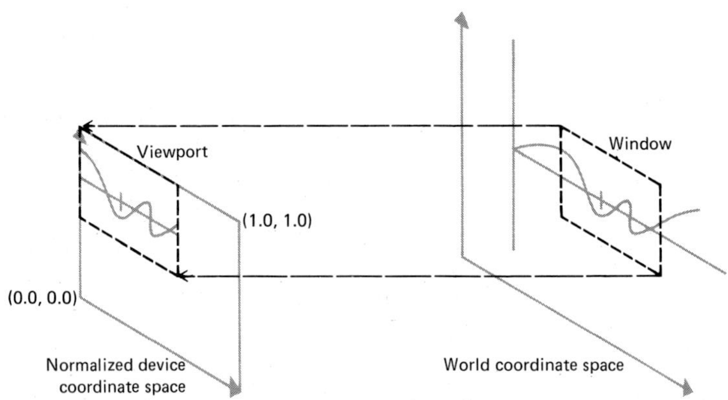

Fig. 2.9 Mapping of window (world coordinates) to viewport (normalized device coordinates) including clipping.

*This restriction could be relaxed in a device-dependent manner to allow the use of a nonsquare NDC space for nonsquare devices.

viewport corners, the world coordinate origin at the center of the world coordinate space in general will not map to the screen origin at the bottom left of the normalized display coordinate (NDC) space.

The *VIEWPORT_2* procedure is used to define a viewport as a portion of the 2D NDC space specified by the x and y values of the corners. (In Chapter 8 we will see the utility of a 3D NDC space and the *VIEWPORT_3* procedure.) For example, suppose we wish to divide the screen into four quadrants and draw a different graph in each quadrant. We can do this by designating four consecutive window-viewport pairs, each followed by its associated graphical data. Thus the statement below defines a viewport in the upper left quadrant of the screen:

VIEWPORT_2(0.0, 0.5, 0.5, 1.0)

If this call were placed immediately after the *WINDOW* call in Example 2.1 of Section 2.6, the clipped graph shown in Fig. 2.10(a) would be displayed. The plot in Fig. 2.10(b) could then be produced by changing the viewport specification to each of the remaining quadrants in turn, accessing three additional sets of data, and generating a separate segment for each one using the *PLOT_DATA* procedure.

Note that the windows and viewports used to generate the plots in Figs. 2.9 and 2.10 are both square. It is also possible for the window and/or viewport to be nonsquare rectangles. If the window and viewport *aspect ratios* do not correspond, i.e., if the ratio of the sides of the window does not equal the ratio of the sides of the viewport, the mapping of world coordinates to normalized device coordinates produces a differentially scaled image—one whose shape in one axis is compressed relative to its shape in the other. For example, note that the graphs in Fig. 2.11 (comparing balance of payments graphs for two successive fiscal years) are compressed in y

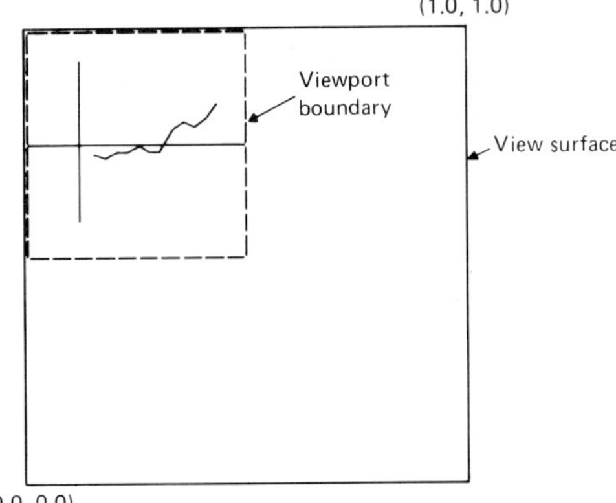

Fig. 2.10(a) Viewport in upper left quadrant of view surface.

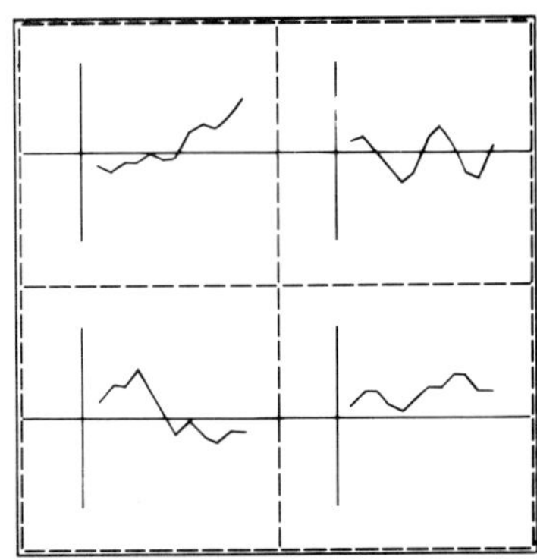

Fig. 2.10(b) Four segments in four viewports.

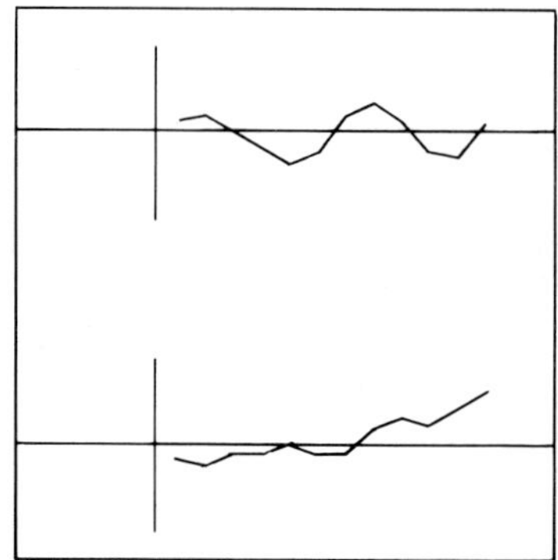

Fig. 2.11 Window and viewport with different aspect ratios.

and stretched in x compared to those of Fig. 2.10. The differential scalings produced by the window-to-viewport mapping can be used to de-emphasize unimportant differences by compressing the data presented on one axis or to bring out details by magnifying an axis.

Note in the program below (which produces Fig. 2.11) that the single window specification is applied to both segments 1 and 2; it will continue in effect until a new window specification is given. The only change is in the viewport specification. It is important for the correct use of the window/viewport mechanism to realize that a change in either specification does not automatically cause a new view to be generated (any more than changing the settings of a camera causes a new picture to be taken). To produce each new picture, the application program must run through the appropriate (part of the) model and (re)describe it to SGP; SGP will then produce a snapshot according to the latest window/viewport *viewing specification*. Thus for each graph in Fig. 2.11 a separate pass through the *PLOT_DATA* model was necessary:

```
begin
  WINDOW(-5.0, 15.0, -10.0, 10.0);   {square window}
  VIEWPORT_2(0.0, 1.0, 0.5, 1.0);    {rectangular top half}
  CREATE_SEGMENT(1);
    PLOT_DATA(months, bop_1980, 12);
  CLOSE_SEGMENT;

  VIEWPORT_2(0.0, 1.0, 0.0, 0.5);    {rectangular bottom half}
  CREATE_SEGMENT(2);
    PLOT_DATA(months, bop_1981, 12);
  CLOSE_SEGMENT
end
```

2.8 CHARACTER STRINGS

In most applications we need to display not only lines but also text, i.e., strings of characters. Text can be essential both to annotate diagrams and to communicate with the user. The application program specifies text by invoking the SGP procedure *TEXT*. Because the first character of the string is positioned with its lower left corner at the CP, invocation of *TEXT* is normally preceded by a *MOVE*.* For example, the statements below specify that the string 'ENTER DATA' is to begin at the world coordinate position (0.0, 0.7):

```
MOVE_ABS_2(0.0, 0.7);
TEXT('ENTER DATA')
```

The SGP programmer cannot control the actual size and spacing of the character strings. This limitation in SGP occurs because SGP is designed for efficiency to invoke, whenever possible, a hardware character generator to generate the character strings appropriate to each specific display (see Chapter 3). Many commonly used commercial packages make provisions not only for whatever hardware character generator exists, but also for the specification of character size, spacing and other text parameters. These facilities in the Core [GSPC79], for example, are based on the generation of individual characters in terms of their component *strokes* (as *software characters*), which can be precisely controlled, or on fine control of tunable hardware character generators. If the SGP programmer needs to control character size and space, specific software characters must be defined in terms of individual strokes. In raster systems each character may be defined in terms of a pixel array (see Chapter 11) which can be copied individually into place in the bit map for appropriate character and word spacing.

To show the use of text to annotate a graph, let us add a title to Example 2.1 to produce a plot like that of Fig. 2.4. The main program has been modified as shown:

```
begin
  WINDOW(-5.0, 15.0, -10.0, 10.0);
  CREATE_SEGMENT(1);
    PLOT_DATA(months, bop_1982, 12, 'x');
    MOVE_ABS_2(5.5, 8.5);
    TEXT('Balance');
    MOVE_ABS_2(8.0, 7.0);
    TEXT('of');
    MOVE_ABS_2(5.0, 5.5);
    TEXT('Payments');
    MOVE_ABS_2(6.0, 4.0);
    TEXT('(FY80)');
  CLOSE_SEGMENT
end
```

*Note that the *TEXT* call in the Core contains the (x, y) origin of the character string explicitly.

Note that *PLOT_DATA* must also be extended by including a fourth parameter, the marker character to be plotted at each data point:

```
procedure PLOT_DATA(x, y: array[1..100] of real;
                         n: integer;
                         character: char);
var
  i: integer;
begin
  {define axes and lines as before but add marker}
  AXES(0.0, 0.0, 15.0, 6.0);
  MOVE_ABS_2(x[1], y[1]);              {first data point}
  TEXT(character);
  for i := 2 to n do                   {remaining data points}
    begin
      LINE_ABS_2(x[i], y[i]);
      TEXT(character)
    end
end;    {PLOT_DATA}
```

2.9 SUMMARY OF SGP'S PICTURE-MAKING FACILITIES

We have seen how the application programmer can produce pictures (i.e., collections of *images* on the screen) of two-dimensional objects from points, straight lines, and character strings. These output *primitives* are grouped together in *segments* which represent the unit of object and picture modification. The programmer now can control what portions of objects in world coordinate space are to be displayed (using *windows*) and where in the screen's NDC space the images will appear (using *viewports*). The window and viewport specifications are together known as the *viewing specification* and correspond to specifying the setting of the SGP synthetic camera and determining where on the bulletin board the snapshot should be placed and at what size.

These capabilities are sufficient for many output-only applications, but in no way represent the full potential of computer graphics. The next sections describe SGP's input capabilities, demonstrate how SGP can be used in an interactive environment, and develop and illustrate the central role of the segment.

2.10 AN INTERACTIVE GRAPHICS PROGRAM—LAYOUT OF SYMBOLS

In the following sections we describe the use of the input facilities of SGP within the context of an application requiring interaction with a model. The example program allows a user to create a model and its picture composed of predefined symbols. Such a program might be useful in the previous office furniture layout example, or in laying out a printed circuit board, or indeed in any application in which a two-dimensional schematic must be interactively prepared with predefined components. The symbols used in the sample output are those used in the furniture layout of Fig. 2.3, but are arbitrary and could easily be changed for another application; thus the program can be adapted without changing any of its structure.*

To keep the sample layout program as simple as possible, we have eliminated or hidden many features that would actually be necessary in practice. For example, in this application each symbol can be individually placed in an office and rotated about its center (this eliminates the need for a large collection of unique symbols for each orientation of the symbol). However, the program doesn't check, for example, whether two symbols "interfere" on the diagram (i.e., occupy the same space) or whether a symbol and the room boundaries interfere—the user will have to check for interference by looking for intersections on the screen as the symbols are moved or rotated.

The symbol placement program maintains a data structure that contains the current status of symbol placement. This data structure would be saved on secondary storage in an actual implementation, but we will not show the associated store and retrieve functions here. The layout program allows the user to:

- Generate a picture of the model described by the current data structure;
- Specify a title for the picture;
- Add a symbol to the data structure and therefore to the picture;
- Delete a symbol from the data structure and therefore from the picture; and
- Change the portion of the room being displayed by redefining the "window" in world coordinates.

2.11 GENERATING A PICTURE FROM THE DATA STRUCTURE

Example 2.2 Before introducing the interaction features of SGP in Sections 2.12–2.14, we present the basic output portion of the sample program. The data structure for the program is very simple; it consists primarily of an array of records, one for each occurrence of a symbol in the data structure. Each record has four elements: a code indicating the symbol type, the (x, y) position of that symbol in world coordinates, and an angular specification of the rotation of the symbol about that (x, y) position. The Pascal declarations below could be used to define the principal data structure elements needed. Note that four parallel arrays for the four different data elements could be used for this same purpose in languages like FORTRAN and BASIC.

*Only the key routines are described—initialization, menu definition and other housekeeping details mentioned below have been omitted for the sake of brevity. The full program may be obtained by writing to the authors.

```
symbols:   array[1..maxsymbol] of
           record
             code:  integer;        {symbol's identifier; 0 => free}
             x, y:  real;           {symbol's location}
             theta: real            {symbol's orientation}
           end;
   title:  packed array[1..80] of char;
           {character string for user-specified title}
```

The procedures for generating a picture from the data structure might be implemented as shown below. Note the natural modularization of the program—all the main loop does is to call the "display the *i*th symbol" routine, which in turn checks the validity of the symbol and then calls the actual symbol generation routine.

To avoid complicating later code with details involved in managing the unused (or used and then freed) entries in the data structure, we adopt the inefficient convention that *DISPLAY_SYMBOL* called by *DISPLAY_D_STR* tests consecutive symbols in the array when the picture is to be generated. A valid code (in the range 1 to 6) indicates that an entry contains a symbol to be displayed. A 0 value in the code field is a "garbage" flag that says the entry may be reused.

The Pascal **with** statement used in the *DISPLAY_SYMBOL* procedure below allows the fields of the record array *symbols*[*i*] to be used within the statement without writing their "fully qualified" names. In other words, it provides the context of the identifiers and thus permits a reference to *code* inside the **with** statement to be shorthand for *symbols*[*i*].*code*; similarly for *x, y,* and *theta.*

We use the SGP procedure *SEGMENT_EXISTS* in *DISPLAY_D_STR* to see if a segment exists, i.e., has been generated previously by SGP (it won't exist, of course, the first time it is generated), and to delete it prior to regeneration if it does (all but the first time). We have to perform this check each time the symbol is regenerated because it is an SGP error to delete a nonexistent segment (as would happen the first time the segment is generated). Each symbol is generated as a separate segment, and segment names from 1 to *maxsymbol,* a symbolic constant defined elsewhere, are reserved for this purpose. Thus the segment name is the location of the symbol in the data structure, a mapping which will be useful later on.

There are six separate procedures that generate the actual primitives representing the symbols, only one of which, *CHAIR,* is shown. A seventh describes the boundary of the room (including doors and windows, which are not considered movable symbols in this application). The routine *XFORM** is used to apply geometric transformations to all specified world coordinates of the six symbols in order to define properly rotated and translated versions of the original symbols. Each

*For generality, *XFORM* manipulates coordinate arrays of ten reals, even though some symbol procedures such as *CHAIR* have fewer coordinate values. The parameter *n* specifies the actual number of values to be transformed.

transformation is therefore a rotation of $\theta°$ about the origin of the coordinate system, followed by a translation to the new position (*xc, yc*)—see Fig. 2.12. In Chapter 7 we discuss such geometric transformations in detail. Here we note that all endpoints of lines and text can be rotated $\theta°$ about the origin using the 2 × 2 matrix:

$$[x1 \quad y1] = [x \quad y] \begin{bmatrix} \cos\theta & \sin\theta \\ -\sin\theta & \cos\theta \end{bmatrix}$$

Note that we declare the arrays that *XFORM* returns as **var** output parameters.

```
procedure DISPLAY_D_STR;
var
  i: integer;                          {array index}
{regenerate the picture of the entire model by checking all symbols in the data structure}
begin
  DISPLAY_ROOM;                        {create segment for room boundary}
  {next loop through consecutive symbols in data structure}
  for i := 1 to maxsymbol do
    begin
      if SEGMENT_EXISTS(i) then
        DELETE_SEGMENT(i);
      DISPLAY_SYMBOL(i)
    end
end;    {DISPLAY_D_STR}


procedure DISPLAY_SYMBOL(id: integer);
{regenerate segment for symbol with segment name = data structure address id}
begin
  with symbols[id] do
    if ((code >= 1) and (code <= 6)) then
      {valid code so create segment, else ignore it}
      begin
        CREATE_SEGMENT(id);
        {call symbol with x, y, theta from symbols definition in the data structure}
        case code of
          1:  CHAIR(x, y, theta);
          2:  DESK(x, y, theta);
          3:  BOOKCASE(x, y, theta);
          4:  LOWDIVIDER(x, y, theta);
          5:  PARTITION(x, y, theta);
          6:  FLOORPLANT(x, y, theta)
        end;    {case}
        CLOSE_SEGMENT
      end    {if}
end;    {DISPLAY_SYMBOL}
```

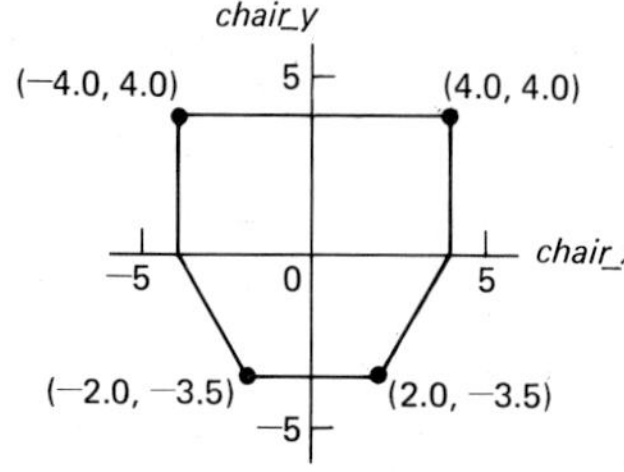

Absolute coordinates

chair_x	chair_y
4.0	4.0
−4.0	4.0
−4.0	0.0
−2.0	−3.5
2.0	−3.5
4.0	0.0
4.0	4.0

(a) Original position

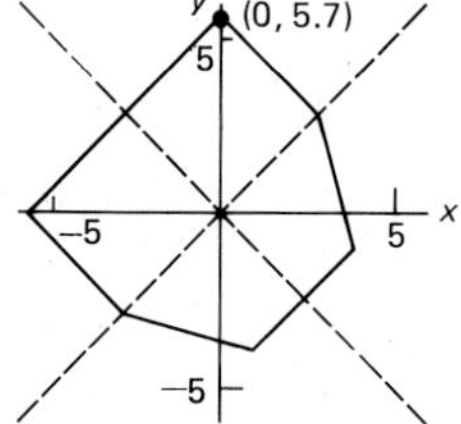

x	y
0.0	5.7
−5.7	0.0
−2.8	−2.8
1.1	−3.9
3.9	−1.1
2.8	2.8
0.0	5.7

(b) Rotated by 45° around origin

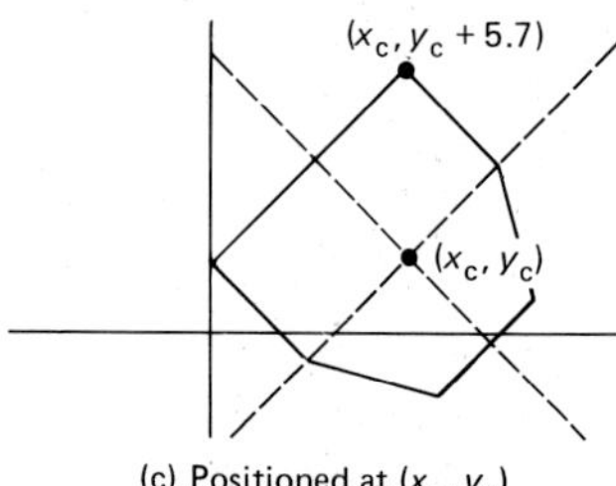

(c) Positioned at (x_c, y_c)

Fig. 2.12 Chair expressed in absolute coordinates rotated by 45° and then positioned at x_c, y_c.

```
procedure CHAIR(xc, yc, rot_angle: real);
{draw symbol for a rotated chair at (xc, yc) and rotated by rot_angle}
var
  chair_x_new, chair_y_new: array [1..10] of real;
begin
  {assume endpoints for chair are predefined in global arrays chair_x, chair_y;
    transform the original coordinates to new, rotated and translated coordinates}
  XFORM(xc, yc, rot_angle, chair_x, chair_y, chair_x_new, chair_y_new, 7);
  {next describe transformed primitives to SGP}
  MOVE_ABS_2(chair_x_new[1], chair_y_new[1]);
  for i := 2 to 7 do
    LINE_ABS_2(chair_x_new[i], chair_y_new[i])
end;
```

```
procedure XFORM(x, y, theta : real; x_old, y_old: array [1..10] of real;
                    var x_new, y_new: array [1..10] of real; n: integer);
{transform x_old, y_old by theta-degree rotation and translation to (x, y)}
var cos_theta, sin_theta: real;
    i: integer;
begin
  cos_theta := COS(theta);
  sin_theta := SIN(theta);
  for i := 1 to n do
    begin
      x_new[i] := x + (cos_theta * x_old[i] - sin_theta * y_old[i]);
      y_new[i] := y + (sin_theta * x_old[i] + cos_theta * y_old[i])
    end
end;
```

2.12 INTERACTIVE PROGRAMMING

2.12.1 Human Factors Considerations

Having dealt with output, we next turn to interaction. The designer of an interactive program must deal with many matters that need not be considered when developing a conventional noninteractive program. He must consider not just the implementation but especially the quality, i.e., the so-called *human factors* aspects, of the user–program interaction. The success or failure of an interactive program is measured at least as much by its ease of use as by its functional capability. The issues involved in proper human factors design are taken up in more detail in Chapter 6.

Some of the guidelines that should be followed in writing interactive programs include:

1. Provide *simple, consistent* interaction sequences.
2. *Do not overload* the user with too many different options and styles for communicating with the program.
3. *Prompt* the novice user at each stage of the interaction (but allow the more experienced user to bypass prompts).
4. Give appropriate *feedback* to the user.
5. Allow the user *graceful recovery* from mistakes.

In the sample program below, we attempt to follow these guidelines and to demonstrate good human factors approaches. For example, the interaction sequences in the sample program are simple and are usually accomplished with one interaction device at a time (rules 1 and 2). At every stage of interaction, the application program displays prompting messages to tell the user what actions can be performed at that point (rule 3). The messages here are designed as reminders to the experienced user rather than as complete descriptions for a novice; one particularly effective technique for assisting novices for whom a given prompt may be too terse is to include a HELP function that generates detailed instructions for the responses and actions available at a given time.

While prompting tells the user what the options are, feedback occurs after a particular option has been selected and before the next prompt is issued. Cogent feedback is especially important in an interactive graphics environment, and feedback is therefore used after *every* user action in the sample program to demonstrate how the system has interpreted the user's actions (rule 4). As in any graphics system, two different kinds of feedback are given. First, SGP produces for each interaction device an application-independent *echo* which is the immediate response to the device's use; for example, typing a character on an alphanumeric keyboard results in the display of that character, so the user can verify that it is correct. SGP provides default echoing facilities for all input devices. The sample program below relies completely on the default echo facilities, and thus appropriate echoing occurs even though there is no explicit code for it in the program. The second type of feedback, which is higher-level than echoing and application-dependent, shows the application program's response to the user's request. For example, if the user requests that an item be deleted from the model represented in the data structure, it is appropriate that the image of that item also be removed from the screen. This feedback is the responsibility of the application program, which uses SGP to create the desired effect on the screen.

In order to minimize the effect of a user's mistake (rule 5), the program has a CANCEL option which allows the user to terminate a partially completed function and, in cases where it makes sense, to "undo" the most recent fully completed function. For consistency, the user completes all functions in the same manner: by use of a DONE option. The implementations of the HELP, CANCEL and DONE options are shown later.

Before presenting the details of the interactive aspects of the sample program, we describe the basic interaction facilities of SGP which it uses.

2.12.2 Logical Interaction Devices

A major goal of the input facilities of SGP, as of output devices, is device-independence. Consequently, SGP defines *logical input devices* [WALL76] for communicating between the application program and its user. Program requests for input functions specify a logical device name which SGP maps to the available physical device with the most naturally corresponding characteristics. This mapping of logical to physical devices is analogous to an operating system's mapping of logical unit numbers or logical file names to appropriate physical file storage devices. Physical input devices commonly available include light pens, data tablets, cursor thumbwheels, control dials (potentiometers), joysticks, and alphanumeric keyboards. They are discussed more fully in Chapters 3 and 5. The logical input devices mentioned in Chapter 1 that correspond to one or more of these physical devices include:

- Button, a choice-indicating device;
- Pick, a device for pointing at information displayed on the screen;

- Keyboard, a device for accepting typed alphanumeric character strings;
- Valuator, a device for generating floating-point values;
- Locator, a device for specifying screen coordinates.

2.12.3 Event-Driven Processing

Any graphics programming system must provide the application program with facilities for *synchronizing* user actions with program responses. Interaction between program and user is best understood as an *event-driven* process in which the events correspond to actions performed by the user via input devices.* The program responds appropriately to an event and then waits for the next event to occur. A session with an interactive program (the *user–computer dialogue*) thus consists of user actions alternating with (typically brief) bursts of computation which arise from the user's request or action. Usually the dialogue is dominated by user "think time" during which the program is in the wait state.

The segment of pseudocode below is a schema for a typical interactive application program. Pseudocode is used here and later as an alternative to our Pascal dialect to avoid distracting details; it is shown as free-standing lower case while comments are still in lower case but enclosed in braces. Note that we check to see if the user's actions are allowed, i.e., useful, at this point in the program.

```
initialize, including generating initial picture;
repeat
  WAIT for user-generated event;
  if event_device = case 1 or case 2 or . . . then      {"legal" action}
    case event_device of
      case 1: action 1;
      case 2: action 2;
        .
        .
        .
    end     {case}
  else else_action
until exit is specified by an event device
```

Normally the action is generation of a prompt for the next parameter to be supplied by the user as part of a command specification dialogue. When a command is fully specified, the action modifies the data structure and then, most likely, the picture as well.

This general schema allows the application program to wait for more than one event-generating device at a time: for example, while typing an input string, the program could also wait on CANCEL and HELP buttons. This generality necessitates

*We use the term *event* here in the sense of a user-generated interrupt that causes a change of state in the system, i.e., from wait to action (and then back to wait). Thus the generation by the application program of a new picture, of feedback or of prompts is not considered an event.

somewhat complex event-decoding logic and status-saving (Exercise 2.12). SGP therefore uses a simpler schema in which the application program can wait on only a single event-generating device at a time. When the application program gains control after the event has taken place, it does a **case** on the *event data* returned by that event-generating device which indicates the exact choice the user made. This simpler schema looks the same, but the **case** is on event data, not the event device:

```
initialize;
repeat
  WAIT for user-generated event;
  if event_data = case 1 or case 2 or . . . then      {"legal" action}
    case event_data of                                {perform appropriate action}
      .
      .
      .
    end     {case}
until exit
```

Even in the more complex situation, the **case** is actually on the event data returned by the event-causing device, not just the device as shown above.

The event-generating devices supported by SGP are the logical button (typically implemented with a programmable function keyboard), the alphanumeric keyboard, and the pick device (usually implemented with a light pen or a data tablet with comparator). Each of these devices is activated by the programmer by having SGP execute the particular *WAIT* procedure for that device; an SGP-defined echo lets the user confirm that the input is being accepted and processed. If the user activates an event-generating device that is not being *WAIT*ed on, the absence of the corresponding echo indicates that the device's input is being ignored.

The *WAIT_BUTTON* procedure is typically used to choose a program option as a reply to a prompt or to specify a global change in mode of operation of the application program. The invocation of the procedure

WAIT_BUTTON(time, button_name)

causes the button device to be enabled and the application program to wait until either time-out occurs (if the user has not pressed a button during the number of seconds specified by the parameter *time*) or the user presses a key.* SGP learns from the hardware which key was pressed (this is the associated event data), returns the key's identifying number in the parameter *button_name,* and lets the application program resume execution at the statement following the *WAIT_BUTTON*. Time-out causes an illegal key number of 0 to be returned. An appropriate echo for button selection might be to turn on or blink the light under the button selected.

Similarly,

WAIT_PICK(time, segment_name)

*This description assumes a physical button keyboard, but the logic is identical if the logical button device is being simulated by another physical device, as discussed in Chapter 5.

will either time-out or return as event data the name of the segment whose primitive is identified on the screen by the user. The appropriate echo might be to blink the selected primitive or the entire segment. *WAIT_PICK* is used, for example, to indicate a segment to be deleted; as we will see, it can also be used in identifying choices as an alternative to buttons. The mechanisms used by SGP to *correlate* the primitive picked by the user to the name of the segment containing the primitive are discussed in the following two chapters.

The procedure

WAIT_KEYBOARD(time, text, length)

allows the user to type characters until an event is caused by hitting the carriage-return key (or its equivalent), and then returns as event data the string (minus the carriage return) in parameter *text* and its length in parameter *length*. An appropriate echo might be to display the typed characters at successive positions of a blinking cursor in a standard *type-in area* on the screen.

2.13 MAINLINE USING BUTTONS FOR FUNCTION INVOCATION

Example 2.3 To begin the demonstration of interactive programming, we first show a preliminary (partially pseudocoded) version of the mainline program for the symbol placement application described earlier. In this version of the mainline the logical button device is used to allow the user to specify the function to be invoked next.

The user of the symbol placement program may choose any of the following functions:

- Specify a new title for the picture;
- Add a symbol to the data structure and the picture;
- Delete a symbol from the data structure and the picture;
- Change the window for the picture; and
- Terminate execution.

In this version of the mainline program, a unique button on the button device is assigned to each of these functions. When a button event occurs, the program performs the function associated with the particular button activated.

The application program procedure *SETUP,* which is called by the mainline, performs all necessary initialization actions. In particular, it reads from secondary storage the data structure information defining the room whose furniture is to be arranged. In addition to reading values into the *symbols* array and *title* variable defined in Section 2.11, *SETUP* reads information describing the size and shape of the room and locations of doorways and windows. This information is used by the *DISPLAY_ROOM* procedure (used in *DISPLAY_D_STR*) to create and display the segment defining the room boundary seen in Fig. 2.3. Finally, *SETUP* initializes the four global variables *room_min_x, room_max_x, room_min_y,* and *room_max_y,* so that they define a window in world coordinates that just surrounds the limits of the room; this is the largest window that can be used to display the room. The application program procedure *CLEANUP* is the opposite of *SETUP*. It performs all necessary termination processing, including writing the updated data structure values to secondary storage.

The interactive portion of the mainline *WAIT*s for a button to be pushed and then invokes the lower-level procedure corresponding to the button. When the user is finished, the function returns from the **case** to the *WAIT*. The mainline therefore shows only the top-level, *dispatcher table* portion of the user dialogue, not the more interesting interactions which accomplish each of the functions. If no event occurs within the period specified by the symbolic constant *wait_time,* say five minutes, the *WAIT* times out and the user is prodded with a prompt or by highlighting the previous prompt—ringing an audible alarm or using some other attention-getting device. The *SCREEN_FEEDBACK* procedure should delete its message from the screen after a short wait and then return to exit in the **case** statement (see Exercise 2.15).

```
{Mainline for Symbol Placement Program—Version 1, using buttons for interaction}
program LAYOUT(input, output);
declare variables;
begin
  {initialize}
  SETUP;
  WINDOW(room_min_x, room_max_x, room_min_y, room_max_y);
  VIEWPORT_2(0.0, 0.8, 0.0, 0.8);        {leave room for prompts}
  {generate initial display}
  DISPLAY_D_STR;
  SCREEN_FEEDBACK('press a button to select a function');

  {main event-driven loop}
  main_done := false;
  repeat
    {wait for user-generated event}
    WAIT_BUTTON(wait_time, button_number);
    if (button number >= 0) and (button_number <= 5) then    {"legal" button}
      case button_number of
        0: SCREEN_FEEDBACK('waiting for you to select a function');
        1: NEW_TITLE;
        2: ADD_SYMBOL;
        3: DELETE_SYMBOL;
        4: CHANGE_VIEW;
        5: main_done := true            {EXIT button}
      end    {case}
    else SCREEN_FEEDBACK('illegal selection, try again')
  until main_done;
  CLEANUP                               {application procedure to terminate}
end.
```

2.14 USING A MENU FOR FUNCTION INVOCATION

2.14.1 Light Buttons

Using buttons to specify functions has some disadvantages. It can be inconvenient and distracting for the user to shift attention from the screen to the box in which the buttons are usually located. Secondly, most function keyboards have no means for labeling the buttons under program control. Although it is possible to show a brief summary of the use of each button on a portion of the screen, the user's attention is still divided.

A technique that many users prefer is to display a *function menu* of *light buttons* on the screen from which the desired function may be indicated with the pick device. A typical menu is composed of the list of text strings and/or graphical symbols that represent the functions available. Figure 2.13 illustrates a typical text string menu. The disadvantage of using light buttons (they take up some valuable screen space) is usually outweighed by the ability to display labeled choices and to change quickly from one menu to another.

For picking purposes, each light button string is defined by the routine *CREATE_FUNC_MENU* (not shown here) in its own uniquely named segment and is displayed in its own viewport. Each segment contains an absolute *MOVE* followed by a *TEXT* primitive, and is created during the *SETUP* initialization phase. The event-driven loop is also altered slightly; instead of

WAIT_BUTTON(*wait_time*, *button_number*);
case *button_number* **of**

Fig. 2.13 Text string menu generated by *CREATE_FUNC_MENU* procedure.

we have the analogous case of

```
WAIT_PICK(wait_time, segment_name);
case segment_name of
```

Note the use of a sequence of symbolic constants for the integer SGP segment names corresponding to the function name light buttons; these have been declared in *CREATE_FUNC_MENU*. The **repeat until** loop now has the form:

```
repeat
  {wait for user-generated event}
  WAIT_PICK(wait_time, segment_name);
  if ((segment_name >= new_t) and (segment_name <= exit)) or
    (segment_name = 0) then
    case segment_name of
                  0: SCREEN_FEEDBACK('waiting for you to select a function');
              new_t: NEW_TITLE;
            addsym: ADD_SYMBOL;
             delsym: DELETE_SYMBOL;
            chngvw: CHANGE_VIEW;
                exit: main_done := true;      {EXIT light button}
    end     {case}
  else SCREEN_FEEDBACK ('illegal selection, try again')
until main_done;
```

2.14.2 Making Segments Visible and Invisible—Menu Switching

The application program can make the image defined by a segment invisible or visible at any time until the segment is deleted. This is a very useful facility for pieces of a screen display that we would like to have appear and disappear repeatedly during a session, such as prompts and function menus.

As an example of the use of selective segment visibility, let us again consider our symbol placement application. Most of the functions of this program let the user perform any of a number of consecutive operations (e.g., to delete five symbols in a row) before returning to the mainline program. The user must therefore be able to exit from a function in order to perform another function. Similarly, with most of the functions the user can cancel or "undo" a partially completed operation, or request more detailed information on how to proceed via the HELP facility. For simplicity of use, we implement these three options in a single consistent manner by creating a global menu available to all the functions with entries DONE, CANCEL, and HELP. Since menu entries should be displayed only when it is legal to pick them, it is necessary to make them selectively visible. In general we create all necessary menu entries, prompts, and feedback messages at the start of the program as individual invisible segments and then make each message and menu entry selectively visible as needed. Making segments visible is sometimes called *posting* them (as one does with snapshots on a bulletin board); making them invisible is then called *unposting.*

The SGP procedure to control segment visibility is

SET_VISIBILITY(segment_name, on/off)

Because most newly created segments are meant to be displayed, the initial (default) visibility setting in SGP is *on*. Segments containing objects not meant to be seen, such as prompts and feedback messages to be made visible later, must be set explicitly to *off*. Chapter 4 describes how SGP implements visibility.

Assume for now that the global menu is generated by the *SETUP* procedure and that the segment names for each of the three options are stored in the global variables *done, cancel,* and *help.* As with *CREATE_FUNC_MENU,* which creates the command menu, we will make them invisible until set. The only exception is the HELP option, which is meaningful in the mainline; it is immediately made visible, while the other segments remain invisible until an appropriate function is chosen.

2.14.3 Revised Mainline

Example 2.4 The facilities described above are all incorporated into the revised version of the mainline shown below. In addition, this revised mainline contains code to generate prompting messages and to invoke a *HELP_USER* procedure that issues more detailed prompting. The *HELP_USER* procedure can be particularized to the mainline and its functions by an appropriate parameter. *HELP_USER* is not detailed here; it typically allows the user to ask for instruction at several levels of detail and, when finished, to return to the previous state. After *HELP_USER* writes on the screen, it must return transparently by erasing its information and regenerating the proper layout display from the data structure (Exercise 2.15).

We assume that the procedure *SETUP* also creates a number of invisible segments containing prompting messages for the mainline and the five user functions, including, for example, the main prompt saying "Please select a function." It is then only necessary to make the appropriate prompt segment visible when needed for each procedure. Finally, we also assume that the *SETUP* procedure calls *CREATE_FUNC_MENU* to create the function menu for mainline *LAYOUT* and creates the global menu used for all but the *NEW_TITLE* and *EXIT* choices.

The global variables *min_x, max_x, min_y,* and *max_y* represent the current window values in world coordinates and are initialized to the values in *room_min_x,* etc., that define a window just surrounding the room. The viewport used to draw the room was defined so that there is surrounding space on the screen available for other purposes: the area above the room viewport is used for the picture title and for prompts, while the area to the right is used for menus.

```
{Mainline for Symbol Placement Program—revised to use pick for interaction}
program LAYOUT(input, output);
declare variables;
begin
  {initialize}
  min_x := room_min_x;   max_x := room_max_x;
  min_y : = room_min_y;  max_y := room_max_y;
  SETUP;      {creates segments for function menu,
    prompts and global DONE/CANCEL/HELP menu}
  WINDOW(min_x, max_x, min_y, max_y);
  VIEWPORT_2(0.0, 0.8, 0.0, 0.8);
  DISPLAY_D_STR;                    {generate initial display}
  SET_VISIBILITY(help, on);         {make HELP visible}

  {main event-driven loop}
  main_done := false;
  repeat
    {turn on prompt and function menu, and wait for user event}
    SET_VISIBILITY(main_prompt, on);
    for i := new_t to exit do
      SET_VISIBILITY(i, on);
    WAIT_PICK(wait_time, segment_name);
    {user made a choice, so turn prompt and function menu off}
    SET_VISIBILITY(main_prompt, off);
    for i := new_t to exit do
      SET_VISIBILITY(i, off);
    if ((segment_name > = new_t) and (segment_name < = help)) or
      (segment_name = 0) then
      case segment name of
              0:  SCREEN_FEEDBACK('waiting for you to select a function');
          new_t:  NEW_TITLE;
         addsym:  ADD_SYMBOL;
         delsym:  DEL_SYMBOL;
         chngvw:  CHANGE_VIEW;
           exit:  main_done := true;     {EXIT light button}
           help:  HELP_USER(mainline);
      end    {case}
    else SCREEN_FEEDBACK('illegal selection, try again')
  until main_done;
  CLEANUP
end.
```

Each of the function procedures typically has the form of the mainline itself:

```
begin
  initialize;
  set visibility of local prompts and menu items on;
  reset the local done flag;
  repeat
    WAIT for user-generated event;
    if event data in case then                {"legal" action}
      case event data of
              time_out: prod user;
        local_action 1: . . . ;
          .
          .
          .
        local_action i: . . . ;
                  help: HELP_USER (local procedure);
                  done: set local done flag;
                cancel: undo local action(s);
      end     {case}
    else prompt user to try again
  until done;
  set visibility of local prompts and menu items off
end;
```

Figure 2.14 shows a complete module (procedure) hierarchy of the application program—we have only encountered the first-level modules thus far. This module decomposition is useful to help us understand the structure of the application program, but it gives us no insight into the user–computer interaction protocols. A common technique for illustrating such dialogue sequences is a *state transition graph* (Fig. 2.15). It is also called a finite-state graph since it represents the behavior of a finite-state machine (also known as a *regular* or *sequential* machine). The state transition graph shows the states of the program that are apparent to the user and the transitions from one state to another caused by the user's input actions. This version of the diagram does not show what actions the program performs in response to user inputs, but is a helpful summary for showing what the valid options are in each state, and to what states the various buttons (shown as labels on transition arrows) lead. The program *WAIT*s in a state until a user input forces a transition to another state.

Note that the internal procedures such as *SETUP* and *CLEANUP* (which *LAYOUT* uses to initialize, plot feedback messages and prompts, and clean up at termination) do not appear in the state transition graph because they do not involve interaction with the user. That is, they don't contain *WAIT*s on user-generated events. Time-out does appear, however, even though it also is not an event caused by user action, strictly speaking. This is because user inaction results in a timer-induced event and a return to the same state. Also, locator and valuator input are shown, although they are not transition-causing event devices. The exact dialogue sequences allowed will be clearer after an examination of the individual functions in the following sections.

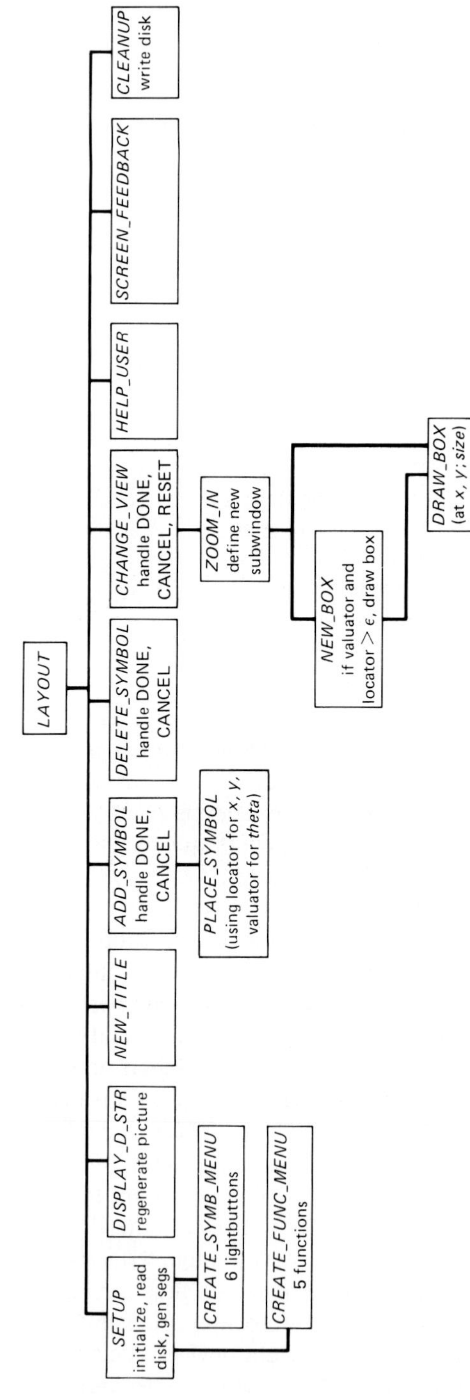

Fig. 2.14 Module hierarchy for layout.

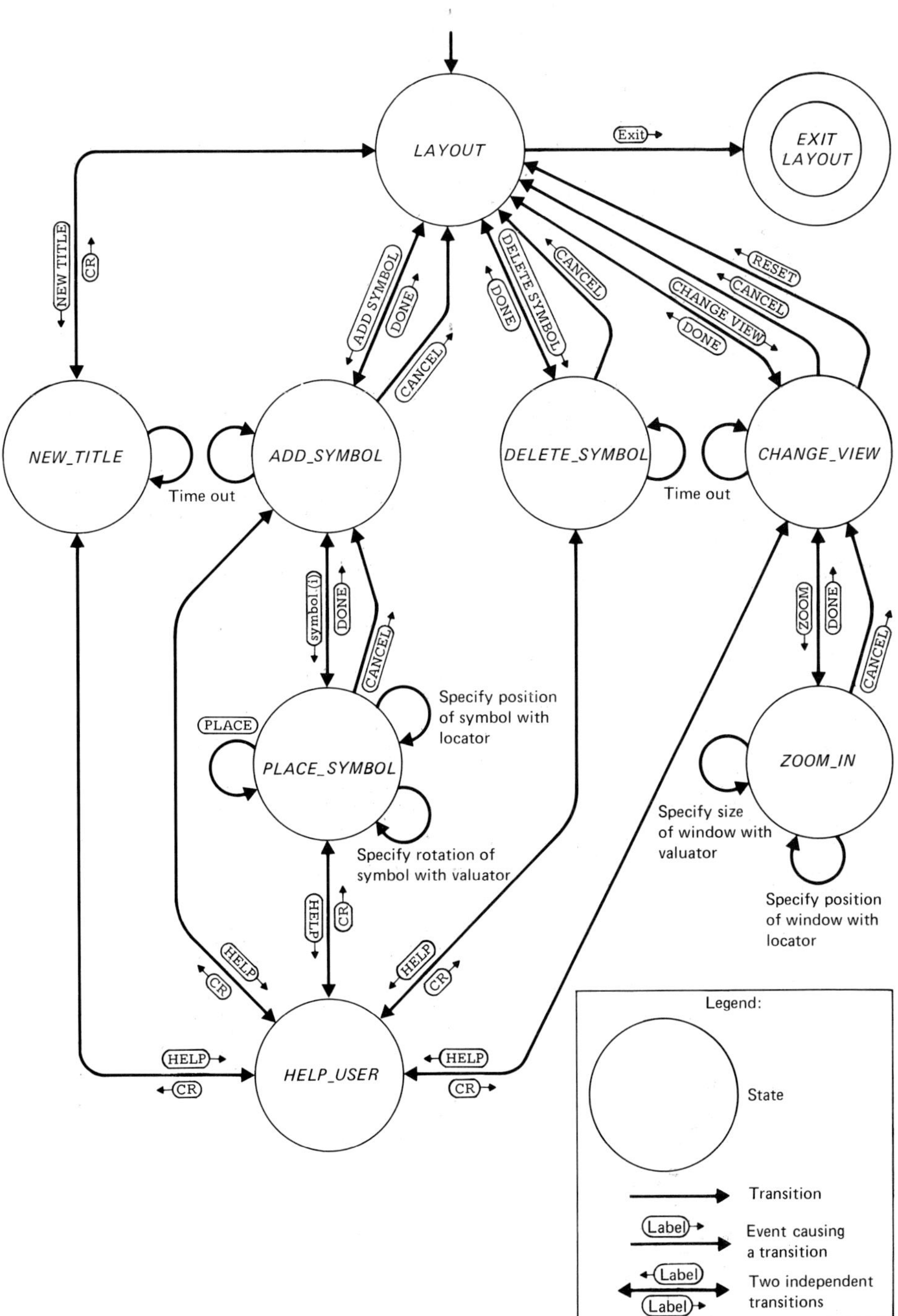

Fig. 2.15 State transition graph for user interaction with *LAYOUT.*

2.15 DEFINING A TITLE

Example 2.5 The simplest function of the symbol placement program allows the user to define a title for the current picture. The program segment below demonstrates the use of the keyboard logical device to implement the *NEW_TITLE* function. The *NEW_TITLE* procedure assumes there is a global variable *title_seg* containing the segment number of the segment currently displaying the title; similarly, *title_x* and *title_y* are constants specifying the origin of the title string. The DONE option is unnecessary for *NEW_TITLE* since this procedure allows only entry of a single title (instead of allowing a sequence of operations as the other functions do). Similarly, CANCEL is not implemented because we may assume that the SGP keyboard routine recognizes the standard special characters for character delete (called *logical backspace*) and line delete (called *logical command kill*) which allow one to edit a line before transmitting it with the (logical) carriage return. (Would you as a user prefer the consistency and safety of CANCEL nonetheless?) The code for *NEW_TITLE* replaces a segment by first deleting the old title segment and then recreating it with updated contents. Note that the time-out at this level below the mainline also results in the repetition of a *WAIT* after a short attention-getting interval. Thus a string must be specified by the user before the function can return to the main *WAIT*.

```
procedure NEW_TITLE;
{define a new title for the picture}
var
  txt_string: array [1..80] of char;
  length: integer;
  done: boolean;
begin
  done := false;
  SET_VISIBILITY(title_prompt, on);
  repeat
    WAIT_KEYBOARD(wait_time, txt_string, length);
    if length = 0 then
      SCREEN_FEEDBACK('waiting for your new title')
    else if txt_string = 'help' then
      HELP_USER(new_t_help)
    else
      begin                              {delete old title and create new}
        if SEGMENT_EXISTS(title_seg) then
          DELETE_SEGMENT(title_seg);
        CREATE_SEGMENT(title_seg);
          MOVE_ABS_2(title_x, title_y);
          TEXT(txt_string);
        CLOSE_SEGMENT;
        done := true
      end
  until done;
  SET_VISIBILITY(title_prompt, off)
end;    {NEW_TITLE}
```

2.16 ADDING SYMBOLS TO THE DATA STRUCTURE

The *ADD_SYMBOL* routine is really the heart of the symbol placement application, in terms both of its complexity and of the number of graphics programming techniques it uses. The algorithm for *ADD_SYMBOL* can be represented by the following pseudocode (which doesn't include checking for a valid pick):

```
display menu of symbols;
repeat
   wait on user event;
   case event of
      picksymbol: place symbol in position specified by user;
            help: HELP_USER(add_symbol);
            done: set done flag to return to mainline;
          cancel: delete previously added symbol
   end      {case}
until done;
remove menu of symbols
```

In each of the following subsections we elaborate pieces of this pseudocode with new techniques and code segments.

2.16.1 A Menu of Symbols

Example 2.6 The program is normally easier to use if the menu displays the symbols available to the user directly rather than merely the text strings representing them. The procedure below generates a symbol menu such as the one shown in Fig. 2.16. For each symbol we use a window which completely encloses the symbol when

Fig. 2.16 Menu of symbols generated by the *CREATE_SYMB_MENU* procedure, each in its own viewport. Dotted boxes surrounding symbols indicate their viewports.

it is placed in an unrotated state at the origin. Each symbol also is mapped to its own viewport which is chosen to scale and position the symbol in the menu area as desired. Note that we could also have defined all symbols in their appropriate sizes and positions in the world coordinate system and then position them all at once with a single window in a single viewport. Instead, by using a separate window and viewport for each symbol, we can more easily control individual relative size and placement by adjusting individual window-to-viewport mappings.

The procedure *CREATE_SYMB_MENU* is called from *SETUP* as part of initialization as *CREATE_FUNC_MENU* was, so that the menu need be created only once. As shown below, the *ADD_SYMBOL* procedure simply makes the menu visible or invisible when appropriate:

```
procedure CREATE_SYMB_MENU;
{Generate a menu of symbols. Each is defined in its own segment, placed in its own
  viewport, and is initially invisible. The window and viewport corner points for each
  symbol are predefined in arrays of 4-component records in the arrays window[i] and
  viewport[i], where the integer components are x_min, x_max, y_min, y_max. The
  consecutive segment names for the symbols are symbolic constants mchair, mdesk,
  etc., declared in SETUP.}
var
  i: integer;
begin
  for i := mchair to mfloorplant do
    begin
      with window[i] do
        WINDOW(x_min, x_max, y_min, y_max);
      with viewport[i] do
        VIEWPORT(x_min, x_max, y_min, y_max);
      CREATE_SEGMENT(i);
        SET_VISIBILITY(i, off);
        case i of
                 mchair:  CHAIR(0.0, 0.0, 0.0);
                  mdesk:  DESK(0.0, 0.0, 0.0);
              mbookcase:  BOOKCASE(0.0, 0.0, 0.0);
            mlowdivider:  LOWDIVIDER(0.0, 0.0, 0.0);
             mpartition:  PARTITION(0.0, 0.0, 0.0);
            mfloorplant:  FLOORPLANT(0.0, 0.0, 0.0)
        end;      {case}
      CLOSE_SEGMENT
    end      {for}
end;      {CREATE_SYMB_MENU}
```

2.16.2 The *ADD_SYMBOL* Procedure

Example 2.7 The *ADD_SYMBOL* procedure first makes the symbol menu visible. It then *WAIT*s for a pick and, when the user picks one of the symbols, calls *PLACE_SYMBOL* (Section 2.16.5) to do the actual work of creating the new symbol and placing it in the data structure and in the picture. Once *PLACE_SYMBOL* returns to *ADD_SYMBOL* via its own DONE or CANCEL, the user can either pick another symbol for *PLACE_SYMBOL* or choose DONE or CANCEL (to return to the mainline). The CANCEL option in *ADD_SYMBOL* allows the user to undo a prior placement before returning to the mainline. If *PLACE_SYMBOL* encounters a condition of no more room in the data structure, it sets the exit flag *add_done* so that both *PLACE_SYMBOL* and *ADD_SYMBOL* are exited. These various options, including multiple placements, are summarized in the state transition graph of Fig. 2.15.

Only the most recently placed symbol may be canceled with the CANCEL option. To implement CANCEL, *ADD_SYMBOL* saves the segment name of the most recently placed symbol (i.e., the symbol's location in its data structure array) in the variable *symb_addr*. When the user invokes CANCEL, this segment and the corresponding entry in the data structure are deleted. The *symb_addr* flag is initialized to 0, indicating that no cancel is yet possible, and is set by the *PLACE_SYMBOL* procedure when a symbol is placed. Also, CANCEL causes *symb_addr* to be reset to 0 in both *PLACE_SYMBOL* and *ADD_SYMBOL* since no second cancellation is possible in the other routine. Procedure *ADD_SYMBOL* is shown on p. 72.

2.16.3 Positioning with the Locator Device

The *PLACE_SYMBOL* procedure in Section 2.16.5 below does the work of creating the new symbol and adding it to the data structure. However, the user must specify the position and orientation of the new symbol: the locator device is used to position the new symbol and the valuator device is used to specify its orientation.

The *locator* device allows the user to specify a position on the screen, typically in order to place symbols at a desired location or to "draw" one or more primitives by indicating (end)points to the application program. The locator device does *not* cause events and is called a *sampled device* because the application program must explicitly ask for (i.e., *sample*) the current (x, y) values of the locator. Some typical physical devices that can be easily used as locators include data tablets, joysticks, and thumbwheel-driven cross-hair cursors. They return two coordinates in the NDC range of 0.0 to 1.0 which can be echoed on the screen by a cross-hair or a blinking cursor at the corresponding screen position. The data associated with the locator can be accessed by the following call:

READ_LOCATOR(x, y)

In most cases the coordinates returned from the locator are of little immediate use because they are given in the normalized device coordinate system and reflect where on the screen the cursor is physically located. However, the program typically views the picture on the screen as a reflection of the model's world coordinate system, and therefore must know where the cursor is in that space. This is important if, for example, the cursor is being used to specify endpoints of lines being constructed by the user, or in the case of our *LAYOUT* program, to specify where a particular furniture symbol is to be located in the (world coordinate) office.

```
procedure ADD_SYMBOL;
{add symbols to the picture and data structure}
var
  i: integer;
  symb_addr, segment name: integer;
  add_done: boolean;
begin
  symb_addr := 0;
  SET_VISIBILITY(done, on);
  SET_VISIBILITY(cancel, on);

  add_done := false;
  repeat
    for i := mchair to mfloorplant do      {symbol menu and prompt visible}
      SET_VISIBILITY(i, on);
    SET_VISIBILITY(add_prompt, on);
    WAIT_PICK(wait_time, segment_name);
    for i := mchair to mfloorplant do
      {since choice picked, make symbol menu and prompts invisible}
      SET_VISIBILITY(i, off);
    SET_VISIBILITY(add_prompt, off);
    if ((segment_name >= help)     and (segment_name <= cancel)) or
      ((segment_name >= mchair)  and (segment_name <= mfloorplant)
      or (segment_name = 0)) then
      case segment_name of       {valid menu pick}
            0: SCREEN_FEEDBACK('waiting for selection');
            mchair, mdesk, mbookcase, mlowdivider, mpartition, mfloorplant:
            {picked a symbol from menu so place a copy; its address is returned in
            symb_addr}
              PLACE_SYMBOL(segment_name, symb_addr, add_done);
         help: HELP_USER(add_help);
         done: add_done := true; {DONE}
       cancel: if (symb_addr > 0) then       {CANCEL only if symb_addr
                 flag on, i.e., no prior CANCEL in ADD_SYMBOL or
                 PLACE_SYMBOL}
                 begin
                   {delete segment, then symbol}
                   DELETE_SEGMENT(symb_addr);
                   symbols[symb_addr].code := 0;
                   symb_addr := 0   {set flag off to prevent second CANCEL}
                 end {CANCEL}
               else SCREEN_FEEDBACK('nothing to cancel')
      end     {case}
    else SCREEN_FEEDBACK('illegal selection, try again')
  until add_done;
  SET_VISIBILITY(done, off);
  SET_VISIBILITY(cancel, off)
end;     {ADD_SYMBOL}
```

To facilitate this *back-mapping* from NDC space to world space, SGP contains the subroutine *INVERSE_2* which transforms a position in normalized device coordinates into a position in world coordinates. The transformation is the inverse of the current *viewing operation,* that is, the inverse of the mapping that takes the world coordinate window into the NDC viewport (discussed in Chapter 4). The statement below is an invocation of the procedure:

INVERSE_2(ndc_x, ndc_y, world_x, world_y)

This procedure must be used carefully because, although a given display on the screen can be generated as a collection of individual images, each specified via its own window–viewport viewing operation, only the current (most recently specified) viewing operation can be used to compute the inverse mapping. In other words, SGP does not remember for each segment what viewing operation was in effect when it was created. Since locator cursor positions are typically used only within the main drawing area, we can program so that this area is the last one drawn; this allows SGP to use the last-specified viewing operation to calculate the inverse.* If multiple drawing areas with multiple viewing operations are required, the application program would have to remember which viewing operation belongs to which viewport and segment combination and would then compute its own inverses.

In our sample program, the mainline's *SETUP* (and some of the procedures it calls) will change the viewport for each menu item; after that, the viewport will be set to the main picture-building area of the screen and left that way to allow *INVERSE_2* to be used for all subsequent operations.

2.16.4 The Valuator Device

The *valuator* logical device allows a user to specify to the application program a single floating-point value between 0.0 and 1.0. Valuators, like locators, are sampled devices and do not cause events. The physical device most often utilized as a logical valuator device is a control dial. A control dial is simply a potentiometer similar to that used as a volume control on a radio or television set. The analog output of the dial is converted to a digital value by hardware, which may be echoed in a control area on the screen or, more likely, by a pointer on a scale attached to the device itself. The *READ_VALUATOR* procedure must be called in order for the application program to obtain the value of a valuator. The valuator specified by the first parameter of this procedure is sampled and the value is returned in the variable specified as the second parameter. The statement

READ_VALUATOR(1, *value*)

sets the variable *value* to the current value of valuator 1.

---

*Note that the locator is not constrained to return values inside a particular viewport; therefore, if the locator returns a point not inside the current viewport, and this point is passed on to *INVERSE_2*, a point lying outside of the current window will be returned as the inverse point.

2.16.5 The *PLACE_SYMBOL* Procedure

Example 2.8 The *PLACE_SYMBOL* procedure called by *ADD_SYMBOL* allows the user to specify the position and orientation of a new symbol as often as desired. It accepts three explicit parameters: the first specifies which symbol is to be added to the picture and data structure, the second is set by the procedure to the segment number (which is also the data structure index) of the symbol added, and the third is a flag which is set when the data structure is full, to allow an exit from *ADD_SYMBOL*. Note that the last two parameters are declared **var** as output parameters whose values may be returned to *ADD_SYMBOL*. Three separate options allow the user to:

- Cause the current values of locator and valuator 1 to be used to position and orient the new symbol;
- Return, leaving the new symbol at its current position; and
- Cancel this iteration of the ADD operation and return without adding a symbol.

These options are invoked by picking a new menu item 'PLACE' or the global options DONE or CANCEL. Each time PLACE is picked the user is allowed to reposition the symbol, until he specifies DONE. We assume that the menu item for 'PLACE' and prompts are created in *SETUP* as invisible segments; the PLACE light button's segment name is stored in the variable *place*.

In order to allow *PLACE_SYMBOL* to signal the user when it is ready to sample the locator and valuator, the program prompts the user and then *WAIT*s for a button to be pushed indicating the user has finished changing the values of the input devices. (In the case that a data tablet is used both to support the logical pick device and the locator, this allows the user to indicate with a stylus press interrupt acting as a button event that the tablet is now to be used as a locator at the place the pen was pressed down—see Exercise 2.10(e) on *associating* an event with sampling.)

Figure 2.17 shows the sequence of pictures that might result from the invocation of the *PLACE_SYMBOL* procedure after the user has picked the desk symbol while the program was in *ADD_SYMBOL*. In Fig. 2.17(a), after picking PLACE and being prompted to activate the sampling button, the user has placed the locator at the desired position on the screen (indicated by the cross) and set the valuator output (which is converted to degrees) at +180°, as indicated by the feedback in the lower right portion of the screen. The program then generates the new symbol at the specified location, as shown in Fig. 2.17(b). The user then picks PLACE again, repositions the locator as shown in Fig. 2.17(c), and, after the button push, gets the picture shown in Fig. 2.17(d). By picking DONE the user indicates satisfaction with this placement and returns to the *ADD_SYMBOL* procedure; this results in the picture shown in Fig. 2.17(e). While this first example of placement is adequate from a user's point of view, it is not as satisfactory as having the desk follow the cursor continually, a technique known as *dragging* (see Section 2.18.2).

The *PLACE_SYMBOL* procedure invokes the procedure *GET_ENTRY*, which returns the first free entry in the *symbols* array available to store a new symbol. (A zero value in the *code* field of an array entry is used to indicate that the entry

(a)

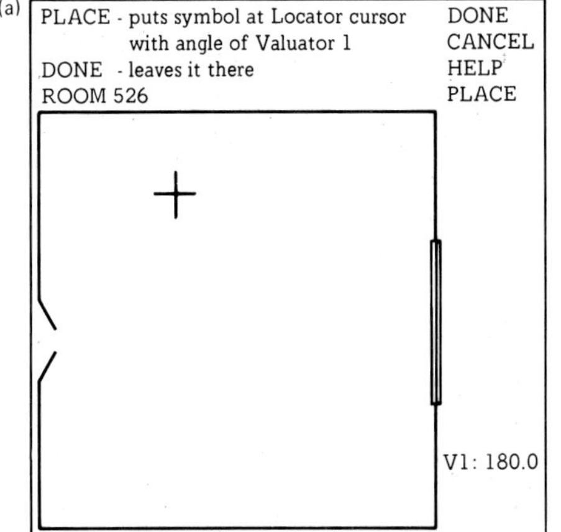

(b)

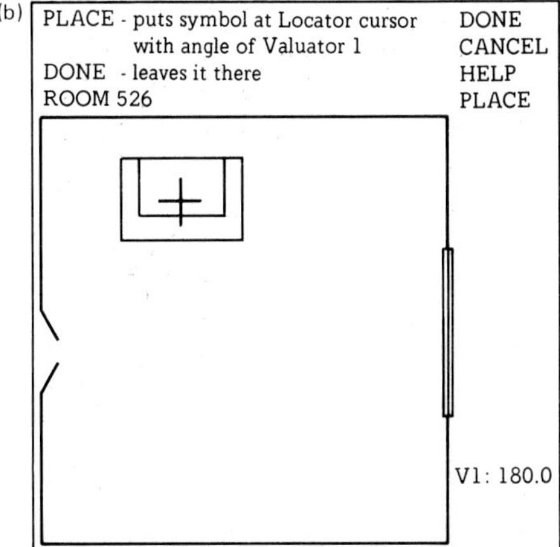

(c)

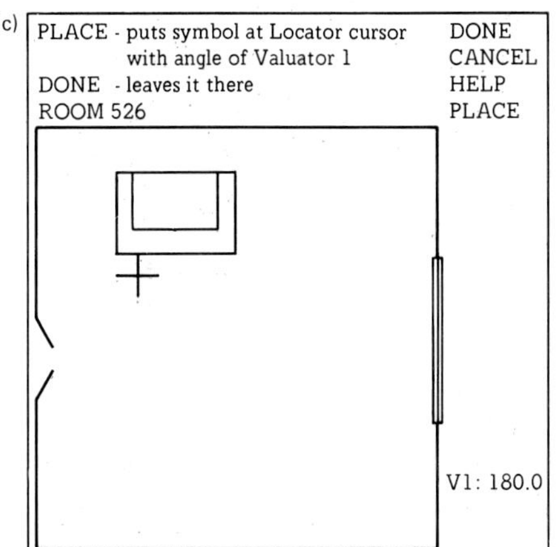

(d)

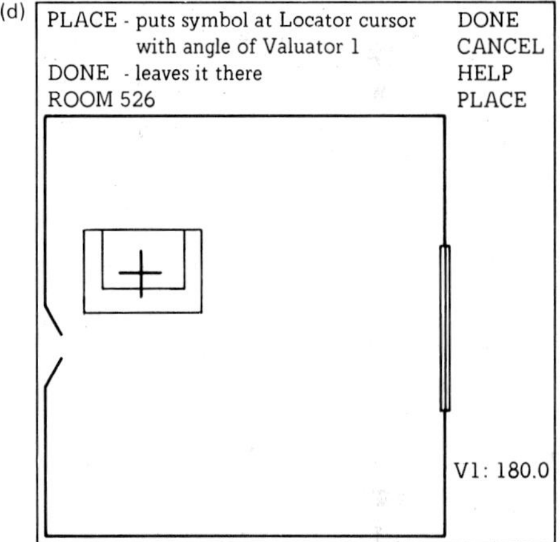

(e)

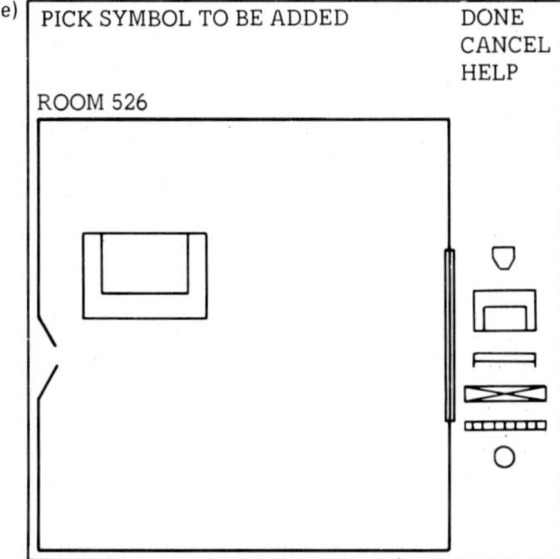

Fig. 2.17 Placing a symbol in *PLACE_SYMBOL* (a) Echo of locator and valuator 1 before PLACE picked; (b) after picking PLACE, symbol is generated; (c) reposition locator; (d) after picking PLACE again, symbol is moved; (e) after DONE picked, return to *ADD_SYMBOL*.

is available.) If an entry is available, its index is returned in the argument. Otherwise, zero is returned, and *ADD_SYMBOL* cannot run until the user deletes some symbols; in this case, an error message is generated and *ADD_SYMBOL*'s global exit flag is set. For ease of reading, two internal procedures involved in the **case** statement are shown separately on the next page.

```
procedure PLACE_SYMBOL (
  picked_segment_name: integer;        {symbol to be placed}
     var new_symb_addr: integer;        {data structure index/segment name}
           var add_done: boolean);      {exit flag for full data structure}
{create and place symbol of type indicated by picked_segment_name in data
  structure and on screen, sampling position and angle each time user picks PLACE}
var ndc_x, ndc_y: real;                 {coordinates returned by locator}
      place_done: boolean;              {exit flag}
    segment_name: integer;              {for picked light button}
{code for internal procedures PLACE_CASE and CANCEL_CASE goes here}
begin
  GET_ENTRY(new_symb_addr);             {get free entry in array}
  if new_symb_addr = 0 then             {no more room in data structure}
    begin
      SCREEN_FEEDBACK('data structure full, please delete some symbols');
      add_done:= true                   {return, and terminate caller}
    end
  else                                  {get user inputs and place symbol}
    {turn on local menu item and prompt—DONE and CANCEL
      already turned on in ADD_SYMBOL}
    begin
      SET_VISIBILITY(place, on);
      SET_VISIBILITY(place_pick_prompt, on);

      place_done := false;
      repeat
        WAIT_PICK(wait_time, segment_name);
        if ((segment_name >= place) and (segment_name <= cancel)) or
          (segment_name = 0) then       {legal pick}
          case segment_name of
                 0: SCREEN_FEEDBACK('waiting for selection');
             place: PLACE_CASE;
              help: HELP_USER (place_help);
              done: place_done := true;     {exit}
            cancel: CANCEL_CASE
          end     {case}
        else SCREEN_FEEDBACK('illegal selection, try again')
      until place_done
    end     {else}
  {turn off local menu item and prompt}
  SET_VISIBILITY(place, off);
  SET_VISIBILITY(place_pick_prompt, off)
end;    {PLACE_SYMBOL}
```

```
procedure PLACE_CASE;
{places symbol in procedure PLACE_SYMBOL:
 places locator and valuator→x, y and theta fields of symbol in
 symbols[new_symb_addr]. First prompt user and wait for him to push any button (or
 time out) to indicate sampling should be done}
begin
  with symbols[new_symb_addr] do
    begin
      SET_VISIBILITY(place_pick_prompt, off);
      SET_VISIBILITY(place_sampling_prompt, on);
      WAIT_BUTTON(wait_time, button_number);
      READ_LOCATOR(ndc_x, ndc_y);
      INVERSE_2(ndc_x, ndc_y, x, y);      {set x, y}
      READ_VALUATOR(1, theta);
      theta := theta*360;      {convert fraction to degrees; set theta field}
      {next convert the picked symbol's segment name passed by
        ADD_SYMBOL to its type code between 1 and 6 and store in the code field:
        the type code is the offset from the first symbol's segment name plus 1}
      code := picked_segment_name - mchair + 1;
      {entry now holds completed symbol, so display it}
      if SEGMENT_EXISTS(new_symb_addr) then
        DELETE_SEGMENT(new_symb_addr);
      DISPLAY_SYMBOL(new_symb_addr);
      SET_VISIBILITY(place_sampling_prompt, off);
      SET_VISIBILITY(place_pick_prompt, on)
    end      {with}
end;      {PLACE_CASE}

procedure CANCEL_CASE;
{delete symbol from data structure and screen in PLACE_SYMBOL and set exit flag}
begin
  if SEGMENT_EXISTS(new_symb_addr) then
    begin
      DELETE_SEGMENT(new_symb_addr);
      symbols[new_symb_addr] . code := 0;
      new_symb_addr := 0
    end
  place_done := true
end;      {CANCEL_CASE}
```

2.17 DELETING SYMBOLS

Example 2.9 The *DELETE_SYMBOL* procedure allows the user to delete any number of symbols from the data structure and the picture. *DELETE_SYMBOL* uses a technique known as a *soft delete,* which allows the user to undo an incorrect deletion: the segment corresponding to the symbol is simply made invisible to show the effect of deleting the symbol, but the segment or the symbol data structure is not actually deleted. If the user decides that the deletion is not wanted, then CANCEL is picked and the symbol is made visible again. If, instead, the user requests another deletion or picks DONE, the deletion becomes permanent: the data structure entry is deleted by having its code set to zero, and the segment is deleted. The segment name of the soft-deleted segment is stored in *del_symb*. *DELETE_SYMBOL* is shown on the next page.

2.18 CHANGING VIEW BY PANNING AND ZOOMING

The *CHANGE_VIEW* procedure shown below allows the user to "zoom in" on successively smaller portions of the currently visible picture, to use RESET to zoom out completely so that the window encompasses the entire scene, or to perform any sequence of these options. In order to zoom in, the user could specify the window size and location by typing in parameters on the keyboard, but that provides no immediate visual feedback and is very cumbersome. Instead, a square on the screen may be specified defining the portion of the current picture that should be shown as the next picture. In effect, this square is not the window itself but its viewable image on the screen, and it is being moved with respect to the current picture, which displays the clipped and mapped contents of the previous window. A new window may be defined, either within the old one or reset to the largest, original enclosing window.

The user specifies the square to be zoomed-in on by positioning the locator at the lower left corner of the new window and using valuator 1 to define its size. The *ZOOM_IN* procedure (Section 2.18.4) called by *CHANGE_VIEW* continually redraws a square box on the screen corresponding to the window defined by the current values of the locator and valuator 1. The user can thus *drag* the box corner with the locator as its size is changed with the valuator. When the desired window is specified, the user picks DONE, the new picture is generated, and control returns to the *CHANGE_VIEW* procedure. The interplay between *CHANGE_VIEW* and *ZOOM_IN* is summarized in the state transition graph of Fig. 2.15.

The continuous redisplay of the box defining the potential new window is a simple form of dynamic graphics that can be extremely effective on refresh devices. With other devices without selective screen update, such as direct-view storage tube (DVST) displays without *write-through mode,** the programming technique shown below is inappropriate for specifying the window. In such a case, it would perhaps be preferable to have the lower left and upper right corners of the new window specified with successive inputs from a locator until the user is satisfied; then the box can be drawn once for a final check before redisplaying the entire scene. Conversely, in systems in which most of the graphics package is implemented in hardware (including clipping and window-to-viewport mapping), the box could be dragged over the

*A limited capability for refreshing a small number of primitives whose images are not stored by the DVST and which may therefore be selectively updated (see Chapter 3).

```
procedure DELETE_SYMBOL;
{delete symbols from data structure and remove the corresponding images from the
  screen}
var
  del_symb, segment_name: integer;
  delete_done: boolean;
begin
  SET_VISIBILITY(done, on);
  SET_VISIBILITY(cancel, on);
  SET_VISIBILITY(delete_prompt, on);
  del_symb := 0;                        {no symbol deletion pending}
  delete_done := false;
  repeat
    WAIT_PICK(wait_time, segment_name);
    if ((segment_name = help) or (segment_name = cancel)) or
      (segment_name = 0) then
      case segment_name of
            0:  SCREEN_FEEDBACK('waiting for your deletion');
         help:  HELP_USER(delete_help);
       cancel:  if del_symb > 0 then    {a symbol was soft-deleted}
                  begin                 {so make it visible again}
                    SET_VISIBILITY(del_symb, on);
                    del_symb := 0       {no pending soft delete now}
                  end
      end    {HELP, CANCEL case}

    else if (((segment_name >= 1) and (segment_name <= maxsymbol)) or
          (segment_name = done)) then
      {DONE or another symbol picked}
      begin    {first make previous soft delete, if any, permanent by deleting segment
                 and clearing its array entry}
        if del_symb > 0 then
          begin
            symbols[del_symb].code := 0;
            DELETE_SEGMENT(del_symb)
          end;
        {now check for DONE or another symbol delete}
        if segment_name = done then
          delete_done := true
        else                            {another delete so soft delete}
          begin
            del_symb := segment_name;
            SET_VISIBILITY(del_symb, off)
          end
      end    {DONE, symbol[i]}
    else SCREEN_FEEDBACK('illegal selection, try again')
  until delete_done;
  SET_VISIBILITY(done, off);
  SET_VISIBILITY(cancel, off);
  SET_VISIBILITY(delete_prompt, off)
end;    {DELETE_SYMBOL}
```

previous picture (typically one of the entire object) in one viewport, while the resultant clipped and mapped new picture could be shown "on the fly" in another. This closely coupled feedback provides an extremely user-friendly mode of interaction.

2.18.1 The *CHANGE_VIEW* Procedure

Example 2.10 The *CHANGE_VIEW* procedure shown on the next page uses two simple menu items to allow the user to indicate either RESET or ZOOM. We again assume that these menu items are generated and made invisible in the mainline initialization and need only be made visible here. We assume also that the variables *reset* and *zoom* contain the segment names of the menu items. The CANCEL operation for this procedure restores the window to the parameters in effect on entry to the procedure. Note that both RESET and ZOOM options force regeneration of the picture from the data structure, including any necessary clipping—the viewport is constant and only the window is reset.

However, before showing the *ZOOM_IN* procedure (on page 86) it is necessary to introduce some additional facilities of SGP.

2.18.2 Dragging via Image Translation

The normal technique for positioning an image on the screen is for the program to define the object at the appropriate position in world coordinate space and then to use the window and viewport specifications to determine the viewing operation which positions the desired image. It is often desirable, however, to allow the user to reposition the image *after* it has been generated without having to run the object definition through SGP with an altered viewing specification in effect. Let us say, for example, that we want to drag the window box by continually repositioning it to follow the locator. In terms of our earlier synthetic camera paradigm, we want to move an existing snapshot on the bulletin board rather than first having to respecify some of the settings of the synthetic camera (which include both window and viewport settings), and then having SGP take a brand new snapshot to be posted in the new position.

With such image repositioning we can avoid the full viewing operation pipeline of SGP which typically includes the time-consuming clipping process. As we will see in Chapter 3, the image can be translated in real time in most refresh displays simply by changing an absolute-move display instruction that precedes the segment's primitives. These primitives are defined with relative coordinates, so that they can be automatically "relocated" when the initial absolute move is altered. Other implementations for image transformations (including image scale and image rotation) are presented in Chapter 8, where 3D image transformations are also discussed. 2D image translation is invoked by

TRANSLATE_IMAGE_2(segment_name, x_rel, y_rel)

where *x_rel* and *y_rel* (needed for dragging) can be obtained from the locator. Note that *x_rel* and *y_rel* specify a translation in *normalized device coordinates.* Succes-

```
procedure CHANGE_VIEW;
{redefine the window and regenerate the picture}
var
  save_min_x, save_max_x, save_min_y, save_max_y: real;
      view_done: boolean;
  segment_name: integer;
begin
  {save the current (global) window parameters in case of CANCEL}
  save_min_x := min_x; save_max_x := max_x;
  save_min_y := min_y; save_max_y := max_y;
  SET_VISIBILITY(done, on);
  SET_VISIBILITY(cancel, on);

  view_done := false;
  repeat
    SET_VISIBILITY(view_prompt, on);
    SET_VISIBILITY(reset, on);          {menu items on}
    SET_VISIBILITY(zoom, on);
    WAIT_PICK(wait_time, segment_name);
    SET_VISIBILITY(view_prompt, off);
    SET_VISIBILITY(reset, off);         {menu items off}
    SET_VISIBILITY(zoom, off);
    if (segment_name = 0) or (segment_name = zoom) or (segment_name = reset) or
      ((segment_name >= help) and (segment_name <= cancel)) then
      case segment name of
            0: SCREEN_FEEDBACK('waiting for selection');
         zoom: ZOOM_IN;                 {define smaller window}
        reset: begin                    {set up original (largest) window}
                 min_x := room_min_x; max_x := room_max_x;
                 min_y := room_min_y; max_y := room_max_y;
                 WINDOW(min_x, max_x, min_y, max_y);
                 DISPLAY_D_STR {regenerate picture}
               end;
         help: HELP_USER(view_help);
         done: begin
                 view_done := true:
                 DISPLAY_D_STR {regenerate picture}
               end;
       cancel: begin                    {restore saved window}
                 min_x := save_min_x; max_x := save_max_x;
                 min_y := save_min_y; max_y := save_max_y;
                 WINDOW(min_x, max_x, min_y, max_y);
                 DISPLAY_D_STR {regenerate picture}
               end
      end     {case}
    else SCREEN_FEEDBACK('illegal selection, try again')
  until view_done;
  SET_VISIBILITY(done, off);
  SET_VISIBILITY(cancel, off)
end;    {CHANGE_VIEW}
```

sive image translations are not cumulative: they specify a translation relative to the *original* position of the image. It may therefore be necessary for an application program to save that original position in order to calculate appropriate offsets.

To drag a specific *anchor point* on the image (such as the bottom left corner of our window box) to the locator, the application program must subtract the anchor point's NDC coordinates from the locator's and then specify these translation offsets to the *TRANSLATE_IMAGE_2* procedure, which moves the entire image by that amount. For example, to drag the bottom left corner of the window box with the locator, we initially define that point to be at (0, 0) in world coordinate space and map it to (0, 0) in normalized device coordinate space. Then the locator values can be used directly in the translation procedure.

We now introduce the procedure *DRAW_BOX* to demonstrate the use of image translations for both positioning and dragging. *DRAW_BOX* draws a square box of dashed lines by using four input parameters: a segment number, the *x* and *y* world coordinates of the position of the lower left corner of the box, and a size in world coordinates. The box is generated invisibly in a new segment with the specified number. Note that a new SGP call is introduced to control the *linestyle attribute* of lines; all LINE primitives have the specified linestyle attribute in effect until it is changed. The default is *solid* and other values include *dashed, dotted,* and *dot-dashed.*

```
procedure DRAW_BOX(box_seg: integer, x, y, size: real);
{create a square box of dashed lines with lower left corner at x, y of size size}
begin
  CREATE_SEGMENT(box_seg);
  SET_VISIBILITY(box_seg, off);
  SET_LINESTYLE(dashed);
  MOVE_ABS_2(x, y);
  LINE_REL_2(0, size);
  LINE_REL_2(size, 0);
  LINE_REL_2(0, -size);
  LINE_REL_2(-size, 0);
  CLOSE_SEGMENT;
  SET_LINESTYLE (solid);
end;     {DRAW_BOX}
```

Suppose we invoke the *DRAW_BOX* procedure to draw the outline of what may become the new window with the following sequence:

```
DRAW_BOX(box, min_x, min_y, 5.0);
SET_VISIBILITY(box, on)
```

Recall that *room_min_x* and *room_min_y* are the world coordinates of the lower left corner of the window and that the main viewport is (0.0, 0.8, 0.0, 0.8). If the original window which maps to the viewport is approximately 10 units wide, the display of the new window's box shown in Fig. 2.18(a) results. If the program now executes

TRANSLATE_IMAGE_2(*box*, 0.50, 0.50)

the display shown in Fig. 2.18(b) results. Here the image translation routine causes the lower left corner of the box to appear at the position on the screen specified in the last two arguments.

The program segment below demonstrates the use of image translation to implement dragging. The coordinates received from the locator device are used to reposition the segment box until DONE is picked. Locator sampling is done every 1/30 of a second on time-out or when the user selects any segment but the DONE button. (The more complete version of *ZOOM_IN* discussed in Section 2.18.4 checks the normal global options as well.)

```
repeat
   {update location}
   READ_LOCATOR(x, y);      {locator position}
   TRANSLATE_IMAGE_2(box, x, y)
   {wait 1/30 of a second to see if user is done}
   WAIT_PICK(.033, segment_name)
until segment_name = done;
   .
   .
   .
```

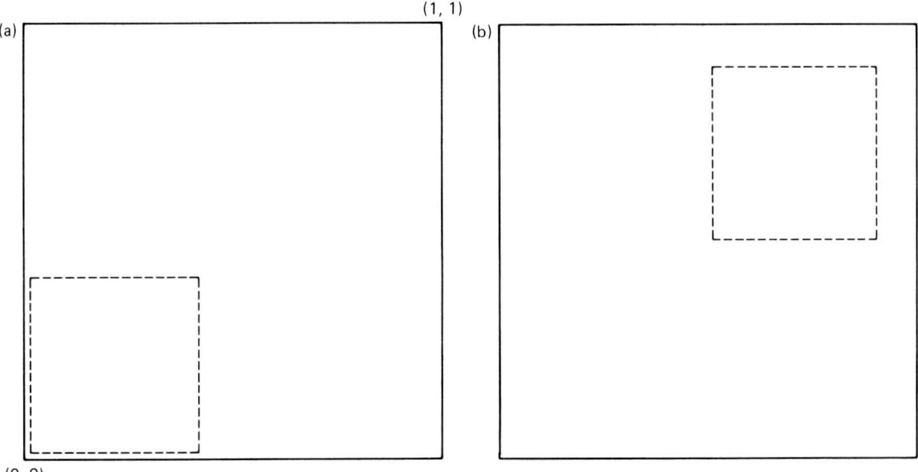

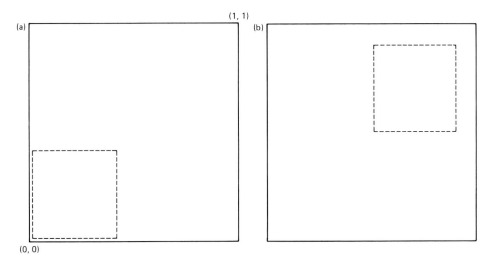

Fig. 2.18 (a) Box with lower left corner at origin at NDC space; (b) box after image translation applied to segment.

2.18.3 Double-Buffering

In Examples 2.2 and 2.5 we replaced visible segments by first deleting the old segment and then creating a new one. If generation of the new segment requires a discernible amount of time, this technique causes a hiatus that can be unpleasant for the user, and it is often preferable to *double-buffer* the image. This is done by generating the new segment (invisibly) before deleting the old one.

Another SGP procedure, *RENAME_SEGMENT,* can be used to simplify the bookkeeping necessary for double-buffering. The first argument to *RENAME_SEGMENT* is the name of an existing segment; the second argument is the new name to be given to that segment. For example, the following procedure call changes to 5 the name of the segment currently named 3:

```
RENAME_SEGMENT(3, 5)
```

The program segment below demonstrates double-buffering techniques in SGP. Because the procedure *DRAW_BOX* here generates an invisible box, the previous box remains visible until the new box is completed (see Exercise 2.19).

```
DRAW_BOX(temp, min_x, min_y, size);
TRANSLATE_IMAGE_2(temp, loc_x, loc_y);
SET_VISIBILITY(box, off);
SET_VISIBILITY(temp, on);
DELETE_SEGMENT(box);
RENAME_SEGMENT(temp, box)
```

2.18.4 The *ZOOM_IN* Procedure

Now we are ready to show the details of the *ZOOM_IN* procedure and its principal subprocedure, *NEW_BOX.* Unless CANCEL is picked, *ZOOM_IN* redefines the global window specification parameters and regenerates the picture (see Exercise 2.14). The variables *loc_x, loc_y, size,* and the symbolic constant *box* define respectively the position (in normalized device coordinates), the size (in world coordinates), and the segment number of the most recently generated box, and these variables are the parameters of the *NEW_BOX* procedure. The *NEW_BOX* procedure recreates the box if its new size specification is different from the previous one, and repositions the box if its new location is different from the previous one. Note that the user may continually move the locator and valuator. They are sampled by *NEW_BOX,* however, only when it is called by *ZOOM_IN* after the user selects the ZOOM option of *CHANGE_VIEW.* In fact, *ZOOM_IN* causes sampling only every 1/30 of a second, by calling *NEW_BOX* after time-out, if HELP, DONE, or CANCEL are not picked.

Figure 2.19 shows a sequence of pictures that might result from the use of the ZOOM option of the *CHANGE_VIEW* function. Figure 2.19(a) shows a view with the window-defining box (here displayed in dashed lines for easy identification). After the valuator is changed, a new, smaller box might result, as shown in Fig. 2.19(b). The locator might subsequently be used to drag the box to the position shown in Fig. 2.19(c). Finally, picking DONE results in the new view shown in Fig. 2.19(d).

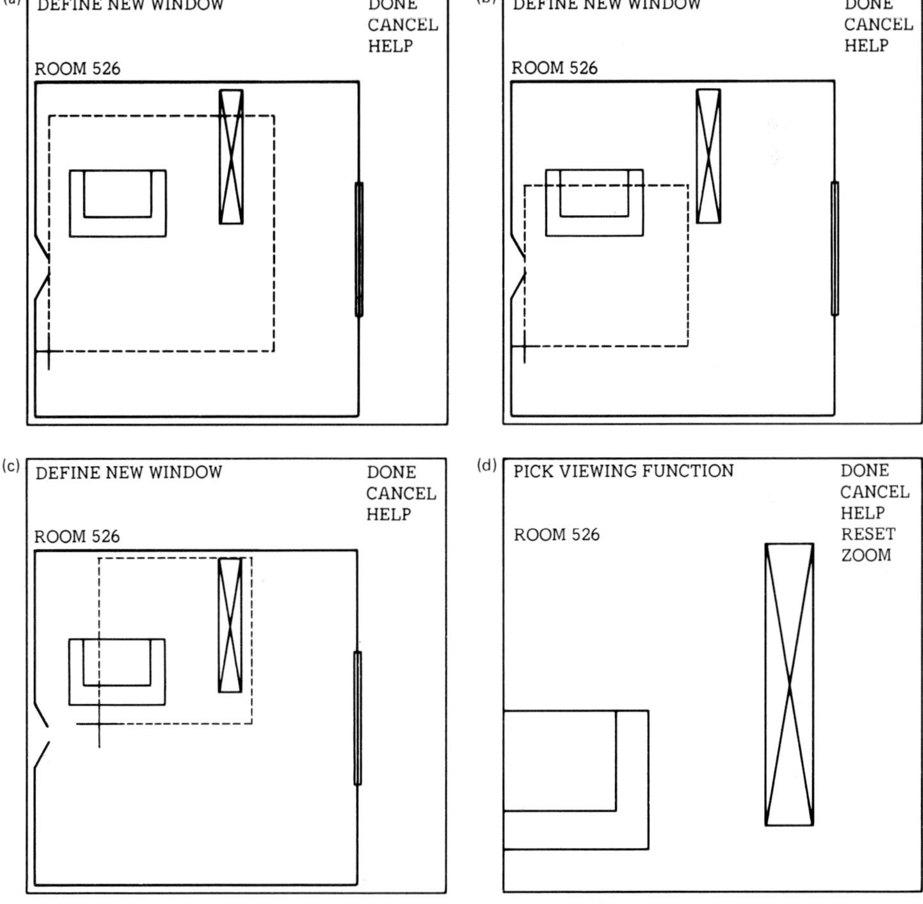

Fig. 2.19 Selecting a window in *CHANGE_VIEW.* (a) Window box; (b) a smaller window box; (c) window box repositioned; (d) DONE picked to define new window.

```
procedure ZOOM_IN;
{define new window as subregion of current window's contents}
var
  loc_x, loc_y, scale, size: real;
  zoom_done: boolean;
begin
  loc_x := 0.0; loc_y := 0.0;
  scale := 1.0;                        {ratio of new window to current window}
  SET_VISIBILITY(zoom_prompt, on);
  {initialize box to correspond to current window}
  DRAW_BOX(box, min_x, min_y, scale * (max_x - min_x));
  SET_VISIBILITY(box, on);

  zoom_done := false;
  repeat
    WAIT_PICK(.033, segment name);  {1/30 sec}
    if ((segment_name >= help) and (segment name <= cancel)) or
       (segment_name = 0) then      {legal pick}
      case segment_name of
             0:  {time-out => check to see if new box is needed}
                 NEW_BOX(box, loc_x, loc_y, scale);
          help:  HELP_USER(zoom_help);
          done:  begin
                   {current box defines new window, lower left corner in NDC => WC}
                   size: = scale * (max_x - min_x);
                   INVERSE_2(loc_x, loc_y, min_x, min_y);
                   max_x := min_x + size;
                   max_y := min_y + size;
                   WINDOW(min_x, max_x, min_y, max_y);
                   SET_VISIBILITY(box, off);
                   DISPLAY_D_STR;
                   zoom_done := true
                 end;
        cancel:  zoom_done := true
      end    {case}
    else SCREEN_FEEDBACK(' illegal selection, please try again')
  until zoom_done;
  DELETE_SEGMENT(box);
  SET_VISIBILITY(zoom_prompt, off)
end;    {ZOOM_IN}
```

```
procedure NEW_BOX(box: integer; var loc_x, loc_y, scale: real);
  {reposition and/or regenerate box}
const
  temp = 999;                    {buffer segment}
  scale_eps = 0.01;              {"epsilon" tolerances}
  loc_eps = 0.01;
var
  new_scale, new_x, new_y: real;
begin
  READ_VALUATOR(1, new_scale);
  {if valuator changed enough from old size, then new box}
  if ABS(new_scale - scale) > scale_eps then
    begin
      scale := new_scale;
      DRAW_BOX(temp, min_x, min_y, (max_x - min_x) * scale);
      TRANSLATE_IMAGE_2(temp, loc_x, loc_y);
      SET_VISIBILITY(box, off);
      SET_VISIBILITY(temp, on);
      DELETE_SEGMENT(box);
      RENAME_SEGMENT(temp, box)
    end;
  WAIT_BUTTON(wait_time, button_number);
  READ_LOCATOR(new_x, new_y);
  {if locator changed enough from old location, then move box}
  if (ABS(new_x - loc_x) > loc_eps)
      or (ABS(new_y - loc_y) > loc_eps) then
    begin
      TRANSLATE IMAGE(box, new_x - loc x, new_y - loc y);
      loc_x := new_x;
      loc_y := new_y;
    end
end;    {NEW_BOX}
```

2.19 ADDING SOLID AREAS FOR RASTER DISPLAYS

Example 2.11 How could we run our sample layout program on a raster display? First of all, such displays support plotting of points, lines, and characters, and therefore the layout program could run without change, thanks to the device-independent nature of SGP. If, however, we wanted to take advantage of the unique ability of raster displays to display solid areas with gray scale or color, we would have to add to SGP the notions of filled enclosed areas. The calls to accomplish this are the *POLYGON* graphic primitive and the *SET_COLOR* attribute setting. The *POLYGON* procedures takes as parameters two arrays of x and y coordinates of vertices of a polygon and the number of vertices to produce a filled polygon in the current color:

POLYGON(x_list, y_list, number)

The COLOR attribute, like the LINE_STYLE attribute, affects subsequent primitives until reset; its default is the foreground color or gray scale, say, white on a gray or green screen or black on a printer.

To color in the shapes of our six standard symbols with specified colors, we alter the routines that plot them by turning the **for** loops which draw successive lines through the vertices forming closed areas into single *POLYGON* calls. This *POLYGON* call is bracketed by appropriate *SET_COLOR* calls using the new color parameter. In order to save the existing color, we make use of INQUIRE routines, one of many which can be used to obtain current values of any attribute, the CP, etc. [GSPC79]. The *CHAIR* procedure of Section 2.11 then simply becomes:

```
procedure CHAIR(xc, yc, rot_angle: real; color: integer)
var chair_x, chair_y, chair_x_new, chair_y_new: array[1..7] of real;
begin
  {transform coordinates by rotation and translation}
  XFORM(xc, yc, rot_angle, chair_x, chair_y, chair_x_new, chair_y_new, 7);
  old_color := INQUIRE_COLOR;
  SET_COLOR(color);
  POLYGON(chair_x_new, chair_y_new, 6);
  SET_COLOR(old_color)
end;
```

2.20 ALTERNATIVE IMPLEMENTATION

The preceding sections have developed an implementation of the symbol placement program that is as straightforward and as easy to explain as possible. It has been described in a top-down fashion and the different procedures have been defined as independently as is feasible with a conventional programming language. The program that results from this implementation is a good program in terms of human factors: it has good HELP features and some CANCEL features. However, one feature is not as convenient for the user as it could be: he must explicitly exit from each function (with a DONE pick) before choosing another function. It would be preferable to leave the main function menu always visible and allow the user to pick a new function at any time.

This minor revision of the program/user interface, however, has a major impact on the implementation of the program, and we must either modify the existing program or create a new implementation scheme. If we choose to modify the existing program, we must provide in each event-handling loop other alternatives to check for a pick of the function menu segments; many of the procedures would have to return an indication of whether they were terminated because DONE was picked, and the mainline would have to invoke the picked function without waiting for another event. The state transition diagram would become more complex as more options are introduced. In general, although the modifications needed are usually obvious, they are also tedious and require introduction of additional explicit parameters and/or global variables.

Alternatively, we can create a completely new implementation scheme based on the revised requirements. The alternative implementation has only *one* event-handling routine in the program which handles all events and invokes the appropriate procedure depending on the value of the *current state* variable.* For example, when the system is in the *add symbol* state, choice of an entry in the symbol menu would initiate an *add symbol* operation, but choice of the *delete symbol* menu item (not requiring a DONE pick to exit) puts the system into the *delete symbol* state. Although this approach can provide a better user interface, the resulting program may not be as well-modularized as the earlier version, since it must rely heavily on global variables to retain important information between subsequent events.

2.21 SUMMARY

In this chapter we have laid the groundwork for the fundamental notions and techniques which are sufficient for writing many straightforward, useful application programs. We paid strict attention to achieving a consistent, uniform user-computer interaction style, as well as a uniform implementation style for the mainline and its subprocedures. We have clearly separated our three major concerns: plotting (producing snapshots of objects), maintaining a data structure which stores the model of the object(s) we wish to view and interact with, and handling the interaction. One procedure might involve all three aspects (*PLACE_SYMBOL* for example), but separate code segments or even subprocedures handle each of the three separately.

One of the key techniques for this separation was putting primitives in *segments* to modify picture pieces selectively or to make them (in)visible. Another was the use of event-driven interaction loops for synchronizing the user-computer dialogue. The programs themselves were high-level and transportable by virtue of being both computer- and device-independent. This was accomplished through the use of Pascal and SGP, a device-independent subroutine package. There have been a number of efforts to extend standard high-level programming languages such as FORTRAN, PL/I, ALGOL 68 and Pascal with graphics data types and operators to provide a more consistent and more elegant interface to the graphics system than provided by a subroutine package [SMIT71, DENE75, SCHR76, MAGN81].

As was noted in Chapter 1, SGP and its parent, the Core package proposed by ACM SIGGRAPH in 1979, have been used as de facto interim standards and many commercial implementations and variations have become available. Meanwhile, the American National Standards Institute (ANSI) and the International Standards Organization (ISO) have been considering official national and international standards derived from the Core [ANSI81, ISO81]. Among the differences likely to result from more recent proposals are the elimination of CP (by explicit specification of starting and ending points) and the inclusion of facilities for hierarchical object definition (as discussed in Chapter 9). Other changes include various mappings of images to physical devices, some of which are not readily explained by the syn-

*This approach is a special case of the more general technique of using a finite-state language processor to define and process interaction sequences. See [NEWM68b] for more details.

thetic camera paradigm (GKS workstation transformations), and far greater attention paid to the special needs of raster graphics (as discussed in Chapters 11 and 12). It should be noted that none of these potential alterations and enhancements will make obsolete the basic approach and programming style presented in this chapter—almost all the concepts and techniques presented are likely to be useful for more sophisticated packages as well. In the next chapter we discuss the spectrum of graphics hardware available today, and in the following chapter we consider how a simple device-independent package (such as SGP) might be implemented on such hardware.

EXERCISES

2.1 Make a high-level symbolic sketch of a suitable model for an application area you are familiar with, using annotated diagrams or high-level abstract data structures in the manner of Section 2.1. Describe the differing types of pictorial representations/views that can be derived from the application data structure. How would interaction be used to change the model and/or its pictorial representations on the screen?

2.2 For three application areas, establish suitable user/world coordinate systems in terms of units and ranges of values that will be occupied by the objects.

2.3 Restate the two purposes of a window declaration.

2.4 How would you use windowing in the application of Exercise 2.1?

2.5 a) Write SGP code to plot an outline of a simple row house; use three segments containing a square wall, a rectangular door in the wall, and a triangular roof, respectively. Do not specify viewports, i.e., use the default of the entire NDC space.

b) Define a viewing window for the house to isolate and magnify the portion from the top of the roof to the top of the door.

c) Write SGP code for the most efficient way to draw a *street* of six row house outlines, one abutting the other. *Hint:* Don't duplicate SGP code unnecessarily and note that segments can't be nested.

2.6 Design and, if possible, implement a simple, nice-to-use offline procedure to plot histograms which uses automatic scaling for maximum and minimum height and width, so the plot fits on a single screen. Would you modify the requirements and/or the program to plot it on a plotter?

2.7 Detail the variables which collectively could be said to comprise the application data structure accessed and modified by *LAYOUT.*

2.8 Write and, if possible, debug a simple variant of the *LAYOUT* program which allows the user to (re)position the row house outlines of Exercise 2.5(c) anywhere on the screen and delete them. You may use whatever input devices you like. What global menu items, such as HELP, CANCEL, DONE in *LAYOUT,* might be useful?

2.9 a) Do you disagree with any of the many human factors criteria in Section 2.2? Have any been omitted? Were any rules violated or not observed in *LAYOUT*?

b) Take the original or your improved list of human factors criteria and critique your least favorite interactive program, such as your text editor. How would you modify the program to be more user-friendly? Note: We aren't dealing here with circumstances beyond our control, such as response time on overloaded time-sharing systems, or with improving functional capability.

2.10 a) Check the physical input devices on the graphics system(s) available to you and categorize them in terms of the five classes of logical devices in SGP.

b) How are their echos handled?

c) How might a logical device for which you do not have a corresponding physical device be simulated by the physical devices available?

d) Is there a physical device that doesn't readily correspond to the five logical ones for which you might like to define a corresponding, new logical device?

e) Explain why it is necessary in *PLACE_SYMBOL* (Section 2.16.5) to use a button to signify the change from pick to locator for the data tablet. (Hint: Suppose the user picked PLACE and the program then sampled without the *WAIT_BUTTON*?) Can you think of other potential conflicts when a single physical device is used to create several logical devices?

Another related problem is that in a time-sharing system there may be a considerable time lag between when the button event has been processed and when the sampling is done. In this interval the user may have changed the state of the sampled device, and the value returned may not be close to the value specified when the event was caused. To eliminate the time lag, the Core allows a sampled device and an event device to be *associated*. This association means that processing the event and doing the sampling are handled as an indivisible operation. How would the code in *PLACE_SYMBOL* be modified if there were an *ASSOCIATION(button, valuator, value)* call?

2.11 Sketch out a high-level design of an interactive graphics display program for a simple version of the application of Exercise 2.1 (or for another simple one of your choice). The application should be no more involved than *LAYOUT*. Start with a precise but readable user's guide (even if only a page long!). Draw both the module hierarchy (or directed graph, if there are multiple callers) and the finite-state graph showing legal interaction sequences. Use mnemonic names for all symbol-plotting routines without defining their output primitives calls, and write other routines with SGP calls or high-level pseudocode, as appropriate. You may also use abstract data structure definitions. Make the listings self-explanatory, using drawings as appropriate. (Passive computer graphics is useful!) Do not take more than three hours and 10–15 pieces of paper for this exercise.

2.12 How would you improve *LAYOUT* if you could enable and WAIT for multiple input devices simultaneously? Check the facilities of the Core or another package you use for such selective WAITs to see how to change *LAYOUT*'s logic. If you think *LAYOUT* isn't amenable to such modification, discuss another application in which it would be useful to have this facility.

2.13 After acquiring some basic experience with programming Exercises 2.6 and 2.8 and after having had your design for Exercise 2.11 reviewed, corrected, and approved, write the program using careful stepwise refinement of your pseudocode and abstract data structures. Keep track of and document where your time was spent, what you had difficulty with, and where your errors were. Discuss your experiences with your peers and your instructor to learn from your mistakes.

2.14 In *LAYOUT,* after zooming in, the data structure is regenerated by deleting a segment and then recreating it with the new viewing specification in effect. What will the user see happening on the display as deletes and replaces occur in succession? How could double buffering be used to switch at once from the old picture to the completed new one?

2.15 Show how to implement the *SCREEN_FEEDBACK* procedure of Section 2.13 and the transparent *HELP_USER* function mentioned in Section 2.14.3.

2.16 In the implementation of *LAYOUT* presented, only one symbol may be added/placed at a time in *ADD_SYMBOL*'s call to *PLACE_SYMBOL*. Show how to modify both procedures to allow adding/placing of multiple symbols without excessive menu picking. What additional *ADD_SYMBOL* options might be user-friendly (unambiguous, yet concise)? Are there any changes you'd like to make to SGP to facilitate this interaction?

2.17 Work out the details of one of the alternate implementations of *LAYOUT* suggested in Section 2.20.

2.18 One of the many extensions of SGP present in richer packages like the Core is the notion of a *segment attribute*. In *LAYOUT* we saw how *visibility* was used as a *dynamic* segment attribute that can be changed after the segment has been created (unlike the static primitive attributes such as color or line styles). The *detectability* dynamic attribute can be used to make visible segments selectively pickable. Show how *LAYOUT* code can be somewhat simplified by selectively turning detectability of segments *on* and *off*. Show also how the *highlightability* dynamic-segment attribute may be used to provide feedback to the user for picked symbols and light buttons. It calls attention to a segment by blinking or intensifying the image.

2.19 On a raster display, changing the visibility of a segment takes much more time than on a vector display, since the segment must be redrawn (in background color to set visibility off). How could the code in Section 2.18.3 be modified slightly to make the transition from the old object to the new a smoother one on a raster display?

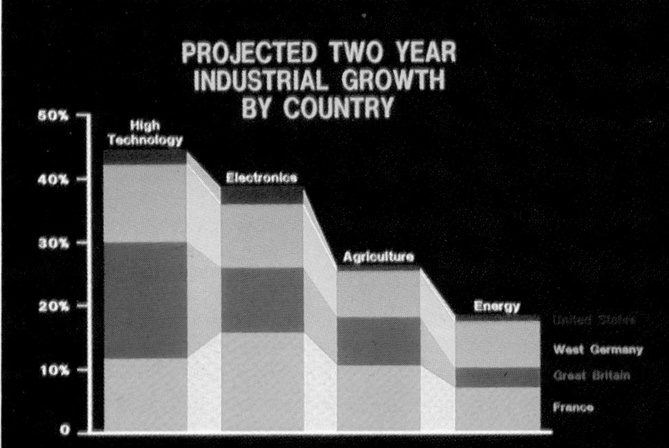

PLATE 1
Business graph produced on the DICOMEDIA II system (courtesy of DICOMED Corporation, Minneapolis, Minn.).

PLATE 2
Logo for Los Angeles PBS television station KCET. (Art Director: Richard Taylor, Art Durinski, John Whitney, Jr.; Technical Director: Gary Demos. Digital scene simulation by Information International, Inc. Copyright 1980. All rights reserved.)

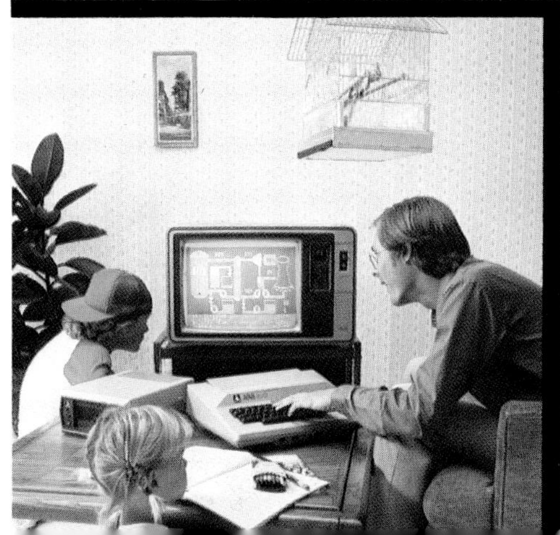

PLATE 3
SCRAM™—a nuclear-power plant simulation as played on ATARI 400™ and 800™ computers (courtesy of ATARI® Inc., Sunnyvale, California).

PLATE 4
Space Invaders (Trade Mark of Taito America Corporation)—one of the world's most popular video games, as played on ATARI 400^{TM} and 800^{TM} computers (courtesy of $Atari^{R}$ Inc., Sunnyvale, California).

PLATE 5
Display of esophagus, spinal cord, and lung surfaces in the upper thoracic region (reconstruction based on five cross-sectional image plates). Red areas show proportions of this anatomy which are in the path of a proposed therapeutic radiation beam (courtesy of D. L. McShan, Ph.D., and A. S. Glicksman, M.D., Department of Radiation Oncology, Rhode Island Hospital, Providence, R.I.).

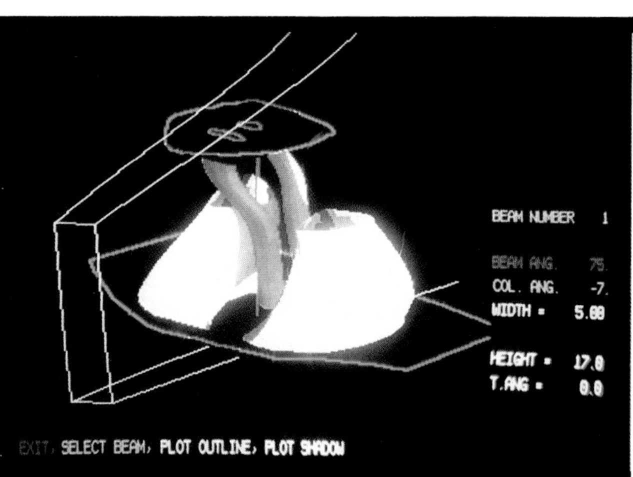

PLATE 6
Simulation of a distorted structural framework consisting of I-beams and a hollow rectangular section. The distorted geometry is represented by a large number (over 1000 elements) of rectangular panels which were generated by a second program. This second program uses node displacements and rotations generated by a third computer program. Color has been used to represent the bending stress in the frame members. The symmetric set of color fringes uses warmer colors to represent the extreme values of stress and has a white fringe at zero stress (courtesy of Prof. Hank Christiansen, Brigham Young University; made by using the MOVIE.BYU system).

PLATE 7

(a) Veronese surface sliced by a hyperplane and projected from 4-space; the slice is white, surface above hyperplane is red, surface below is green (courtesy of Banchoff/Strauss Productions, Providence, R.I.).

(b) Figure-eight torus with six twists. The upper part of the 8 is rendered in copper; the lower part, in obsidian (courtesy of David Salesin, Brown University Computer Graphics Group).

PLATE 8

Cartoon painted interactively on a raster display (courtesy of Evans & Sutherland Computer Corporation, Salt Lake City, Utah).

PLATE 9
Command and control displays (courtesy of U.S. Navy).

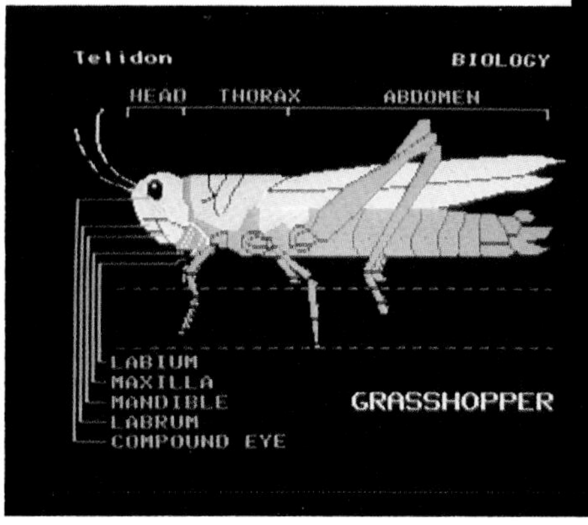

PLATE 10
Example of high-quality Videotex graphics: the Canadian Telidon system (courtesy of Communications Research Centre, Ottawa, Ontario).

PLATE 11
A view of the Spatial Data Management System (courtesy of Prof. Nicholas Negroponte, Architecture Machine Group, MIT).

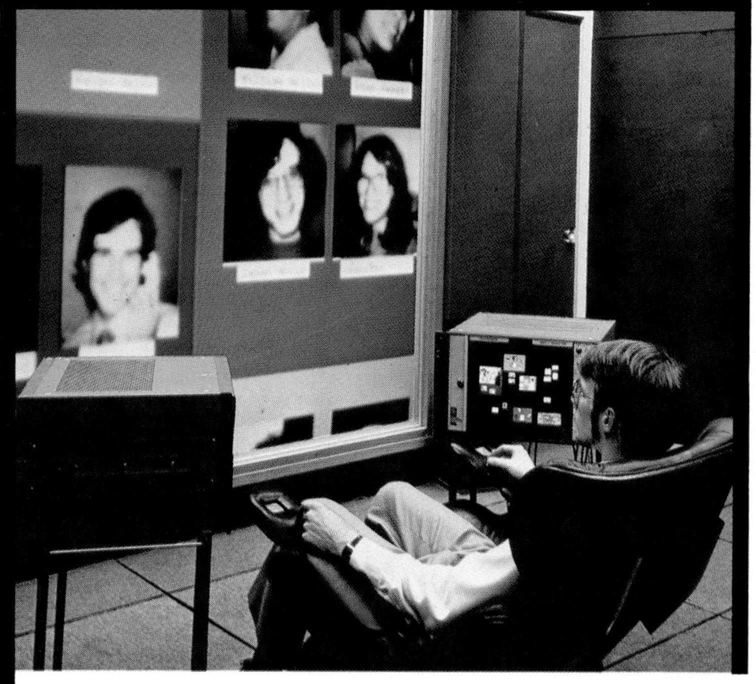

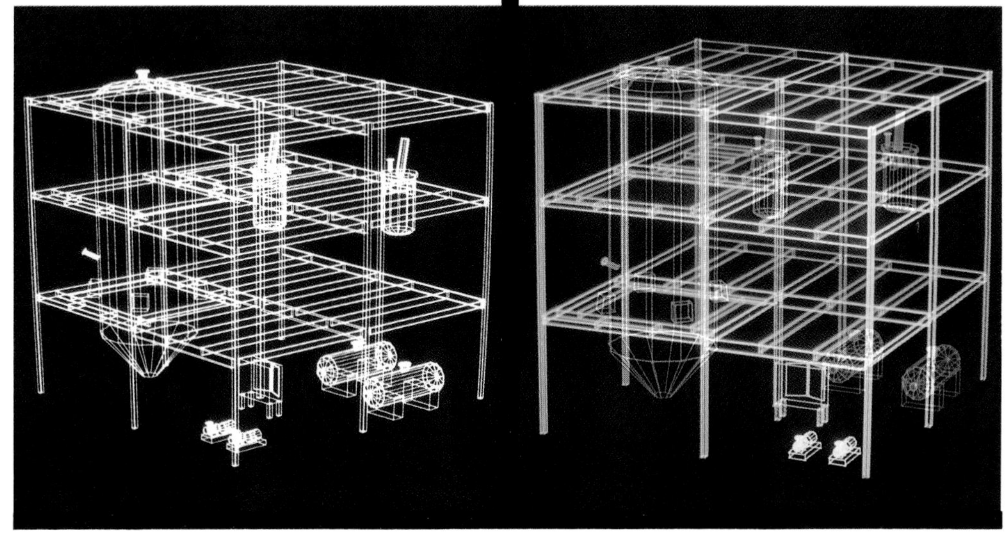

PLATE 12
A building framework. Color helps show different substructures (courtesy of Evans & Sutherland Computer Corporation).

PLATE 13
Scene from "The Works" (1980): a giant mechanical ant and its robot driver (courtesy of New York Institute of Technology).

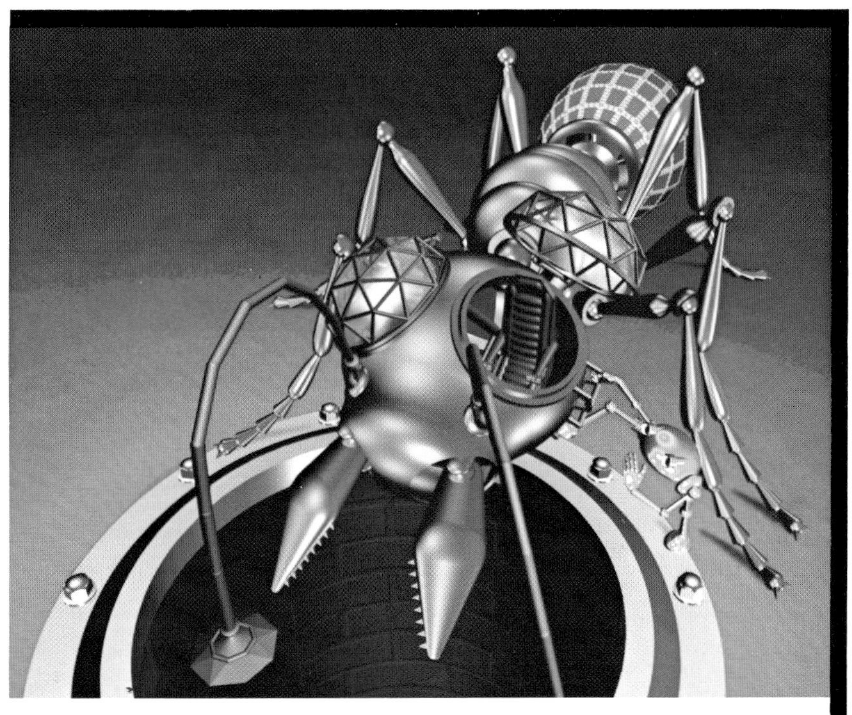

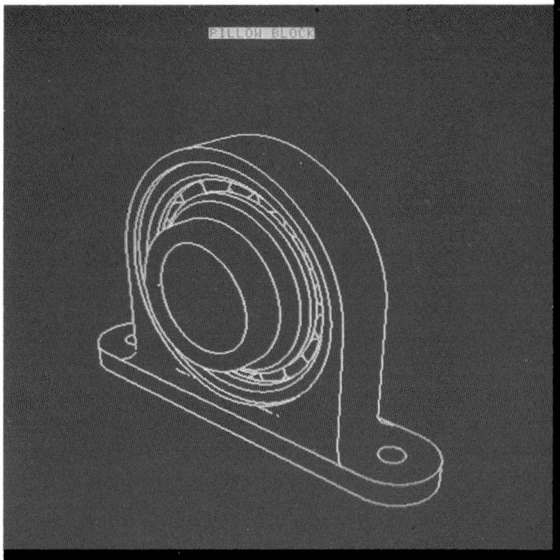

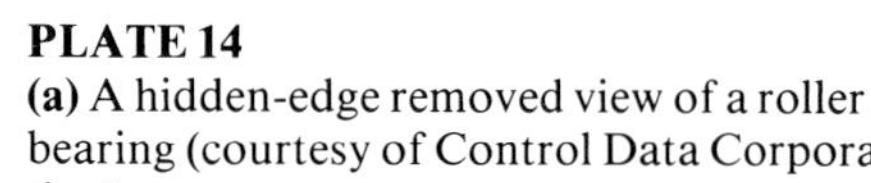

PLATE 14

(a) A hidden-edge removed view of a roller bearing (courtesy of Control Data Corporation).

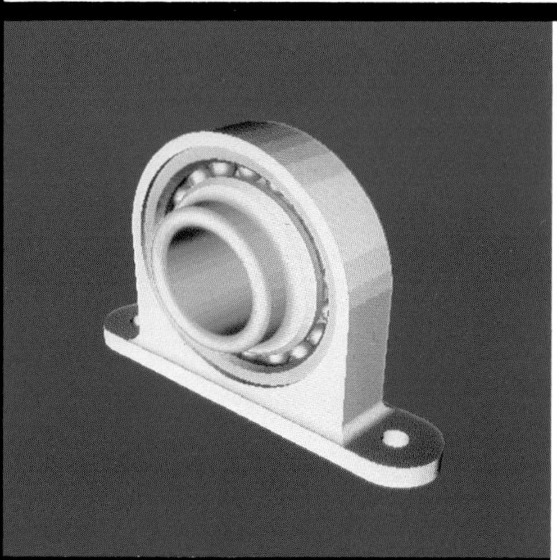

(b) A hidden-surface removed view of a roller bearing (courtesy of Control Data Corporation).

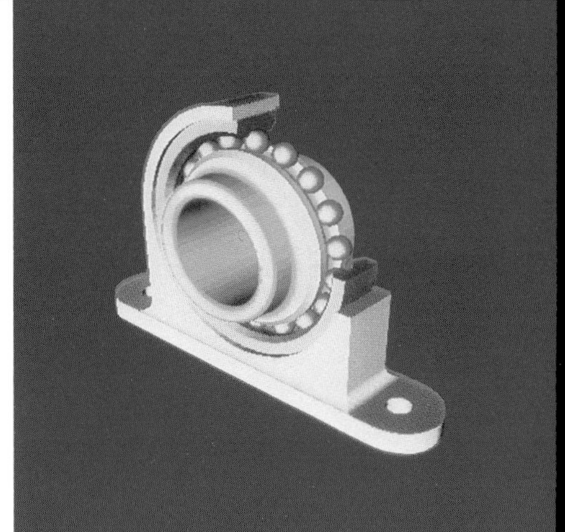

(c) A cut-away view of a roller bearing (courtesy of Control Data Corporation).

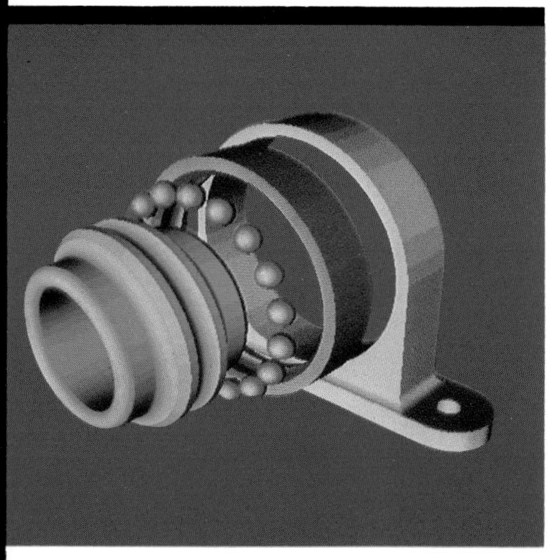

(d) An exploded view of a roller bearing (courtesy of Control Data Corporation).

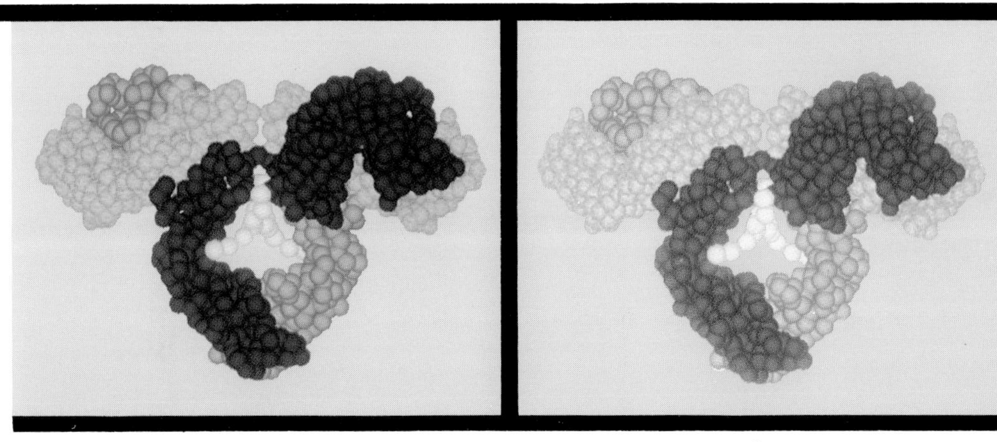

a b

PLATE 15
Stereo pairs of a molecule (courtesy of R. Feldmann and T. Porter, National Institute of Health).

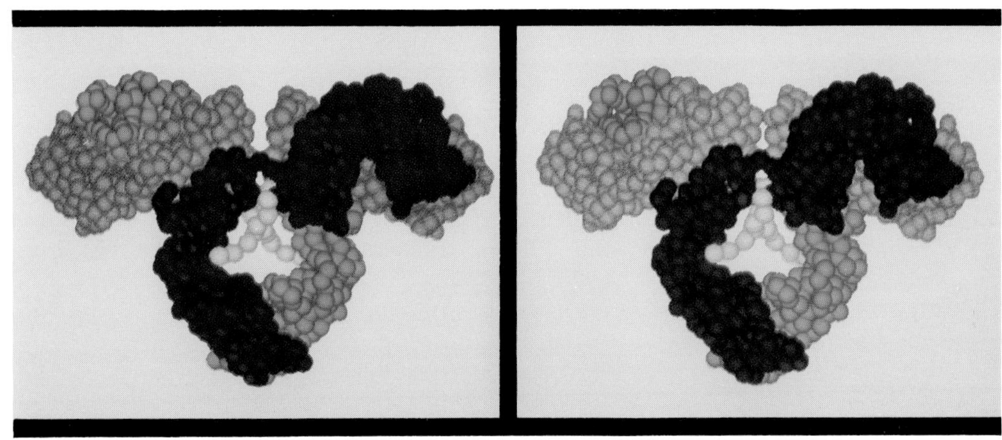

c d

PLATE 16
Hidden-surface-removed view of NASA space shuttle (courtesy of Evans & Sutherland Computer Corporation).

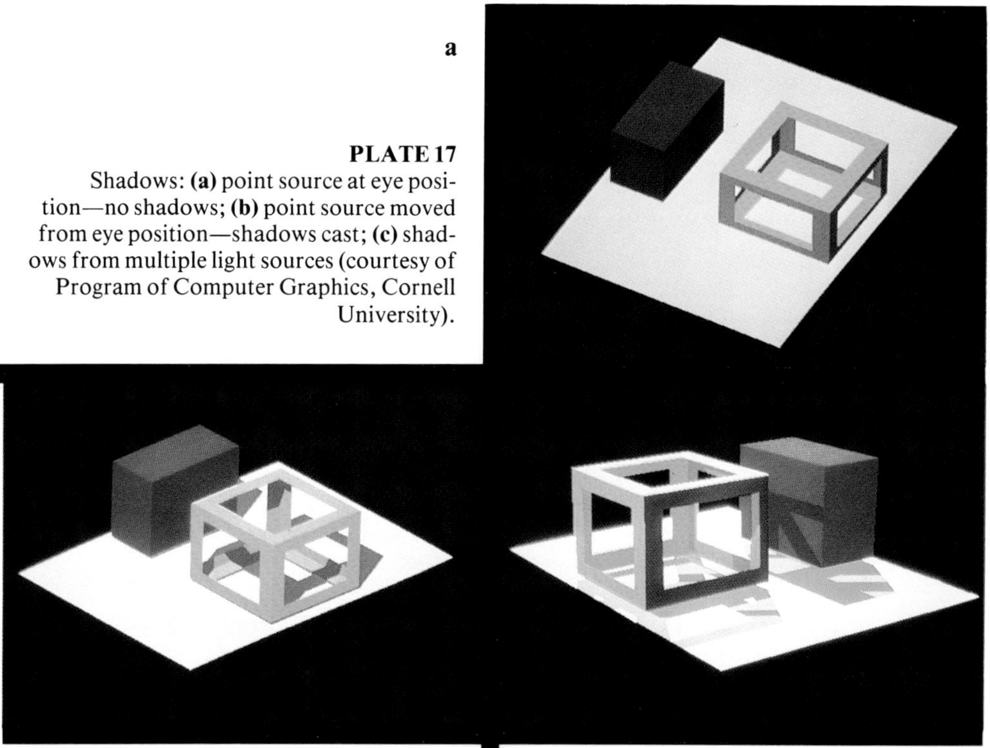

a

PLATE 17
Shadows: **(a)** point source at eye position—no shadows; **(b)** point source moved from eye position—shadows cast; **(c)** shadows from multiple light sources (courtesy of Program of Computer Graphics, Cornell University).

b

c

PLATE 18
A toroid whose textured surface shows both diffuse and specular reflection (by J. Blinn, courtesy of University of Utah).

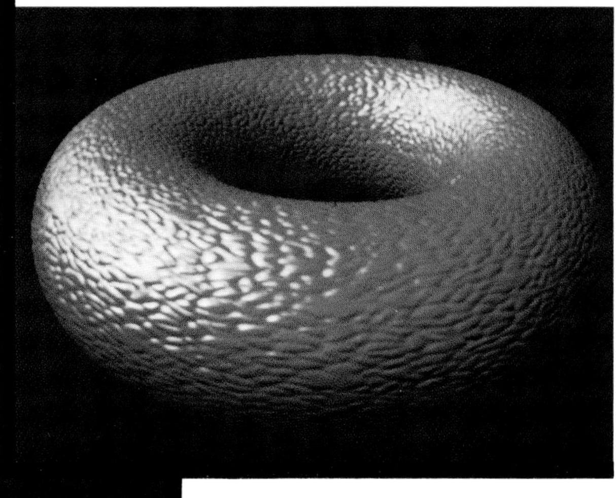

PLATE 19
A computer-generated strawberry, showing both diffuse and specular reflection (by J. Blinn, courtesy of University of Utah)

PLATE 20
Red–yellow checker table with ball (courtesy of Turner Whitted, Bell Laboratories).

PLATE 21
Mountain scenes created with fractal surfaces (courtesy Boeing Computer Services Co.). For more details on the many applications of fractals, see [MAND 77, MAND 82].

a

b

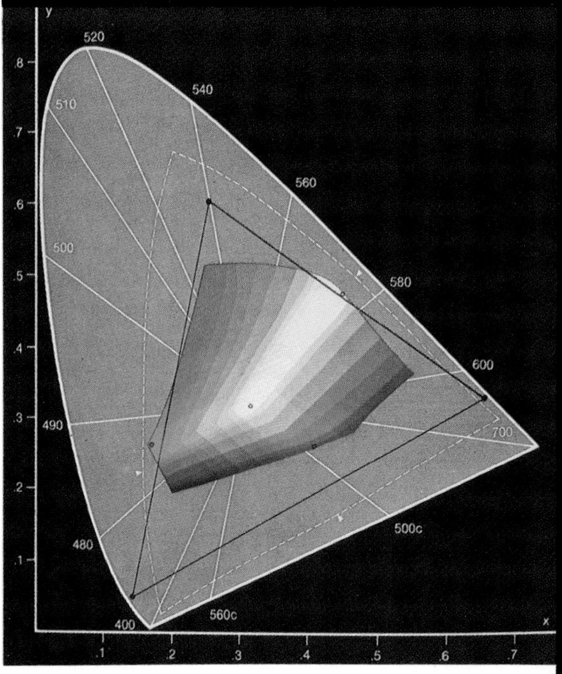

COLOR PLATE 22
The CIE chromaticity diagram from "How Light Interacts With Matter", by V.F. Weisskopf (copyright 1968 by Scientific American, Inc. All rights reserved).

PLATE 23
Three views of RGB color space: **(a)** the R, G, and B axes; **(b)** the RB, BG, and GR planes filled in; **(c)** the outline of the RGB cube; black is obscured by white (courtesy of Tektronix, Inc.).

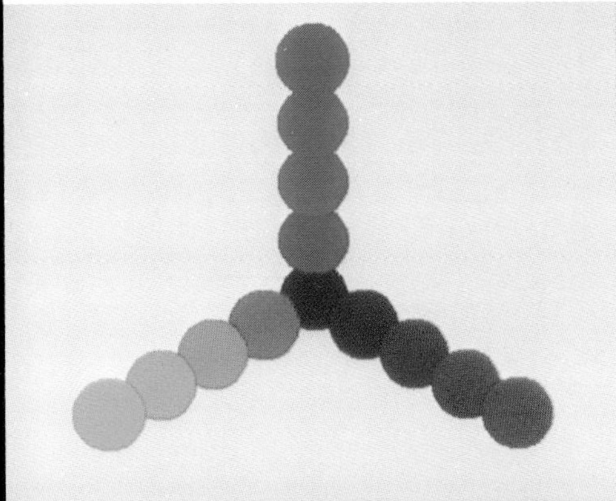

a

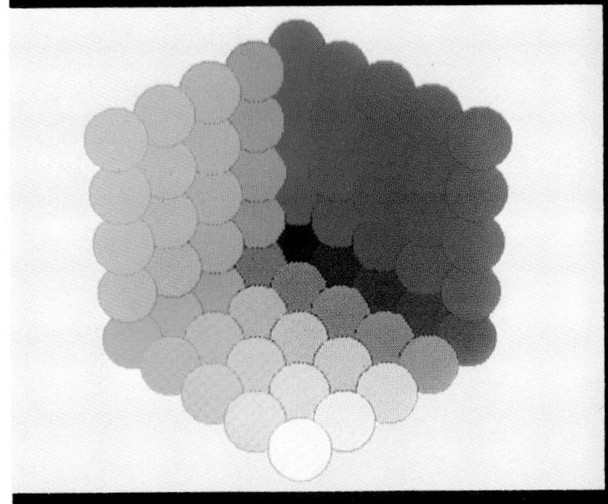

b

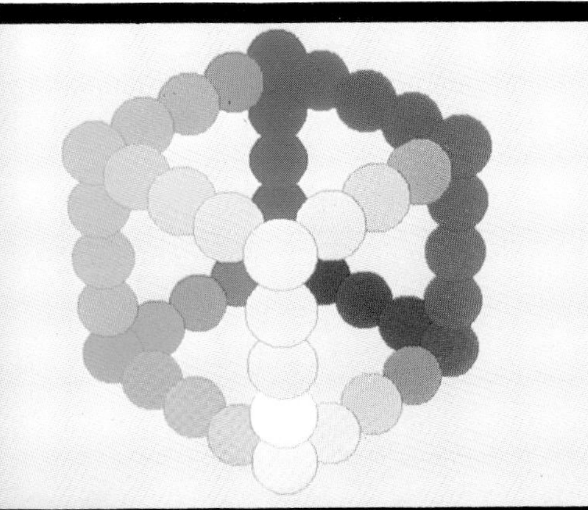

c

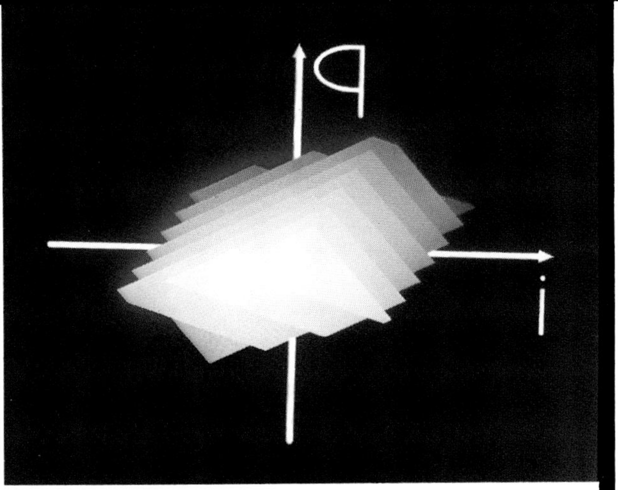

PLATE 24
YIQ color space (courtesy of Alvy Ray Smith).

PLATE 25
Exploded view of HLS color space, with double hexcone deformed into double cone (courtesy of Tektronix, Inc.).

PLATE 26
An enlarged halftone color picture.

PLATE 27
A total of 125 colors generated on Tektronix 4027 by using 2×2 pixel patterns for each primary. Each 5×5 grid is a plane of constant R in the RGB color space (courtesy of Tektronix, Inc.).

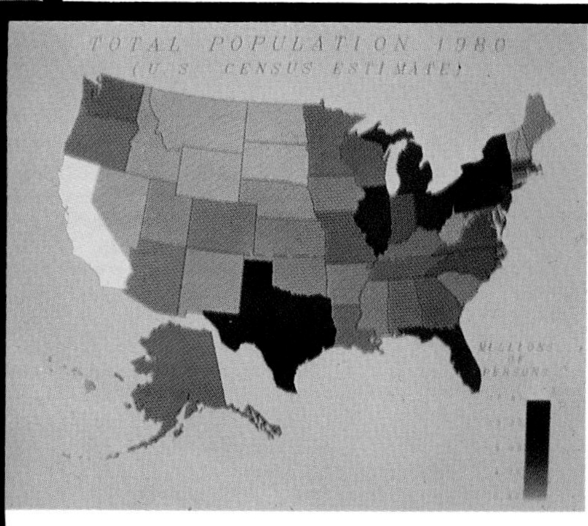

PLATE 28
A continuous-tone chloropleth map of the United States. Colors are taken from RGB space, along a path that starts along the red axis (in the region that appears brown), goes through the cube to the $R = 1$ plane, and continues toward partially saturated yellow (courtesy of John Sibert, The George Washinton University).

3
Graphics Hardware

In this chapter we describe, primarily with regard to hardware, the organization and operation of a complete interactive graphics system. The typical system that will be examined is shown in Fig. 3.1. There are four major subsystems: computer, display processing unit (DPU), display device, and user input devices. Associated with the computer are two hard-copy devices: a printer and a plotter. The computer is, of course, the heart of the system. Some basic knowledge of computer hardware will be helpful in reading this chapter.

The display device used in interactive graphics is usually a cathode ray tube (CRT). New display devices are emerging, some of which are already in limited use, but CRTs are likely to be dominant for quite a few more years. The newer technologies are discussed briefly in Sections 3.2.5 and 3.2.6.

As described in Chapter 1, the two basic types of CRTs are refresh and storage. With a refresh CRT, the drawing must be refreshed, i.e., regenerated 30 to 60 times per second from the digital representation stored in the buffer to avoid flicker. Storage CRTs store the image as an internal charge distribution, and thus neither a digital buffer nor a refresh cycle is necessary.

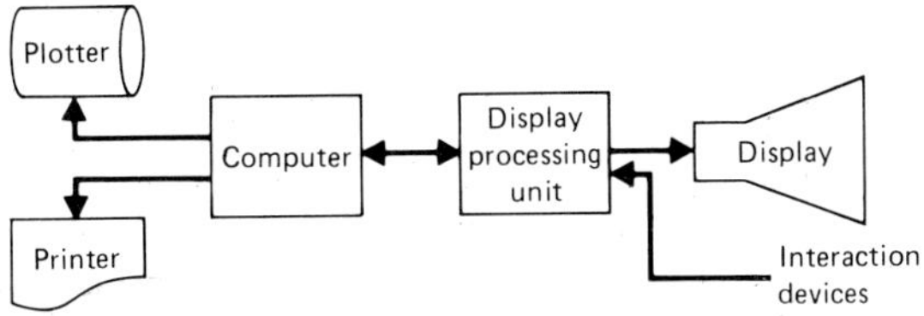

Fig. 3.1 Block diagram of typical interactive graphics system.

The DPU can be viewed as a special-purpose CPU, with its own set of commands, data formats, and an instruction counter. It executes a sequence of display instructions (the display file, which hereafter will be called a *display program or DPU program*), to create a drawing on the display device. Individual DPU instructions typically draw a point, line, or character string. Interaction devices, with which the user inputs commands and other information, are attached to the DPU. A few basic devices are described here and many more are presented in Chapter 5.

The DPU can be organized to create a drawing either by random scan or raster scan. In a *random-scan* (also called *vector, stroke,* or *calligraphic*) system, parts of the drawing can be depicted on the display in any order. The house in Fig. 3.2 was drawn by moving (deflecting) the beam to the starting point, turning it on and continuously deflecting it between successive line endpoints to trace the house outline. In a *raster* (TV-type) *scan* system, the drawing is divided into horizontal lines; all parts of the drawing appearing in the first line are reproduced in left-to-right order, then all parts of the drawing in the second line, etc. Hard-copy devices also operate with either a random or raster scan. The printer is a simple raster-scan hard-copy device. The print head moves from left to right, top to bottom. The pen plotter, in which a pen can be moved in any direction over a piece of paper, is a random-scan device.

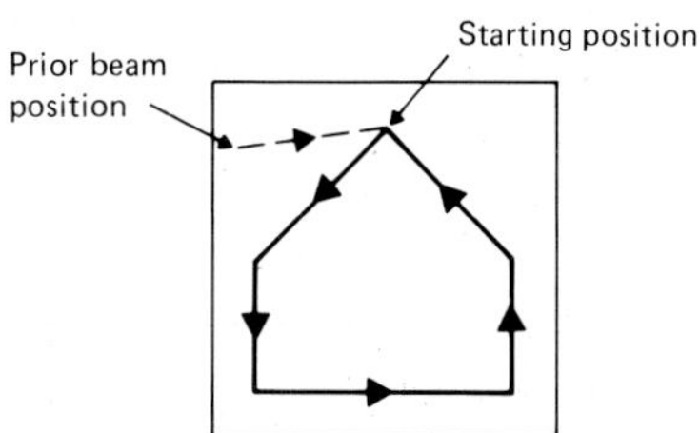

Fig. 3.2 House displayed with random scan.

Figure 3.3 shows a basic raster scan starting at the upper left of the screen. During the left-to-right sweep the beam intensity is modulated to create different shades of gray. At the right edge the beam is blanked (turned off), repositioned (dashed line) at the left edge, one unit down from the previous scan line, and un-

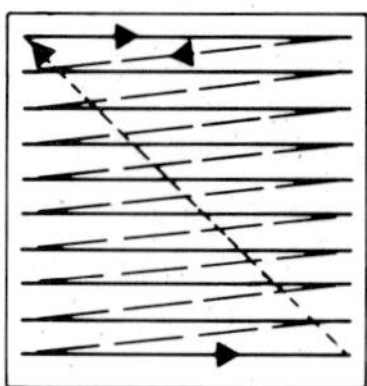

Fig. 3.3 Raster-scan pattern.

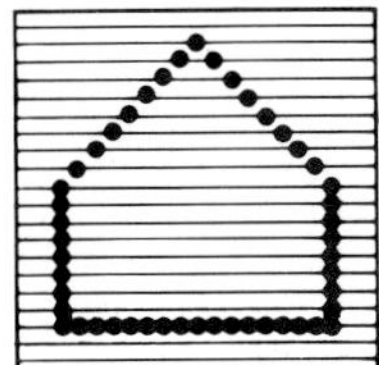

Fig. 3.4 House displayed with raster scan.

blanked. After all scan lines have been drawn, the beam returns to the upper left corner. U.S. broadcast TV operates with 525 scan lines, but common raster graphics systems use anywhere from 256 to 1024 lines. The more lines, the higher the picture quality. A raster-display outline of the house would be drawn as depicted in Fig. 3.4, showing the scan lines and the points at which they are intensified.

In this chapter we first discuss printers and plotters as graphic output devices. We treat the important display technologies and then turn to a detailed discussion of the architecture of basic vector DPUs. Advanced vector DPUs are presented in Chapter 10. Raster DPUs are introduced briefly and are discussed in much greater detail in Chapter 12. Sections marked with a star ★ are strongly hardware-oriented and may easily be skipped without loss of continuity. Readers interested in further technology details are referred to [SHER79].

3.1 OUTPUT-ONLY TECHNOLOGY

Computers were used in drawing pictures long before the development of interactive graphics. The two principal output devices used for this purpose are the printer and the plotter.

3.1.1 Printers as Graphic Output Devices

The major areas in which line printers are practical for graphic output are flowcharting (and other block diagrams), plotting of functions of a single variable (including bar graphs, etc.), and plotting functions of two variables, with the function values being indicated by the darkness of characters at each point.

The main factor determining whether a graphic output device is appropriate for a particular application is its *resolution,* which is the number of distinguishable elements per unit of distance. The low resolution of the printer (usually 10 points per inch horizontally and 6 points per inch vertically) limits its usefulness. Balanced against the poor resolution are the printer's speed, accessibility, and low cost per page of output. The flowchart in Fig. 3.5 lacks nothing essential despite the low resolution and costs much less to produce than would have been possible with a plotter. Some printers use dot matrix techniques to print discrete dots at resolutions of up to 100 points per inch. When equipped with multicolor ribbons, these printers produce reasonable color hard copy.

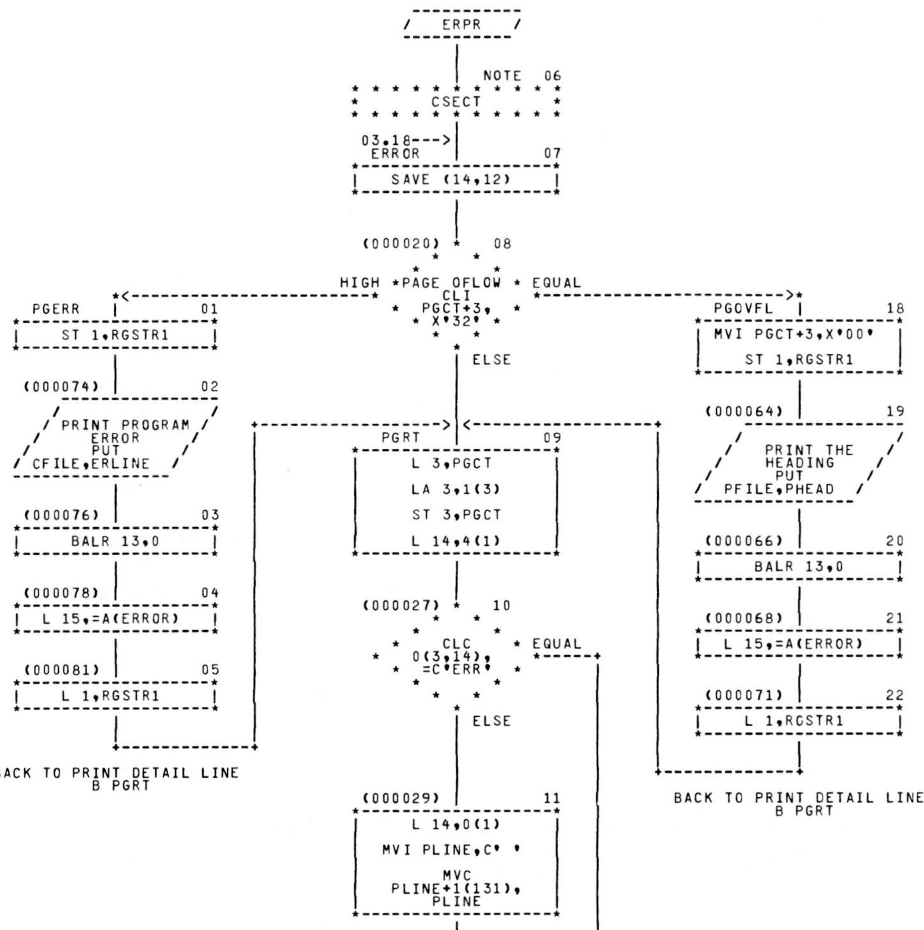

Fig. 3.5 Flowchart produced on line printer. AUTOFLOW II chart set (courtesy Applied Data Research, Inc., Princeton, N.J.).

Figure 3.6 shows data plotted on a set of labelled axes. The plotting of a function requires that the function be evaluated for as many values of the independent variable as there are print positions along the length of the horizontal axis. Each function value must be rounded or truncated to a print position along the vertical axis. If the plot covers only a single printer page of about 50 vertical print positions, rounding can introduce errors of up to 1%. Furthermore, unwanted visual effects, such as the jagged "staircase" appearance of lines, easily occur.

Plotting functions of two variables is useful in several distinct application areas, including spatial distribution maps (Fig. 3.7) and computer-generated pictures (Fig. 3.8). Whatever the application, the technique involves choosing a set of characters sufficient to represent the desired number of intensity levels, ranging from very light

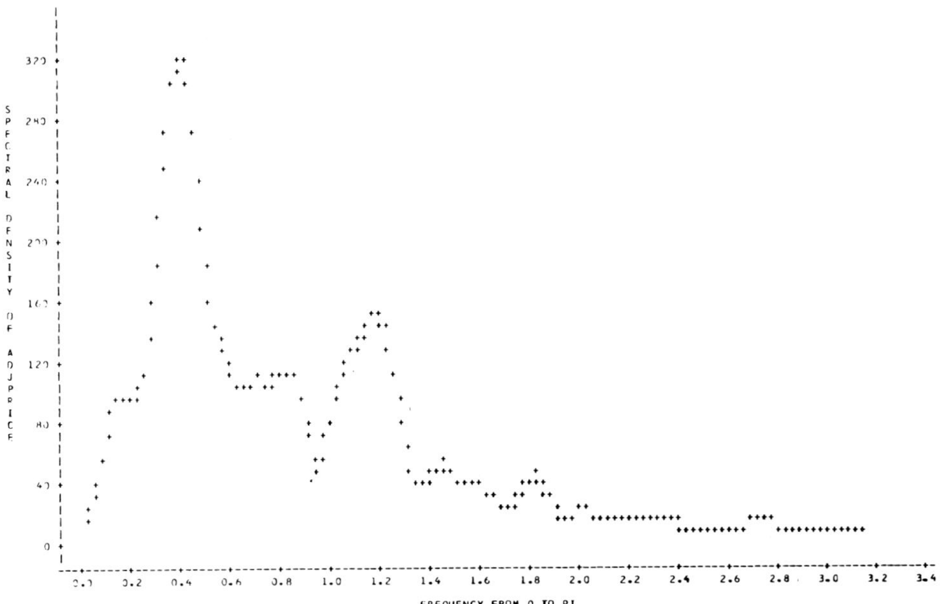

Fig. 3.6 Data plotted on line printer.

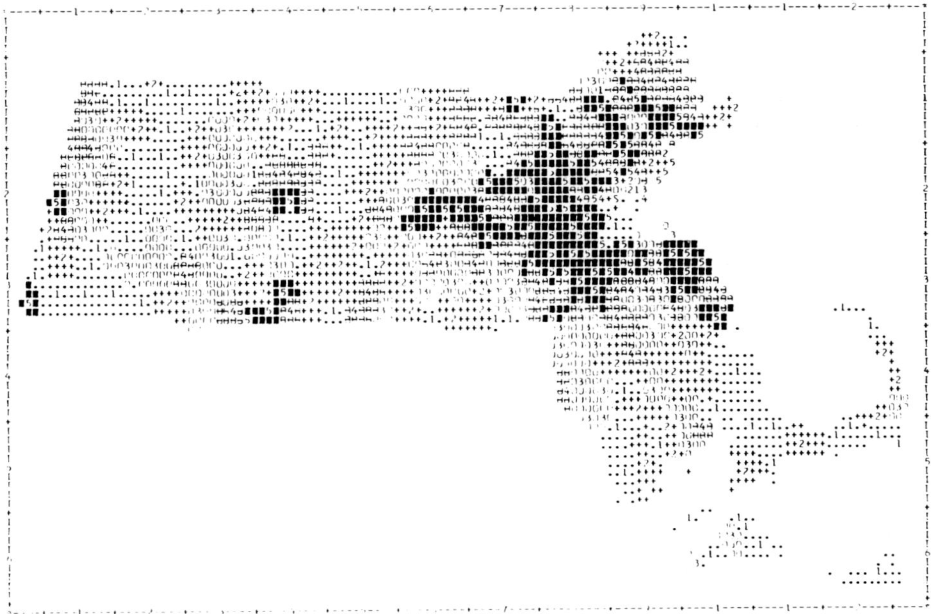

Fig. 3.7 Median family income in Massachusetts for 1968. Map produced by the SYMAP software program created by the Laboratory for Computer Graphics and Spatial Analysis (Harvard Graduate School of Design, Cambridge, Mass., 02138).

Fig. 3.8 Picture generated on line printer.

to very dark, so that the resulting image is meaningful to the viewer. With some printers it is possible to increase the number of intensity levels available by overprinting with one or more characters. Some dot matrix printers allow individual dots to be controlled, so the number of dots printed in a character cell can be used to give different intensities.

Programs producing plots like the ones we have shown often accumulate the characters to be printed in a two-dimensional array, whose size corresponds to the number of columns and lines on a printer page (the array can be larger if a single plot is to cover more than one page). The array is initialized to contain only blanks (spaces), and then selected elements of the array are filled in with nonblank characters. To plot single-variable functions, the characters to print axes, axis labels, axis values, plot name, and function values are inserted in the corresponding array elements. After this, the array is printed out row by row.

What we are really dealing with here are *scan conversion* algorithms that convert the specification of a plot in terms of points, lines, and functions into the sequential row-at-a-time form of a raster scan. Scan-conversion algorithms are fundamental to all raster graphics devices and are discussed in detail in Chapter 11.

3.1.2 Plotters

Just as there are random and raster displays, so too there are random and raster plotters. *Flatbed plotters* draw at random on a sheet of paper spread out on a table and held down by electrostatic charge, by vacuum, or by being stretched tightly (Fig. 3.9). A carriage moves longitudinally over the table. On the carriage is a pen mount that moves latitudinally along the carriage; the pen can be raised and lowered. Flatbed plotters are available in sizes from 12 × 18 inches to at least 6 × 10 feet. In some cases the "pen" is a light source for exposing photographic negatives or a knife blade for scribing. Often pens of multiple colors or widths are used.

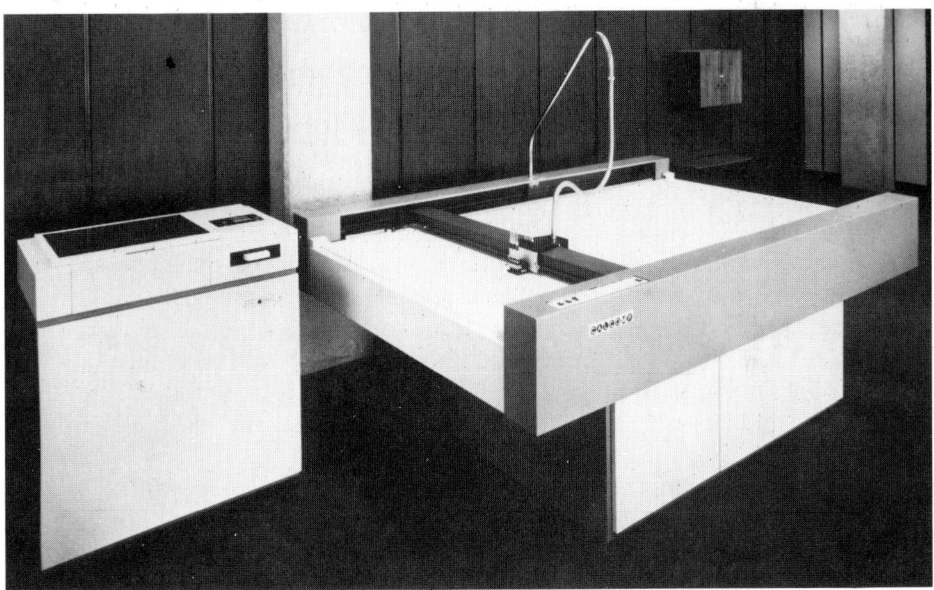

Fig. 3.9 Flatbed plotter (courtesy CalComp—California Computer Products, Inc.).

Drum plotters, another kind of random plotter, draw on a roll of paper stretched tightly across a drum, as shown in Fig. 3.10. Pins on the drum engage prepunched holes in the paper to prevent slipping. The drum can rotate both forward and backward; feed and take-up rolls maintain the paper's tension across the drum. The pen moves transversely across the paper and can be raised and lowered. Paper width varies from 12 to 36 inches.

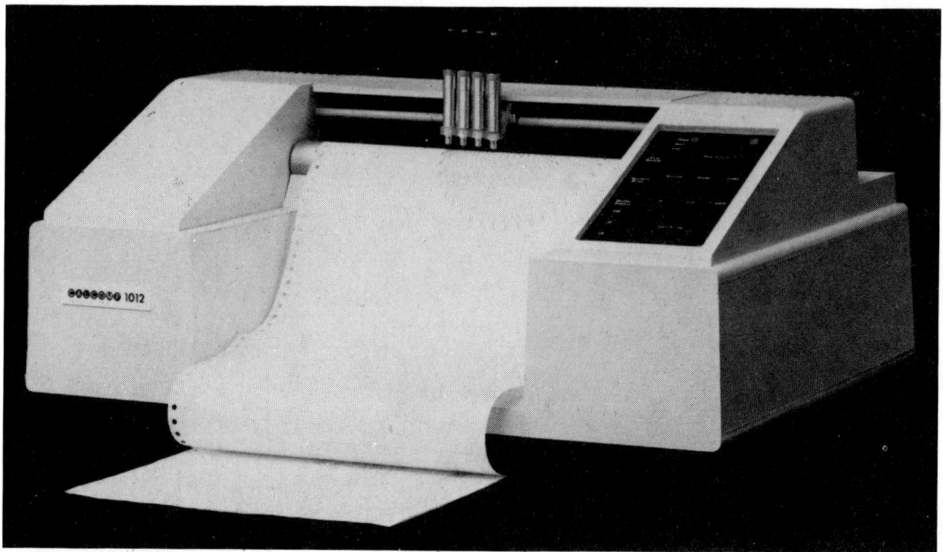

Fig. 3.10 Drum plotter (courtesy CalComp—California Computer Products, Inc.).

All random plotters accept the general commands *lower pen, raise pen, move one unit left (right),* and *move one unit up (down).* A feedback system consisting of position sensors and servomotors implements the motion commands, and the pen is raised and lowered by an electromagnet. More sophisticated plotters can make unit moves in any of 8 or even 16 directions and also allow moves of more than one unit. Plotters that incorporate microprocessors typically accept commands to draw circles, arcs, and characters; the microprocessor generates the low-level hardware commands.

The most common raster plotter—the *electrostatic plotter*—works by first depositing a negative charge on those parts of a white paper strip that are to be black and then flowing positively charged black toner over the paper (Fig. 3.11). The particles adhere to the paper where the charge was deposited. The charge is placed on the paper, which can be up to 72″ wide, one row at a time. The paper moves at speeds up to three inches per second under a fine comb of electric contacts spaced horizontally 100 to 250 to the inch. Each contact is either *on* (to impart a negative charge) or *off* (to impart no charge). From 100 to 250 vertical rows per inch are produced. Each dot on an electrostatic plot is either black or white, although limited gray levels can be obtained by defining small texture patterns with different numbers of black dots (see Chapter 17 for further discussion of this technique).

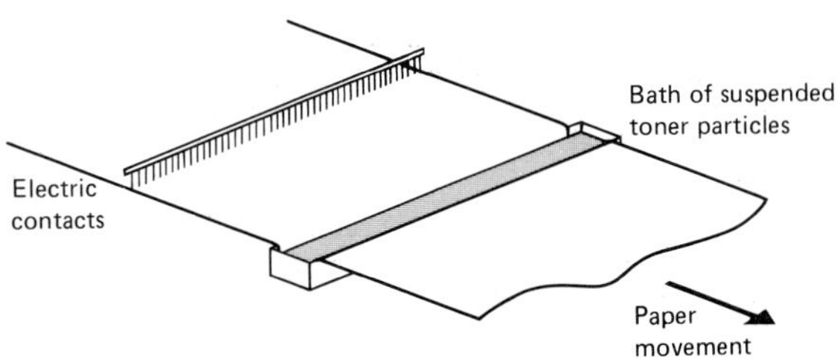

Fig. 3.11 Electrostatic plotter.

Comparison of electrostatic and pen plotters. Pen plotters produce sharp, high-contrast images, and can use pens of different colors and thicknesses. Electrostatic plotter images have lower contrast, because a slight toner residue adheres to the uncharged part of the paper, and they are currently limited to black and white. The electrostatic plotter is typically 10 to 20 times faster than a pen plotter. However, the scan conversion takes time, and can be done either by a general-purpose computer or by a specialized processor optimized for this specific task. Electrostatic plotters can double as medium-speed line printers.

Other technologies. Several other hard-copy technologies are coming into increasing use. Perhaps the most important is the xerographic technique developed by Xerox. A standard *Xerox copier* reproduces a page by creating, on a selenium drum, an electrostatic charge of electrons wherever the document is black. Dry toner adheres to the drum where there is a charge and is then transferred to blank paper to form the copy. In color xerography this process is repeated three times, once for each primary color. The powdered colored pigments mix on the paper to form other colors.

This idea has been extended to computer-controlled image creation, in which a laser beam is scanned across the rotating selenium drum, creating the same charge distribution as if the original document had been placed in the copier. Once the charge is established, the process continues as in the conventional copier. Resolution of several hundred points per inch can be achieved.

The *ink-jet plotter* "shoots" ink of three colors at a paper stretched on a rapidly rotating drum (Fig. 3.12). The ink jets move slowly along a track from one end of the drum to the other. In basic concept, this process is similar to the xerographic process: a raster scan is done, but in this case the three colors are deposited at the same time rather than on separate passes.

A camera used to photograph an image displayed on a cathode ray (TV) tube is another hard-copy device. Simple "homemade" systems use a standard still or movie camera aimed at a display in a darkened room. Commercial systems use the same idea, but with high-precision CRTs and color filters (Fig. 3.13). The image to

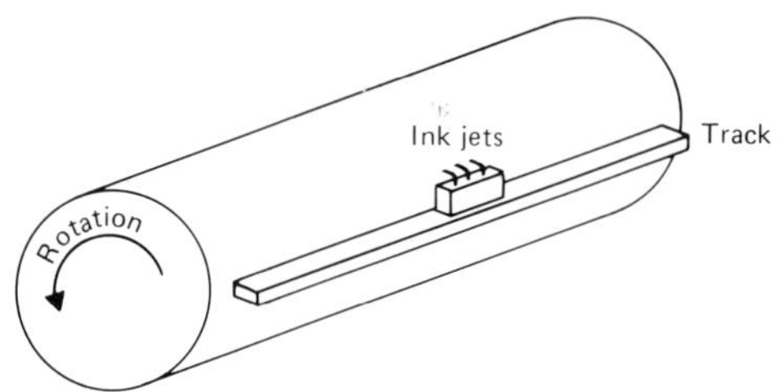

Fig. 3.12 Ink-jet plotter.

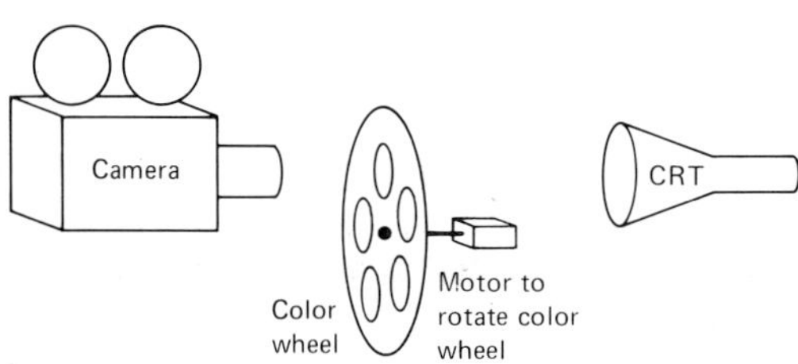

Fig. 3.13 Film recorder.

be displayed is sorted by color, to avoid extraneous and time-consuming color-filter changes. Color mixtures are created by double exposing parts of the image through two or more colors, perhaps with different CRT intensities. Several moderately priced systems for color raster images use the signals which drive the CRT to drive a "slaved" higher-quality monitor. This eliminates duplication of much hardware. Photography is through color filters, eliminating any jaggedness caused by the shadow-mask itself (Section 3.2.4).

3.2 DISPLAY TECHNOLOGY

Interactive computer graphics demands display devices whose images, unlike those drawn on plotters, can be changed very quickly. Nonpermanent image displays allow an image to be changed, making possible movement of portions of an image. The CRT is by far the most common display device and will remain so for many years. However, solid-state technologies are being developed which may, in the long term, have a substantial impact on the dominance of the CRT.

3.2.1 Refresh Cathode Ray Tubes

The CRTs used in black-and-white home television sets are, in most respects, the same as those used for monochrome graphics displays. Figure 3.14 gives a highly stylized sectional view of a CRT. The electron gun emits a stream of electrons which

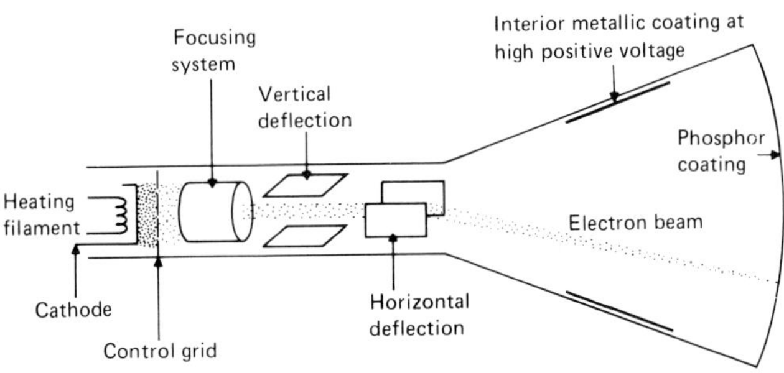

Fig. 3.14 Cross section of CRT.

is accelerated toward the phosphor-coated screen. On the way to the screen, the electrons are forced into a narrow beam by the focusing mechanism and are directed toward a particular point on the screen by the electrostatic or magnetic field produced by the deflection system. When the electrons hit the screen, the phosphor emits visible light. Character and vector generators trace a picture on the screen by deflecting the beam along the desired path. Since the phosphor's light output decays exponentially with time, the entire picture must be redrawn many times per second, so that the viewer sees what appears to be a constant unflickering picture.

The stream of electrons is generated by *thermionic emission:* in a vacuum, a heated metal or metal oxide surface "bubbles off" electrons. The high voltage (thousands of volts) applied to a metallic coating on the interior of the sides of the tube then drives the electrons toward the front of the CRT. The final velocity the electrons attain depends on this voltage; hence it is usually referred to as the *acceleration voltage.*

The control-grid voltage determines how many electrons are actually attracted to the screen. As the voltage becomes more negative, fewer electrons are attracted through it to the screen, and the beam current becomes smaller. This provides a convenient way to control the picture's intensity, because the phosphor's light output decreases with the number of electrons striking it. If the grid's voltage is sufficiently negative, no electrons pass through, and the beam is blanked.

The focusing system uses either electric or magnetic fields to focus the electron beam so it converges to a small point on the screen's surface. In *electrostatic* focusing elements are mounted inside the tube's neck (Fig. 3.14) while in *magnetic* focusing coils are placed around the outside of the neck. A fine parallel beam of electrons would diverge because of electron repulsion, so the focusing must actually force the electrons to converge. With the exception of this tendency to diverge, however, focusing an electron beam is analogous to focusing light. An optical lens and an electron lens both have a focal distance, which in the case of the CRT is adjusted so that the beam converges as it hits the screen.

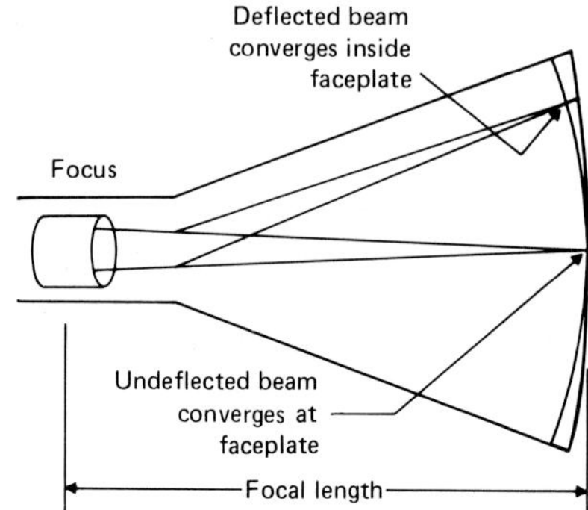

Fig. 3.15 Focusing an electron beam.

Figure 3.15 illustrates focusing while depicting a problem with CRTs. The beam is shown in two positions. In one case the beam converges at the point where it strikes the screen. In the second case, however, the convergence point is not on the screen, and the resulting image is therefore somewhat blurred. Why has this happened? Most CRTs have a radius of curvature far greater than the distance from the lens to the screen, and thus not all points on the screen are equidistant from the lens. If the beam is in focus when directed at the center of the screen, it will not be in focus anywhere else on the screen. The further the beam is deflected from the center, the more defocused it will be. In high-precision displays this problem is solved by dynamically focusing the lens as a function of the beam's position, rather than by maintaining a fixed focus.

★ **The deflection system.** From the point of view of computer graphics, the most crucial part of a CRT is the deflection system, which is used to trace a picture on the screen. As with focusing, either an electrostatic or magnetic field controls the deflection of the electron beam. With electrostatic deflection, two sets of plates are built into the CRT neck, as shown in Fig. 3.14. The electron beam first passes between the two vertical deflection plates (which are parallel to each other and lie in horizontal planes) and is bent toward the plate with the higher voltage. The magnitude of the deflection is easily controlled because it is directly proportional to the difference in voltage between the two plates. The second set of plates controls the horizontal deflection.

Electromagnetic deflection systems have two coils around the tube's neck. As the beam passes through, the field from one coil deflects the electron beam horizontally, while the field from the other deflects it vertically. The magnitude of each deflection is only approximately proportional to the current in the corresponding coil: for a flat-faced tube the relation between the coil current I and the resulting deflection D is:

$$D = \frac{L \cdot k \cdot I}{\sqrt{1 - (k \cdot I)^2}}$$

where k is a constant and L is the distance from the deflection coils to the screen. Either deflection compensation circuitry or permanent magnets strategically placed around the tube's neck can be used to correct for this nonlinear relation between I and D. Without the correction, a regular square grid has a ''pin cushion'' appearance, as in Fig. 3.16. Two separate distortion effects are actually noticeable in this figure. Along the horizontal and vertical centerlines, grid points which should be equally spaced are not. In addition, deflections off the centerline are greater than on the centerline. This is because the above equation gives D along one axis under the assumption that there is no simultaneous deflection on the other axis. This is actually not the case, and the figure illustrates the cross-coupling that exists. As the deflection increases along the x axis, a given y deflection current actually results in an increased y deflection.

★ **Deflection systems compared.** Magnetic deflection has many assets and few liabilities when compared to electrostatic deflection. Tube construction is simpler because of the external deflection system. Intensity modulation is simpler, and smaller spot sizes can be achieved. Also, the higher acceleration voltages that can be attained in magnetic systems make brighter images possible, since brightness is proportional to both the number of electrons in the beam and their velocity. Higher acceleration voltages are possible with magnetic deflection because the power needed to produce a given deflection is only linearly proportional to the acceleration voltage, while in electrostatic systems it is proportional to the square of the acceleration voltage. This fact also allows magnetically deflected tubes to be shorter than electrostatic tubes.

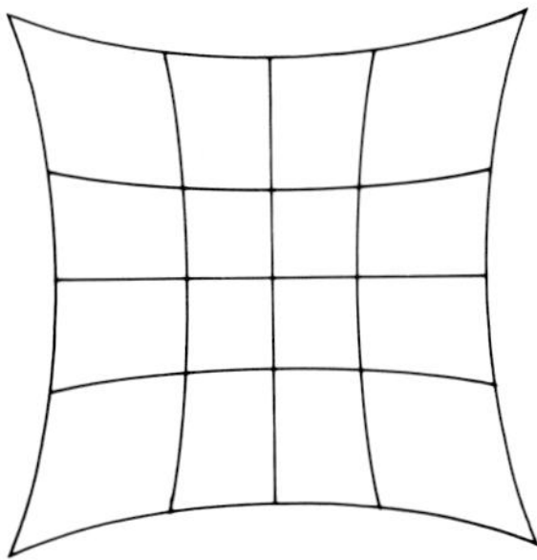

Fig. 3.16 Uncompensated magnetic deflection.

Electrostatic systems are superior in three respects. Writing speed can be substantially faster (and thus a denser picture can be displayed without flicker), positioning accuracy is superior, and there is no pin-cushion distortion problem. Despite these advantages, most interactive random displays and all raster displays use magnetic systems because of their relative simplicity.

The phosphor. When the electron beam strikes the phosphor-coated screen of the CRT, the individual electrons are moving with kinetic energy proportional to the acceleration voltage. Some of this energy is dissipated as heat, but the rest is transferred to the electrons of the phosphor atoms, which then jump to higher quantum energy levels. These excited electrons return to their previous quantum levels by giving up their extra energy in the form of light, at frequencies predicted by the quantum theory. In a given phosphor there are several different quantum levels to which electrons can be excited. Each of the levels corresponds to a light color associated with the return to an unexcited state. Further, electrons on some levels are less stable and return to the unexcited state more rapidly than others. Phosphor's *fluorescence* is the light emitted as these very unstable electrons lose their excess energy while the phosphor is being struck by electrons. *Phosphorescence* is the light given off by the return of the relatively more stable excited electrons to their unexcited state once the electron beam excitation is removed. This light output decays exponentially with time. There are many phosphors, each with its own characteristics. Phosphors known as P1, P4 (used in black-and-white TV), P7, and P31 are commonly used for graphics.

A phosphor's *persistence* is the time from the removal of excitation to the moment when phosphorescence has decayed to 10% of the initial light output. The range of persistence of different phosphors can reach many seconds, but for most phosphors used in graphics equipment it is usually 10 to 60 microseconds. The persistence is the main determinant of the *refresh rate* (number of times per second a picture is redrawn) required to produce a *flicker-free* picture. The longer the persistence, the lower the required refresh rate. A flicker-free picture appears constant or steady to the viewer even though in reality any given point is "off" much longer than it is "on". The refresh rate above which a picture stops flickering and fuses into a steady image is called the *fusion frequency*. The process of fusion is familiar to all of us: it occurs whenever we watch television or motion pictures.

The refresh rate for a raster-scan display is fixed, at 30 or 60 per second, independently of picture complexity. The refresh rate for vector systems depends directly on picture complexity (number of lines, points and characters): the greater the complexity, the longer the time for a single refresh cycle and the lower the refresh rate.

If the refresh rate can be decreased as persistence increases, why not use a very "long" phosphor? The problem with this solution can be seen by considering what would appear on the screen after changing pictures: a bright new picture, plus the less bright but clearly visible old picture, slowly fading away over a period of a minute or more. A moving image would thus leave an objectionable smear of previous images. In general, highly dynamic applications need low-persistence phosphors, while some computer-aided design applications tend to trade off dynamics for a larger number of flicker-free picture elements to produce complex, relatively static drawings.

The relation between fusion frequency and persistence is strictly nonlinear: doubling persistence from 10 to 20 microseconds does not halve fusion frequency. Of course, as persistence increases into the several-second range, the fusion frequency will become quite small. At the other extreme, even a phosphor with absolutely no persistence at all can be used, since all the eye really requires is to see some light for a short period of time, repeated at a frequency above the fusion frequency. With typical phosphors, most of the light is caused by phosphorescence, because the excitation and hence the fluorescence usually last just a fraction of a microsecond. With a zero-persistence material, the electron beam would have to dwell much longer on each point, and this would decrease the number of points the beam could intensify during a refresh cycle.

Persistence is not the only factor affecting fusion frequency. Fusion frequency also increases with image intensity and with ambient room lighting, and varies with different wavelengths of emitted light. Finally, it depends on the observer: fusion is, after all, a physiological phenomenon. Therefore, any quoted fusion frequencies are usually averages for a large number of observers.

★ **Evaluation criteria.** The quality of a display's deflection and focusing system is commonly measured in terms of resolution, spot size, repeatability, linearity, and speed. For vector graphics, *resolution* and *spot size* (the diameter of the focused beam) are reciprocals: a resolution of 100 lines per inch (about the best attainable) implies a spot size of 0.01″. Resolution is usually measured with a *shrinking raster:* a known number of equally spaced parallel lines is displayed, and the interline spacing is uniformly decreased until the lines just begin to merge together. Resolution is the distance between the two outermost lines, divided by the number of lines in the raster. As the intensity of the electron beam increases, resolution tends to decrease because a more intense line will be wider. This is due to *bloom,* the tendency of a phosphor's excitation to spread somewhat beyond the area being bombarded. Resolution for raster graphics displays is more often cited as a total number of lines (i.e., scan lines) than as lines per inch.

Repeatability measures the deflection system's ability to move the beam to the same spot on the CRT with repeated application of a given deflection signal, especially when the beam is moved to the spot from different starting positions. It is usually measured in absolute distance and can be as low as 0.01″ on contemporary high-quality systems. Repeatability pertains primarily to vector graphics.

A display is *linear* if lines that should be straight really are straight. Linearity is specified either in absolute or relative form. *Absolute linearity* is the maximum perpendicular distance between the displayed line and a truly straight line connecting the same endpoints. *Relative linearity* is the ratio between the absolute linearity and the line's length, expressed as a percentage. One percent linearity on full screen lines can be achieved.

The *speed* of a display can be measured in several ways. As we discuss more details of display operations, more precise definitions of speed will evolve: for now we define it to be the average time needed to move the beam to a given point on the screen and display a dot there. The amount of flicker-free information that can be displayed is inversely proportional to this time.

★ 3.2.2 Direct-View Storage Tube

The direct-view storage tube (DVST) is similar to the standard CRT, except that the DVST does not need to be refreshed. The image is stored inside the DVST as a distribution of charges on the inside surface of the screen. Figure 3.17 shows the basic parts of the tube. The writing electron gun, focusing system, and deflection system are functionally identical to those in the conventional system. The primary function of the focused electron gun is creation of the stored image, while the flood beam makes the stored image visible.

Initially, the storage surface has a uniform negative charge. When the high-velocity (high-kinetic-energy) electron beam strikes this storage surface, many electrons are dislodged and are attracted by the more positively charged collector grid. Thus, the area struck experiences a net decrease in the number of electrons, so that a relative positive charge is created. Because the storage surface is nonconducting, other electrons cannot migrate and the charge pattern is stored. Just how many electrons are lost depends on the storage surface's exact voltage and the number of incident electrons. In the direct-view bistable storage tube used in the well-known Tektronix displays, the number of electrons lost per unit area is constant, so only two intensities, on and off, are possible. Continuous-tone DVSTs have also been made, but are not widely used.

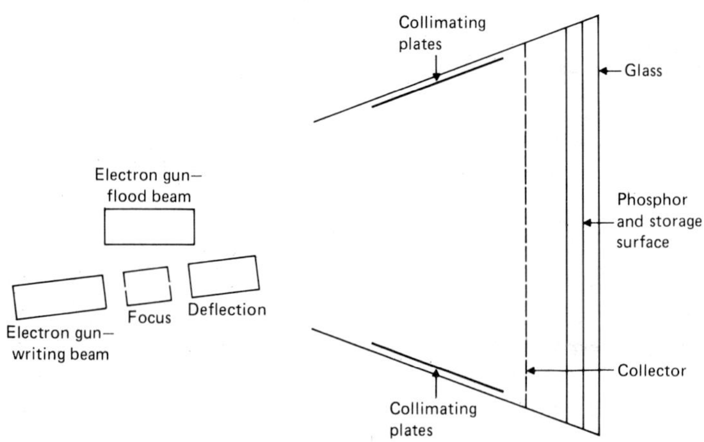

Fig. 3.17 Cross section of DVST.

The writing beam can be deflected at speeds up to 8000 inches per second and still create a stored image. This high speed has been exploited in the IBM 3277 Graphics Attachment, which can accept display instructions fast enough to display at this rate [MCMA80].

Decreasing the energy of the writing beam makes "write-through" possible: the writing beam excites the phosphor and creates an image on the screen, but does not affect the stored-charge distribution. This feature is useful to display cursors and to allow characters or vectors to be refreshed from a buffer, to provide dynamics for part of the picture while other parts are stored as a charge distribution.

Independently of "writing" charges onto the storage mesh, the flood gun emits low-velocity electrons which are also attracted toward the screen. This flood beam is not focused and deflected: rather it "floods" (uniformly covers) the entire screen with electrons. Constant voltages are applied to collimating plates which cause the flood beam's electrons to approach the storage surface at right angles. Flood electrons approaching a relatively positively charged part of the storage surface (where the number of electrons has been decreased) pass through, strike the phosphor, and cause light emission. Electrons approaching other areas of the surface are repelled and do not pass through. The charge pattern on the surface is thereby faithfully reproduced as a visible image on the display surface.

The charge pattern, and hence the image, is erased in a two-step process. First, a positive voltage is applied to the storage surface. This attracts floodgun electrons and causes the entire surface to be "written" (and produces the flash of light when a storage tube is erased). With the entire display written, the storage surface has lost some of its electrons. To replenish the supply, a negative voltage is applied to the surface, so incident floodbeam electrons are retained. The operating voltages are then returned to normal, and a new picture can be written.

DVSTs have several disadvantages, but also some major advantages. Selective erasure of just some parts of the picture is not normally possible, and the contrast between the dark and bright picture areas is low. These relative disadvantages are mitigated because the cost of DVST display systems is lower than that of random (and many raster) refresh systems because no refresh buffer is needed, and the deflection electronics need not be as fast as for refresh graphics. Most important, arbitrarily complex pictures with sharp lines and characters can be displayed without concern for flicker. For instance, on a 19″ diagonal DVST with 4096 units of addressability, in excess of 40,000 characters can be displayed.

3.2.3 Beam-Penetration Color CRT

Beam-penetration color CRTs are sometimes used with random drawing systems to obtain color. The inside of the tube's viewing surface is coated with layers of two different phosphors (normally red and green), each of which has a different excitation energy level. Thus, the acceleration voltage of the electron beam determines which phosphor is excited and hence which of several colors appears. Mixtures of red and green are produced by acceleration voltages in between those which excite each individual phosphor.

One disadvantage of this type of CRT is that the time needed to change the acceleration voltage is long, typically 20 to 200 microseconds. Making many color (hence voltage) changes in the 1/30 second refresh time can significantly limit the amount of information that can be displayed without flicker and can also burn out the power supply. Thus it is necessary to sort output primitives by color, so that all lines, points, and characters of one color are displayed in sequence.

The quality and range of colors (four at most, typically red, orange, yellow, and green) available with penetration CRTs are limited, but this is currently the least expensive way to obtain color with a random display. Shadow-mask CRTs, described next, have been used recently for random displays, but so far their cost in this mode of use is at least twice that of the penetration CRT, and their line width is greater.

3.2.4 Shadow-Mask Color CRT

Home color TV sets use some form of shadow-mask CRT. The inside of the tube's viewing surface is covered with phosphor dots arranged in triangular patterns. Each group of three dots, called a triad, has one dot whose phosphor emits red when excited, one for blue, and one for green. The triads are so small that, when viewed from a sufficient distance, light emanating from their individual dots mixes together and is perceived by the viewer not as individual dots of red, green, and blue, but as a mixture of the three colors. Thus a wide range of colors can be produced at each triad depending on how strongly each component of the color mixture is excited. Color is discussed in more detail in Chapter 17.

How are the individual phosphor dots excited by electrons? Three different electron guns, arranged in the same triangular shape as the triad, are used (see Fig. 3.18). The guns are deflected synchronously and are focused on the same point on the view surface. Just behind the view surface is the shadow mask, with one small hole for each triad. The holes are precisely aligned with respect to both the triads and the electron guns, so that each dot in the triad is exposed to electrons from only one gun. Thus the number of electrons in each beam controls the amounts of red, green, and blue light generated by the triad.

The need for the shadow mask and triads imposes a limit on the resolution of these CRTs that is not present with monochrome CRTs. In very high-resolution tubes the triads are placed on centers of about 0.35 mm, while in home TV tubes the triads are on about 0.60 mm centers.

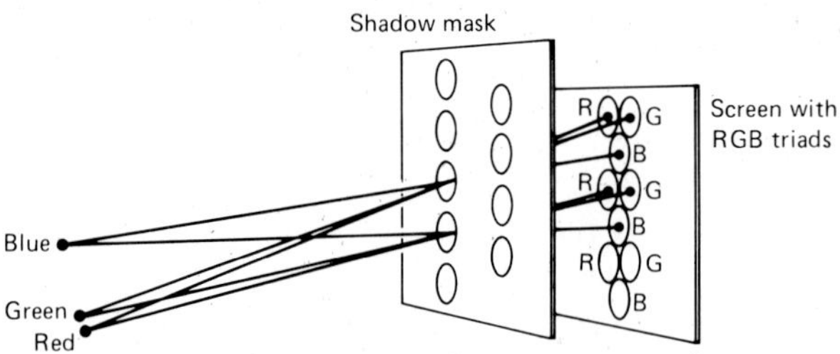

Fig. 3.18 Shadow-mask color CRT.

3.2.5 Plasma Panel Display

Not all interactive displays are based on CRT technology. The plasma panel, for instance, is an array of tiny neon bulbs. Each bulb can be put into an "on" (intensified) state or an "off" state, and remains in the state until explicitly changed. The most common plasma panel has 64 cells (bulbs) per inch and is 8 inches square, so that it has one-quarter million cells. Panels up to 40 inches square have been made. The plasma panel is thus in essence a medium-resolution "storage" display without need of a refresh buffer.

The bulbs are not discrete separate units, but rather are part of a single integrated panel made of three layers of glass, as seen in Fig. 3.19. The inside surface of the front layer has thin vertical strips of an electrical conductor; the center layer has a number of holes (the bulbs), and the inside surface of the rear layer has thin horizontal strips of an electrical conductor. To turn on bulb (*2,a*) in the figure, the voltages on lines *2* and *a* are adjusted so their difference is large enough to fire the neon in the cell and make it glow. This happens when the voltage is sufficiently high to pull electrons from the neon molecules, allowing a current to flow. Once the glow starts, a lower voltage is applied to sustain the glow. To turn off the same bulb, the voltages on lines *2* and *a* are momentarily made less than the sustaining voltage. Bulbs can be turned on or off in about 20 microseconds. In some panel designs the individual cells are replaced with an open cavity, because the neon glow can be contained in a localized area. The front and back glass layers are simply separated by spacers.

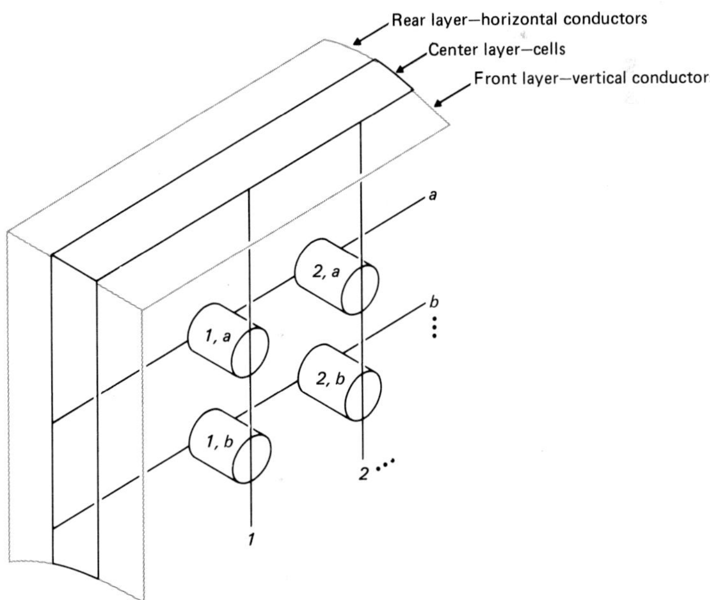

Fig. 3.19 Plasma panel display.

The plasma panel is flat, transparent, and rugged, and needs no refresh buffer. It has been used with a rear projection system to mix photographic slides as static background for computer-generated dynamic graphics. However, its cost, while continually decreasing, is still relatively high for its limited resolution. The development of plasma panels is described in two recent review articles [SLOT76, TANN78].

3.2.6 Other Display Techniques

At least two solid-state technologies show promise for use in displays of the future: light-emitting diodes (LED) and liquid-crystal displays (LCD), both already used in wristwatch and calculator read-out panels. It is possible to arrange either LED or LCD cells in an array of closely spaced dots and to turn each dot on or off. An array of, say, a million cells in an area 10 inches square would be a very attractive display device. The LCD is particularly attractive for portable displays because it is not an active light source but rather reflects ambient light. Its power requirements are thus quite low.

Lasers have been used in several types of displays. Laser beams can be deflected electromechanically by mirrors mounted on sensitive galvanometers, or by passing the beam through a material whose index of refraction can be controlled by an applied electrical potential. However, only limited amounts of graphics can be refreshed by these methods. One commercial system avoids this refresh problem by using the laser beam to etch an image in a film of photochromic material which darkens when exposed to the laser light's wavelength. Light of another wavelength is used to project the etched image onto a large (39 × 27″) screen. A very complex image can be drawn in a few seconds. The photochromic material is not selectively erasable, so that making deletions necessitates redrawing the remaining image, just as with the DVST [WOOD76].

3.3 RANDOM-SCAN DISPLAY PROCESSING UNIT

Display processing units (DPUs) may be viewed as special-purpose CPUs. They decode opcodes and data, and have instruction counters and registers. In this section we first describe a trivial DPU with just two registers, then add functions until it becomes typical of a class of currently used random-scan DPUs. In this process of expanding the DPUs' capabilities, we will also gain some insight into the rationale behind the design of many commercially available DPUs. We start with a very simple DPU and build up to a more realistic one in Section 3.3.6.

3.3.1 Point-Plotting System

The simplest DPU randomly plots individual discrete points under CPU control. Let us think of the display surface, i.e., the CRT's face, as a grid of 1024 × 1024 positions, with the origin in the screen's lower left corner. We would like to be able to draw a point at any grid position. Doing this requires that 10-bit x and y values be made available to the DPU. A system organization like that in Fig. 3.20 is satis-

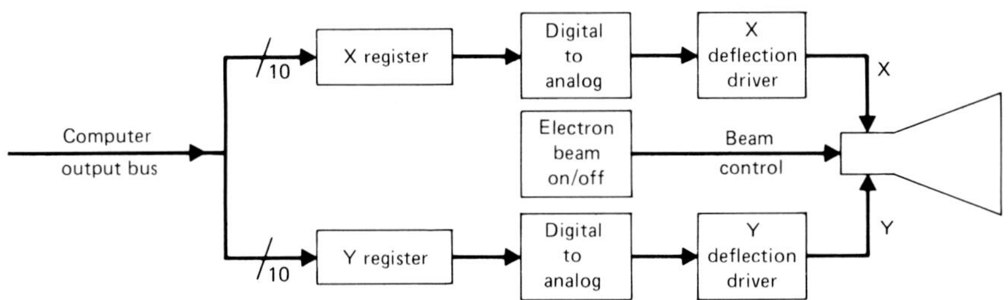

Fig. 3.20 Point-plotting display.

factory for this purpose. The computer uses I/O commands to load the x and y registers with coordinate values. The analog (voltage) equivalents of the coordinate values go to the deflection system. The current amplifiers for the magnetic deflection coil (or voltage amplifiers for deflection plates) produce the appropriate current (voltage), and once the current (voltage) has stabilized, the electron beam is unblanked (turned on) for a few microseconds, then blanked again so that the next point can be moved to and then drawn. The whole process can take from 5 to 20 microseconds per point with a fast deflection system, or as much as 50 microseconds per point with a slow deflection system. In a given system, the time between display of successive points is usually nearly proportional to the distance between them. A refresh rate of 30 per second allows 33000 microseconds per refresh cycle, resulting in display capacities from 33 000/50 = 660 to 33 000/5 = 6600 points.

How can the computer drive the DPU? Figure 3.21 outlines a program which plots points at the n coordinate pairs in the x and y arrays.

```
repeat                                {refresh loop}
  TICK_WAIT(.0333);                   {wait for the next tick of a 1/30 second clock}
  for i := 1 to n do
    begin
      repeat                          {wait here until DPU refresh is done}
      until dpu_ready;
      DPU_XREG(x[i]);                 {procedure to load DPU X-register}
      DPU_YREG(y[i])                  {procedure to load DPU Y-register}
    end                               {of one refresh cycle}
until terminate_flag        {flag set by operating system when refresh is to stop}
```

Fig. 3.21 Program segment to display points stored in arrays x and y of length n.

If n is less than the number of points which can be displayed without flicker, then all is well. Indeed, the CPU will in that case have some time left over to do some other work. If n is close to the flicker limit, the CPU must spend essentially all its time refreshing the display. If the CPU is expensive or has other, more productive work to do, it is being badly used. Further, if a request is made for some computation to be done, the CPU must abandon its refresh task, leaving the user with a blank screen. This system will thus become unpleasant to use, to the point of being unacceptable.

Displaying lines. To display a line from $(x1,y1)$ to $(x2,y2)$, we must fill in the x and y arrays with the coordinates of points that lie approximately on the line. We say "approximately" because for an integer value of x the corresponding value of y on the line may not be an integer, and thus rounding or truncating is necessary. Figure 3.22 shows a basic line-drawing algorithm *DRAW*; more sophisticated algorithms are presented in Chapter 11. All points are specified in display screen coordinates, with (0,0) at the lower left. The algorithm assumes that $x1 < x2$, steps along the x-axis from $x1$ to $x2$, calculates the y coordinate, and rounds it to the nearest integer value. The expression for y is based on the slope–intercept form of the line equation $y = mx + b$. The *ROUND* function is used rather than truncation, so that the points which do not fall exactly on a grid point appear sometimes above the line and sometimes below.

```
procedure DRAW(
  x1, y1,                                  {starting point of line}
  x2, y2: integer);                        {ending point of line}
var m, b, dx, dy, x, y: real;
  inty: integer;
begin
  {compute coefficients m and b of y = mx + b}
  dx := FLOAT(x2 - x1);
  dy := FLOAT (y2 - y1);
  if dx<>0, then                                {avoid division by zero}
    begin
      m := dy/dx;                               {slope}
      b := FLOAT(y1) - m * FLOAT(x1);           {y-intercept}
      x := x1
      repeat
        y := m * FLOAT(x) + b;
        inty := ROUND(y);
        PLOT(x, y);                        {fill in output array with (x, y)}
        x := x + 1
      until x > x2
    end
end    {DRAW}
```

Fig. 3.22 Program to calculate points on a line.

DRAW has several faults. First, it works well enough for lines with absolute slope of 1 or less, but not very well for other lines. This is because the calculated points will be separated in y by more than one unit. In the extreme case, if the line's slope is infinite ($x2 - x1 = 0$), then an error condition (division by zero) exists. This problem is easily resolved by modifying the algorithm so that it increments along the x-axis only if $x2 - x1 > y2 - y1$ and along the y-axis otherwise. Second, if $x2 < x1$, the loop is never executed. This problem is solved by making sure that $x2 > x1$ (by swapping endpoints if necessary). These modifications to the algorithm are straightforward and are not shown.

Another modification to *DRAW* is possible and often desirable, since it is computationally somewhat faster. The slope m of a line is of course just $m = dy/dx$; rearranging, $dy = m*dx$, where dy is just the change in y that corresponds to a change of dx in x. Now let $dx = 1$; then $dy = m$ is the change in y for a unit change in x. When incrementing along the x-axis, each unit change in x just causes an incremental change of m in y. That is, in the inner loop of *DRAW* we use $x = x + 1$ and $y = y + m$. If instead we increment along y, then $dy = 1$ and $dx = 1/m$, so $x = x + 1/m$ and $y = y + 1$ are used. *DRAW* is a scan conversion algorithm; more sophisticated algorithms are discussed in Chapter 11.

There is a general problem with displaying lines as points on a random-scan display. If we assume that 100 points are plotted per inch of line and that 6600 points can be displayed without flicker, then only 66 inches of flicker-free lines can be displayed. The higher estimate for the number of points displayable is used in this calculation because nearly all points are adjacent to the previous point and thus will be drawn with minimum delays.

Displaying curves. The line-drawing procedure can be generalized to plot some function $y = f(x)$ on the display. If $f(x)$ has already been scaled so that its units are display coordinates, all that need be done is to increment along the x-axis, evaluating $f(x)$ at each point. The resulting value must then be rounded or truncated, just as with *DRAW*. The only difficulty, as with lines, is that whenever the slope $f'(x)$ is large, the distance between plotted points will be large too. If the inverse of f, that is, $x = g(y)$, is available, then $y = f(x)$ is plotted in regions where $f'(x) < 1$, and $x = g(y)$ is plotted in other regions, in direct analogy to the line-plotting situation.

Displaying characters. Each character to be displayed is defined as a pattern of dots on a small grid, as in Fig. 3.23. In order to display all upper-case characters, digits, and punctuation marks, at least a 5×7 grid is needed for each character. Such a grid contains 35 points, so each possible character can be represented with 35 bits. Figure 3.24 is an algorithm which uses the 35-bit representation of a character to fill in the x and y arrays which in turn are used by the refresh program. The variable *code* is the integer character code of the symbol to be displayed, and (*x_org*, *y_org*) are the coordinates of the lower left corner of the screen position at which the character is to be displayed; *character_definition* is a two-dimensional array of bits, indicating which points in the 5×7 grid are to be intensified.

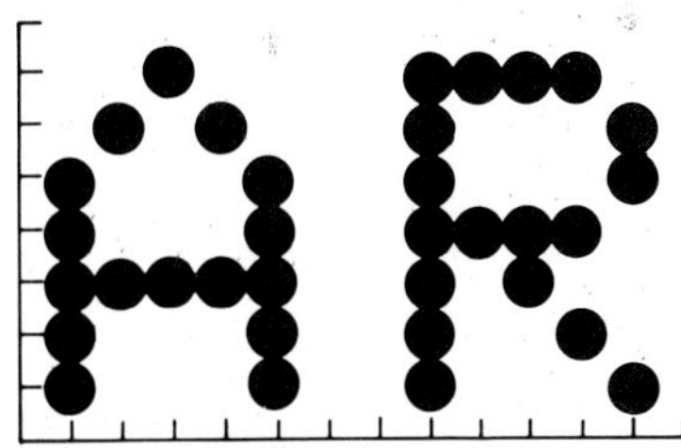

Fig. 3.23 Characters created by displaying points.

```
procedure CHAR(
  code, x_org, y_org: integer,
  character_definition: array[1..5, 1..7] of boolean);
  {plot a 5 × 7 character matrix with lower left corner at x_org, y_org on screen}
var i, j: integer;
begin
  for i := 1 to 7 do
    for j := 1 to 5 do
      if character_definition[i, j]
        then PLOT(x_org + i, y_org + j)
        {PLOT puts coordinates in x and y arrays of Fig. 3.21}
end     {CHAR};
```

Fig. 3.24 Program to display characters.

The average number of points displayed per character in typical text is around 20, so the display can present only about 6600/20 = 330 characters without flicker.

Summary of point-plotting displays. The major problems with this simple point-plotting display system are: (1) most of the CPU's time is devoted to just refreshing the display, which is often an inefficient use of a valuable resource; (2) the amount of information that can be presented without flicker is limited; (3) much of the CPU's memory is used to store the x and y arrays and the programs that build the arrays. All of these problems can be solved by placing more functionality in the DPU. The slight modification made to the DPU in the next section removes the first of these three problems.

3.3.2 DPU Instruction Counter

If a processor is defined as a computing device that has its own instruction counter and control logic and follows the customary *instruction fetch—instruction counter increment—instruction execute* cycle, then the DPU described in the previous section is not really a processor at all: it is just a special I/O device, not unlike a printer or card punch. We can transform it into an independent processor by adding an instruction counter and the requisite control logic, as in Fig. 3.25. To use the display, a CPU program builds a DPU program in its memory, loads the DPU's instruction counter with the address at which the DPU program starts, and tells the DPU to begin executing instructions. The DPU then "cycle steals" from the CPU's memory whenever it needs a new instruction; that is, it pauses the CPU, in mid-execution if necessary, for a single memory access.

The result of this enhancement is to free the CPU of the refresh task. The CPU needs only two instructions relating to the DPU:

1. Load DPU instruction counter and start DPU;
2. Stop DPU.

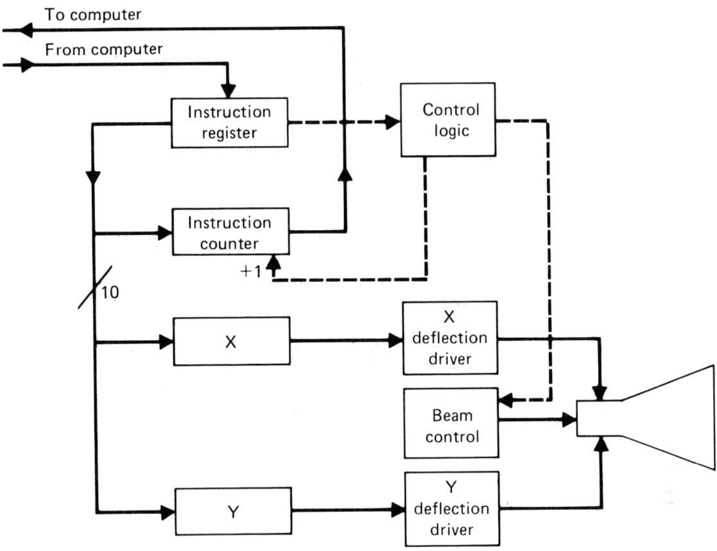

Fig. 3.25 DPU with instruction counter.

The DPU must be able to execute either two or three instructions, depending on the number of bits in the instruction. If 21 or more bits are available, two instructions will suffice. The first, called *draw point,* has one opcode bit, a 10-bit x coordinate, and a 10-bit y coordinate. The second, called *jump,* has one opcode bit plus an address to be loaded into the instruction counter. Jump is used primarily to maintain picture regeneration—the last instruction in the DPU program is a jump to the first instruction. It can also be used to link together several parts of the display program which are noncontiguous in memory.

If fewer than 21 bits are available, then three instructions, requiring two opcode bits, are needed. They are:

1. Load X register;
2. Load Y register, draw point at (x, y);
3. Jump.

3.3.3 Line-Drawing Display

Converting the display to an autonomous processor relieves the CPU of the refresh task, but does not address the other objections to a point-plotting display for drawing lines and characters: large DPU program size and limited display capacity due to slow speed.

Removing these limitations is simple. We specify only endpoints in the DPU program and add sufficient DPU hardware to do the actual line drawing (Fig. 3.26).

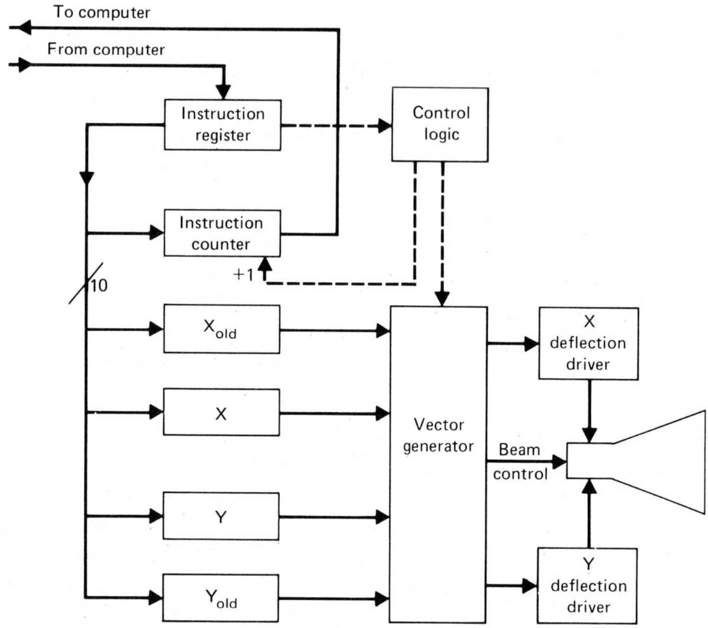

Fig. 3.26 DPU with vector generator; indicates a 10-bit data path.

The hardware added to the DPU is an extra pair of registers (X_{old}, Y_{old}), in which to hold a line's endpoint, and a vector generator, whose main task is moving the CRT beam in a straight line from one point to another. Vector-generator technology is the subject of the next section. Here it suffices to say that a line can be drawn in anywhere from 2 to 50 microseconds, depending on the speed of the vector generator and the length of the line. This contrasts markedly with the point-plotting display, where a 1000-unit line might take 5000 microseconds to draw.

Including a vector generator means that more instructions must be added to the DPU's repertoire. The functions that can be performed by the DPU have expanded beyond drawing a point and jumping, and include moving the beam's position (without drawing anything) and drawing a line. In all beam manipulation instructions, the end position is loaded into the X and Y registers; after the beam has moved to the end position, the control logic automatically moves X into register X_{old} and Y into register Y_{old}. With the most common instruction length for displays, 16 bits, there are five required instructions:

1. Load X;
2. Load Y, move beam to (x, y);
3. Load Y, move beam to (x, y), draw point;
4. Load Y, draw line to (x, y) from (x_{old}, y_{old});
5. Jump.

The instructions can be used in various combinations to draw points, connected line segments, and disconnected line segments.

The vector generator can also be used to draw straight-line parts of characters and piecewise linear approximations to curves. This is an improvement over drawing numerous individual dots. For curve drawing, the only precaution to be observed is that in regions where the curve has a small radius of curvature the line segments should be shorter than in regions where the radius of curvature is relatively large.

★ **Vector generators.** The task facing a vector generator, when carefully analyzed, is rather demanding. The requirements are:

1. Move the CRT beam from (X_{old}, Y_{old}) to (X,Y) in a straight line, or at least in what appears to the viewer to be a straight line.
2. Draw all lines with the same brightness. The slower the beam moves, the more electrons will bombard a given area of the phosphor, making the area brighter. Constant brightness can be achieved either by moving the beam with a constant velocity for all vectors, by adjusting beam intensity for different vectors, or by some combination of these two. The objective is to hit each point along the line with the same *number* of electrons, depending on how fast the beam moves.
3. Turn on the beam exactly as it leaves the start point and turn it off again exactly at the endpoint—not before, not after.
4. Do all this as rapidly as possible.

The vector generator must produce three outputs: x-deflection, y-deflection, and intensity. If intensity compensation is not needed (i.e., all vectors are drawn at essentially the same speed), then the intensity signal is just an on–off indicator. The various drawings in Fig. 3.27 show what is required to draw several different lines at constant velocity. The x and y deflection graphs are calibrated vertically in raster units, and horizontally in time. The time origin is the start of vector generation, and T_{max} is the maximum time that is needed to draw the longer vectors. Examination of the figure shows that the actual time taken to draw a vector is proportional to the change in x or in y, whichever is larger.

Two different techniques are used to generate the deflection signals. *Analog vector generators* use an analog integrator to produce a reference voltage ramp which varies linearly from 0 to a maximum in some time T_{max} (in some systems T_{max} varies for vectors of different length; in others it is constant). The x and y deflection signals are then generated by multiplying the reference ramp by signals derived from the desired changes in x and y. This produces a smooth signal to drive the deflection amplifiers, and a smooth straight line results. Current high-performance systems using this general technique can draw a short vector in 1 or 2 microseconds, and a full-screen vector in 15 to 20 microseconds.

The second technique, *digital vector generation,* is to increment (or decrement, as the case may be) the X_{old} and Y_{old} registers at rates proportional to the changes in x and y. Whichever register requires the largest change is incremented at a constant rate of r units per second. The other register is incremented at a lower rate r' which

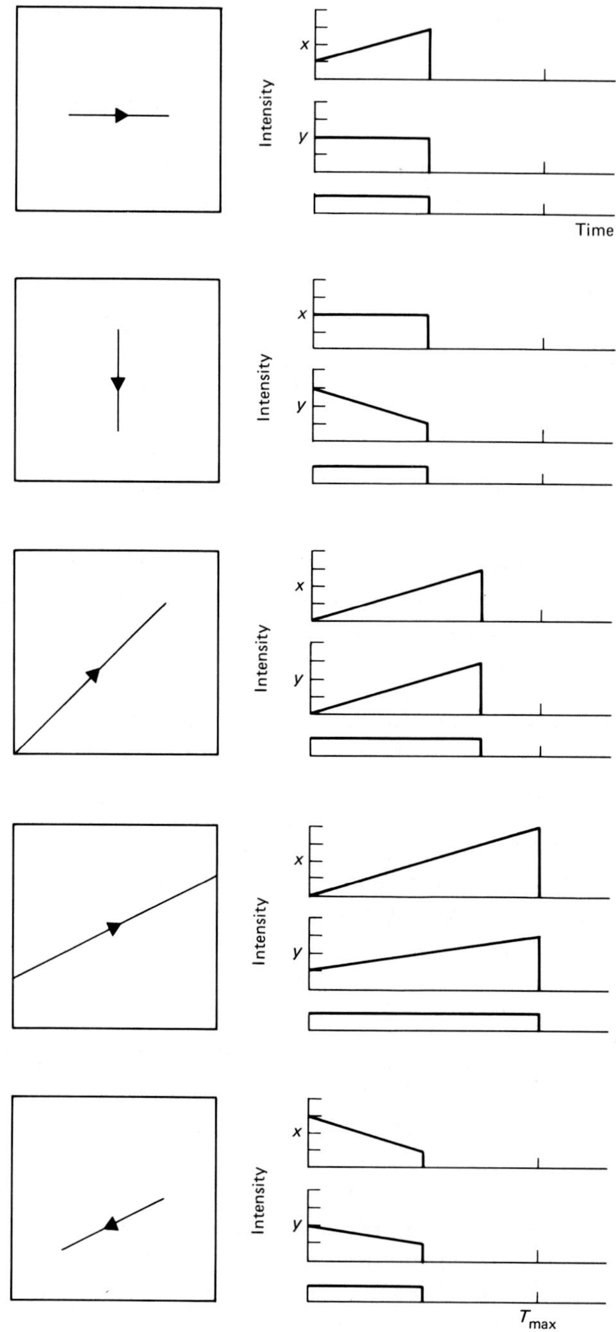

Fig. 3.27 Five vectors and their control signals.

is proportional to the ratio of the smaller to the larger change. (Notice that this technique is merely a hardware implementation of the incremental line-drawing algorithm discussed in Section 3.3.1.) The two registers are continually fed through digital-to-analog converters and thence to the deflection amplifiers. Notice, however, that the signals driving the amplifiers are no longer smooth—they are now step functions and produce a slightly staircased vector because the beam is now directed only to addressable points on the CRT. This problem does not arise in the analog vector generator.

With current technology, the increment rate r can be at least 30 million units per second. A full-screen vector on a display addressed with 10-bit registers needs 1024 incrementations and is therefore drawn in about 30 microseconds, somewhat slower than with the analog vector generator. On the other hand, a contemporary high-performance display which uses digital vector generation can draw short vectors in 0.1 microseconds, i.e., considerably faster than analog generators. Digital vector generators require fewer calibration adjustments and are becoming less expensive than analog vector generators. As digital logic speeds continue to increase, they will begin to match analog performance.

★ **Evaluation criteria.** Vector generators are judged on linearity, speed, brightness uniformity, and endpoint matching. Linearity was defined in an earlier section. *Speed* is typically either a constant or some function of vector length. In the latter case, the time for short vectors is constant because the set-up time for loading the registers becomes the dominating factor. Many vector generators have poor *brightness uniformity:* there is often a bright area at one or both ends of the line, since the beam is moving more slowly than normal and hence is directing more electrons per unit time to a small area of the phosphor. *Endpoint matching* is a measure of how precisely the beam is unblanked at the vector's starting point and blanked at the ending point. One test of matching is to draw a point at B, a line from A to B, and then a point at A. The points and the ends of the vectors should match closely. Another test is to draw several lines from various points to one common center point P: the lines should all end exactly at P.

3.3.4 Relative Coordinates

Our display processor is now able to run by itself, asynchronously from the CPU, but still lacks one important and common feature. Consider Fig. 3.28, which shows a display of a triangle and the DPU program needed to draw it. All is well until the application program (under user control) wants to relocate the triangle elsewhere on the screen, say left 50 and up 100 units from its current position. There are two basic ways to do this. First, the application program could find the triangle's description in the application data structure, modify the endpoint values appropriately, and call the graphics package to create a new DPU program. Alternatively, and more efficiently, the application program could request the graphics package to subtract 50 from all x-coordinates and add 100 to all y-coordinates in the triangle's DPU program segment. This can be done quickly for the triangle, but can be slow for more complex objects.

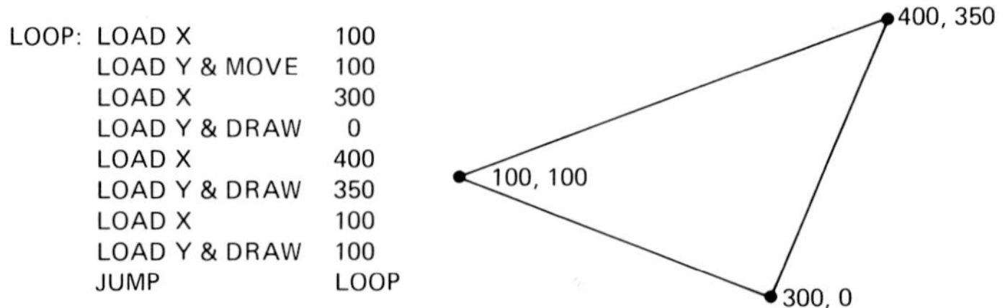
LOOP: LOAD X 100
LOAD Y & MOVE 100
LOAD X 300
LOAD Y & DRAW 0
LOAD X 400
LOAD Y & DRAW 350
LOAD X 100
LOAD Y & DRAW 100
JUMP LOOP
400, 350
100, 100
300, 0

Fig. 3.28 Triangle drawn with absolute coordinates.

Objects can be moved even more easily than this if coordinates can be specified as either absolute or relative to the current contents of X_{old} and Y_{old}. The DPU program in Fig. 3.29 uses absolute coordinates to move the beam to one corner of the triangle and then uses relative coordinates to draw the triangle itself. Thus moving the triangle is just a matter of modifying the initial *x* and *y* values stored in the first two instructions in the DPU program.

```
LOOP: LOAD X ABSOLUTE              100
      LOAD Y ABSOLUTE & MOVE       100
      LOAD X RELATIVE              200
      LOAD Y RELATIVE & DRAW      −100
      LOAD X RELATIVE              100
      LOAD Y RELATIVE & DRAW       350
      LOAD X RELATIVE             −300
      LOAD Y RELATIVE & DRAW      −250
      JUMP                        LOOP
```

Fig. 3.29 The same triangle drawn with relative coordinates.

The DPU instruction codes now need an extra bit to indicate whether a coordinate is relative or absolute. If the current instruction specifies relative coordinates, then the adder is used to add the increment to the X and Y registers (Fig. 3.30). Relative coordinates must be specified with 11 bits, so that quantities from -1024 to $+1023$ can be represented, allowing any point on the screen to be reached from any other point in one move.

If the current instruction specifies absolute coordinates, only adder input A is enabled, so that the adder's output is the same as its input. For incremental moves, adder inputs A and B are both enabled, with B coming from the appropriate register. In either case, the adder output is directed into the register designated by the instruction. Note that the instruction counter is seen by the adder as just another register. A jump is an absolute load of the instruction counter, and a relative jump is an add into the instruction counter. Relative jumps are convenient in allowing a DPU program to be easily repositioned in main memory.

Relative coordinates, while convenient, are also potentially dangerous. Consider the program in Fig. 3.29. Suppose the triangle were moved right 720 units by adding 720 to the existing starting-point *x*-coordinate of 100. The triangle now starts at (820,100) and its other two vertices are at (1020,0) and (1120,350). This last vertex

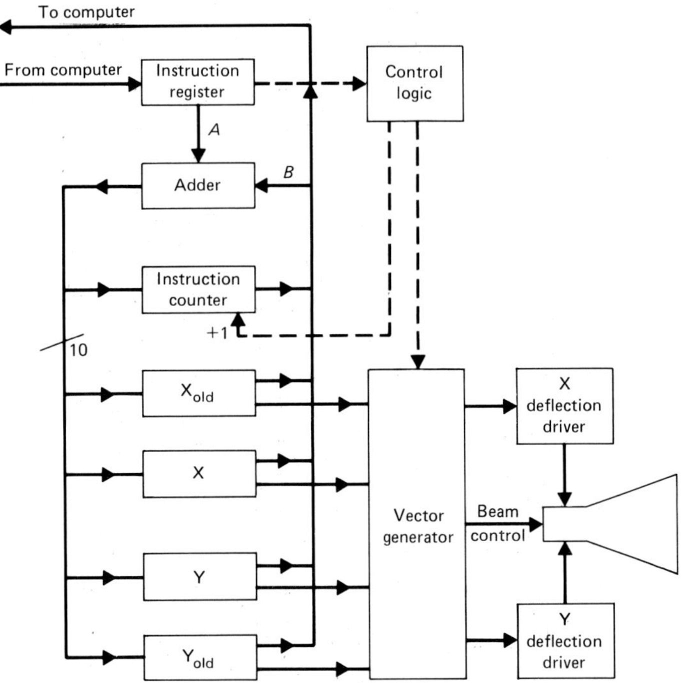

Fig. 3.30 DPU with adder.

is outside the screen area, and the image displayed is distorted because the X register contains not 1120 but rather 96 (the decimal equivalent of the low-order 10 bits of the binary representation of 1120). The line from (1020,0) goes not to (1120,350) but to (96,350). This annoying result, called *wraparound* in Chapter 2, may be eliminated in two ways. First, because the X and Y registers are each only 10 bits wide, the graphics package should allow the triangle to be moved on the screen only in such a way that its vertex coordinates remain in the range 0 to 1023. A second solution is to design DPUs which remove this restriction without causing wraparound (see Chapter 10).

Having introduced relative coordinates, we can now easily add another useful feature. Recall that vectors can be used to display characters and curves. To do this normally requires very short moves and draws—typically no more than 10 or 20 units along each axis. Because these incremental moves are small, they can be encoded with 5 or 6 bits each, instead of the current 11 bits (10 if absolute). This coding inefficiency of about 100% makes the display program take up more space than necessary. The solution is simple: we introduce a new instruction type, the *short incremental load,* with which a short move, a short point (move and intensify), or a short line can be specified in a single instruction. A slight disadvantage of this solution, however, is that it does make additional opcodes necessary.

3.3.5 Character Generator

The display program for applications requiring the display of substantial amounts of text will contain many short moves and draws, as suggested in the previous section. While this is certainly preferable to the use of the long form of move and draw, and far preferable to the use of individual points, it is nevertheless relatively inefficient in terms of DPU program space and DPU execution time. This latter commodity is usually the more precious, since it determines the amount of flicker-free information displayable and hence must be used carefully.

A hardware character generator reduces the time and space consumed by characters. In our system the generator's input is an 8-bit character code, and its outputs are signals to the x and y deflection systems, the intensity system, and the "current position" registers X_{old} and Y_{old}. The "draw character" command accepts a character string that ends with a nondisplayed terminating code. The characters are displayed starting at the current position. After each character is displayed, the generator increments X_{old} by the sum of the character's width and the intercharacter spacing. When X_{old} becomes greater than 1023 (that is, gets to the right screen edge), it resets to zero and Y_{old} is decremented by the sum of the characters' height and the interline spacing.

Most commercial character generators fit this general functional description. Some do not automatically decrement Y_{old}, but instead require the equivalents of explicit carriage return and line feed codes in the character string. Some permit characters of different sizes and allow their display either in a horizontal or vertical orientation. Fast character generators require 4 to 5 microseconds per character, while slower ones take 10 to 20 microseconds.

★ **Character generator technology.** The character generator, when given a character code, must decide how to direct the CRT beam and how to modulate its intensity so the required character is traced on the screen. The information necessary to do this is stored in read-only memory, read–write memory, or in the CPU's main memory. In either of the latter two cases, the meanings of character codes can be altered to define special-purpose characters and small symbols.

The simplest approach to storing character definitions is to store the dot matrix used earlier. For characters defined on a 5 × 7 grid, 35 bits per character code must be stored. For higher-quality characters, a 7 × 9 or larger grid must be used. Another way to store the character definitions, while complex, offers in return characters of even better quality. The concept of a 5 × 7 (or larger) grid is retained, but now each grid point is assigned a number. A character is defined as a sequence of short lines (called strokes or segments) and short moves between the grid points. Thus, the beam's motion is controlled in a manner similar to that used in drawing lines, but with a more efficient encoding for each move: 6 bits are used for the grid point and 1 bit to control beam on–off. The information may be stored in a fast-access memory, and in any event is not duplicated in the DPU program for each occurrence of the character on the screen. What we have, in a very real sense, are display subroutines to draw the characters, and the character generator is the subroutine invocation mechanism.

3.3.6 The DPU Instruction Set

We now have a random-scan DPU with much the same functionality and architecture as simple, commercially available systems. In this section we define the instruction formats for the DPU, assuming a 16-bit word length. Figure 3.31 shows a set of instructions and mnemonics for the instructions, and Fig. 3.32 is a simple DPU program which uses many of these instructions. The final instruction jumps back to the start of the DPU program. Because the *frame lock bit* is set, the instruction is delayed until the next tick of a 30-Hz clock, in order to allow the DPU to refresh at 30 Hz but prevent more frequent refreshing of small DPU programs which could burn the phosphor.

Mnemonic	Meaning	Instruction format (bits 15 … 0)
LD{X/Y}{R/A}M	Load & move	0 0 0 X/Y R/A ← X OR Y OR ΔX OR ΔY →
LD{X/Y}{R/A}P	Load & point	0 0 1 X/Y R/A ← X OR Y OR ΔX OR ΔY →
LD{X/Y}{R/A}L	Load & line	0 1 0 X/Y R/A ← X OR Y OR ΔX OR ΔY →
LD{X/Y}{R/A}	Load	0 1 1 X/Y R/A ← X OR Y OR ΔX OR ΔY →
SM	Short move	1 0 0 — | ΔX | ΔY
SP	Short point	1 0 1 — | ΔX | ΔY
SL	Short line	1 1 0 — | ΔX | ΔY
CHAR	Characters	1 1 1 0 ———— | Char 1 Char 2 | Char 3 etc. to terminate code
JMP{R/A}LI	Jump	1 1 1 1 R/A L I ———————— Absolute or relative address

Key to notation

X/Y: 0 ⇒ Load X, 1 ⇒ Load Y

R/A: 0 ⇒ 11 bits of ΔX or ΔY, 1 ⇒ 10 bits of X or Y

{ }: Choose one of, for use in mnemonic code

L: Frame lock bit, 1 ⇒ delay jump until next clock tick

I: Interrupt bit, 1 ⇒ interrupt CPU

Fig. 3.31 DPU instruction set.

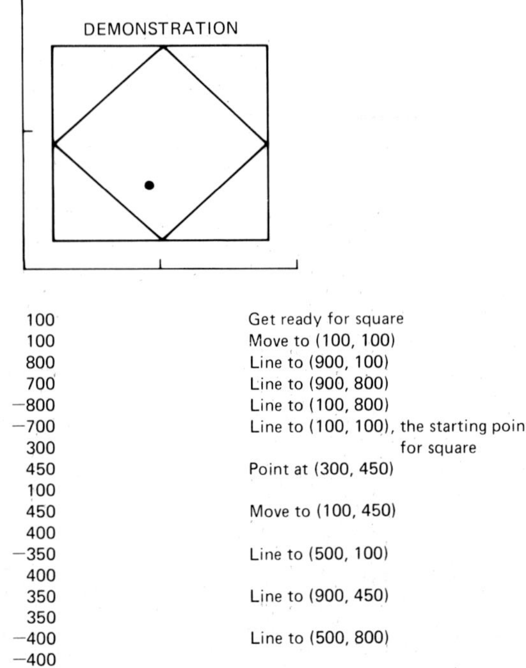


```
SQUARE:   LDXA    100               Get ready for square
          LDYAM   100               Move to (100, 100)
          LDXRL   800               Line to (900, 100)
          LDYRL   700               Line to (900, 800)
          LDXRL   -800              Line to (100, 800)
          LDYRL   -700              Line to (100, 100), the starting point
POINT:    LDXA    300                                  for square
          LDYAP   450               Point at (300, 450)
DIAMOND:  LDXA    100
          LDYAM   450               Move to (100, 450)
          LDXR    400
          LDYRL   -350              Line to (500, 100)
          LDXR    400
          LDYRL   350               Line to (900, 450)
          LDYR    350
          LDXRL   -400              Line to (500, 800)
          LDXR    -400
          LDYRL   -350              Line to (100, 450), the starting point
TEXT:     LDXA    200                                  for diamond
          LDYAM   900               Move to (200, 900) for text
          CHAR    'DEMONSTRATION t' t is terminate code
          JMPRL   SQUARE            Regenerate picture, frame lock
```

Fig. 3.32 DPU program.

Notice that with this instruction set, only one load command is needed to draw or move either horizontally or vertically, because the other coordinate is held constant; oblique movements, however, require two loads. The two loads can be in either x-then-y or y-then-x order, with the second of the two always specifying a move, draw-point, or draw-line operation. For the char opcode, a character string in single quotes follows, and the last character is the character generator's terminate code.

There are two main differences between DPU instructions and the instruction set for a general-purpose computer. With the exception of the jump command, all of the instructions are rather special-purpose: a register can be loaded and added to, but the result cannot be stored; the register only controls the beam. The second difference, again excluding jump, is that all data is immediate, i.e., part of the instruction. LDXA 100 means "load the data value 100 into the X-register," not "load the contents of address 100 into the X-register," as might be expected in a computer instruction. This restriction is removed in some of the more advanced DPUs described in Chapter 10.

3.3.7 DPU Organization for the DVST

The DVST is used in several Tektronix products, such as the 4054 depicted in Fig. 3.33. The 4054 has a local refresh buffer for displaying images in write-through mode and can also store images on the DVST. Our DPU could be modified to operate in a similar way by adding just two more instructions: "set display mode" (either store or write-through) and "erase."

To adapt our DPU for use in a DVST-based display without a refresh buffer, several modifications are appropriate. Again, an erase command must be added. The instruction counter and jump command can be deleted, since they were introduced to allow autonomous refresh. Elimination of refresh also implies that it is reasonable for the CPU to output DPU commands under program control, one at a time, waiting for a "done" flag from the DPU to send the next command. The vector generator and character generator can be relatively slow and thus less expensive, because fast refresh is no longer critical.

Fig. 3.33 Storage-tube display (courtesy Tektronix, Inc).

3.4 INPUT DEVICES FOR OPERATOR INTERACTION

Thus far, the DPU has been described as purely an output-only device. How can the user interact with the application program to delete a line, add a new line, move a line, or analyze the object whose picture is displayed? In this section we briefly mention the input devices described in Chapter 2: the sampled valuators and locators and the event-causing alphanumeric and button keyboards and the (light pen) pick. These and other devices are described in detail in Chapter 5.

Our DPU will be assumed to contain a number of registers in which input devices store the appropriate values. Event (interrupt-) generating devices load their device registers and interrupt the CPU; the CPU then reads the associated registers. The sampled devices load their registers with data whenever they are interrogated by the CPU; the CPU then reads the associated registers. Many sampled devices require analog-to-digital converters to load the registers with digital data.

3.4.1 Keyboards

The alphanumeric keyboard is used to enter commands, text, and parameter values. Each keystroke causes a 7-bit code to be stored in a character register, after which the CPU is interrupted. The interpretation or meaning given the code is determined by the CPU program, which might accumulate consecutive characters into a buffer until a termination character is typed, and thereby give the application program a character-string input device such as SGP provides.

The button device is often implemented with a so-called *programmed function keyboard* (PFK), a keyboard with typically 16 or 32 pushbuttons. Depression of each button generates a unique 4- or 5-bit code which is stored in the button register, after which the CPU is interrupted. Alternatively, 16 or 32 bits are stored to provide the status of all buttons and to allow multiple simultaneous depressions. Some PFKs have lights, controllable by the CPU, in each button. The lights are useful for operator feedback or to indicate which buttons are currently eligible for use.

3.4.2 Tablet as Locator

A tablet, pictured in Fig. 1.14 is a convenient way for the user to enter x and y locator positions. The tablet stylus is held like a pencil and moved over the tablet surface. In some tablets, electrical coupling between the stylus and a 2D grid of wires in the tablet is used to sense the stylus position. With most tablets, the position may be determined whenever the stylus is within a half inch or so of the tablet surface. Downward pressure on the stylus closes a microswitch and interrupts the computer. Hence the tablet can serve as a sampled locator with a single event-causing button.

3.4.3 Light Pen as Pick Device

Light pens (Fig. 1.14) are inherently element-indicating or picking devices. The name *light pen* is, in fact, a misnomer—the pen does not emit light to draw a picture as a fountain pen emits ink. Rather, it senses (detects) light from picture elements (lines, points, characters) drawn on the screen. The name probably arose because some light pens do have a narrowly focused light source (the *finder beam*) directed toward the screen to tell the user just what picture elements are in the pen's field of view.

The pen sees the sharp burst of fluorescent light emitted when the electron beam is actually bombarding the phosphor, that is, the light emitted during the short period the DPU is drawing the picture element; it is not sensitive to the more prolonged phosphorescence or to ambient room light. The pen's output is usually connected to the DPU's control logic in such a way that the DPU stops executing commands as soon as the pen reports that it has seen light.

When the DPU stops, its instruction counter contains the address of the next instruction after the one that drew the detected element (the counter is incremented immediately after the instruction fetch). As will be explained in the next chapter, this address can be used by the graphics package to give the application program the name of the segment containing the detected element. The application program can then operate on the segment (delete it or move it) or the (piece of the) object in the *application data structure* corresponding to the element detected. In order for the graphics package to actually use the light pen, the CPU must be able to read the DPU's instruction counter.

As is discussed in detail later, the light pen acts as a locator with a raster display, stopping the raster scan at the detected pixel. The (x, y) address of this pixel provides a location.

3.4.4 Valuator

Control dials (see Fig. 1.14), levers, and sliding potentiometers are sampled devices whose analog values are converted and stored in device registers when read by the CPU. The values read from the registers are then converted to equivalent floating-point numbers before being used in the application program.

3.5 RASTER-SCAN DISPLAY PROCESSING UNIT

Images to be displayed by a random-scan system are encoded as commands to draw each output primitive by using endpoints of lines as coordinate data values. The encoding for raster-scan systems is much simpler: output primitives are broken up into their constituent points for display.

The major difference between simple point-plotting random-scan displays (which also store sequences of points) and raster-scan displays is in the organization of the stored points. In point-plotting displays, the component points of each successive output primitive are stored sequentially in memory and are plotted in that order, one picture element at a time, since the beam may be moved randomly on the screen. In the raster display, on the other hand, the refresh memory is arranged as a two-dimensional array. The entry at a particular row and column stores the brightness and/or color value of the corresponding (x, y) position on the screen in the simple one-to-one relationship shown in Fig. 3.34, i.e, each screen location and memory location is referenced by an x-coordinate (ranging from 0 to $M - 1$) and a y-coordinate (ranging from 0 to $N - 1$). The top row of memory corresponds to the top scan line, etc., and image refreshing is done by a sequential raster scan through the buffer by scan line (rather than by output primitive, as in the random scan).

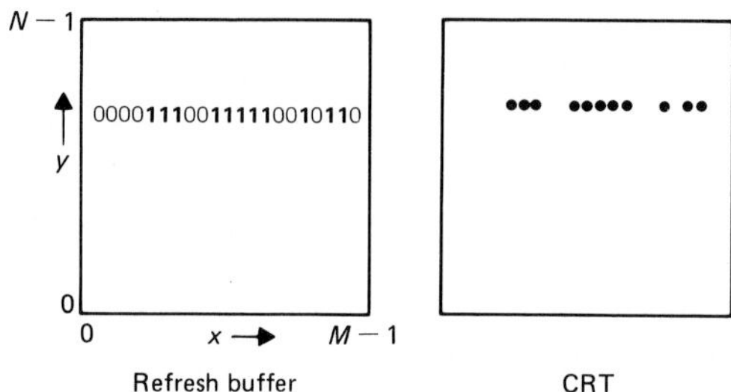

Fig. 3.34 A row in the refresh buffer corresponds to a scan line on the CRT. A "1" in the buffer maps onto a dot on the screen.

Since each memory location defines one point-sized element of an image (or picture), each screen location (and its corresponding memory location) is often called a *pixel* or *pel,* both short for the image processing term *picture element.* In computer graphics, we reserve the term *pixel* for points on the raster display and the terms *picture elements* and *output primitives* for higher-level primitives such as lines, points, and characters. A simple refresh buffer has one bit per pixel and thus defines a two-color (usually black and white) image. Modern refresh buffers, also called frame buffers or bit maps, are implemented with solid-state random-access semiconductor memories. Earlier raster displays used mechanical drums, delay lines, or solid-state shift registers to store images.

The job of the image refresh system (Fig. 3.35) is to cycle through the refresh buffer row by row (hence scan line by scan line), typically 30 or 60 times per second. Memory reference addresses are generated in synchronism with the raster scan, and the contents of the memory are used to control the CRT beam's intensity. The image refresh system has the general organization shown in Fig. 3.36. The raster-scan generator produces deflection signals which generate the raster scan, and also controls the X and Y address registers, which in turn define the location of image storage to be fetched next to control the CRT beam.

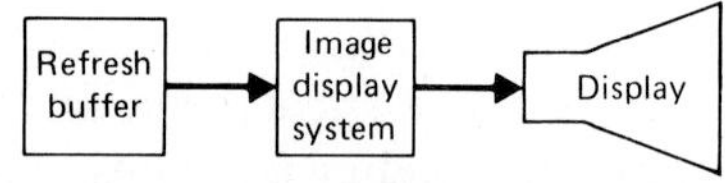

Fig. 3.35 Image display system cycles through refresh buffer and displays contents on CRT.

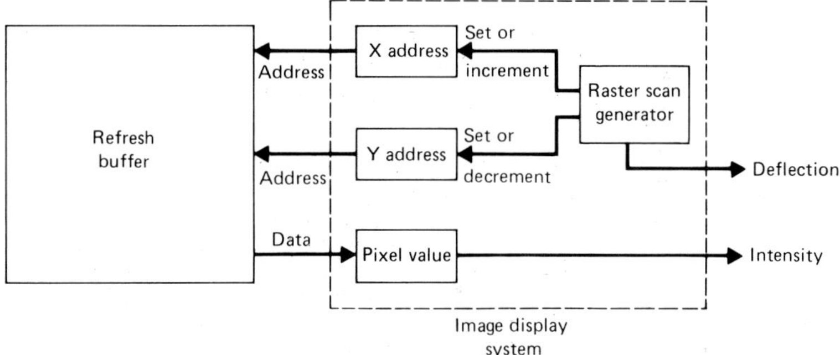

Fig. 3.36 Refresh buffer and image display system.

At the start of a refresh cycle, the X address register is set to zero and the Y register is set to $N - 1$ (the top scan line). As the first scan line is generated, the x address is incremented up through $M - 1$. Each pixel value is fetched and used to control the intensity of the CRT beam. After the first scan line, the x address is reset to zero and the y address is decremented by one. The process continues until the last scan line ($y = 0$) is generated.

The image refresh system is sometimes able to interrupt the computer when the raster scan is completed. The computer can then make changes in the image storage during the 1.3 millisecond *flyback* time in which the CRT beam is moved from the lower right to the upper left of the screen; alternatively, it can stop the image refresh if the changes will take longer than does the flyback. Changes can also be made while image refresh is in process, but it is sometimes preferable not to distract the viewer with a partially updated display.

The image refresh system often performs an interlaced scan of two fields, as is done in commercial TV. The refresh cycle is broken into two phases, each lasting 1/60 of a second: thus a full refresh still lasts 1/30 of a second. In the first phase, all odd-numbered scan lines (the first field) are displayed; in the second phase, all even-numbered scan lines (the second field) are displayed. The purpose of the interlaced scan is to place some new information in all areas of the screen in 1/60 of a second, eliminating the tendency of a raster-scan image to otherwise flicker at the 1/30 of a second refresh rate. The net effect is to produce a picture whose effective refresh rate is closer to 60 than to 30 Hz. This works as long as adjacent scan lines display similar information.

Some raster displays use a repeat-field scan: the entire image is displayed 60 times a second. This is easily possible at 512 × 512 resolution, and becomes increasingly difficult at higher resolutions. For 30-Hz refresh of a 512 × 512 display, each scan line must be displayed in about 60 microseconds, or about 100 nanoseconds per pixel. With repeat-field, this figure drops to about 50 nanoseconds per pixel. A high-resolution 1280 × 1024 image must be displayed at about 30 microseconds per scan line, or about 25 nanoseconds per pixel. Halving this pixel time for repeat-field display requires display of one pixel each 12 nanoseconds. These fast times mean that the deflection amplifiers and intensity control amplifier must have very high bandwidths, and the refresh buffer transfer rate must be increased.

The reason for the low cost of simple raster displays should now be evident: the basic components are semiconductor memory, some logic, a scan generator, and a TV monitor. We avoid random vectors and their need for fast, linear, accurate vector generators and corresponding high-current deflection amplifier technology. Indeed, the well-developed and inexpensive deflection and beam control technology of commercial TV can be used for medium-quality (256 × 256) resolution. Additionally, with raster displays we gain solid areas for *continuous* grey scale or color, and video mixing with standard TV signals from video cameras, video recorders, and video disks. Finally, there is no flicker, regardless of picture complexity. Except in applications needing arbitrary motion, rapid update, and very high resolution, raster technology today dominates vector technology in price/performance ratio.

3.5.1 Color and Grey-Level Raster-Display Systems

Two-intensity images are fine for some applications but grossly unsatisfactory for others. Additional control over the intensity of each pixel is obtained by storing multiple bits for each pixel: two bits yield four intensities, etc. The bits can be used to control not only intensity, but color as well.

How many bits per pixel are needed for a stored image to be perceived as having continuous shades of grey? Five or six bits are often enough, but up to eight bits can be needed. Thus for color displays, a somewhat simplified analysis suggests that three times as many bits would be needed; eight bits for each of the three additive primary colors red, blue, and green (see Chapter 17).

Systems with 24 bits per pixel are still relatively expensive, despite the dramatic decreases in cost of random-access solid-state memory. Furthermore, many color applications don't require up to 2^{24} different colors in a single picture (which typically has only 2^{14} to 2^{20} pixels). On the other hand, there is frequent need for both a relatively small number of colors in any one picture or application and the ability to change colors from picture to picture or from application to application. Also, in many image analysis and enhancement applications, it is desirable to change the visual appearance of an image without changing the underlying data defining the image; for example, one might want to display all pixels with values below some threshold as black, to expand an intensity range, or to create a pseudo-color display of a monochromatic image.

For these various reasons the image refresh system of raster displays often includes a so-called *video look-up table* (also called a *color table* or *color map*). A pixel's value is not routed directly to the intensity digital-to-analog converter, but is instead used as an index into this look-up table. The table entry's value is used to control the intensity or color on the CRT. A pixel value of 67 would cause the contents of table location 67 to be accessed and used to control the CRT beam. This look-up operation is done for each pixel on each display cycle, so the table must be accessible quickly; for a 512 × 512 image, about 100 nanoseconds is available to process each pixel. The associated computer must be able to load and change the look-up table on program command. The look-up table has as many entries as there are pixel values.

We can diagram systems with n bits per pixel and a look-up table w bits wide as shown in Fig. 3.37. For a monochromatic CRT, 2^w intensity levels are therefore defined. With color, the w bits are typically divided into three equal groups, one for each of the red, blue, and green electron guns of the shadow-mask CRT. Sometimes other color representations with more intuitive appeal (such as intensity and chrominance) are used in the application program and are stored in the refresh buffer. This representation is then converted into red, green, and blue control signals by a fixed-content intensity/chrominance to red/green/blue look-up table. These and other color representations are discussed further in Chapter 17.

3.5.2 Image Creation

How is an image created in the first place? The images of real objects come directly or indirectly from a scanning device of some sort: film scanner, TV scanner, ultrasound scanner, etc. Here, however, we concentrate instead on the creation of synthetic images: images of objects which exist as abstract collections of lines, points, curves, areas, etc. in the computer's memory. This is the usual domain of interactive computer graphics.

There is a fundamental mismatch between the two-dimensional array of pixel values used to drive a raster system and the line, point, and area representation of objects stored and manipulated by the application program. We first saw this mismatch in our discussion of printers as hardcopy raster-scan devices (Section 3.1.1). The process of converting a line, point, and area representation to the pixel array of the image storage is called *scan conversion.* Figure 3.22 is a simple scan-conversion algorithm. Other algorithms for scan-converting lines, as well as areas and circles, are discussed in Chapter 11. For now it is sufficient to say that the algorithms exist and must be executed each time some or all of the displayed image changes. Scan conversion can therefore be a major bottleneck in updating the picture.

Because the scan-conversion algorithms are universally needed in raster-scan systems for interactive graphics, they are often incorporated into the raster-display system as another functional unit, the *image creation system* shown in Fig. 3.38. The entire raster system now loosely corresponds to a random-display DPU. The system accepts a DPU program having the general form of the one discussed in Section 3.3.6. Instead of driving a vector CRT directly, the instructions are converted into a simpler representation—the refresh buffer. Of course, the image creation system need not reprocess its input commands each 1/30 of a second.

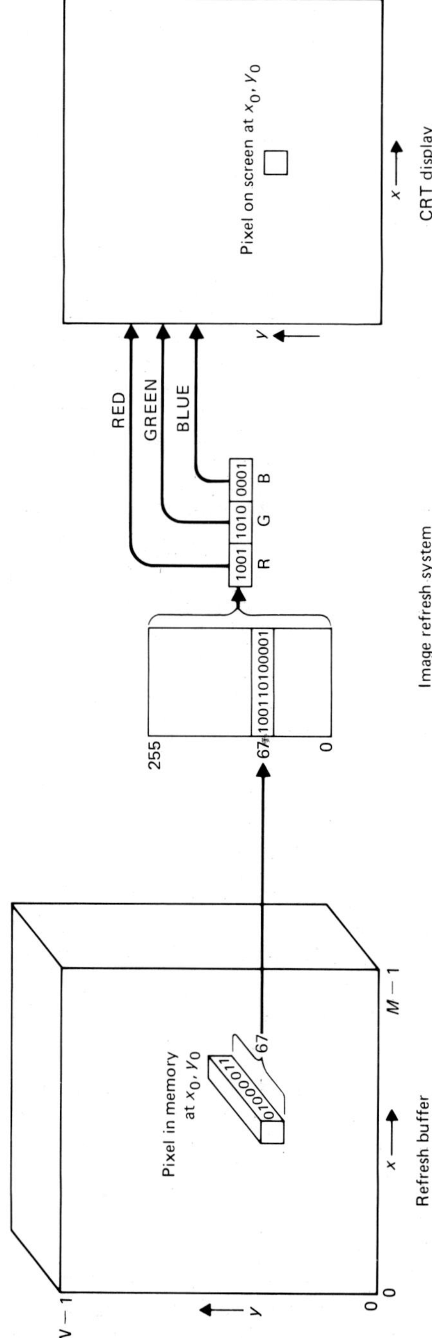

Fig. 3.37 Video look-up table. A pixel with value 67 is shown.

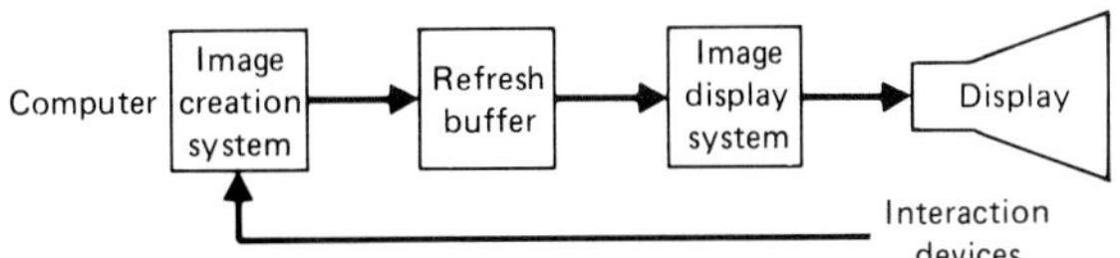

Fig. 3.38 Complete raster-display system.

A raster-display instruction set usually includes points, lines, conic sections, solid areas, and text. Various attributes of these output primitives can be controlled, such as color or intensity, line style (solid, dashed, dotted, etc.), and text spacing, orientation, font, and size. Coordinates are usually given in the coordinate system of the refresh buffer itself: if the buffer is 512×512, then the coordinates range from 0 to 511 in each dimension.

The image creation system is also typically able to accept images which already exist in pixel form, such as images of real objects or images of synthetic objects that have already been scan converted. Often a rectangular area of the image storage can be moved around in the buffer. The image creation system can usually load the video look-up table, start and stop image refresh, and deal with interaction devices in much the same way as vector displays.

While there are certainly nontrivial differences between raster and vector displays (discussed further in Chapters 10 and 12), our discussion in the next few chapters considers them as essentially equivalent from the user's and application programmer's points of view. Thus for the time being we will not deal with the ability of a raster display to show solid areas.

EXERCISES

3.1 Modify the line-drawing algorithm in Fig. 3.22 to draw lines with all slopes. Implement the algorithm and test it, observing the visual results for lines with different slopes.

3.2 Design a DPU instruction set in which each opcode (move, point, line) includes both an x and y coordinate, perhaps using multiple words. Do this for a 16-bit and 24-bit instruction length.

3.3 Extend the DPU instruction set from Section 3.3.6 to include two line styles (such as solid and dotted) and four intensity levels. Do this in two different ways: (i) include the style and intensity with each line, point, or text string display instruction; (ii) design instruction(s) to load style and intensity registers. The register values affect all following output primitives until the values are changed.

3.4 Make a list of the advantages and disadvantages of random refresh displays, random DVST displays, and raster refresh displays.

3.5 In some raster systems the image storage is part of the image creation system's memory address space, while in others the image storage and the image creation system's memory are separate. Describe the possible advantages and disadvantages of each arrangement.

3.6 Prepare a report on technologies for large-screen displays.

3.7 Redesign the simple DPU instruction set of Fig. 3.31 for a 16-bit word, assuming that all opcodes are equal in length.

3.8 Modify the character-drawing routine of Fig. 3.24 to include scaling and orientation of characters.

3.9 If long-persistence phosphors decrease the fusion frequency, why not routinely use them?

3.10 For an electrostatic plotter with 9″-wide paper, a resolution of 200 units to the inch in each direction, and a paper speed of 3 inches per second, how many bits per second must be provided to allow the paper to move at full speed?

3.11 Consider means for picking (as with a light pen) a line on a raster display when all that can be detected is a single pixel.

3.12 Given a 1024 × 1280 raster refresh buffer, calculate the number of pixels accessed per second and the inverse, access time per pixel.

3.13 How long would it take to load a 512 × 512 by 1-bit refresh buffer, assuming that the pixels are packed eight to a byte and that bytes can be transferred and unpacked at the rate of 100,000 per second?

3.14 How long would it take your favorite microprocessor to scan convert 1000 lines, each 512 pixels long, into a refresh buffer?

4 Implementation of a Simple Graphics Package (SGP)

4.1 OVERVIEW OF SGP

4.1.1 Introduction

In Chapter 2 we saw how to write a high-level, computer- and device-independent graphics application program by using a device-independent subroutine package, the *simple graphics package* (SGP). SGP allows the user to display pictures of two-dimensional objects and transmits input actions from the user to the application program in order to establish user–computer interaction. The architecture of simple refreshed vector and raster display devices was described in Chapter 3; the purpose of this chapter is to show how SGP can be implemented to use these displays. The internal design and structure of device-independent graphics packages is an important subject in the study of interactive graphics. We will describe here the program and data structures typical of well known device-independent packages such as GINO-F [GINO76], GPGS [VAND77], and the ACM Core [GSPC79]. Additional, more complex graphics package features, such as display of 3D objects and support of more sophisticated display devices, will be discussed in later chapters.

The implementation considerations discussed below apply to both refreshed vector displays and raster displays, unless otherwise noted. This is because, as we saw in Section 2.19, raster displays can be programmed essentially as if they were vector displays, with the additional capability to provide *area fill* of closed polygons. More sophisticated use of features peculiar to raster displays is discussed in Chapters 11 and 12. Because raster displays usually do their own scan conversion of the individual output primitives into their internal bit map representations, SGP need not concern itself with that process.

The functional facilities of SGP (and most other subroutine packages) available to the application programmer can be divided into the six distinct classes summarized below and defined in Table 4.1.

1. *Graphic output primitives*—the functions that result in DPU instructions which either write on the view surface or help SGP control the generation and structure of the DPU code.
2. *Attribute-setting*—the functions that determine the line style of subsequent lines and the color of all subsequent output primitives.
3. *Segment control*—the functions that group logically related output primitives into *segments* (the units of selective modification of the display program). Functions are available to delete, rename, or change the visibility of segments, and to translate the image on the screen which was produced by a segment.
4. *Viewing operation*—the two functions that together specify to the package what part of the world coordinate system to display on what portion of the screen.
5. *Input*—the functions that control user interaction with the application program.
6. *Control*—the *INITIALIZE* function helps the package initialize its own tables and the DPU status and mode flags/registers; it also initializes the default values for the window (the unit square) and the viewport (the entire screen). The *TERMINATE* function (used by *CLEANUP* in Chapter 2) clears the screen and closes out the graphics device to provide an orderly exit. *INQUIRE_COLOR* is used for saving and restoring color values. (Other *INQUIRE* functions are not listed.)

In later chapters we will add further facilities to SGP, primarily for 3D viewing and for operations specific to raster graphics systems.

TABLE 4.1. SGP SUBROUTINES—GENERAL FORMAT

1. Graphic output primitives	*Function*
MOVE_ABS_2(x, y)	move the CP to (x, y)
MOVE_REL_2(dx, dy)	move the CP to $(CP_x + dx, CP_y + dy)$
POINT_ABS_2(x, y)	define a point at (x, y)
POINT_REL_2(dx, dy)	define a point at $(CP_x + dx, CP_y + dy)$
LINE_ABS_2(x, y)	define a line from CP to (x, y)
LINE_REL_2(dx, dy)	define a line from CP to $(CP_x + dx, CP_y + dy)$
POLYGON(x_array, y_array, n)	define a closed polygon with *n* vertices starting and ending at (*x_array*[1], *y_array*[1])
TEXT(string)	define a string specified by *string* at the CP

TABLE 4.1 (continued)

2. Attribute setting	*Function*
SET_LINESTYLE(style)	set the line style for all following primitives until reset
SET_COLOR(color)	set the color for all following primitives until reset
3. Segment control	
CREATE_SEGMENT(segment_name)	start a new segment with an integer name
CLOSE_SEGMENT	close the currently open segment
DELETE_SEGMENT(segment_name)	delete *segment_name*
RENAME_SEGMENT(old_name, new_name)	rename segment *old_name* to *new_name*
SET_VISIBILITY(segment_name, on/off)	make *segment_name* visible or invisible
TRANSLATE_IMAGE_2(segment_name, dx, dy)	translate *segment_name*'s image by *dx* and *dy* in NDC units
4. Viewing operation	
WINDOW(x_min, x_max, y_min, y_max)	specify window in world coordinates
VIEWPORT_2(x_min, x_max, y_min, y_max)	specify viewport in NDC units
5. Input	
READ_LOCATOR(x, y)	sample locator position on screen, return NDC value in *x, y*
READ_VALUATOR(n, value)	sample the *n*th valuator, return fraction between 0 and 1 in *value*
*WAIT_BUTTON(time, button_name)**	return 0 or name of button pressed in *button_name*
*WAIT_PICK(time, segment_name)**	return 0 or name of segment containing picked primitive in *segment_name*
*WAIT_KEYBOARD(time, text, length)**	read typed characters into *text,* return 0 or number of characters typed in *length*
INVERSE_2(x_ndc, y_ndc, x_wc, y_wc)	convert an *x, y* in normalized device coordinates (typically read from locator) to world coordinates using current window and viewport specification

(*Continued*)

*Each of the *WAIT* procedures waits for either time-out (in which case it returns 0) or the user-activated event (and returns the associated event data).

TABLE 4.1 (continued)

6. Control	*Function*
INITIALIZE	clear screen; set default window, viewport; display cursor at locator x, y
TERMINATE	clear screen and close the graphics device
INQUIRE_COLOR	return current color attribute

4.1.2 Block Diagram of the Graphics System

The block diagram of Fig. 2.1 is expanded in Fig. 4.1 to give a high-level summary of the major components of a typical graphics system: hardware, software, and data modules. The two principal hardware components are the host computer and the DPU; the host's CPU and the memory shared by CPU and DPU are not shown here to reduce the complexity of the diagram. The two important data modules shown are both stored in the shared memory. The first is the DPU display program (also called display file/list) which is written by the graphics package and is read by the DPU as it refreshes the image on the screen. The second is the application data structure (or data structure for short) which contains, among other things, a description of the objects whose images are to be displayed and is said to *model* the objects.

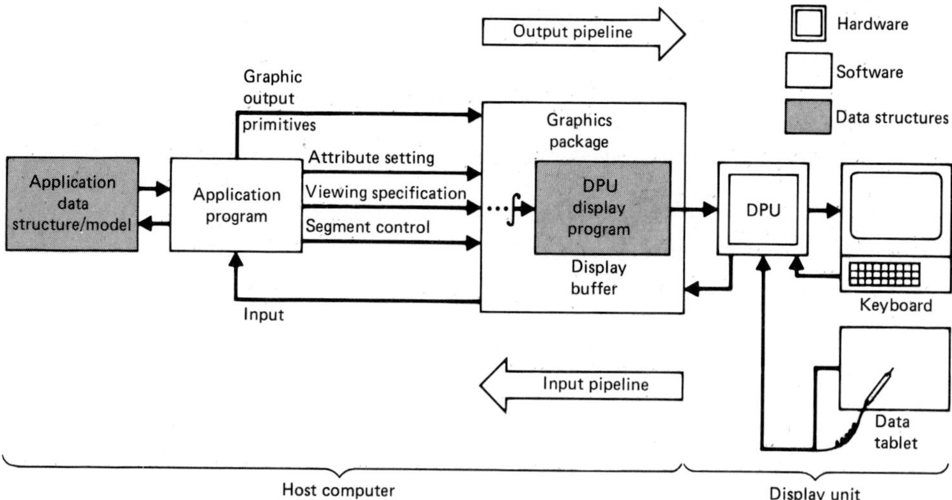

Fig. 4.1 Major hardware, software, and data modules of a graphics system.

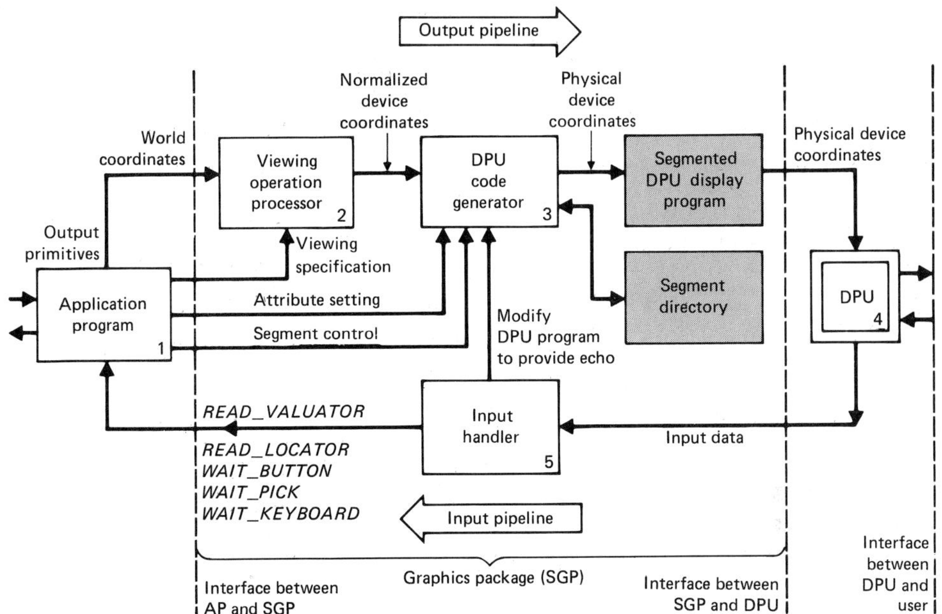

Fig. 4.2 High-level block diagram of graphics package.
Output pipeline: application data structure → · · · image.
Input pipeline: input actions → · · · application data structure.

Fig. 4.2 expands a portion of Fig. 4.1 to give a more detailed view of the structure of SGP. The three major SGP processes, numbered 2, 3, and 5, are shown implemented as software modules, although pieces of these processes may actually be implemented in hardware or firmware in more complex systems. The interaction between the five processes is best understood by looking at the two major data flows going in opposite directions within the graphics system: one is from a data structure description of an object to its image on the screen, and the other is from the user-supplied input to the data structure and/or display program.

There are several useful conceptualizations of the object-to-image transformation sequence. One is that of a four-stage *output pipeline* which transforms the object description into successively more machine-dependent representations and finally to an image on a screen. Stage 1 of this pipeline, the application program, transforms a piece of the data structure modeling the *geometry* (layout) and *topology* (connectivity) of an object (such as an electronic circuit) into a sequence of calls to SGP using parameters derived from the data structure. As shown in Chapter 2, these calls describe the object in terms of its point, line, and text output primitives. Other calls specify the division of the object into logical units, i.e., segments, as well as the desired view of the object. The specification of the viewing operation may be thought of as adjusting the settings of a *synthetic camera*.

Stage 2 in the pipeline, the viewing operation processor, uses the viewing specification to clip the object's primitives against the user-supplied or default window boundaries and then maps the visible portion of the object into the current viewport. Stage 3, the DPU code generator, transforms the still device-independent specifications of (clipped) primitives from normalized device coordinates into the device-dependent hardware instructions and device coordinates of the DPU. The SGP segment functions control the segmentation of this DPU "machine code" and specify to the DPU code generator which segments are to be added, made visible/invisible, translated, or deleted. Stage 4 in the pipeline, the DPU itself, transforms DPU output primitives to light on the screen or ink or toner on a piece of paper. (In raster systems, this transformation will typically include an additional scan conversion transformation, followed by refresh from the bit map.)

A second paradigm for the output pipeline is suggested by the discussion in the previous paragraph: a "display program compiler" generates code from a machine-independent high-level language description (the SGP-based graphics program) into machine-dependent low-level code for a specific DPU. Segments then correspond roughly to object code load modules which may be linked, unlinked, and deleted at run time. As we shall see in Section 4.3, SGP may use a *segment directory* as an auxiliary data structure for managing this dynamically changing segment structure.

The compilation of the DPU code, unlike normal compilation, takes place at the run time of the application program, as the state, the flow of control, or the parameters of calls in the SGP-based "source" program are changed as a result of user interaction. Repeatedly compiling changed segments is somewhat similar to incremental compilation. Another significant difference from normal compilation is that ordinary source code is compiled to equivalent target code in its entirety, while SGP "source" code may be clipped to a subset before being compiled to equivalent DPU "target" code.

Note that we do not specify whether or not execution of the viewing operation processor and of the DPU code generator are interleaved. There are two alternate strategies: a clipped normalized device coordinate primitive can be mapped from window to viewport and immediately converted to a DPU code primitive, or the two processors can respectively write to and then read from an intermediate data structure of clipped normalized device coordinate primitives. Such an intermediate representation would be analogous to a compiler's intermediate code representation. In either case, the decomposition of the display program compiler into the two independent viewing and code generation modules is a useful conceptual and structural division that allows us to add modularly any new device-dependent code generators for additional display devices. These generators can then share the device-independent viewing operation processor, as discussed in Section 4.8 below.

The *input pipeline* has fewer stages and has no ready analogies to compilation. The DPU records input device use, and either interrupts the CPU (for event-causing devices such as pick, button, keyboard) or transmits data on request (for sampling devices, i.e., locator, valuator). The input data is collected from the DPU by the input handler which typically passes it on to the application program. The data changes the state or flow of control of the application program; it may also cause the application program to modify either the data structure (and probably the corresponding SGP call parameters) or to change the viewing operation parameters. The input may also be used directly by the code generator to perform segment manipulation operations.

As stated in Chapter 2, we tend today to emphasize programmer efficiency more than program efficiency; yet it behooves designers and implementers of graphics packages and application programs to make the output and input pipelines function as efficiently as possible. In essence, the user at the terminal is less productive if noticeable delays (greater than a fraction of a second) cause discontinuities in the closely coupled user–computer interaction cycle. (Cursor tracking must, of course, be done without any visible delay at all.) In short, the results of user actions should be available almost immediately, so that smooth, "kinesthetic" feedback involving close hand/eye coordination can develop. Both user-controlled motion and update dynamics in refresh vector displays provide good examples of this principle. Even when such dynamics cannot be implemented we can attempt by careful design to minimize annoying discontinuities in the picture caused by flicker or abrupt changes from one image to another, and give immediate feedback to any input action to show the user his request is being processed.

4.2 VIEWING OPERATION

Processes 2 and 3 of the output pipeline in Fig. 4.2 serve to transform a device-independent description of an object to a device-dependent display program which generates an image that is a particular view of the object. Fig. 4.3 shows the three steps performed by these two processes in greater detail: clipping, window-to-viewport mapping, and generating display code in device-dependent physical screen coordinates. The first two steps are conventionally considered part of the viewing operation, while the third step is part of the DPU code generation process. (The viewing operation can also convert primitives directly to physical device coordinates

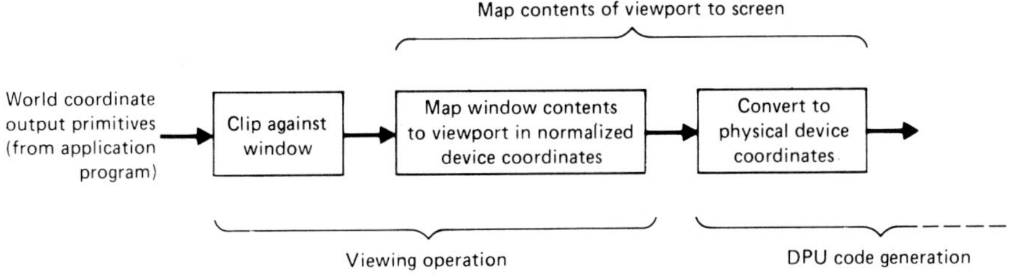

Fig. 4.3 Mapping object's world coordinates to screen device coordinates.

—see Section 4.2.2.) In this section we discuss the first two steps: clipping, and window-to-viewport mapping of clipped world coordinate primitives to normalized device coordinate primitives.

4.2.1 Clipping Output Primitives

Clipping of points, lines, and character strings is illustrated in Fig. 4.4 for the usual case of an upright rectangular window. Point *A* is within the window, and thus is displayed within the viewport on the view surface. Point *B* is outside the window and thus is not displayed. Line segment *EF* is displayed, *GH* and *IJ* are partly displayed (clipped), and *CD* and *KL* are not displayed. The text string YES is not displayed, HELLO is, and WAIT is clipped and then displayed. Text is shown here as rotated and clipped on an individual character basis; below we see that the hardware or even software may not support such accuracy. Note that lines intersecting a rectangular window (or any convex polygon) are always clipped to a single resulting line segment, such as *I′J′* on *IJ*. Points and lines lying on the window border are considered inside and hence displayed.

We treat first clipping of points and lines and then clipping of text. Chapters 8 and 11 contain additional discussion of clipping in 3D and clipping to polygonal windows, respectively.

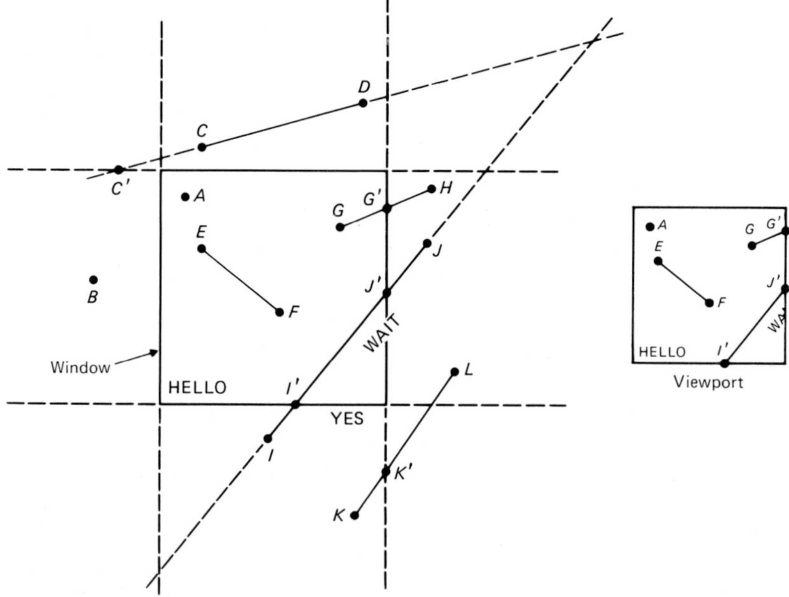

Fig. 4.4 2D clipping; several lines and window edges are extended (dashed lines) for intersection calculations.

Points. Clipping points is a straightforward process. If the x-coordinate boundaries of the window are at *xmin* and *xmax* and the y-coordinate boundaries are at *ymin* and *ymax,* then for a point at (x, y) to be visible, four inequalities must be satisfied:

$$xmin \leq x \leq xmax \quad \text{and} \quad ymin \leq y \leq ymax.$$

If any of the four inequalities does *not* hold, the point is not displayed.

Lines. The clipping of lines takes more testing and calculation, in general, than the clipping of points. Fortunately, we need only to consider the endpoints of a line, not its infinitely many interior points. First, we can deal quickly with the special case of a line like *EF,* whose endpoints both lie inside the window. Such lines are known to be entirely inside the rectangular window because their endpoints are, and can therefore be *trivially accepted* without clipping calculations. Other lines require clipping because they intersect the window with one endpoint in and one out (*GH*). Lines neither of whose endpoints lie inside, require testing and calculations for potential intersection and clipping (*CD* and *KL* are not displayed, while *IJ* needs to be clipped).

The brute-force approach to clipping lines that cannot be trivially accepted is to intersect the line with each of the four window edges to see if any intersection points lie on the window edges; if so, the line cuts the window and is partially inside. For each line segment and window edge, one therefore takes the two mathematically infinite lines that contain them and intersects them. Next, one tests if this intersection point is *interior,* i.e., lies on both the window edge and the line segment; if so, there is an intersection with the window (in Fig. 4.4, I' and G' are interior, C' and K' are not).

With this approach, unfortunately, two simultaneous equations must be solved for each (edge, line) pair using multiplication and division. A parametric formulation for lines is useful:

$$x = x_1 + t(x_2 - x_1),$$
$$y = y_1 + t(y_2 - y_1).$$

These equations describe points (x, y) on the directed line segment from (x_1, y_1) to (x_2, y_2) for parameter t in the range $[0,1]$. Two sets of simultaneous equations of this parametric form can be solved for parameters t_{edge} for the edge and t_{line} for the line. The values of t_{edge} and t_{line} can then be checked to see if both lie in $[0,1]$; if so, the intersection point lies within both segments and is a true window intersection. Furthermore, the special case of a line parallel to a window edge must also be considered by testing prior to solving the simultaneous equations. Altogether, the brute-force approach involves considerable calculation and testing and is not very efficient.

Clipping efficiency is of major concern in interactive graphics because a typical display includes hundreds or even thousands of lines that must be processed as quickly as possible to provide the next view of the object as smoothly as possible. A more efficient algorithm would perform some initial tests on a line to determine whether intersection calculations are really necessary. First, endpoint pairs would be checked to see if they both are within the window so the lines can be trivially accepted. Next, *region checks* would be done. For instance, two simple comparisons on y show that both endpoints of line CD in Fig. 4.4 have a y-coordinate greater than *ymax* and thus lie in the region above the window, and therefore CD can be *trivially rejected* and need be neither clipped nor displayed. Similarly, we can trivially reject lines with both endpoints in regions below *ymin,* left of *xmin,* or right of *xmax.*

a) *The Cohen–Sutherland clipping algorithm.* The Cohen–Sutherland clipping algorithm is designed to identify efficiently those lines that can be trivially accepted or rejected by using region checks. Intersection calculations are required only for those lines for which neither case occurs. The algorithm is especially efficient in the two extreme cases of a large window including most of the primitives, or a relatively small window and a large, dense picture in which most primitives lie outside the window; most lines can then be trivially accepted or trivially rejected, respectively.

The algorithm starts by assigning to each endpoint of a line a four-bit *outcode* based on the nine regions shown in Fig. 4.5, with bit 1 leftmost. Each bit in the outcode is set to 1 (TRUE) if a given relation between the endpoint and window is true:

Bit 1—point is above window,
Bit 2—point is below window,
Bit 3—point is to right of window,
Bit 4—point is to left of window;

otherwise the bit is 0 (FALSE).

A particularly efficient way to calculate the outcode in languages allowing bit manipulation derives from the observation that bit 1 is the sign bit of $(ymax - y)$; bit 2 is the sign bit of $(y - ymin)$; bit 3, $(xmax - x)$; bit 4, $(x - xmin)$. A point is inside the window (outcode 0000) if all these differences are nonnegative. A line can

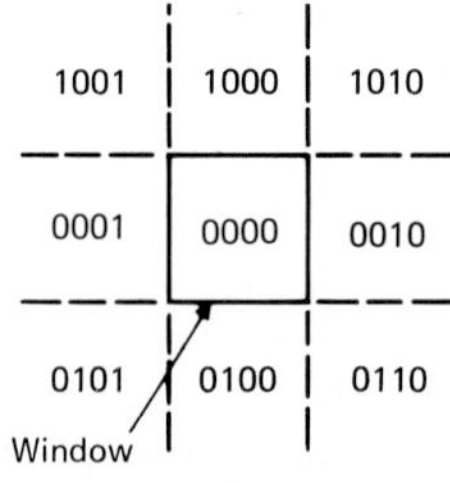

Fig. 4.5 Outcodes for endpoints.

be trivially accepted if both ends are in the window (corresponding to outcodes of 0000). A line is trivially rejected if both endpoints are in a region above, below, to the left, or to the right of the window. This will be the case if the corresponding bits in the outcodes for both endpoints are 1, and this can easily be tested by taking the logical **and** of the outcodes and testing for "**not** = 0000".

If the result of the logical **and** is 0000, the line can be neither trivially rejected nor accepted—it may intersect the window. (In Fig. 4.6, *AD* and *EH* both **and** to 0000, but only *EH* intersects the window.) The algorithm does not use brute force to determine intersection (test for parallelism, then solve two simultaneous equations, then test whether the intersection point is interior to both line segments). Rather, it uses an iterative "divide and conquer" strategy to home in on the intersection point—a process that requires few calculations. It takes advantage of the fact that each line is intersected by a window edge which is vertical or horizontal. This provides the intersection point's x or y coordinate without calculation. It also uses the fact that the part of a line segment on the side of the edge away from the window can be discarded; the remaining line segment is then tested for trivial acceptance or rejection. If it cannot yet be accepted, the process is repeated for the remaining line segment and a different window edge. An endpoint with a nonzero outcode is replaced by an endpoint lying on a window edge or the infinite line containing a window edge in each iteration.

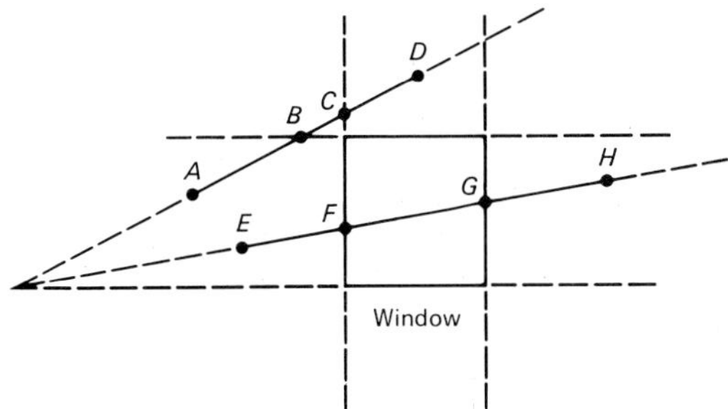

Fig. 4.6 Clipping illustration.

The choice of the order of window edges is completely arbitrary: no matter what order is used, clipping some lines will require four iterations to compute intersections with all four edges. We pick the following order because it corresponds to the bit order in the outcode and makes bookkeeping easy:

1. Top—discard line segment part above;
2. Bottom—discard line segment part below;
3. Right side—discard line segment part on the right;
4. Left side—discard line segment part on the left.

As an example, there are two lines in Fig. 4.6 that must be subdivided. For line *DA,* the sequence would be:

1. Test outcodes of *A,* of *D,* and their **and;** can't accept or reject;
2. Calculate intersection point *B;* make *BA* new line and discard *BD* because it is above window;
3. Test outcodes of *A, B;* trivially reject.

For line *EH,* the sequence is slightly longer:

1. Test *EH* outcodes; can't accept or reject;
2. Calculate intersection point *G;* discard *GH;*
3. Test *EG;* can't accept or reject;
4. Calculate intersection point *F;* discard *EF;*
5. Test *FG;* trivially accept.

The complete algorithm is shown below. The real role of the outcodes becomes apparent after studying the algorithm: they are used both in the trivial accept/reject tests and as a simple device for remembering the locations of successive endpoints of divided lines in order to avoid repeated testing within the loop of endpoint coordinates against all four window boundaries. They also direct the endpoint replacement.

```
procedure CLIPPER(x1, y1, x2, y2, xmin, xmax, ymin, ymax: real);
{Cohen–Sutherland Clipping Algorithm for line P1 = (x1, y1) to P2 = (x2, y2)}
type outcode = array [1..4] of boolean;
var accept, reject, done: boolean;
  outcode1, outcode2: outcode; {outcodes for P1 and P2}
{Definitions for SWAP, REJECT_CHECK, ACCEPT_CHECK and OUTCODES go
  here. OUTCODES takes CLIPPER's window parameters and a point and returns a
  4-bit outcode (see also Exercise 4.2)}
begin
  accept := false;
  reject := false;
  done := false;
```

```
repeat
  OUTCODES(x1, y1, outcode1);
  OUTCODES(x2, y2, outcode2);
  reject := REJECT_CHECK(outcode1, outcode2);    {check trivial reject}
  if reject then done := true
  else
    begin    {possible accept}
      accept := ACCEPT_CHECK(outcode1, outcode 2);    {check trivial accept}
      if accept then done := true
      else
        begin    {subdivide line since at most one endpoint is inside}
          {First, if P1 is inside window, exchange points 1 and 2 and their outcodes
            to guarantee that P1 is outside window, using SWAP}
          if not ((outcode1[1]) or (outcode1[2]) or (outcode1[3]) or (outcode1[4]))
            then SWAP;

          {Now perform a subdivision, move Pl to the intersection point; use the
            formulas y = y1 + slope * (x - x1), x = xl + (l/slope) * (y - y1).}
          if outcode1[1] then
            begin                              {divide line at top of window}
              x1 := x1 + (x2 - x1) * (ymax - y1) / (y2 - y1);
              y1 := ymax
            end
          else if outcode1[2] then
            begin                              {divide line at bottom of window}
              x1 := x1 + (x2 - x1) * (ymin - y1) / (y2 - y1);
              y1 := ymin
            end
          else if outcode1[3] then
            begin                              {divide line at right edge of window}
              y1 := y1 + (y2 - y1) * (xmax - x1) / (x2 - x1);
              x1 := xmax
            end
          else if outcode1[4] then
            begin                              {divide line at left edge of window}
              y1 := y1 + (y2 - y1) * (xmin - x1) / (x2 - x1);
              x1 := xmin
            end
        end    {subdivide}
    end    {possible accept}
until done;
if accept then
  DRAW(x1, y1, x2, y2)
end;    {CLIPPER}
```

b) *Midpoint subdivision with the clipping divider.* In the Cohen–Sutherland clipping algorithm one coordinate calculation is trivial, but (floating-point) multiplications and divisions are still needed to calculate successive intersections for the other coordinate. This can be very time-consuming if the computer's instruction repertoire lacks these operations, as today's microprocessors often do. The following midpoint subdivision algorithm eliminates the need for these operations, although at the expense of additional iterations. It estimates that the window intersection point of lines that cannot be trivially accepted or rejected lies at the midpoint of the line segment; if that estimate is wrong, it then divides the line and tests both halves. A line's midpoint is easily expressed as $((x2 + x1)/2, (y2 + y1)/2)$, and can be calculated for integer coordinates with two simple additions and right shifts. This algorithm was originally intended for use in *clipping divider* hardware [SPRO68], where avoiding multiplies and divides was important and integer (or fractional) arithmetic and shifts (binary division) were very fast.

The midpoint subdivision algorithm is predicated on the reversal of the SGP order of clipping in world coordinates and then mapping the clipped primitives to the viewport in normalized (or even physical) device coordinates. The algorithm first maps all primitives in the world to device coordinates and then clips them to the viewport boundaries; the equivalence of the two orders is illustrated in Fig. 4.7. For software clipping it usually makes sense to reduce the number of primitives to be mapped by clipping all invisible elements first, but with fast clipping hardware it may pay either to use device coordinates as world coordinates directly or to do a floating-point to fixed-point conversion of each coordinate before passing a primitive to the clipper. (The new generation of VLSI-based floating-point clippers now being designed [CLAR80] will make the Cohen-Sutherland algorithm especially efficient.)

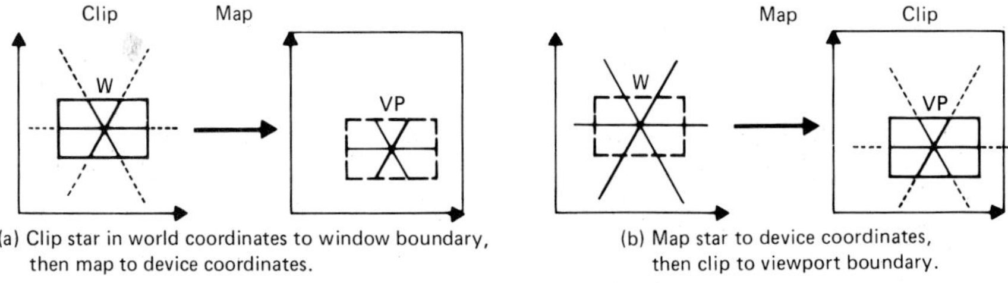

(a) Clip star in world coordinates to window boundary, then map to device coordinates.

(b) Map star to device coordinates, then clip to viewport boundary.

Fig. 4.7 Equivalence of the clip, map and map, clip orders of operation.

In the midpoint subdivision algorithm, the outcodes are used as before. If a line is neither trivially accepted nor rejected, it is divided into two equal parts. The general strategy is to keep on doing this, in binary search fashion, until one segment of the original line is trivially accepted (if there is an intersection) and the other is trivially rejected. At each iteration we can typically accept and/or reject half the remaining line. For lines like *GI* and *JL* in Fig. 4.8, for example, half the line is either accepted (*GH*) or rejected (*KL*) and the algorithm iterates.

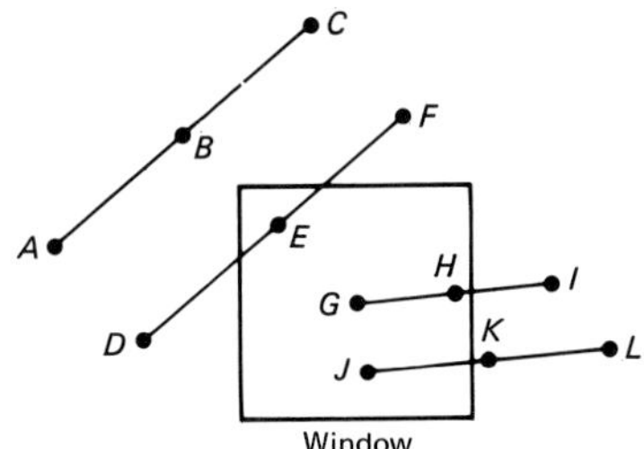

Fig. 4.8 Midpoint subdivision clipping.

There is only one slight complication. In clipping lines like *AC* and *DF* in Fig. 4.8, either zero or two intersections must be calculated. Which case pertains is easily determined during the subdivision process. At some step, either both halves are rejected (as *AB* and *BC*) or are not (as *DE* and *EF*). In the latter case, one line (say *DE*) is temporarily set aside and the other (*EF*) is further subdivided until an intersection is found. Then the intersection's coordinates are saved and the process is repeated with the other line (*DE*).

Just as a binary search terminates in at most $\log_2 N$ steps, where N is the length of the list being searched, so too will this algorithm terminate when the midpoint coincides with one of the endpoints, in $\log_2 N$ steps. Here N is interpreted as the longer of the horizontal and vertical components of the line, as measured in the device's resolution units. Thus a line of maximum length with one endpoint visible can be clipped by our DPU in at most 10 steps ($\log_2 1024$).

Other clipping algorithms have been used [FRYE72, JARV75] and evaluated [JARV75]. Their basic approach is to spend more time performing initial tests on the line and its endpoints than the Cohen–Sutherland algorithm does, in order to save time by minimizing unnecessary intersection calculations.

c) *Rotated windows.* All the algorithms mentioned above, whether based on outcodes or on other methods, assume a window whose sides are parallel to the principal axes. What if a rotated window had been specified (as is possible in some graphics packages)?

We may again be reduced to calculating all four intersections of the line with the edges of the window. Some preliminary screening is possible, however. The rotated window W can be surrounded by an upright window W' that contains W (see Fig. 4.9), and a line's outcodes can be calculated using W'. Any lines that are trivially rejected for W' are also trivially rejected for W. The converse, for trivial acceptance, obviously does not hold, and any line that is not trivially rejected must be clipped against W by using simultaneous equations. Alternatively, in the typical case when the viewport is upright, it might be more efficient to transform all primitives to device coordinates and then clip to the upright viewport by using either the Cohen–Sutherland or midpoint algorithms. The trade-offs in the order of clipping and mapping are examined further in Chapter 9.

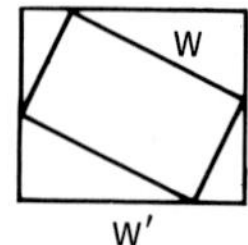

Fig. 4.9 Upright window surrounding a rotated one.

Text. Text may be clipped in one of several ways, briefly described here in order of increasing crudeness and computing efficiency. If each character is thought of as a collection of short straight lines (strokes), then each line must be individually clipped. This produces attractive results (see Fig. 4.10) but is slow and incompatible with conventional hardware character generators.(Raster characters are typically drawn as small bit maps, not as strokes—see Chapter 11.)

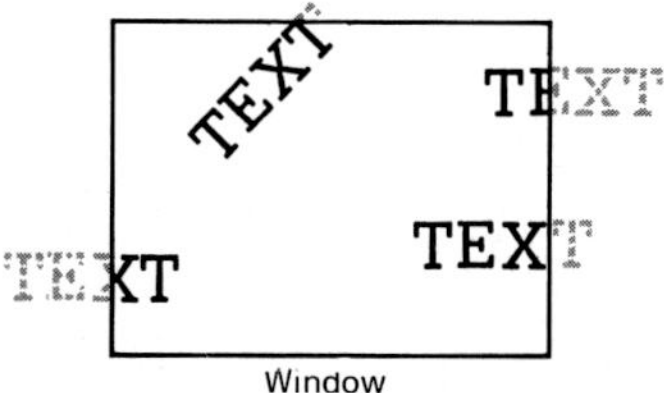

Fig. 4.10 Clipping individual lines in each character.

Characters can be treated as indivisible entities and a text string can then be clipped character by character. We think of each character as being enclosed in a rectangle known as the *character box* and then compare some point in the box—the center or one of the corners—to the window: if the point is inside, the character is displayed. Alternatively, one can test either the whole character box or, as a shortcut, a diagonal against the window and then display the character only if the character box or diagonal is completely within the window. Fig. 4.11 shows the results of using these two methods; corner point and box/diagonal clipping are equivalent only if the character box does not intersect the window. Furthermore, clipping to the character box and clipping to its diagonal are equivalent only when the sides of the window are parallel to the sides of the character box. Otherwise, the character box itself, rather than just the diagonal, must be clipped.

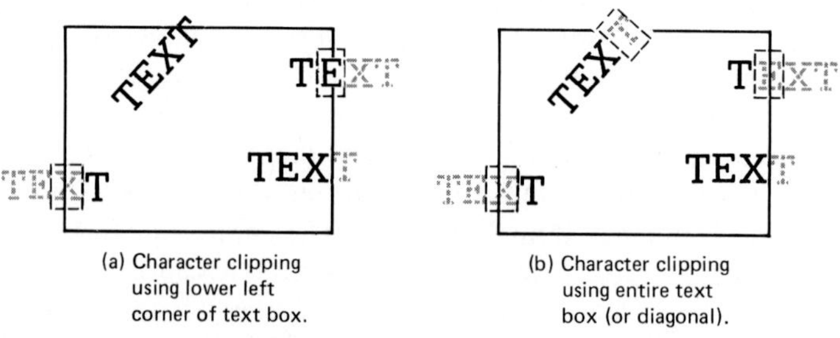

Fig. 4.11 Clipping entire characters.

The third and cheapest way to clip text is to treat the entire character string as indivisible, so that either all or none of it is displayed. For this approach, one might test some point on the box surrounding the text string, the diagonal of the box, or the box itself (Fig. 4.12).

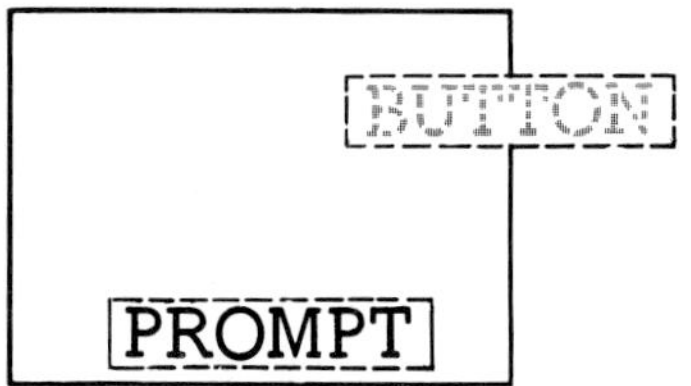

Fig. 4.12 Clipping character-string box.

For our simple graphics package and simple DPU we will use characters of a single size (that provided by the hardware character generator) and do the simplest kind of ''all or none'' clipping on the string as a whole using the surrounding string box. Note that this implies that characters, unlike lines, don't get larger or smaller as the application program changes window/viewport size ratios—the string either appears or doesn't, at its constant, hardware-generated size. Typically, handling the visually more attractive cases allowed by more versatile character generators is far from easy (especially for 3D!), since most DPUs have separate facilities for handling vectors and characters (see Chapter 10). If the SGP programmer wanted higher-quality text he could either use the facilities of the Core or implement software characters as a set of line-drawing subroutines on top of SGP.

4.2.2 Window-to-Viewport Mapping

Having clipped a primitive to the window boundary, the viewing operation processor next maps it to the viewport (see Fig. 4.7(a)). In Fig. 4.13 the point (x_w, y_w) maps to the point (x_v, y_v) in such a way as to preserve proportions, i.e., its relative position within the enclosing rectangle. To be more precise, the ratio of the distance of the point from the y boundary to the length of the x boundary, and the ratio of the distance of the point from the x boundary to the length of the y boundary, should be the same in window and viewport. This condition requires, in terms of Fig. 4.13, that:

$$\frac{x_{\text{w.dist}}}{x_{\text{w.leng}}} = \frac{x_{\text{w}} - x_{\text{w.min}}}{x_{\text{w.max}} - x_{\text{w.min}}} = \frac{x_{\text{v}} - x_{\text{v.min}}}{x_{\text{v.max}} - x_{\text{v.min}}} = \frac{x_{\text{v.dist}}}{x_{\text{v.leng}}},$$

and

$$\frac{y_{\text{w.dist}}}{y_{\text{w.leng}}} = \frac{y_{\text{w}} - y_{\text{w.min}}}{y_{\text{w.max}} - y_{\text{w.min}}} = \frac{y_{\text{v}} - y_{\text{v.min}}}{y_{\text{v.max}} - y_{\text{v.min}}} = \frac{y_{\text{v.dist}}}{y_{\text{v.leng}}}.$$

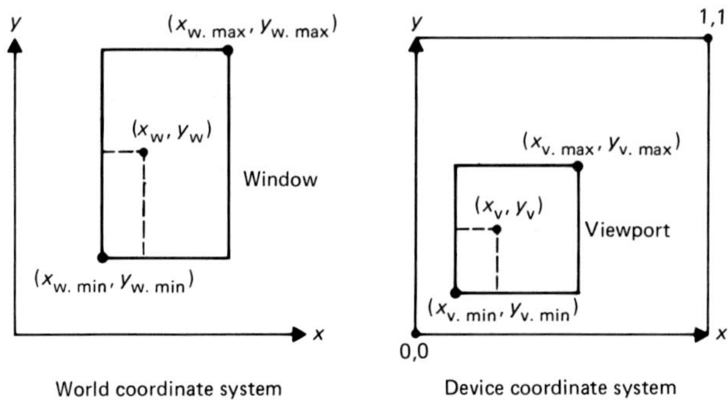

Fig. 4.13 Preserving proportions in window-to-viewport mapping.

These reduce to the mapping equations:

$$x_v = x_{v.min} + \frac{x_{v.max} - x_{v.min}}{x_{w.max} - x_{w.min}} (x_w - x_{w.min}),$$

$$y_v = y_{v.min} + \frac{y_{v.max} - y_{v.min}}{y_{w.max} - y_{w.min}} (y_w - y_{w.min}),$$

which are of the form

$$x_v = s_x(x_w - x_{w.min}) + x_{v.min},$$
$$y_v = s_y(y_w - y_{w.min}) + y_{v.min}.$$

Here s_x and s_y are *scale factors* to scale from window to viewport size and $x_{v.min}$ and $y_{v.min}$ are *translation factors* which take the scaled (relative) *window coordinates* $(x_w - x_{w.min}, y_w - y_{w.min})$ to the bottom left corner of the viewport. These equations can be further simplified to the linear forms

$$x_v = s_x x_w + a \qquad \text{and} \qquad y_v = s_y y_w + b,$$

which involve only a multiplication and an addition, each with predetermined coefficients. The geometric scaling and translation transformations are discussed in more detail in Chapter 7.

The equations can yield either fractional normalized device coordinates or, by scaling those results by 1024, physical device coordinates for our DPU. For graphics packages that support only a single DPU, it is of course most efficient to convert directly from world coordinates to physical device coordinates. For packages that must drive multiple display units, it is convenient to produce a low-level, but still machine-independent, normalized device coordinate (NDC) representation of the image that can then be translated by multiple DPU code generators to the appropriate physical device coordinates. The device-independent NDC representation can easily be stored in a file or transmitted over communications lines as a low-level but still device-independent picture representation. This possibility is discussed further in Section 4.8.

4.3 DPU PROGRAM CODE GENERATION

4.3.1 Introduction

Having clipped and mapped output primitives to NDC space, SGP must next convert the primitives, which are still device-independent, to actual DPU commands with opcodes, modes, and beam displacement fields with physical device coordinates. There are three subprocesses:

1. The conversion of normalized device coordinates to physical (integer) device coordinates (if not already performed as part of the window-to-viewport mapping);
2. Generation of DPU-specific code;
3. Segmentation of the DPU program.

The first subprocess is just trivial scaling. The second, DPU code generation, is naturally DPU-dependent, but is quite straightforward and therefore needs little explanation (see Exercises 4.9 and 4.10). The only device-independent technique that needs mentioning is the conversion of both absolute and relative primitives specified by the application program to relative DPU primitives, prefaced by an initial absolute move at the start of each segment. This is done in preparation for dragging, which is done using *TRANSLATE_IMAGE_2;* to cause an image to move, SGP simply changes the coordinates of the initial absolute move.

The third subprocess, segmentation, concerns the organization of device-dependent DPU code, but it can be discussed as a collection of primarily device-independent techniques. Because these techniques can be quite complex and are implemented in a variety of ways, the topic merits considerable discussion.

4.3.2 Segmentation Background

In Chapter 2 we discussed collecting logically related output primitives in segments for convenient modularization and for selective identification (picking) and modification of the image. Fast, selective modification is a sine qua non of high-quality interactive graphics because it provides rapid response to the user for closely coupled feedback. Segments are easily implemented with a refresh DPU of the type covered in Chapter 3 because, as we shall see, the refresh buffer and DPU jump instruction allow the buffer to be organized for easy segment storage and manipulation. For other devices, it is not essential but nonetheless useful to keep a stored, segment-structured DPU program, as further explained in Section 4.6. Thus segmentation is a generally useful technique.

For example, selective modification with stored segments can be used with flat panel and raster displays because, unlike DVSTs without write-through mode, they have selective erase: the package deletes the segment by redrawing its stored primitives with a background intensity.* Even for DVSTs connected over low-speed telephone lines, it is often preferable to delete a stored segment by crossing out its "erased" primitives with dashed Xs rather than to erase the whole screen and retransmit the visible primitives.

In order to design proper data structures for handling segmentation efficiently, we must understand what is required for segment manipulation. In general, the programmer must be able to use SGP to construct a segment (initialize it and then "grow" it by adding primitives), to delete individual segments, to display only the visible ones, and to find and manipulate a user-identified (picked) segment efficiently. The segment is both a programmer-defined grouping of the application program describing (a piece of) the object, and a DPU program structure of *logically contiguous* DPU primitives (the primitives need not be *physically contiguous* in the buffer or on the screen). The visible segments must be sequentially and cyclically accessible by the DPU for refresh and randomly accessible by the CPU for update. Segments in SGP may contain an arbitrary number of output primitives, so that there are no constraints on the application programmer. Similarly, there are no restrictions on the number of segments allowed (except in the amount of memory available and the size of the integer segment name space).

The *explicit*, programmer-specified segment operations permitted in SGP are *CREATE_SEGMENT, CLOSE_SEGMENT, DELETE_SEGMENT, RENAME_SEGMENT, SET_VISIBILITY,* and *TRANSLATE_IMAGE_2.* We permit neither internal modification (editing) of output primitives in a segment nor appending of new primitives to a previously closed segment. These operations are usually quite difficult and costly to implement in the general case because of the amount of bookkeeping that would be required to record the internal device-dependent structure of the segment, status of attributes and global variables, etc. (see Exercise 4.12 and also [MICH78a] for a detailed discussion). Furthermore, they are not needed to make a basic but functionally complete set of segment operations. Even a *REPLACE_SEGMENT* of one segment by another is not explicitly available in SGP because the programmer (or a higher-level package built on top of SGP) can easily provide this function with a *CREATE_SEGMENT/DELETE_SEGMENT/RENAME_SEGMENT* combination.

The *implicit* segment operations are those invoked indirectly by the programmer and include adding a new primitive to the currently open segment, determining what segment contains the primitive just picked by the user, and searching for a

*This technique, in fact, produces results which are only approximately correct in that the intersections of erased primitives with non-erased primitives are erased, leaving holes in the non-erased primitives. (When the picture becomes confusing, it can be regenerated from the up-to-date and correct DPU program by invoking the SGP *NEW_FRAME* operation described in Section 4.6.) Chapter 11 discusses this problem in more detail.

given segment (verifying whether the segment whose name is supplied by the application program exists and, if it does, accessing it in the buffer). The segment search operation should be as efficient as possible, since it is invoked by every explicit segment operation—even *CREATE_SEGMENT* must check to see if a segment with the name specified already exists.

Given this brief statement of operational requirements for segmentation, how do we impose a segment data structure on the DPU program which meets all these requirements in some "optimal" fashion? There is no single "right" or best answer—there are many possibilities and trade-offs which depend on the relative frequency of use and the priority of functions invoked by the typical user dialogue. These trade-offs also depend on the implementation environment, that is, the programming language and run-time environment supplied by the operating system. We present here two of several alternative structures—contiguous versus linked-list allocation—and discuss their advantages and disadvantages. The discussion should seem familiar to those who have studied data structures and storage management.

4.3.3 Explicit Operations

Array of contiguous segments. In an environment without dynamic storage allocation (such as FORTRAN), SGP can reserve a large (integer) array to use for segment storage. The array is divided into two areas: the active segment area for all the segments defined thus far and the free area.

Figure 4.14 shows that to do a *CREATE_SEGMENT,* SGP starts a new segment at the end of the active segment area and adds output primitives sequentially to this segment. The new segment becomes the current segment. The final instruction of the current segment, which is pushed down by each new primitive added, is a jump back to the top to start the next refresh cycle. Note that the frame lock bit in the jump instruction is set to prevent phosphor burn, a classical problem for refresh vector displays. Also, SGP can omit this jump for raster displays, since they don't refresh directly from the display list used only for scan conversion to the bit map representation. Once a *CLOSE_SEGMENT* is done, the programmer cannot change it; the next *CREATE_SEGMENT* starts the new current segment below the one just closed. To do a *TRANSLATE_IMAGE_2,* SGP simply changes the initial absolute move preceding the remaining relative DPU primitives.

Each segment's output primitives are preceded by a header containing a relative jump (JMPR) instruction, and the segment's name and its length. Fig. 4.15 shows that to do a *SET_VISIBILITY* of a segment SGP sets the jump to bypass the rest of the header and point to the segment's first primitive (to make the segment visible), or to jump to the header of the next segment (to make the segment invisible by skipping all its primitives). SGP can first check the current visibility by testing if the first instruction is a JMPR 3. Segments are thus delimited by the consecutive JMPRs in the headers. To do a *RENAME_SEGMENT,* SGP follows the JMPRs from segment to segment, looking for the old name and altering it if it is found. For proper error-checking, it should search the entire list to make sure the new name doesn't already exist.

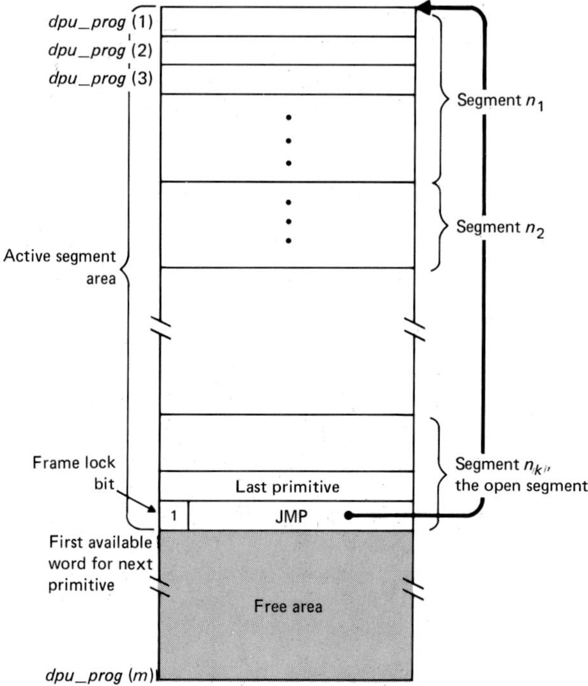

Fig. 4.14 Segment stored in array called *DPU_PROG*.

To do a *DELETE_SEGMENT,* SGP could use one of two strategies. The first is to compact the array every time a segment is deleted ("on the fly") by moving up the remainder of the segment area below the deleted segment to the first word of the deleted segment. The second is to leave the segment in place but flag it as available for reuse, as was done in the *LAYOUT* program of Chapter 2. This technique, which leads to a more complex storage allocation mechanism with list processing, is discussed in the next section.

How inefficient is deleting by on-the-fly compaction? The linear search for the right segment and other bookkeeping would normally be dominated by the compaction itself. For example, for a large DPU program of 32k 16-bit words, deleting the topmost segment (an unusual worst case) could take up to 1/3 of a second (estimating the move-memory compaction loop at 10 microseconds per word). This estimate is quite high for the types of dedicated mini- and microcomputers now common in graphics systems. The average single delete in a large DPU program would take half of the worst case, or less than 1/6 of a second.

These conservative figures still seem entirely acceptable in terms of common human-factors criteria for response time, which range from 0.1 to 0.5 seconds per typical user operation (see Chapter 6). However, there is another, more stringent cri-

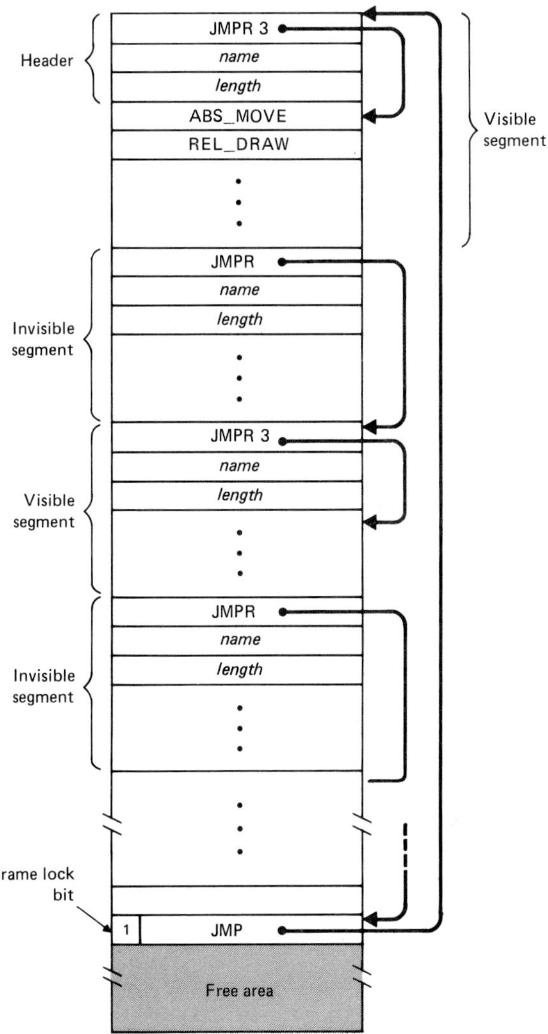

Fig. 4.15 Compacted array off consecutive segments with relative jumps for visibility/invisibility.

terion for vector displays, that of preventing flicker. As we will see in Section 4.4., while the CPU is in the process of updating the DPU program, the DPU must be stopped from reading and executing it, in order to avoid unexpected effects due to incorrect DPU code. Therefore, for this example, the DPU will be stopped during the entire delete compaction. This is 1/6 of a second on the average, which implies that approximately five 30-Hz refresh frames will be missed, producing a momentary but noticeable flicker.

If multiple segments are deleted in succession, the problem is worse because of the amount of memory movement. Such multiple deletes, however, are not very common during a user session, arising almost exclusively when the user changes program modes or pictures. The application programmer can readily handle these situations by double-buffering (building the new DPU program before deleting the old one) if there is room, or by flashing a prompt showing "work in progress." Multiple deletes might appear to present a problem in the *LAYOUT* program of Chapter 2 every time the window is changed and the data structure is regenerated. In fact, *DISPLAY_D_STR* replaces the segments one at a time by deleting and recreating them: segment deletes and creates thus are interleaved. Given adequate storage, it would be a minor change to double-buffer the two complete images instead, and this also produces a more natural-looking change (see Exercise 2.14).

What are the approximate timings of these operation sequences? Let's assume a rather complex room layout with an average of 10 double-word primitives per symbol segment for each of 150 symbols. Then the part of the segment area to be compacted for deleting all symbols is only 3000 words, and deletion takes 30 milliseconds. This figure is approximately equal to the time to refresh a single frame and is therefore acceptable. In terms of response time for the user, this time is also acceptable because it is likely to be dominated anyhow by the time required to pass each primitive in each replacement segment through the entire viewing/code generation pipeline. This pipeline operates in parallel with refreshing and thus does not cause flicker. For simple package implementations on fast hardware, the time to pass through this pipeline might be from several hundred to as much as 1000 microseconds per primitive, because of levels of internal subroutining, error-checking, and expensive clipping. (For more complete packages with full 3D viewing pipelines these figures might be worse by a factor of 10.)

We conclude that the criterion of flicker prevention gives us a moderate upper bound of some 3000 words to be moved, at 10 microseconds per word on the average, to miss only a single frame.

Noncontiguous linked list. While the contiguous storage scheme has the advantage of simplicity and is satisfactory for modest applications, it does present two problems. First, it ties up a significant amount of memory (enough to hold the maximum allowable display file size), which today is still a precious resource. Second, for vector displays flicker due to delete compaction may be noticeable for large display files with many hundreds of segments. Standard list processing/free storage management techniques may be used to solve both of these classical problems by allocating and freeing storage blocks as needed. SGP can either manage its own storage located in a dynamically extensible area or make use of the operating system's standard dynamic storage allocator. Instead of overlaying the deleted segment for each deletion, SGP then deletes the segment simply by flagging it as deleted, if it does its own storage management, or by passing its location to the storage allocator. After several deletions, the storage would have the familiar pattern of Fig. 4.16(a), and a linked-list structure of Fig. 4.16(b) would be necessary to connect valid segments.

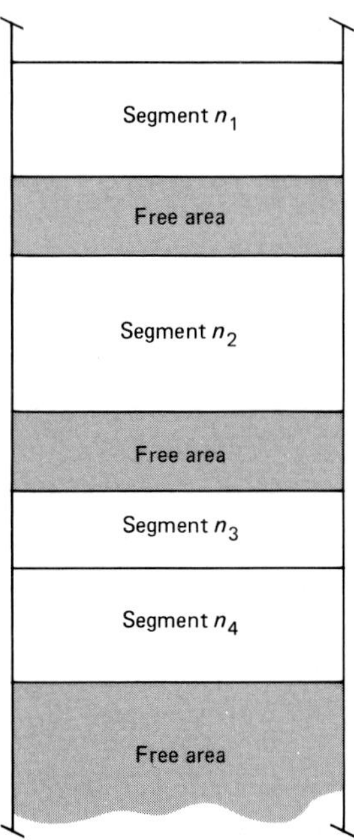

Fig. 4.16(a) Storage with valid and deleted segments.

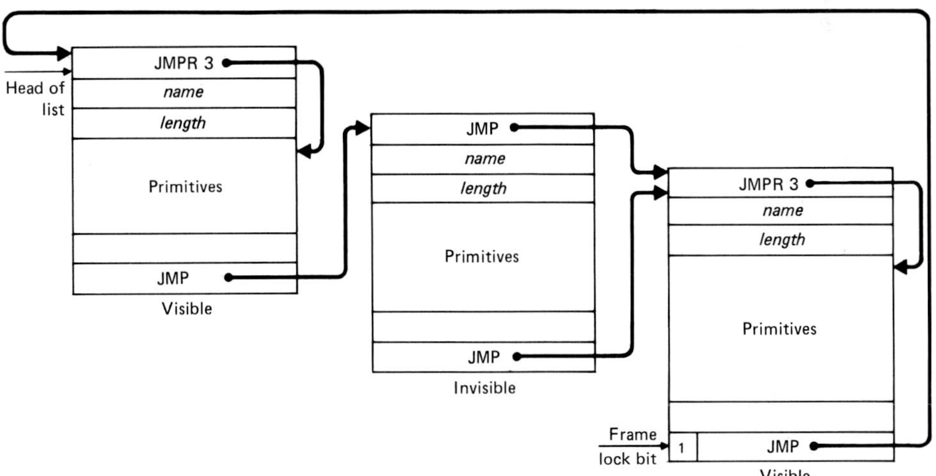

Fig. 4.16(b) Circularly linked list of segments in noncontiguous memory.

The jump at the bottom of each segment is used by the DPU to move from segment to segment, while the jump's address field can be used by the CPU as a data structure linked-list pointer. The list is circular to provide cyclical refreshing. The initial jump in each segment is set either to JMPR 3 (segment is visible) or to a copy of the linking jump at the bottom (segment is invisible).

To delete a segment, the list is searched linearly with each segment's list predecessor being temporarily saved. When the specified segment is found, it is unlinked by setting the link in its predecessor to jump to its successor.

When a new segment is needed for *CREATE_SEGMENT,* two strategies are possible, depending on whether an allocator or SGP manages storage. If an allocator is used, SGP simply requests a block of the proper size. Otherwise, it checks segments with delete flags for one of the proper size. But in either case, what in fact *is* the proper size? SGP can't know the segment's size when it is created. SGP could simply start to grow the segment in a free block and, if and when it were about to overflow, request a larger block, copy the overflowing block in it, return the overflowing block, and so on, until the *CLOSE_SEGMENT* was done. But then, what would have been done with any unused space in the final, largest block? A block of the correct size could be requested upon *CLOSE_SEGMENT,* so that SGP can copy all the preliminary blocks into it, but the free block of the closest size would probably still be larger than needed and this would leave space unused. There are then two possible strategies. The oversized block can either be used and eventually freed (upon segment deletion) by SGP in its entirety or the unused subblock can be added to the free list. In the first case, the allocator could run out of memory because each time more space was handed out than needed. In the second case, the unused subblock might well be too small for any new segment and thus be unavailable for reuse. The first strategy is often preferred, because it simplifies bookkeeping and one assumes that used blocks will be deleted and returned often enough to prevent running out of space.

In either case, after a number of additions and deletions have been made, the array will be full of unused or unusable noncontiguous subblocks of free memory—a standard situation in dynamic storage allocation called *fragmentation.* If at some time there were no free block large enough for a newly opened segment and if SGP did its own storage management, it would have to run a simple form of *garbage collection* by rewriting all valid blocks contiguously to eliminate the free space between them. While the deletion marking phase of a general garbage-collection scheme would have been done by flagging each segment as it was "deleted," a lot of data movement will still be necessary for the compaction phase, and the user will definitely notice that the program is temporarily too busy to interact. In effect, this linked-list scheme trades heavy batch compaction once in a while, as needed, for the contiguous storage scheme's much lighter on-the-fly compaction for each delete.

If SGP uses a system storage allocator, the fragmentation problem will be much worse since the system allocator cannot compact an application program's space because it can't know whether it contains nonrelocatable addresses. When no more free space was available, the application program would have to inform the user that he should either perform some deletes or reinitialize the program. Neither is a pleasant alternative. (Modern virtual memory systems obviate many of these concerns.)

A third storage allocation strategy is for SGP to manage fixed-length blocks. Then it can grow the segment in a free block and, when a segment becomes too large to fit, overflow to the next free block, etc. The use of fixed-length blocks avoids memory fragementation [KNUT73], but at the cost of fragmenting the segment over multiple blocks and adding extra jumps to connect the fragments. This slows most segment operations and, for vector refresh displays, the refresh process. Also, extra bookkeeping is required to figure out where the next segment starts, in order to (re)set the (in)visibility jump. Further, not all fragmentation is eliminated, since there is unused free space in the last block. Because of these disadvantages, this scheme is not recommended, except possibly for storage tube and raster displays.

Summary. What, then, are the approximate tradeoffs between contiguous and linked-list segment structures? At the cost of using free-list storage management routines of the standard first-fit variety, of potentially fatal memory fragmentation, and of an extra linked-list jump, we can provide essentially instantaneous response to deletes with linked lists. Having SGP do its own storage management means that more implementation code must be written and stored, but SGP then has the ability to recover from fragmentation by compaction. Certainly, fewer total cycles are needed to do occasional "batch" compactions when SGP runs out of space than to do on-the-fly compaction. An important and difficult question to answer is how often fatal fragmentation will occur. This will be a function of the amount of memory available and the frequencies and types of updates in the application programs that the system will handle, and is naturally very difficult to predict.

What rules of thumb may we infer from the above? In general, if there is typically little extra space available beyond what is needed for the display file, the simpler contiguous mechanism is preferable because it is easy to implement and uses the least storage for programs: in essence, in a classic space-time trade-off, it trades the inelastic resource (space) for the elastic resource (time). If somewhat more memory is available, SGP can do its own memory management to handle fragmentation, at a cost of more bookkeeping and extra space. Finally, if genuinely adequate memory and a dynamic storage allocator are available, SGP should use the system's allocator, relying on the assumption that most user sessions will terminate before total fragmentation occurs.

4.3.4 Implicit Operations

Segment searching. Having treated two alternatives for the explicit segment operations, we now take a closer look at the process of locating segments for these operations. Previously, we saw that segments are identified by name and, for convenience, also contain their length. We can either store this control information in the header of the segment itself (Figs. 4.15 and 4.16(b)) or create a separate table (directory) for it (Fig. 4.17). Both techniques may be used with either contiguous or linked-list allocation. With a separate directory, the visibility field allows a quick check to see if a segment is visible; with the header attached to the segment, the initial jump can be tested to see whether the segment is invisible.

If we store the control information in the attached header, looking for a specified name to locate the corresponding segment in a sequence of segments involves only a simple linear search through the list. With randomly ordered segments, the average number of segments searched, therefore, is $n/2$ if the segment is found, n if it is not. The segment length is used in this linear search to locate the start of the next successive segment for contiguous allocation, or the jump to the next segment for linked allocation.

To improve average search time, segments could also be ordered by their segment name in either the contiguous or the linked-list storage scheme; this allows the search to stop as soon as the search name is larger than the segment name in the list. With a reasonably uniform distribution of names, this maintains the search time for existing segments at $n/2$, since on the average the segment will still be found halfway. For nonexistent segments, however, search time is decreased from n to $n/2$. On the other hand, searching is now required to locate the proper place to insert a new segment in the ordered list, and furthermore, for contiguous storage, data movement of segments below the insertion point is required. This cost is usually not worth the increased search efficiency, especially considering that, for many applications, there are fewer than 100 segments to be searched and most searches are successful.

For application programs with many hundreds of segments, searching for segment names can be made somewhat more efficient by maintaining a separate segment directory. While segments themselves can then be left in arbitrary order (usually the order induced by the sequence of *CREATE_SEGMENTs*), the directory can be easily ordered by segment names to facilitate searching. Because the directory entries are of fixed length, a binary search algorithm can be used to locate particular segments; such algorithms have an average search time proportional to $\log_2 n$.

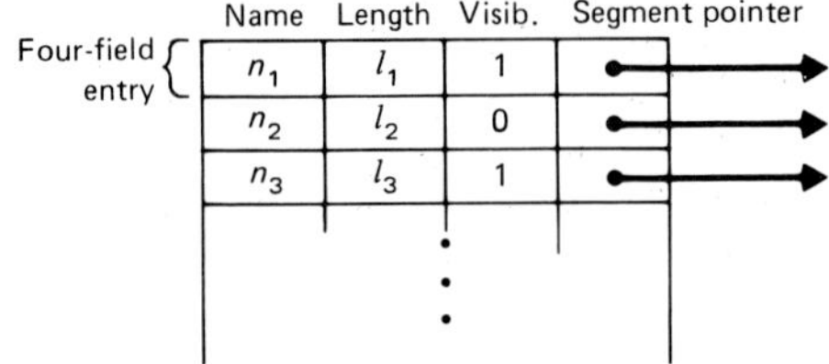

Fig. 4.17 Segment directory.

What are the costs of a separate directory? We still need an initial jump in each segment (JMPR or JUMP to next segment) to control visibility, while a visibility field and one extra pointer are needed in each directory entry, the latter to locate a segment. SGP no longer needs the length for locating the next segment, but it is still convenient for storage management. Adding a segment is somewhat more work than before: it again requires a search for duplicate names and then an insert of the entry into the directory. If the directory is stored as a table, this requires moving down the entries below the insert point; if the directory is stored as a binary tree of entries, the new entry need only be linked in, but additional pointers are required, as is more dynamic storage management. The segment itself is inserted either at the end of the segment area (for contiguous allocation) or at the beginning of the circular list. Deletion requires deleting the segment and also moving up the entries below the segment's entry in the directory table by three words to compact the directory. (For a binary tree directory, only unlinking the entry is required.)

We may conclude that in most cases a separate segment directory is not worthwhile: the number of searches without subsequent data movement in the segment area and in the directory (only for *RENAME_SEGMENT, SET_VISIBILITY,* and *TRANSLATE_IMAGE_2*) and the search time per linear search for a large number of segments would both have to be comparatively large in order to justify the added complexity and expense. Distributing the segment directory control information in the segment headers suffices for most common cases.

Pick identification. Finally, how does SGP identify which segment the user selected during a pick operation? If the DPU supports a light pen, typically either a *name register* or the DPU instruction counter is available for readout by the CPU when a pen detect occurs. In the best case, a name register is available. Then the first DPU instruction in a visible segment is not the absolute move output primitive but a *load name register* instruction that uses the segment's name as immediate data (Fig. 4.18). When the DPU is stopped by a pen detect, the CPU interrupt handler sends the contents of this DPU name register to SGP's *WAIT_PICK* procedure, which returns it in the *segment_name* parameter.

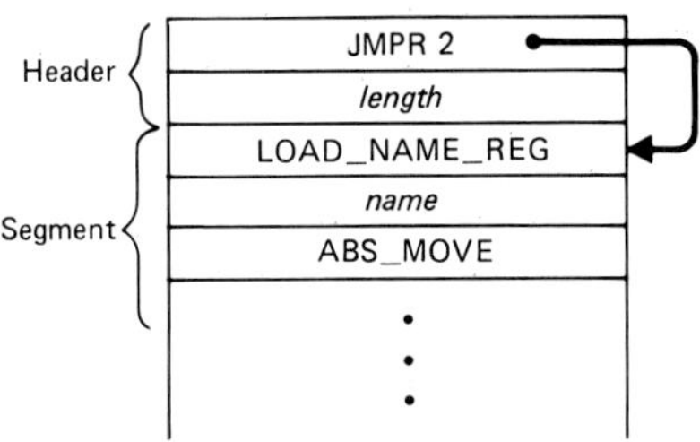

Fig. 4.18 Revised header and segment for name register.

When the DPU has no name register, one of several equivalent techniques can be used to map (*correlate*) the buffer address read out from the DPU instruction counter to the segment whose primitives occupy the region of the buffer where the DPU stopped. For example, the buffer address of the picked primitive is compared to each segment's starting address and to its ending address (the starting address plus the segment length): the segment whose starting and ending addresses bracket the primitive's address is the one picked. If SGP maintains distributed control headers on segments (i.e., there is no segment directory table), the segments must be checked sequentially, with an average search time again proportional to $n/2$. If SGP maintains a separate segment directory, this directory could be sorted on buffer address rather than on segment name, to allow use of a binary search to speed up pick identifications to $\log_2 n$. Such a segment directory used for mapping is often called a *correlation map* (Fig. 4.19). Since picking, especially of large numbers of menu items, often dominates other (construction) operations, it may be advisable for rapid selection of alternatives to have such a dual-purpose correlation map/segment directory.

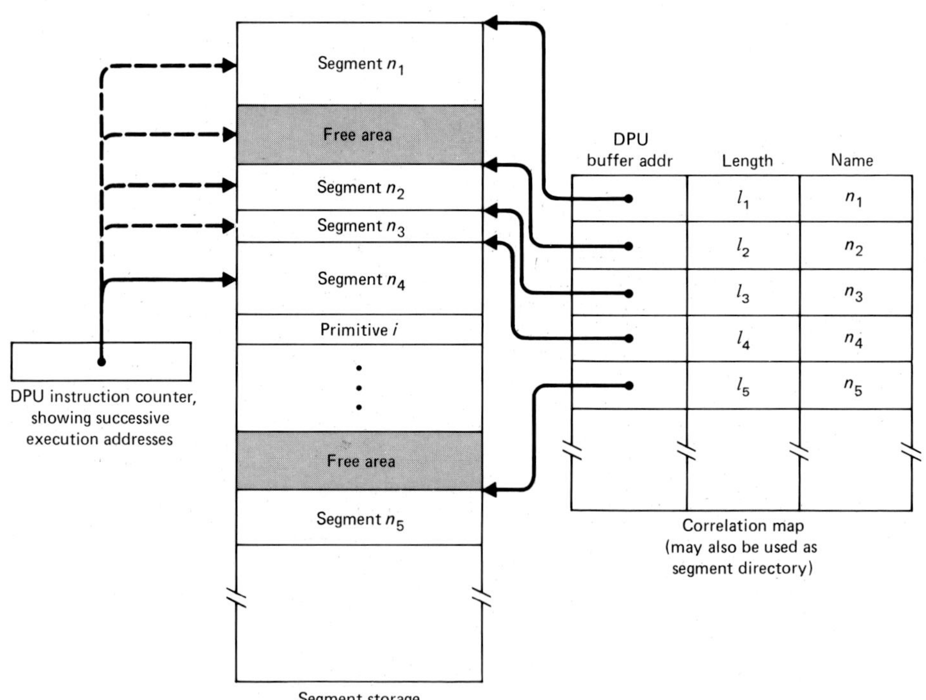

Fig. 4.19 Linear correlation map used in absence of name register.

If neither a name register nor instruction counter readout is available, as in the case of a data tablet locator being used to simulate a pick, the DPU X, Y registers containing (x, y) values of the cursor may be used. Correlation then consists of a laborious process of scanning primitives sequentially in consecutive visible segments until one is found whose (x, y) values lie at a distance less than some predetermined distance from the cursor position. When this software comparison is successful, SGP returns the name of the corresponding segment (which it retains each time it accesses a new segment for this comparison).

We can avoid the computational complexity of an exhaustive search through all visible primitives if we are willing to sacrifice a bit in the accuracy with which picks are correlated. For each segment, SGP can compute the size and location of the upright rectangle in normalized device coordinate space which just surrounds the segment's image on the view surface. We call this rectangle the *screen extent* of the segment. A linear list ordered by increasing area of these rectangles is maintained. Thus, segments whose screen extents are small are near the head of the list. To correlate a point on the view surface with a segment, we search through the list until we find the first segment whose screen extent includes the point.

This scheme easily handles cases in which segments occur "within" other segments on the screen, but it is not without problems. In particular, since each segment is approximated as a rectangular region on the screen, segments for which this is a poor approximation may cause difficulties. A worst-case example is depicted in Fig. 4.20. Point A correlates to segment 1, but so does point B, even though B lies directly on the diagonal line which comprises segment 2! To pick segment 2, the user would have to take a point, such as C, that lies outside of segment 1's screen extent. Since the screen extents do not actually appear on the view surface, situations such as the one depicted may prove a source of confusion to the user (see Exercise 4.17).

Despite these potential problems, this correlation technique is surprisingly effective in many cases, and its comparatively small computational cost makes it

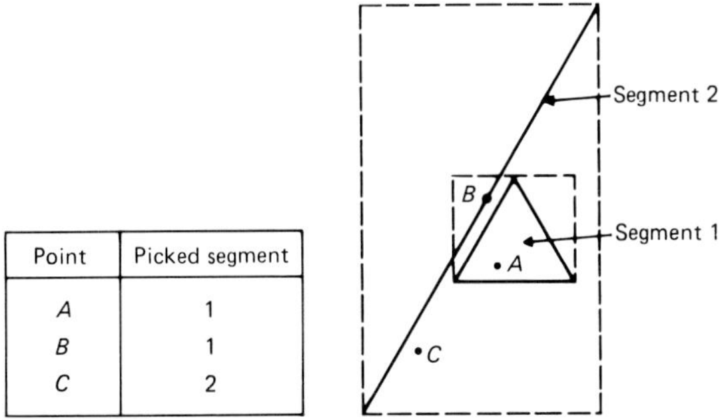

Point	Picked segment
A	1
B	1
C	2

Fig. 4.20 Dashed rectangles show the segments' screen extent.

attractive. SGP can minimize the effects of any confusion that may arise by momentarily highlighting the picked segment. This useful form of feedback allows the user to confirm the accuracy of the correlation. We will discuss additional techniques in Section 5.3.2 and a similar use of extents in world coordinate space in Chapter 9.

4.4 CPU–DPU SYNCHRONIZATION

In the previous section we saw several possible alternative segment organizations which are designed to optimize for both fast execution of all visible segments by the DPU and for fast segment locating and updating by the CPU. We now consider the classic problem of synchronizing these two processors as they read from and write to a common buffer containing the segmented DPU program.* This problem first became apparent when we discussed the effects of rewriting segment storage when deleting segments. Our overall goal is to have the CPU and DPU delay each other as little as possible, subject to the constraint that the DPU must always execute a sequence of display instructions which is at least correct, if not entirely up-to-date.

The goal of minimal delay means, for example, that when we create a new segment, we cannot have the DPU stop and wait until SGP has passed an entire segment through the viewing operation and DPU code generation processes. Nor can we defer linking a new segment into the DPU's refresh list until after the segment has been completely defined. Since the programmer normally expects immediate visibility of output primitives (the default in SGP), each new primitive generated by SGP must be added to the DPU program as soon as possible.

How do we prevent the DPU from executing the same part of the DPU program that the CPU is modifying? This is a very real concern: for example, if the CPU has just overwritten a DPU register load instruction with a jump opcode but has not yet had time to write the correct jump address when the DPU executes the jump, the DPU would jump to the wrong place and start interpreting non-DPU "instructions" there. Clearly some form of synchronization is necessary to prevent such situations.

The synchronization in our simple graphics system is accomplished by having the writer (SGP) control the reader (the DPU) using the hardware facilities of the CPU/DPU interface. After SGP has done all preparation to update either a segment or a directory entry, it signals the DPU to stop with the STOP DPU command and waits for it to signal that it has stopped. Before actually stopping in response to the STOP command, the DPU completes any instruction in progress (including multiword instructions such as text display and jump instructions) and then waits to be restarted. As soon as the DPU signals the CPU that it has stopped, the CPU makes the necessary changes to the DPU program and then restarts the DPU. This synchroniz-

*This assumes a shared-memory configuration. When the DPU has a private display memory, there may be a microprocessor in the DPU for handling communications and synchronization between CPU and DPU.

ation protocol is required, for example, for adding primitives to a segment. After each new primitive's code has been generated, the CPU stops the DPU, adds the primitive's DPU code word(s) to the growing segment (displacing the jump at the bottom of the segment), and then restarts the DPU.

In order for the synchronization to work properly, the part of SGP that runs after the DPU stops must be an *indivisible* operation, i.e., of sufficiently high priority that it runs to completion before any operating system task switching can take place. If the code generator is not run indivisibly, the DPU could be stopped indefinitely. Whenever a few words are being changed, as in adding a primitive to a segment or starting a new segment, this presents no problem, but if segment deletion is done by compaction, *DELETE_SEGMENT* would have to run with highest priority to insure its running to completion without interruption. Conversely, for one-word changes, such as resetting the address words of jumps for visibility or list linkage, the CPU's memory write operation is a single indivisible hardware operation which need not even force a DPU halt: memory contention logic will prevent the DPU and CPU from competing for the same memory location.

What are the synchronization implications of adding primitives to a current segment (probably the most common SGP operation)? Luckily, they are not very severe. Each primitive is, of course, first passed through the entire viewing operation and code generation processes. This pipeline may take several hundred to more than 1000 microseconds. Even a time period of several hundred microseconds dominates the "stop DPU, insert a few words of code, restart DPU" sequence, which only takes tens of microseconds (equivalent to the time to display a few vectors). There are thus relatively few and very short unnoticeable interruptions in each frame. (For DVST and raster displays, momentary delays in the DPU process aren't a problem at all.)

Another type of synchronization problem arises with linked-list allocation, when deleting a segment and freeing the deleted block. If the DPU was interpreting a segment at the moment it was deleted and freed, and then the block was immediately reused, SGP or another process might modify the block, with the result that the DPU could end up executing invalid commands. SGP handles this highly unlikely case simply by freeing unlinked segments at the end of the refresh cycle (marked by the frame lock WAIT) rather than when the segment deletion command is in progress. This requires that the DPU interrupt the CPU when it enters the WAIT. When the CPU finishes, it restarts the DPU, which must first serve any remaining time in the frame lock WAIT instruction.

4.5 INTERACTION HANDLING

Since sampling and event-causing devices are different by nature, SGP must handle them with somewhat different techniques. The *READ_LOCATOR* routine simply samples the DPU's X, Y locator registers and returns the values in normalized device coordinates as the routine's *x* and *y* parameters. *INVERSE_2* can then be used to provide the equivalent world coordinates. SGP must independently sample the locator from 10 to 30 times per second to provide an echo, usually a cursor. This typically involves updating the absolute move's *x, y* values of a special segment displaying the cursor. Some DPUs do this automatically when the locator is logically enabled by the package.

READ_VALUATOR similarly samples the appropriate DPU register and returns a fractional value as a parameter for the application program's use. Again SGP must echo the sampled value. Since there are typically multiple valuators (from 8 to 16) on a system, the user would like to suppress the echo of valuators not used in the program. SGP can track which valuators were specified in the program and turn on the echo for those only. In more sophisticated packages such as the Core, individual input devices, such as a single valuator, can explicitly be enabled and disabled by the programmer. The form of echo also may be adjusted at run time.

The *WAIT_PICK, WAIT_KEYBOARD,* and *WAIT_BUTTON* routines are more complex in that they implicitly enable their respective event-generating devices, put the application program in a WAIT state, and then return control to the operating system dispatcher. Meanwhile the DPU continues to refresh as normal. When the user next causes an event to occur (or when time-out occurs), the DPU reports the event to the CPU by interrupting it. The operating system's interrupt service routine (ISR), entered in response to the interrupt, returns control to the appropriate SGP procedure and provides it with event data. This data is then formatted by the SGP procedure to be returned to the application program in the appropriate output parameter(s). For example, when the operator pushes a button, the ISR transfers the button number, which it obtained from the DPU, to the *WAIT_BUTTON* routine, and *WAIT_BUTTON* returns it in its *button_name* parameter. Actually, the ISR first must signal the dispatcher that the application task is ready to be dispatched. Then, when *WAIT_BUTTON* is reactivated at the statement following its low-level operating-system WAIT call, it copies an operating-system variable containing the button number into the *button_name* variable and returns control to the application program statement following the *WAIT_BUTTON* call. Thus, there is transfer of both data (the button number) and control from the DPU to the operating system (ISR), from there to SGP's *WAIT_BUTTON* routine, and finally back to the application program.

Similarly, when the operator presses the logical "carriage return" on the keyboard, the interrupt generated causes *WAIT_KEYBOARD* to return to the application program the character string which was input and the number of characters it contains via the parameters *text* and *length,* respectively. Finally, an operator pick generates an interrupt which causes the *WAIT_PICK* routine to be reactivated and to perform the correlation discussed in Section 4.3.4 above. It then returns the appropriate segment name to the application program in the *segment_name* parameter.

All event routines must check for time-out and return the reserved value of zero for the button name, character string length or segment name, as appropriate. A time-out condition should be tested for by the application program's "**case** event data" statements in each user action-handling procedure, as shown in the *LAYOUT* example of Chapter 2.

All event routines must also provide an appropriate echo. *WAIT_BUTTON* may turn a light on under a physical button by adding a "load button register with mask" DPU instruction. For buttons simulated by the keyboard (and for *WAIT_KEYBOARD* itself), SGP would add DPU code to echo the characters in a reserved system area of the screen which is not in the NDC space accessible to the program. This is convenient on rectangular displays where the unit square of NDC space leaves some unused screen area. For square screens, however, the NDC space either must be shared or must be somewhat smaller than the full addressable screen area to make a border area *available for* use as a reserved area.

Characters typed in during a *WAIT_KEYBOARD* are passed one at a time to *WAIT_KEYBOARD* by the ISR, and *WAIT_KEYBOARD* will typically provide some reserved screen area for echoing, as for simulated buttons. In addition, when the logical carriage return is typed, the application program can position the entire returned character string (minus the carriage return) at an appropriate point in the NDC space for additional user feedback. To achieve effects such as having the characters appear as they are typed at the cursor or at the CP, a *SET_ECHO_POSITION* command could be added to SGP. SGP could then build a special segment for the characters being received, using the specified position for the initial absolute move.

For buttons simulated with a light button menu and for *WAIT_PICK* itself, picked segments are blinked or otherwise highlighted for example by having the DPU make them alternately visible and invisible for, say, 10 frames at a time, using a simple timer interrupt. SGP may do this automatically or the application programmer may use the highlightability segment attribute of Exercise 2.18.

Altogether, then, handling input devices to provide convenient user–computer interaction takes some careful design and implementation. Suitable echoes, in particular, are not trivial to implement.

4.6 SEGMENTED DPU PROGRAMS FOR OTHER DEVICES

While segmented DPU programs are clearly oriented towards vector refresh displays because of the ease of editing and seeing the results of the updated display in the next refresh cycle, they have been routinely applied to storage displays such as DVSTs and raster displays as well. Not only does this allow more compatibility between refresh and storage display packages, but there are also significant performance advantages in trading off the additional memory used for the segmented DPU program for update modification time.

The key idea is to avoid running through the entire picture generation pipeline from data structure to display code every time the user requires a selective modification involving deleting part of the image. On a DVST without write-through mode, for example, it is easy to add new primitives but it is essentially infeasible (that is, too time-consuming) to drag an image, make it invisible or delete it and then see an up-to-date picture on the screen. This is because the application program must first clear the screen and then run through the object's entire description in order to redraw the modified object. Obviously, one would like to save all of the previous work done in clipping and mapping for the parts of the picture that are unchanged.

By storing a segmented DVST program, we can redraw all but the deleted or invisible segments directly from previously compiled DPU code rather than from higher-level descriptions which must first be compiled to code. For a plasma panel or raster display, use of a segmented DPU program provides even faster changes, since the graphics package can execute the code in the deleted segment in erase mode and then delete the segment. Thus all display systems, whether they have built-in storage or not, can be made more efficient by storing segmented DPU programs. For refresh vector displays, this display file is used both for update dynamics and for refreshing, while for storage displays it is used only for updating. Note that when the display file need not be used for refreshing, the CPU/DPU synchronization problem and the need to WAIT to free deleted segments are avoided.

In order to make the update process even more efficient for storage displays, we introduce the notion of *batching* successive updates so that SGP doesn't automatically erase and regenerate the screen after every segment delete to keep the display up to date. For example, for a DVST one would like to batch the deletion of a series of segments, rather than having to wait while the screen is cleared and the picture is redrawn for each successive deletion. After a *BEGIN_BATCH* is specified, all DPU operations on the *DPU program* will proceed normally, but no changes will be made to the screen until *END_BATCH* is called (typically specified before a *WAIT_PICK, _KEYBOARD* or *_BUTTON* for user input is specified, when an up-to-date picture is required). A new SGP function, *NEW_FRAME,* may be used by the programmer to erase the screen at any time outside a batch and have the current picture redrawn. On hard-copy plotters, *NEW_FRAME* is used to advance the medium to the next frame and redraw the current picture. True refresh displays can ignore the *BATCH* and *NEW_FRAME* commands, since the image always reflects the up-to-date display file.

The batch update process can be made even more efficient by recording whether any segments in the batch were made invisible, were deleted, or had image translation applied. If so, the screen is cleared and the DPU runs through the up-to-date display file. If not, i.e., if only additions were specified, the screen need not be cleared and the DPU need draw only the newly added segments. An extra control bit for each segment can record whether the segment is to be drawn because it was new or because it was changed from invisible to visible; when the segment is drawn, the bit is reset.

Finally, let us consider applications which require only infrequent interaction but do make use of the storage display's ability to display an arbitrarily large number of flicker-free output primitives. An example of such an application is interactive plotting when plots are previewed on the DVST or raster display before being plotted on a hard-copy device. Another such application is displaying dynamically modified objects drawn in write-through mode on a DVST over an unchanging background (such as a map, legend, or standard form) drawn in store mode. In the first application there is no point in using the display file as an intermediate data structure, since each plot is likely to be different, while in the second application one could store only the repeated background in a DPU program segment and draw the changing elements directly onto the screen. Naturally, if the background is sufficiently elaborate, the cost of the storage may be prohibitive. The Core has a facility for "one-shot" plotting, called *temporary segments,* which are not saved in the segmented DPU program.

4.7 ERROR HANDLING

In Chapter 2 little mention was made of what would constitute incorrect use of SGP and how SGP would handle such errors. Errors at the lexical and syntactic level (such as missing or extra parentheses or parameters, or parameters of the wrong data type) would normally be handled by the compiler. Other syntactic or semantic errors resulting from inappropriate sequences of SGP calls would be handled by SGP itself.

The question arises in package design of how strict the notion of a semantic error should be. For example, is it an error to specify an operation on a nonexistent segment? We believe that a good design should enforce the notion that operations do only what they are intended to do, have no side effects (implicit, extra results), and generate warnings to the user if they are applied incorrectly. In other words, we do not endorse the strategy of "trying to do something useful" with whatever the programmer specifies, let alone "fixing up" his mistakes, as some (student) programming languages and systems do. Experience shows that the results of such supposed helpfulness are rarely what the programmer intended and that the strategy may lead to confusion because operations may accomplish different purposes at different times depending on the context of the call. SGP should, of course, always try to keep running in order to give maximum useful feedback, after having bypassed the procedure in error.

In short, there is but one simple rule to remember: only if the single function of each SGP procedure can be accomplished in the standard, prescribed way is the procedure properly specified; all else is an error condition. Thus in Chapter 2 we saw that SGP issues a warning if the programmer tries to do a *DELETE_SEGMENT* on a nonexistent segment. Similarly, SGP won't allow him to *SET_VISIBILITY, TRANSLATE_IMAGE_2* or to do a *RENAME_SEGMENT* of a nonexistent segment. He may not do a *CREATE_SEGMENT* of an already existing segment or do a *CREATE_SEGMENT* of a new one before the current one is explicitly *CLOSE_SEGMENT*ed. (Some other packages, in contrast, allow a *CREATE_SEGMENT* to have the side effect of doing a *CLOSE_SEGMENT* of any open segment.) Conversely, a current segment must be explicitly opened with *CREATE_SEGMENT* before an output primitive may be specified.

It is also considered a semantic error to reset the viewing transformation by calls to *WINDOW* and/or *VIEWPORT* in the middle of a segment definition (between *CREATE_SEGMENT* and *CLOSE_SEGMENT*): such a change would conflict with the principle that an entire (sub)object is defined in a segment after the viewing operation has been appropriately set up—one does not change the setting of a camera while taking a snapshot! On the other hand, input handling is considered *orthogonal* both to segment operations and to specifying output, so that input calls may be interspersed freely anywhere in the program.

As each SGP procedure is entered, it does its own error checking; if an error is found, it is logged to an appropriate logical device. A run-time binding or I/O redirection mechanism (such as a job control language processor or the operating system's command language interpreter) may be employed. It can allow the logical device to be assigned to a disk file, printer, alphanumeric CRT used for communicating with the operating system, or even a system message area on the display surface itself. When a program is being debugged, it is helpful to see error messages immediately; in production use, off-line printing will probably suffice. An SGP error routine may also be made available to test return codes/error flags set by each routine.

To implement error checking for segment operations, the search process need only check for valid segment names. Context-dependent errors (generating primitives without a current segment, mismatched *CREATE_SEGMENT*s and *CLOSE_SEGMENT*s, or viewing operation changes in the wrong place) can be easily handled with a few global state variables. Note that there are no fatal programming errors and only one halting condition: only when SGP runs out of space and cannot continue to generate primitives, or when some other system error takes place, is its processing halted.

4.8 DEVICE-INDEPENDENT GRAPHICS

In this chapter we have touched on many issues involved in making graphics packages as independent as possible of the display surface and input devices. For example, we saw that one can split SGP between the device-independent viewing operation processor and the device-dependent DPU code generator in order to create a special-purpose segmented display file for each DPU (Fig. 4.21). We could go a step further and create an intermediate, device-independent *pseudo display file* for an abstract pseudo-DPU (Fig. 4.22). This strategy is analogous to the P-code used for device-independent but low-level intermediate representation of Pascal programs. By using NDC coordinates, the pseudo display file could be shared for

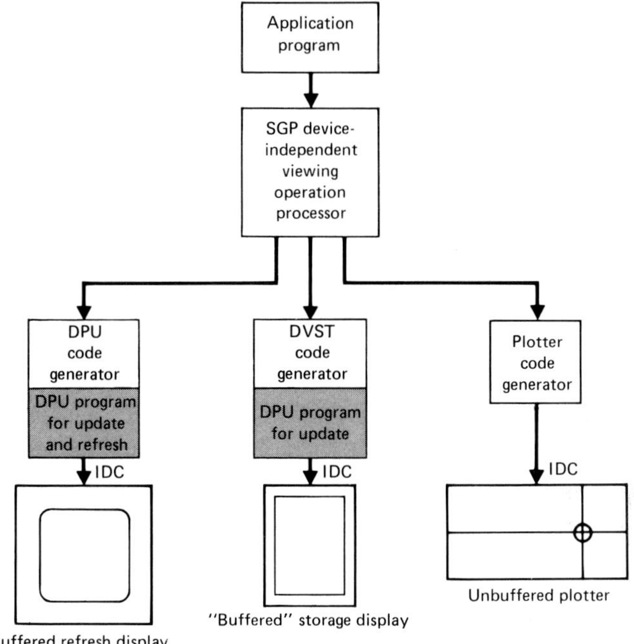

Fig. 4.21 SGP output showing device-independent common front end and device-dependent code generators.

updating purposes by all display devices except the refresh vector display, which additionally needs the speed of a DPU-specific display file for the refresh cycle. (The raster display with its integral bit map refresh buffer is again considered as a storage display.) The desirability of using a pseudo display file depends primarily on the number of devices to be driven from a single picture description. Using such a file pays off, for example, if several storage displays, a pen plotter, and a microfilm plotter are all copying the same images because they can all be driven from the same file. In short, pseudo display files allow greater device-independence, but at the cost of an extra representation and two code generation phases in sequence.

A pseudo display file which can be stored as a self-sufficient low-level but still device-independent picture description is referred to as a *metafile.* A graphics package which can write and read metafiles can use them to save "compiled code" between sessions and to transport the graphical information between installations as well as between application programs in the same installation.

When we add device-dependent low-level input handlers for each display to the output pipeline of Fig. 4.21, we can partition all of each device's device-dependent code and data in a module called the *logical device driver* (Fig. 4.23). This includes the code generator and input handler and the DPU program and its segment control

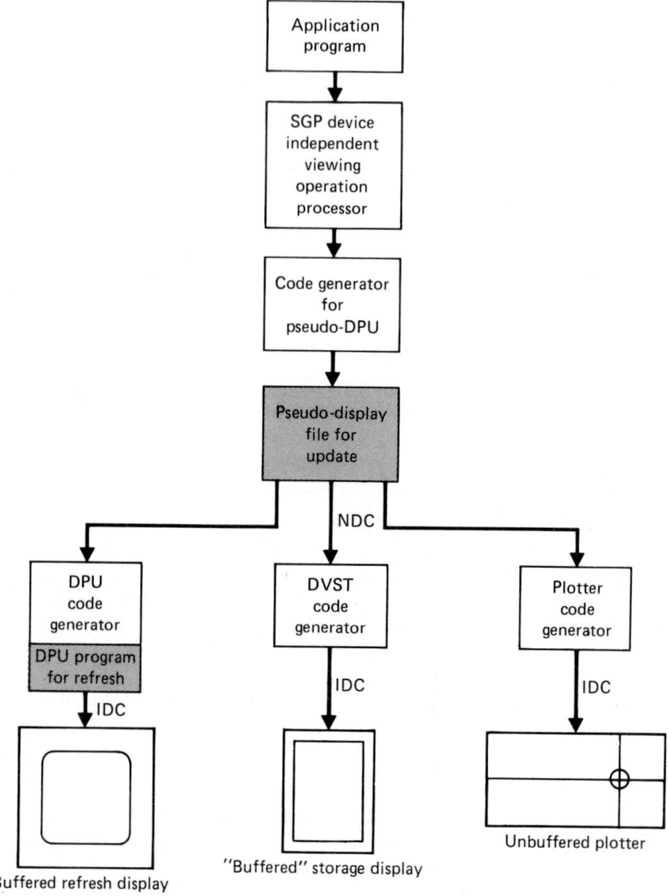

Fig. 4.22 Alternate SGP output; common pseudodisplay file and a simpler device-dependent display file for refresh display.

information. Each such logical device driver makes use of *physical device drivers* or "access methods" in the operating system to control the flow of data and control to and from the physical input and output devices. In order to build a device- and machine-independent package like SGP, we implement the device-independent part and logical device drivers for each display in a high-level transportable language. With this modularization, it is primarily the lowest-level physical device drivers that must be changed as we move the package from machine to machine, device to device.

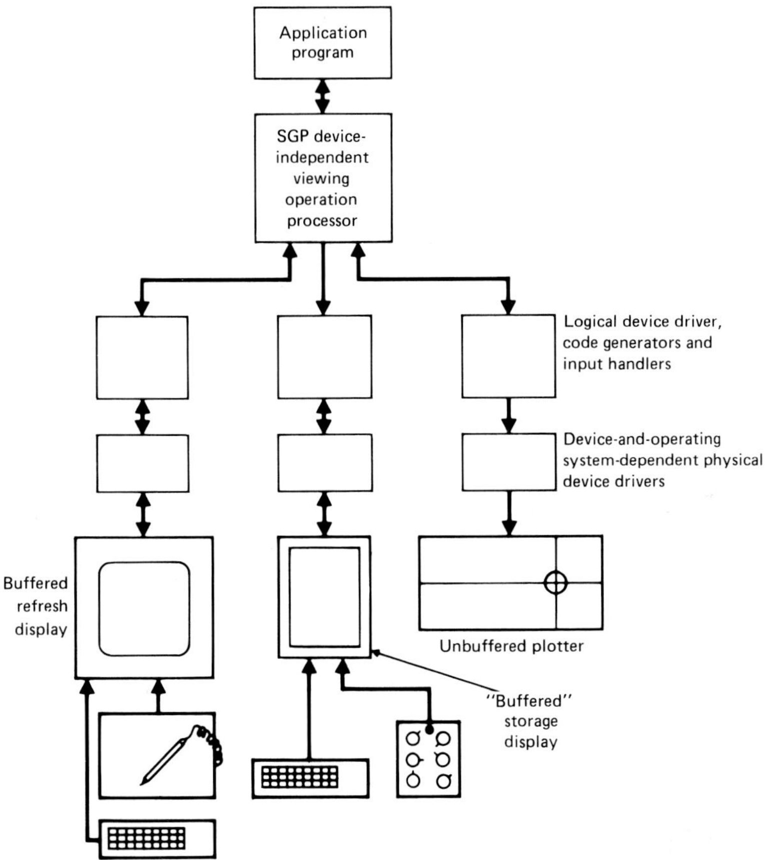

Fig. 4.23 Three parts of a graphics system: common SGP device-independent front end, SGP specialized logical-device drivers, and low-level physical input/output drives (display files not shown).

4.9 SUMMARY

In the first four chapters we have taken our first look at interactive graphics applications, programming, hardware, and software. We have focused on the use and design of a simple device-independent subroutine package callable from within standard high-level languages in order to make application programs transportable among all computer systems supporting the subroutine package. SGP provides a basic but functionally complete set of line-drawing and interaction-handling primitives, and will be extended to 3D and additional raster (solid-area) primitives in Chapters 8 and 11 respectively. SGP does not, however, deal with application-dependent modeling (discussed in Chapter 9) or higher-level utilities such as graph-plotting packages or typesetting packages which can be implemented "on top of" the core facilities of SGP. It also may not allow access to the special, nonstandard features of a particular display device and will not, in general, take optimal advantage of facilities for run-time dynamics provided by the most powerful displays. In most cases, the loss of some efficiency and flexibility is more than outweighed by the ease of writing and transporting graphics applications, thereby protecting the software investment. The case for such standard high-level subroutine packages and the design trade-offs are discussed in [NEWM78] and companion articles in the December 1978 issue of *ACM Computing Surveys,* as well as in [GSPC79].

While we emphasize the Core and its subset SGP in this book, the limitations of the subroutine approach must be kept in mind. These include the clumsy "parameter list" syntax and the lack of compile-time checking (since the graphic subroutines can "compile" pictures only when the package is invoked, at run time of the application program). It would be far preferable to extend a compiled (or, better yet, an interpreted) language with graphic data types and operators for immediate checking of a more natural, more expressive syntax (see, for example, [NG78]). "Standard" language extensions are typically not as easy as might be supposed: agreement must occur on the host (base) language as well as on the extensions themselves, and major modification of the compiler is usually necessary. Interpreting such a language for maximum interaction with the programmer and user, while most desirable, is in general still prohibitively expensive on time-sharing systems. With the age of powerful personal computers with integral bit-map displays dawning, we can look forward to a gradual demise of the world of compiled sequential FORTRAN enhanced with graphics subroutines and to the large-scale introduction of interactive, graphics-based languages employing parallelism at the programmer level. The design of such languages is still an object of much-needed research (even the newly created Ada [WEGN80] is oriented towards conventional batch or time-sharing systems and has no built-in graphics facilities). Smalltalk [BYTE81] treats graphical communication and parallel processes as intrinsic to an object-oriented, integrated language and run-time environment. It is a significant new paradigm for thinking about and implementing interactive graphics, and merits considerable attention.

In this chapter, we discussed the implementation of SGP for a simple refresh DPU. Several alternatives for other display devices were also treated briefly. All of the techniques for handling each of the stages in the output and input pipelines have been covered in sufficient detail that the reader should now be in a position to use or implement such a graphics package effectively. Naturally, there are a great many issues still to be explored for more powerful features and hardware. Before starting more advanced topics, however, we complete this basic shell by taking a closer look at the physical and logical implementation of input devices (Chapter 5) and then at the human-factor aspects of interactive graphics programs (Chapter 6).

EXERCISES

4.1 Propose another model of graphics input/output that you might find more appropriate than the one advocated in this chapter, and discuss the trade-offs between the two.

4.2 Complete the procedures left unspecified in the Cohen–Sutherland clipping algorithm (Section 4.2.1). Improve the efficiency of that clipping algorithm by eliminating the evaluation of both outcodes each time through the **repeat** loop.

4.3 After a careful study of the possible cases of intersections with the window, write the midpoint division algorithm of Section 4.2.1.

4.4 Discuss whether the midpoint subdivision algorithm of Section 4.2.1 is worth implementing in software.

4.5 a) For the Cohen–Sutherland and the midpoint subdivision algorithms (Section 4.2.1), discuss which types of lines (as characterized by the outcodes of their endpoints and their intersections with the window) take the longest to clip.

b) Show with simple algebra that clipping may be done equivalently in world coordinate space, normalized device coordinate space, and (integer) device coordinate space.

c) For either of the two clipping algorithms of Section 4.2.1, contrast the work involved in processing a line in each of the two sequences: map, then clip against an upright viewport; clip against a non-upright window, then map. Consider four cases for each sequence: (i) Trivial accept; (ii) Trivial reject; (iii) Line cuts one edge; (iv) Line cuts two edges.

d) Summarize the trade-offs for clipping in world coordinate space, normalized device coordinate space, and (physical) device coordinate space as a function of the distribution of the lines with respect to the window, the hardware available, the rotation of window and/or viewport, and any other factors you may deem relevant. What space is most likely to be right for "most" circumstances?

4.6 Investigate some of the other clipping methods in [JARV75] and characterize the testing versus computation trade-offs with the algorithms of Section 4.2.1.

4.7 The batch update process of Section 4.6 deferred all screen updates until the end of batch was encountered. Describe a modification that defers updates more effectively for storage displays. Does it have any side effects?

4.8 Text handling is one of the most difficult aspects of graphics package design, as the designer is caught between conflicting goals of aesthetic rendition and efficient use of software and hardware. For example, producing a perspective projection of a moving truck with lettering on its side certainly poses far more stringent requirements than producing a prompt message to the user. Characterize various requirements for text which you feel are important and then give a critical analysis of the Core's [GSPC79] facilities (in time to be submitted for presentation at the next SIGGRAPH conference!)

4.9 Write an "assembly code" generator for the DPU of Chapter 2 for output primitives. Show how to generate CPU code for the other functions and show how the DPU program is modified.

4.10 Consider the simple, ancient 10-bit integer-coordinate Tektronix 4006–1, which has only three instructions, transmitted as one or more 7-bit ASCII characters:

(i)	ENTER graphics mode	00	11101
(ii)	LEAVE graphics mode	00	11111
(iii)	VECTOR graphics mode (the five high- and five low-order bits for 10-bit x and y are in consecutive 7-bit bytes)	01	*y_high*
		11	*y_low*
		01	*x_high*
		10	*x_low*

To compress the byte stream transmitted to the terminal for short vectors, either or both of the high-order bytes may be left off, e.g.,

11*y_low*, 01*x_high*, 10*x_low*

The first vector after an ENTER is used as an absolute move to position the beam, while the following ones are used to draw. After a LEAVE character, the terminal is in alphanumeric text mode at the current beam position, and the beam is automatically spaced from character position to character position until the ENTER character. Write a simple code generator for this device and show how to handle the problems of mode switching between text and graphics (and between application program and system use of the screen).

4.11 Discuss what the optimization of DPU code might entail and how it might be implemented. Give specific examples using the DPU of Chapter 3.

4.12 The ability to modify an existing segment is available neither in SGP nor in the Core.

a) Many package designers wish to provide for selective addition by using an *APPEND(segment_name)* function that would serve to reopen the named segment and allow new primitives at the bottom. Discuss in what situations such a function would be useful or preferable to a *DELETE_SEGMENT,* (re)*CREATE_SEGMENT* sequence and what is required to implement it. *Hint:* Consider problems with CP, line style, and other attributes. Which of the two data structures of Section 4.3 would make it easier to implement *APPEND*?

b) How would you specify and implement segment editing?

4.13 Discuss in more detail than in Section 4.3 the advantages and disadvantages of fragmenting segments over fixed-length and variable-length blocks for the segment operations.

4.14 Show how back pointers could be used in the linked list of Section 4.3.3 to simplify segment deletion and changing visibility, as well as to obviate having invisible segments in the linked list. Is the cost of back pointers worth the (potential) benefits?

4.15 What are the trade-offs in having the segment directory stored as a binary tree? How could hashing be used and what would be its advantages and disadvantages?

4.16 Work out the details of a *SET_ECHO_POSITION* procedure which would allow SGP to echo characters as they are typed at a point chosen by the application program rather than in the standard echo area.

4.17 The pick identification algorithm (described in Section 4.3.4) that uses screen extents is ambiguous if identically sized screen extents overlap. Show how this ambiguity may arise and trade off two alternative strategies: (i) the user interactively resolves the ambiguity; (ii) the correlation routine does exact distance-to-nearest-primitive calculations for all the primitives in the competing segments (see Chapter 5, Section 5.3.2).

4.18 Advocate a "universal" DPU architecture for maximum transportability and show how its pseudodisplay file might be structured. Is this desirable?

4.19 As a medium-sized (e.g., three- to four-week) software engineering project, do a top–down design and implementation of the SGP output pipeline for the line printer or (glass) teletype. Handle the problems of aspect ratio (differing numbers of print positions in the horizontal and vertical directions) and making lines look as smooth (continuous) as possible. *Hint:* Use different sequences of characters as a function of the slope of the line to make the smoothest (least jagged) approximation to a straight line. Conversely, to show color attributes of primitives use single character abbreviations for forming primitives.

5
Interaction Devices and Techniques

We have already introduced, in the preceding chapters, a number of interaction devices and techniques. The devices include the light pen, data tablet with stylus, and alphanumeric and function keyboards. Techniques for using the devices include selecting commands from a menu with the light pen or tablet and positioning symbols with a tablet. In this chapter we describe more (but not all) of the available devices and techniques and touch on their relative merits.

Our objective is to impart an understanding of how the devices work and how they can be used. The devices and techniques are the building blocks from which an interactive dialogue is constructed. In Chapter 6 we consider methodology and guidelines to help in selecting the set of devices and techniques to be used in a specific application and in integrating these building blocks into a usable dialogue.

5.1 LOGICAL CLASSES OF DEVICES AND TECHNIQUES

There is a large variety of interaction devices and techniques. Fortunately, we can impose some organization on them and thereby structure our study and use of the techniques. The organization employed is that of *logical devices,* introduced in Chapter 2 as part of SGP. There are five basic logical devices: the *locator,* to indicate a position and/or orientation; the *pick,* to select a displayed entity; the *valuator,* to input a single value in the space of real numbers; the *keyboard,* to input a character string; and the *button,* to select from a set of possible alternative actions or choices.

Each logical device has a natural prototype in a specific physical device or class of devices. In SGP, for example, the pick device was discussed in terms of its natural prototype, the lightpen. Other natural prototypes are: locator—tablet; valuator—potentiometer; keyboard—alphanumeric keyboard; button—programmed function keyboard. However, any of these logical devices can be simulated by any input device: many of the interaction techniques we will discuss are such simulations.

The concept of logical input devices is rather like that of logical files in an operating system. A sequential input file may be implemented physically by means of a card reader, a magnetic tape drive, a disk drive, or a terminal keyboard. The application programmer doesn't care which one it is—the operating system makes them all "look alike" functionally, despite their physical differences.

The essence of the logical-device idea is found in a 1968 paper by Newman [NEWM68b]. In 1971 the *general-purpose graphic system* (GPGS) subroutine package [VAND77] implemented interaction by using logical devices and showed the utility of simulating input devices, such as picks, on simple display devices lacking physical pick mechanisms. A series of articles by Cotton [COTT72], Wallace and Foley [FOLE74] and Wallace [WALL76] elaborates on the concept. In addition, several higher-level devices (such as a *sketch* device) for specifying a sequence of positions are described in [WALL76]. Logical devices are found not only in GPGS but also in the proposed *Core System* [GSPC79] and in the *ARPA network graphics protocol* [SPRO74].

5.2 PHYSICAL INTERACTION DEVICES

In this section we describe how some interaction devices actually work. Many devices are in use, so we focus on those which are more common or more innovative. The devices are grouped by the logical-device category which matches the inherent physical operation of each device—the logical device which the physical device implements with a minimum of support software. Realize, however, that ease of implementation may not be equivalent to ease of use. We are thus not proposing that the physical devices are best used to implement the logical device under which they are here categorized. Throughout this chapter the reader will find comparisons and contrasts among different logical device implementations, meant to help in the actual process of selecting the appropriate interaction technique for implementing a logical device.

5.2.1 Locators

The most commonly used locator, the *tablet,* is a flat surface over which a *stylus* (like a pencil) or *hand cursor* is moved; the position of the hand cursor or stylus is available to the computer. A tablet with a stylus is shown in Fig. 1.14; a back-lit tablet with a hand cursor is shown in Fig. 5.1. The stylus typically incorporates a pressure-sensitive switch which closes when the user pushes down on the stylus, thus indicating to the application program that the stylus is at a position of interest. Most hand cursors have several buttons which can be operated by the user to input commands. The stylus switch and the hand cursor buttons are really separate logical button devices, physically but not necessarily logically integrated into the locator device.

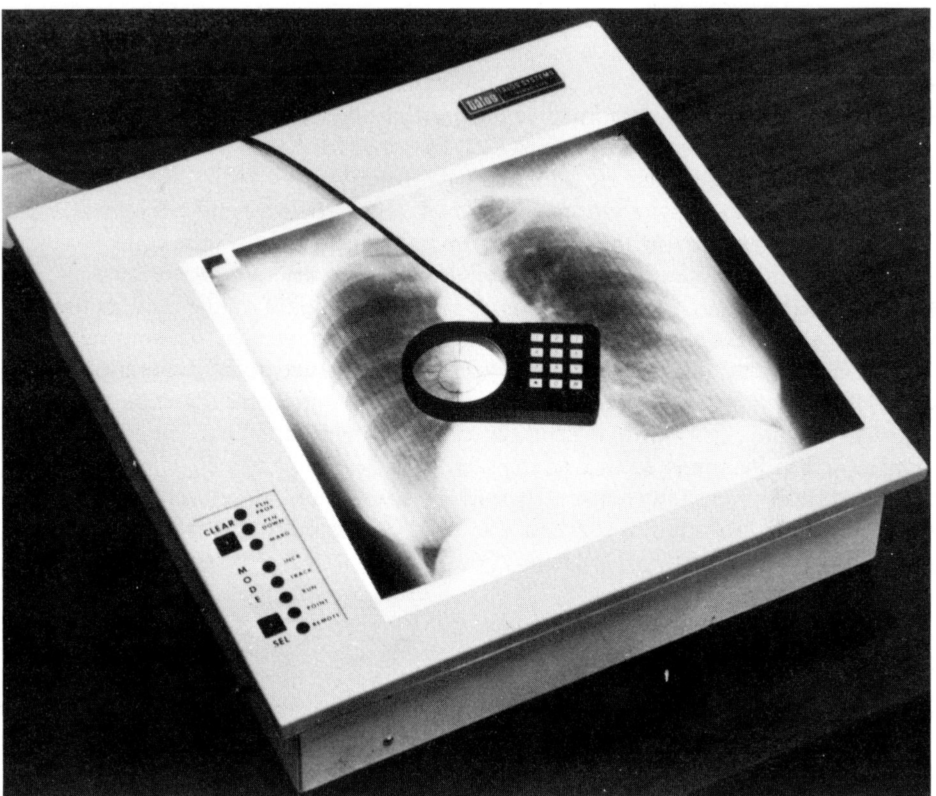

Fig. 5.1 Back-lit tablet with 12-button cursor (courtesy Talos Systems, Inc.).

Most tablets use an electrical sensing mechanism to measure the stylus or hand cursor position. In one such arrangement, a grid of wires is embedded in the tablet surface. Electromagnetic coupling between electrical signals in the grid and in the stylus or cursor induces an electrical signal in a wire coil in the stylus or cursor. The strength of the electromagnetic coupling can be used to determine roughly how far the stylus or cursor is from the tablet (''far'', ''near'', ''on''). When the answer is ''near'' or ''on'', a *screen cursor* is usually displayed (by the display hardware or graphics package) to track the position being read from the tablet and thus to provide visual feedback to the user.

Information is typically obtained from a tablet controller in one of three ways: on demand, when the computer makes a request; every *t* units of time; and each time the hand cursor or stylus is moved more than some distance *d*. The time-interval sampling is helpful if a screen cursor is being displayed to reflect the position of the tablet cursor or stylus. The distance-interval sampling is appropriate for digitizing drawings in order to avoid recording an excessive number of points.

Relevant parameters of tablets and other locator devices are their resolution, linearity, repeatability, and size or range. These parameters are particularly crucial for digitizing maps and drawings, but are of less concern when the device is used only to position a screen cursor, since the user has the feedback of the screen cursor position to guide his hand movements. Tablets of at least 48 × 72 inches with accuracy of 200 points per inch are commercially available.

Another locator is the *mouse* shown in Fig. 5.2. It is a hand-held device with rollers on its base. Moving the mouse across a flat surface causes the rollers to turn, and potentiometers coupled to one roller sense the relative movements in two orthogonal directions. The motion is converted to digital values and is used to determine the direction and magnitude of the mouse's movement. The mouse can be picked up, moved, and then put down without any change in the apparent position of its screen cursor. Thus the mouse reports relative movement, while the tablet reports absolute positions. The computer must maintain a "current mouse position" which is incremented or decremented by mouse movements. The mouse, like most hand cursors, usually has several push buttons which can be used to input commands or other information and hence serve as logical buttons; the pick function is thus easily implemented.

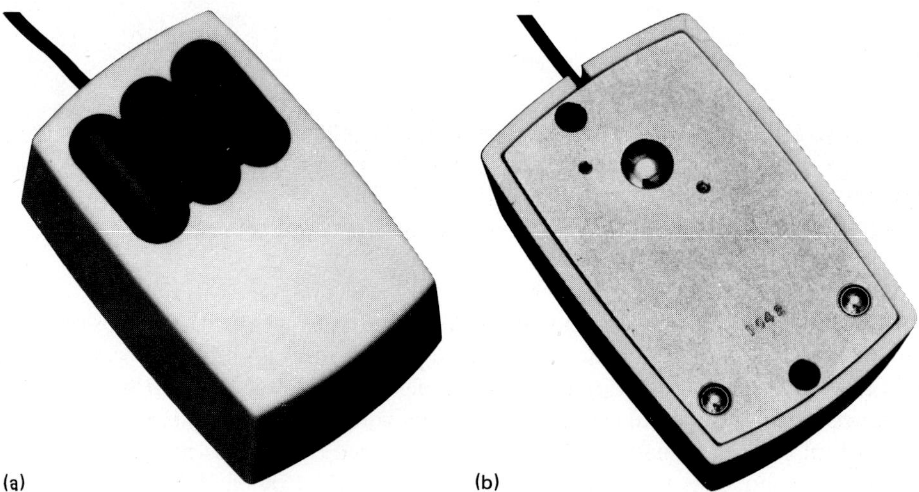

(a) (b)

Fig. 5.2 The mouse: (a) top view; (b) bottom view (courtesy Xerox Corporation).

While the accuracy of the mouse is comparable to that of a tablet, very fine and precise sketching is more difficult than with a tablet and stylus because fine fingertip motor control is more difficult. On the other hand, a mouse requires only a small table area to use and is inexpensive to manufacture.

Fig. 5.3 Trackball (courtesy Ramtek Corporation).

Trackballs, sometimes called *crystal balls,* are another form of locator (Fig. 5.3). The ball's motion turns potentiometers, whose output is converted into digital form. The ball rotates freely within its mount, and is typically moved by drawing the palm of one's hand across it. Large and rapid position changes are difficult to make with a trackball.

The *joystick* is simply a stick which can be moved left or right, forward or backward (Fig. 5.4). Again, potentiometers sense the movements. Very often, sets of springs are used to return the joystick to its home center position. Some joysticks, including the one pictured, have a third degree of freedom: the stick can be twisted clockwise and counterclockwise. The *isometric joystick,* shown in Fig. 5.5, is rigid: strain gauges on the shaft measure slight deflections caused by force applied to the shaft.

It is difficult to use a joystick to control the absolute position of a screen cursor directly, because a slight hand movement is amplified five or ten times in the position of the screen cursor. This makes the screen cursor's movements quite jerky and doesn't allow quick and accurate fine positioning. Thus the joystick is often used to control the *velocity* of the screen cursor's movement rather than its absolute position. This means that the current position of the screen cursor is changed over time at rates determined by the joystick. It is important that a small *dead zone* of zero

Fig. 5.4 Joystick with rotating shaft to provide third axis (courtesy Vector General).

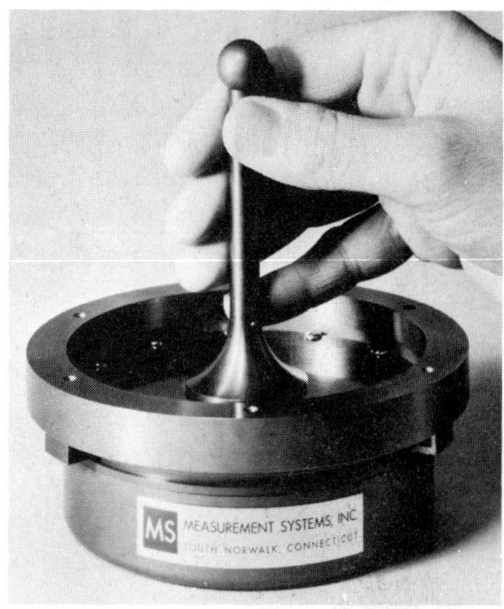

Fig. 5.5 Rigid joystick (courtesy Measurement Systems, Inc.).

velocity be established to allow for drift in the joystick's home center position. To further enhance ease of use, the relation of cursor velocity to joystick displacement is often made nonlinear, as shown in Fig. 5.6. This velocity curve, along with the spring return on the joystick, makes positioning fairly fast, but not as fast as with a tablet or mouse.

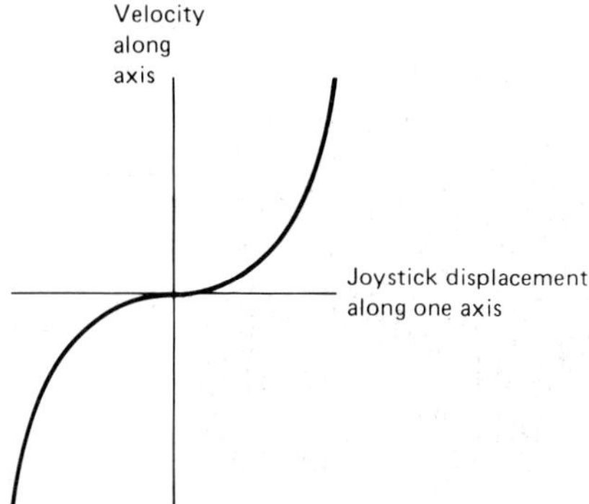

Fig. 5.6 Nonlinear velocity control.

The *joyswitch,* a variant of the joystick, can be moved in any of eight directions: up, down, left, right, and in the four diagonal directions. The switch hence has nine states. In each of the eight "on" states, the position of the screen cursor is changed at a *constant* rate, in the appropriate direction. The difficulty with this is in moving the screen cursor over large distances.

The joystick can also be used conveniently as a 3D orientation device (logical locators can provide both position and orientation), especially if the shaft rotates with a third degree of freedom. The three values from the joystick can be used to control the rate of rotation about each of the three axes. If the joystick does not have spring return to zero, its values can be used as absolute rotations rather than as rates of rotation.

These locator devices are manipulated with the user's hands, while the screen cursor is watched with the eyes. The *touch panel,* on the other hand, is a locator device which allows the user to give full attention to the screen and to indicate positions on it directly rather than by driving a screen cursor to the desired location. The transparent panel is mounted across the face of the CRT: when the user's finger touches the panel, the position touched is detected.

Several different technologies are used for touch panels. Low-resolution panels (from 10 to 50 resolvable positions in each direction) use a series of light sources (light-emitting diodes) and light sensors (photodiodes or phototransistors) to form a grid over the display area. Touching the screen breaks one or two vertical and horizontal light beams, thereby revealing the finger's position. If two parallel beams are broken, the finger is presumed to be centered between them; if one is broken, the finger is presumed to be on the beam. One high-resolution panel (about 500 resolvable positions in each direction) uses sonar-style ranging. Bursts of high-frequency shock waves traveling alternately horizontally and vertically are induced in a flat glass plate. The touch of a finger on the glass causes part of the wave to be reflected back to its source. The distance to the finger can be calculated from the time interval between emission of the wave burst and its arrival back at the source. Another high-resolution panel uses two slightly separated layers of transparent material, one coated with a thin substrate of conducting material; the other, resistive. Finger-tip pressure forces the layers to touch, and the voltage drop across the resistive substrate is measured and used to calculate the coordinates of the touched position.

The *sonic tablet* uses sound to couple the stylus to strip microphones along two sides of the tablet. An electrical spark is generated at the tip of the stylus. The time delay between when the spark occurs and when its sound arrives at each microphone is proportional to the distance of the stylus from each microphone, as suggested by Fig. 5.7.

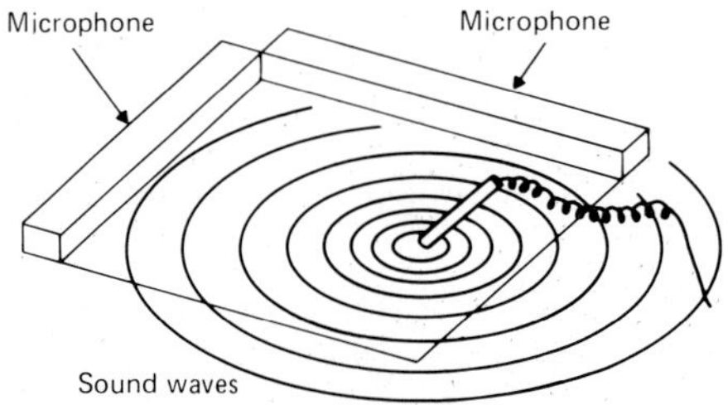

Fig. 5.7 2D sonic tablet.

All the devices we have discussed are 2D locators. It is often convenient to have 3D devices as well, even though 2D devices can be used in sequence to specify 3D locations. The sound coupling concept can be easily extended to create a 3D *sonic pen*. In one approach, three orthogonal strip microphones are used, as illustrated in Fig. 5.8. Each microphone fixes the position of the stylus on a cylinder of known radius (determined by the "time of flight" of the sound to the microphone) centered on the microphone. The intersection of the three cylinders determines the position of the stylus. The equations of the three cylinders are:

$$x^2 + y^2 = r_z^2, \qquad y^2 + z^2 = r_x^2, \qquad z^2 + x^2 = r_y^2, \tag{5.1}$$

where r_x, r_y, and r_z are the measured radii. Another way to use strip microphones for 3D is to arrange four of them in a square.

An earlier sound-based locator, the *Lincoln Wand* (so named because it was developed at Lincoln Labs), had four point microphones at the corners of the display

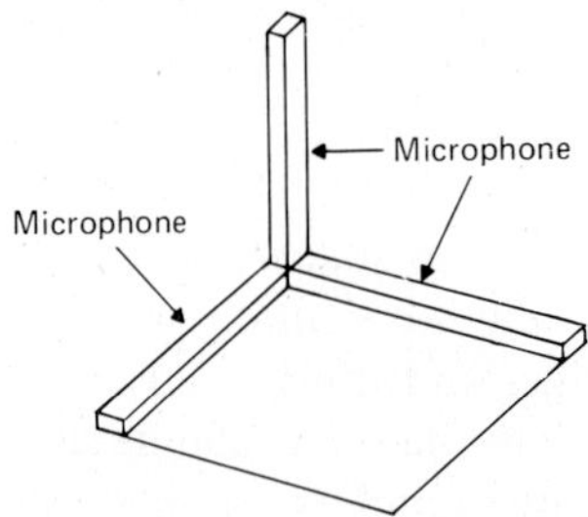

Fig. 5.8 3D sonic tablet.

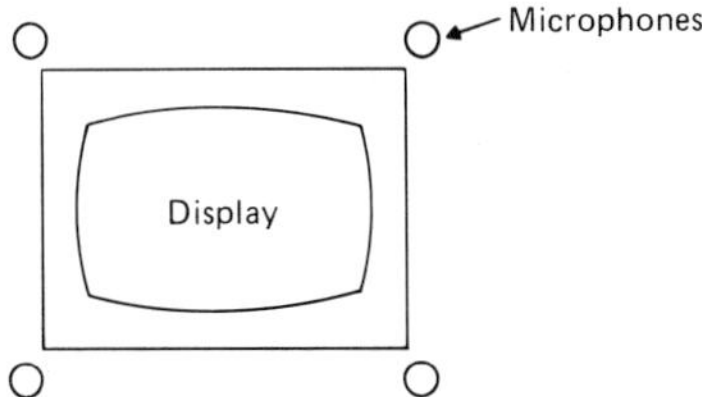

Fig. 5.9 Microphone arrangement for the Lincoln Wand.

area (Fig. 5.9). Again, time of flight is measured, but now the times determine the radii of four spheres. Each sphere is centered on one microphone. (Actually, only three spheres are needed to determine a position; the fourth sphere can be used for error checking or in case the sound path to one microphone is blocked.) The spherical equations are all of the form

$$(x - x_i)^2 + (y - y_i)^2 + (z - z_i)^2 = r_i^2, \qquad i = 1,2,3,4. \tag{5.2}$$

The (x_i, y_i, z_i) are the positions of the four microphones. Solving the equations is left as an exercise for the reader.

Several mechanically coupled 3D locator devices have been developed. One, the *Noll Box* (after its developer, Michael Noll), is just a large box with slide mechanisms allowing the knob to be moved anywhere in a 12-inch cube (Fig. 5.10). The vertical shaft is counterbalanced so that it maintains any established position, and long slide potentiometers are used to record the position along each axis. Another mechanically coupled 3D locator is described in [GEYE75].

These 3D locators all work in relatively small volumes—several cubic feet at most. One of the dreams of computer graphics researchers has been to sense the 3D motion of the user's hands and fingers, so that they can be used to define positions and even shapes in 3D. This has been accomplished through the use of optical coupling between active light sources on the user (light-emitting diodes) and sensors mounted high in the corners of a small room.

Two different sensor mechanisms have been developed [BURT74, FUCH77a]. The sensor is organized to provide the parameters of a plane on which the light source is located. Three sensors defining three planes are therefore sufficient to determine the position of the light source; again, a fourth sensor can be used for error-checking and for cases when one of the light sources is obscured from a sensor. The equations for the planes are of the form:

$$a_{i1}x + a_{i2}y + a_{i3}z + a_{i4} = 0, \qquad i = 1,2,3,4. \tag{5.3}$$

Mechanical, sound, and light coupling to determine 3D positions are subject to noise and obstructions in the work area. The Polhemus Navigation Sciences ROPAMS system generates electromagnetic fields which are detected by a small sensor mounted on a hand or other part of the body. The position and orientation of the sensor can be determined very precisely. This technology is still too expensive for all but experimental use.

Fig. 5.10 3D locator device.

5.2.2 Picks

The only device which is inherently a pick device is the light pen. As we saw in Chapter 3, the pen's output is usually connected to the DPU's control logic, so that the DPU stops executing commands when the pen sees light. The DPU stops with its instruction counter containing the address of the instruction following the one that drew the detected output primitive.*

What will the DPU's X and Y position registers contain if the light-pen "hit" occurred while a vector was being drawn? With an analog vector generator, the endpoints of the vector will be in the registers, because points along the vector are never in digital form. With a digital vector generator (increasingly common with contemporary vector displays), the coordinates of a point on the vector a little past the point seen by the light pen will be in the register, and can be made available to the CPU. These coordinates can be used, for instance, in creating a connecting line somewhere in the middle of an existing line.

*In some high-performance displays, the time for the light pen to halt the DPU may be longer than the time required to draw one or more short vectors or characters, so that the address counter could point to an element further down in the DPU program. Also, the DPU may be pipelined, beginning the processing of one instruction before the preceding one is completed. To get precise pen detects, the graphics package may have to insert graphic "no-op" commands after each group of elements which is to be uniquely identifiable.

The light pen, which implements a logical pick on a vector display, implements a locator on a raster display. When a pixel is detected, the image display system can make the x and y coordinates of the raster scan's current position available to the associated computer.

Figure 5.11 shows several light pens, while Fig. 5.12 shows a cross-section of a light pen and the fundamentals of its associated electronics. The pen's field of view can be controlled by putting different sizes of apertures in front of the lens or by adjusting the lens focus. The switch can be used to enable and disable the light pen. It is shown here as controlling an electrical circuit, but on some pens it is linked to a mechanical shutter. Also, some pens place the photomultiplier tube in the pen barrel and dispense with the fiber optics bundle.

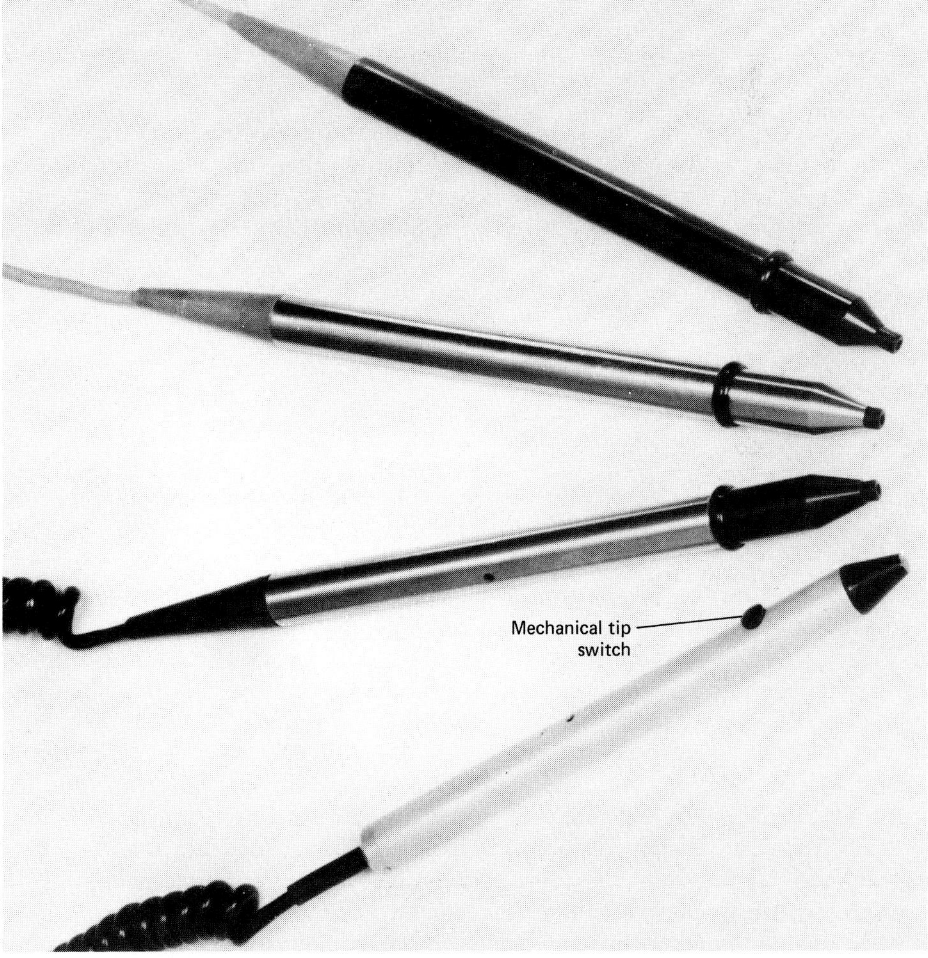

Fig. 5.11 Several light pens. One pen has mechanical tip switch; the others, capacitive.

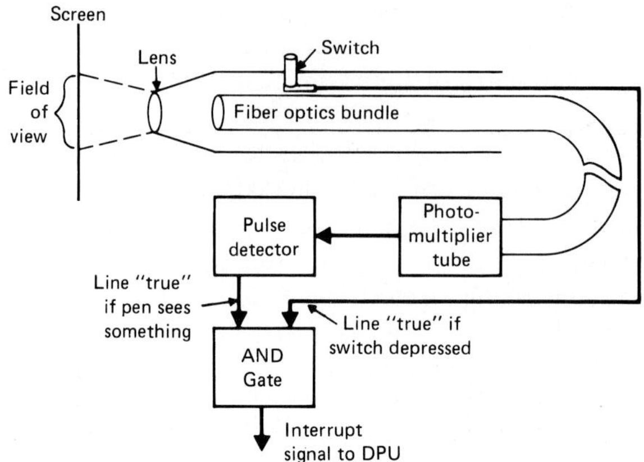

Fig. 5.12 Diagram of light pen.

Light pens were developed very early in the history of interactive computer graphics, originally for use in the SAGE air defense system to point at targets on a radar screen. Unless properly adjusted, light pens may detect false targets, such as fluorescent lights or nearby primitives (e.g., adjacent characters) and fail to detect intended targets. When used over a period of several hours, a pen can be tiring to the user, who must pick it up, point it, and set it down for each use. As a consequence, more and more systems employ the tablet or mouse to simulate the picking capability of a light pen. As raster graphics grows, the popularity of light pens can be expected to decrease even further.

5.2.3 Valuators

Most valuators, devices which provide scalar values, are based on the potentiometer. The volume, balance, and tone controls on a stereo set, for instance, are potentiometers.

Most valuators are rotary potentiometers (dials), typically mounted in a group of eight or ten, as pictured in Fig. 1.14. Rotary potentiometers are especially appropriate for controlling object rotation. Slide potentiometers, in which linear movement replaces rotation, are appropriate for specifying values with no angular interpretation. The current setting of a slide potentiometer is much easier for the user to deduce than that of a rotary potentiometer; unfortunately, most graphics system manufacturers offer only rotary potentiometers. Availability of both types of potentiometers can help users remember what functions are associated with each valuator. When designing a system involving potentiometers, one must be sure to adopt a consistent interpretation for increasing and decreasing values: for instance, clockwise or upward movements normally increase a value.

An analog-to-digital converter and a power supply can determine the potentiometer's position by measuring the voltage $V1$ (Fig. 5.13). The voltage is propor-

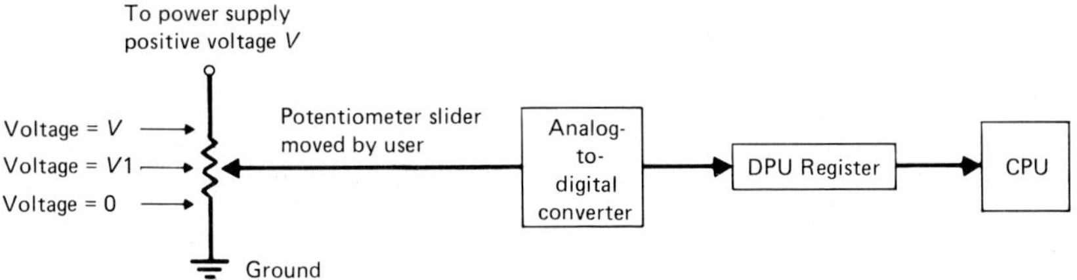

Fig. 5.13 Potentiometer interfaced to DPU.

tional to the amount of the shaft rotation about the corresponding axis. If the converter is properly adjusted, zero rotation will correspond to a digital reading of all zeros, while full rotation will correspond to all ones. We assume that the converted values are placed into DPU device registers which can then be read by the CPU.

For some applications, it is convenient to have the graphics package poll the valuator to see if it has been changed more than some small amount, and then to generate an event which is placed on the graphics package event queue. This means the application program need not monitor the valuator via a polling loop to see if it has changed. Both programmer effort and CPU time are saved by supporting polling at the lower, more efficient level. Notice too that the same technique could be applied to locator devices.

5.2.4 Keyboards

The alphanumeric keyboard is our prototype (and only) text device. Several different technologies are used to detect a key depression: some of these are mechanical contact closure, change in capacitance, and magnetic coupling. The important functional characteristic of a keyboard device is that it creates a code (ASCII, EBCDIC, etc.) uniquely corresponding to a depressed key.

There are many factors which make one keyboard preferable to another: interkey spacing, slope of the keyboard, shape of the key caps, pressure needed to depress a key, and a feeling of contact when a key is fully depressed. Many keyboard design issues are summarized in [KLEM71] and [KROE72]. Other considerations, dealing not with hardware but with software design, are making frequently used delimiter or correction keys easily reachable *without* the need to simultaneously depress the control or shift keys, and separating dangerous keys (such as line delete) from other frequently used keys (such as return).

5.2.5 Buttons

The *programmed function keyboard* (PFK) is the most common button device. It is sometimes built as a separate unit, but more often the buttons are integrated with a keyboard. Other button devices are the keys found on many tablet cursors and on the "mouse." Buttons are generally used to enter commands or menu options to a graphics program. Dedicated-purpose systems can use buttons with permanent labels. To allow changing or "soft" labels, some PFKs can be used with coded overlays on which command names are printed. The presence or absence of tabs on the edge of the overlay is sensed, so the system knows which overlay is in place. The operator inserts the overlay containing the desired command and then depresses the appropriate button. Knowlton's keyboard, which uses mirrors to superimpose labels from a CRT on top of an unlabeled keyboard, provides a more general sort of soft label capability [KNOW75]. Another way to have soft labels is by having the buttons at the edge of the view surface, allowing labels to be displayed.

How does a button device differ from a text device? The text device provides input from buttons which are prelabeled. The button device keys have no predefined character meanings, and the number of keys may vary from one to many. Further, some button devices report button releases as well as button depresses. This makes it easy to start an activity (such as rotation of a displayed object) when a button is depressed and then to terminate the activity when the button is released. One can consider the text device to be a special type of button device, but because text devices are so common, we give them a separate identity.

Another button device is the *chord keyboard.* It has just five keys shaped like thin piano keys (Fig. 5.14). The device is operated by depressing several keys at once, thus "playing a chord." With five keys, 31 chords can be generated. Learning the chords takes much time, but skilled users can "play" quite rapidly, since the hand can stay in one place, resting on a table; this allows fast "touch typing" which is much harder with a standard PFK. However, chord keyboards are *not* suitable substitutes for the standard alphanumeric keyboard [KLEM71].

5.2.6 Nontraditional Devices

A number of other interaction devices are useful for graphics systems but do not easily fit into the categories we have used. For instance, speech recognizers can be used to input commands, values, etc., and are available in versions recognizing from 10 to over 1000 words. Words are defined as discrete utterances preceded and followed by 100 to 200-millisecond pauses. Continuous speech recognition, on the other hand, is mostly still in the research stage [KAPL80], although a few commercial systems have appeared.

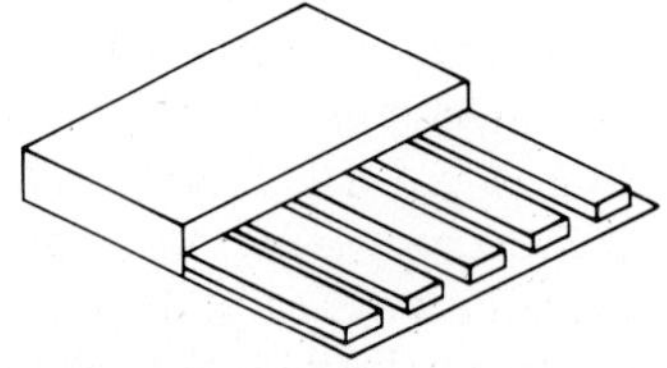

Fig. 5.14 Chord keyboard.

Most word recognizers are trained to the characteristics of an individual's speech. A word is filtered into several frequency bands. Patterns in the relative loudness of the sound of each band are matched against a dictionary of such patterns. Training the recognizer consists of establishing a dictionary of such patterns by having the user speak each word several times. Once established, a dictionary can be saved for later use. However, if a user has a cold, retraining is necessary. Speaker-independent recognizers are limited to 10 or 20 words, typically including the digits 0–9.

The converse of speech input is speech output from digitized patterns, which is eminently usable for prompts, feedback, and error messages. Synthesizers have become quite common and inexpensive and are found in several contemporary home computers. Texas Instruments' *Speak and Spell* "toy" exemplifies the capabilities becoming available. In general, we expect the use of speech input-output to increase enormously during this decade because it is natural, easy, and fast, and requires no manual dexterity.

5.3 TECHNIQUES FOR SIMULATING LOGICAL DEVICES

Many graphics programs have a need for locator, pick, valuator, keyboard and button devices, but in many graphics systems not all of these physical devices are available. It is possible, however, to provide the logical function of any of these devices with a device from any other class, although some of the simulations can be rather awkward. On the other hand, we are not advocating that separate physical devices should always be made available for each of the required logical devices. Many very easily used interactive systems have only a positioning device (usually a mouse or tablet), a keyboard, and sometimes a few special-purpose function buttons on the keyboard. These three physical devices are used to implement all the logical devices. Our purpose in the following sections is to describe some of the more common and useful input device simulations. More extensive descriptions and human factors evaluations of these techniques are found in [EMBE81, FOLE81a].

Sometimes the implementations are part of the graphics package. For example, since a direct-view storage tube cannot be used with a light pen, the cross-hair cursor locator is used as a pick: the cursor is placed on top of the item to be picked. Then, when the user depresses any key, its character code and the cursor position are sent to the CPU. That position is then compared against the positions of all displayed items to find which item is closest. In other cases, the implementation will be part of the application program. One can consider the light button menu selection used in Chapter 2 to be an implementation of a button device by a pick device.

Graphics packages such as GPGS and the Core System define all five types of devices to be available and guarantee that a reasonable implementation will be provided by the package if the corresponding physical device is not available. "Reasonable" here means (a) approximately the best that can be done with the given input tools, but (b) typically less user-friendly and convenient, i.e., more time-consuming, and (c) logically identical, so that the application program is unaware of the physical realization. This promotes program portability, but does remove control of some of the detailed, low-level interaction techniques from the application programmer. Also, certain implementations may require considerable CPU intervention, for example when simulating interrupting logical devices by using polling loops. Nevertheless, it is very cost-effective to be able to debug an application on an inexpensive storage tube, one of many in an installation, prior to running the program in production mode on one of the few more expensive high-performance displays.

5.3.1 Locator Device Simulations

Light pen. The light pen is frequently used as a locator on a vector display. A tracking cross is initially displayed somewhere on the CRT screen (Fig. 5.15). To indicate a position, the light pen is first pointed at the cross and is then used to "move" it to the desired position. This is made possible by a feedback loop which continually (each refresh cycle) moves the cross so that it is always under the light pen. The light pen's new position, at which the tracking cross is displayed, is calculated by determining which dots on the previous tracking cross were just within the pen's field of view, as in Fig. 5.16. The new center position is found by averaging the x and y coordinates of each point detected by the pen.

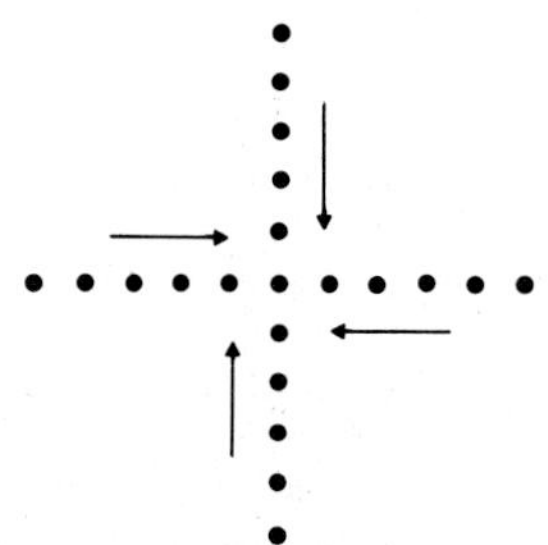

Fig. 5.15 Light-pen tracking cross: arrows show order of display. Typical height and width are one inch.

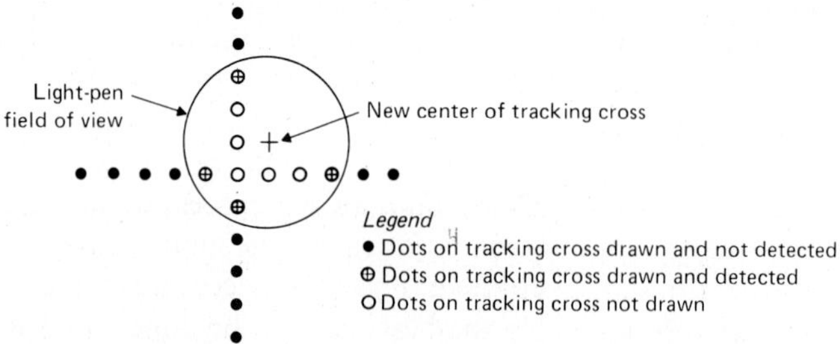

Fig. 5.16 Example of tracking.

If no points on the cross are detected, tracking has been *lost*. This can happen accidentally (if the user moves the pen faster than the tracking algorithm can move the cross) or intentionally (if the user moves the pen away from the CRT). In the latter case, the user may be indicating that the tracking cross is at its final position and that it is desired to proceed to the next interaction step.

When tracking is lost, the display system can automatically attempt to reestablish tracking to determine whether the tracking loss was accidental or intentional, that is, to try to find where the light pen is now. If the pen really has been moved away from the screen, it will not be found, and the system knows that the loss of tracking was intentional. One way to reestablish tracking is to draw a square spiral of points around the last known pen position, until the entire screen has been covered or the pen has been found, as is shown in Fig. 5.17. Another technique is to do what is effectively a raster scan of the entire screen, with scan-line spacing just slightly less than the diameter of the pen's field of vision. If the pen is still pointed at the screen, a scan line will be detected. If the vectors are drawn digitally, the detected coordinates will be immediately available, while with analog vector generators, a finer search along the scan line must be initiated in order to find the pen's horizontal position. A third approach is the *character blast*—filling the screen with consecutive characters (or points, or short lines), and stopping when one is seen by the pen. Notice that all three of these techniques can be used independently of pen-tracking to determine where on the screen the pen currently is.

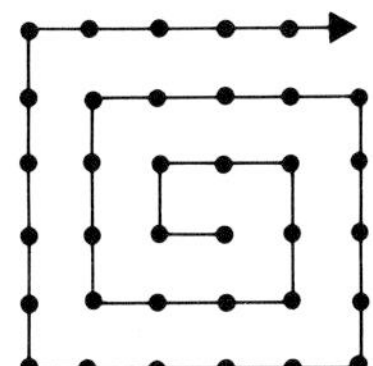

Fig. 5.17 Spiral of points used to re-establish pen tracking.

It is important that the tracking algorithm be able to move the cross at a reasonable speed, so that tracking is not easily lost. The maximum distance the cross can move per iteration of the algorithm is the length of an arm on the cross. The diagonal distance will be less. If the arms of the cross are one inch from end to end, and the cross is repositioned 30 times a second, then the maximum horizontal or vertical velocity at which the cross can be moved is 15 inches per second (one half inch per step).

One way to decrease the probability of losing tracking is to increase the speed at which the cross can move, by predicting where the pen will be during the next cycle on the basis of where it has been during the last two or three cycles. Then the cross is placed at this predicted position rather than at the position calculated by the simple averaging method described above. In the prediction it is assumed that the pen moves with constant velocity. Thus at refresh cycle $i + 1$, the cross is placed not at the position calculated during step i, but rather at the position found by linear extrapolation from the positions of the cross at steps $i - 1$ and i, as shown in Fig. 5.18.

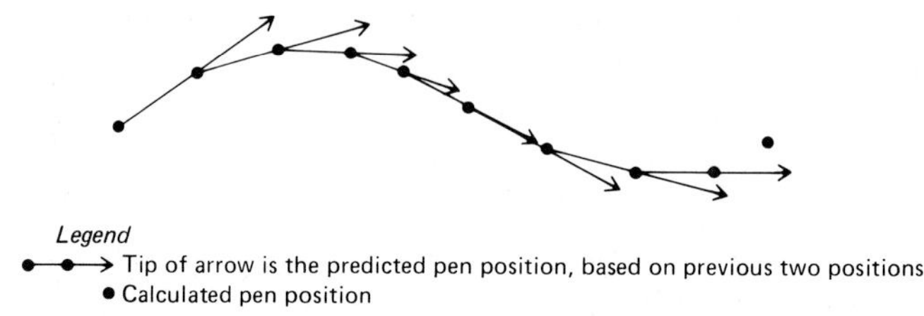
Legend
Tip of arrow is the predicted pen position, based on previous two positions
Calculated pen position

Fig. 5.18 First-order light-pen tracking prediction.

Cursor control from keyboard. A locator can also be simulated by four keys on a keyboard which control cursor movements going up, down, left, and right. Some keyboards have specially designated keys for this purpose. Holding a key down might cause rapid continuous motion of the cursor, while a quick key depression might cause only a unit move (a unit being no less than the unit of display resolution). Rapid positioning is facilitated by allowing the cursor's speed to increase as long as the key is down: when the key is released, the cursor should stop.

Position type-in. We can always simulate a locator by typing the position or orientation coordinates on a keyboard. This obviously works, but the user is forced into a very analytic approach in which desired visual results must be translated into numbers. Also, the immediate feedback of smooth dynamic position or rotation is replaced by long interaction cycles, each ending with a static display presentation. With a storage display lacking local refresh, this is the best one can expect. Otherwise, this method is very painful unless the coordinates are already precisely specified.

5.3.2 Pick Device Simulations

Cursor pick. Picks are most commonly simulated with a physical locator—tablet, mouse, etc.—with which the user moves the screen cursor to the object of interest and then pushes a button. The graphics package then searches through the (pseudo) display file for the segment closest to the cursor position. This technique is especially attractive if one of the several buttons on the mouse or tablet cursor is used to trigger the search: each button can have a different meaning, such as select, delete, move, rotate, etc. Of course too many buttons can become confusing, in which case the locator can also be used for menu selection.

The search process can be done in several ways, one of which was discussed in Chapter 4. Another is to extend the graphics package correlation table to include the *screen extent* of each segment. This screen extent is just an upright rectangle surrounding the image of a segment, and thus can be defined by $(x_{min}, x_{max}, y_{min}, y_{max})$. In the rest of this section we refer to it simply as an extent. Use of the correlation table is simple: given the simulated pick device position (x_p, y_p), search the table for all segments such that:

$$x_{min} < x_p < x_{max} \qquad \text{and} \qquad y_{min} < y_p < y_{max}.$$

If only one segment satisfies the conditions, we are done. Otherwise, further processing is needed. Figure 5.19 shows why several segments might satisfy the test conditions. There are of course many cases when segments will not overlap, such as with light button symbols in a menu.

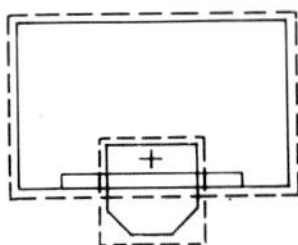

Fig. 5.19 Overlapping extents for the chair and desk symbols.

If the extents of several segments do overlap, what then? The next step is to consider the individual output primitives that make up each of the segments whose extents overlap. This will generally be a small fraction of all segments. The notion of extents can again be used, this time for individual primitives. Consider the point at (x_p, y_p) in Fig. 5.20. The extent is defined by $x_{min} = x_p - d$, $x_{max} = x_p + d$, $y_{min} = y_p - d$, and $y_{max} = y_p + d$. This extent could also be stored in a correlation table or could be computed each time it is needed by reinterpreting the DPU program. The *tolerance factor d* is chosen to allow for some reasonable amount of inaccuracy in positioning the cursor. The greater d, the less precise the user need be, but the greater the possibility that several points might be within range of the simulated pick device.

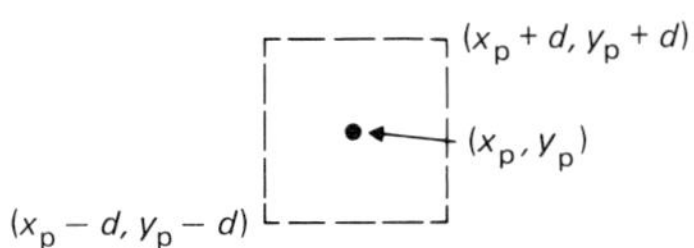

Fig. 5.20 Point extent.

For the line from $(x1, y1)$ to $(x2, y2)$ shown in Fig. 5.21, the extent is defined by

$$x_{min} = \min(x1, x2) - d, \qquad x_{max} = \max(x1, x2) + d,$$
$$y_{min} = \min(y1, y2) - d, \qquad y_{max} = \max(y1, y2) + d.$$

If the application program needs to know whether an endpoint of the line or the line itself is being picked, it is simple enough first to compare the simulated pick device's position to the extents surrounding the points $(x1, y1)$ and $(x2, y2)$. Only if the endpoint comparison fails is the line comparison made.

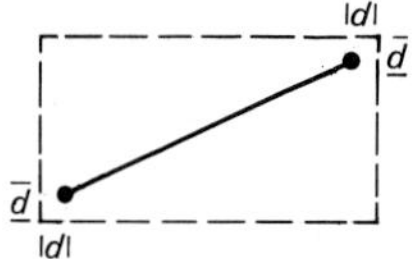

Fig. 5.21 Line extent.

This second screening, which compares the extent of each primitive to (x_p, y_p), can also fail if there are overlapping primitive extents (Fig. 5.22). When this is the case, the final step is to determine more precisely which of the primitives is closest to the simulated pick device. For a point (x,y) this is simple:

$$D^2 = (x_p - x)^2 + (y_p - y)^2. \tag{5.4}$$

Since only comparisons of relative distances are of interest (to find which of the selected points is actually closest to (x, y)), taking the square root of this equation is unnecessary: squared distances can be compared to find a minimum just as well as the distances themselves.

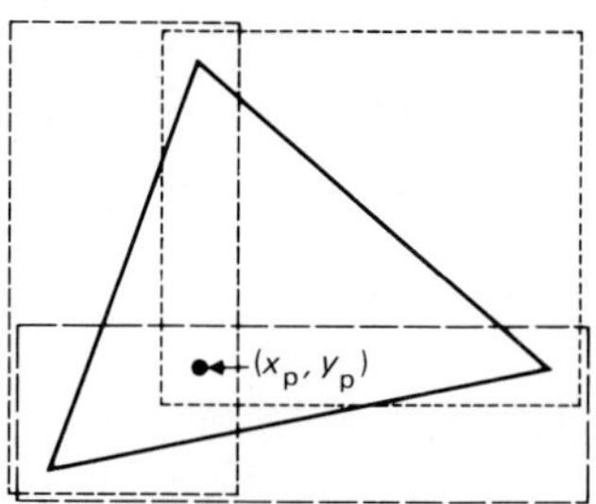

Fig. 5.22 Overlapping extents for three lines, each in separate segments.

Calculating the shortest distance from a line to a point P takes several multiplications and divisions. It is equivalent to first finding the point P' on the line which is nearest P, and then finding the distance between P and P'. One approximation is to use the minimum of the horizontal and vertical distances from the locator position to the line; this is easier to compute, but can be incorrect by $\sqrt{2}$. Forming the sum of squares to calculate D^2 can itself be time-consuming, particularly if done on a computer which lacks multiplication hardware. An excellent approximation [PIZE75] to D (not D^2) is given by:

$$\frac{|x_p - x| + |y_p - y| + 2*\max(|x_p - x|, |y_p - y|)}{3}. \tag{5.5}$$

Its average error is only about 3.5%, and its maximum error is only slightly greater than 5%—quite acceptable for the approximation's intended use. Because only comparisons between distances will be made, the division by 3 need not be performed. Thus the calculation of this approximation can be faster than that of D^2.

Whatever method is used, we compute distances from each output primitive to the simulated pick position. The first primitive found to be within d of the position is reported as having been picked. If no such primitive is found, no pick is reported.

This three-step screening process avoids detailed examination of most segments and output primitives which are far from the simulated pick's position by first examining segment extents, then primitive extents, and finally actual distances. Another approach, simpler to implement but slower in execution, examines each output primitive. The basic idea is to clip each output primitive against a small *pick window,* measuring $2d$ on a side. The first output primitive which passes through the pick window is "detected." DPUs with hardware windowing can use this approach to great advantage. As discussed in Chapter 9, extents can also be used to speed up the clipping process, by determining whether the extent and pick window overlap. Garrett reviews several of these methods in detail [GARR80a].

Many physical devices can be used to move a screen cursor to a desired target either in order to simulate a pick or as a locator. Which one is best? In a 1978 experiment, Card, English, and Burr found that a mouse is faster than an isometric joystick or cursor control keys in selecting characters and character groups from a full-page display [CARD78]. They also showed that the time to move the cursor corresponds to *Fitts' law,* which predicts that the time is proportional to the log of the ratio of the distance moved to the size of the target. The (not surprising) implication of this finding is that pick targets, be they light buttons or symbols, should be made as large as possible.

In a 1967 experiment by English, Engelbart, and Berman, the mouse was also found superior to a light pen and joystick [ENGL67]. In 1975 Goodwin found the lightpen superior to cursor control keys on a keyboard [GOOD75]. Mehr and Mehr found the trackball superior to joysticks with and without spring return and to isometric joysticks [MEHR72]. While one must be careful in generalizing experimental results, the mouse certainly ranks high and the joystick low, over the range of devices studied.

Name type-in. Yet another way to simulate a pick is to assign and display names with each segment or other logical grouping of output primitives. The user then types in the name of interest. This technique is found in several commercial drafting systems; however, it is slower than the cursor pick simulation and is susceptible to typing errors. Ease of use is enhanced if the names are assigned by the user, so that they are natural to the application rather than contrived.

Successive intensification. Three buttons can simulate a pick. In this technique, each pickable entity is successively increased in intensity for a short period. When the entity to be picked brightens, the user activates one button. However, in the brief moment between the entity's brightening and the button activation, several subsequent entities are likely to have brightened, so the second button is depressed to reverse the brightening sequence, one step at a time. When the correct entity is again brightened, the third button is depressed to make the pick. This simulation has been applied successfully to pick a single molecular bond from several thousand on the screen—a case where the proximity of individual bonds precludes use of any other method. It is also appropriate with stereoscopic three-dimensional displays, as discussed in Chapter 14 [ORTO71].

5.3.3 Valuator Simulations

In graphics applications, the user must often enter numeric values which are unrelated to world coordinates. A resistor's value, Young's modulus for a beam, and a shock absorber's damping factor are all examples.

Locator axis. A single axis of a joystick, tablet, or other locator device can simulate a low-resolution valuator. Thornton has shown how to use a tablet to simulate a valuator of essentially infinite range [THOR79].

Value type-in. A value can be directly entered from a keyboard, possibly in scientific notation for very large or very small values.

Dial interaction. One of the variety of dials and scales illustrated in Fig. 5.23 can be displayed. A pick, perhaps simulated with a locator, is then used to manipulate the dial in various ways, such as dragging the pointer to a new position or picking a new tickmark on a scale. The utility of any of these valuators is often enhanced by echoing in numeric form whatever value is currently indicated. All such gauges or dials should be laid out in a natural way: we normally associate left-to-right, bottom-to-top, or clockwise movement with increasing values, and the opposite directions with decreasing values.

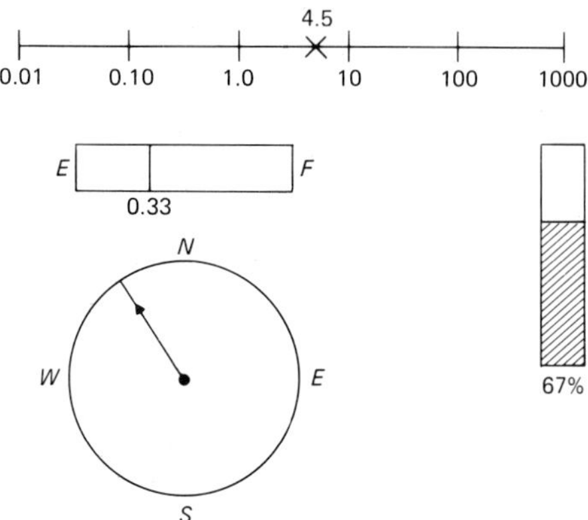

Fig. 5.23 Dials and scales.

5.3.4 Keyboard Simulations

Pattern recognition. Character recognizers have been used with interactive graphics since the early 1960s [BROW64, TEIT64]. Program and data typically occupy less than four Kbytes: several commercial microprocessor-based implementations exist. A simplified adaptation of *Teitelman's recognizer* [TEIT64], developed by Ledeen, is described in [NEWM79]. Recognition is done by comparing characteristic *features* (slopes, points of inflection, quadrants crossed, etc.) of characters drawn with a locator against a stored dictionary of each character's features. The recognizers can be trained to recognize different styles of block printing: the parameters of each feature are calculated from sample characters drawn by the user.

The rate at which we print is relatively slow compared to typing or writing in script—it is difficult to block print more than two or three characters a second (try it!), so recognition would not be appropriate for massive input of text. We can write script faster than we can print, but there are as yet no simple algorithms to recognize continuous script.

Keyboard menu. A menu of characters can be displayed and selected with a pick device. This technique is slow and can be considered only for very short character sequences or for operators who are known to be poor typists. The menu need not be on the screen: a keyboard can be printed on a tablet, and the tablet stylus can then be used to point at sequences of characters. This latter technique can also be used for commands, given that they change infrequently.

5.3.5 Button Simulations

Pattern recognizers. A powerful application of a locator is to recognize certain movement patterns as button activations, as illustrated in Fig. 5.24 for a queueing analysis system [IRAN71]: the eight different motions are easily recognized by a

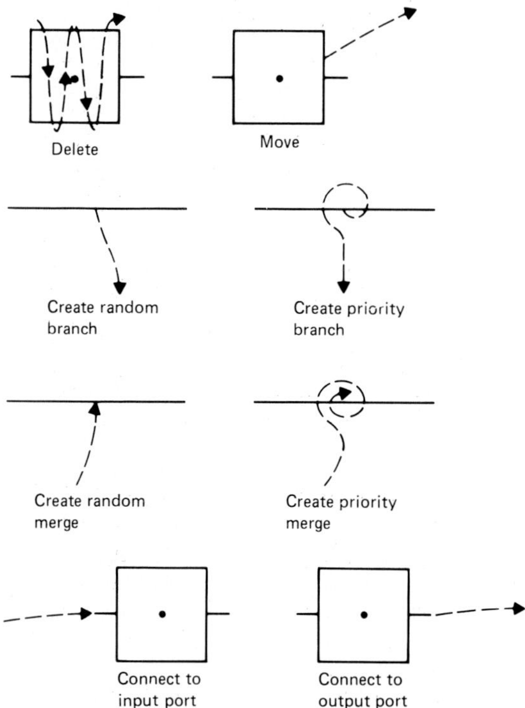

Fig. 5.24 Motions recognized as commands.

simple algorithm. Some of the meanings in this example are specialized to queueing networks, while others are quite general. A design drafting system made by Applicon recognizes several dozen such motions. The technique is especially attractive because the motion is normally performed on top of the object to be operated upon or at the position where something is to be placed, so that several parts of a complete command are input to the system at once. There are commercially available *intelligent tablets* with built-in microprocessors to recognize patterns and characters.

Menus. The menu, used in Chapter 2, is a common button simulation. The command menu contains character strings, while the furniture menu uses *icons,* or symbols, representing the various pieces of furniture. Command menus can use icons too: a straight arrow can indicate translation, a curved arrow can indicate rotation, a red paintbrush can mean MAKE IT RED.

Menus are a very important interaction technique, because memorization of command names or options is replaced by recognition. Icons are appropriate if they can be recognized more quickly than equivalent text. For example, the Xerox Star office automation workstation uses symbolic representations of in and out baskets, printers, file folders, and documents. To print a report, the user simply selects the icon for the report and moves it on top of the printer icon [SEYB81].

Menus can contain many selections. In the limit, the entire screen may be taken to show the menu (Fig. 5.25). This has devastating effects on visual continuity and maintenance of a sense of "place" in the interaction dialogue, because the visual context is lost each time the menu is shown. An abbreviated, terser menu (Fig. 5.26) is generally preferable, although the entries can be harder to understand. A *static* menu is always displayed in the same position on the screen and may or may not appear at all times. A *dynamic* (pop-up) menu appears on the screen at different locations, typically wherever the screen cursor (controlled by a tablet or other locator) happens to be. The presumption is that the operator's eyes will be on the screen cursor, so the dynamic menu is displayed there to minimize hand and eye movements.

Dynamic menus are easily implemented with raster displays: the menu replaces a rectangular part of the displayed image. With a vector display, the menu may be on top of the image, causing confusion. There are conflicting reports on the advantages of static versus dynamic menus: static menus allow use of "muscle memory" to position the pen or tablet and don't cause drastic changes to the display, while dynamic menus usually are displayed where the operator is looking, and thus visual search is minimized.

SET ENDPOINTS
SET INPUT VALUES
ORIENTATION–WITHOUT FORCE
ORIENTATION–WITH FORCE
DIRECT LINEAR FORCE
INVERSE LINEAR FORCE
DIRECT SQUARE FORCE
INVERSE SQUARE FORCE
DIRECT CUBE FORCE
INVERSE CUBE FORCE
VELOCITY DEPENDENT FORCE
PERPENDICULAR VELOCITY DEPENDENT FORCE
ARBITRARY CHARGE DISTRIBUTION
CAPACITOR
DIODE
TRIODE
NUCLEAR FORCE
TWO PLANETS
PLANE CAPACITOR
CYLINDRICAL CAPACITOR
SPHERICAL CAPACITOR
METER–FINE
METER–COARSE
SET INPUT VALUES
CHANGE PROPORTIONALITY CONSTANT
DOUBLE PROPORTIONALITY CONSTANT
HALVE PROPORTIONALITY CONSTANT
REPULSIVE FORCE
ATTRACTIVE FORCE
FIND POSITION OF GROPE DEVICE
TERMINATE

Fig. 5.25 Full-screen menu (Foley and Wallace, Proc.IEEE, Vol. 62, No. 4, 1974).

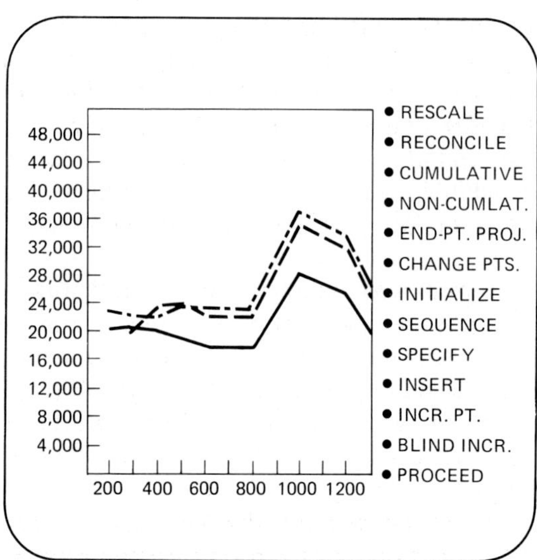

Fig. 5.26 Abbreviated menu (Foley and Wallace, Proc. IEEE, Vol. 62, No. 4, 1974).

Command type-in. Command names can be typed on a keyboard. A shorthand, useful both for poor typists and to minimize input, is used to display the commands with numbers: only the number is typed. Abbreviations can be used: they should be easy to remember, and preferably be of uniform length. The simplest rule for forming abbreviations is "fixed length," with "shortest unambiguous" abbreviations also being accepted.

5.4 INTERACTION TECHNIQUES

Interaction techniques are higher-level functions implemented through the basic devices and device simulations we have already discussed. These techniques, which are general, application-independent ways of interacting with a computer, are routinely used in many graphics application programs. The devices, device simulations, and interaction techniques are the basic building blocks from which complete interactive dialogues are designed.

5.4.1 Construction Techniques

We think of picture construction as the process of creating (or modifying) a model of an object whose image we are viewing. Common operations in this process are defining points and lines, and moving, rotating, or scaling objects. We manipulate the object by indirectly manipulating its physical appearance on the screen. *Drag-*

ging, a technique of dynamically moving an object around with a locator, was used in Chapter 2 to position furniture symbols. The locator is read frequently, preferably each refresh cycle, and its position is used to reposition the displayed object. With a vector display, the repositioning is effected relatively easily by manipulating the DPU program. The task is not quite so easy with a raster display, but can be done in a way discussed in Chapter 12. Dragging an image stored on a direct-view storage tube is impossible without using write-through mode and a refresh buffer, as found in the Tektronix 4054.

An extension of dragging is dynamic scaling and rotation of objects to a desired size and orientation. In 2D this requires that two valuators be continually read and their values used to control size and angle. Of course, if horizontal and vertical size are to be controlled simultaneously, or if a model of a 3D object is being developed, more valuators will be needed. The application of *image transformations* to clipped primitives is discussed in Chapter 8, while *geometric transformations* of world coordinate objects are discussed in Chapter 7.

Because the orientation of some complex 3D objects is difficult to perceive in a 2D projection, a *gnomon* may be used to show the orientation of the principal axes, as in Fig. 5.27. The gnomon helps facilitate 3D rotation tasks.

Lines are often constructed by *rubberbanding.* With the push of a button, the starting point of a line is read from a locator and a line is drawn from this starting point to wherever the screen cursor is positioned by the locator. As the cursor moves, so moves the line endpoint. Another push of a button or even better, release of the button depressed to start rubberbanding, and the locator is no longer coupled to the endpoint. Tablets which use a stylus with a tip switch work especially well here, as the starting and ending button pushes can come from the stylus itself. Figure 5.28 illustrates a rubberband sequence.

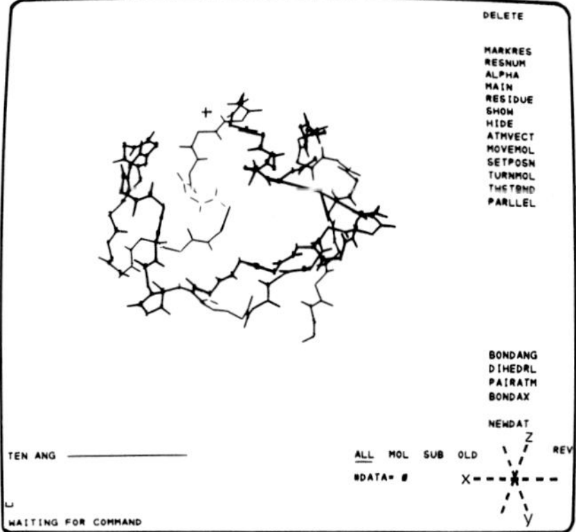

Fig. 5.27 Gnomon (lower right) helps show orientation of molecule (picture taken on Wright's GRIP system [WRIG72]).

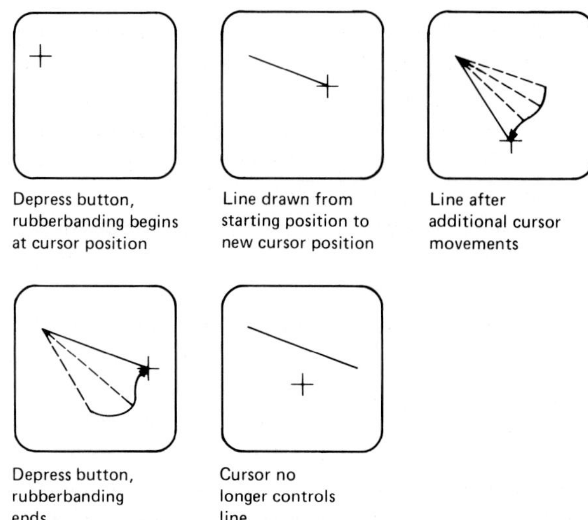
Depress button,
rubberbanding begins
at cursor position
Line drawn from
starting position to
new cursor position
Line after
additional cursor
movements
Depress button,
rubberbanding
ends
Cursor no
longer controls
line

Fig. 5.28 Rubberband line drawing.

Constraints can be applied to the line resulting from rubberbanding. Figure 5.29 shows a sequence of lines drawn by using the same cursor positions as in Fig. 5.28 but with a horizontal constraint in effect. A vertical line, or a line at some other orientation, can also be drawn in this way, as can part of a circle, ellipse, or any other curve: the curve is initialized at some position, then cursor movements control how much of the curve is displayed. In general, the locator position is used as input to a constraint function which forces the appropriate feedback to be generated.

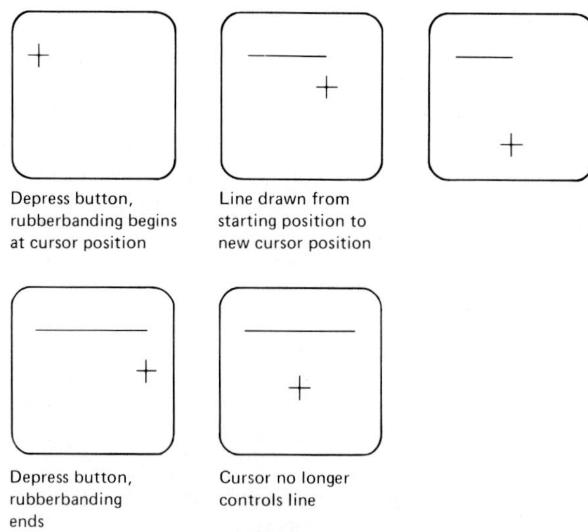
Depress button,
rubberbanding begins
at cursor position
Line drawn from
starting position to
new cursor position
Depress button,
rubberbanding
ends
Cursor no longer
controls line

Fig. 5.29 Horizontally constrained rubberband line drawing.

Another form of constraint, applied not only in rubberbanding, is *gridding*. All endpoints of lines, etc., are constrained to fall on a grid of points (sometimes displayed as lines or dots). Gridding helps generate drawings with a neat appearance. To enforce gridding, the application program simply rounds locator coordinates to the nearest grid point. Gridding usually is applied in world coordinates. Thus the spacing of grid lines displayed on the view surface will depend on the window-to-viewport mapping. While grids are often regular and span the entire display, irregular grids, different grids in different areas, and rotated grids are all useful in creating figures and illustrations [FEIN81].

When constructing drawings, one frequently wants a new line to begin at the endpoint of or on an existing line. Positioning a cursor at such an exact point can be difficult unless gridding is in use. The difficulty is avoided by placing a programmed *gravity field* around each existing line, so that the cursor is attracted to the line as soon as it enters the gravity field. Figure 5.30 shows a line with a gravity field. The field is larger around the line's endpoints, so that matching of endpoints is especially easy. As with light-pen picking, a cluttered display makes the use of this technique difficult. A gravity field can be implemented through an approach similar to that described for simulating a pick with a locator. The tolerance factor is simply made larger for endpoints than for lines.

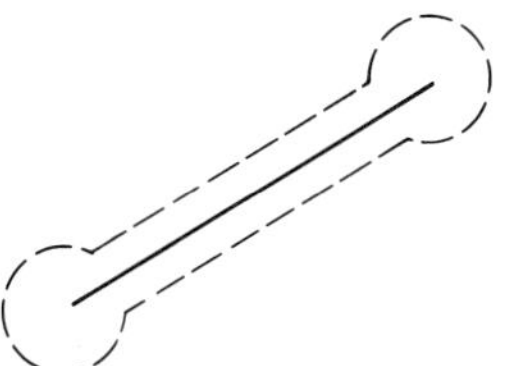

Fig. 5.30 Line surrounded by gravity field.

It is sometimes necessary to trace or draw freehand a curve or contour. *Sketching* is a technique in which a trail of lines is "sketched" along the path of a cursor, as though one were drawing a line with a pencil. In *discrete* sketching, the user pushes a button each time one line is to end and the next is to start, as in Fig. 5.31. This allows specific points to be connected by straight lines. If smooth curves are desired, then

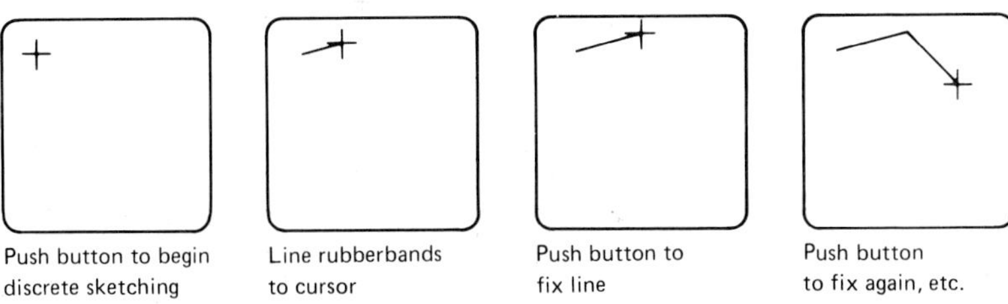

Push button to begin discrete sketching
Line rubberbands to cursor
Push button to fix line
Push button to fix again, etc.

Fig. 5.31 Discrete sketching.

continuous sketching is used. With this technique, no explicit user action is required to terminate one line and start another: a series of short lines approximating a smooth curve is displayed along the path of the cursor, as in Fig. 5.32. More short lines are used where the radius of curvature is small, to give a smoother appearance.

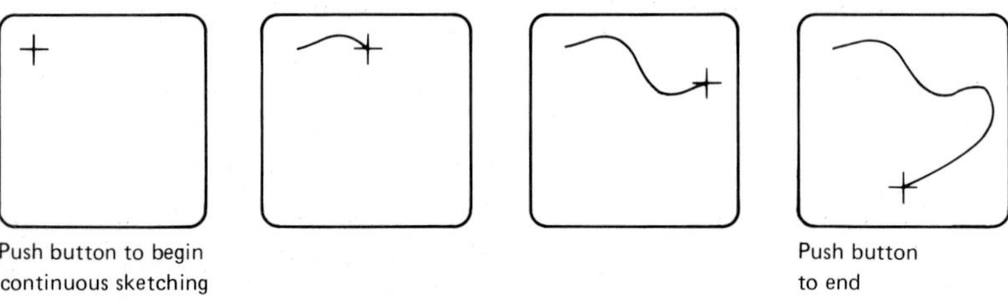
Push button to begin continuous sketching
Push button to end

Fig. 5.32 Continuous sketching.

Dragging dynamically moves a selected symbol from one position to another, under control of a locator, as in Fig. 5.33. Typically, a button is pushed to start the dragging (in some cases it may be possible to have the button push also do the selecting), and then either another button push or a release of the button freezes the symbol in place, so that further movements of the locator have no effect on the symbol.

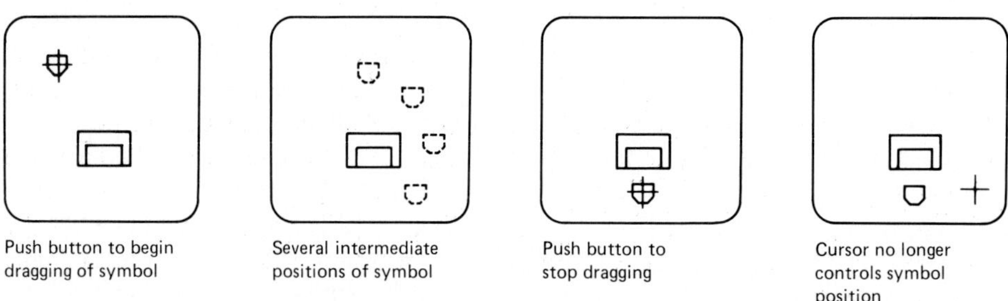
Push button to begin dragging of symbol
Several intermediate positions of symbol
Push button to stop dragging
Cursor no longer controls symbol position

Fig. 5.33 Dragging a symbol into position.

All of these construction techniques make heavy use of immediate dynamic feedback, which can be provided only if the computer can give rapid and regular service or if the DPU has sufficient computation capability to provide the feedback on its own (see Chapter 10). This can easily be done with a small personal computer, but is often difficult with a timeshared computer. In the absence of dynamic feedback, slower and more cumbersome interaction techniques are used. For instance, rubberbanding is replaced by the capability to specify the line's endpoints, see the line drawn, and then respecify one or both of the endpoints if the line is unsatisfactory. Respecifying can continue until the results are satisfactory. In essence, the dynamic feedback of rubberbanding is replaced by a much slower and less satisfactory static feedback. Consequently, the user either takes longer to complete construction tasks or produces less satisfactory results.

5.4.2 Command Techniques

We saw, in Chapter 2, the use of menus and programmed function keyboards for command entry. Many real-world applications have dozens and even hundreds of different commands—many more than can be displayed in a menu or assigned to the 16 or 32 buttons on a PFK. This plethora of commands can be dealt with by grouping them into different *phases,* or *modes.* Each phase contains a group of logically related commands, or *subphases,* which are further groupings of commands.

If a PFK is used for command entry, then the commands for each phase can be associated with a separate overlay. Designing phases which are made up of logically related commands should help minimize the frequency with which overlays need to be changed. If the application has a small nucleus of often-used commands, they should be made available in each phase and should be invoked by the same key on each overlay. Naturally, the name of the current phase or subphase should be prominently displayed, so that the operator can easily remember the context in which commands will be performed. The method of changing from one mode to another needs to be simple and obvious.

If a menu is used for command entry, then the "main" or highest-level menu will be used to select a phase. Then a second menu, with all commands in the selected phase, is shown. Several levels of phases and subphases can be used if needed: in some application programs there are as many as four or five levels in the *command hierarchy* (tree) defined by the phases. This means that four or five successive menu selections must be made in order to actually specify a command. Hierarchical menu selection can be slow and tedious for experienced users if successive menus are not displayed nearly instantaneously. One possible alternative is to allow any command name to be typed at the keyboard, whether or not it is in the currently displayed menu: now new users can pick from a menu while experienced ones can use the keyboard-oriented method. Powerful personal computers can display menus quickly, so the keyboard alternative is less attractive unless the user's hands are already on the keyboard.

5.4.3 Picking Techniques

An important part of many graphics interaction sequences is selecting the displayed object to be operated upon. Often, picks are used with a hierarchical object structure, allowing the user to pick a basic object (like a house window), a collection of basic objects (a house made up of several windows, walls, and a roof), or perhaps a collection of collections (several houses).

A pick device has no inherent notion of hierarchy, yet the user's intent must somehow be made known to the application program. One way to achieve this goal is to design the interaction commands so that the level of object to be operated on can be inferred without explicit operator action. For example, in a phase having to do with placing houses in a subdivision, the entire house would be designated, while in a phase for designing individual houses, the house components would be selected.

If the intent is not implicit, then the command language must provide the user with explicit means for conveying his purpose. Commands like MOVE WINDOW and MOVE HOUSE illustrate such means. On the other hand, if the hierarchical level at which the user operates changes relatively infrequently, it is more convenient to have a separate command which sets the level at which all ensuing picks will be made. The user respecifies the level whenever necessary.

Another approach is required if the number of hierarchical levels of objects is unknown to the system designer and is potentially large (as in a drafting system where templates can be defined to contain both other templates and basic objects like lines, points, and arcs). Two user commands are required: TRAVEL UP THE HIERARCHY and COME BACK DOWN. When the user picks something, the system highlights the lowest-level object seen. If this is what the user wants to pick, he can proceed. If not, he issues the first of the two commands: TRAVEL UP THE HIERARCHY. The entire first-level object (the house, say) of which the detected object is a part is highlighted. If this is not what the user wants, he travels up again and still more of the picture is highlighted. If he should accidentally travel too far up the hierarchy, he reverses direction with the COME BACK DOWN command.

In some text editors, there is a hierarchy of character–word–sentence–paragraph. Using the Xerox Star text editor, one selects a character by positioning the screen cursor on the character and pushing the "select" button (one of two) on the mouse. To choose the word, the user simply pushes "select" again. Further moves up the hierarchy are accomplished by further pushes.

EXERCISES

5.1 Solve Eqs. (5.1) for x, y, and z.

5.2 Solve three equations from (5.2) for x, y, and z.

5.3 Solve three equations from (5.3) for x, y, and z.

5.4 Develop an algorithm that uses all four of the Eqs. (5.2) to calculate the "best guess" position (x, y, z) of the light source. Start by solving all four combinations of three equations. This will give four different solutions for (x, y, z). If all four are "close," an average is a good estimate. What if the solutions differ considerably?

5.5 Can a light pen be used with a direct-view storage tube? Why or why not?

5.6 How can a light pen be used as a pick device with a raster display?

5.7 Write a pen-tracking algorithm to do (a) tracking with spiral search if tracking is lost or (b) first- and second-order prediction.

5.8 Implement a simple feature-comparison character recognizer.

5.9 Simulate a light-pen pick with the locator and experiment with x–y correlation techniques.

5.10 Write a procedure to find the extent of a series of lines and points, allowing a tolerance of d around the outside.

5.11 Show that if we approximate distances from a point to a line by the minimum of the horizontal and vertical distances, the worst-case approximation is wrong by a factor of $\sqrt{2}$.

5.12 Describe at a high level techniques for simulating any logical device with a device from any other logical device class. Repeat this exercise, assuming the availability of a single physical device (keyboard, light pen, tablet). Devise reasonable protocols for the user to tell the system how the physical device is currently being used—as a pick, locator, etc. (This is necessary because some graphics packages allow the user to perform any one of several different actions constituting a complete command specification in any sequence: If a pick and button are both required, either may be done first.)

5.13 Write a continuous sketching subroutine which reads a locator and displays short line segments to approximate the path followed by the locator. A parameter to the subroutine is A, the smallest angle which two successive line segments are permitted to make. That is, a sufficient number of short lines is used so that the constraint on angles is met without using more than are needed. Think of the subroutine as a filter: many points are read, and in general only some of the points become endpoints of lines.

5.14 Review and critique several experiments with interaction devices [ENGL67, GOOD75, CARD78]. Conduct a similar experiment with devices available to you.

6 The Design of User–Computer Graphic Conversations

We have now described the fundamental building blocks from which the interface to an interactive graphics system is crafted—the interaction devices and techniques. The question now is how to put the building blocks together into a form which is pleasing and usable. In a sense, we are somewhat like aspiring architects who have just learned about the properties of windows, doors, trusses, etc., and who now want to know how to put these components together into an appealing and habitable house.

Like architecture, the design of user interfaces is at least partly an art rather than a science. We hope that the design of user interfaces will someday become more science than art, but the climb to reach this goal is long; the ascent has begun, but there are many hard traverses ahead. In the meantime, we offer an attitude toward the design of interactive systems, and some specific dos and don'ts for the designer which, if applied creatively, can help focus attention on the *human factors,* also called the *ergonomics,* of an interactive system.

Why is a proper understanding of human factors important? What if a designer simply selected interaction techniques and devices in an *ad hoc* fashion? Numerous studies have shown the strong effect of different devices and techniques on speed of use and operator error rates. A classic study [ENGL67] demonstrated 100% differences in speed and 200% differences in error rates among several techniques for picking displayed words. Two different interactive graphics drafting systems, designed to do the same job, have shown differences of 100% in the overall time to complete a given task. Each of us in our use of computer systems has undoubtedly experienced some unnecessary loss of productivity and considerable aggravation caused by bad human factors. As more interactive graphics systems of similar functional capabilities become available, their success in the marketplace will be based increasingly on ease of use. Systems whose use is not mandatory must be particularly attractive, lest their users not return for a second try. Ease of use, not ease of implementation, is becoming the crucial design consideration.

Human factors have not been a traditional concern in the formal study of computers. The emphasis in the past has been on optimizing the use of two scarce resources, computer time and memory space. Program efficiency was the highest goal. Now, with plummeting hardware costs and increasingly powerful graphics-oriented personal computing environments (as discussed in Chapter 1), we can afford to optimize user efficiency rather than computer efficiency. Many of the ideas presented in this chapter do require additional computer resources—both time and memory space—to implement, but the potential rewards in user productivity and satisfaction more than outweigh the low additional cost of these resources.

The design of user–computer interfaces is not the domain of computer scientists alone. Elements of perceptual psychology (how we see), cognitive psychology (how we acquire knowledge), and human factors (how we interact with equipment) are all crucial to a successful design. Thus interdisciplinary design teams are appropriate for major projects, and some familiarity with all these areas is important even to modest design projects. Some of the papers in the Proceedings of the Seillac-II Workshop on Methodology of Interaction [GUED80] deal with the interdisciplinary aspects of user-interface design. The basic challenge is to design a system whose capabilities are both understandable to its users (not merely to its designers) and readily invoked. Methodologies for doing this are still poorly developed. One general approach, described here, is to apply concepts and insights from person-to-person communication and language theory to the design process. This approach was first developed by Wallace, and is briefly described in [FOLE74].

6.1 THE LANGUAGE ANALOGY

The terms *user–computer dialogue* or *man–machine dialogue* are common in discussions of interactive systems, because anyone who designs an interactive graphics program is at the same time designing a graphical user–computer dialogue. There is a helpful analogy between user–computer dialogue and interpersonal communication. To be sure, the language of computer graphics seldom involves spoken or written words; rather, pictures and actions such as button pushes, picks, and locator positionings serve as "words" for the language. Nevertheless, there are various desirable attributes of interpersonal conversation and language which should be preserved in a graphic user–computer dialogue.

What are some of these desirable attributes? The language of the conversation should be the language of the user and not be slanted towards the computer; it should be natural to the user. To help understand the analogy, recall your own first attempts at learning a foreign language. Your first sentences came slowly, as you struggled with vocabulary and grammatical rules. Later, as the rules became more familiar and natural through practice, your effort was concentrated on building vocabulary. The new user of an interactive system must go through a similar learning process. The process can be even more difficult than learning a foreign language if the user must learn not only new grammar rules and vocabulary, but new concepts as well. The designer's task, then, is to keep the rules and vocabulary simple, and to use concepts which the user already knows or can easily learn. For instance, a biochemist studying molecular conformations (geometric structures) is familiar with concepts such as atoms, bonds, dihedral angles, and residues, but does not know and should not have to know concepts such as linked lists, iteration, and segments. The former are concepts familiar to the user, while the latter are foreign notions which the user has neither time nor inclination to master.

The language of the user–computer dialogue should be *efficient* and *complete* and should have a *natural grammar.* With an efficient language, the user can convey commands to the computer effectively and concisely. A complete language allows expression of any idea relevant in the domain of discourse. A natural grammar has a minimum number of simple, easy-to-learn rules. This helps minimize user training and allows the user to concentrate on the problem to be solved. The idea is to avoid complex grammatical rules which will introduce discontinuities and distractions into the user's conscious thought processes.

A complete language may be quite concise: for example, a language for logic design need provide only a single building block, either the NOR or the NAND, with which any logic circuit can be built. On the other hand, a language like this will be very laborious to use, and thus inefficient. It is better to include in the language a facility for building up more complex commands from the few basic ones. *Extensibility* is a technique for making a complete language efficient by allowing new terms to be defined as combinations of existing terms. Extensibility is usually made available in operating systems as *scripts, catalogued procedures,* or *command files,* and in programming languages as *macros,* but is less commonly found in graphics systems.

Let us go beyond these considerations and examine an interpersonal conversation. One person asks a question or makes a statement, and the other responds, usually quite quickly. If a reply is not given immediately, the speaker usually at least sees some signs of attentiveness to his statement, such as facial or body gestures. These are both forms of *feedback,* a very important component of interaction.

Occasionally, too, someone makes a mistake, says "Oops, I didn't mean that," and the listener immediately adjusts accordingly. Being able to undo mistakes is also important in user–computer dialogues. Similarly, in conversation the speaker might ask the listener for help in expressing a thought or to explain the various possible next actions. These same capabilities should also be present in user–computer dialogues.

A characteristic of interpersonal dialogues which has been hard to replicate in user–computer dialogues is the use of the previous context of the dialogue to resolve ambiguities, understand indirect references, and make other similar inferences. These problems are now beginning to be solved by artificial-intelligence techniques [HAYE81].

6.2 THE LANGUAGE MODEL

Having set the general framework, let us more specifically define the components of the user–computer interface. There are really two languages at this interface. With one, the user communicates to the computer; with the other, the computer communicates to the user. The first language is expressed with actions applied to various interaction devices, while the second language is expressed graphically through lines, points, character strings, filled areas, and colors combined to form displayed images and messages.

Each of these languages can be broken down into four major parts: the *conceptual, semantic, syntactic,* and *lexical* designs. Each part can be analyzed or designed in sequence, beginning at the conceptual design.

The *conceptual design* is the definition of the key application concepts which must be mastered by the user, and is hence also called the *user model* of the application. The conceptual design typically defines objects or classes of objects, relationships between the (classes of) objects, and operations on the (classes of) objects. In a simple text editor, the objects are lines and files, the relation between objects is that files are sequences of lines, the operations on the line object are insert, delete, move, and copy, and the operations on the file object are create, delete, insert, rename, and copy.

The conceptual model of the application program in Chapter 2 has one object (the room), and one class of objects (different pieces of furniture). The relation between objects is that a room contains furniture, and operations on the furniture are move, rotate, etc.

The *semantic design* specifies detailed functionality: what information is needed for each operation on an object, what semantic errors may occur and how they are handled, and the results of each operation. Note that the semantic design defines meanings, not form or sequence—these are left to subsequent design steps.

The *syntactic design* defines the sequence of inputs and outputs. For input, sequence is grammar—the rules by which sequences of *tokens* (words) in the language are formed into proper (but not necessarily semantically meaningful) sentences. The types of tokens in an input sentence are typically commands, quantities, names, coordinates, and arbitrary text. As in natural and artificial languages, tokens are the units of meaning and cannot be further decomposed without losing their meaning.

For output, the notion of sequence is extended to include spatial and temporal factors. Therefore the output syntax includes the 2D and 3D organization of a display as well as any temporal (time) variation in the form. The tokens in the output sequence, by analogy to input, represent the units of meaning and cannot be further decomposed. The tokens are often conveyed graphically as symbols and drawings rather than as sequences of characters, and have no meaning if broken up into individual lines or characters. For example, a transistor symbol has meaning to a circuit designer, while the individual lines making up the symbol do not.

The *lexical design* determines how input and output tokens are actually formed from the available hardware primitives, or *lexemes*. Input lexemes are whatever are provided by available input devices, and output lexemes are the primitive shapes (such as lines and characters) and their attributes (such as color and font) provided by the graphics subroutine package. Thus for input, lexical design is the design of an interaction technique, such as discussed in Chapter 5, for each input token. For output, similarly, lexical design is the combining of output primitives and attributes to form the output units of meaning, or tokens. We see, then, that lexical design represents the binding of hardware capabilities to the hardware-independent tokens of the input and output languages. As in other top-down designs, binding to physical representations or implementations is deferred to the last stage of the design.

In the furniture layout program, the input language's semantics are create, delete, and move. The syntax of a sentence is prefix, with an initial imperative, followed by zero, one, or two operands, always in a specified order. In some cases an explicit terminating action (a "period") is necessary; in other cases the terminating action is implicit. The ADD SYMBOL operation, for example, is invoked by the follow sequence of actions:

1. Enter ADD SYMBOL command;
2. Pick furniture symbol to be added;
3. Drag symbol to new position;
4. Terminate by entering "DONE."

The lexical component of the input language for the furniture layout program is defined by the binding of the tablet (as opposed to some other physical device) to serve the functions of picking commands from the menu, picking templates to be deleted, and providing locations. Had a keyboard-oriented language been used, then one of the lexical components of the language would be the definition of the string of characters *PLACE* to be the token (word) for the command having the meaning "place symbol." With a PFK, the binding of a particular key to the token "place symbol" would be the corresponding lexical component.

The semantic content of the application's output language is the state of the room layout, plus prompt and control information (such as the menu). The syntax of the output language defines the screen arrangement, including the partitioning into different areas and the exact placement of menus, prompts, and error messages. The lexical level of the output language includes the font of the text, the line thicknesses and color, color of filled regions and the way in which output primitives are combined to create the output language's primitive symbols, such as those representing the furniture objects being manipulated.

An alternative output syntax to convey the semantics of the furniture layout would be a tabular presentation of the position, orientation, and type of each furniture piece in the room. Then the lexical component of the output would be the character sizes, fonts, and spacings used in the table.

In addition to the input and output languages, there is a conversation protocol which defines how the user-to-computer and computer-to-user conversations are temporally related. For instance, input commands can either be executed immediately and their results displayed, or they can be batched into groups for execution. Some systems have "type-ahead," the ability to enter new commands while the old ones are still being executed, but without any explicit batching of commands. Response times are also part of the protocol, as is the feedback which the computer typically provides in response to lexical, syntactic, and semantic input.

What then constitutes a design for an interactive graphics system's user–computer interface? It is a specification of the conceptual model, a complete specification of the semantic, syntactic, and lexical components of the input and output languages, and of the conversation protocol. We will say more about how to develop a design in Section 6.4. First, we need to understand some of the considerations which affect the quality of the user–computer interface.

6.3 DESIGN PRINCIPLES

In this section we describe a number of design principles which can help ensure good human factors in a design. While mere application of these principles alone carries no guarantee of success in design, their application, either conscious or unconscious, is generally considered necessary for a successful design. The principles outlined here are discussed more fully in [CHER76, ENGE75, FOLE74, FOLE80, HANS71, MART73, and SHNE79].

6.3.1 Give Feedback

Imagine conversing with someone who never smiles or nods, and who responds only when forced to: it is a frustrating experience, because there is little or no indication that the listener is really hearing what is being said. Feedback is as essential an ingredient in conversation with a computer as it is in human conversation. The difference is that in normal conversation with another person there are many sources of feedback (gestures, body language, facial expressions, eye contact) which are usually provided without conscious action by either of the participants in the conversation. By contrast, a computer graphics terminal gives little automatic feedback (the "power on" light is an exception), so the only feedback the user will have is that which is planned and programmed.

In interactive systems there are three possible levels of feedback corresponding to the levels of the language: lexical, syntactic, and semantic. The designer must consciously consider each level and explicitly decide whether feedback should be present, and if so, what form it should take. The lowest level of feedback is lexical. Each lexical action in the input language can be provided with a lexical response in the output language: for instance, echoing characters typed on a keyboard and moving a screen cursor as the user changes the position of a locator.

Feedback to a syntactic input occurs as each unit (word) of the input language (command, position, picked object, etc.) is accepted by the system. A command picked from a menu or an object picked to be moved is highlighted, so the user can know that the actions have been accepted (that is, the "words" have been understood). Similar forms of feedback to syntactic inputs are prompting for the next input, lighting the PFK button which has just been depressed, and echoing verbal (speech) input with verbal output. The furniture layout program in Chapter 2 uses several such feedback mechanisms.

Another form of feedback on the syntactic level occurs not as each syntactic token is input, but rather when a complete syntactic sequence (a sentence in the command language) has been input and been found to be well-formed. This is acknowledgement of receipt of a proper sentence, and is generally needed only if performing the semantics of the sentence (the actions specified by the command) will take more than a second or two. The layout program does not use this form of feedback.

The most useful and welcome form of semantic feedback tells the user that the requested operation has been completed. This is usually done with a new or modified display which explicitly shows the results. The furniture program uses only this type of semantic feedback, because each command can be carried out quite quickly. In some cases, as when the user asks that a drawing be filed for later use, such explicit graphical feedback is not appropriate, and prompts or completion messages (either text or icons) are used instead.

Another type of semantic feedback, necessary only if completion of the semantics will take more than a few seconds, is some indication that the computer is at least working on the problem. (In the absence of such feedback, users have been known to express their frustration physically on the graphics terminal or even on the designer of the application!) Such feedback can take many forms; a particularly attractive one is a 360° dial whose rotating indicator completes one revolution by the time the problem is solved. The user can quickly extrapolate from the dial's progress whether a coffee break is in order.

Another form of semantic feedback, again given before any of the semantics have been carried out, is to display a precise and definitive statement of what the interactive system believes has been requested. Such feedback is a poor substitute for seeing the actual results and should be used only if performing the semantics immediately will consume unacceptable amounts of time or other resources, or if several commands must be batched together before their semantics are performed. Given these circumstances, the feedback is particularly helpful for new users if ambiguity or context dependencies are possible. Figure 6.1 is an example: the command language accepts keywords, such as TITLE, X, Y, AXIS, and BAR, in a free-form way. Figure 6.2 shows the graph resulting from this sequence. If the feedback indicates that the system has misunderstood the input, the incorrect commands can be changed before the chart being requested is drawn. In Fig. 6.3, we see changes being requested to the original graph, while Fig. 6.4 shows the new graph. Only those parts of the chart specification which are being changed need be modified.

GENERATE LEVEL . . ENTER
create a monthly bar chart.
GENERATING A MONTHLY BAR CHART.
ENTER:
title of the chart is "SALES VOLUME BY DISTRICT".
TITLE TEXT IS "SALES VOLUME BY DISTRICT".
ENTER:
label on the x axis is "MONTHS OF 1978".
X AXIS LABEL TEXT IS "MONTHS OF 1978".
ENTER:
the label on the y axis is "MILLIONS".
Y AXIS LABEL TEXT IS "MILLIONS".
ENTER:
input data.
"WEST"
3 49.7 4 63.8 5 77.9 6 68.3
"EAST"
3 64.9 4 68.7 5 62 6 58.7
end of the data
ENTER:
go

Fig. 6.1 Interactive dialog with immediate command feedback. Computer output is on upper-case lines; user input is on lower-case and quoted lines. Dialog is with TELL_A_GRAF®, a proprietary software product of Integrated Software Systems Corporation (ISSCO), San Diego, California.

Sometimes semantic feedback can profitably take the form of partial results slowly appearing on the screen. If the results appear in some rational order, the resulting "animation" this produces actually helps the user understand the final graphical presentation better than if, after some delay, the entire presentation were to appear instantaneously on the screen.

The positioning of feedback is important. There is a natural tendency to designate a fixed area of the screen for feedback and error messages. This can have a bad effect on *visual continuity*, however, because the user's eyes must move between the work area and the message area. Audio feedback eliminates this problem, as does the technique of placing the feedback where the user is looking. This position is easy to predict in those systems in which a tablet and cursor is the major interaction tool: the user's eyes will generally be at or near the cursor, particularly when some action is being initiated. Building on this principle, Sneeringer's OCCAM screen-oriented editor places error messages, in color, at the current text insertion point on the screen [SNEE78]. Baecker and Tilbrook's NEWSWHOLE newspaper layout system uses the form of the cursor itself for feedback: a "thumbs-down" symbol means the user has made an error, and a small Buddha symbol "encourages the user to be patient" while the system is carrying out a task [TILB76, DEFA80].

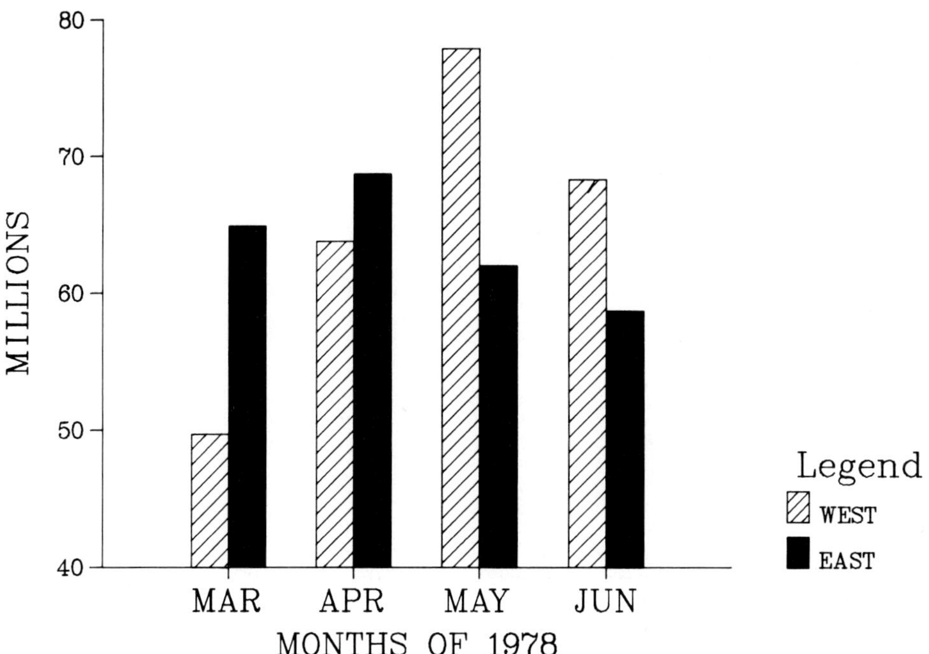

Fig. 6.2 Results from dialog of Fig. 6.1.

GENERATE LEVEL . . ENTER:
continue.
ENTER:
change the title to "SALES VOLUME"
ENTER MORE OR PERIOD:
"EASTERN AND WESTERN DISTRICTS".
TITLE TEXT IS "SALES VOLUME" "EASTERN AND WESTERN DISTRICTS".
ENTER:
put a frame around the plot. draw a grid for the y axis.
AXIS FRAME IS ENABLED.
ENTER:
Y AXIS GRID IS ENABLED.
ENTER:
don't put any tick marks on the x axis.
X AXIS TICK-MARKS EXISTENCE IS NO.
ENTER:
go.

Fig. 6.3 Interactive dialog to modify plot of Fig. 6.2.

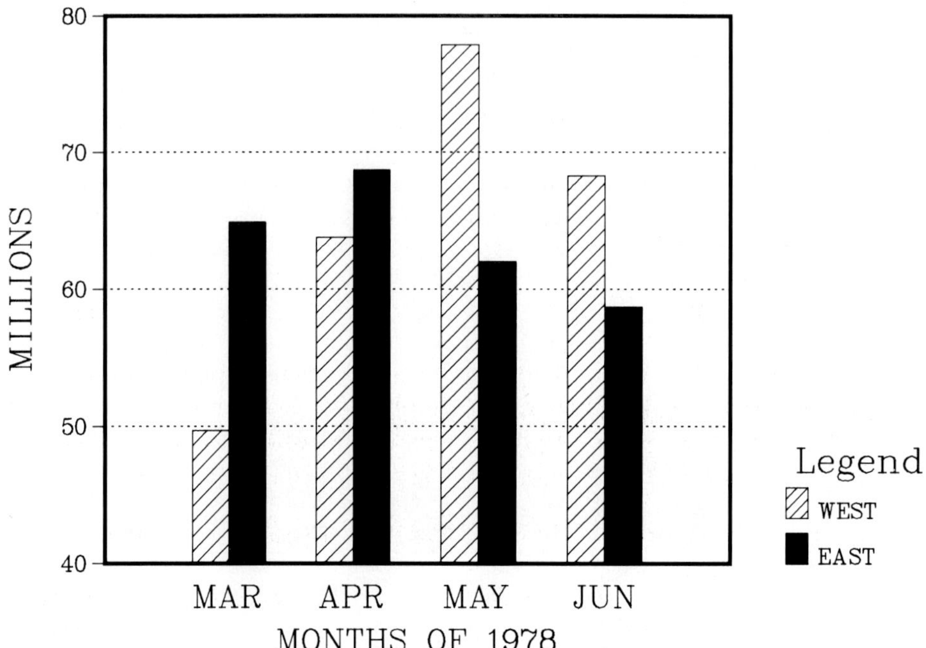

Fig. 6.4 Modified plot.

6.3.2 Help the User Learn the System

Many interactive graphics systems must be designed for a spectrum of users which ranges from the completely new and inexperienced user up through those who work with the system for hundreds or thousands of hours. User experience level is, of course, a continuum, but a rough three-part categorization is helpful: *novice users,* who are just learning the basic concepts and mechanics of the system; *intermediate users,* who have learned how to do at least some productive work and are now building proficiency and learning additional system capabilities; and *experienced users,* who are proficient in all or most system aspects and who know all of the system capabilities (some systems have so many capabilities that users are experienced only with certain sets of frequently-used capabilities).

How can we design an interactive system to meet the needs of such a diverse group? The novice user's first need is for a computer-guided "tour" of the system facilities with examples of what the system does, and for computer-guided instruction in the use of basic commands, perhaps in a computer-aided instruction style. In the most simplistic form of such interaction, the user is simply presented with a series of yes–no or multiple-choice questions.

Beyond this step, we have two basic tools: *prompting* and *help.* Unlike feedback, which acknowledges specific user actions, the purpose of prompts is to suggest to the user what to do next. The more experienced the user, the less prompting is appropriate, especially if the prompting is done in an obtrusive way which slows down the pace of the interaction. Many systems provide several levels of prompting, controllable by the user; those who are inexperienced can be "led by the hand", while those who are experienced can proceed without the distracting prompts.

Prompting takes many forms. The most direct is a displayed message explicitly explaining what to do next, such as SPECIFY LOCATION. A speech synthesizer gives explicit verbal instructions to the user. More subtle forms of prompting, less obtrusive to the user, are also available. On a PFK, buttons eligible for selection can be illuminated. A prominent tracking cross or cursor can be displayed when a position must be input; a blinking cursor can indicate that a text string is to be input; a scale or dial can be displayed when a value is desired. These unobtrusive prompts are appropriate for intermediate and advanced users, but may be too subtle for new users.

User–computer dialogues which employ menus and other prompts are called *computer-initiated* dialogues, because the computer takes the initiative in guiding the user through the intricacies of specifying input. They are popular for novice users. As discussed in Section 5.3.5, menus are also appropriate for experienced users *if* the menus can be presented very quickly. Conversely, dialogues in which the user has control and invokes one of many different alternatives, typically without being presented with an explicit set of alternatives, are called *user-initiated* dialogues, and are suitable for experienced users. Unfortunately, most of today's timesharing systems use this style of dialogue—it is easily implemented using keyboard input, whereas the most effective forms of menu selection require high-resolution displays and pointing devices.

A help facility allows the user to obtain additional information about various commands and how to invoke them. The user typically does this by specifying a HELP command, and it should be possible to invoke HELP at any point in the user–computer dialogue, always with the same mechanism. The return from HELP must leave the system at exactly the same state as it was when HELP was invoked. If HELP is invoked while the system is awaiting a command, a list of commands available in this state should be shown (with menus or PFKs, this may be unnecessary). Entering HELP and then a command name gives more information about what the command does. If a command has been specified and HELP is then requested, details of how to enter the command's first parameter should be given to the user. A second invocation of HELP would produce more detailed information on the same subject, and perhaps allow more general browsing through on-line documentation.

For example, the *UNIX*™ operating system has all its documentation on line, accessible to users with the "manual" command:

man <command name> .

A help capability is appropriate even if prompts and menus are normally displayed, because the user is provided with an opportunity to receive more detailed information than can be provided in a short prompt. Even experienced users can be expected occasionally to forget some detail, particularly in a large and complex application, and they should be able to turn to HELP as a fast way to get the needed information.

Figure 6.5 summarizes these and other considerations for various types of users (see [MART73] for further discussion of user categories).

Type of user	Implications for design of user–computer interface
Casual–uses system irregularly	Prompting and menus are especially appropriate.
Regular–uses system often enough so that details of use are not forgotten	Terse command language or fast menu selection, few steps to complete a task.
Motivated–user *wants* to use the system	User will invest time in learning how to use system, even if difficult.
Unmotivated–user does not really want to use the system	Any flaw in design will give user an excuse to criticize or stop using the system.
Stressed–user under time or other pressure to get job done quickly	Simplicity especially important, so work can be done by instinct or reflex.

Fig. 6.5 Types of users.

6.3.3 Allow Backup and Accommodate Errors

We all make mistakes when working with computers and need to have easy and convenient ways to correct these mistakes in order to prevent us from making even worse ones. Most, if not all, interactive systems provide a backspace key to delete the last character entered. Imagine how frustrated we would be without this simple error-correction mechanism! Many systems also allow the entire current input line to be deleted, and there is often a way to abort execution of the current command before it has been completed. The system is usually restored to its stage *before* the aborted command was entered, unless changes to files have been made. Less customary is the ability to completely undo the effects of the most recent command, even when file changes have been made. Multiple versions of files are saved in some systems, a strategy which partially alleviates this problem. As an extreme, a few systems record all user inputs for an entire session: if need be, the session can be "replayed" up to the point where an error was made.

These are illustrations of error accommodation at three levels: lexical, syntactic and semantic. A system designer should consider providing each type of recovery, while recognizing that the cost of semantic recovery can be quite high: the application program must continually save either the system state or changes made to the system state, and provide logic to restore the previous state. The cost of not accommodating errors is user frustration and lessened productivity. In particular, the availability of semantic recovery frees the user to explore unlearned system facilities without "fear of failure," since recovery is so easy.

Many of the dynamic interaction techniques discussed in the previous chapter provide backup: for instance, the trial position of an object being dragged into place is easy to change, thus many positions can be tried. This is syntactic backup, in that many different values of one syntactic unit (the position, in the case of dragging) of the overall command can be easily changed. Semantic backup in this case would be to have the system return the object to its exact starting position—undoing the effect of the command.

Another form of backup is involved in picking. When picking is done with a light pen, the item currently being sensed by the pen is typically highlighted. The user moves the pen around until the item desired is highlighted and then presses a button. The sequence of positioning the pen and pushing a button forms a syntactic unit—a picked item. Once an item has been so picked, designating another item in its place would require additional backup capabilities, this time at the semantic level.

The opportunity to cancel the effect of a complete command is provided in some systems by asking the user to explicitly verify the command—to accept or reject the results of the operation. However, this adds to the number of user actions required to accomplish a unit of work. A good alternative is to require explicit action only to reject the results of a command: the command is implicitly accepted when the next command is entered. Cancellation is easily understood by the user if the interaction language has a clear *sentence structure* which denotes the start and end of commands, since the unit to which cancellation applies is clearly the whole command.

Providing cancellation of commands requires extra programming effort, especially for commands which involve major changes to data structures. An alternative to cancellation is to require the user to confirm commands which, when performed, would require a major user effort to undo. File deletion is perhaps the best example of this. When deletion confirmation, standard in many interactive systems, is lacking, one is not surprised by the following news report about a newspaper text-editing system [TIME73]:

> One of these keys [on the CRT keyboard], the "kill" button, even whisks the story off the screen and erases it from computer memory . . . When stories began vanishing into electronic limbo, the (Detroit) News was forced to modify its CRTs so that the "kill" button must be hit twice before a story dies.

A popular microcomputer system has the reset key just above the return key. Until a recent product modification, hitting reset by accident cleared the current program from memory. In both these examples, considerable effort is needed to recover. Thus, in the absence of command cancellation, confirmation of commands is the next best alternative.

6.3.4 Control Response Time

The response time of a program is of critical importance to the program's usability, although in time-sharing systems it often cannot be directly controlled by the application designer. But when response times can be controlled, what should they be? There is unfortunately no single answer. Consider again interpersonal communication: if you ask someone for the time of day, you expect an answer in a matter of seconds, and become quite annoyed if you receive a blank stare for 30 seconds. On the other hand, 30 seconds is not at all long to wait for the answer to a question requiring a complicated series of computations. Consider, too, the machines we use. When we strike a key on a typewriter, we expect to hear the sound of type ball on paper quite quickly. Indeed, if we perceive any delay, we are often quite startled.

The point is, then, that response time requirements relate to the user's expectations. Miller [MILL68] suggests that there is a hierarchy of required response times, corresponding to different levels of psychological "closure," the feeling of having completed a task. The larger or more substantial the task being completed, the greater the tolerable response time.

Two costs are incurred by systems whose response times are noticeable to the user. The first is the time the user wastes waiting for the computer to respond. The second is the time the user wastes regaining the train of thought once the computer finally does respond, so that the work at hand can be continued.

There appear to be fairly rigid response-time requirements in two areas: response to reflex actions and to "simple" interactions. By "reflex actions" we mean those actions performed by either learned or natural reflex, such as typing a character or moving a display cursor. In each case the system response must appear to be immediate or nearly so, which means no more than a 100-millisecond delay between typing or moving a stylus and seeing the result [WOOD54].

"Simple" interactions are defined as those which the user believes the computer should be able to do without any substantial processing and for which the user is therefore not willing to wait. The question then is one of how long the response time can be before the user realizes a delay is occurring, begins to wonder why the computer is taking so long, and thereby loses his train of thought. The answer to the question used to be "about two seconds" [MILL68]. This two-second delay was generally considered to be appropriate for much of the syntactic-level feedback discussed above and for "simple" semantics such as deleting a line when using time-shared computers.

Part of the reason for this satisfaction with two-second response time is user expectation. The problem is that as personal computers and dedicated single-user graphics systems become more and more common, more and more computer users experience increasing expectations because these systems are capable of faster response to most user actions, with the possible exception of requests requiring massive numeric calculations or file searching. Thus we expect more of our interactions to occur instantaneously, and therefore within 100 to 200 milliseconds.

Another response-time requirement is consistency. Indeed, some experiments suggest that users are more productive with a somewhat slower system having low response-time variance than with a somewhat faster (on the average) system having a high response-time variance [BOEH71, MILL76]. Predictability is preferable to variability, at least within limits.

6.3.5 Design for Consistency

A consistent system is one whose conceptual model, semantics, command language syntax, and display formats are uniform and lack exceptions and special conditions. Simple examples of consistency in the output language are:

- The same codings are always employed. All circle center lines have the same intensity and dot–dash structure. Colors always code information in the same way, just as red always means stop and green always means go.
- System status messages are shown at a logically (though not necessarily physically) fixed place on the display surface.
- Menu items are displayed in the same relative position within a menu, so that users can allow "muscle memory" to help in picking the desired item.

Examples of consistency in the input language are:

- Keyboard characters, such as carriage return, line feed, and backspace, always have the same function, and can be used whenever text is being input.
- Global commands, like HELP, STATUS, and CANCEL, can be invoked at any time.
- Keywords in a character-string-oriented language can be abbreviated with a constant-length string.

One of the most important applications of the consistency principle is the syntactic and lexical definition of the input language. In terms of formal language theory, many of the languages are *regular* and can therefore be represented by state transition graphs (see Section 2.14.3). Input events are user actions, and the outputs are the computations and resulting changes to the display. Each arc of a graph is labeled with the user action which causes the transition and the system action (if any).

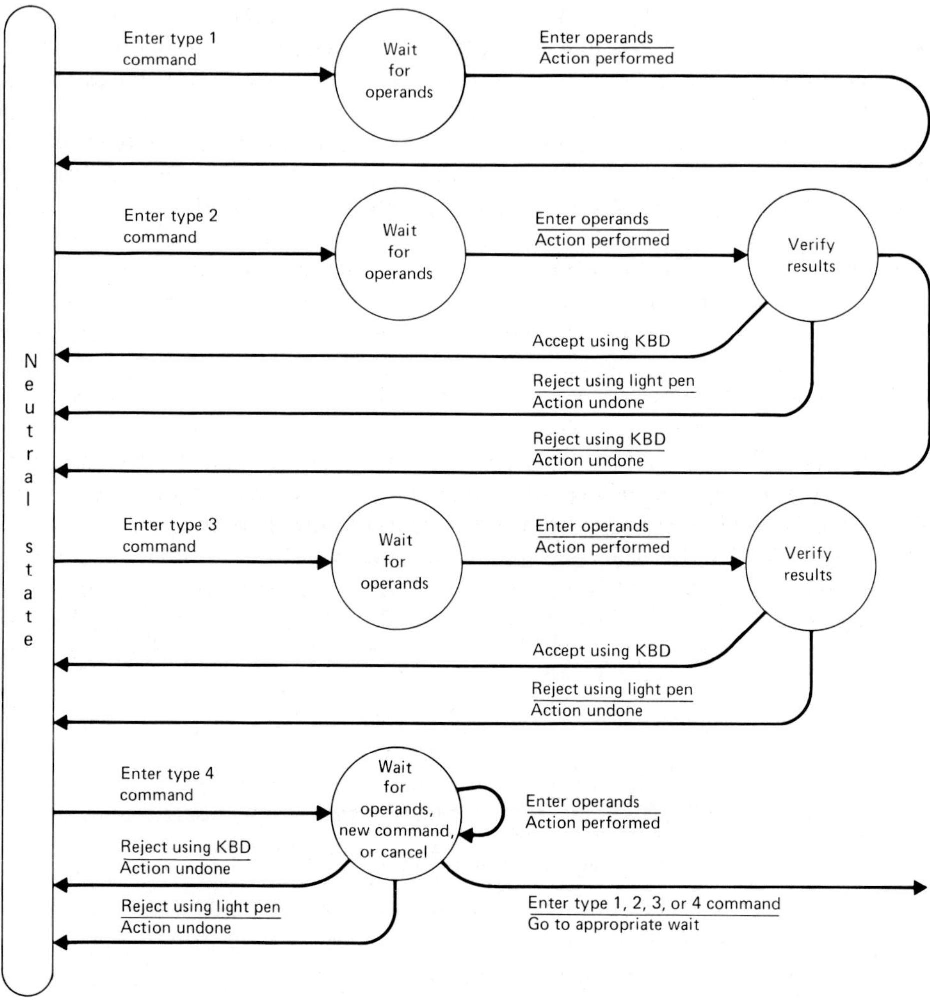

Fig. 6.6 Transition graph showing a complex inconsistent command language.

Figure 6.6 is the transition graph representation of classes of commands for an actual command language which is not particularly consistent. In the *neutral state,* which is also the initial starting state, any command may be entered. This causes a transition to an operand *wait state* in which the user is prompted to input appropriate information. There are four sentence structures (which is too many): each corresponds to one of the five major loops in the figure. Command types 2 and 3 illustrate the concept of explicit acceptance or rejection of a command's effect, while command type 4 shows explicit rejection and implicit acceptance. There is a particularly troublesome inconsistency between structures 2 and 3: the only difference is in how the effect of a command can be canceled. Needless to say, users who wish to cancel a command of type 3 must remember not to attempt to do so with the keyboard. This increases the possibility of errors.

Representing all the commands of an inconsistent system can create large and complex transition graphs. This is an additional incentive to seek after consistency. Consider, for example, the simple case of explicit versus implicit acceptance of results. Figure 6.7 represents a one-operand command with explicit acceptance and rejection of its results. Figure 6.8 shows implicit acceptance and explicit rejection. In the first case, three steps are required to carry out all commands, while in the latter case only two steps are required. Minimizing steps per task is one goal of designing an interface, especially for experienced users, since (not surprisingly) the speed with which experienced users can input commands is nearly linearly related to the number of discrete steps (keystrokes, hand movements) required [CARD80].

Reisner has demonstrated experimentally an intuitively expected result: given two functionally equivalent systems, the one with simpler syntactic structures produces fewer errors and is more quickly learned [REIS81]. Thus another design objective to apply is simply to minimize the number of different sentence structures.

At the semantic level, consistency requires, for example, that an operation which can be applied to one class of objects (such as the move operation applied to desks) be equally applicable to other "similar" objects (such as the move operation applied to chairs).

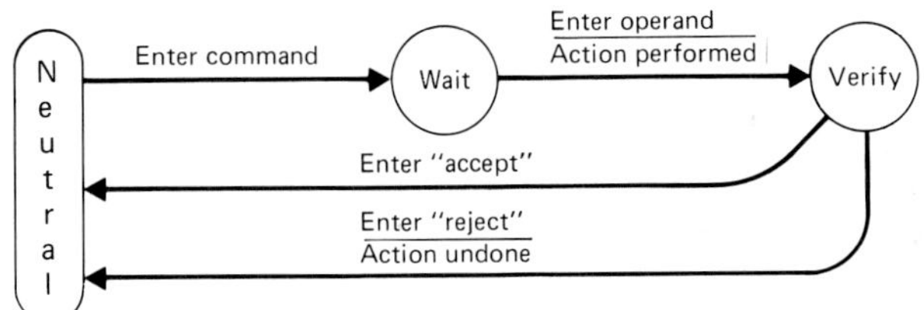

Fig. 6.7 Explicit rejection and acceptance.

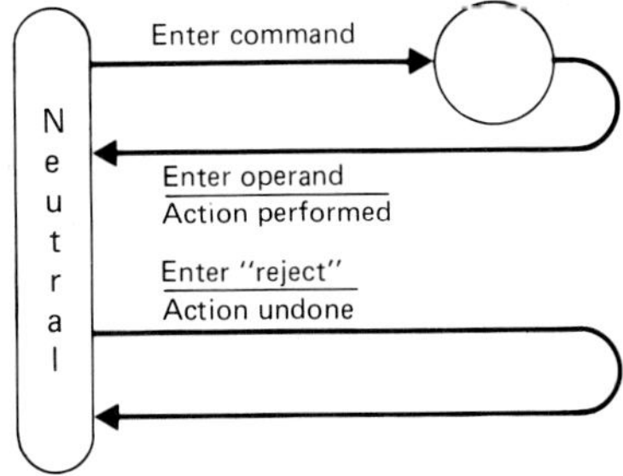

Fig. 6.8 Explicit rejection, implicit acceptance.

We see, in retrospect, that one purpose of consistency is to allow the user to *generalize* knowledge about one aspect of the system to other aspects. Consistency also helps avoid the user frustration which occurs if the system does not behave in an understandable and logical way. The best way to achieve this consistency is through a careful top–down design of the overall system.

6.3.6 Structure the Display

Often a great deal of information must be displayed to the user, and if it is presented in an unstructured form it can be difficult to perceive and understand. To help structure the information, it is helpful to divide the view surface into different areas where different specific types of information are presented. Prompts, error messages, system status, and graphical representation of the information of interest to the user each has its own area. This helps provide an uncluttered and organized display presentation and allows the user to locate relevant information. A few systems even allow the user to arrange various feedback areas on the screen [TEIT77,

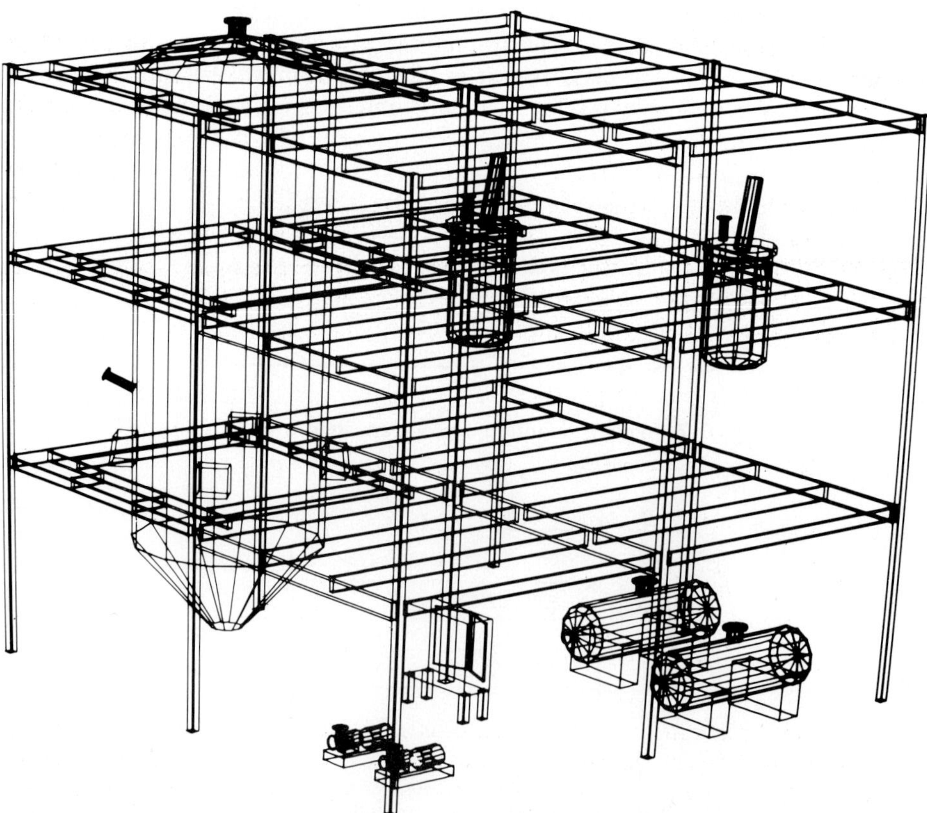

Fig. 6.9 Industrial structure (courtesy of Evans & Sutherland).

HERO80]. While areas can overlap, their borders set one off from another and provide a strong logical grouping. As mentioned in the discussion of feedback, visual continuity is not necessarily best served with fixed display areas.

The perception of the structure of displayed items can be enhanced by various visual encodings, such as color, line style, or intensities. Figure 6.9 shows a structure with some details that are hard to make out. Color Plate 12 uses color to display the same structure, and the major parts of the structure are easily distinguished. Figure 6.10 gives more specific information about ways to encode information, listed approximately in decreasing order of effectiveness. Color is the most easily perceived distinction between items (for users who are not strongly color-blind) and is readily available with raster displays.

The coding methods can be combined to increase discrimination (by redundant coding) or to increase the number of discernible items [CHRI75]. For instance, red boxes and green triangles are easier to pick out and discriminate one from the other than any of the pairs: (red box, red triangle), (green box, green triangle), (red box, green box), (red triangle, green triangle). Although the shape coding and color coding are redundant (either coding contains sufficient information), they allow the user to key on either one or both coding methods.

The structure of the presentation of 3D objects can be enhanced by providing various depth cues, as will be discussed in Chapter 14. The user's attention can be directed to a specific part of the display by using methods such as displaying objects in that area in a different color, by blinking the objects (2 to 3 times per second, with an on-time of at least 50 milliseconds), or by pointing to the objects with a large colored blinking overlay. Any of these methods would help the user, for instance, to locate and keep track of an object which is moving or has just been modified. Other aspects of structuring displays to aid perception and understanding are described in [KRIL76]. Marcus explains well-known graphic design principles and their application to computer-generated charts and graphs [MARC80].

Coding method	Maximum number of codes for nearly error-free recognition
Color	6
Geometric shapes	10
Line width	2
Line type	5
Intensity	2

Fig. 6.10 Coding methods.

An obvious means of creating more apparent structure in order to decrease visual clutter is selective display. Two ways to display a molecule are shown in Figs. 6.11 and 6.12. If one's primary interest is the gross overall structure of the molecule, Fig. 6.11 is much to be preferred, while if detailed information is desired, Fig. 6.12 is recommended. A zoom capability also permits a user to decrease visual clutter by

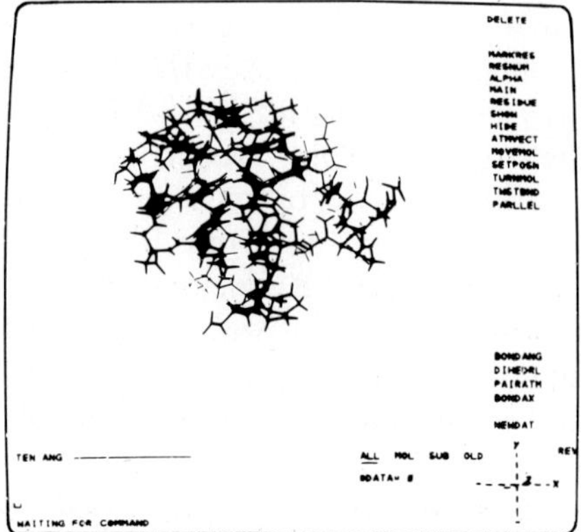

Fig. 6.11 Complete molecule (picture from the GRIP system [WRIG72]).

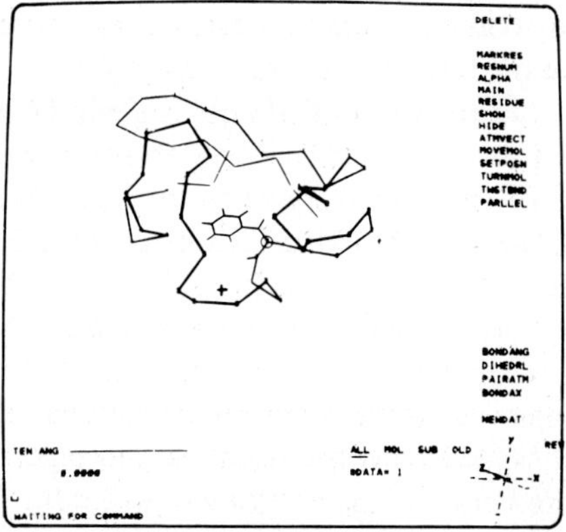

Fig. 6.12 Partial molecule showing backbone and just one side chain (picture from GRIP).

enlarging a small area of the display to expose details not otherwise distinguishable. However, when an enlarged part of a larger drawing is being shown, some way to have a sense of "place" in the overall drawing is necessary, so that the enlarged part is put into its overall context. Figure 6.13 shows one way of giving an overall spatial context: the small square inside of the larger square area indicates which part of the overall drawing is being shown. This can be done even more effectively with two displays: one for the overview, the other for the blowup. Pairing of a DVST for overview with a refresh vector or raster display for blowup has been very effective for VLSI chip design, where as many as 100,000 high-resolution vectors can be required to display the entire chip.

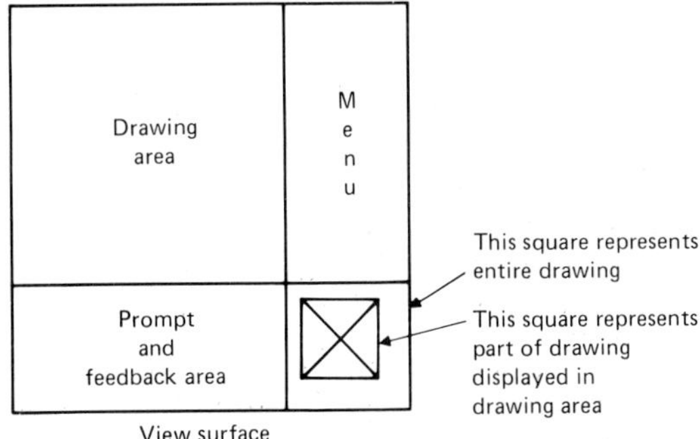

Fig. 6.13 Use of feedback to provide spatial context.

6.3.7 Minimize Memorization

Learning to use a system involves memorization of information. An important design principle is to make the memorization as simple as possible and indeed to avoid it whenever possible. Consistency is one way to do this, as is the provision of menus and prompting, but there are other ways as well. Many keyboard-oriented systems have full-word commands which express the meaning of the command, such as DELETE. Short forms of such commands are obviously best designed to be abbreviations of the words. The need to remember the order of positional parameters is also to be avoided.

Interface designs sometimes force unnecessary memorization. In one design drafting system, objects are referred to by numeric rather than by alphanumeric names. To appreciate what this means, imagine an interactive operating system in which file names must be numeric. In both cases, the remembering/learning tool of mnemonic names is unavailable to the user, whose productivity will surely suffer. Of course explicit picking of displayed objects or icons further eliminates the need for memorization. One prefers that the user's recognition rather than recall memory be used whenever possible.

In an interactive graphing system, a command such as PLOT YEARS GROSS NET produces a trend chart of yearly gross income and net income on a single set of axes. A reasonable way to allow the style of one line to be controlled would be with a command like LINESTYLE NET DASH (to make the net income be plotted with a dashed line). Unhappily, the actual command is of the form LINESTYLE 3 DASH. The "3" refers to the third variable named in the most recent PLOT command: in this case, NET. Since the most recent PLOT command is not generally on the screen, the user must remember the order of the parameters.

In many context-oriented text editors, a two-step process is required to change a text string because the CHANGE command operates only on the current line. First a SEARCH command is issued to locate the line containing the string to be deleted; then a CHANGE command is issued, giving the old string and new string. The user must remember the old string from one command to the next. At least one editor removes the need for this remembering by allowing the change command to first search forward from the current line until a matching string is found and then perform the change, all in one step [FRES76].

Memorization is required when the help facilities on many systems are used. The act of obtaining help information often leads to substantial changes to the display area, causing the user to lose sight of the context within which the help was required. Therefore the user has to remember the circumstances, such as the error message or display layout, surrounding the situation which led to seeking help. Once the help information is understood, it must be remembered while the user returns to the previous context within which the error occurred. One of the advantages of user interfaces based on window managers, such as in Xerox Star and Smalltalk [BYTE81, KAY77a, KAY77b], is that several windows are displayed at the same time (Figs. 1.6, 1.9). Each window shows a different context, such as a help facility in one and an interactive application in another. Switching between use of the application and obtaining help in use of the application is as simple as moving the screen cursor from one window to another.

Similarly, copying part of one document into another can be accomplished quite easily with multiple windows. One window shows part of the document being copied from, and the other shows part of the document being copied into. Scrolling and other positioning commands can be issued to either window: when the text to be copied and the insertion point have been located in their respective windows, the copy is actually invoked. There is no need to remember one context when switching to another, as they are *both* visible. Tesler, in his description of the Smalltalk environment [BYTE81], very convincingly argues the utility of this approach.

Using dynamic window management is not without cost. A high-performance personal computer is needed to do a really effective job, and there is much more software complexity than found in a more traditional environment such as SGP and the room layout application of Chapter 2. We expect window managers to increasingly become a standard part of the basic support software on personal computers, so application programmers will routinely use them, just as graphics packages like SGP are used today.

6.3.8 Summary

To those familiar with interactive systems, these rules may seem obvious. However, when the time comes to design an interactive system, the rules are all too often forgotten or given lip service only. The reasons for this are clear enough. Typically, there is pressure to get a system running as soon as possible, which leaves insufficient time for a thoughtful design to be developed. Thus the user interface is consequently designed for ease of implementation rather than for ease of use. Sometimes the design is insufficiently detailed, and programmers unknowingly introduce inconsistency. Thus one phase of the application may require commas between input parameters, while another phase may require blanks instead.

But while the reasons for bad design are understandable, the resulting systems can be deplorable. To design an interactive system, a complete, well-thought-out and well-documented design is necessary, prepared with clear guidelines (like the ones presented here or others) in mind.

6.4 THE DESIGN PROCESS

How is the user–computer interface for an interactive graphics application program designed? The first step is to understand the problem area and the prospective users. While this statement may sound trite, the step is often not well-done. It can be accomplished in part by studying the way in which the problem area is currently treated. As Hornbuckle says, "observing what man does normally during his creative efforts can provide a starting point for the . . . designer. In particular, a mathematician does not manipulate equations at a typewriter, nor does a circuit designer prefer a keypunch" [HORN67]. Hansen is even more succinct: his advice is "Know the user" [HANS71]. Watch, study, interact with prospective users, learn to understand how they think, why they do what they do.

This does not imply that the computer graphics system should necessarily mimic the way in which the user works manually or with nongraphics computer tools. Computer graphics often provides the means for making major improvements in the methods by which a problem is solved or a job is done. Of course, any potential increase in efficiency from changing methods must be balanced against the training and adaptation costs of switching users over to the new methods. A typical strategy is to first computerize the current methods, then switch to better, more efficient methods once the users have become familiar with the computer.

The process of understanding the application and users is often called *task analysis.* It results in a set of functional requirements, or capabilities, which are to be made available through the user–computer interface. The analysis can also provide insight into how the capabilities of the system might be presented to the user. Finally, the analysis identifies the types of users for which the system is to be designed (a concern whose importance was discussed in the preceding section).

Having completed a task analysis, what next? A reasonable approach, proven useful in practice, is to perform a top–down design following the language model of Section 6.2. Thus we:

- Specify the conceptual design of the system;
- Design the semantics—the operations performed on objects in the conceptual model, the changes caused to the objects, and the information to be displayed;
- Design the syntax—the user's logical action sequences which effect each operation, and the organization of the display;
- Perform the lexical design—each logical token (word) is bound to physical action(s) with specific interaction devices, and the visual encodings are bound to the capabilities of the display device.

The principles described in the preceding section are applied at each step of this design process. It may be necessary to iterate through the process several times before a completely satisfactory design is achieved.

The conceptual, semantic, syntactic, and lexical components of the design were initially discussed as part of the language analogy in Section 6.1. We now expand on these central concepts.

The conceptual model defines the general form of the set of capabilities to be provided to the user. It includes the types of objects the user will know about and the types of actions which can be performed on these objects. For instance, alternative models for an interactive drafting system might be:

- Mimic the tools and techniques used by a draftsman;
- Extend the tools and techniques to three dimensions;
- Depart from traditional drafting tools—allow the user to manipulate directly (position, add, subtract) 3D volumes;
- Depart from traditional drafting tools—provide capabilities to describe procedurally (as with a program) how to draw/construct the 2D or 3D object of interest.

Possible models for an interactive text editor are:

- A line-number-oriented editor, with operations performed on a line or sets of lines;
- A string-oriented editor, with operations performed on arbitrary strings of text;
- A window editor, with operations performed on strings in rectangular areas of the screen.

Clearly, the detailed semantics of an application are highly dependent on the conceptual model, which must therefore be selected with great care. Unfortunately, there are few guidelines. It may well be desirable that the conceptual model be similar to the concepts with which the user is already familiar. On the other hand, some other model may be more powerful and efficient. The more adaptable the user community is to new ideas, the more the designer can opt for power over familiarity.

We use the task analysis along with the conceptual model to define the application's semantics. Each necessary operation is identified, and the information needed to carry out the operation is detailed. In Chapter 2, the entities are the furniture symbols and a title; actions on the symbols are ADD and DELETE; on the title, REPLACE. Adding a symbol requires that both the symbol and its desired location be designated. Replacing the title requires a character string input.

The users of the application will need to understand the conceptual model and the semantics. In large and powerful applications, there are typically many kinds of objects and actions. The conceptual model and semantics are best structured so that beginning users can do some productive work without first understanding all of the semantics, and thus are able to grow into the entire system. One way to examine rigorously the complexity of the relationships between the various concepts in a system is to create a graph showing connections and dependencies. Moran has also suggested a formal way to define the semantics and their interrelationships [MORA81].

Having completed the semantic design, we proceed to the syntactic design. Considerable variety is possible, even for a simple command such as adding a symbol, for which at least six syntaxes are possible:

1. ADD	ENTITY	POSITION
2. ADD	POSITION	ENTITY
3. ENTITY	ADD	POSITION
4. ENTITY	POSITION	ADD
5. POSITION	ADD	ENTITY
6. POSITION	ENTITY	ADD

With the command prefix forms 1 and 2, complete prompting is possible. Only forms 1 and 3, in which the command and entity are entered first, readily permit dragging as the positioning technique. In general, prefix forms can allow the command to be easily respecified if it was chosen incorrectly, while postfix forms allow operands to be respecified.

Another syntactic consideration is the use of *open-ended* commands, which accept an arbitrary number of complete operands. For example, we could have an add command which, once specified, allows multiple furniture symbols to be added to the drawing, one after the other, until another command is selected. A typical input sequence would be

```
ADD
  ENTITY  POSITION
  ENTITY  POSITION
DELETE
  ENTITY
  ENTITY
   .
   .
   .
```

This can reduce the number of user actions required to complete a task.

Another way to reduce the number of user actions for the furniture layout application, though at the cost of more commands, is to have a different ADD command for each furniture symbol: ADD_CHAIR, ADD_DESK, etc. Now rather than selecting the ADD command and then the chair symbol, the user just selects the ADD_CHAIR command, perhaps simply by picking the chair symbol from the menu.

Lexical design entails binding of specific hardware capabilities to tokens of the input and output languages. For the input language, this means associating actions or sequences of actions by using input devices with "words" of the language. For the output language, it is the association of display primitives of line, characters, curves and filled areas, as well as attributes such as color, line style and character font, with data for display. As in other top-down designs, binding to physical representations or implementations is left to the latest possible stage of the design.

The logical devices described in Chapter 5 can be thought of as types of syntactic units (like different parts of speech in a language). The various interaction techniques, which are realizations of the logical devices by using tablets, keyboards, speech input and output, etc., represent the associations of physical user actions (or sequences of physical actions) with words at the syntactic level.

Various formalisms can help in the syntactic and lexical design process. The state diagrams discussed in Section 6.3.5 are one example. Reisner used BNF to formally define the two systems she studied [REIS81]. Given a formal definition, two next steps can be taken. The first is to use the definition to drive a simulation of the user interface [HANA80] or the actual interface [NEWM68b]. The input tools of van den Bos use modified regular expressions to achieve similar goals [VAND78]. LANGPAK [HEIN75] and the combined YACC and LEX [JOHN78] systems are examples of similar capabilities for keyboard input. The second step which can be taken with a formal definition is to use metrics to predict user interface characteristics. Reisner did this to predict error rates, while Card, Moran and Newell did this to predict the time taken by skilled users to input command sequences by means of different devices and interaction techniques [CARD80].

Thus a design results from a process which begins with task analysis and a conceptual model and progresses down toward hardware details. Given a design, what next? Just as with a program design, so too a user interface design should be precisely documented and formally reviewed. Part of the review should be to determine how well principles (such as those of Section 6.3) have been applied in the design. After the design review (and only then) does implementation of the user–computer interface begin.

A word of caution: experience shows that even the most carefully thought-out design may, when implemented, not be just right. Thus the implementation of the user interface should be highly modularized, particularly to facilitate changes at the lexical and syntactic level. Such *human-factors fine-tuning* is often needed to make the system truly productive for its user community.

Designing a finely tuned user interface can be time-consuming, but the results justify the effort. The Xerox Star user interface reportedly represents an investment of 20 to 30 person-years [SEYB81], including experimentation with various alternative designs. The result is one of the nicest user interfaces yet seen!

EXERCISES

6.1 Analyze an existing interactive system, preferably an interactive graphics system. What is the conceptual model and what are the semantic, syntactic and lexical components of the input and output languages? Identify all the input and output tokens and lexemes. Critique the application by using the guidelines of this chapter and your own personal experience.

6.2 Study a simple task, such as flowcharting, drawing circuit diagrams, or "painting" with a raster system. Synthesize a user interface by applying the top–down design methodology described in this chapter. Explicitly identify the four levels in the design: conceptual model, semantics, syntax, lexical. Show a typical scenario of user–computer interaction by using a state diagram and cartoons of what is on the screen.

6.3 Formally define the command (input) language syntax of the application program described in Chapter 2. Use production rules or state transition diagrams.

6.4 Which interaction techniques from Chapter 5, when employed by skilled users, would include reflex actions and hence require very fast response times?

6.5 List some dos and don'ts in the design of interactive systems which are omitted in our treatment (preferably based on your own experience) and discuss them. Also list any points you disagree with and explain why. Mail the results to us for possible use in a second edition (with appropriate credits, of course!).

6.6 Critique the human factors of an interactive system, such as a text editor, with which you are familiar.

6.7 Choose a task from Exercise 2 and define the data structures required to allow the effects of any command to be undone. Develop an approach more sophisticated than simply saving the entire data structure at each step.

6.8 Design a computer-controlled introduction to the furniture layout system for naive users. Assume that your users know a lot about furniture arranging and nothing about computers: all they can do is log on to the graphics terminal. Your job is to introduce the relevant concepts, show some typical results, and provide drill in the use of each command.

6.9 Examine several interactive systems. What types of unobtrusive prompts are used?

6.10 Design a user interface for a sketching system which uses just a tablet as the interaction device. The capabilities needed are: (a) approximate a curve with a series of short lines; (b) edit (that is, correct) part of a curve which has been entered; (c) delete a curve; and (d) move a curve. First design an interface for novice users, then design a second interface for experienced users. Now try to design an interface which is adaptable to either novice or experienced users.

6.11 Revise the user interface in the furniture placement program to make the ADD and DELETE commands open-ended, as in Section 6.4.

7
Geometrical Transformations

The purpose of this chapter is to introduce the basic two-dimensional (2D) and three-dimensional (3D) geometrical transformations used in computer graphics. The translation, scaling, and rotation transformations discussed here are at the heart of many graphics applications and will be referred to extensively in succeeding chapters.

The transformations are typically applied both within a graphics package and directly by the application program itself. For example, the viewing operation processor of SGP (Chapter 4) uses 2D translation and scaling to effect the mapping from world coordinates to screen coordinates. When we introduce 3D world coordinates in Chapter 8, 3D rotation and translation will be used for the same purpose. In Chapter 9 we will see how to apply geometric transformations to change the position, orientation, and size of objects (also called *symbols* or *templates*) in a drawing. The transformation used to place furniture symbols in Chapter 2 is a very simple example of this use.

7.1 2D TRANSFORMATIONS

Points in the xy-plane can be *translated* to new positions by adding translation amounts to the coordinates of the points. For each point $P(x, y)$ which is to be moved by Dx units parallel to the x-axis and by Dy units parallel to the y-axis to the new point $P'(x', y')$, we can write:

$$x' = x + Dx, \qquad y' = y + Dy. \tag{7.1}$$

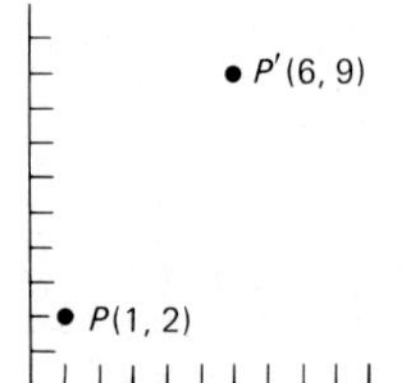

Fig. 7.1 Translation of a point.

This is illustrated in Fig. 7.1, in which the point (1, 2) is translated by (5, 7) to become the point (6,9). Defining the following row vectors as

$$P = [x \quad y], \qquad P' = [x' \quad y'], \qquad T = [Dx \quad Dy],$$

we can rewrite Eq. (7.1) in vector form as

$$[x' \quad y'] = [x \quad y] + [Dx \quad Dy], \tag{7.2}$$

and even more concisely as

$$P' = P + T. \tag{7.3}$$

An object can be translated by applying (7.1) to *each* point of the object. Because each line in an object is made up of an infinite number of points, this process would take infinitely long. Fortunately, all the points on a line can be translated by translating only its endpoints and drawing a new line between the translated endpoints. This is also true for scaling (stretching) and rotation. Proof of this is left as an exercise to the reader. Figure 7.2 shows the effect of translating the outline of a house by (3, −4).

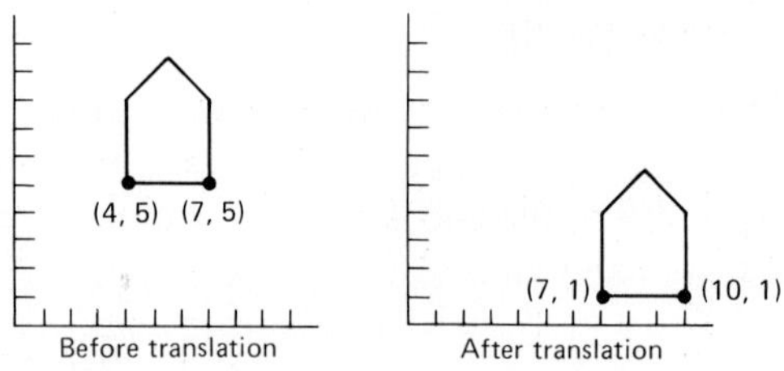

Fig. 7.2 Translation of an object.

Points (as endpoints of vectors) can be *scaled* (stretched) by Sx along the x-axis and by Sy along the y-axis into new points by the multiplications:

$$x' = x \cdot Sx, \qquad y' = y \cdot Sy. \tag{7.4}$$

Defining S as $\begin{bmatrix} Sx & 0 \\ 0 & Sy \end{bmatrix}$, we can write in matrix form

$$[x' \quad y'] = [x \quad y]\begin{bmatrix} Sx & 0 \\ 0 & Sy \end{bmatrix} \tag{7.5}$$

or

$$P' = P \cdot S. \tag{7.6}$$

In Fig. 7.3 the single point (6, 6) is scaled by 1/2 in x and 1/3 in y. Figure 7.4 shows the house outline scaled by 1/2 in x and 1/4 in y. Notice that the scaling is about the origin: the house is smaller *and* closer to the origin. If the scale factors were greater than one, the house would be larger and further from the origin. Techniques for causing the scaling to occur about some point other than the origin are discussed in a later section of this chapter. The proportions of the house have also changed: a *differential* scaling, for which $Sx \neq Sy$, has been used. With a *uniform* scaling, $Sx = Sy$, so the proportions are unaffected.

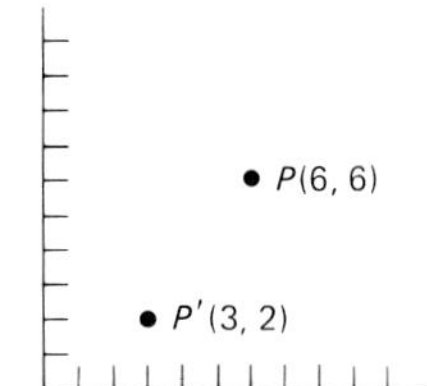

Fig. 7.3 Scaling of a point.

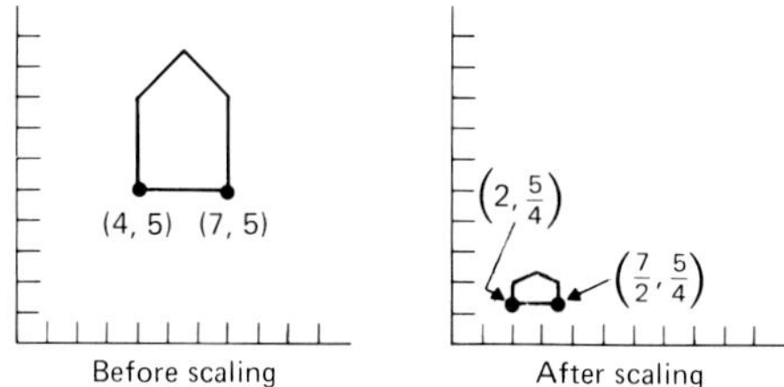

Fig. 7.4 Scaling of an object.

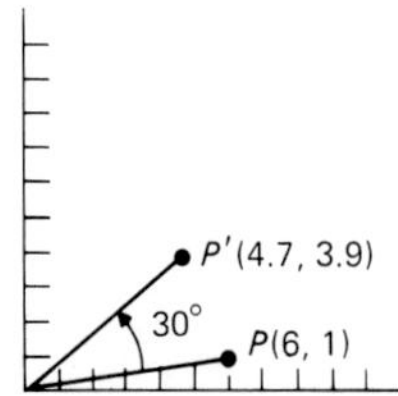

Fig. 7.5 Rotation of a point.

Points (as end points of vectors) can be *rotated* through an angle θ about the origin, as illustrated in Fig. 7.5 for the point $P(6, 1)$ and angle $\theta = 30°$. The rotation is defined mathematically as:

$$\begin{aligned} x' &= x \cdot \cos\theta - y \cdot \sin\theta, \\ y' &= x \cdot \sin\theta + y \cdot \cos\theta. \end{aligned} \tag{7.7}$$

In matrix form, we have

$$[x' \quad y'] = [x \quad y] \begin{bmatrix} \cos\theta & \sin\theta \\ -\sin\theta & \cos\theta \end{bmatrix} \tag{7.8}$$

or

$$P' = P \cdot R \tag{7.9}$$

where R represents the rotation matrix in (7.8). Figure 7.6 shows a square rotated by 45°. As with scaling, the rotation is about the origin. Rotation about an arbitrary point is discussed in a later section.

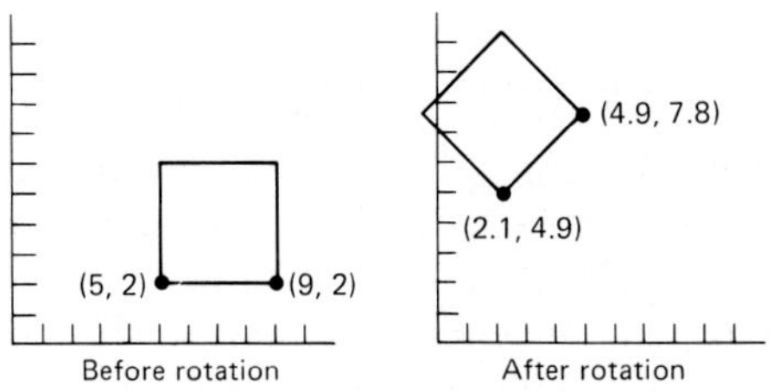

Fig. 7.6 Rotation of a square.

Positive angles are measured *counterclockwise* from x toward y. For negative (clockwise) angles, the identities $\cos(-\theta) = \cos\theta$ and $\sin(-\theta) = -\sin\theta$ can be used to modify (7.7) and (7.8).

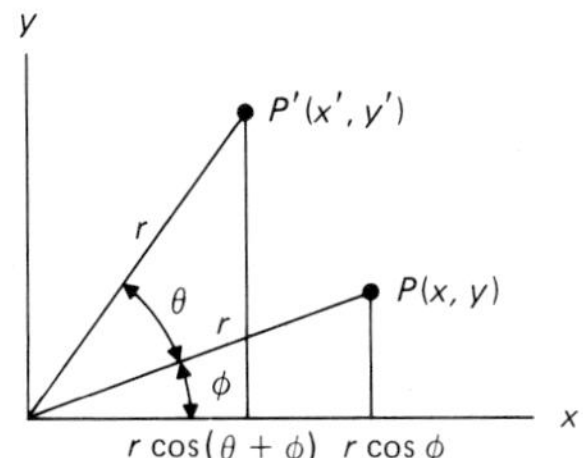

Fig. 7.7 Deriving the rotation equation.

Equation (7.7) is easily derived from Fig. 7.7, in which a rotation by θ transforms $P(x, y)$ into $P'(x', y')$. Because the rotation is about the origin, the distances from the origin to P and to P' are equal and are labeled r in the figure. By simple trigonometry, we note that

$$x = r\cos\phi, \qquad y = r\sin\phi \tag{7.10}$$

and

$$\begin{aligned} x' &= r\cos(\theta + \phi) &&= r\cos\phi\cos\theta - r\sin\phi\sin\theta, \\ y' &= r\sin(\theta + \phi) &&= r\cos\phi\sin\theta + r\sin\phi\cos\theta. \end{aligned} \tag{7.11}$$

Now we substitute (7.10) into (7.11) and obtain (7.7).

7.2 HOMOGENEOUS COORDINATES AND MATRIX REPRESENTATION OF 2D TRANSFORMATIONS

The matrix representations for translation, scaling, and rotation are, respectively,

$$P' = P + T, \tag{7.3}$$

$$P' = P \cdot S, \tag{7.6}$$

$$P' = P \cdot R. \tag{7.9}$$

Unfortunately, translation is treated differently (as an addition) from scaling and rotation (multiplications). We would like to be able to treat all three in a consistent or homogeneous way, so that all three basic transformations can be easily combined together, as is done later in this section.

If we express points in *homogeneous coordinates,* all three transformations can be treated as multiplications. Homogeneous coordinates were developed in geometry [MAXW46, MAXW51] and have subsequently been applied in graphics [ROBE65, BLIN77b, BLIN78a]. Numerous graphics subroutine packages and some display processors work with homogeneous coordinates and transformations. In some cases the application program uses them directly in passing parameters to the graphics package, while in other cases they are applied only within the package and are not visible to the programmer.

In homogeneous coordinates, point $P(x, y)$ is represented as $P(W \cdot x, W \cdot y, W)$ for any scale factor $W \neq 0$. Then, given a homogeneous-coordinate representation for a point $P(X, Y, W)$, we can find the 2D cartesian coordinate representation for the point as $x = X/W$ and $y = Y/W$. In this chapter, W will always be 1, so the division will never be required. One can think of homogeneous coordinates as embedding the 2D plane, scaled by W, in the $z = W$ (here $z = 1$) plane in three-space.

Points are now 3-element row vectors, so transformation matrices, which multiply a point vector to produce another point vector, must be 3×3. In the 3×3 matrix form for homogeneous coordinates, the translation equations (7.1) are represented as:

$$[x' \quad y' \quad 1] = [x \quad y \quad 1] \cdot \begin{bmatrix} 1 & 0 & 0 \\ 0 & 1 & 0 \\ Dx & Dy & 1 \end{bmatrix}. \tag{7.12}$$

Expressed differently,

$$P' = P \cdot T(Dx, Dy), \tag{7.13}$$

where

$$T(Dx, Dy) = \begin{bmatrix} 1 & 0 & 0 \\ 0 & 1 & 0 \\ Dx & Dy & 1 \end{bmatrix}. \tag{7.14}$$

What happens if a point P is translated by (Dx_1, Dy_1) to P' and then translated by (Dx_2, Dy_2) to P''? The result expected intuitively is a net translation of $(Dx_1 + Dx_2, Dy_1 + Dy_2)$. To confirm this, we start with the givens:

$$P' = P \cdot T(Dx_1, Dy_1), \tag{7.15}$$

$$P'' = P' \cdot T(Dx_2, Dy_2). \tag{7.16}$$

Now, substituting (7.15) into (7.16), we obtain

$$P'' = (P \cdot T(Dx_1, Dy_1)) \cdot T(Dx_2, Dy_2) = P \cdot (T(Dx_1, Dy_1) \cdot T(Dx_2, Dy_2)). \tag{7.17}$$

The matrix product $T(Dx_1, Dy_1) \cdot T(Dx_2, Dy_2)$ is

$$\begin{bmatrix} 1 & 0 & 0 \\ 0 & 1 & 0 \\ Dx_1 & Dy_1 & 1 \end{bmatrix} \cdot \begin{bmatrix} 1 & 0 & 0 \\ 0 & 1 & 0 \\ Dx_2 & Dy_2 & 1 \end{bmatrix} = \begin{bmatrix} 1 & 0 & 0 \\ 0 & 1 & 0 \\ Dx_1 + Dx_2 & Dy_1 + Dy_2 & 1 \end{bmatrix}. \tag{7.18}$$

The net translation is indeed $(Dx_1 + Dx_2, Dy_1 + Dy_2)$. The matrix product is variously referred to as the *compounding, catenation, concatenation,* or *composition* of $T(Dx_1, Dy_1)$ and $T(Dx_2, Dy_2)$. In this text, the term *composition* will normally be used.

Similarly, the scaling equations (7.4) are represented in matrix form as

$$[x' \quad y' \quad 1] = [x \quad y \quad 1] \cdot \begin{bmatrix} Sx & 0 & 0 \\ 0 & Sy & 0 \\ 0 & 0 & 1 \end{bmatrix}. \tag{7.19}$$

Defining

$$S(Sx, Sy) = \begin{bmatrix} Sx & 0 & 0 \\ 0 & Sy & 0 \\ 0 & 0 & 1 \end{bmatrix}, \tag{7.20}$$

we have

$$P' = P \cdot S(Sx, Sy). \tag{7.21}$$

Just as successive translations are additive, one expects that successive scalings should be multiplicative. Given:

$$P' = P \cdot S(Sx_1, Sy_1), \tag{7.22}$$

$$P'' = P' \cdot S(Sx_2, Sy_2), \tag{7.23}$$

then, substituting (7.22) into (7.23), we get

$$P' = (P \cdot S(Sx_1, Sy_1)) \cdot S(Sx_2, Sy_2) = P \cdot (S(Sx_1, Sy_1) \cdot S(Sx_2, Sy_2)). \tag{7.24}$$

The matrix product $S(Sx_1, Sy_1) \cdot S(Sx_2, Sy_2)$ is

$$\begin{bmatrix} Sx_1 & 0 & 0 \\ 0 & Sy_1 & 0 \\ 0 & 0 & 1 \end{bmatrix} \cdot \begin{bmatrix} Sx_2 & 0 & 0 \\ 0 & Sy_2 & 0 \\ 0 & 0 & 1 \end{bmatrix} = \begin{bmatrix} Sx_1 \cdot Sx_2 & 0 & 0 \\ 0 & Sy_1 \cdot Sy_2 & 0 \\ 0 & 0 & 1 \end{bmatrix}. \tag{7.25}$$

Thus the scalings are indeed multiplicative.

Finally, the rotation equations (7.7) can be represented as

$$[x' \quad y' \quad 1] = [x \quad y \quad 1] \cdot \begin{bmatrix} \cos\theta & \sin\theta & 0 \\ -\sin\theta & \cos\theta & 0 \\ 0 & 0 & 1 \end{bmatrix}. \tag{7.26}$$

Letting

$$R(\theta) = \begin{bmatrix} \cos\theta & \sin\theta & 0 \\ -\sin\theta & \cos\theta & 0 \\ 0 & 0 & 1 \end{bmatrix}, \tag{7.27}$$

we have

$$P' = P \cdot R(\theta). \tag{7.28}$$

Showing that two successive rotations are additive is left as an exercise for the reader.

In the 2×2 submatrix of (7.27) containing the sines and cosines, consider each of the two columns as vectors. The vectors can be shown to have three properties:

1. Each is a unit vector.
2. Each is perpendicular to the other (their dot product is zero).
3. The directions specified by the vectors are rotated by $R(\theta)$ so as to lie on the positive x and y axes.

The first two properties are also true of the rows of the 2×2 submatrix. The two directions are those to which vectors along the positive x and y axes are rotated. These properties suggest two useful ways to go about deriving a rotation matrix, when one knows the effect desired from the rotation.

7.3 COMPOSITION OF 2D TRANSFORMATIONS

The idea of composition was introduced in the preceding section. The purpose of this section is to show how composition can be used to combine the fundamental R, S, and T matrices so as to produce desired general results. The basic purpose of composing transformations is that it is more efficient to apply a single composed transformation to a point than to apply a series of transformations, one after the other.

Consider, for example, the rotation of an object about some arbitrary point P_1. Because we only know how to rotate about the origin, we convert our original (hard) problem into three different (easy) problems. Thus to rotate about P_1, a sequence of three fundamental transformations is necessary:

1. Translate so that P_1 is at the origin.
2. Rotate.
3. Translate so that the point at the origin returns to P_1.

This sequence is illustrated in Fig. 7.8, in which the house outline is rotated about $P_1(x_1, y_1)$. The first translation is by $(-x_1, -y_1)$, while the later translation is by the inverse (x_1, y_1). The result is rather different than what would result from applying just the rotation.

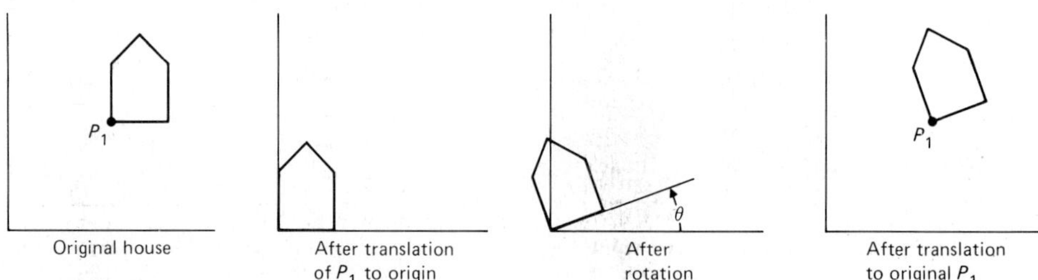

Fig. 7.8 Rotation about point P_1.

The net transformation is:

$$\begin{bmatrix} 1 & 0 & 0 \\ 0 & 1 & 0 \\ -x_1 & -y_1 & 1 \end{bmatrix} \cdot \begin{bmatrix} \cos\theta & \sin\theta & 0 \\ -\sin\theta & \cos\theta & 0 \\ 0 & 0 & 1 \end{bmatrix} \cdot \begin{bmatrix} 1 & 0 & 0 \\ 0 & 1 & 0 \\ x_1 & y_1 & 1 \end{bmatrix}$$

$$= \begin{bmatrix} \cos\theta & \sin\theta & 0 \\ -\sin\theta & \cos\theta & 0 \\ x_1(1-\cos\theta) + y_1\sin\theta & y_1(1-\cos\theta) - x_1\sin\theta & 1 \end{bmatrix}. \tag{7.29}$$

This composition of transformations by matrix multiplication is an example of how homogeneous coordinates lend simplicity.

A similar approach is used to scale an object about an arbitrary point P_1: translate P_1 to the origin, scale, translate back to P_1. In this case the net transformation is:

$$\begin{bmatrix} 1 & 0 & 0 \\ 0 & 1 & 0 \\ -x_1 & -y_1 & 1 \end{bmatrix} \cdot \begin{bmatrix} Sx & 0 & 0 \\ 0 & Sy & 0 \\ 0 & 0 & 1 \end{bmatrix} \cdot \begin{bmatrix} 1 & 0 & 0 \\ 0 & 1 & 0 \\ x_1 & y_1 & 1 \end{bmatrix}$$

$$= \begin{bmatrix} Sx & 0 & 0 \\ 0 & Sy & 0 \\ x_1(1-Sx) & y_1(1-Sy) & 1 \end{bmatrix}. \tag{7.30}$$

Suppose we wish to scale, rotate, and position the house shown in Fig. 7.9, with P_1 being the center for the rotation and scaling. The sequence would be to translate P_1 to the origin, perform the scaling and rotation, and then translate from the origin to the new position P_2, where the house is to be placed (the sequence is shown in Fig. 7.9). A data structure which records this transformation might contain the scale factor(s), rotation angle, and translation amounts, or might simply record the composite transformation matrix:

$$T(-x_1, -y_1) \cdot S(Sx, Sy) \cdot R(\theta) \cdot T(x_2, y_2).$$

Given that M_1 and M_2 each represent a fundamental translation, scaling, or rotation, when is $M_1 \cdot M_2 = M_2 \cdot M_1$, that is, when do M_1 and M_2 commute? In gen-

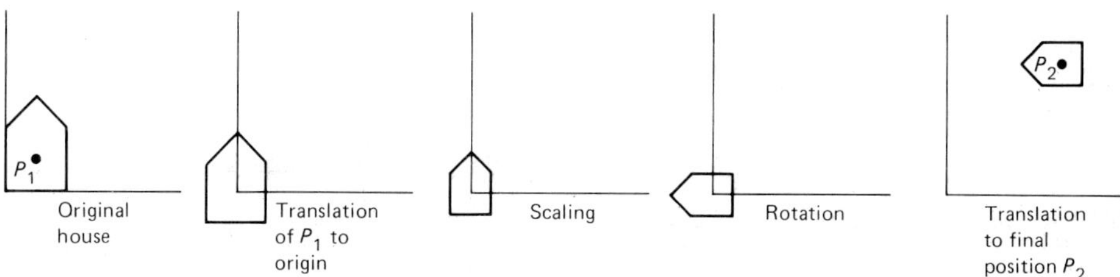

Fig. 7.9 Transformation of template.

eral, of course, matrix multiplication is *not* commutative. However, it is easy to show that in the following special cases, commutativity holds:

M_1	M_2
Translate	Translate
Scale	Scale
Rotate	Rotate
Scale (with $Sx = Sy$)	Rotate

It is in these cases that we need not be concerned about the *order* of matrix multiplication.

7.4 EFFICIENCY CONSIDERATIONS

The most general composition of *R, S,* and *T* operations will produce a matrix of the form:

$$M = \begin{bmatrix} r_{11} & r_{12} & 0 \\ r_{21} & r_{22} & 0 \\ t_x & t_y & 1 \end{bmatrix}. \tag{7.31}$$

The upper 2×2 is a composite rotation and scale matrix, while the t_x and t_y are composite translations. Calculating $P \cdot M$ as a vector times a 3×3 matrix takes nine multiplies and six adds. The fixed structure of the last column of (7.31) simplifies the actual operations to

$$\begin{aligned} x' &= x \cdot r_{11} + y \cdot r_{21} + t_x, \\ y' &= x \cdot r_{12} + y \cdot r_{22} + t_y, \end{aligned} \tag{7.32}$$

reducing the process to four multiplies and four adds—a significant speedup, especially because the operation might be applied to hundreds or even thousands of points per picture. Thus while 3×3 matrices are convenient and useful for composing 2D transformations, the final matrix can be applied most efficiently in a program by recognizing its special structure. Some hardware matrix multipliers have parallel adders and multipliers, thereby diminishing or removing this concern.

Another area where efficiency is important is creating successive views of an object, such as a molecule or airplane, with the object rotated a few degrees between each successive view. If each view can be created and displayed sufficiently quickly (in 30 to 60 milliseconds each), then the object will appear to be dynamically rotating. To achieve this speed, each individual point and line of the object must be transformed as quickly as possible. The rotation equations (7.7) require four multiplies and two adds. This can be improved by recognizing that because θ is small (just a few degrees), then $\cos\theta$ is very close to 1. In this approximation, Eq. (7.7) becomes

$$x' = x - y\sin\theta, \qquad y' = x\sin\theta + y, \tag{7.33}$$

which requires just two multiplies and two adds. The saving of two multiplies can be significant on computers lacking hardware multipliers. An even better approximation is to use x' instead of x in the second equation:

$$x' = x - y\sin\theta, \qquad y' = x'\sin\theta + y. \tag{7.34}$$

The determinant of the corresponding 2×2 matrix is now 1, as are the determinants of all rotation matrices.

There is one problem, however. The formulas represent an approximation to the correct values of x' and y': a small error is built in. Each time the formulas are applied to the new values of x and y, the error gets a bit larger. Repeated indefinitely, the error will overwhelm the correct values, and the displayed rotating image will begin to look like a collection of randomly drawn lines.

This problem can be completely eliminated by keeping the original list of (x, y) coordinates. After each rotation of 360°, the rotated data is discarded, and the original data is used once more to restart the rotation. This of course means that space is needed for the extra list of coordinates. Not surprisingly, there is a space–time tradeoff between incremental and absolute rotation! Incremental rotation does not provide something for nothing.

7.5 MATRIX REPRESENTATION OF 3D TRANSFORMATIONS

The representation of 2D transformations as 3×3 matrices has a parallel for 3D transformations, which are represented as 4×4 matrices. To permit this, the 3D point (x, y, z) will be represented in homogeneous coordinates as $(W \cdot x, W \cdot y, W \cdot z, W)$, with W not equal to zero. If $W \neq 1$, then W is divided into the first three homogeneous coordinates to obtain the 3D cartesian coordinate point (x, y, z). This implies, incidentally, that two homogeneous coordinate points H_1 and H_2 represent the same 3D point if and only if $H_1 = cH_2$, for any nonzero constant c.

The 3D coordinate system used in this text is *right-handed,* as shown in Fig. 7.10. We adopt the convention that positive rotations are such that, when looking from a positive axis toward the origin, a 90° *counterclockwise** rotation will transform one positive axis into the other. The following table, usable for either right-handed or left-handed coordinate systems, follows from this convention:

If axis of rotation is	Direction of positive rotation is
x	y to z
y	z to x
z	x to y

These positive directions are also depicted in Fig. 7.10.

*This convention, also used in vector algebra, is the reverse of that used in [NEWM79].

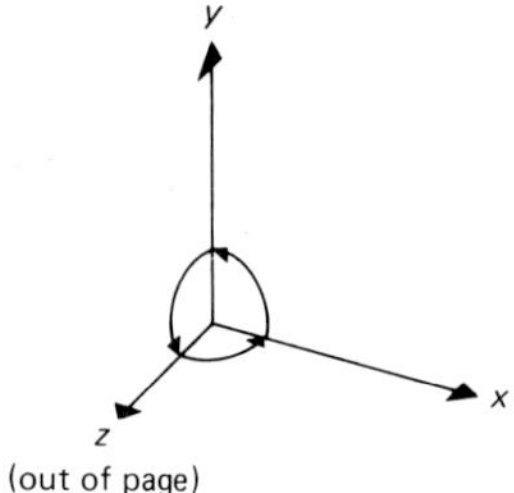

Fig. 7.10 Right-handed coordinate system.

A right-handed system is used here because it is familiar to most people, even though in 3D graphics the left-handed system is often desirable, since it is more convenient to think of a left-handed system superimposed on the face of a display, as shown in Fig. 7.11. This then gives the natural interpretation of larger z values being further from the viewer. Notice that in a left-handed system, positive rotations are *clockwise,* when looking from a positive axis toward the origin.

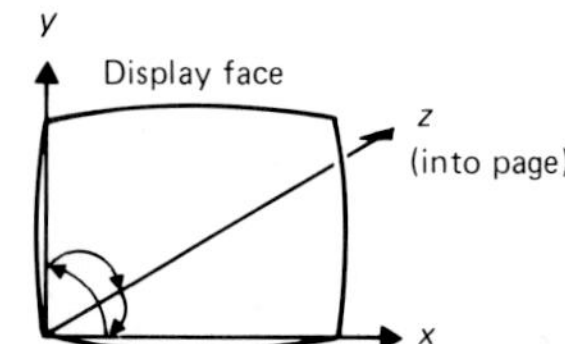

Fig. 7.11 Left-handed coordinate system.

Translation in 3D is a simple extension from 2D:

$$T(Dx, Dy, Dz) = \begin{bmatrix} 1 & 0 & 0 & 0 \\ 0 & 1 & 0 & 0 \\ 0 & 0 & 1 & 0 \\ Dx & Dy & Dz & 1 \end{bmatrix}. \tag{7.35}$$

That is, $[x \quad y \quad z \quad 1] \cdot T(Dx, Dy, Dz) = [x + Dx \quad y + Dy \quad z + Dz \quad 1]$.

Scaling is similarly extended:

$$S(Sx, Sy, Sz) = \begin{bmatrix} Sx & 0 & 0 & 0 \\ 0 & Sy & 0 & 0 \\ 0 & 0 & Sz & 0 \\ 0 & 0 & 0 & 1 \end{bmatrix}. \tag{7.36}$$

Checking, $[x \quad y \quad z \quad 1] \cdot S(Sx, Sy, Sz) = [Sx \cdot x \quad Sy \cdot y \quad Sz \cdot z \quad 1]$.

The 2D rotation of (7.26) is just a rotation about the z-axis in 3D. In 3D, a rotation about the z-axis is:

$$Rz(\theta) = \begin{bmatrix} \cos\theta & \sin\theta & 0 & 0 \\ -\sin\theta & \cos\theta & 0 & 0 \\ 0 & 0 & 1 & 0 \\ 0 & 0 & 0 & 1 \end{bmatrix}. \qquad (7.37)$$

This is easily verified: a 90° rotation of [1 0 0 1], which is the unit vector along the x-axis, should produce the unit vector [0 1 0 1] along the y-axis. Evaluating the product

$$[1 \quad 0 \quad 0 \quad 1] \cdot \begin{bmatrix} 0 & 1 & 0 & 0 \\ -1 & 0 & 0 & 0 \\ 0 & 0 & 1 & 0 \\ 0 & 0 & 0 & 1 \end{bmatrix} \qquad (7.38)$$

gives the predicted result of [0 1 0 1].

The x-axis rotation matrix is:

$$Rx(\theta) = \begin{bmatrix} 1 & 0 & 0 & 0 \\ 0 & \cos\theta & \sin\theta & 0 \\ 0 & -\sin\theta & \cos\theta & 0 \\ 0 & 0 & 0 & 1 \end{bmatrix}. \qquad (7.39)$$

The y-axis rotation matrix is:

$$Ry(\theta) = \begin{bmatrix} \cos\theta & 0 & -\sin\theta & 0 \\ 0 & 1 & 0 & 0 \\ \sin\theta & 0 & \cos\theta & 0 \\ 0 & 0 & 0 & 1 \end{bmatrix}. \qquad (7.40)$$

The columns (and the rows) of the upper left 3 × 3 submatrix of $Rz(\theta)$, $Rx(\theta)$, and $Ry(\theta)$ are mutually perpendicular unit vectors with the same interpretation as for 2D.

All these transformation matrices have inverses. The inverse for T is obtained by negating Dx, Dy, and Dz; for S, by replacing Sx, Sy, and Sz by their reciprocals; for each of the three rotation matrices, by negating the angle of rotation.

Composing an arbitrary sequence of rotations about the x, y, and z axes will create matrix A of the form:

$$A = \begin{bmatrix} r_{11} & r_{12} & r_{13} & 0 \\ r_{21} & r_{22} & r_{23} & 0 \\ r_{31} & r_{32} & r_{33} & 0 \\ 0 & 0 & 0 & 1 \end{bmatrix}. \qquad (7.41)$$

The 3×3 rotation submatrix is said to be *orthogonal,* because its columns are mutually orthogonal unit vectors. These unit vectors are rotated by the matrix into the x, y, and z axes. Finding the appropriate rotation matrix given such directions is sometimes necessary, so this observation can be helpful. Rotation matrices preserve both lengths and angles, while scaling and translation matrices do not.

For any orthogonal matrix B, the inverse of B is just its transpose: $B^{-1} = B^T$. Finding the inverse of a rotation matrix is often necessary, so this is a useful result. In fact, taking the transpose need not even involve exchanging elements in the array that stores the matrix—it is only necessary to exchange row and column indexes when accessing the array. Notice that this method of finding an inverse is consistent with the result of negating θ to find the inverse of Rx, Ry, and Rz.

An arbitrary number of rotation, scaling, and translation matrices can be multiplied together. The result will always be of the form:

$$\begin{bmatrix} r_{11} & r_{12} & r_{13} & 0 \\ r_{21} & r_{22} & r_{23} & 0 \\ r_{31} & r_{32} & r_{33} & 0 \\ t_x & t_y & t_z & 1 \end{bmatrix}. \tag{7.42}$$

As in the 2×2 case, the 3×3 upper-left submatrix R will give the aggregate rotation and scaling, while T will give the subsequent aggregate translation. Some computational efficiency is achieved by performing the transformation explicitly as

$$[x' \quad y' \quad z'] = [x \quad y \quad z] \cdot R + T, \tag{7.43}$$

where R and T are submatrices from (7.42).

7.6 COMPOSITION OF 3D TRANSFORMATIONS

Basic 3D transformations can be composed to obtain many different results. This section illustrates how to do this, to obtain a result which will be useful in Section 8.4. The task is to transform the lines $\overline{P_1P_2}$ and $\overline{P_1P_3}$ of Fig. 7.12 from the starting position to the ending position. Point P_1 has been translated to the origin, $\overline{P_1P_2}$ lies on the negative z-axis, and $\overline{P_1P_3}$ lies in the positive y-half of the yz-plane. The lengths of the lines are unaffected by the transformation.

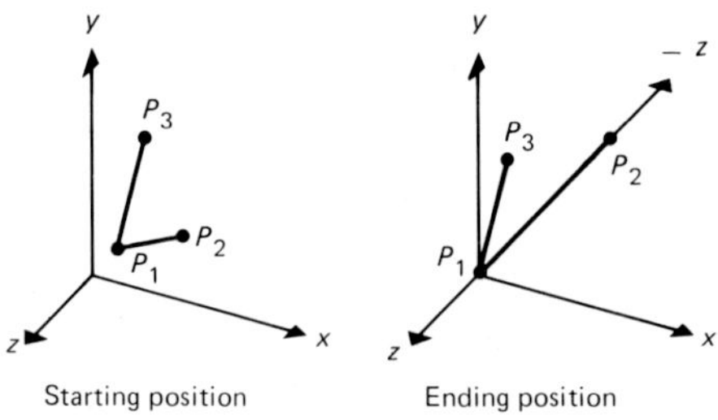

Fig. 7.12 Transformation of P_1, P_2, and P_3 from the starting position to the ending position.

Again, we break a hard problem into simpler problems. In this case, the transformation can be done in four steps:

1. Translate P_1 to the origin.
2. Rotate about the y-axis, so that $\overline{P_1P_2}$ lies in the yz-plane.
3. Rotate about the x-axis, so that $\overline{P_1P_2}$ lies on the negative z-axis.
4. Rotate about the z-axis, so that $\overline{P_1P_3}$ lies in the yz-plane.

Step 1: Translate P_1 to the origin.

$$T(-x_1,\ -y_1,\ -z_1) = \begin{bmatrix} 1 & 0 & 0 & 0 \\ 0 & 1 & 0 & 0 \\ 0 & 0 & 1 & 0 \\ -x_1 & -y_1 & -z_1 & 1 \end{bmatrix}. \tag{7.44}$$

Applying T to P_1, P_2, and P_3 gives:

$$P_1' = P_1 \cdot T(-x_1,\ -y_1,\ -z_1) = [\,0 \quad 0 \quad 0 \quad 1\,], \tag{7.45}$$

$$P_2' = P_2 \cdot T(-x_1,\ -y_1,\ -z_1) = [x_2 - x_1 \quad y_2 - y_1 \quad z_2 - z_1 \quad 1], \tag{7.46}$$

$$P_3' = P_3 \cdot T(-x_1,\ -y_1,\ -z_1) = [x_3 - x_1 \quad y_3 - y_1 \quad z_3 - z_1 \quad 1]. \tag{7.47}$$

Step 2: Rotate about the y-axis. Figure 7.13 shows $\overline{P_1P_2}$ after step 1, along with the projection of $\overline{P_1P_2}$ onto the xz-plane. The rotation is by the positive angle θ, for which

$$\cos\theta = \frac{-z_2'}{D_1} = \frac{-(z_2 - z_1)}{D_1}, \tag{7.48}$$

$$\sin\theta = \frac{x_2'}{D_1} = \frac{x_2 - x_1}{D_1}, \tag{7.49}$$

where

$$D_1 = \sqrt{(z_2 - z_1)^2 + (x_2 - x_1)^2}. \tag{7.50}$$

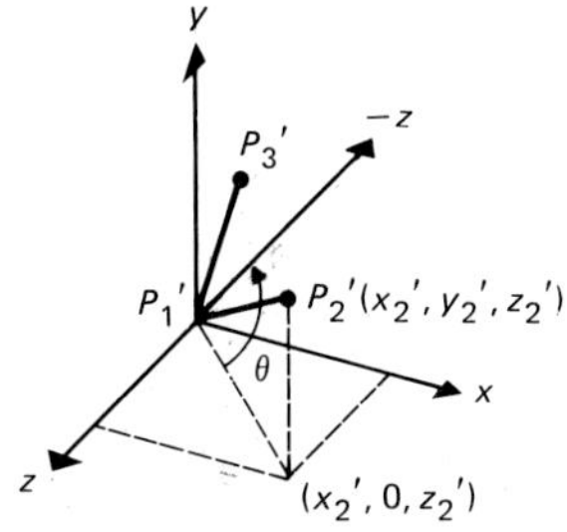

Fig. 7.13 Rotation about y-axis; the projection of $\overline{P_1'P_2'}$ rotates into negative z-axis.

These values are to be substituted into (7.40). Then

$$P_2'' = P_2' \cdot Ry(\theta) = \left[0 \quad y_2 - y_1 \quad -\frac{(x_2 - x_1)^2}{D_1} - \frac{(z_2 - z_1)^2}{D_1} \quad 1 \right]. \tag{7.51}$$

As expected, the x-component of P_2'' is zero.

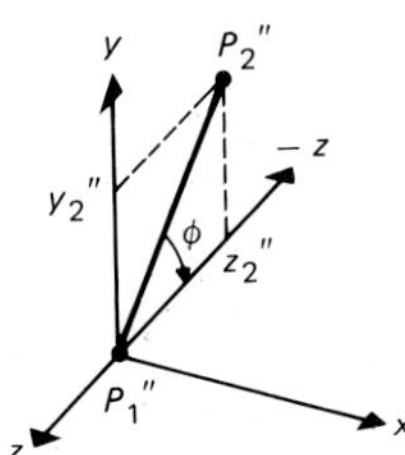

Fig. 7.14 Rotation about x-axis; $\overline{P_1''P_2''}$ rotates into negative z-axis.

Step 3: Rotate about the x-axis. Figure 7.14 shows $\overline{P_1P_2}$ after step 2. The rotation is by the negative angle ϕ, for which

$$\cos(-\phi) = \cos\phi \quad = \frac{-z_2''}{||\overline{P_1P_2}||}, \tag{7.52}$$

$$\sin(-\phi) \ = -\sin\phi \ = \frac{-y_2''}{||\overline{P_1P_2}||}, \tag{7.53}$$

where

$$||\overline{P_1P_2}|| = \sqrt{(x_2 - x_1)^2 + (y_2 - y_1)^2 + (z_2 - z_1)^2}. \tag{7.54}$$

The notation $||\overline{P_1P_2}||$ just means "the length of $\overline{P_1P_2}$." The result of the rotation in step 3 is

$$\begin{aligned} P_2''' &= P_2'' \cdot Rx(\phi) = P_2' \cdot Ry(\theta) \cdot Rx(\phi) \\ &= P_2 \cdot T \cdot Ry(\theta) \cdot Rx(\phi) = [\, 0 \quad 0 \quad -||\overline{P_1P_2}|| \quad 1]. \end{aligned} \tag{7.55}$$

That is, $\overline{P_1P_2}$ now coincides with the negative z-axis.

Step 4: Rotate about the z-axis. Figure 7.15 shows $\overline{P_1P_2}$ and $\overline{P_1P_3}$ after step 3, with P_2''' on the negative z-axis and P_3''' at the position

$$P_3''' = [x_3''' \quad y_3''' \quad z_3''' \quad 1] = P_3 \cdot T(-x_1, -y_1, -z_1) \cdot Ry(\theta) \cdot Rx(\phi). \tag{7.56}$$

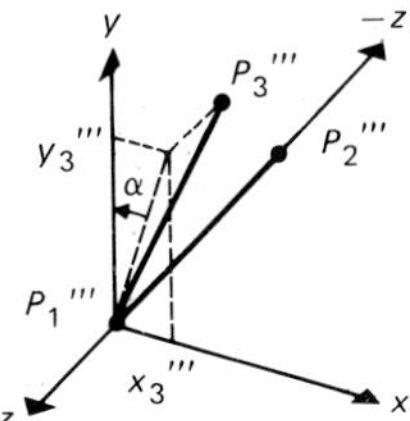

Fig. 7.15 Rotation about z-axis; the projection of $\overline{P_1'''P_3'''}$ rotates into y-axis.

The rotation is through the positive angle α, with:

$$\cos\alpha = y_3'''/D_2, \qquad \sin\alpha = x_3'''/D_2, \qquad D_2 = \sqrt{(x_3''')^2 + (y_3''')^2}.$$

Step 4 is the final step in achieving the final result depicted in Fig. 7.12.

The composite matrix

$$T(-x_1, -y_1, -z_1) \cdot Ry(\theta) \cdot Rx(\phi) \cdot Rz(\alpha) = T \cdot R \tag{7.57}$$

is the required transformation, with $R = Ry(\theta) \cdot Rx(\phi) \cdot Ry(\alpha)$. Applying this transformation to P_1, P_2, and P_3 to verify that P_1 is transformed to the origin, P_2 is transformed to the negative z-axis, and P_3 is transformed to the positive y-half of the yz-plane is left as an exercise for the reader.

A computationally simpler way to obtain the same matrix R is to use the properties of orthogonal matrices discussed on p. 258. We define

$$r_z = [\, r_{1z} \quad r_{2z} \quad r_{3z} \,] = \frac{-\overline{P_1P_2}}{||\overline{P_1P_2}||}. \tag{7.58}$$

This is the unit vector along $\overline{P_1P_2}$ which will rotate into the positive z-axis. Also,

$$r_x = [\, r_{1x} \quad r_{2x} \quad r_{3x} \,] = \frac{\overline{P_1P_2} \times \overline{P_1P_3}}{||\overline{P_1P_2} \times \overline{P_1P_3}||}. \tag{7.59}$$

This unit vector is perpendicular to the plane of P_1, P_2, and P_3 and will rotate into the positive x-axis. Finally,

$$r_y = [\, r_{1y} \quad r_{2y} \quad r_{3y} \,] = r_z \times r_x$$

will rotate into the positive y-axis. Then the composite matrix is given by

$$T(-x_1, -y_1, -z_1) \cdot \begin{bmatrix} r_{1x} & r_{1y} & r_{1z} & 0 \\ r_{2x} & r_{2y} & r_{2z} & 0 \\ r_{3x} & r_{3y} & r_{3z} & 0 \\ 0 & 0 & 0 & 1 \end{bmatrix} = T \cdot R, \tag{7.60}$$

where T and R are the same as in Eq. (7.57).

7.7 TRANSFORMATION AS A CHANGE OF COORDINATE SYSTEMS

We have been discussing transforming a set of points belonging to an object into another set of points, with both sets in the same coordinate system. Thus the coordinate system stays unaltered and the object is transformed with respect to the origin of the coordinate system to obtain proper size. An alternative but equivalent way of thinking of a transformation is as a change of coordinate systems. This view is useful when multiple objects, each defined in its own (local) coordinate system, are combined and we wish to express their coordinates in a single, global coordinate system. Before we see why this is so, let us verify that a point defined in one coordinate system can have its position specified in any other coordinate system. For example, the point in Fig. 7.16 has coordinates (10,8), (6,6), (8,6), and (4,2) in coordinate systems 1 through 4, respectively.

The transformation from coordinate system 1 to 2 is $T_{12} = T(-4,-2)$; from 2 to 3, $T_{23} = T(-2,-3) \cdot S(2,2)$; from 3 to 4, $T_{34} = T(-6.7,-1.8) \cdot R(-45°)$. In general, the coordinate system transformation T_{ij} transforms the axes of coordinate system j into the axes of coordinate system i with respect to coordinate system i.

If P_i represents a point whose coordinates are given in coordinate system i, then we can write $P_2 = P_1 T_{12}$. Checking this for the case at hand, we have

$$[6 \quad 6 \quad 1] = [10 \quad 8 \quad 1] \cdot T(-4,-2).$$

Transformation T_{21} from coordinate system 2 to 1 is of course $T_{12}^{-1} = T(4,2)$. Similarly,

$$\begin{aligned} T_{32} = T_{23}^{-1} = (T(-2,-3) \cdot S(2,\ 2))^{-1} &= S^{-1}(2,\ 2) \cdot T^{-1}(-2,-3) \\ &= S(0.5,\ 0.5) \cdot T(2,\ 3). \end{aligned}$$

Furthermore, $T_{13} = T_{12} \cdot T_{23}$, etc. Hence, $T_{13} = T(-6,-5) \cdot S(2,\ 2)$.

When we assemble objects into a higher-level object, as with the room symbols in Chapter 2, we can think of transformations in one of two ways. In Chapter 2, we thought of the symbols as being defined in world coordinates and transformed them

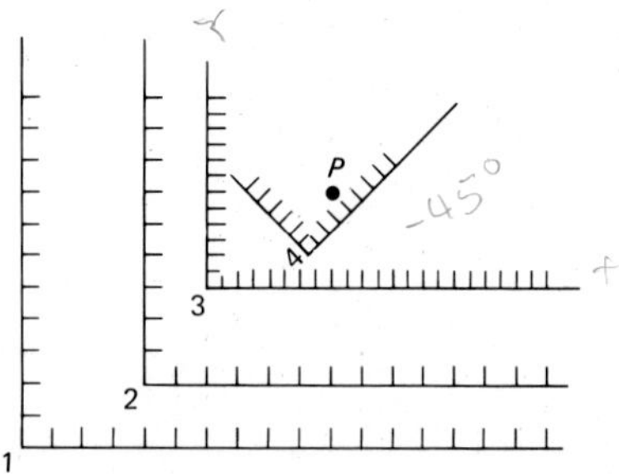

Fig. 7.16 Point P and four coordinate systems.

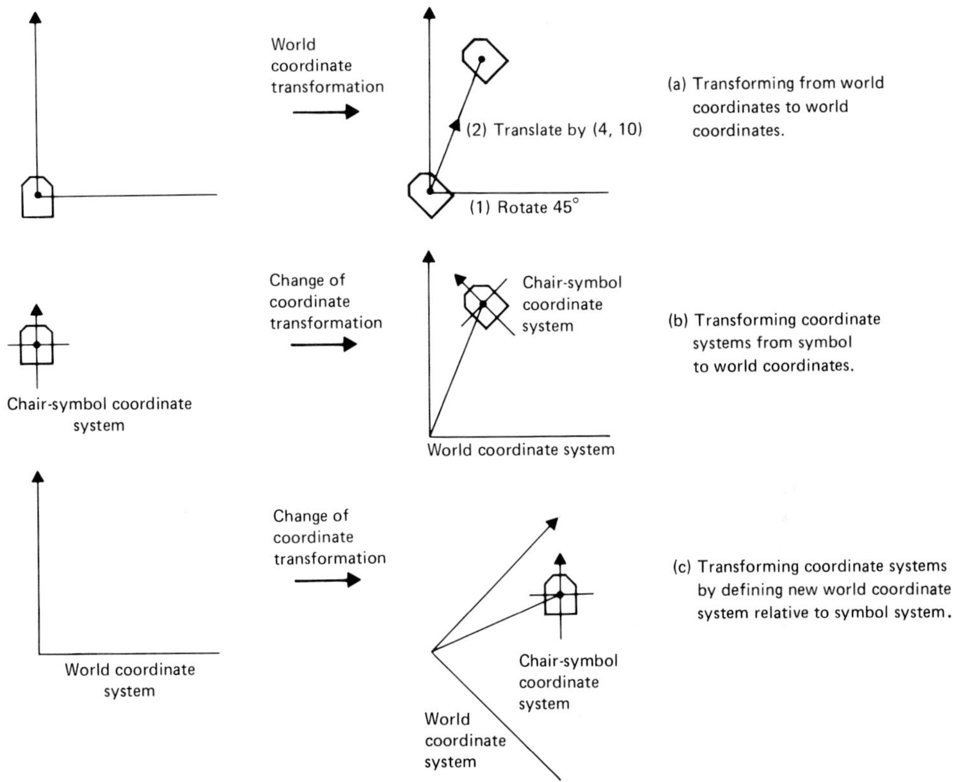

Fig. 7.17 Three ways of transforming coordinate systems.

to new positions and orientations in the same world coordinate system, as in Fig. 7.17(a). More generally, placing symbols can be considered as transforming points defined in their local *symbol* coordinate system to equivalent points in the room (that is, world) coordinate system by transforming the symbol coordinate system to the world coordinate system, as in Fig. 7.17(b). (Note that, strictly speaking, the new room coordinate system is defined with respect to the old symbol coordinate system shown in Fig. 7.17(c), although, of course, we think of having had the room coordinate system all along and placing successive symbol coordinate systems with respect to it. These two approaches, of course, give identical results.) The coordinates of points on the symbol expressed in room (world) coordinates are $P_{\text{room}} = P_{\text{chair}} \cdot T_{\text{chair,room}}$, where $T_{\text{chair,room}}$ is the transformation that takes the chair axes into the world axes: $R(45°) \cdot T(4,10)$. This can be seen by applying the definition of $P_{\text{chair,room}}$ to Fig. 7.17(b). Not surprisingly, this is the same transformation as the one that takes the original world coordinates of the symbol into transformed world coordinates in Fig. 7.17(a).

Taking the first point of view, of defining all objects/symbols in the world coordinate system and then transforming them to the desired place, gives a somewhat unrealistic view of all symbols initially defined on top of each other in the same world coordinate system. It is more natural to think of each symbol defined in its own symbol coordinate system and then scaled, rotated, and translated by having its coordinates redefined in the new world coordinate system. In this second point of view, one thinks naturally of separate pieces of paper, each with a symbol on it, being shrunk or stretched, rotated and placed on the world coordinate plane (or alternatively having the plane shrunk or stretched, tilted, and slid relative to each piece of paper). Mathematically, all these views are identical.

The change of coordinate system point of view is useful when additional information is specified for subobjects in their local coordinate system. For example, if torque is applied to the front wheel of the tricycle in Fig. 7.18, all wheels have to be rotated appropriately and we need to find out how the tricycle as a whole is moved in the world coordinate system. This problem is a bit more complex than the symbol placement problem because there are several successive changes of coordinate systems. First, the tricycle and front-wheel coordinate systems have initial positions in the world coordinate system. As the bike moves forward, the front wheel rotates about the z axis of the wheel coordinate system, while simultaneously the wheel and tricycle coordinate systems move relative to the world coordinate system. The wheel and tricycle coordinate systems are related to the world coordinate system by time-varying translations in x and y plus a rotation about y. The tricycle and wheel coordinate systems are related to each other by a time-varying rotation about y as the handlebars are turned. (The tricycle coordinate system is fixed to the frame, not to the handlebars.)

To make the problem a bit easier, we assume that the wheel and tricycle axes are parallel to the world coordinate axes and that the wheel moves in a straight line parallel to the world coordinate x axis. As the wheel rotates by an angle α, a point on the wheel (which we denote as P_{wh}) rotates through a distance αr, where r is the radius of the wheel. Because the wheel is on the ground, the tricycle therefore moves

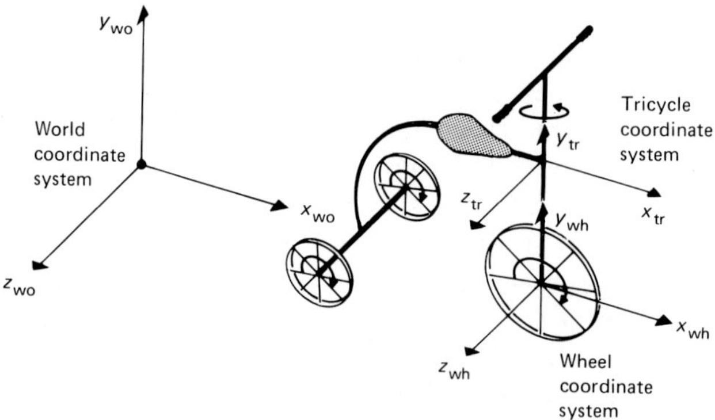

Fig. 7.18 Stylized tricycle with three coordinate systems.

forward αr units. Therefore the rim point P_{wh} on the wheel moves and rotates with respect to the initial wheel coordinate system with a net effect of translation by αr and rotation by α, so that it has new coordinates in the original wheel coordinate system of

$$P'_{wh} = P_{wh} \cdot R_z(\alpha) \cdot T(\alpha r, 0, 0), \tag{7.61}$$

or coordinates in the new (translated) wheel coordinate system of

$$P'_{wh'} = P_{wh} \cdot R_z(\alpha). \tag{7.62}$$

To find the points P_{wo} and P'_{wo} in the world coordinate system, we transform from the wheel to the world coordinate system:

$$P_{wo} = P_{wh} \cdot T_{wh,wo} = P_{wh} \cdot T_{wh,tr} \cdot T_{tr,wo}. \tag{7.63}$$

In this case $T_{wh,tr}$ and $T_{tr,wo}$ are simple translations given by the initial positions of the tricycle and wheel. P'_{wo} is computed by using Eqs. (7.61) and (7.63):

$$P'_{wo} = P'_{wh} \cdot T_{wh,wo} = P_{wh} \cdot R_z(\alpha) \cdot T(\alpha r, 0, 0) \cdot T_{wh,wo}. \tag{7.64}$$

Alternatively, we recognize that $T_{wh,wo}$ has been changed to $T_{wh',wo}$ by the translation of the wheel coordinate system, and write the same result as (7.64):

$$P'_{wo} = P'_{wh'} \cdot T_{wh',wo} = (P_{wh} \cdot R_z(\alpha)) \cdot (T(\alpha r, 0, 0) \cdot T_{wh,wo}). \tag{7.65}$$

In general then, we derive the new $T_{wh',wo}$ and $T_{wh',tr'}$ from their previous values by applying the appropriate transformations based on the equations of motion of the tricycle parts and then apply these updated transformations to updated points in local coordinate systems and derive the equivalent points in world coordinate systems. It is left as an exercise to the reader to treat the case of turning the tricycle's front wheel to change direction and to compute rotation angles for the rear wheels based on their radius and the trajectory of the tricycle.

EXERCISES

7.1 Prove that a line can be transformed by applying the transformation to the endpoints of the line and then constructing a new line between the transformed endpoints.

7.2 Prove that two successive 2D rotations are additive: $R(\theta_1) \cdot R(\theta_2) = R(\theta_1 + \theta_2)$.

7.3 Prove that 2D rotation and scaling commute if $Sx = Sy$. Prove that otherwise they do not.

7.4 Find an expression relating the accumulated error in Eq. (7.33) to θ and the number of incremental rotations performed. Do the same for Eq. (7.34).

7.5 Write a program for your favorite minicomputer to perform 2D incremental rotation. How much time is needed per endpoint? Compare this to the time needed per endpoint for absolute 2D rotation.

7.6 You have a drawing consisting of N endpoints. It is to be dynamically rotated about a single axis by using software. Multiplication on your computer takes time t_m; addition, t_a. Write expressions for the time needed to rotate the N points by using both absolute and relative rotation. Ignore control steps. Now evaluate the expressions with N as a variable and using the actual instruction times for your computer.

Suppose the slowest rate at which an object can be rotated without being annoyingly slow is a 360° revolution in 30 seconds. Suppose also that, to be smooth, the rotation must be in steps of at most 4°. How many points can be rotated in the time available by using absolute rotation? Incremental rotation?

7.7 Apply the transformations developed in Section 7.6 to the points P_1, P_2, and P_3, to verify that the points do transform as intended.

7.8 Rework Section 7.6, assuming that $||\overline{P_1P_2}|| = 1$ and $||\overline{P_1P_3}|| = 1$, and that direction cosines for $\overline{P_1P_2}$ and $\overline{P_1P_3}$ are given. The direction cosines for a line are the cosines of the angles the line makes with the x, y, and z axes. For a line from the origin to (x,y,z) the direction cosines are $(x/d,\ y/d,\ z/d)$, where d is the length of the line.

7.9 Another reason why homogeneous coordinates are attractive is because 3D points at infinity in cartesian coordinates can be explicitly represented in homogeneous coordinates. How?

7.10 Show that Eqs. (7.57) and (7.60) are equivalent.

7.11 Given a unit cube with one corner at (0,0,0) and the opposite corner at (1,1,1), derive the transformations necessary to rotate the cube by θ degrees about the main diagonal (from (0,0,0) to (1,1,1)) in the counterclockwise direction when looking along the diagonal toward the origin.

7.12 Suppose the window might have its base rotated at an angle θ from the x axis, as in the Core system [GSPC79]. What is the window-to-viewport mapping? Verify your answer by applying the transformation to each corner of the window, to be sure that they are transformed to the appropriate corners of the viewport.

7.13 You are given a line from the origin of a right-handed coordinate system to the point $P(x,y,z)$. Rotate the line into the positive z-axis in three different ways and prove by algebraic manipulation that the results are equivalent.

a) Rotate about the x-axis into the xz-plane, then rotate about the y-axis into the z-axis.
b) Rotate about the y-axis into the yz-plane, then rotate about the x-axis into the z-axis.
c) Rotate about the z-axis into the xz-plane, then about the y-axis into the z-axis.

For each method calculate the sines and cosines of the angles of rotation.

7.14 An object is to be scaled by a factor S in the direction whose direction cosines are (α, β, δ). Derive the transformation matrix.

7.15 Prove that the properties of $R(\theta)$ described at the end of Section 7.2 are true.

7.16 Extend the incremental rotation discussed in Section 7.4 to 3D, forming a composite operation for rotation about an arbitrary axis.

8 Viewing in Three Dimensions

The 3D viewing process is inherently more complex than the 2D process. In 2D, we simply specify a window on the 2D world and a viewport on the 2D view surface. Conceptually, objects in the world are clipped against the window and are then transformed into the viewport for display. The extra complexity introduced with 3D viewing is caused by the fact that display devices are only 2D.

The solution to the mismatch between 3D objects and 2D displays is solved by introducing *projections,* which transform 3D objects onto a 2D *projection plane.* Much of this chapter is devoted to projections: what they are, their mathematics, and how they are used and specified in SGP (the Simple Graphics Package) and the Core.

In 3D viewing we specify a *view volume* in the world, a projection onto the projection plane, and a viewport on the view surface. Conceptually, objects in the 3D world are clipped against the 3D view volume and are then projected. The contents of the window, which is itself the projection of the view volume onto the projection plane, are then transformed (mapped) into the viewport for display. Figure 8.1 shows this conceptual model of the 3D viewing process, which is the model presented to the users of numerous 3D graphics subroutine packages. Just as with 2D viewing, a variety of models can be used for actually implementing the viewing process. The normal implementation approach is described in Section 8.4.

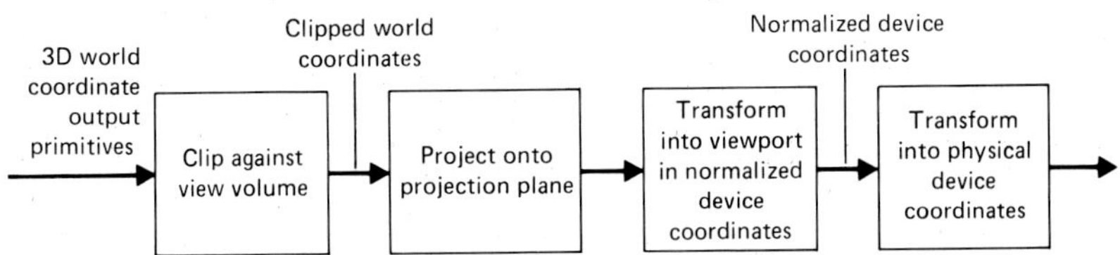

Fig. 8.1 Conceptual model of the 3D viewing process.

8.1 PROJECTIONS

In general, projections transform points in a coordinate system of dimension n into points in a coordinate system of dimension less than n. In the case at hand the projection is from 3D to 2D. The projection of a 3D object (which is just a collection of points) is defined by straight projection rays (called *projectors*) emanating from a *center of projection,* passing through each point of the object, and intersecting a projection plane to form the projection. Figures 8.2 and 8.3 show two different projections of the same line, along with projectors through the endpoints of the line. Fortunately, the projection of a line is itself a line, so only line endpoints need actually be projected.

The class of projections so defined is known as *planar geometric projections* because the projection is onto a plane rather than onto some curved surface and uses straight rather than curved projectors. Many cartographic projections are either nonplanar or nongeometric, as discussed in [RICH72].

Planar geometric projections, hereafter referred to simply as *projections,* can be divided into two basic classes: *perspective* and *parallel.* The distinction is in the relation of the center of projection to the projection plane. If the distance from the one to the other is finite, then the projection is perspective, while if the distance is infinite, the projection is parallel. Figures 8.2 and 8.3 illustrate these two cases. The parallel projection is so named because, with the center of projection infinitely distant, the projectors are parallel. When defining a perspective projection, we explicitly specify its *center of projection,* while for a parallel projection we give its *direction of projection.*

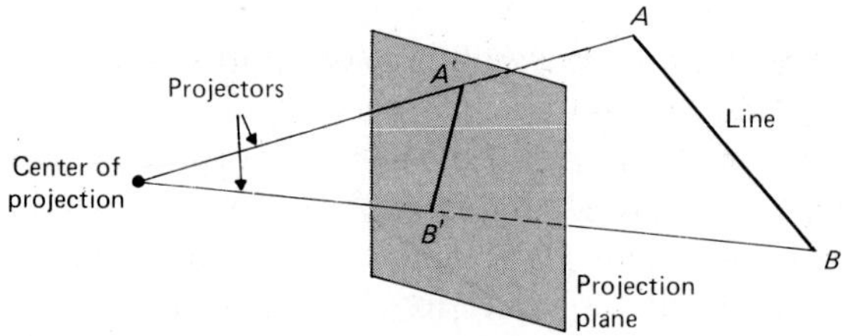

Fig. 8.2 Line *AB* and its perspective projection *A′B′*.

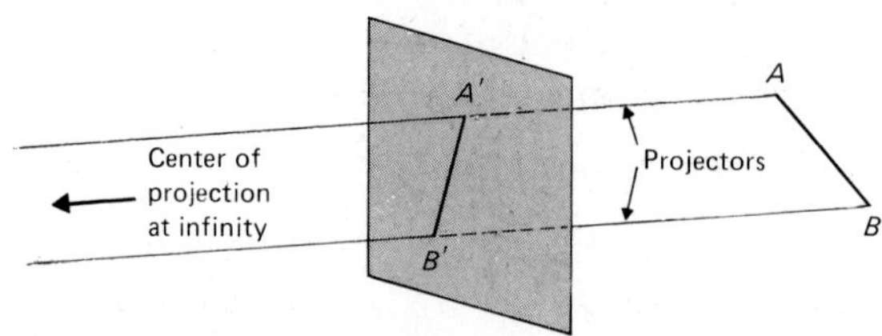

Fig. 8.3 Line *AB* and its parallel projection *A′B′*. Projectors *AA′* and *BB′* are parallel.

The perspective projection creates a visual effect similar to that of photographic systems and the human visual system, and hence is used when some degree of realism is desired. The effect is known as *perspective foreshortening*: the size of the perspective projection of an object varies inversely with the distance of the object from the center of projection. This means that while the perspective projection of objects may be realistic, it is not particularly useful for recording the exact shape and measurements of the objects: distances cannot be taken from the projection, angles are preserved only on those faces of the object which are parallel to the projection plane, and parallel lines generally do not project as parallel lines.

The parallel projection is a less realistic view because perspective foreshortenings is lacking, although there can be different constant foreshortenings along each axis. The projection does record exact measurements (to within a scale factor) and parallel lines do remain parallel. As with the perspective, angles are preserved only on faces of the object which are parallel to the projection plane. Parallel projections are also somewhat easier than perspectives for a draftsman to draw, but this is a moot issue in computer graphics.

The different types of perspective and parallel projections are discussed and illustrated at length in the comprehensive paper by Carlbom and Paciorek [CARL78]. In the following two subsections we summarize some of the basic definitions and characteristics of the more commonly used projections; we then move on in Section 8.2 to the mathematics of the projections.

8.1.1 Perspective Projections

The perspective projection of any set of parallel lines which are not parallel to the projection plane will converge to a *vanishing point*. In 3D the parallel lines meet only at infinity, so the vanishing point can be thought of as the projection of a point at infinity. There is of course an infinity of vanishing points.

If the set of lines is parallel to one of the three principal axes, the point is called a *principal vanishing point*. There are at most three such points, corresponding to the number of principal axes cut by the projection plane. For example, if the projection plane cuts just the z-axis (and is therefore normal to it), only the z-axis has a principal vanishing point, because lines parallel to either the y- or x-axes are also parallel to the projection plane and have no vanishing point.

Perspective projections are categorized by the number of principal vanishing points they have and therefore by the number of axes the projection plane cuts. Figure 8.4 shows two different one-point perspective projections of a cube. It is clear that they are one-point projections because lines parallel to the x- and y-axes do not converge; only lines parallel to the z-axis do so. Figure 8.5 shows the construction of a one-point perspective with some of the projectors and with the projection plane cutting only the z-axis. Figure 8.6 shows the construction of the two-point perspective. Notice that lines parallel to the y-axis do not converge in the projection.

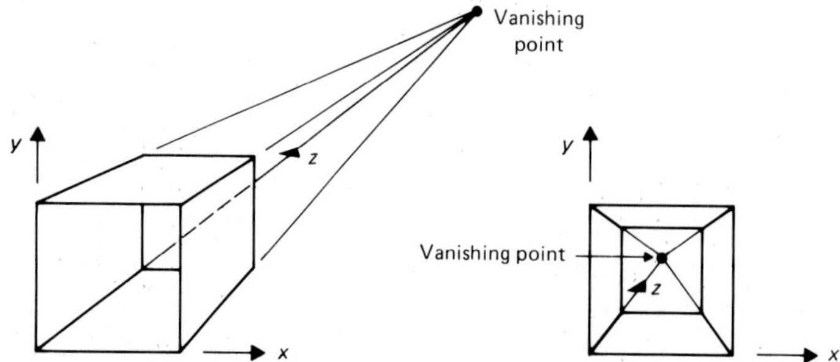

Fig. 8.4 One-point perspective projections of a cube onto a plane cutting the *z*-axis with vanishing point of lines that are perpendicular to projection plane.

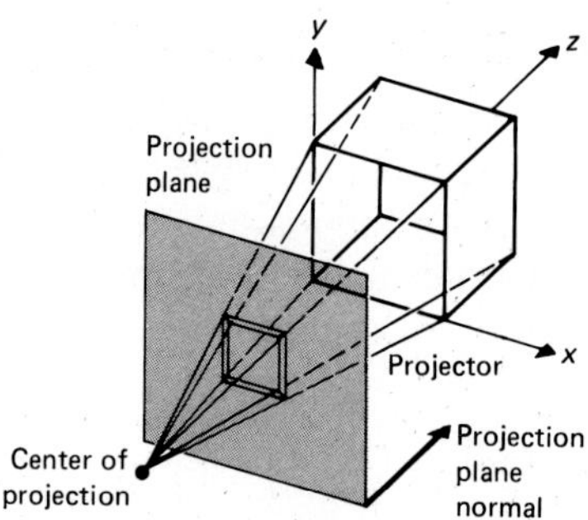

Fig. 8.5 Construction of one-point perspective projection of cube onto plane cutting the *z*-axis. Projection-plane normal is parallel to *z*-axis (adapted from [CARL78], Association for Computing Machinery, Inc.; used by permission).

The two-point perspective is commonly used in architectural, engineering, industrial design, and advertising drawings, with vertical lines projecting as parallel and hence not converging. Three-point perspectives are not used nearly so much, in part because they are hard to construct and in part because they don't add much realism beyond that afforded by the two-point perspective.

8.1.2 Parallel Projections

Parallel projections are categorized into two types, based on the relation between the direction of projection and the normal to the projection plane. In *orthographic* parallel projections, these directions are the same, while in *oblique* parallel projections, they are not. That is, in an orthographic projection the direction of projection is normal to the projection plane.

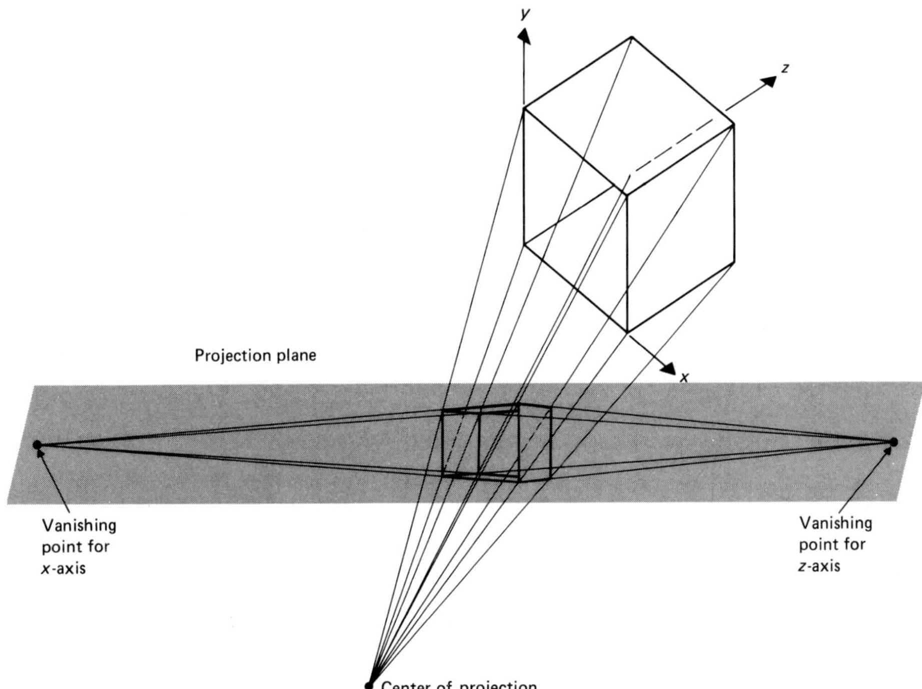

Fig. 8.6 Two-point perspective projection of a cube. The projection plane cuts the x- and the z-axes.

The most common types of orthographic projections are the *front* (elevation), *top* (plan), and *side* (elevation) projections, in which the projection plane is perpendicular to a principal axis, which is therefore the direction of projection. Figure 8.7 shows the construction of each of these three projections; they are often used in engineering drawings to depict machine parts, assemblies, and buildings because distances and angles can be measured from them. But since each depicts only one face of an object, the 3D nature of the projected object can be difficult to deduce, even if several projections of the same object are studied simultaneously.

The *axonometric* orthographic projections use projection planes which are not normal to a principal axis and therefore show several faces of an object at once, just like the perspective projection, except that the foreshortening is uniform rather than being related to the distance from the center of projection. Parallelism of lines is preserved but angles are not, while distances can be measured along each principal axis (in general, with different scale factors).

The *isometric* projection is a commonly used axonometric projection. The projection-plane normal (and therefore the direction of projection) makes equal angles with each principal axis. If the projection-plane normal is (a, b, c), then we require

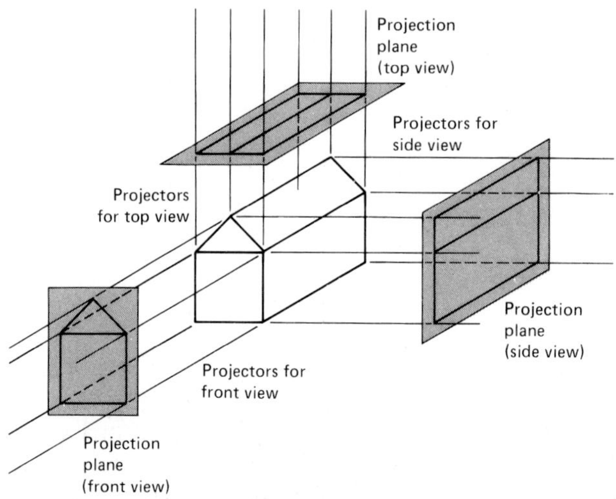

Fig. 8.7 Constructing three orthographic projections.

that $|a| = |b| = |c|$ or $\pm a = \pm b = \pm c$. There are just eight directions (one in each octant) that satisfy this condition, but there are only four different isometric projections (unless hidden line removal is considered): the directions (a, a, a) and $(-a, -a, -a)$ are normal to the same projection plane, leaving (a, a, a), $(-a, a, a)$, $(a, -a, a)$, and $(a, a, -a)$ as the unique normals. Figure 8.8 shows the construction of an isometric projection along the direction $(1, -1, 1)$.

The isometric projection has the useful property that all three principal axes are equally foreshortened, allowing measurements along the axes to be made with the same scale (hence the name: *iso* for equal, *metric* for measure). In addition, the prin-

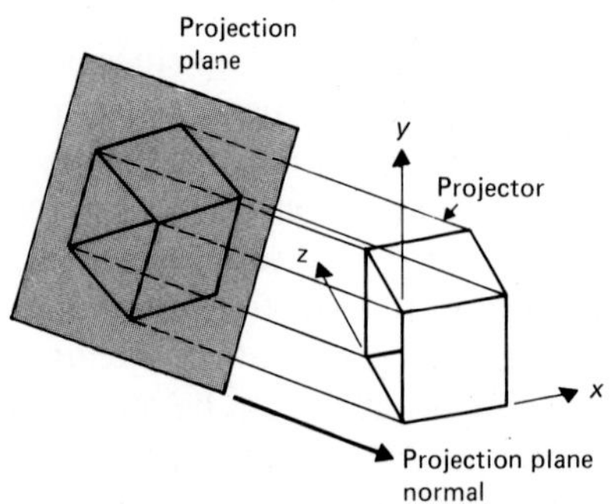

Fig. 8.8 Construction of an isometric projection of a unit cube (adapted from [CARL78], Association for Computing Machinery, Inc.; used by permission).

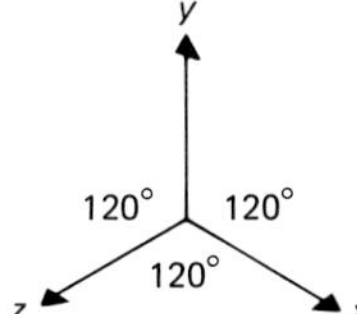

Fig. 8.9 Isometric projection of unit vectors.

cipal axes project so that they make equal angles one with another, as shown in Fig. 8.9.

Oblique projections, the second class of parallel projections, combine properties of the front, top, and side orthographic projections with those of the axonometric projection: the projection plane is normal to a principal axis, so the face of the object parallel to this plane projects to allow measurement of angles and distances. Other faces of the object project also, allowing distances along principal axes (but not angles) to be measured. Oblique projections are widely (but not exclusively) used in this text because of these properties and because they are easy to draw. Figure 8.10 shows the construction of an oblique projection. Notice that the projection-plane normal and the direction of projection are not the same.

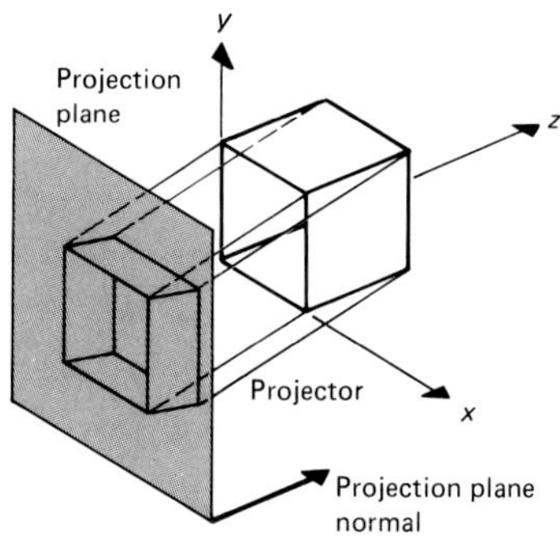

Fig. 8.10 Construction of oblique projection (adapted from [CARL78], Association for Computing Machinery, Inc.; used by permission).

Two important oblique projections are the *cavalier* and the *cabinet*. For the cavalier projection, the direction of projection makes a 45° angle with the projection plane. As a result, the projection of a line perpendicular to the projection plane is the same length as the line itself; that is, there is no foreshortening. Figure 8.11 shows several cavalier projections of the unit cube onto the *xy*-plane: the receding lines are the projections of the cube edges that are perpendicular to the *xy*-plane, and they form an angle α to the horizontal. This angle is typically 30° or 45°.

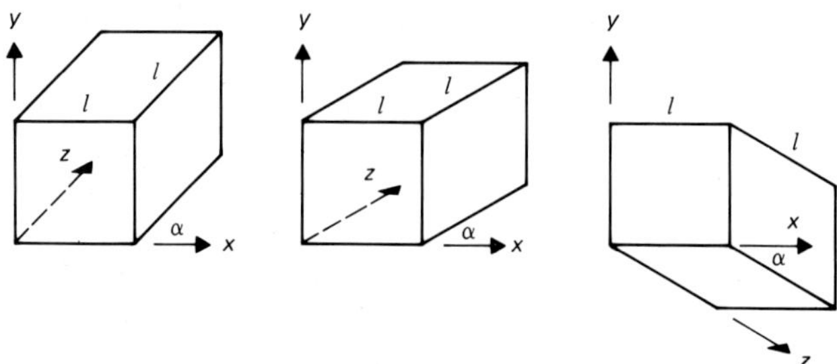

Fig. 8.11 Cavalier projection of unit cube onto plane $z = 0$.

Cabinet projections, such as those in Fig. 8.12, have a direction of projection that makes an angle of arccot(1/2) with the projection plane, so that lines perpendicular to the projection plane project at 1/2 their actual length. Cabinet projections are a bit more realistic than cavalier, because the foreshortening by 1/2 is more in keeping with our other visual experiences.

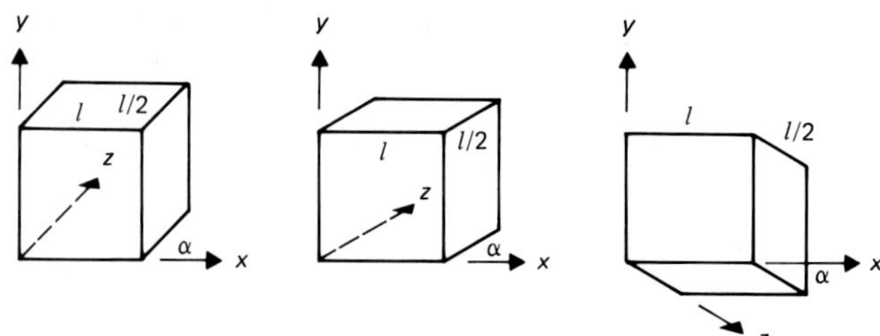

Fig. 8.12 Cabinet projection of unit cube onto plane $z = 0$.

In the next section we develop the mathematics needed for actual calculations of perspective (one-point) and parallel (orthographic, cabinet, and cavalier) projections, and then proceed in ensuing sections to integrate the projections into a graphics package.

8.2 THE MATHEMATICS OF PLANAR GEOMETRIC PROJECTIONS

The purpose of this section is to introduce the basic mathematics of planar geometric projections. For simplicity we assume the projection plane for the perspective projection to be normal to the z-axis at $z = d$, and for the parallel projection to be the $z = 0$ plane. In a later section we discuss the case of arbitrary projection planes. The projections are developed in the *viewing coordinate system,* which, as discussed in Section 7.5, is left-handed because of the natural correspondence to a display, with x oriented to the right, y upwards, and z into the screen. In a later section we discuss the transformation of objects defined in the right-handed world coordinate system into the left-handed viewing coordinate system.

Each of the projections can be defined by a 4 × 4 matrix. This is convenient because the projection matrix can be composed with transformation matrices, allowing two operations (transform, project) to be represented as a single matrix. In this section we derive the 4 × 4 matrix for several projections, beginning with the perspective projection. Figure 8.13 shows three views of a left-handed coordinate system with the projection plane at a distance d from the origin and a point P to be projected onto the projection plane. To calculate the projection of (x,y,z), with coordinates x_p and y_p, the similar triangles in each of the lower figures are used to write the ratios:

$$\frac{x_p}{d} = \frac{x}{z}, \quad \frac{y_p}{d} = \frac{y}{z}. \tag{8.1}$$

Multiplying each side by d yields:

$$x_p = \frac{d \cdot x}{z} = \frac{x}{z/d}, \quad y_p = \frac{d \cdot y}{z} = \frac{y}{z/d}. \tag{8.2}$$

The distance d is just a scale factor applied to x_p and y_p. The division by z is what causes the perspective projection of more distant objects to be smaller than that of closer objects. Note that all values of z are allowable, except $z = 0$. Points can be behind the center of projection on the negative z-axis or between the center of projection and the projection plane.

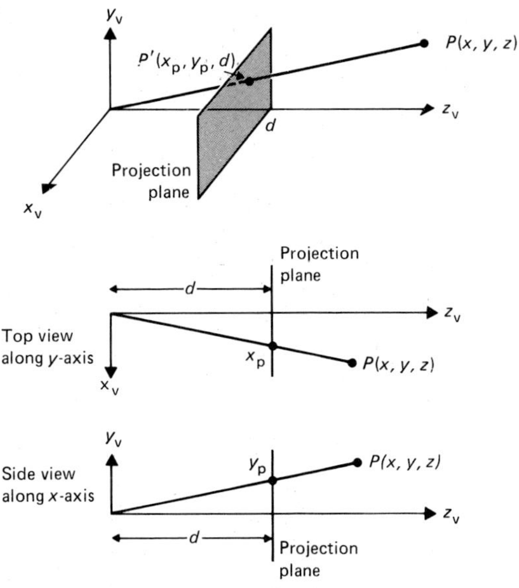

Fig. 8.13 Perspective projection.

These transformations can be expressed as a 4 × 4 matrix:

$$M_{\text{per}} = \begin{bmatrix} 1 & 0 & 0 & 0 \\ 0 & 1 & 0 & 0 \\ 0 & 0 & 1 & 1/d \\ 0 & 0 & 0 & 0 \end{bmatrix}. \tag{8.3}$$

Multiplying the point $P = [x \quad y \quad z \quad 1]$ by the matrix M_{per}, we get the general homogeneous point $[X \quad Y \quad Z \quad W]$:

$$[X \quad Y \quad Z \quad W] = P \cdot M_{\text{per}} = [x \quad y \quad z \quad 1] \begin{bmatrix} 1 & 0 & 0 & 0 \\ 0 & 1 & 0 & 0 \\ 0 & 0 & 1 & 1/d \\ 0 & 0 & 0 & 0 \end{bmatrix} \tag{8.4}$$

or

$$[X \quad Y \quad Z \quad W] = \begin{bmatrix} x & y & z & \dfrac{z}{d} \end{bmatrix}. \tag{8.5}$$

Now, dividing by W (which is z/d) to come back to 3D, we have

$$\begin{bmatrix} \dfrac{X}{W} & \dfrac{Y}{W} & \dfrac{Z}{W} & 1 \end{bmatrix} = [x_p \quad y_p \quad z_p \quad 1] = \begin{bmatrix} \dfrac{x}{z/d} & \dfrac{y}{z/d} & d & 1 \end{bmatrix}, \tag{8.6}$$

which is the correct result, including the transformed z coordinate of d, which is the position of the projection plane along the z-axis.

An alternative formulation for the perspective projection, used in some references, places the projection plane at $z = 0$ and the center of projection at $z = -d$, as seen in Fig. 8.14. Similar triangles now give:

$$\frac{x_p}{d} = \frac{x}{z + d}, \qquad \frac{y_p}{d} = \frac{y}{z + d}. \tag{8.7}$$

Multiplying by d, we get:

$$x_p = \frac{d \cdot x}{z + d} = \frac{x}{(z/d) + 1}, \qquad y_p = \frac{d \cdot y}{z + d} = \frac{y}{(z/d) + 1}. \tag{8.8}$$

The matrix is

$$M'_{\text{per}} = \begin{bmatrix} 1 & 0 & 0 & 0 \\ 0 & 1 & 0 & 0 \\ 0 & 0 & 0 & 1/d \\ 0 & 0 & 0 & 1 \end{bmatrix}. \tag{8.9}$$

This matrix can be derived from M_{per} by translating the center of projection to the origin, applying M_{per}, and translating back:

$$T(0, 0, d) \cdot M_{\text{per}} \cdot T(0, 0, -d). \tag{8.10}$$

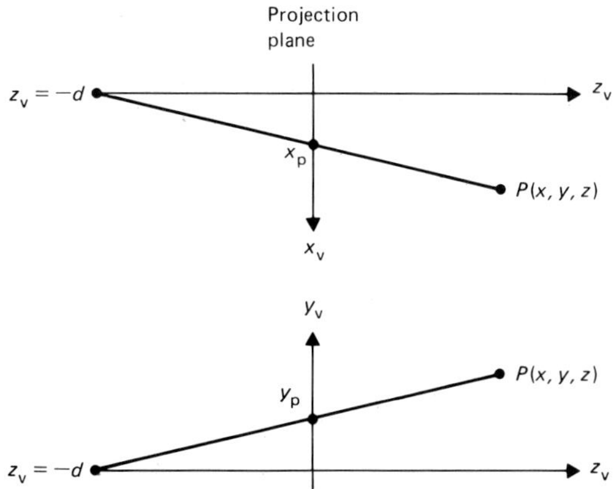

Fig. 8.14 Alternative perspective projection.

The orthographic projection onto a projection plane at $z = 0$ is straightforward. The direction of projection is the same as the projection-plane normal, i.e., the z-axis in this case. Thus point P projects as:

$$x_p = x, \qquad y_p = y, \qquad z_p = 0. \tag{8.11}$$

This projection is expressed by the matrix:

$$M_{ort} = \begin{bmatrix} 1 & 0 & 0 & 0 \\ 0 & 1 & 0 & 0 \\ 0 & 0 & 0 & 0 \\ 0 & 0 & 0 & 1 \end{bmatrix}. \tag{8.12}$$

Consider now the oblique projection, the matrix for which can be written in terms of α and l shown in Fig. 8.15, which is the unit cube projected onto the xy-plane. From this figure we see that the point $P(0, 0, 1)$ on the back of the unit cube projects onto $P'(l \cos \alpha, l \sin \alpha, 0)$ on the xy-plane. By definition, this means the direction of projection is that of a line $\overline{PP'}$ passing through these two points, as shown in Fig. 8.16. This direction is $P' - P = (l \cos \alpha, l \sin \alpha, -1)$. The direction of projection makes an angle β with the xy-plane.

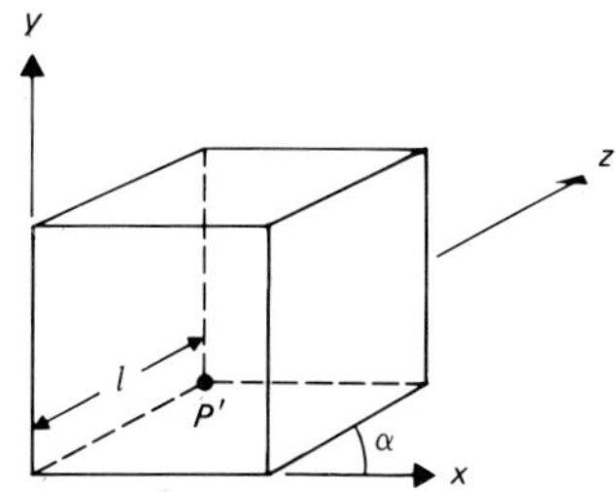

Fig. 8.15 Oblique parallel projection of unit cube. Here P' is projection of $P(0, 0, 1)$.

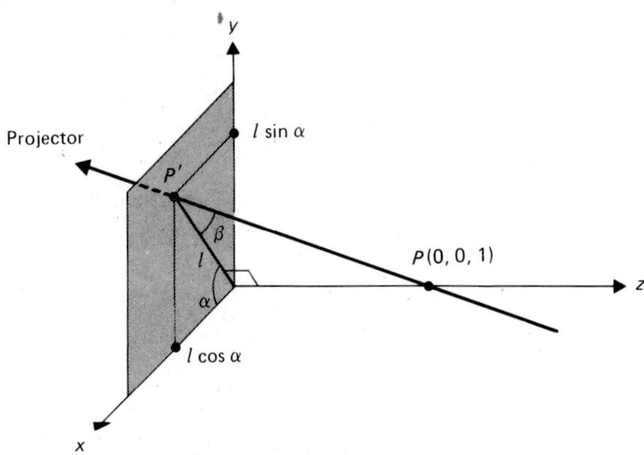

Fig. 8.16 Oblique parallel projection of $P(0, 0, 1)$ into $P'(l \cos \alpha, l \sin \alpha, 0)$.

Now consider a general point x,y,z. What is its oblique projection (x_p, y_p) onto the xy-plane? Figure 8.17 shows two views of the point and the projector, which is parallel to the projector of Fig. 8.16. The equations are for the projector's x and y values as a function of z and are of the generic form $y = mz + b$. Solving the two equations for x_p and y_p in Fig. 8.17, we get:

$$x_p = x + z\,(l \cos \alpha), \qquad y_p = y + z\,(l \sin \alpha). \tag{8.13}$$

The 4×4 matrix that performs these operations and hence represents the oblique projection is:

$$M_{ob} = \begin{bmatrix} 1 & 0 & 0 & 0 \\ 0 & 1 & 0 & 0 \\ l \cos \alpha & l \sin \alpha & 0 & 0 \\ 0 & 0 & 0 & 1 \end{bmatrix}. \tag{8.14}$$

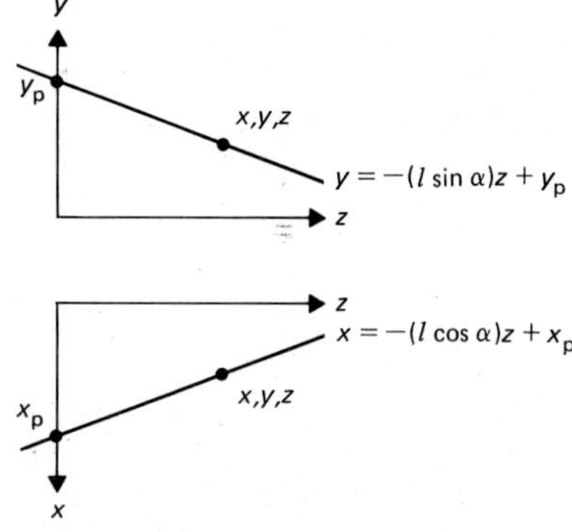

Fig. 8.17 Oblique parallel projection of (x, y, z) into $(x_p, y_p, 0)$.

The effect of this is to shear and then project the object: planes of constant $z = z_1$ are translated in x by $z_1 l \cos \alpha$ and in y by $z_1 l \sin \alpha$, and are then orthographically projected to $z = 0$. The shear preserves all parallel lines and preserves angles and distances in planes parallel to the z-axis. The reader may refer ahead to Fig. 8.31 to see the effect of a shear along the y-axis.

For a cavalier projection $l = 1$, so the angle β in Fig. 8.16 is 45°. For the cabinet projection, $l = 1/2$ and β is arctan(2), or about 63.4°. For an orthographic projection, $l = 0$ and $\beta = 90°$, so M_{ob} reduces to the trivial M_{ort} from the previous section.

8.3 SPECIFYING AN ARBITRARY 3D VIEW

In the development of projection matrices in the preceding section we have assumed a left-handed viewing coordinate system and a projection plane normal to the z-axis (Fig. 8.10). By contrast, we have defined the world coordinate system to be right-handed (Fig. 8.18), and we want to view objects by using *any* projection plane. We also want the center of projection (for perspective projections) or the direction of projection (for parallel projections) to be arbitrary, rather than being restricted as in the preceding section.

In this section we show one way, based on the Core System, of defining *any* planar geometric projection [GSPC79].* This very general capability is unlike that found in many other graphics packages, which place restrictions either on the types of projections or on the position of the projection plane and center of projection. These restrictions force application programmers to assume responsibility for providing the missing generality.

We require ways to specify a projection plane (hereafter called a *view plane,* as in [GSPC79]), a view volume, and a window. Recall that we clip in 3D against the

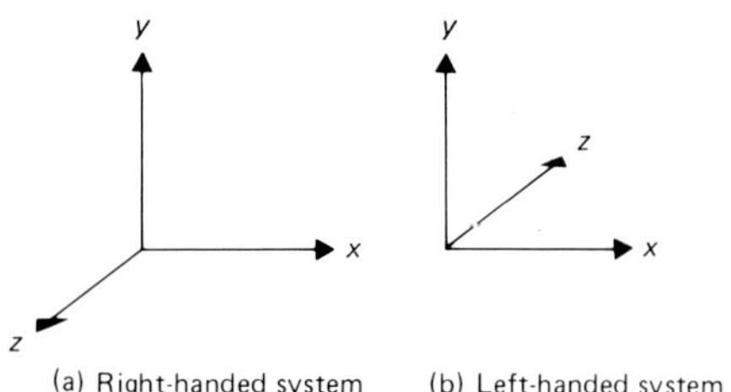

Fig. 8.18 Coordinate systems.

*We are consistent with [GSPC79] so long as the view plane passes through the view reference point. That is, we require the Core System parameter *view_distance* to be zero. The mathematics for the more general case are treated in [MICH79, MICH80]. An APL implementation of Core System viewing based on the general case is listed in [FREI79], and an APL implementation of perspective projection at Level 2 (output only) is described in [NAGE79].

view volume and then project onto the view plane. Finally, the window to viewport transformation* is used to display the projected objects.

The view plane is defined by a point on the plane called the *view reference point* (VRP) and a normal to the plane called the *view plane normal* (VPN). The view plane may be anywhere with respect to the world objects to be projected: it may cut through, be in front of or be behind the objects.

To define a window we need a coordinate system in the view plane called the *uv coordinate system*. The origin of the coordinate system is the VRP. The *view up* vector (VUP) determines the v-axis direction on the view plane: the projection of VUP parallel to VPN onto the view plane is coincident with the v-axis (Fig. 8.19). (Some graphics packages use the y-axis as VUP, but this is too restrictive and fails if VPN is parallel to the y-axis, in which case VUP is undefined.) In any event, the u-axis direction is defined so that u, v and VPN form a left-handed coordinate system. The view reference point and the two direction vectors (VPN and VUP) are specified in the right-handed world coordinate system.

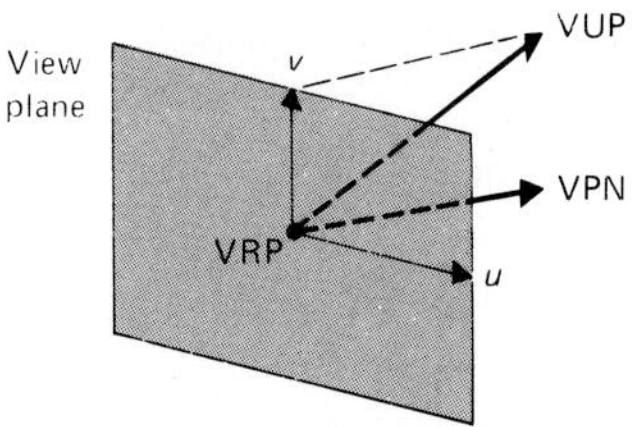

Fig. 8.19 *uv*-system in the view plane.

With the *uv*-system defined on the view plane, we can now specify the window's minimum and maximum u and v values, as in Fig. 8.20. Note that the window need not be symmetrical about the view reference point.

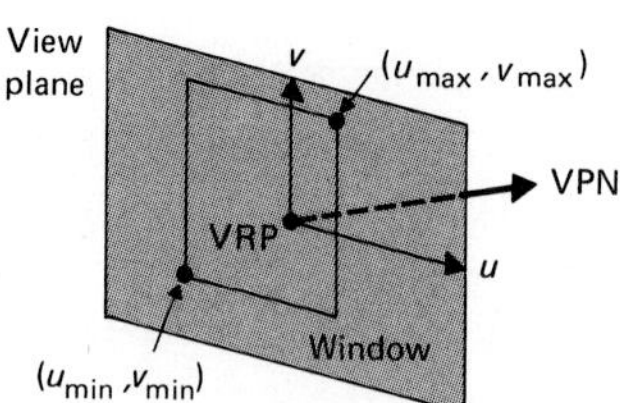

Fig. 8.20 Window in *uv*-coordinates.

---

*The term *window to viewport mapping* is also used.

The *view volume* bounds that portion of the world which will be clipped out and projected and is defined in part by the window. For perspective projections, the center of projection (COP) also helps define the view volume. The center of projection is specified in world coordinates relative to the view reference point. The view volume is the semi-infinite pyramid with apex at the center of projection and sides passing through the window.* Figures 8.21 and 8.22 show two different perspective projection view volumes. Positions behind the center of projection are not included in the view volume, so they will not be projected.

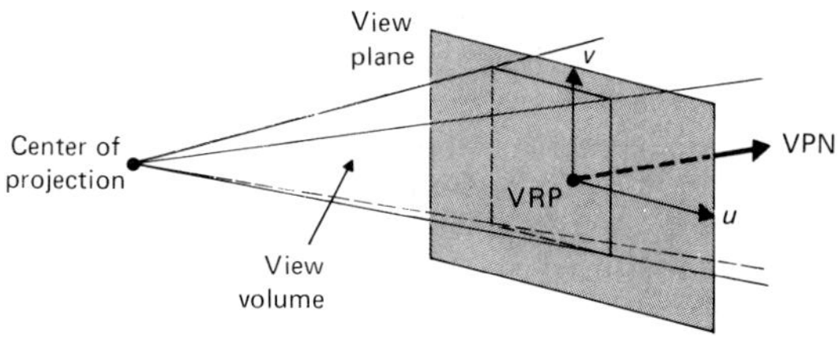

Fig. 8.21 Semi-infinite pyramid view volume for perspective projection.

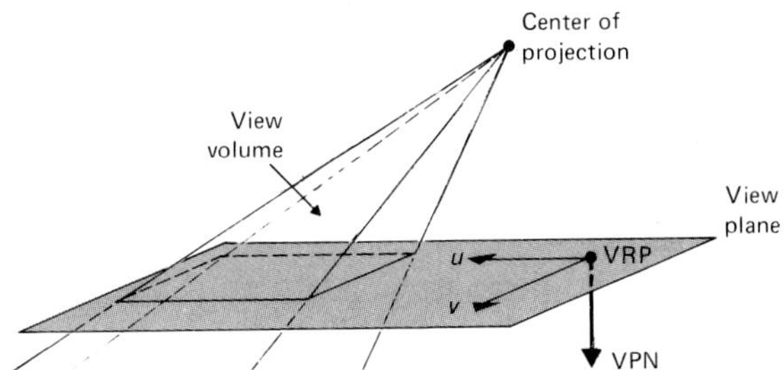

Fig. 8.22 Another semi-infinite pyramid view volume for perspective projection.

For parallel projections, the direction of projection (DOP) helps define the view volume, which is an infinite parallelepiped with sides parallel to the direction of projection. Figures 8.23 and 8.24 show parallel projection view volumes and their relation to the view plane and window. In orthographic parallel projections, but not in oblique parallel projections, the sides of the view volume are normal to the view plane.

*While our eyes "see" a cone-shaped view volume, the pyramid is mathematically more tractable for clipping and lends itself to rectangular viewports.

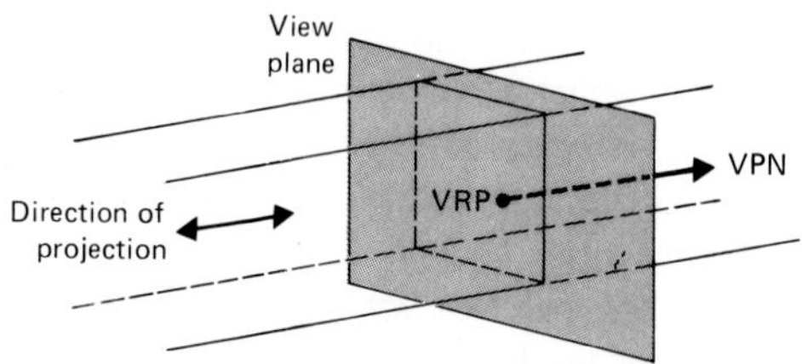

Fig. 8.23 Infinite parallelepiped for orthographic parallel projection. The VPN and direction of projection are the same.

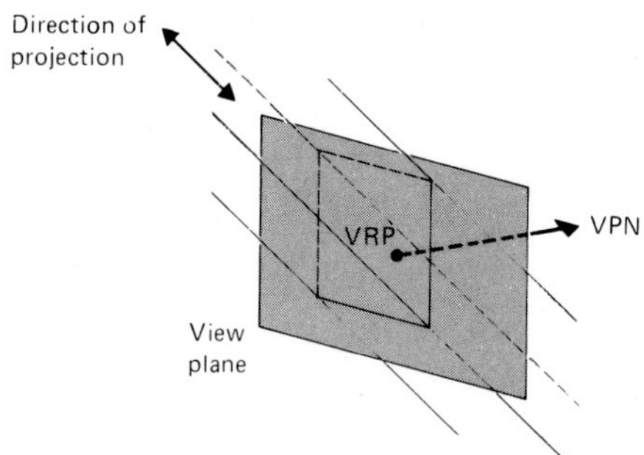

Fig. 8.24 Infinite parallelepiped for oblique parallel projection. The VPN and direction of projection are different.

There are times when we might want to make the view volume finite, in order to limit the number of output primitives projected onto the view plane. This might be necessary to eliminate extraneous objects, allowing the user to concentrate on a particular portion of the world. For perspective projections there is additional motivation. An object which is very distant from the center of projection will project onto the view surface as a "blob," with no distinguishable form. On a plotter the pen might wear through the paper, and on a CRT the phosphor might be burned by the electron beam. Also, an object very near the center of projection may extend across the window like so many disconnected pick-up sticks with no discernible structure.

Figures 8.25 to 8.27 show how the view volume is made finite with a *front clipping plane* and *back clipping plane.* These planes, sometimes called the *hither* and *yon* planes, are specified with signed quantities called *front distance* (F) and *back distance* (B) relative to the view reference point and along the VPN with positive distances in the direction of the view plane normal. These planes are parallel to the view plane; their normal is the VPN.

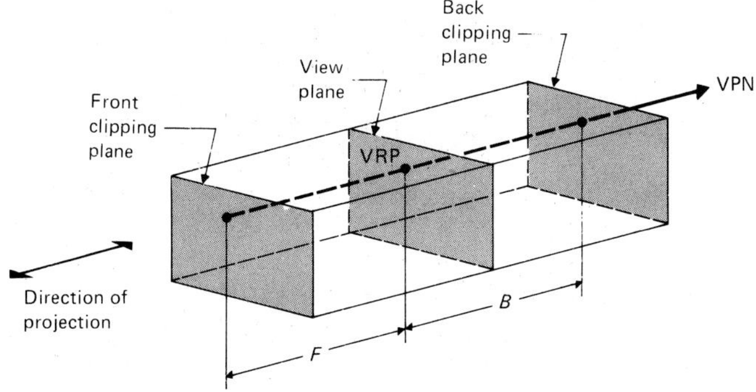

Fig. 8.25 Truncated view volume for orthographic parallel projection.

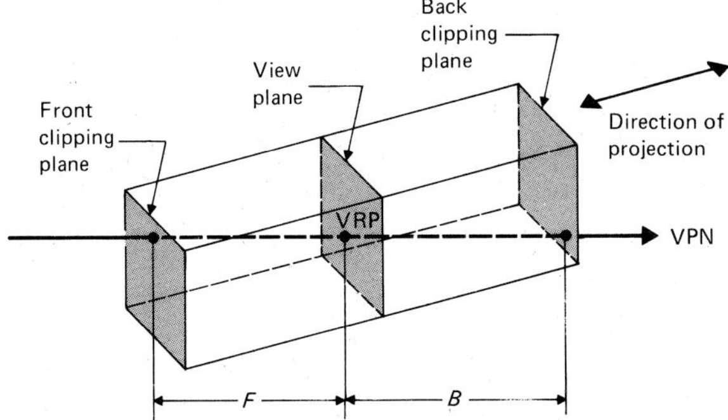

Fig. 8.26 Truncated view volume for oblique parallel projection showing VPN oblique to direction of projection; VPN is also normal to the front and back clipping planes.

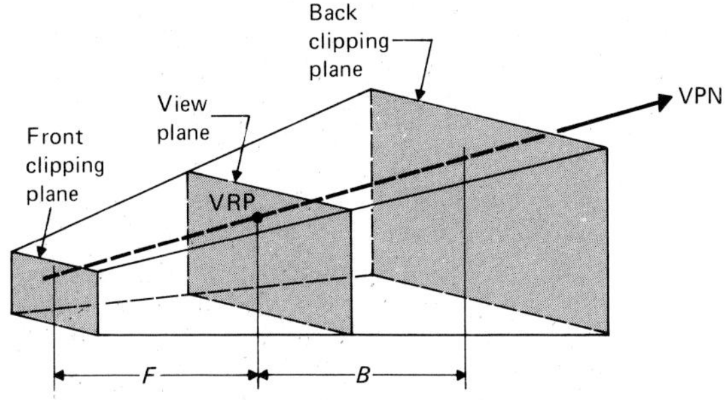

Fig. 8.27 Truncated view volume.

8.4 CALCULATING THE PLANAR GEOMETRIC PROJECTIONS

Given the specification of a view volume and a projection, we want to understand how the clipping is actually done and how the projection is applied. As suggested by the conceptual model for viewing (Fig. 8.1), we could clip lines against the view volume by first calculating their intersections with each of the six planes that define the view volume. Lines remaining after the clipping would be projected onto the view plane by calculating the intersection of the projectors through their endpoints with the view plane, by solving simultaneous equations. The coordinates would then be transformed from 3D world coordinates to 2D device coordinates. The large number of calculations required for this process, repeated for many lines, calls for considerable computing. Happily, there is a more efficient procedure, based on the general philosophy of dividing a hard problem into a series of simpler problems.

Some view volumes are easier to clip against than the general one (the actual algorithms are discussed in Section 8.5). For instance, calculating the intersections of a line with the planes of a parallel projection view volume defined by the six planes

$$x = 0, \quad x = 1, \quad y = 0, \quad y = 1, \quad z = 0, \quad z = 1 \tag{8.15}$$

involves a minimum of calculation. This is also true for the perspective projection view volume defined by the planes:

$$x = z, \quad x = -z, \quad y = z, \quad y = -z, \quad z = z_{\min}, \quad z = 1. \tag{8.16}$$

We call these the *canonical view volumes.*

Our strategy will be to find the *normalizing transformations* N_{par} and N_{per} which transform an arbitrary parallel or perspective projection view volume into the parallel and perspective canonical view volumes, respectively, thus transforming from world to viewing coordinates. Clipping will be done in viewing coordinates, followed by projection (by using matrices from Section 8.2) into 2D. With this strategy we do run the risk of investing effort in transforming points which are subsequently discarded by the clip operation, but at least the clipping is easy to do.

Figure 8.28 shows the sequence of processes involved in using this strategy. The processes can be reduced to a transform–clip–transform sequence, by composing steps 3, 4, and 5 into a single transformation matrix for use as the second transform in the sequence. In the case of a perspective projection, a division is also needed to map from homogeneous coordinates back to 3D coordinates. This could be done following the second transformation of the combined sequence.

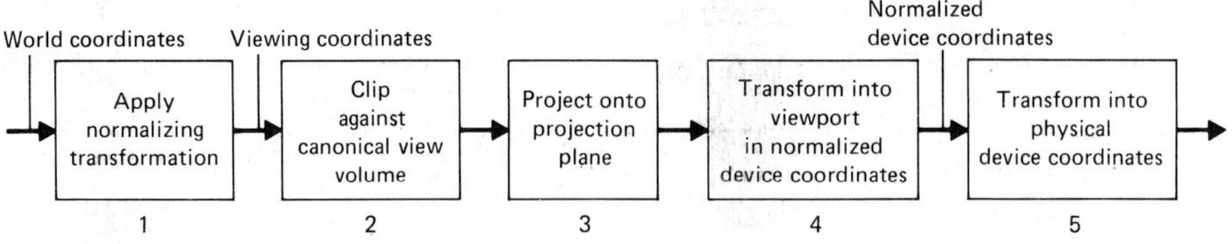

Fig. 8.28 Implementation of 3D viewing.

In the next two subsections we derive the normalizing transformations for perspective and parallel projections, which are used as step 1 in the transform–clip–transform sequence for their respective type of projection.

8.4.1 Parallel Projection

In this section we derive the normalizing transformation N_{par} for parallel projections, to transform world coordinate positions (x, y, z) into viewing coordinate positions (x_v, y_v, z_v), so that the view volume is transformed into the unit cube defined by Eq. (8.15). The transformed coordinates are clipped against this canonical view volume, and the results are projected onto the $z_v = 0$ plane and transformed into the viewport for display.

Transformation N_{par} is derived for the most general case, which is the oblique (rather than orthographic) parallel projection. Therefore, N_{par} includes a shear transformation which has the effect of causing the direction of projection in viewing coordinates to be parallel to z_v, even though in world coordinates it is not parallel to VPN. By including this shear, the projection onto the $z_v = 0$ plane can be done simply by setting $z_v = 0$. If the parallel projection is orthographic, the shear component of the normalizing transformation becomes the identity.

The series of transformations that make up N_{par} is:

1. Translate the VRP to the origin;
2. Rotate so that VPN becomes the negative z-axis;
3. Rotate so that the projection of VUP onto the view plane becomes the y-axis;
4. Change from right-handed (world) to left-handed (viewing) coordinates;
5. Shear so that all the planes defining the view volume become normal to axes of the viewing coordinate system;
6. Translate and scale the view volume into the unit cube.

Figure 8.29, created with the aid of BUMPS [GURW80], shows this sequence of transformations being applied to a parallel projection view volume and to an outline of a house, while Fig. 8.30 shows the parallel projection which would result with no clipping against the back plane of the view volume.

Steps 1, 2, and 3 of N_{par} were developed in Section 7.6. To apply the results, we make the associations:

View reference point:	VRP $= P1$,	
View plane normal:	VPN $= \overline{P1P2}$	(the directed line segment from $P1$ to $P2$),
View up:	VUP $= \overline{P1P3}$	(the directed line segment from $P1$ to $P3$).

The transformation is the composition:

$$T \cdot Ry(\theta) \cdot Rx(\phi) \cdot Rz(\alpha) = T \cdot R, \tag{8.17}$$

where R was computed in Section 7.6.

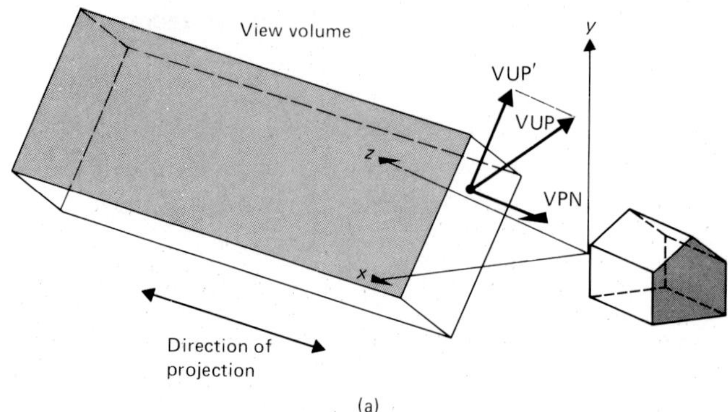

Fig. 8.29(a) The initial viewing situation with the right-handed world coordinate system. VUP′ is the projection of VUP onto the view plane. In subsequent drawings, only VUP′ will be shown. The VRP is at the base of VUP and VPN. Note that VPN is not parallel to the edges of the view volume (the direction of projection). For clarity, the house is not in the view volume—none of the house will actually be visible after clipping.

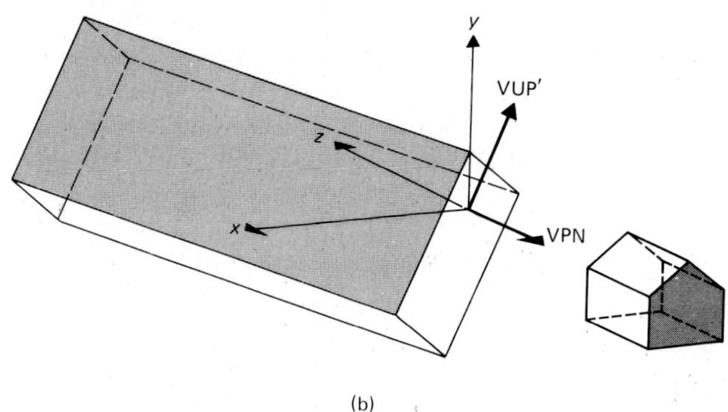

Fig. 8.29(b) The view reference point has been translated to the origin, taking with it VUP′, VPN, and the view volume. This is step 1 of N_{par}.

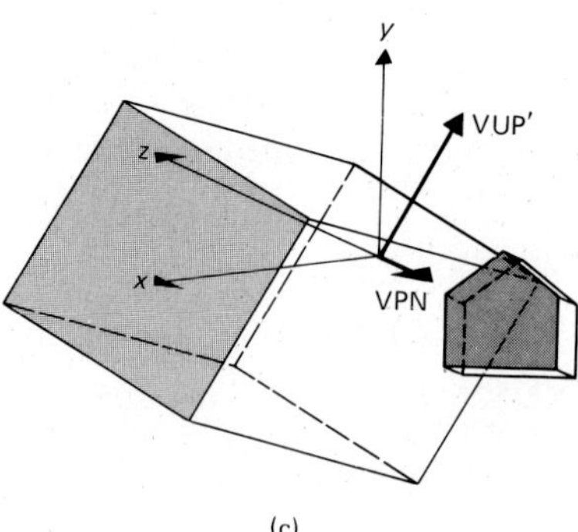

Fig. 8.29(c) Rotation about the *y*-axis and then the *x*-axis, making VPN the negative *z*-axis and accomplishing step 2 of N_{par}.

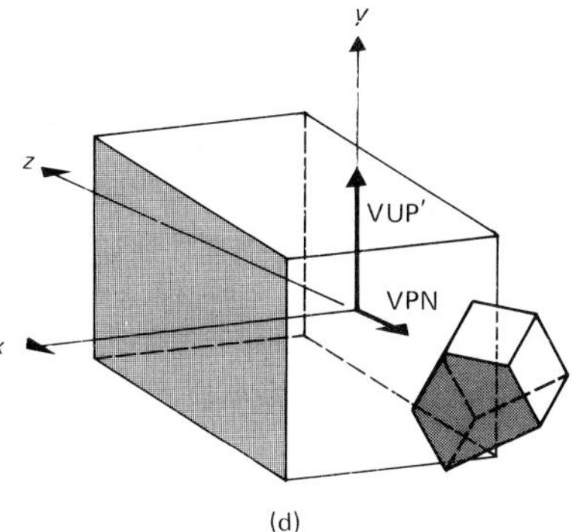

Fig. 8.29(d) Rotation about the *z*-axis to make VUP′ the *y*-axis; this is step 3 for N_{par}. Here VPN remains as the negative *z*-axis.

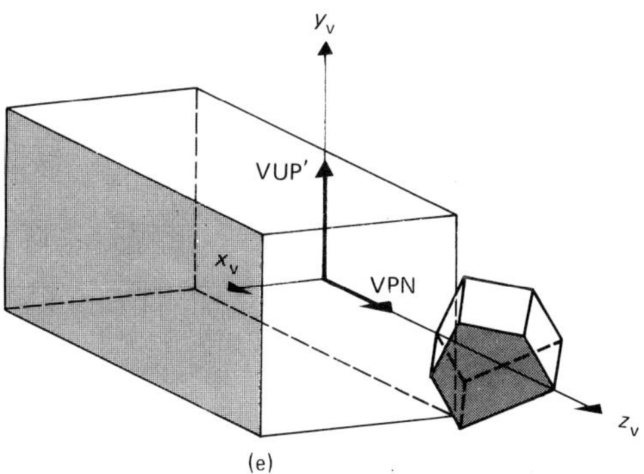

Fig. 8.29(e) Change to left-handed viewing coordinates and shear. The edges of the view volume are now parallel to the principal axes and VPN remains coincident with the *z*-axis; these are steps 4 and 5 of N_{par}.

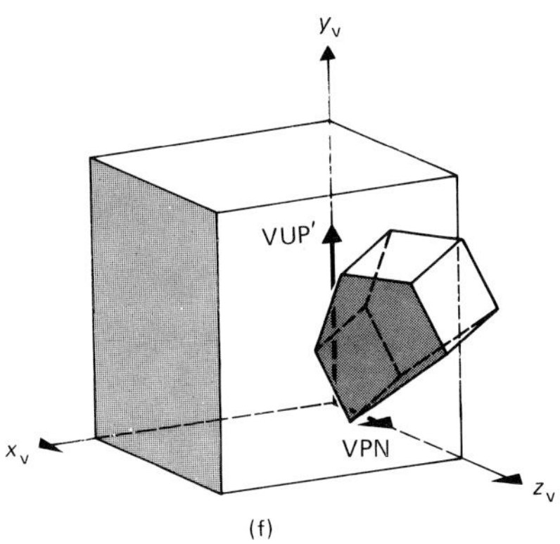

Fig. 8.29(f) Scale and translate, so VRP is coincident with the corner of view volume, which is now the canonical view volume, the unit cube; this is step 6 of N_{par}.

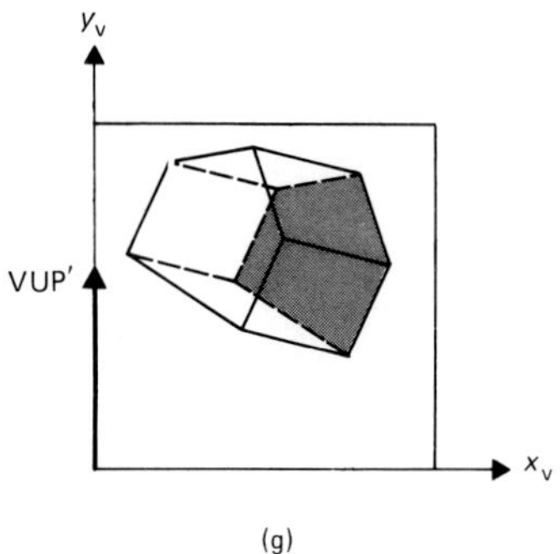

Fig. 8.29(g) The house and view volume as seen in the direction of the positive z-axis, after step 6 of N_{par} has been applied.

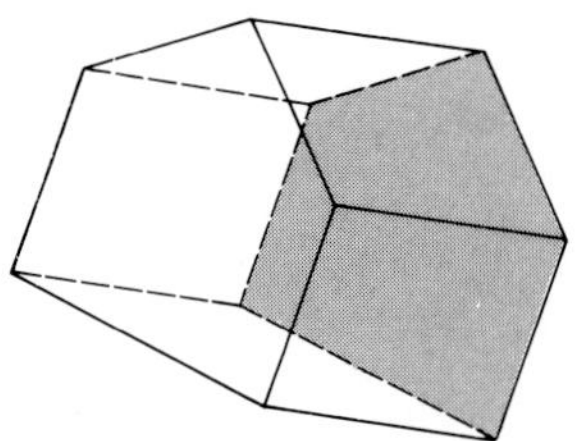

Fig. 8.30 Final view of house with no clipping assumed.

The fourth step in developing N_{par} is to convert from right-handed to left-handed coordinates. In Fig. 8.18 we note that if the direction of the z-axis were opposite, we would have a left-handed system. This is done with the matrix:

$$T_{RL} = \begin{bmatrix} 1 & 0 & 0 & 0 \\ 0 & 1 & 0 & 0 \\ 0 & 0 & -1 & 0 \\ 0 & 0 & 0 & 1 \end{bmatrix}. \tag{8.18}$$

The fifth step is to shear the view volume along the z-axis so all of its planes are normal to one of the coordinate system axes. The z-axis shear matrix is:

$$SH_z(a_1, b_1) = \begin{bmatrix} 1 & 0 & 0 & 0 \\ 0 & 1 & 0 & 0 \\ a_1 & b_1 & 1 & 0 \\ 0 & 0 & 0 & 1 \end{bmatrix}. \tag{8.19}$$

In the case at hand we want to shear the direction of projection (DOP) vector, after it is transformed by $Ry(\theta) \cdot Rx(\phi) \cdot Rz(\alpha) \cdot T_{RL}$, so its x and y components are zero (Fig. 8.31). Note that this transformation of DOP excludes the initial translation of step 1, because we are transforming a direction, not a position.

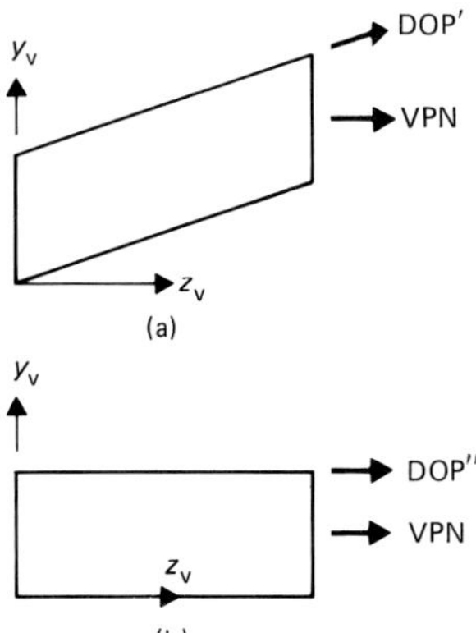

Fig. 8.31 Illustration of shearing with side view of view volume as example. The parallelogram in (a) is sheared into the rectangle of (b); VPN is unchanged because it is parallel to the z-axis.

Representing the transformed direction of projection vector by

$$\mathrm{DOP}' = [\mathrm{DOP}'_x \quad \mathrm{DOP}'_y \quad \mathrm{DOP}'_z \quad 1] = \mathrm{DOP} \cdot Ry(\theta) \cdot Rx(\phi) \cdot Rz(\alpha) \cdot T_{\mathrm{RL}},$$

we want to find a_1 and b_1 such that:

$$\mathrm{DOP}' \cdot SH_z(a_1, b_1) = [0 \quad 0 \quad \mathrm{DOP}'_z \quad 1]. \tag{8.20}$$

Algebraic manipulation shows that this will occur if:

$$a_1 = -\frac{\mathrm{DOP}'_x}{\mathrm{DOP}'_z}, \qquad b_1 = -\frac{\mathrm{DOP}'_y}{\mathrm{DOP}'_z}. \tag{8.21}$$

Notice that in the case of an orthographic projection, $\mathrm{DOP}'_x = \mathrm{DOP}'_y = 0$, so $a_1 = b_1 = 0$, and the shear matrix reduces to the identity.

Figure 8.32 shows the view volume after these five transformation steps have been applied. The bounds of the volume are:

$$u_{\min} \le x \le u_{\max}, \qquad v_{\min} \le y \le v_{\max}, \qquad F \le z \le B. \tag{8.22}$$

The final step in the process is transforming the sheared view volume into the unit cube. This is accomplished by translating the point $(u_{\min}, v_{\min}, F)$ to the origin and then scaling. The matrices are:

$$T_{\mathrm{par}} = T(-u_{\min}, -v_{\min}, -F), \tag{8.23}$$

$$S_{\mathrm{par}} = S\left(\frac{1}{u_{\max} - u_{\min}}, \frac{1}{v_{\max} - v_{\min}}, \frac{1}{B - F}\right). \tag{8.24}$$

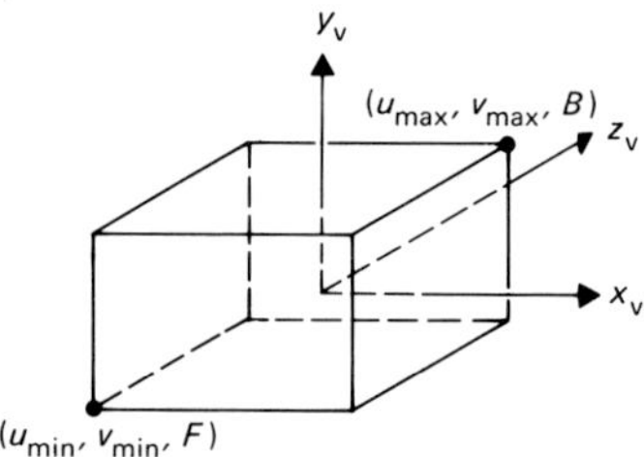

Fig. 8.32 View volume after transformation steps 1 to 5 (corresponds to Fig. 8.29(f)).

Summarizing, we have:

$$N_{par} = T \cdot Ry(\theta) \cdot Rx(\phi) \cdot Rz(\alpha) \cdot T_{RL} \cdot SH_z(a_1,b_1) \cdot T_{par} \cdot S_{par}. \tag{8.25}$$

This N_{par} transforms world coordinate positions into viewing coordinate positions, where they can be easily clipped against the unit cube.

8.4.2 Perspective Projection

We turn now to developing a normalizing transformation N_{per} for perspective projections. N_{per} transforms world coordinate positions into the viewing coordinate system so that the view volume becomes the canonical perspective projection view volume, which is a truncated pyramid with apex at the origin, as defined by (8.16). After N_{per} is applied, clipping is done against this canonical volume, and the results are projected onto the view plane by using M_{per} (derived in Section 8.2).

The series of transformations which make up N_{per} are:

1. Translate the center of projection to the origin;
2. Rotate so that the VPN becomes parallel to the negative z-axis;
3. Rotate so that the projection of VUP onto the view plane becomes parallel to the y-axis;
4. Change from right-handed (world) to left-handed (viewing) coordinates;
5. Shear so the center line of the view volume becomes the z-axis;
6. Scale so the view volume becomes the truncated right pyramid defined by the six planes of Eqs. (8.16).

Figure 8.33 shows this sequence of transformations being applied to a perspective projection view volume and to a house. Figure 8.34 shows the resulting perspective projection, provided that clipping against the back plane is not performed.

To determine the initial translation of the center of projection to the origin, we define:

$$\text{VRP} = (\text{VRP}_x, \text{VRP}_y, \text{VRP}_z). \tag{8.26}$$

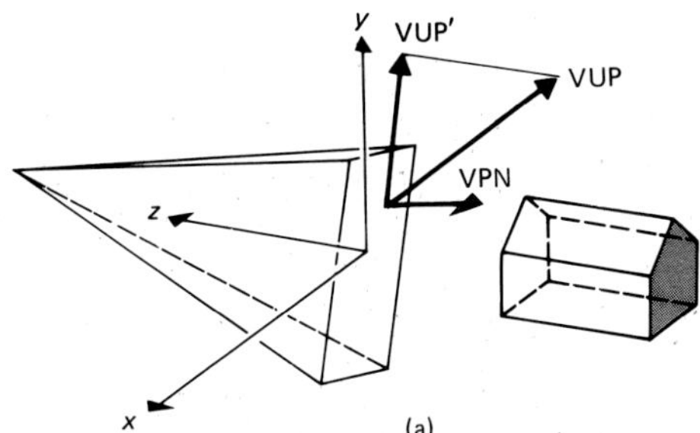

Fig. 8.33(a) The initial viewing situation, with the right-handed world coordinate system. VUP′ is the projection of VUP onto the view plane. In subsequent drawings, only VUP′ will be shown. The VRP is at the base of VUP and VPN. VPN is parallel neither to the *z*-axis nor to the center line of the pyramid, i.e., the pyramid is skewed. For clarity, the house is outside the view volume.

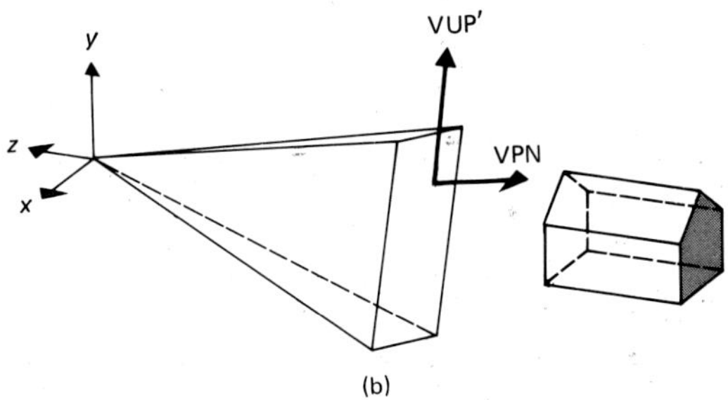

Fig. 8.33(b) The center of projection has been translated to the origin, moving with it VUP′, VPN, and the view volume. This is the first step of N_{per}.

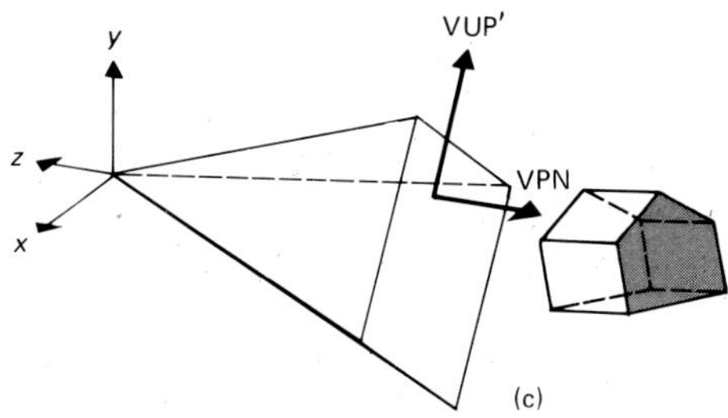

Fig. 8.33(c) Rotation about the *y*-axis and then the *x*-axis to make VPN parallel to the negative *z*-axis and accomplishing step 2 of N_{per}.

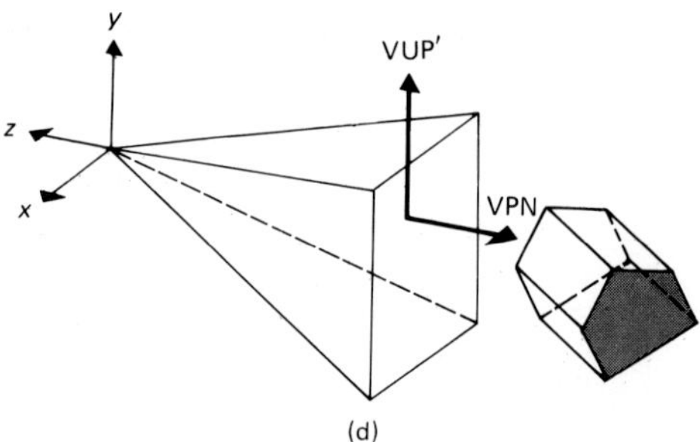

Fig. 8.33(d) Rotation about the *z*-axis, to make VUP′ parallel to the *y*-axis: step 3 of N_{per}; VPN remains parallel to the *z*-axis.

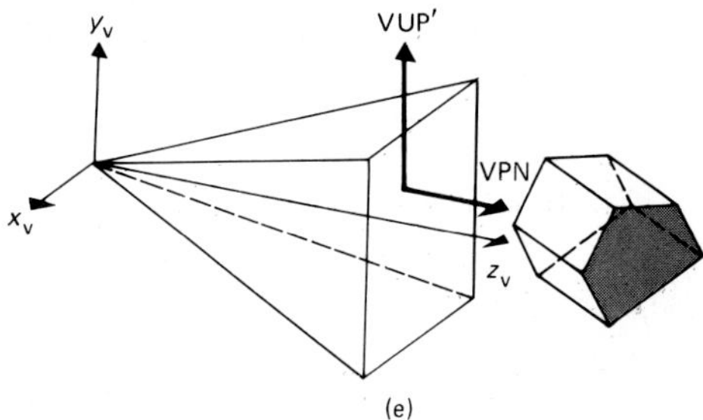

Fig. 8.33(e) Change to left-handed viewing coordinates and shear. The center line of the pyramid becomes the *z*-axis, VPN remains parallel to the *z*-axis, and VUP′ remains parallel to the *y*-axis: steps 4 and 5 of N_{per}.

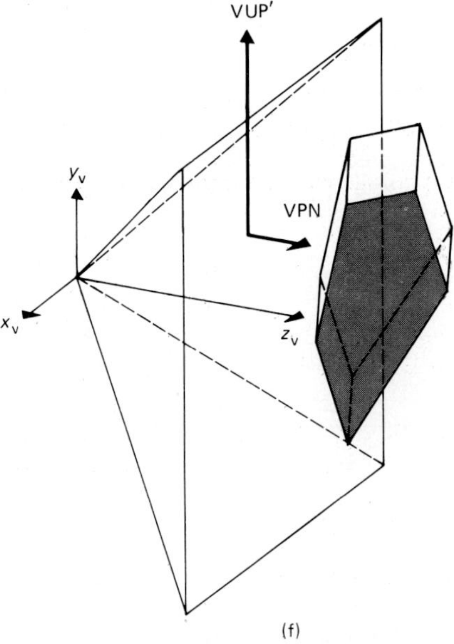

Fig. 8.33(f) The view volume is scaled into the canonical view volume: step 6 of N_{per}.

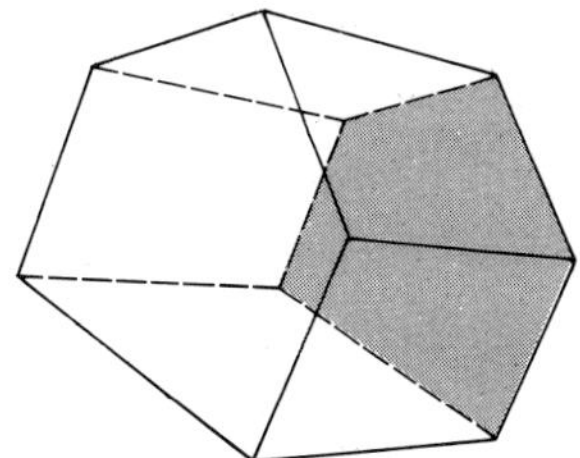

Fig. 8.34 Perspective projection of house.

The center of projection is specified relative to the VRP by

$$\text{COP} = (\text{COP}_x, \text{COP}_y, \text{COP}_z). \tag{8.27}$$

Therefore the center of projection is at

$$(\text{VRP}_x + \text{COP}_x,\ \text{VRP}_y + \text{COP}_y,\ \text{VRP}_z + \text{COP}_z),$$

so the initial translation is:

$$T_{\text{per}} = T\big(-(\text{VRP}_x + \text{COP}_x),\ -(\text{VRP}_y + \text{COP}_y),\ -(\text{VRP}_z + \text{COP}_z)\big). \tag{8.28}$$

The rotations of steps 2 and 3 are again those calculated in Section 7.6, with the same associations as for parallel projections:

View reference point: VRP = $P1$,
View plane normal: VPN = $\overline{P1P2}$ (the directed line segment from $P1$ to $P2$),
View up: VUP = $\overline{P1P3}$ (the directed line segment from $P1$ to $P3$).

The translation of $P1$ to the origin in Section 7.6 is applied only to calculate θ, ϕ, and α, but does not become part of N_{per}: only the rotations are used.

The right-to-left conversion for step 4 is T_{RL}, as given by (8.18) in the preceding section. To compute the shear for step 5, we examine Fig. 8.35 which shows a side view of the view volume after transformation steps 1 to 4. Notice that the center line of the view volume, which goes through the origin and through the center of the window, is not the same as z_v. The purpose of the shear is to transform the center line into the z_v axis. To calculate this shear, we start with the coordinates of the center of the window which in the uv coordinate system of the projection plane is still at $\big((u_{\min} + u_{\max})/2,\ (v_{\min} + v_{\max})/2\big)$ since none of the transformation steps have affected the lengths of lines.

The origin of the uv-coordinate system, the VRP, after transformation steps 1 to 4 is:

$$\text{VRP}' = \text{VRP} \cdot T_{\text{per}} \cdot Ry(\theta) \cdot Rx(\phi) \cdot Rz(\alpha) \cdot T_{\text{RL}} = \text{VRP} \cdot T_{\text{per}} \cdot R \cdot T_{\text{RL}}, \tag{8.29}$$

where R was derived in Section 7.6.

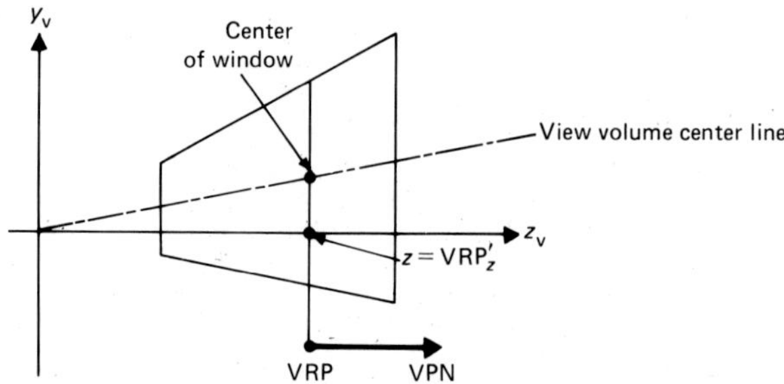

Fig. 8.35 Cross section of view volume after transformation steps 1 to 4.

Thus the center of the window, through which the view volume center line passes, is now at:

$$\begin{aligned} \mathrm{CW}_x &= \mathrm{VRP}'_x + \tfrac{1}{2}(u_{\min} + u_{\max}), \\ \mathrm{CW}_y &= \mathrm{VRP}'_y + \tfrac{1}{2}(v_{\min} + v_{\max}), \\ \mathrm{CW}_z &= \mathrm{VRP}'_z. \end{aligned} \tag{8.30}$$

We want to shear the center of the window to $(0, 0, \mathrm{VRP}'_z)$. We readily find that the coefficients for SH_z are

$$\begin{aligned} a_2 &= -\frac{\mathrm{CW}_x}{\mathrm{CW}_z} = -\frac{\mathrm{VRP}'_x + \frac{1}{2}(u_{\min} + u_{\max})}{\mathrm{VRP}'_z}, \\ b_2 &= -\frac{\mathrm{CW}_y}{\mathrm{CW}_z} = -\frac{\mathrm{VRP}'_y + \frac{1}{2}(v_{\min} + v_{\max})}{\mathrm{VRP}'_z,}. \end{aligned} \tag{8.31}$$

After applying the shear, the window (and hence the view volume) is centered on the z_v-axis and is defined by

$$\begin{aligned} -\tfrac{1}{2}(u_{\max} - u_{\min}) \le x_v \le \tfrac{1}{2}(u_{\max} - u_{\min}), \\ -\tfrac{1}{2}(v_{\max} - v_{\min}) \le y_v \le \tfrac{1}{2}(v_{\max} - v_{\min}). \end{aligned} \tag{8.32}$$

The final step is a scaling along all three axes to create the canonical view volume defined by Eq. (8.16). Figure 8.36 shows the view volume before and after this final step. The scaling is best thought of as being done in two substeps. In the first substep we scale differentially in x_v and y_v, so the sloped planes of the view volume have unity slope. This is accomplished by scaling the window so its half-height and half-width are both equal to VRP'_z. The appropriate x_v and y_v scale factors are $2 \cdot \mathrm{VRP}'_z/(u_{\max} - u_{\min})$ and $2 \cdot \mathrm{VRP}'_z/(v_{\max} - v_{\min})$, respectively. In the

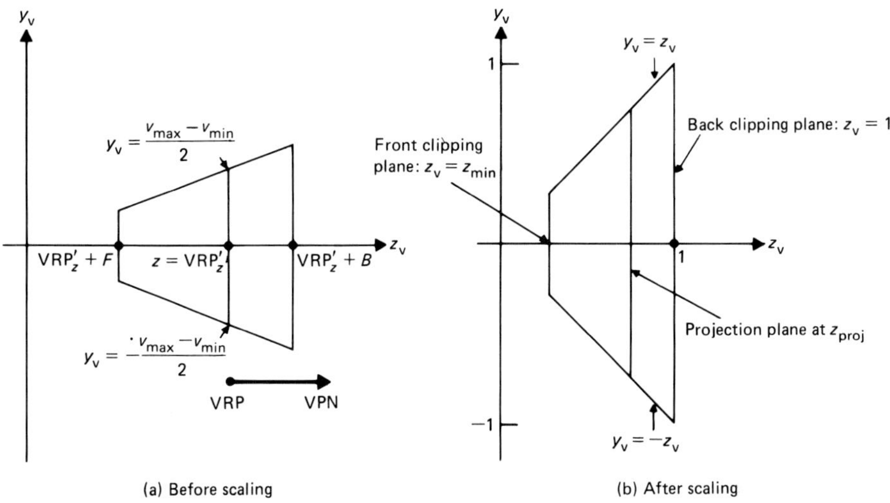

Fig. 8.36 Cross section of view volume before and after final scaling steps.

second substep we scale uniformly so that the back clipping plane at $z_v = VRP'_z + B$ becomes the $z_v = 1$ plane. The scale factor for this is $1/(VRP'_z + B)$.

Bringing these two substeps together, we define the scale as:

$$S_{per} = S\left(\frac{2 \cdot VRP'_z}{(u_{max} - u_{min}) \cdot (VRP'_z + B)}, \frac{2 \cdot VRP'_z}{(v_{max} - v_{min}) \cdot (VRP'_z + B)}, \frac{1}{VRP'_z + B}\right). \quad (8.33)$$

The scale applied to z_v changes the positions of the front clipping plane and of the projection plane to the new positions:

$$z_{min} = \frac{VRP'_z + F}{VRP'_z + B}, \qquad z_{proj} = \frac{VRP'_z}{VRP'_z + B}. \quad (8.34)$$

The overall viewing transformation for the perspective projection is

$$N_{per} = T_{per} \cdot Ry(\theta) \cdot Rx(\phi) \cdot Rz(\alpha) \cdot T_{RL} \cdot SH_z(a_2,b_2) \cdot S_{per}. \quad (8.35).$$

8.5 CLIPPING AGAINST A CANONICAL VIEW VOLUME

In the previous section normalizing transformations were developed to map arbitrary 3D view volumes into canonical ones ready for clipping: the unit cube for parallel projections and the truncated right regular pyramid for perspective projections. Clipping for both cases is treated similarly, with only the intersection calculations and inside/outside tests varying.

The algorithm for clipping against the unit cube exactly parallels the 2D Cohen–Sutherland algorithm from Section 4.2, but the out-code is now six bits, with a bit being true (1) when the appropriate condition is satisfied:

bit 1 — point is above view volume:	$y_v > 1$,
bit 2 — point is below view volume:	$y_v < 0$,
bit 3 — point is right of view volume:	$x_v > 1$,
bit 4 — point is left of view volume:	$x_v < 0$,
bit 5 — point is behind view volume:	$z_v > 1$,
bit 6 — point is in front of view volume:	$z_v < 0$.

As in 2D, a line is trivially accepted if both endpoints have a code of all zeros and trivially rejected if the bit-by-bit logical **and** of the codes is not all zeros. Otherwise, the process of line subdivision begins. Up to six intersections may have to be calculated: one for each side of the view volume.

The intersection calculations make use of the parametric representation of a line from $P_1(x_1, y_1, z_1)$ to $P_2(x_2, y_2, z_2)$:

$$\left.\begin{aligned} x_v &= (x_2 - x_1) \cdot t + x_1, \\ y_v &= (y_2 - y_1) \cdot t + y_1, \\ z_v &= (z_2 - z_1) \cdot t + z_1. \end{aligned}\right\} \quad 0 \le t \le 1 \tag{8.36}$$

As t is allowed to vary from 0 to 1, the three equations give the coordinates of all points on the line. To calculate the intersection of a line with the top of the unit cube view volume, we replace the variable y_v with the constant 1 and solve for t:

$$t = \frac{1 - y_1}{y_2 - y_1}. \tag{8.37}$$

If t is outside the interval from 0 to 1, the intersection is outside the cube. Otherwise, t is then substituted into the equations for x_v and z_v, giving the intersection's coordinates:

$$x_v = \frac{(1 - y_1)(x_2 - x_1)}{y_2 - y_1} + x_1, \qquad z_v = \frac{(1 - y_1)(z_2 - z_1)}{y_2 - y_1} + z_1. \tag{8.38}$$

Other intersections are calculated in a similar manner.

To clip against the canonical view volume for perspective projection, we again use a six-bit outcode, with the bits defined by:

bit 1 — point is above view volume:	$y_v > z_v$,
bit 2 — point is below view volume:	$y_v < -z_v$,
bit 3 — point is right of view volume:	$x_v > z_v$,
bit 4 — point is left of view volume:	$x_v < -z_v$,
bit 5 — point is behind view volume:	$z_v > 1$,
bit 6 — point is in front of view volume:	$z_v < z_{min}$.

Calculation of intersections of lines with the sloping planes is simple: consider the $y_v = z_v$ plane for which:

$$(y_2 - y_1) \cdot t + y_1 = (z_2 - z_1) \cdot t + z_1. \tag{8.39}$$

Then:

$$t = \frac{z_1 - y_1}{(y_2 - y_1) - (z_2 - z_1)}. \tag{8.40}$$

Substituting t into (8.36) for x_v and y_v gives:

$$x_v = \frac{(x_2 - x_1)(z_1 - y_1)}{(y_2 - y_1) - (z_2 - z_1)} + x_1, \qquad y_v = \frac{(y_2 - y_1)(z_1 - y_1)}{(y_2 - y_1) - (z_2 - z_1)} + y_1. \tag{8.41}$$

We know from the problem being solved that $z_v = y_v$. The reason for choosing this canonical view volume is now clear: the unit slopes of the planes make the intersection computations simpler than would arbitrary slopes.

The midpoint subdivision algorithm (Section 4.2.1), which does not involve division and multiplication, can easily be extended to 3D. However, the increasing availability of fast and inexpensive multiply/divide capabilities for microcomputers makes it less attractive than using the 3D generalization of the Cohen–Sutherland algorithm.

8.6 IMAGE TRANSFORMATIONS

Many graphics applications require a sequence of views of the same object to be displayed in succession. Often the goal is to display the sequence sufficiently rapidly so that real-time dynamics results, as in the simple case of "dragging" (i.e., translating) an image across the view surface in response to locator movements. In Chapter 2, the SGP subroutine *TRANSLATE_IMAGE_2* was used to drag furniture symbols on the screen.

An extension of this goal to other dynamic transformations (2D or 3D scaling and rotation) is also often desired. A need for 2D rotation is found in drafting systems, in which a predefined pattern may have to be rotated into the proper orientation. Rotation in 3D would be needed to fit a stick-figure molecule into an electron density map. In other cases, where real-time dynamics are either simply unattainable because of hardware restrictions (e.g., a direct-view storage tube display) or are not desired, each successive view in the sequence might be requested explicitly. In such cases the goal is to display each new view as quickly as possible.

A sequence of views can be produced by using either a sequence of *modeling* transformations, a sequence of *viewing* transformations, or a sequence of *image* transformations. Modeling transformations are applied in world coordinates to transform objects prior to the viewing transformation (see Chapter 9). Viewing transformations (a clip, projection, and geometric transformation) convert an object from world coordinates to normalized device coordinates. Image transformations (another geometric transformation) are applied *after* the viewing transformation, in normalized device coordinates.

The key problem in using modeling or viewing transformations to achieve real-time dynamics is to perform the entire image-creation process (wherein the application program describes output primitives to the graphics package, which then transforms, clips, projects, and displays the output primitives) at a rate of at least 10 picture updates per second. This rate can be achieved only in a few special cases:

1. The number of output primitives is quite small, so that viewing transformation software can process all primitives quickly enough, or
2. The transformation and clipping capabilities of high-performance, expensive graphics hardware are used by the graphics package, and the definitions of the output primitives can be kept in memory which is directly accessible to the DPU.

If neither of these cases is true (which is most of the time), real-time dynamics is not possible with modeling or viewing transformations. The situation is especially difficult if the display terminal is connected to the main computer by a communication link. Even transmission rates of 10,000 or 20,000 bits per second simply do not allow transmission of a complex new image each 1/10 of a second.

The potential to overcome these problems is increased by including image transformations in a graphics package, as in GPGS[VAND77] and the Core System. Image transformations are inherently faster than viewing transformations, because the latter perform clipping, discarding some output primitives, whereas the former do not clip and do not process discarded primitives. Furthermore, if many primitives are discarded during clipping, sufficient main storage might be available to hold the clipped primitives, whereas the unclipped primitives might have to reside in secondary storage. In such cases, image transformations have an additional speed advantage, even if hardware support for modeling and viewing is available. The graphics workstation concept of GKS represents a generalization of this notion of post-viewing transformations to include a second level of windowing, thereby further delaying the binding of what part of an image will be displayed [ENCA80].

We begin our implementation discussion with 2D image transformations and then generalize to 3D. Figure 8.37 shows how the viewing process can be extended to include 2D image transformations, which are performed after clipping and mapping into normalized device coordinates.

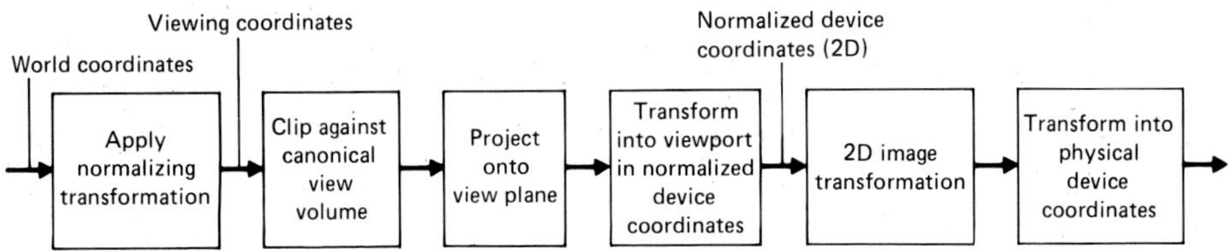

Fig. 8.37 3D viewing process extended to include 2D image transformations.

Any 2D image transformation can be represented as a 3×3 matrix by using compositions of the matrices from Chapter 7. To apply a 2D image transformation, a procedure such as

SET_IMAGE_XFORM(*segment_name*, *matrix*)

is called.* The segment is located in the pseudo display file and the coordinates therein are transformed by the composition of the image transformation matrix and the normalized-to-physical device coordinate transformation matrix. The resulting physical device coordinates are used to create DPU instructions to display the new image. Each time a new image transformation is given, the *original* segment definition is transformed and displayed.

3D image transformations require the implementation of more fundmental changes to the viewing process, as shown in Fig. 8.38. The first two steps are the same as in the 2D case. The next step transforms the canonical view volume into a 3D viewport, which is a rectangular parallelepiped embedded in 3D normalized device coordinate space. (This space, which is just the unit cube, is 3D, so the pseudo display file must be 3D.)

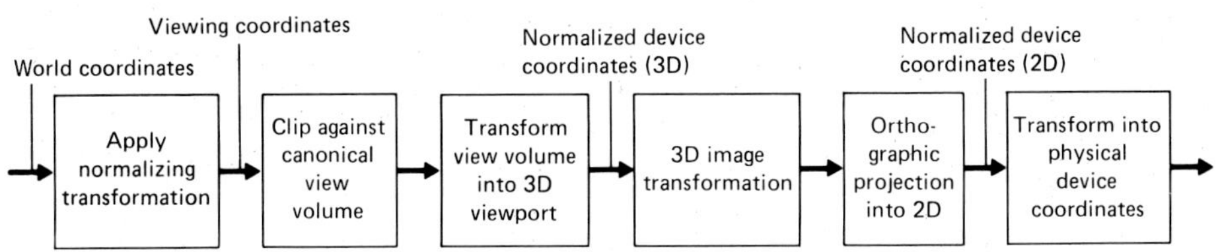

Fig. 8.38 3D viewing process extended to include 3D image transformations.

*This procedure is more general than that used in the Core System, which involves explicit scale, rotate, and translate parameters.

Image transformations are next applied to the 3D coordinates of output primitives, which are then displayed by being orthographically projected along the z-axis of 3D NDC space and transformed into physical device coordinates; Fig. 8.39 shows this projection.

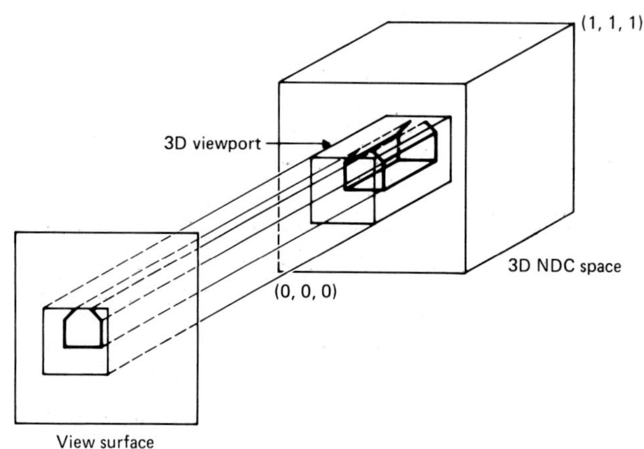

Fig. 8.39 3D NDC and 3D viewport with projection onto display.

The first step in implementing 3D image transformations is transforming the view volume to the 3D viewport, bounded in x by $x_{v.min}$ and $x_{v.max}$ and with similar bounds in y and z. For a parallel projection's canonical unit cube view volume, the transformation is just a scale followed by a translate. The scale shrinks the unit cube to the size of the 3D viewport; the translate moves the scaled-down cube to the appropriate position. The scale is:

$$S_1 = S(x_{v.max} - x_{v.min},\quad y_{v.max} - y_{v.min},\quad z_{v.max} - z_{v.min}). \tag{8.42}$$

The following translation is:

$$T_1 = T(x_{v.min},\quad y_{v.min},\quad z_{v.min}). \tag{8.43}$$

The transformation from the perspective projection canonical view volume to a 3D viewport is more complex. There is, however, a simple 4×4 matrix which will transform the truncated pyramid into the volume defined by:

$$-1 \leq x \leq 1, \qquad -1 \leq y \leq 1, \qquad 0 \leq z \leq 1. \tag{8.44}$$

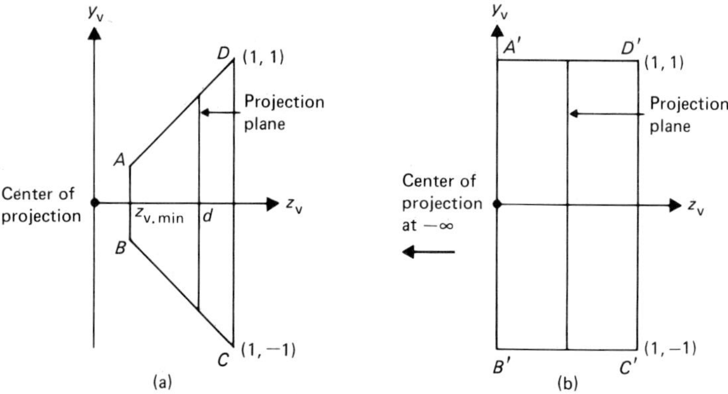

Fig. 8.40 Side views of normalized perspective view volume (a) before and (b) after application of matrix *M*.

Figure 8.40 shows the desired results of the transformation, with point A being transformed to A', etc. The matrix performing the transformation is:

$$M = \begin{bmatrix} 1 & 0 & 0 & 0 \\ 0 & 1 & 0 & 0 \\ 0 & 0 & \dfrac{1}{1 - z_{v.min}} & 1 \\ 0 & 0 & \dfrac{-z_{v.min}}{1 - z_{v.min}} & 0 \end{bmatrix}. \tag{8.45}$$

More will be said about M, called the *perspective transformation* (as opposed to the perspective projection), in Chapter 15 on hidden-surface removal. For the moment, simply notice that

$$[x \quad y \quad z \quad 1] \cdot 2d \cdot M \cdot M_{ort} = [x \quad y \quad z \quad 1] \cdot M_{per} \cdot M_{ort}, \tag{8.46}$$

where d is the position of the projection plane. This means that by using $2d \cdot M$ in place of M_{per} before the orthographic projection into 2D, we can obtain the same visual results as with the perspective matrix M_{per}. However, if we apply a 3D image rotation about the x- or y-axis, the resulting view will be distorted from what might be expected, because objects close to the front of the view volume are enlarged by M. That is, M and 3D rotations do not commute.

With the perspective projection's canonical view volume transformed into the volume defined by Eq. (8.44), the next three steps to transform into the 3D viewport are simple: translation of the volume defined by Eq. (8.44) so that the corner at (−1, −1, 0) goes to the origin; scale to the size of the 3D viewport; and translation to the viewport position. The steps are:

$$T_a = T(1, 1, 0), \tag{8.47}$$

$$S_a = S\left(\frac{x_{v.max} - x_{v.min}}{2}, \frac{y_{v.max} - y_{v.min}}{2}, z_{v.max} - z_{v.min}\right), \tag{8.48}$$

$$T_1 = T(x_{v.min}, y_{v.min}, z_{v.min}). \tag{8.49}$$

In summary, the results for 3D image transformations are:

$$I_{par} = S_1 \cdot T_1 \qquad \text{(parallel projection)}$$
$$I_{per} = M \cdot T_a \cdot S_a \cdot T_1 \quad \text{(perspective projection)}.$$

What happens when $z_{v.min} = z_{v.max}$? This means the 3D viewport has no depth and a z-axis scale of zero is created in S_1 and S_a. Then the final translation T_1 sets $z = z_{v.min}$ in 3D NDC space. If in addition it happens that $z_{v.min} = 0$, then the result is mapped into our standard 2D viewport in 2D NDC space. Thus we are assured that 3D image transformations also work appropriately for 2D.

The 3D image transformation itself can be represented as a 4×4 matrix. Just as in the 2D case, a graphics package subroutine call such as

SET_IMAGE_XFORM_3(segment_name, matrix)

is used to cause a segment to be image transformed. Each time the procedure is called, the 3D NDC coordinates in the pseudo display file are multiplied by the matrix computed by compounding the image transformation, orthographic projection, and normalized-to-physical device conversion matrices. Alternatively, the pseudo display file could store clipped viewing coordinates, prior to application of the mapping into the 3D viewport. Then all the transformations following the clip in Fig. 8.38 would be combined into a single composite matrix. In any case, each time the image transformation is changed, the composite matrix is recalculated and reapplied to the pseudo display file, with the transformed output primitives being displayed.

8.7 3D VIEWING IN SIMPLE GRAPHICS PACKAGE (SGP)*

We now want to add 3D viewing operations to SGP to make it a full 3D graphics package. Two sets of capabilities must be added to achieve this:

- Output primitives in 3D,
- Specification of planar geometric projections.

*This section has been adapted from Section 3 of [BERG78].

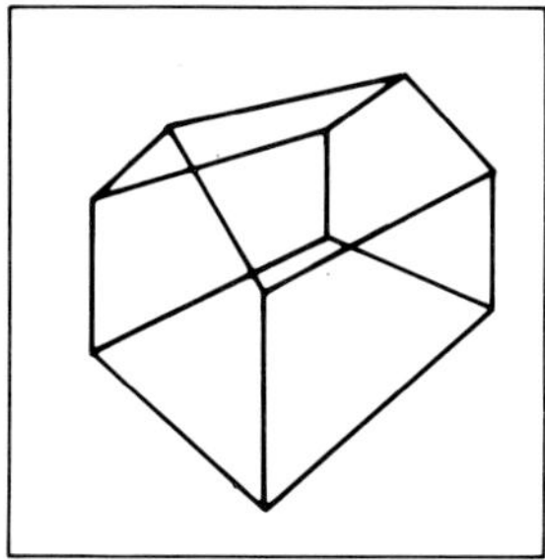

Fig. 8.41 Two-point perspective projection of a house.

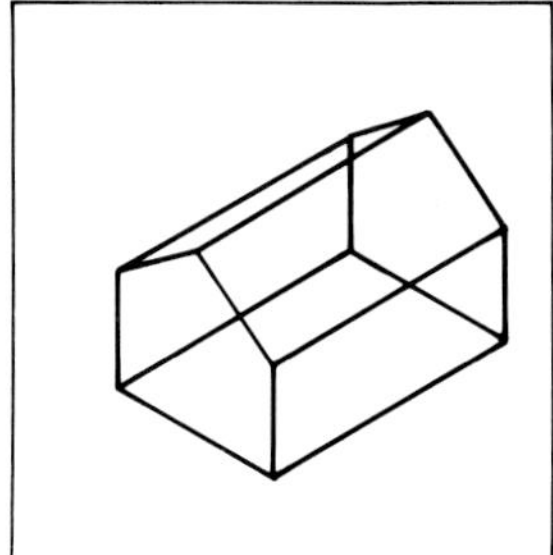

Fig. 8.42 Isometric projection of a house.

With these capabilities, we will be able to create views such as depicted in Figs. 8.41 and 8.42. As was the case in Chapter 2, the extensions to SGP will be patterned after the Core System [GSPC79]. The procedures which provide the extensions will be introduced as needed throughout this section.

Output primitives in 3D world coordinates, which in SGP is a right-handed coordinate system, are straightforward extensions from the 2D primitives. In the procedure name the "2" changes to "3", and a third parameter, the z-coordinate, is added. For instance, we have *LINE_ABS_3*(x, y, z). Also, the *current position* (CP) is extended to include a z-component.

It is possible to intermingle 2D and 3D output primitives. The 2D primitives simply do not affect the z-component of the CP. Thus, if the CP is (5.0, 10.0, 4.0) and

LINE_ABS_2(12.0, 17.0)

is called, a line is drawn from the CP to (12.0, 17.0, 4.0), which becomes the new CP. This shorthand is convenient for describing objects on a plane of constant z.

The procedure in Fig. 8.43 defines the house shown in Fig. 8.44 and illustrates how 2D and 3D output primitives can be mixed. The house is 16 feet wide, 24 feet deep, and 16 feet high at the peak (in this example we assume that one foot is one world coordinate unit).

```
procedure HOUSE;
begin
{draw front face of house in z = 30.0 plane}
  MOVE_ABS_3(0.0, 0.0, 30.0);
  LINE_REL_2(16.0, 0.0);
  LINE_REL_2(0.0, 10.0);
  LINE_REL_2(-8.0, 6.0);
  LINE_REL_2(-8.0, -6.0);
  LINE_REL_2(0.0, -10.0);
{draw face in z = 54.0 plane}
  MOVE_ABS_3(0.0, 0.0, 54.0);
  LINE_REL_2(16.0, 0.0);
  LINE_REL_2(0.0, 10.0);
  LINE_REL_2(-8.0, 6.0);
  LINE_REL_2(-8.0, -6.0);
  LINE_REL_2(0.0, -10.0);
{now connect front and rear faces}
  MOVE_ABS_3(0.0, 0.0, 30.0);
  LINE_REL_3(0.0, 0.0, 24.0);
  MOVE_ABS_3(16.0, 0.0, 30.0);
  LINE_REL_3(0.0, 0.0, 24.0);
  MOVE_ABS_3(16.0, 10.0, 30.0);
  LINE_REL_3(0.0, 0.0, 24.0);
  MOVE_ABS_3(8.0, 16.0, 30.0);
  LINE_REL_3(0.0, 0.0, 24.0);
  MOVE_ABS_3(0.0, 10.0, 30.0);
  LINE_REL_3(0.0, 0.0, 24.0);
end    {HOUSE}
```

Fig. 8.43 Procedure to draw 3D house.

8.7.1 Perspective Projections

How can the house be viewed with a perspective projection? In SGP a perspective projection is defined by:

- A center of projection;
- A view plane (the projection plane);
- A window on the view plane, and
- A viewport on the view surface.

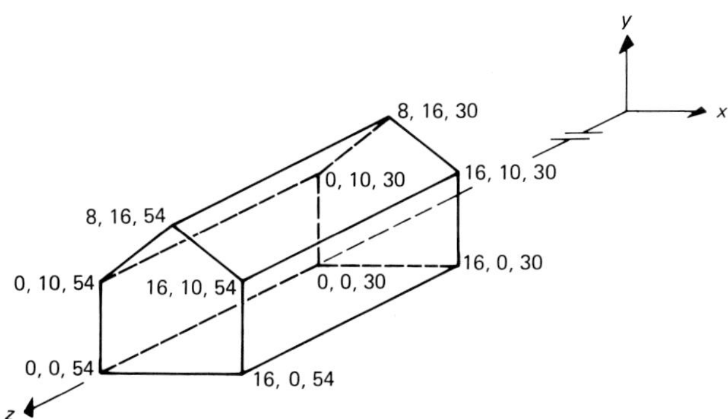

Fig. 8.44 House drawn by procedure defined in Fig. 8.43.

These are exactly the general concepts of Sections 8.1 and 8.2, and in turn imply the use of concepts like the VRP, VPN, VUP, and the *uv* coordinate system from Section 8.3.

Readers who seek aid in understanding how all these concepts interrelate are encouraged to buy a set of Tinker Toys™ to use in constructing a house, the world coordinate system, and the *u, v,* VPN coordinate system, as pictured in Fig. 8.45. The VRP is the origin of the *u, v,* VPN coordinate system. The idea is to position this coordinate system in world coordinates in the same way as done in the viewing example and to imagine projectors from points on the house intersecting the view plane. Experience shows that this is a useful way to understand (and to teach) 3D viewing concepts.

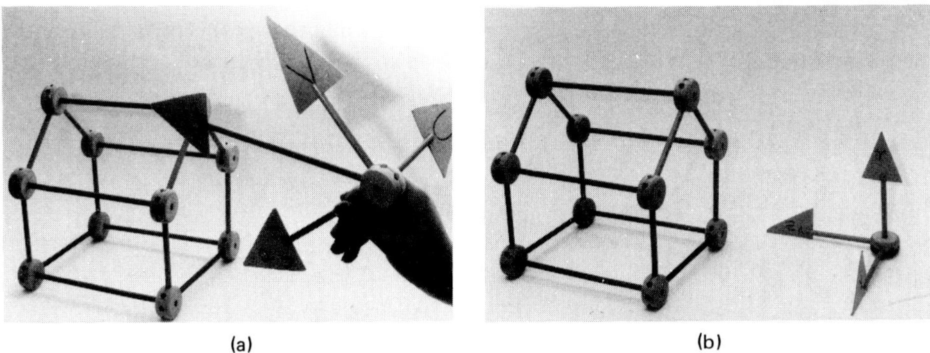

Fig. 8.45 Stick models useful for understanding 3D viewing: (a) house and right-handed coordinate systems; (b) house and left-handed coordinate system (courtesy JDF and MHF).

In SGP, as in the Core System, there are defaults for all of the viewing specifications. The view reference point defaults to the origin, and the view plane normal defaults to the negative z-axis. Therefore, the default view plane is the $z = 0$ plane. Furthermore, the default view-up vector is the positive y-axis, and the default projection is parallel, along the z-axis. Therefore, the u- and v-axes correspond to the x- and y-axes, respectively. These defaults mean that 2D viewing is just a special case of 3D viewing. All 2D output primitives are in the $z = 0$ plane, which is the projection plane. The default window and viewport each range from 0 to 1 along both axes. Unless explicitly specified otherwise, these defaults are assumed to be in use in each of the following examples.

To obtain a front one-point perspective view of the house (that is, looking along the positive z-axis toward the origin), we could position the center of projection (which can be thought of as the position of the viewer) at $x = 8.0$, $y = 6.0$, and $z = 84.0$. The x value is selected to be at the horizontal center of the house, the y value to correspond to the approximate eye level of a tall viewer standing on the xz-plane, while the z value is arbitrary. In this case, z is removed 30 units from the front of the house ($z = 54$ plane).

The call

SET_PROJECTION("PERSPECTIVE", 8.0, 6.0, 84.0)

specifies a center of projection relative to the view reference point. With the default view reference point, this call places the center of projection at $x = 8.0$, $y = 6.0$, and $z = 84.0$. The call

WINDOW(−50.0, 50.0, −50.0, 50.0)

specifies a window in the view plane (the $z = 0.0$ plane, in this case) with sides 100 units long. The window determines which part of the view plane is displayed in the viewport. A large window is needed because the house is between the center of projection and the view plane. The house is therefore enlarged by the projection onto the view plane. These two calls can be used as shown below to create the view of Fig. 8.46:

```
SET_PROJECTION("PERSPECTIVE", 8.0, 6.0, 84.0);
WINDOW(-50.0, 50.0, -50.0, 50.0);
CREATE_SEGMENT(1);
  HOUSE;
CLOSE_SEGMENT
```

Although Fig. 8.46 is indeed a perspective projection of the house, it is too small and not centered on the view surface. We would prefer to have a more centered projection of the house and have the projection more nearly span the entire view surface, as seen in Fig. 8.47. We could more easily produce this effect if the view plane and the front plane of the house coincided. Then, because the front of the house extends from 0.0 to 16.0 in both x and y, a window extending from −1.0 to 17.0 in x and y would produce reasonable results.

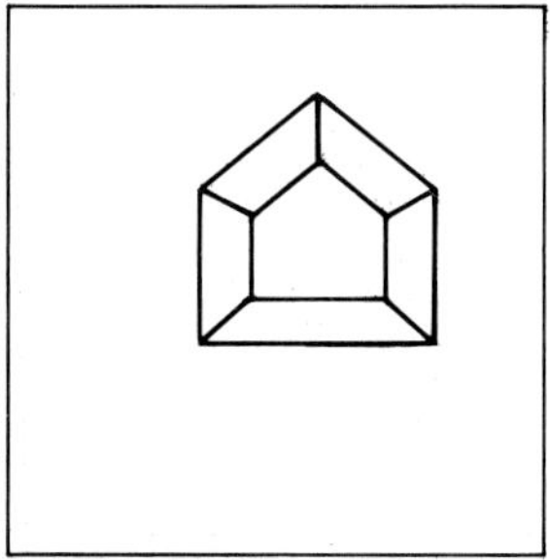

Fig. 8.46 Uncentered perspective projection of a house.

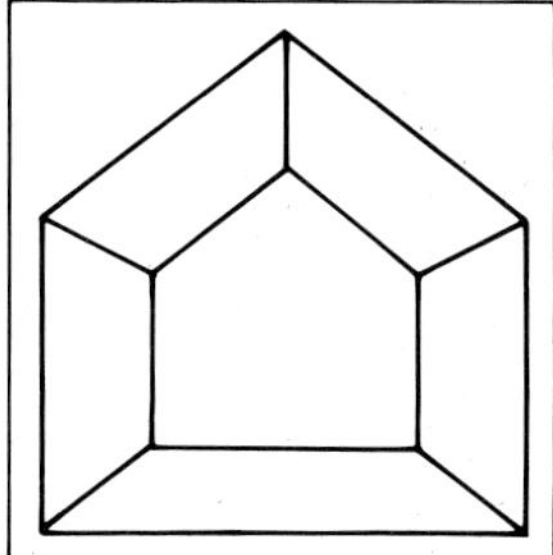

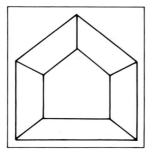

Fig. 8.47 Centered perspective projection of a house.

To reposition (but not to reorient) the view plane to coincide with the front of the house, we change the view reference point with the procedure call:

```
SET_VIEW_REFERENCE_POINT(0.0, 0.0, 54.0)
```

The center of projection, which is specified relative to the view reference point, can continue to be at the same position, but relative to the new reference point. The following program segment produces Fig. 8.47:

```
SET_VIEW_REFERENCE_POINT(0.0, 0.0, 54.0);
SET_PROJECTION("PERSPECTIVE", 8.0, 6.0, 30.0);
WINDOW(-1.0, 17.0, -1.0, 17.0);
CREATE_SEGMENT(2);
  HOUSE;
CLOSE_SEGMENT
```

This same result can be obtained in many other ways. For instance, if the view reference point were placed at (8.0, 6.0, 54.0), the center of projection would be at (0.0, 0.0, 30.0) relative to this point. The window would also have to be respecified, because its definition is based on the *u, v,* VPN coordinate system, the origin of

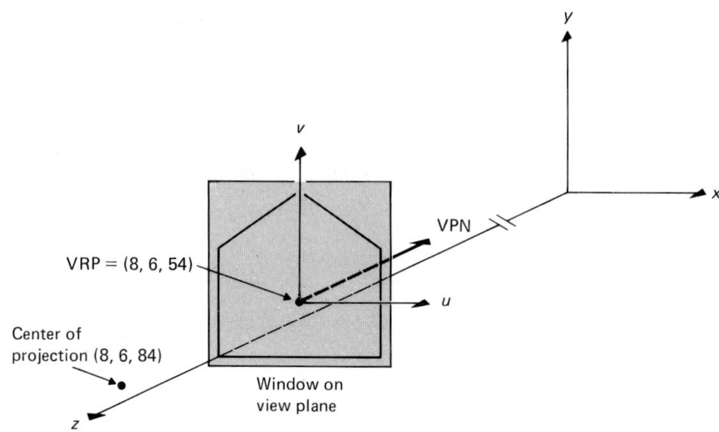

Fig. 8.48 The *u*, *v*, VPN coordinate system.

which is the view reference point. (In the Core System, but not in SGP, this origin can be anywhere along the line through the VRP and parallel to the VPN.) Figure 8.48 shows the *u*, *v*, and VPN axes forming the *u*, *v*, VPN coordinate system, the front face of the house, the center of projection, and a window extending from –9.0 to 9.0 in *u* and from –7.0 to 11.0 in *v*. With respect to the house, this is the same window used in the previous example, but specified now in a different *uv* coordinate system. In this case, the *u*-axis and *x*-axis are parallel, as are the *v*-axis and *y*-axis, because the view-up direction defaults to the *y*-axis.

The program segment below gives this new viewing specification:

```
SET_VIEW_REFERENCE_POINT(8.0, 6.0, 54.0);
SET_PROJECTION("PERSPECTIVE", 0.0, 0.0, 30.0);
WINDOW(-9.0, 9.0, -7.0, 11.0);
CREATE_SEGMENT(3);
  HOUSE;
CLOSE_SEGMENT
```

Incidentally, these viewing parameters can be specified in any order: whatever viewing parameters are in effect when a segment is created are used.

Next, let us work toward obtaining the view shown earlier in Fig. 8.41. The center of projection can be thought of as being analogous to the position of the synthetic camera which takes snapshots of world coordinate objects. With this analogy in mind as we examine Fig. 8.41, it appears that the center of projection is somewhat higher than the house and to the right of the house, as viewed from the positive *z*-axis. The exact center of projection is (36.0, 25.0, 74.0).

If the corner of the house at (16.0, 0.0, 54.0) is chosen as the view reference point, then this center of projection is at (20.0, 25.0, 20.0) relative to the view reference point. With the view plane coincident with the front of the house (the $z = 54.0$ plane), and the viewing coordinate system origin at the view reference point, a window ranging from −20.0 to 20.0 in u and from −5.0 to 35.0 in v is certainly large enough to contain the projection. The following program segment embodies this viewing specification and corresponds to the view of Fig. 8.49:

```
SET_VIEW_REFERENCE_POINT(16.0, 0.0, 54.0);
SET_PROJECTION("PERSPECTIVE", 20.0, 25.0, 20.0);
WINDOW(−20.0, 20.0, −5.0, 35.0);
CREATE_SEGMENT(4);
  HOUSE;
CLOSE_SEGMENT
```

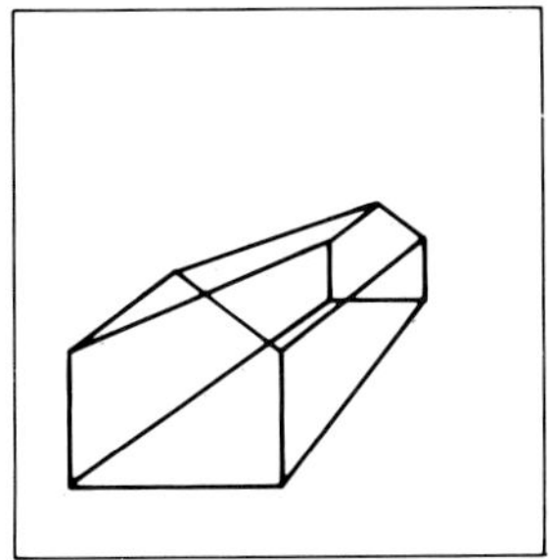

Fig. 8.49 Perspective projection of a house from (36.0, 25.0, 74.0) with VPN parallel to z-axis.

This view has some similarity to Fig. 8.41, but is clearly not the same. For one thing, Fig. 8.41 is a two-point perspective projection, while Fig. 8.49 is a one-point perspective. It is apparent that simply moving the center of projection is not sufficient to produce Fig. 8.41. It is, in fact, necessary to reorient the view plane so that it cuts the x- and z-axes. With

```
SET_VIEW_PLANE_NORMAL(−1.0, 0.0, −1.0)
```

a new normal is established such that the view plane cuts the z- and x-axes at 45° angles and remains parallel to the y-axis. Figure 8.50 shows the view plane established with this VPN.

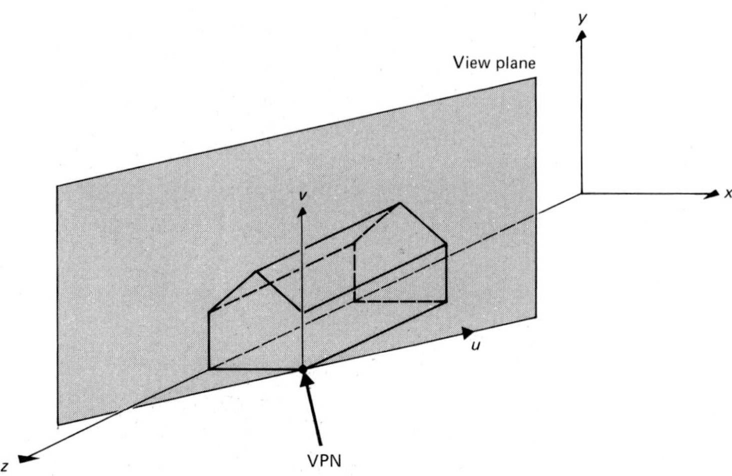

Fig. 8.50 View plane and u, v coordinate system.

There are two general ways to choose a satisfactory window that completely surrounds the projection, as does the window in Fig. 8.41. The size of the projection of the house onto the view plane can be calculated or the trial-and-error method can be used. In this case, the sketch presented in Fig. 8.51 was used to calculate the intersections of the view plane with two projection rays. This yielded the appropriate window bounds along the u-axis from -12 to $+13$. Trial and error was then used to find satisfactory bounds along the v-axis, from -2 to $+23$.

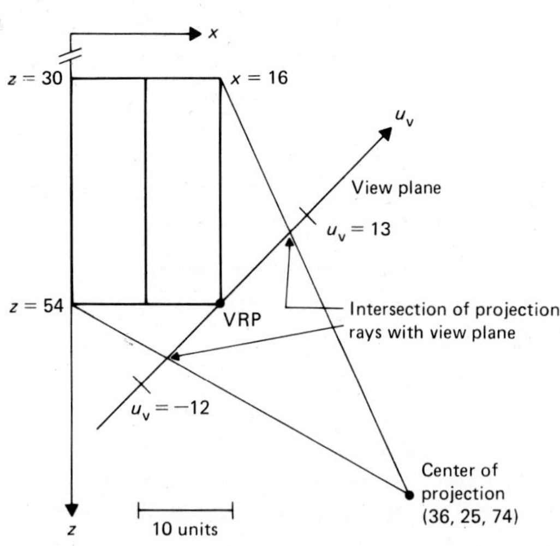

Fig. 8.51 Top (plan) view of a house for determining an appropriate window size.

This next program segment does produce Fig. 8.41:

```
SET_VIEW_REFERENCE_POINT(16.0, 0.0, 54.0);
SET_VIEW_PLANE_NORMAL(-1.0, 0.0, -1.0);
SET_PROJECTION("PERSPECTIVE", 20.0, 25.0, 20.0);
WINDOW(-12.0, 13.0, -2.0, 23.0);
CREATE_SEGMENT(5);
  HOUSE;
CLOSE_SEGMENT
```

Figure 8.52 is nearly the same as Fig. 8.41. It is as though Fig. 8.52 were obtained from exactly the same projection, but with a window at a different orientation. This is indeed the case. In all previous examples, the v-axis of the viewing coordinate system was parallel to the y-axis of the world coordinate system. Therefore, the window (two of whose sides are parallel to the v-axis) was nicely aligned with the vertical sides of the house. While we do not show the code here, Fig. 8.52 was actually produced with the aid of the *SET_VIEW_UP_3* call to rotate the v-axis by defining a new view-up vector.

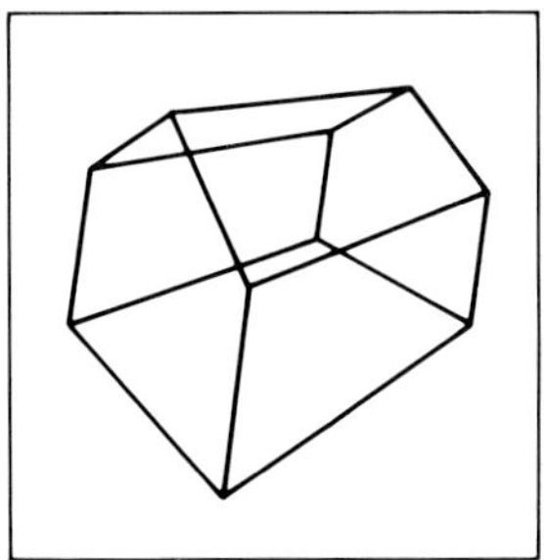

Fig. 8.52 Rotated two-point perspective projection of a house.

8.7.2 A Programming Example

Computing viewing parameters to obtain a desired view can be difficult, as the previous example suggests. Part of the power of interactive graphics is in allowing the user to change views interactively to obtain the one that is just right (as typically done in plot preview packages) to orient a view for best visualization before creating hard copy. Suppose we need the basic view of Fig. 8.41 but want the user to control the distance of the center of projection from the view plane. The program example in Fig. 8.53 reads a value ranging from 0.0 to 1.0, scales it by 100, and uses the result to adjust the x- and z-components of the center of projection. The y-component remains fixed at 25.0. Operator interaction ends when a button is pressed.

```
SET_VIEW_REFERENCE_POINT(16.0, 0.0, 54.0);
SET_VIEW_PLANE_NORMAL(-1,0, 0.0, -1.0);
root_2 := SQRT(2.0);
{Create an initial perspective projection with the center of
projection 50 units (in xz-plane) from view reference point}
SET_PROJECTION(''PERSPECTIVE'', 50.0/root_2, 25.0, 50.0/root_2);
WINDOW(-20.0, 20.0, -5.0, 35.0);
CREATE_SEGMENT(10);
  HOUSE;
CLOSE_SEGMENT;
{Now loop to react to valuator changes; exit when button is pushed}
old_distance := 50.0;
temp := 20;                              {name of temporary segment}
repeat                                   {interactive loop}
  READ_VALUATOR(1, distance);
  distance := distance *100              {scale into range 0 to 100}
  if ABS(distance - old_distance) > 1.0 then
    begin
      SET_PROJECTION(''PERSPECTIVE'', (distance/root_2, 25.0,
        distance/root_2));
        old_distance := distance;
      CREATE_SEGMENT(temp);
        SET_VISIBILITY(temp, false);
        HOUSE;
      CLOSE_SEGMENT;
      SET_VISIBILITY(10, false);
      SET_VISIBILITY(temp, true);
      DELETE_SEGMENT(10);
      RENAME_SEGMENT(temp, 10)
    end;
    WAIT_BUTTON(0.033, number)   {wait 1/30 second}
until number<>0      {end interaction loop when a button is pushed}
```

Fig. 8.53 Interaction program to change center of projection.

Double buffering between segments 10 and 20 is done using *RENAME* so that an image is nearly always displayed. The speed and frequency with which the image changes in response to valuator changes depend on many details of the SGP implementation, the capabilities of the display device, and the configuration of the host computer. For a few systems the changes would be nearly instantaneous and therefore apparently continuous, while for many more systems there would be discernable discontinuities from the display of one image to the next. Figure 8.54 shows three views of the house for different values of *distance*.

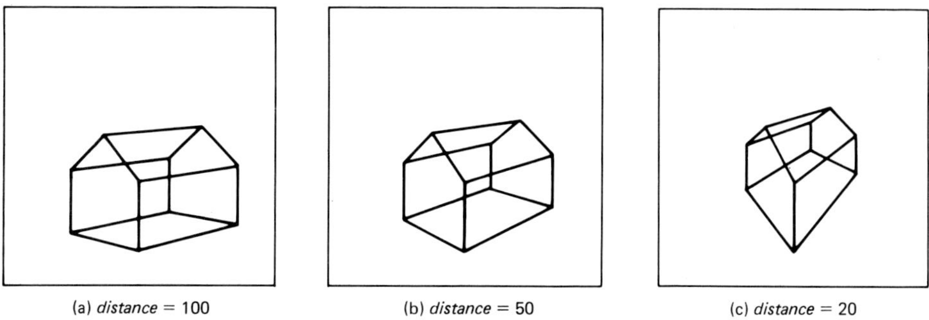

(a) *distance* = 100 (b) *distance* = 50 (c) *distance* = 20

Fig. 8.54 Views of a house created by interaction program with various distances.

8.7.3 Parallel Projections

A parallel projection is specified with

SET_PROJECTION("PARALLEL", *dx*, *dy*, *dz*)

where (*dx*, *dy*, *dz*) is the direction of projection. A front view of the house (Fig. 8.55) can be created with:

```
SET_PROJECTION("PARALLEL", 0.0, 0.0, -1.0);
WINDOW(-1.0, 17.0, -1.0, 17.0);
CREATE_SEGMENT(6);
  HOUSE;
CLOSE_SEGMENT
```

Fig. 8.55 Front view of the house.

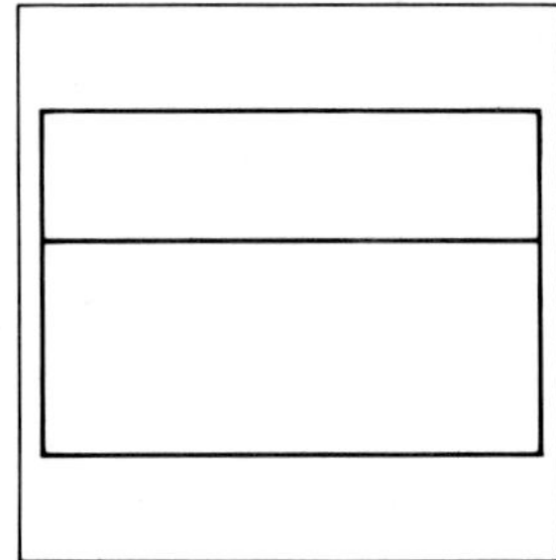

Fig. 8.56 Parallel projection from the side of the house.

A side view of the house (Fig. 8.56) is created with:

```
SET_VIEW_REFERENCE_POINT(0.0, 0.0, 54.0);
SET_VIEW_PLANE_NORMAL(−1.0, 0.0, 0.0);
SET_PROJECTION("PARALLEL", −1.0, 0.0, 0.0);
WINDOW(−1.0, 25.0, −5.0, 21.0);
CREATE_SEGMENT(7);
  HOUSE;
CLOSE_SEGMENT
```

A top view of the house is created by using the $y = 0$ plane as the view plane. Thus, VPN is the negative y-axis. This means that the default view-up direction of $+y$ no longer works, so the new view-up direction must be explicitly specified—we chose the negative x-axis. The VRP is specified as a corner of the house, so an appropriate window is easily calculated. The code is:

```
SET_VIEW_REFERENCE_POINT(16.0, 0.0, 54.0);
SET_VIEW_PLANE_NORMAL(0.0, −1.0, 0.0);
SET_VIEW_UP_3(−1.0, 0.0, 0.0);
SET_PROJECTION("PARALLEL", 0.0, −1.0, 0.0);
WINDOW(−1.0, 25.0, −5.0, 21.0);
CREATE_SEGMENT(8);
  HOUSE;
CLOSE_SEGMENT
```

Figure 8.42 is an isometric (parallel orthographic) projection in the direction (−1.0, −1.0, −1.0), which is one of the four possible directions for an isometric (see Section 8.2). The following code segment would create the figure:

```
SET_VIEW_REFERENCE_POINT(10.0, 8.0, 54.0);
SET_VIEW_PLANE_NORMAL(−1.0, −1.0, −1.0);
SET_PROJECTION("PARALLEL", −1.0, −1.0, −1.0);
WINDOW(−15.0, 25.0, −15.0, 25.0);
CREATE_SEGMENT(9);
  HOUSE;
CLOSE_SEGMENT
```

A cavalier projection onto the default view plane with angle *alpha* is specified with

SET_PROJECTION("PARALLEL", *COS*(*alpha*), *SIN*(*alpha*), −1.0)

If some other view plane is used, then the application program must transform the direction of projection by the rotation matrix which transforms from *x, y, z* world coordinates into *u, v,* VPN coordinates: this is the $Ry \cdot Rx \cdot Rz$ sequence used in Section 8.4. If SGP were to interpret the direction of projection as already being in *u, v,* VPN coordinates, the application program would not need to perform this transformation.

8.7.4 Finite View Volumes

The front clipping plane and back clipping plane, described in an earlier section, help determine a *finite view volume.* These planes, both of which are parallel to the view plane, are specified as *front_distance* and *back_distance* from the view reference point. These distances are specified with

SET_VIEW_DEPTH(*front_distance, back_distance*)

and are measured from the VRP along the VPN. To avoid errors, it is required that *front_distance* does not exceed *back_distance.* Clipping against the front and back planes can be turned on and off by using the procedures:

SET_FRONT_PLANE_CLIPPING(*flag*), and
SET_BACK_PLANE_CLIPPING(*flag*)

The default value is no clipping against these planes.

A front perspective view of the house with the rear wall clipped away (Fig. 8.57) results from the following code segment:

```
SET_BACK_PLANE_CLIPPING(true);
SET_VIEW_REFERENCE_POINT(0.0, 0.0, 54.0);
WINDOW(−1.0, 17.0, −1.0, 17.0);
SET_PROJECTION("PERSPECTIVE", 8.0, 6.0, 30.0);
SET_VIEW_DEPTH(−1.0, 23.0);
CREATE_SEGMENT(10);
  HOUSE;
CLOSE_SEGMENT
```

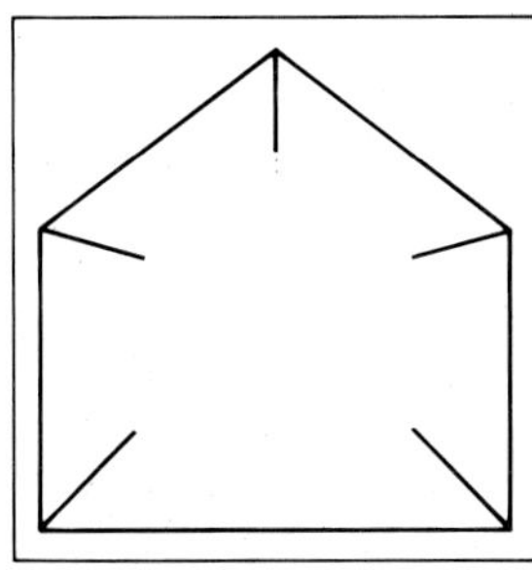

Fig. 8.57 Perspective projection of the house with back clipping plane at $z = 31$.

8.7.5 Using Image Transformations

In this section we show how to use 3D image transformations (discussed in Section 8.6) to rotate a clipped portion of a molecule in 3D NDC space about the line parallel to the screen's y-axis and passing through $x = 0.5$, $z = 0.5$. The program segment is in Fig. 8.58. The molecule is initially displayed by using a parallel projection and a view volume which is $10.0 \times 10.0 \times 10.0$. We presume that the molecule is larger than this. The view volume is mapped into a 3D viewport sufficiently smaller than 3D NDC space so that the rotated clipped molecule will always be completely contained in 3D NDC space.

In the program, a valuator is used to read an angle. Each 1/30 of a second a new image transformation is calculated and used, until the interaction is stopped by pushing a button. The image transformation used is the composition of a translation of the center of rotation to the origin, a rotation about the y-axis, and another translation back to the center of rotation.

```
{Program segment to tumble a molecule using image transformations.
First, establish a view volume which is 10×10×10}
SET_VIEW_DEPTH(30.0, 40.0);
WINDOW(15.0, 25.0, 23.0, 33.0);
{Establish other viewing parameters}
SET_FRONT_PLANE_CLIPPING(true);
SET_BACK_PLANE_CLIPPING(true);
SET_PROJECTION("PARALLEL", 0.0, 0.0, -1.0);      {parallel along z axis}
SET_VIEWPORT_3(0.15, 0.85, 0.15, 0.85, 0.15, 0.85);
CREATE_SEGMENT(molecule);
  MOLECULE;                          {procedure which describes the molecule to}
CLOSE_SEGMENT                        {SGP}
repeat                               {interaction loop}
    READ_VALUATOR(1, angle);
    angle := angle*6.28;             {convert to radians}
    {Calculate the 4×4 matrix consisting of}
    xform := T(-0.5, 0.0, -0.5)*RY(angle)*T(0.5, 0.0, 0.5);
    SET_IMAGE_XFORM_3(molecule, xform);
    WAIT_BUTTON(0.033, number);  {wait 1/30 second}
until number<>0      {interaction loop ends when a button is pushed}
```

Fig. 8.58 Program segment to tumble a molecule.

8.8 SUMMARY

This chapter has presented a complete discussion of 3D viewing, beginning with the definitions of planar geometric projections and moving through the basic mathematics of the projections to their actual implementation and use in a contemporary graphics package. Unfortunately, not all graphics packages provide the complete set of projections, so that in some cases the application programmer may be actually forced to implement some of the mathematics described here.

EXERCISES

8.1 Write a program which accepts a viewing specification and calculates either N_{par} or N_{per}.

8.2 Program 3D clipping algorithms for parallel and perspective projections.

8.3 Assuming that $F = -\infty$ and $B = +\infty$, show that the result of 3D solid rectangle clipping and then parallel projecting is the same as from parallel projecting and then 2D clipping.

8.4 Show that if all objects are in front of the center of projection and if $F = -\infty$ and $B = +\infty$, then the result of 3D truncated pyramid clipping followed by perspective projection is the same as from first doing a perspective projection and then doing 2D clipping.

8.5 Verify that S_{per} (Section 8.4.2) does transform the view volume of Fig. 8.36(a) into that of Fig. 8.36(b).

8.6 Write the code for 3D clipping against the unit cube. Generalize the code to clip against any rectangular solid with faces normal to the principal axes. Is the generalized code more or less efficient than for the special unit cube case?

8.7 Write the code for 3D clipping against the canonical perspective projection view volume. Now generalize to the view volume defined by:

$$-a \cdot z_v \le x_v \le b \cdot z_v, \qquad -c \cdot z_v \le y_v \le d \cdot z_v, \qquad z_{min} \le z_v \le z_{max}.$$

This is the general form of the view volume after steps (1) to (4) of the perspective normalizing transformation. Which case is more efficient?

8.8 Write the code for 3D clipping against a general six-faced view volume whose faces are defined by:

$$A_i x + B_i y + C_i z + D = 0, \qquad 1 \le i \le 6.$$

Compare the computational effort needed:

a) With that required for clipping against either of the canonical view volumes;

b) With that required to apply N_{par} and to clip against the unit cube.

8.9 You are given a line in 3D going from $P1(6, 10, 3)$ to $P2(-3, -5, 2)$ and a viewing pyramid defined by the planes

$$z = +x, \qquad z = -x, \qquad z = +y, \qquad z = -y.$$

The projection plane is at $z_v = 1$.

a) Clip the line in 3D (using parametric line equations), then project it onto the projection plane. What are the clipped endpoints on the plane?

b) Project the line onto the plane, then clip the lines using 2D computations. What are the clipped endpoints on the plane?

If the answers to (a) and (b) disagree, you have a problem!

8.10 Show what happens when an object is "behind" the center of projection if the object is projected by M_{per} and then clipped.

8.11 Show that if $z_{v.min} = z_{v.max} = 0$, then the 3D transformations used to map the canonical view volume into a 3D viewport produce the same result in NDC space as when image transformations are not used at all.

8.12 Write an interactive program, similar to that in Fig. 8.53, to "fly" through the world by controlling the VRP and VPN with six input values. Use a fixed-size window with the center of projection a fixed distance from the VRP and on the line that goes through the VRP and is parallel to VPN. Consider the three values used to control "heading" (the VPN) as direction cosines: this makes calculation of the center of projection's position with respect to the VRP trivial.

8.13 Write a procedure whose inputs are ℓ, α (for specifying an oblique parallel projection), VUP, and VPN, and whose outputs are the direction of projection needed to create the desired oblique projection on the plane normal to VPN, with "up" determined by VUP. Note that VRP is *not* needed, because only rotations are used in the solution, not translations.

8.14 Consider the 2D viewing operation with a rotated window. Devise a normalizing transformation to transform the window into the unit square. The window is specified by $u_{\min}$, $v_{\min}$, $u_{\max}$, $v_{\max}$ in the uv coordinate system, as in Fig. 8.59. Show that this is the same result as for the general 3D N_{par}, when the projection plane is the xy-plane and VUP has an x-component of $-\cos\theta$ and a y-component of $\sin\theta$.

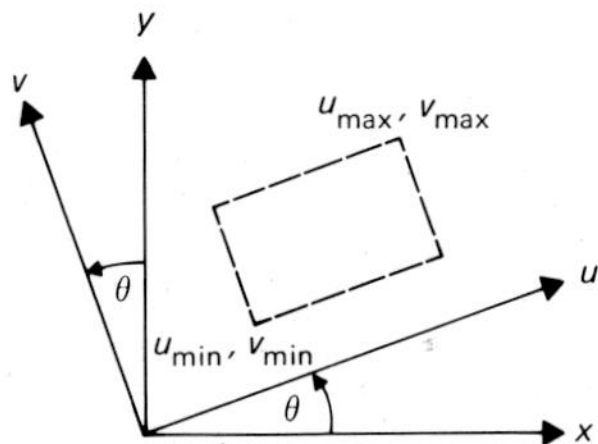

Fig. 8.59 Rotated window.

8.15 The matrix M_{per} in Section 8.2 defines a one-point perspective projection. What is the form of the 4×4 matrix that defines a two-point perspective? A three-point perspective? *Hint:* Try multiplying M_{per} by various rotation matrices.

8.16 What is the effect of applying M_{per} to points whose z-coordinate is less than zero?

8.17 Devise a clipping algorithm for a cone-shaped (circular) view volume. The cone's apex is at the origin and has a 90° interior angle. The axis of the cone is the positive z-axis. Consider using a spherical coordinate system.

8.18 Design and implement a set of utility subroutines to generate a 4×4 transformation matrix from an arbitrary sequence of R, S, and T primitive transformations.

8.19 Draw a decision tree to be used when examining a projection to determine its type. Apply this tree to the various figures in this chapter.

8.20 In the concluding discussion of image transformations, we described two alternative times to apply T_{per} or T_{par} (whichever is appropriate). In one case, it is applied just once, when the primitives are clipped; in the other case, it is applied each time an image transformation is specified. When is each case more efficient?

8.21 Evaluate the speed trade-offs of performing 3D clipping by using the Cohen–Sutherland and the midpoint subdivision algorithms for different assumptions about the relative speeds of shift/add operations as opposed to multiply/divide operations.

9 Modeling and Object Hierarchy

In Chapter 2 we introduced the *application model,* or *model* for short, as that component of the programmer's conceptual model of interactive graphics applications which holds object descriptions and application data. In the office layout application, for example, the model was used to hold the definitions of the basic components or objects (chairs, desks, etc.), as well as the geometric placement information for positioning them. The objects were then described to the graphics system to create particular views, both during and after construction of the floor plan. In Chapter 2, the application model was implicitly equated with the application data structure or data base. The purpose of this chapter is to generalize that simplified notion of the model by showing that it is typically a mixture of both data and procedures, and to examine a number of representations of models and their trade-offs. We will be especially interested in models which encode object hierarchy of the type briefly introduced in Chapter 2.

9.1 WHAT IS A MODEL?

Models are used to represent physical or abstract entities and phenomena not just for the purposes of making pictures (creating views) but, in general, to represent their structure and/or behavior. Models are used, for example, in physical, social, and life sciences, in engineering, and in mathematics. They allow simulation, testing, and prediction of the behavior of the entities modeled for such purposes as understanding, visualization, experimentation, and learning. Models help in the understanding of complex systems with many interacting components and allow prediction of the effects which varying input parameters will have on the system and its outputs.

As an example of modeling, the Federal Reserve may check the effect of raising interest rates on inflation by using a macroeconomic model. Financial models are used by universities to compute how much net income would be produced by a tuition increase and how financial aid would have to be increased commensurately. Weather forecasting is done by feeding real-time measurements into a complex model of local weather systems, typically on a very powerful computer, which then is used to compute the probabilities of various weather conditions. In a similar fashion, appropriate modeling allows astronauts to practice navigation for deep-space missions, pilots to learn to fly in animated simulators, nuclear-reactor safety experts to predict the effects of various plant malfunctions and their remedies, and automobile safety designers to test the integrity of the passenger compartment with simulated crashes. In these (and many other) instances, it is far easier, cheaper, and safer to experiment with a model than with a real entity. In fact, in many situations, such as space-shuttle pilot training and nuclear-reactor safety studies, modeling and simulation provide the only feasible method for learning about and experimenting with the system. For these reasons, computer modeling is replacing more traditional techniques, such as building of scale models in wind-tunnel testing or measurement. For example, simulated car crashes are augmenting precomputer modeling techniques involving real cars, occupied by dummies and much instrumentation, which are actually crashed into barriers.

While models need not, of course, be computerized, we will restrict ourselves in this book to the discussion of computer models: computer-based representations of the component objects and processes of an entity. In particular, we are most interested in those models which lend themselves to graphic interpretation. Among common types of models for which computer graphics has been used are:

- Organizational models: institutional bureaucracies and taxonomies (library classification schemes, biological taxonomies);
- Quantitative models: econometric, financial, sociological, demographic, climatic, chemical, physical, and mathematical systems;
- Geometric models: engineering and architectural structures, molecules and other chemical structures, vehicles.

The key concern in modeling is, of course, to design and implement models which adequately reflect the properties of the entities by using suitably precise (quantitative) formalisms. When possible, the model must be checked against reality; where they differ, the modeler will try to adjust the model to improve its predictive accuracy and utility. Models are often represented as systems of equations, with input and output variables and adjustable parameters such as coefficients and exponents.

Models need not necessarily have *intrinsically* geometric data associated with them; abstractions such as organizational models are not spatially oriented. Nonetheless, most such models can be represented geometrically: for example, an organizational model may be symbolized by an organization chart. Even when a model contains intrinsically geometric information, no particular graphical representation of that geometry is dictated—we can decide from which viewpoint the object is to be "photographed" with the synthetic camera and indeed with which type of geometric projection. In addition to these standard viewing options, there might be others for hidden-line removal, cross-hatching or shading, and other "rendering" techniques. Also, the presentation may be enriched with nongeometric information such as textual annotation.

The main question for our purposes is to determine *what* geometrical and nongeometrical information is to be encoded in the model; once that is clear, one may decide *how* to encode that information. Among the necessary ingredients to be represented are:

- Basic data elements and their interrelationships;
- Spatial layout and shape of components (i.e., their *geometry*) and other information relating to their appearance such as color and shading;
- Connectivity of components (i.e., the structure or *topology* of the entity). Note that the connectivity information may be specified abstractly (say, in a connectivity matrix for flowchart boxes) or may have its own intrinsic geometry (as with the dimensions of channels or runs in an integrated circuit);
- Application-specific data values such as electrical or mechanical characteristics, or descriptive text; and
- Processing algorithms such as linear-circuit analysis for discrete circuit models or finite-element analysis for mechanical structures.

The model is thus a rich description of components and processes which together specify both the *structure* and the *behavior* of the entity being modeled. We may choose to show either or both of these two aspects pictorially. For example, we may want to see both a circuit's physical layout on a board and its electrical behavior as a function of inputs and time. Determining what structural and behavioral information needs to be encoded typically involves many compromises between the simplicity and intellectual tractability of the model on the one hand, and its accuracy or degree of "realism" (and its attendant computational resource requirements) on the other. Another difficult trade-off is between what is stored explicitly and what must be computed—a classical space–time trade-off. For example, a flowchart model could store the connecting lines explicitly or it could recompute them from a connectivity matrix with a simple graph layout algorithm each time a new view is requested. Similar choices must be made with respect to schemes for organizing the model, so that it allows fast analysis or fast display. In short, enough information must be kept with the model to allow both analysis and display, but the exact format and the choices of encoding techniques are dependent on the application and on space–time trade-offs.

In general, then, the model consists of the application data structure plus a collection of application program procedures that help define structure and/or behavior. Figure 9.1 symbolizes the interrelation between the model, the application program, and the graphics system (SGP in our case). We have divided the application programs into four subsystems:

a) Programs which build, modify, and maintain the model by adding, deleting, and replacing information in it;
b) Programs which traverse the model in order to extract information to be displayed;
c) Programs which traverse the model to extract information used in the analysis of the model's behavior/performance;
d) Programs which are used in common by the other three subsystems to display information from the model (the output of the analysis program, prompts, and menus) and to handle the user-generated inputs that drive the interaction dialogue.

Application code refers to a collection of routines which are not part of the interactive dialogue but do housekeeping, postprocessing, etc. The term *subsystem* above should not be construed as implying major modules of code: only a few calls or a short procedure may be sufficient to implement a given subsystem. Furthermore, a subsystem may be distributed throughout the application program rather than being gathered in a separate program module. Thus the diagram as a concep-

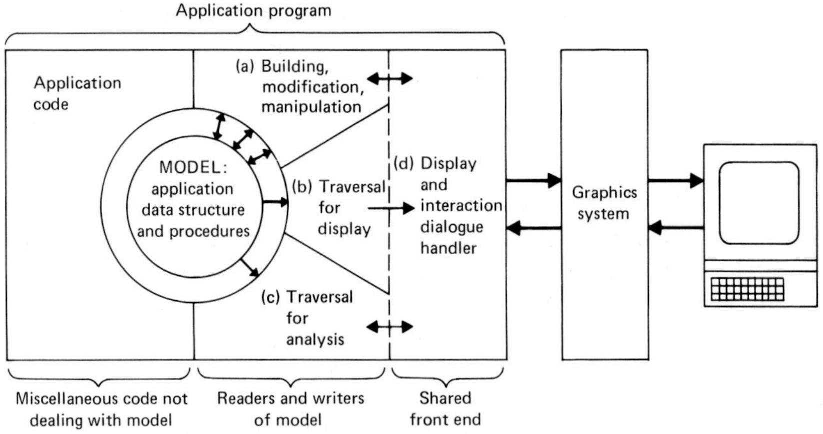

Fig. 9.1 The model and its readers (display, analysis) and writers (building, modification, and analysis procedures).

tual division simply singles out logical components, not necessarily program structure components. As Fig. 9.1 shows, we do not include the procedures which build, modify, analyze or display the model as part of the model itself, although it is not always clear what part of an application program is part of the model and what part is external to it and manipulates it. A case could be made, for example, that the circuit analysis module is really part of the model's definition because it describes how the circuit behaves. Figure 9.1 works best if one thinks of the model as containing primarily data. The mixture of data and procedures which encode our model will be further examined in the remainder of this chapter.

While in the early days of computer graphics the modeling activity was tightly integrated with graphic display and input handling [SUTH63], it should be realized that modeling is primarily an activity of the application program. The synthetic camera paradigm of graphics leads us to a clear distinction between the activities of building and modifying models of entities, on the one hand, and taking pictures of them, on the other. Indeed, modeling applications can be totally designed without involving any graphics. However, the use of modern modeling packages (see below) is predicated on the presence of a graphics package to make pictures and supply interaction.

Furthermore, in many application programs, especially industrial ones, an "80/20" rule holds: the major portion, say 80%, of the program deals with modeling of entities and only 20% with taking pictures of them. In other words, graphics applications tend to be data and processing intensive but not picture-making intensive. Naturally, there are also many applications for which "the picture is the thing": sketching, painting, drafting, film animation, making realistic synthetic photographs, and animating scenes for flight simulators. However, most applications, such as computer-aided design (CAD), treat pictorial representation of models as a means to an end such as analysis, construction, numerical control, or other types of postprocessing. In this chapter we deal with typical applications involving a nontrivial amount of modeling.

9.2 GEOMETRIC MODELS AND OBJECT HIERARCHY

Geometric, or *graphical* models describe entities with inherent geometrical properties and thus lend themselves naturally to graphical representation. As with the *LAYOUT* program of Chapter 2, they often have a hierarchical structure that is induced by a bottom-up construction process: components are used as building blocks to create higher-level entities which in turn may be used as building blocks for yet higher-level entities, and so on.

Object hierarchies are very common because few entities are monolithic (indivisible); as soon as we see how an entity can be decomposed into a collection of parts, we have at least a one-level hierarchy.

In engineering design, the object–subobject hierarchy is also known as an assembly–subassembly hierarchy. It is very common to use standard components as the basic building blocks in hierarchies. These are often drawn by using templates of standard symbolic shapes (called *symbols* in Chapter 2). Plastic flowchart and digital logic templates for 2D objects are common examples; in 3D, shapes such as cylinders, parallelepipeds, spheres, and pyramids might be basic building blocks. We reserve the term *object* for those 2D or 3D standard components which are defined in their own world coordinates and usually have not only geometrical data but also associated application data. However, we will bow to common custom and use the term *symbol* as well, especially for 2D objects which have only geometric (shape) data. Note that this usage is somewhat misleading in that, strictly speaking, the term *symbol* then should, like *object* or *component,* refer to the original 2D or 3D object, and not (as is customary) to a particular graphical representation (icon) on a view surface that is the result of the synthetic camera interpretation.

In the model of an entity we must capture not only which components are present, but also how they are connected in physical or causal interrelations. A hierarchy, then, is created for a variety of related purposes, such as:

- Constructing complex objects in a modular fashion, as in *LAYOUT,* typically by repetitive use of standard components;
- Storage economy, since it suffices to store only references to objects which are repeatedly used, rather than redefining them each time;
- Modification of the entity on the basis of its component structure. For example, if we change the definition of one fundamental component, that change will automatically be propagated to all higher-level components which make use of it (since they will refer henceforth to the updated version). Thus on the next call to *DISPLAY_D_STR* all chairs in the room layout will be automatically updated if the coordinates or the primitive calls of the *CHAIR* procedure are changed.

A convenient pictorial representation of intrinsic or induced object hierarchy is, of course, the familiar tree diagram. Figure 9.2 shows several standard objects from the large class of 2D block diagrams and 3D mechanical objects. Most consist of components connected to form a network. Note that the hierarchical (de)composition is a matter of the designer's choice. For example, the flowchart of Fig. 9.2(a) could be conveniently decomposed into a two-level hierarchy of an assignment box followed by a **repeat until** box and an **if then else** box, the latter with a nested **repeat until.** The tricycle of Fig. 7.18 could be decomposed into a two-level hierarchy containing at the first level (below the root node) the rear end, the body, and the front wheel, with the rear end containing two wheels and the axle, etc. Alternatively, we could model it directly as a one-level hierarchy of three wheels, axle, frame, saddle, and handlebars. Similarly, in the **nor** circuit of Fig. 9.3(a), one could define the standard resistor, diode, and transistor symbols to be the lowest-level components, as in Fig. 9.3(b), a natural choice from the *electronic-circuit* point of view. Alterna-

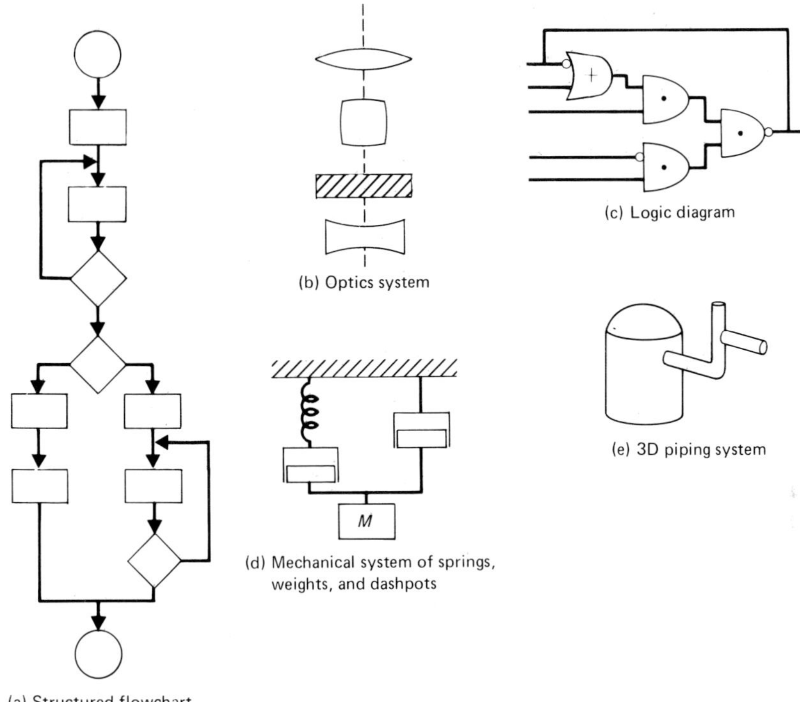

(a) Structured flowchart

(b) Optics system

(c) Logic diagram

(d) Mechanical system of springs, weights, and dashpots

(e) 3D piping system

Fig. 9.2 Common examples of 2D and 3D block diagrams.

tively, one could decompose the **nor** in terms of lowest-level *logical* building blocks, the inverter, filter, and **or** components, as in Fig. 9.3(c). Finally, one could decompose each circuit symbol, such as the transistor, even further for *drawing* purposes into lower-level components such as a circle, an arrow, a T-bar and an angle, as in Fig. 9.3(d). (Both hierarchies (b) and (c) could have the expected graphical representation for each node.) In a sense, an object is a user-defined primitive, and one typically picks as lowest-level objects those which are meaningful, logical entities to the user of the application. This consideration suggests that the hierarchies of Figs. 9.3(b) and 9.3(c) are reasonable but that the hierarchy of Fig. 9.3(d) is probably too low-level!

9.3 OBJECT PLACEMENT AND INSTANCE TRANSFORMATIONS

In many hierarchies, objects are placed in specified locations and/or with specified connections, either interactively by the user or automatically by the application program. In Chapter 2, furniture symbols were placed by the user without connecting them, by having the application program do simple geometrical transformations for

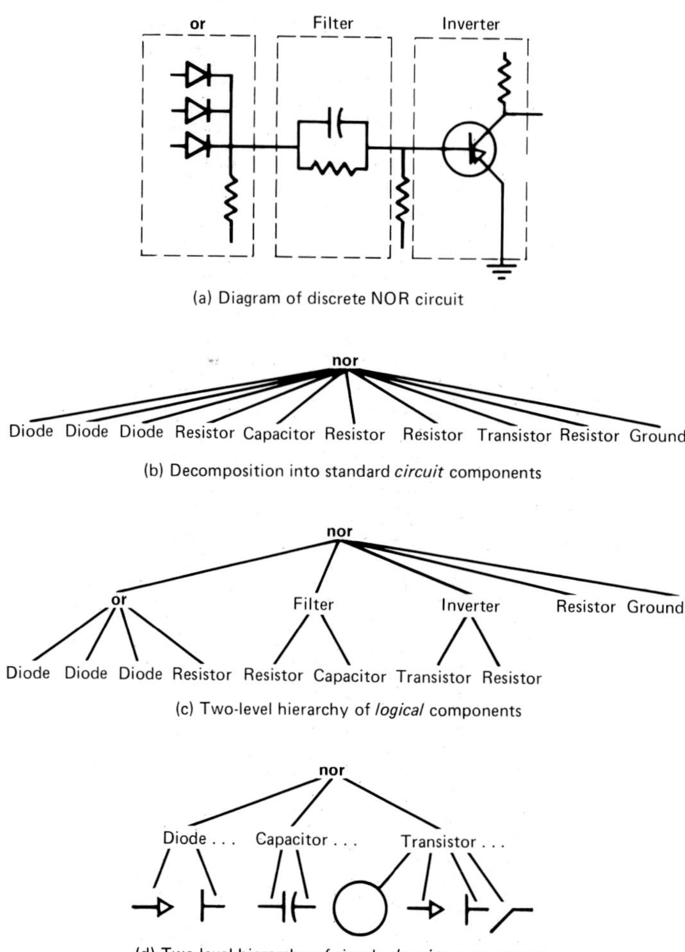

Fig. 9.3 Decompositions of the **nor** components.

rotating and positioning them in the world coordinate system prior to taking a snapshot. In an integrated circuit layout application we would expect to have the user fine-tune the layout of components and the routing of connections explicitly after having the bulk of this work done algorithmically on a trial basis. In a PERT chart scheduling application (and many other graph-drawing applications as well), the program does the layout of both nodes (symbolizing tasks) and edges (annotated with completion times) automatically from textual information specified by the user. Note again that connections may be described and stored explicitly or they may be specified procedurally by the application program, to be computed on the fly. In either case, connections often have their own geometric properties and *constraints* (e.g., line segments must have horizontal or vertical orientation regardless of how the attached components are moved).

In Chapter 7 we discussed the homogeneous coordinate formulation of the geometric transformations (translation, rotation, and scaling) which are used to transform primitives and objects in the world coordinate system. In a hierarchy we can think of objects as being defined in their own coordinate systems which are then transformed into the coordinate system of the higher-level object (Section 7.7). In terms of Sketchpad [SUTH63] terminology, we apply a (geometric) *instance transformation* to a *master* definition of an object defined in its own master coordinate system, to create an *instance* of the master object in the higher-level master coordinate system.

Figures 9.4(a) and 9.4(b) show the *LAYOUT* hierarchy as symbolized in Chapter 2 and with explicit instance transformations, respectively. Each instance transformation that is applied to a component of the root maps the corresponding master into the world coordinate system. Thus the first instance transformation, $IT_{c,r}$, maps primitives from the chair master coordinate system to the room master coordinate system; since room is the root object, its master coordinate system is also the world coordinate system. (Note that the $IT_{c,r}$, etc. symbolism represents arbitrary instance transformations, not specific ones.)

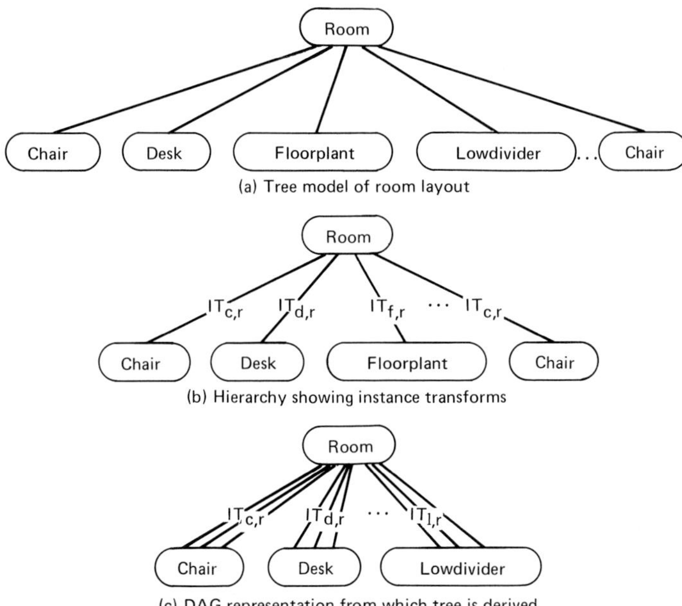

Fig. 9.4 Room layout as a one-level hierarchy.

There is a convenient analogy between abstract object hierarchy and procedure hierarchy in a program: the root object "calls" the subobject by instancing it, passing it as the "parameters" for that "call" the geometric instance transformation values. These transformations tailor the subobject for use by the calling object. Since objects are typically instanced more than once (as with procedure hierarchy), the tree representations for the hierarchies of Figs. 9.2, 9.3, and 9.4(b) are really expansions of the directed acyclic graphs (DAGs) whose nodes are (sub)objects and whose edges are labeled with the instance transformations which make each instance unique (Fig. 9.4(c)). In some modeling systems objects may not only be instanced but copied as well. To copy an object means that the definition of the copied object (potentially subject to geometric transformation) is placed in the body of the copying object. While instances thus act like references to independent subroutines, copies act like macros whose (parameterized) text is included at the point of invocations, thereby losing their identity, i.e., their relation to the master. Thus if a master definition is altered at run time, the next time the hierarchy is traversed to define the root object for display, all instances will automatically show the updated version of the master, while all copies are unaffected, having no identity and no ties to the master.

In addition to instance transformations applied to master objects comprising the root object, geometric transformations (such as a uniform scale or a rotate) may be used to adjust the root itself in the world before a snapshot is taken. Similarly, prior to instancing, all primitives in an individual master may be manipulated with geometric transformations in their local master coordinate system to achieve a desired effect. Both geometric transformations used to manipulate objects in their own (local) coordinate systems and those used to instance an object in a higher-level coordinate system are referred to as *modeling transformations,* since they are used to construct the world coordinate model. They are not to be confused with the geometric transformations used for normalizing view volumes and doing window-to-viewport mapping in the postmodeling viewing operation of the graphics system. Mathematically, all modeling and viewing geometric transformations have, of course, the same form and use the same translation, rotation, scale (and shear) matrix formulations, but they are conceptually applied at different times and under the control of different subsystems. In Section 9.11 we will see how to combine as many geometric modeling and viewing transformations as possible for greater efficiency.

9.4 TRANSFORMING OBJECTS WITH THE CURRENT TRANSFORMATION MATRIX

The instance transformation applied to objects such as chairs in *LAYOUT* is accomplished by having the chair-defining procedure itself transform its own master coordinates stored in the application data structure *chair_x* and *chair_y* arrays. *CHAIR* calls the internal procedure *XFORM,* which maps these stored master coordinates to transformed instance coordinates in temporary arrays. These coordinates are then used by *CHAIR* to call SGP primitives. Thus two successive transformations are done, one by the programmer and one by SGP—an inefficient strategy. Because instancing is a very common process, we would like to design a systematic strategy which eliminates the need to program each procedure to do the repetitive work of its own instancing. Thus we introduce a new facility, the *current transformation matrix* (CTM). The CTM is a system-defined global variable which the application programmer will set to the appropriate homogeneous instance transformation matrix prior to invoking object-defining procedures. The system will then cause each coordinate vector X to be transformed by the CTM before the coordinate is passed to SGP's output primitive procedure: $X_{\text{world}} = X_{\text{master}} \cdot \text{CTM}$. In other words, master coordinates are preprocessed automatically by the CTM mechanism to become world coordinates before being used in the viewing operation applied to each output primitive.

How does this mechanism fit in the instancing/procedure-calling analogy? The geometric instancing parameters are now "passed" from the higher-level instancing procedure to the lower-level master procedure via the CTM global variable and preprocessing mechanism, rather than by an explicit parameter-passing mechanism as in *LAYOUT.* Since this preprocessing takes place on the model prior to the graphics system's picture-making process, we should think of the CTM mechanism not as part of the graphics system itself, but as the beginning of an embryonic modeling system which will be interfaced to the graphics system (Fig. 9.5). (Note that this "modeling" system deals only with geometric parameters and not with more general application-related modeling data, as a full modeling system would.) The application program now calls on the CTM modeling system as well as on the graphics system to manage object descriptions and present views of them, respectively.

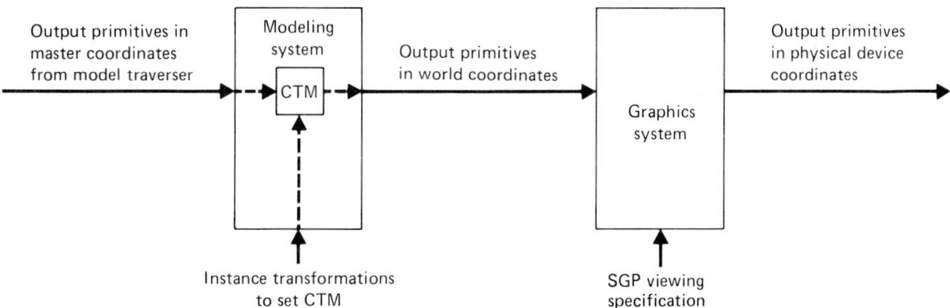

Fig. 9.5 Embryonic modeling system: using the CTM to interface directly to the graphics system.

Before investigating these interfaces a bit further, let us examine the functions of the CTM manipulation package. First we need to be able to set (load) the CTM from a specified matrix and, for symmetry, to store it into a specified matrix as well. Second, we shall see that it is very useful, when dealing with multiple instance transformations and multilevel hierarchies, to be able to alter the CTM incrementally by premultiplying it with a specified matrix. Because this premultiplication allows matrix composition for successive transformations, the CTM is also called the composite, cumulative, or compound transformation matrix. Since we now have both absolute and incremental modification of the CTM and since we want to uphold consistent naming conventions, we use the *ABS* and *REL* modifiers which were previously used for absolute and incremental modification of the SGP line primitive definitions. Finally, in order to spare the application program the bother of calculating homogeneous coordinate matrices for the CTM for specific translation, rotation, or scale factors, we add CTM functions which compute the proper matrices and reset or premultiply the CTM automatically.

Table 9.1 lists first the three procedures for the 2D case which form a functionally complete basic set of operations on the CTM. Below those three are the six 2D procedures using the *SET_CTMs* which have been added for convenience; the 3D variants are obvious. Finally, *PUSH* and *POP* are additional procedures which make use of *COPY;* their function is explained in Section 9.5.

TABLE 9.1. CTM MANIPULATION FUNCTIONS*

SET_CTM_ABS_2(m)	set *ctm* to 3 by 3 matrix *m*
SET_CTM_REL_2(m)	replace *ctm* by *m* · *ctm*
COPY_CTM(m)	copy *ctm* into *m*
TRANSLATE_CTM_ABS_2(x, y)	replace *ctm* by translation matrix formed by *x, y*†
TRANSLATE_CTM_REL_2(x, y)	premultiply *ctm* by translation matrix formed by *x, y*
SCALE_CTM_ABS_2(sx, sy)	replace *ctm* by scale matrix formed by *sx, sy*†
SCALE_CTM_REL_2(sx, sy)	premultiply *ctm* by scale matrix formed by *sx, sy*
ROTATE_CTM_ABS_2(theta)	replace *ctm* by rotation matrix formed by *theta*-degree rotation†
ROTATE_CTM_REL_2(theta)	premultiply *ctm* by rotation matrix formed by *theta*-degree rotation
PUSH(ctm, stk)	push *ctm* onto *stk*
POP(ctm, stk)	pop top of *stk* into *ctm*

*When referring to the system CTM in a general, descriptive way, we use capital letters, but when a CTM procedure accesses it, we use lower-case italics to denote that it is a (system) variable.

†Other components of the matrix are set to provide the identity transformation.

Having briefly discussed CTM manipulations, we next look at an example of their use. The procedure *DISPLAY_SYMBOL* appears schematically in Example 9.1(a) in the form in which it was discussed in Chapter 2, while it is revised to use the CTM operations in Example 9.1(b). Three points should be noted. First, there is an obvious simplification in having the calling procedure set up the instancing "parameters" via the CTM, so that the object-defining procedures are no longer responsible for their own instance transformations. Thus the CTM package takes care of the *XFORM* function, and we no longer need the local arrays of instanced coordinates either. Second, the relative CTM specifications are useful for multiple instance transformations, as will be shown later (the compounding is done automatically by the CTM package).

Example 9.1(a) ***DISPLAY_SYMBOL*** **scheme for** ***LAYOUT*.**

```
procedure DISPLAY_SYMBOL(id: integer);
{Chapter 2 version which calls appropriate symbol procedure,
  passing it instance transformation parameters}
begin
  with symbols[id] do
    if valid code then
      begin
        CREATE_SEGMENT(id);
        {next call proper symbol procedure with x, y, theta and based on
          the code field in symbols[id]}
          case code of
            1: CHAIR(x, y, theta);
            .
            .
            .
            6: FLOORPLANT(x, y, theta)
          end;     {case}
        CLOSE_SEGMENT
      end     {if}
end; {DISPLAY_SYMBOL}

procedure CHAIR(xc, yc, rot_angle: real);
{Chapter 2 version of the chair symbol procedure, which calls
  XFORM with the number of coordinate data values to be transformed (here 7), with
  the global coordinate data arrays, and with the instance parameters}
var chair_x_new, chair_y_new: array[1..10] of real;
    i: integer;
begin
  XFORM(xc, yc, rot_angle, chair_x, chair_y, chair_x_new, chair_y_new, 7);
  MOVE_ABS_2(chair_x_new[1], chair_y_new[1]);
  for i := 2 to 7 do
    LINE_ABS_2(chair_x_new[i], chair_y_new[i]);
end;     {CHAIR}
```

Example 9.1(b) ***DISPLAY_SYMBOL*** **revised to use CTM.**

```
procedure DISPLAY_SYMBOL(id: integer);
begin
  with symbols[id] do
    if valid code then
      begin
        CREATE_SEGMENT(id);
        {set up CTM using instancing parameters from symbols[id], then call proper
          symbol procedure}
          TRANSLATE_CTM_ABS_2(x, y);
          ROTATE_CTM_REL_2(theta);
          case code of
            1: CHAIR;
            .
            .
            .
            6: FLOORPLANT
          end;    {case}
        CLOSE_SEGMENT
      end   {if}
end;   {DISPLAY_SYMBOL}

procedure CHAIR;
{CTM has been properly set, so define untransformed primitives in master coordinates;
  no instancing parameters need be passed}
var i: integer;
begin
  MOVE_ABS_2(chair_x[1], chair_y[1]);
  for i := 2 to 7 do
    LINE_ABS_2(chair_x[i], chair_y[i])
end;   {CHAIR}
```

Finally, it is most important to understand the proper *lexical* order in which to specify instance transformations to the CTM package so that the transformations are applied to the object master coordinates in the correct *logical* order. In general,

$$X_{\text{instance}} = X_{\text{master}} \cdot \text{ITM}_{\text{master, instance}}.$$

Here $\text{ITM}_{\text{master, instance}}$ is the instance transformation matrix* (typically stored in the CTM) which maps an object's master coordinates to the instanced coordinates in

---

*IT in Fig. 9.4 refers to a general sequence of one or more instance transformations, while ITM refers specifically to such a set composed in a homogeneous coordinate matrix.

higher-level master or world coordinate system in which the instanced object is placed. In *LAYOUT,* for example, for the desk symbol this is

$$X_{room} = X_{desk} \cdot \text{ITM}_{desk,\ room};$$

here $\text{ITM}_{desk,room}$ is the instance transformation matrix which instances the desk in the room master coordinate system. When using the CTM, and for the current case of one-level hierarchy where the higher-level master coordinate system is also the root's world coordinate system, the general formulation is equivalent to

$$X_{world} = X_{master} \cdot \text{CTM},$$

as in Example 9.1(b) before. The $\text{ITM}_{master,\ instance}$, stored in the CTM, is a compound matrix consisting of any combination of translation, rotation and scale ITMs. These may be compounded by premultiplication of the CTM, which means that the most (lexically) recently specified ITM is logically applied first to the master coordinates. Thus the lexical order is the reverse of the logical order. For the *LAYOUT* case of a single rotation (specified in ITM_θ) followed by a translation (specified in $\text{ITM}_{(x,\ y)}$), we want the effect of

$$X_{room} = (X_{symbol} \cdot \text{ITM}_\theta) \cdot \text{ITM}_{(x,\ y)} = X_{symbol} \cdot (\text{ITM}_\theta \cdot \text{ITM}_{(x,\ y)}) = X_{symbol} \cdot \text{CTM}$$

by matrix associativity. Therefore the CTM operations are specified in Example 9.1(b) in the lexical order:

TRANSLATE_CTM_REL_2(*x*, *y*);
ROTATE_CTM_REL_2(*theta*);

Assuming that the CTM is initialized to the identity matrix I, this premultiplication produces the desired

$$\text{CTM} = \text{ITM}_\theta \cdot (\text{ITM}_{(x,\ y)} \cdot \text{I}) = (\text{ITM}_\theta \cdot \text{ITM}_{(x,\ y)}).$$

In the same vein, if geometric transformations mapping the master object to its own master coordinate system prior to any instancing were also present (as $\text{ITM}_{master,master}$), they would be applied logically before and lexically after the instance transformations:

$$\begin{aligned} X_{instance} &= X_{master} \cdot \text{ITM}_{geo} \cdot (\text{ITM}_\theta \cdot \text{ITM}_{(x,\ y)}) \\ &= X_{master} \cdot \text{ITM}_{master,\ master} \cdot \text{ITM}_{master,\ instance}. \end{aligned}$$

Neither *LAYOUT* nor the examples below use geometric master-to-master transformations.

In Section 9.9 we add another facility for postmultiplying the CTM so that the lexically *first* transformation takes logical effect first, a seemingly more natural order. Premultiplication is necessary, however, for a multilevel hierarchy, as we shall see in Section 9.5.3.

Returning to the interface between the CTM/modeling package and the graphics package, we see that the output primitives in *CHAIR* must now be viewed, strictly speaking, as modeling primitives which are passed as output primitives to the graphics package only after the modeling transformations have been applied via the CTM. Since the graphics package is likely to transform the primitives' world coordinates further either with the normalizing transformations discussed in the previous chapter for 3D, or indeed with the entire set of transformations induced by the viewing specification for the simple 2D case, it would be most efficient if the modeling transformations in the CTM and the normalizing/viewing transformations could be combined and then applied to the original master coordinates. Figure 9.6 shows how this may be accomplished by the introduction of a *hook,* a calling convention with which the modeling package can pass the CTM-setting parameters to the graphics package. The graphics package compounds the CTM values with composite viewing transformations and then transforms the master coordinates by the total composite matrix. Other combinations of modeling and viewing are discussed in Sections 9.10 and 9.11.

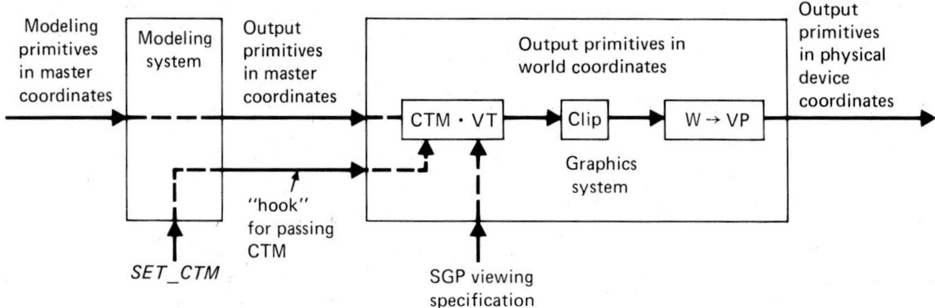

Fig. 9.6 Passing the CTM via the "hook" to allow maximum compounding of matrices.

9.5 GENERALIZING TO TWO-LEVEL AND *n*-LEVEL HIERARCHIES

9.5.1 Two-Level Fixed (Static) Hierarchy

Let us now make *LAYOUT* a bit more realistic by recognizing that interior decorators placing furniture in a room tend to think of clusters or groupings of pieces of furniture (often called modules in industrial design) rather than just of individual pieces. Thus, in our furniture layout program we would like to be able to place a module consisting of a desk and a chair, for example, since they have a fixed relationship with respect to each other, rather than individually placing these two symbols each time. To produce exactly the same types of room layouts as pictured in Chapter 2, we will now use a two-level model (Fig. 9.7). (This example once again illustrates that one should not confuse a model of an object with a particular visual

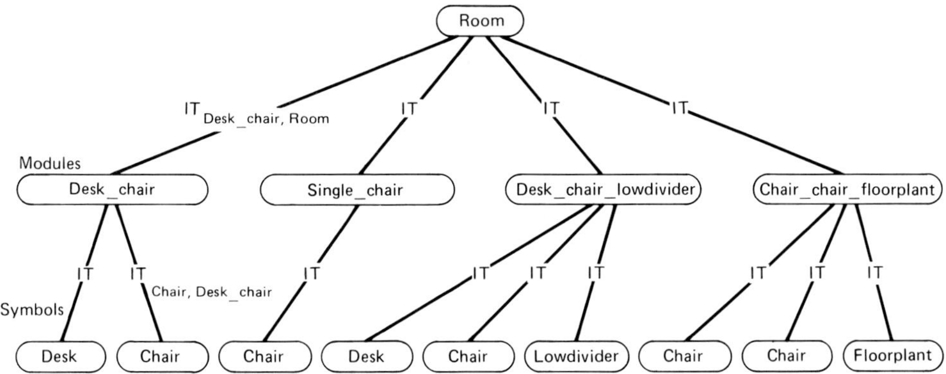

Fig. 9.7 Two-level fixed hierarchy for layout. The IT's, in general, are all different.

representation: any number of models may yield the same view.) The application programmer uses instance transformations to place standard symbols as lowest-level subobjects in standard module definitions, and the user then interactively places modules with their own instance transformations in the room. In order to preserve a strict two-level hierarchy of modules and symbols, we will need to define simple modules such as *single_chair* to place a single chair—the symbol-to-module instance transformation for this case is simply the identity matrix. This clumsy, rather wasteful restriction will be removed shortly.

Figure 9.8 shows a modification of the original *LAYOUT* data structure adapted to the two-level hierarchy. The array of module instance blocks generated by user interactions with a new procedure, *ADD_MODULE,* takes the place of *LAYOUT*'s original array of symbol instance blocks, and *module_type* is used to index into an array of module definitions instead of into the symbols themselves. Several of these index pointers are shown in the drawing. Each piece of a module definition is again an instance block containing the *symbol_type* used to **case** the symbol by the two-level programs of Example 9.2(a) which traverse the data structure. The pseudocode* of Example 9.2(a) shows a revised, brute-force version of *LAYOUT* that does not use the CTM/modeling mechanism: the procedure *DISPLAY_ D_STR* loops through the array of module instance blocks, and each module definition in turn causes looping through each of the symbol definitions.

*For purposes of conciseness and clarity, pseudocode and Pascal are intermixed, and declarations of parameters and variables are symbolic or largely absent from the pseudocode in the remainder of this chapter.

Example 9.2(a) Displaying the module-symbol hierarchy by explicitly composing and transforming.

```
procedure DISPLAY_D_STR;
var i: integer;
begin
  DISPLAY_ROOM;                          {create segment for room boundary}
  for i := 1 to max_module do
    with module[i] do
      begin
        if SEGMENT_EXISTS(i) then
          DELETE_SEGMENT(i);
        CREATE_SEGMENT(i);
          DISPLAY_MODULE(module_type, x, y, theta);    {from data structure}
        CLOSE_SEGMENT
      end
end;    {DISPLAY_D_STR}

procedure DISPLAY_MODULE(module_type: integer; x, y, theta: real);
  var itm: instance transformation matrix (3 × 3);
  for all symbol[i]s in module_def_table[module_type] do
    with symbol[i] do
      begin
        {pick up symbol's instance transformation parameters from data structure and
          compose their ITMs with ITMs for module's parameters passed to
          DISPLAY_MODULE}
        itm := symbol's (ITM_θ · ITM_(x, y)) * module's (ITM_θ · ITM_(x, y));
        case symbol_type of
          1: DISPLAY_CHAIR(itm);
          :
          :
          6: DISPLAY_FLOORPLANT(itm)
        end    {case}
      end    {with}
end;    {DISPLAY_MODULE}

procedure DISPLAY_CHAIR(itm: matrix);
var i: integer;
begin
  {first apply instance transformation matrix itm to stored coordinates to get trans-
    formed coordinates; this procedure differs from Chapter 2's CHAIR only in that a
    full matrix itm is passed rather than separate x, y, and theta parameters; XFORM is
    similarly changed to accept a matrix and is now called TRANSFORM}
  TRANSFORM(itm, chair_x, chair_y, chair_x_new, chair_y_new, 7);
  MOVE_ABS_2(chair_x_new[1], chair_y_new[1]);
  for i := 2 to 7 do
    LINE_ABS_2(chair_x_new[i], chair_y_new[i])
end;    {DISPLAY_CHAIR}
```

Example 9.2(b) Displaying the module-symbol hierarchy by using CTM facilities.

```
procedure DISPLAY_D_STR;
var stk: stack to save CTMs;
  i: integer;
begin
  EMPTY(stk);                    {procedure to initialize stack}
  TRANSLATE_CTM_ABS_2(0, 0);     {set translation, rotation and scale entries of
                                   CTM to identity transformation}
  DISPLAY_ROOM;                  {create segment for room boundary}
  for i := 1 to max_module do
    with module[i] do
      begin
        if SEGMENT_EXISTS(i) then
          DELETE_SEGMENT(i);
        CREATE_SEGMENT(i);
          TRANSLATE_CTM_ABS_2(x, y);
          ROTATE_CTM_REL_2(theta);
          DISPLAY_MODULE(module_type);
        CLOSE_SEGMENT
      end    {with}
end;    {DISPLAY_D_STR}

procedure DISPLAY_MODULE(module_type: integer);
begin
  for all symbol[i]s in module_def_table[module_type] do
    with symbol[i] do
      begin
        {save and then set up CTM by premultiplying module instance
          parameters by symbol instance parameters}
        PUSH(ctm, stk);
        TRANSLATE_CTM_REL_2(x, y);
        ROTATE_CTM_REL_2(theta);
        {next, as in Example 9.1(b), call untransformed symbol
          procedures; the CTM implicitly affects each coordinate of a primitive
          routine before the graphics package receives the primitive}
        case object_type of
          1: CHAIR;
          .
          .
          .
          6: FLOORPLANT
        end;    {case}
        POP(ctm, stk)    {restore module instance parameters}
      end    {with}
end;    {DISPLAY_MODULE}
```

Note that we have assumed that each symbol consists of a list of endpoints which represents a sequence of connected line segments. In the general case a flag would be used to indicate the end of such a sequence, and the next endpoint would result in a *MOVE*.

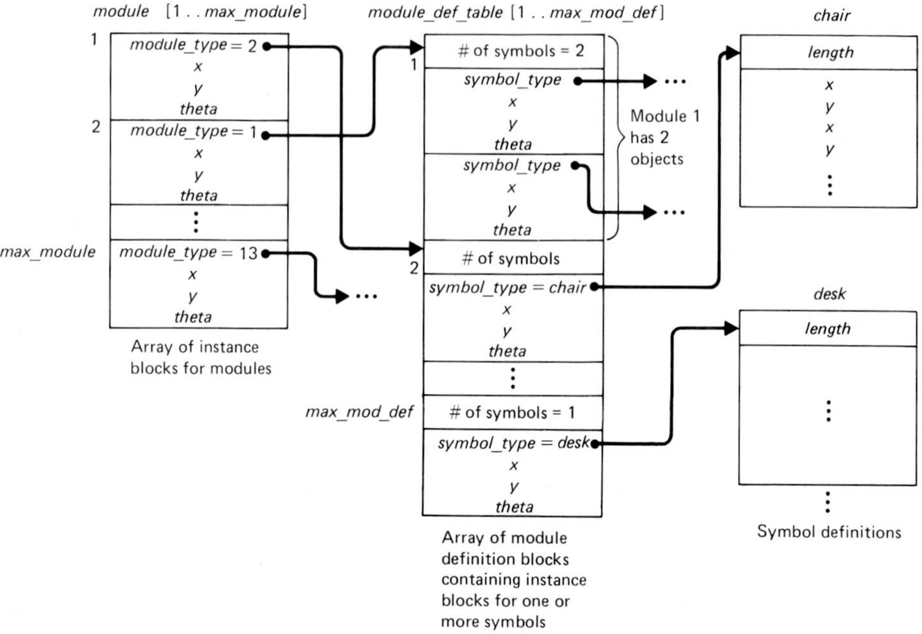

Fig. 9.8 Application data structure for two-level fixed hierarchy.

A symbol is called in Example 9.2(a) with the composite instance transformation that is the result of multiplying the instance transformation which maps the symbol to the module with the one that maps the module to the room. In other words, to display primitives in a symbol node in the hierarchy, the program composes all the instance transformations in the path from the node to the root, and due to matrix associativity, applies the lowest one first, directly to the symbol primitives. Thus to calculate the room coordinates of a particular chair in a particular desk-chair module in Fig. 9.7, the composite $\mathrm{ITM}_{\mathrm{chair,\ room}}$ is used to map the chair to the room:

$$X_{\mathrm{room}} = X_{\mathrm{chair}} \cdot \mathrm{ITM}_{\mathrm{chair,\ room}} = X_{\mathrm{chair}} \cdot (\mathrm{ITM}_{\mathrm{chair,\ desk\_chair}} \cdot \mathrm{ITM}_{\mathrm{desk\_chair,\ room}}).$$

Each of the individual ITMs has the form $(\mathrm{ITM}_\theta \cdot \mathrm{ITM}_{(x,\ y)})$. Symbol-defining procedures such as *CHAIR* take the composite matrix $\mathrm{ITM}_{\mathrm{chair,\ room}}$ and, in the manner of the Chapter 2 *LAYOUT,* call a *TRANSFORM* routine before invoking output primitives.

By using the CTM in the program of Example 9.2(b), however, we can again obviate the need to have symbols do their own coordinate transformations in temporary local arrays. Furthermore, we have also taken care of the work of computing and composing matrices. In Example 9.2(b) the CTM and a stack remember prior history so that at any one time access only to the data of the current level in the tree is needed. As we descend a level in the tree of Fig. 9.7 from module to symbol in *DISPLAY_MODULE*, for each symbol we:

1. *PUSH* to save the higher-level CTM (the module's instance transformation);
2. Compose this module's instance transformation with the lower-level symbol's instance transformation;
3. Call primitives with the new CTM in effect, and
4. *POP* to restore the higher-level CTM to get ready for the next symbol.

When all symbols for a module are exhausted, the CTM is loaded with the instance transformation of the next module in *DISPLAY_D_STR*. Note that in this code the restoring *POP* is followed immediately by a *PUSH* of the CTM just *POP*ped; although this allows easy generalization to *n*-level hierarchy, it seems a bit inefficient. In the two-level case, we could instead save the matrix in a local array rather than a stack at the top of *DISPLAY_MODULE* and restore it at the bottom of the **for** loop, eliminating the *PUSH* at the top of the **for** loop. An *n*-level hierarchy would then require local arrays at each level, which is the reason for preferring the stack mechanism.

It is important to note that *DISPLAY_D_STR* traces out the canonical "prefix" or preorder tree traversal of the two-level hierarchy to access all nodes in a left-and-down pattern. (This is the same traversal done, for example, through a syntax tree built by a compiler's parser, but in our case there is typically no left–right order significance.) Also, it is interesting that the hierarchy is manifested not only in the user-level abstraction of Fig. 9.7, but also in *both* the application data structure of Fig. 9.8 (via the multipurpose fields *module_type* and *symbol_type* which serve both as type codes and as index pointers to lower-level components) and the dynamic trace of procedure calls. This procedure hierarchy is produced by *DISPLAY_D_STR* calling *DISPLAY_MODULE(i)* which in turn calls the *j*th symbol definition procedure. Below we will see that it is possible to encode hierarchy exclusively in either the application data structure or in the object-defining procedures.

9.5.2 Dynamically Alterable Two-Level Hierarchy

Before we make the two-level *LAYOUT* program even less restricted, we should observe that the tree traversal above serves to linearize the hierarchy to just output primitives in the world coordinate system of the root object and to define this linear world to the graphics package so it can take a snapshot. While traversing the model and taking a snapshot are conceptually two distinct processes, they are in practice interleaved. As soon as a primitive has been transformed and clipped, it is put in a segment to be displayed. This process takes place at the run time of the application program, after a compile-time binding of all the immediate data for the data structure which defines symbols and modules. At run time (also called *picture-compile time*), the only things the user can change in this version of the program are the number and placement of modules.

In fact, the application programmer could have built an extremely simple data structure for this restricted case at the cost of more procedural code. He could have written each module-defining procedure so that it contained the explicit calls to its symbols which would be preceded by the proper CTM settings, using immediate data for the transformation parameters (Example 9.3). This eliminates the module definition table and the corresponding **case** on *symbol_type* in *DISPLAY_MODULE,* and lets *DISPLAY_D_STR* do a **case** directly on the module type in the module instance block. This strategy would mean, however, that we could never modify a module's definition interactively, since we cannot edit the procedure at run time to insert or delete additional symbol procedure calls. By using the "table-driven" data structure of Fig. 9.8 to define the object in each module, however, it is a simple matter to allow interactive editing of module definitions in the data structure without run-time modification of the associated code. All that is required is to delete or insert new instance blocks for symbols in the module definition table, as was done for adding symbols in *LAYOUT.* To prevent having to update pointers in the module array after such an alteration, it is preferable to change from contiguous allocation to linked-list allocation, in the manner of the segment management scheme described in Chapter 4. All levels of the data structure may then be edited at run time with relative ease, at the cost of a list pointer.

Fig. 9.9 is equivalent to Fig. 9.8, except that the arrays of Fig. 9.8 have been replaced by linked lists. This very regular data structure makes it obvious that a room consists of a set of instanced modules, each being a set of instanced symbols. The

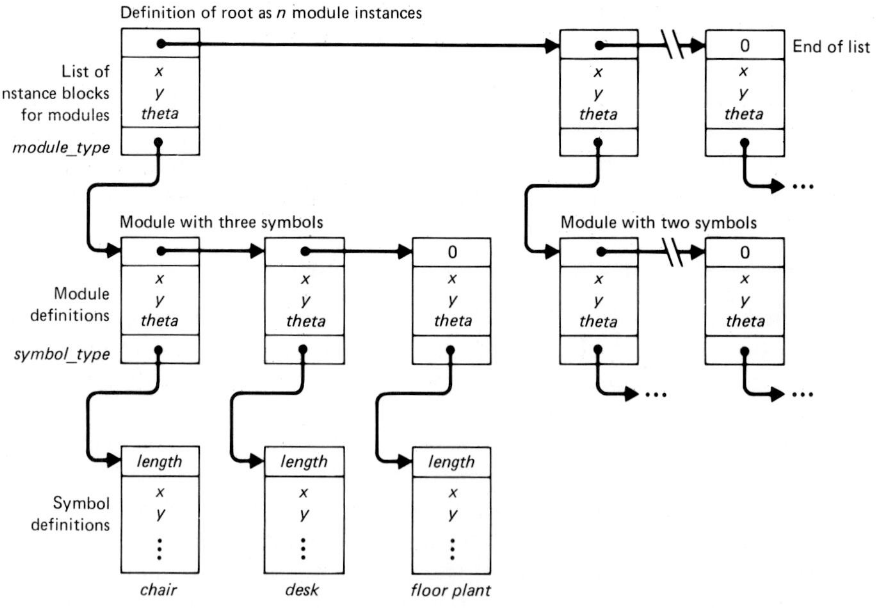

Fig. 9.9 Application data structure for a two-level dynamically alterable hierarchy.

code of the procedures of Example 9.2 would be changed for Fig. 9.9 only by the replacement of array element enumeration by a test for the EOL (end-of-list) flag (the null-pointer **nil** in Pascal) and subsequent pointer chasing to the next linked-list block (Exercise 9.5).

Example 9.3 Alternate two-level fixed procedure hierarchy with explicit calls and immediate data.

```
procedure DISPLAY_D_STR;
var i: integer
begin
  for i := 1 to max_module do
      with module[i] do
        begin
          TRANSLATE_CTM_ABS_2(x, y);
          ROTATE_CTM_REL_2(theta);
          if  SEGMENT_EXISTS(i) then
              DELETE_SEGMENT(i);
          CREATE_SEGMENT(i);
            case module_type of
              1: DESK_CHAIR;
              2: DESK_CHAIR_DIVIDER;
              .
              .
              .
              n:
            end;      {case}
          CLOSE_SEGMENT
        end     {with}
end;     {DISPLAY_D_STR}

procedure DESK_CHAIR;
{"hardwired" module procedure with symbolic constants as immediate data for
  instance parameters}
begin
  {first the desk}
  PUSH(ctm, stk);
  TRANSLATE_CTM_REL_2(a, b);
  ROTATE_CTM_REL_2(c);
  DESK;
  POP(ctm, stk);
  {then the chair}
  PUSH(ctm, stk);
  TRANSLATE_CTM_REL_2(d, e);
  ROTATE_CTM_REL_2(f);
  CHAIR;
  POP(ctm, stk)
end;     {DESK_CHAIR module}
```

9.5.3 Dynamically Alterable *n*-Level Hierarchy

Given the regularity of the two-level data structure of Fig. 9.9, it is easy to modify it slightly to allow any number of levels in the hierarchy, as well as the free mixing of primitives, objects, and modules at any level in the tree. Figure 9.10(a) shows the tree symbolism* for a general *n*-level hierarchy, while Fig. 9.10(b) shows the two types of data structure blocks needed: one for leaf nodes in the tree containing only primitives (L type code) and one for a compound object containing one or more instances of lower-level (possibly compound) objects or leaf nodes (I type code). Note that a collection of primitives can now be either an identified object suitable for instancing or an unidentified collection of primitives present only at a given level. Also, we have replaced individual *x, y,* and *theta* parameters with a composite instance transformation matrix (*itm*) in order to allow the composition of an arbitrary number of instance transformations for a given object rather than just a rotation followed by a translation. This generality costs a few extra words per instance block (9 for the 2D 3 × 3 homogeneous matrix, 16 for 3D, versus 3 in the current 2D scheme), but simplifies CTM setting during traversal of the data structure. Many other, more elaborate data structures can be used to encode additional features of object structure such as attachment points of objects (like connectors on flowcharts or on logic blocks, or pins on integrated circuits), the geometry or topology of connections between such attachment points, and application data associated with components [VAND72b, WILL71].

The interesting question now becomes how one can traverse this more general type of tree without knowing in advance how many levels it has and what type of component is found where. The predefined two-level procedure hierarchy of our

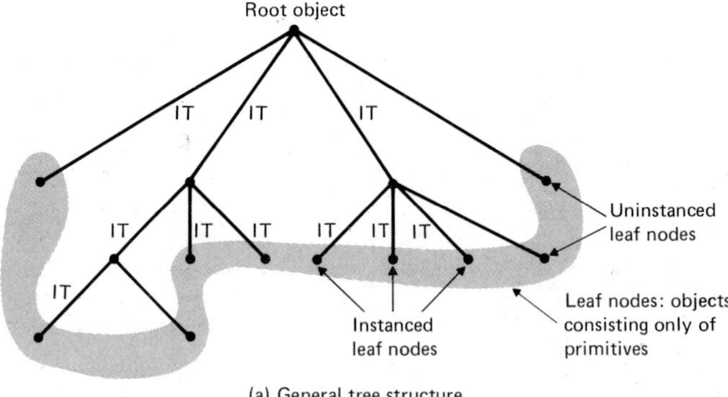

Fig. 9.10 Application data structure for a general *n*-level hierarchy. Leaf nodes may be included "as is" or instanced. (a) A general tree structure; (b) linked list structure for this tree with instance and leaf blocks (p. 343).

*As with Fig. 9.4(b), it is an expansion of the DAG actually represented by the list structure and hierarchy.

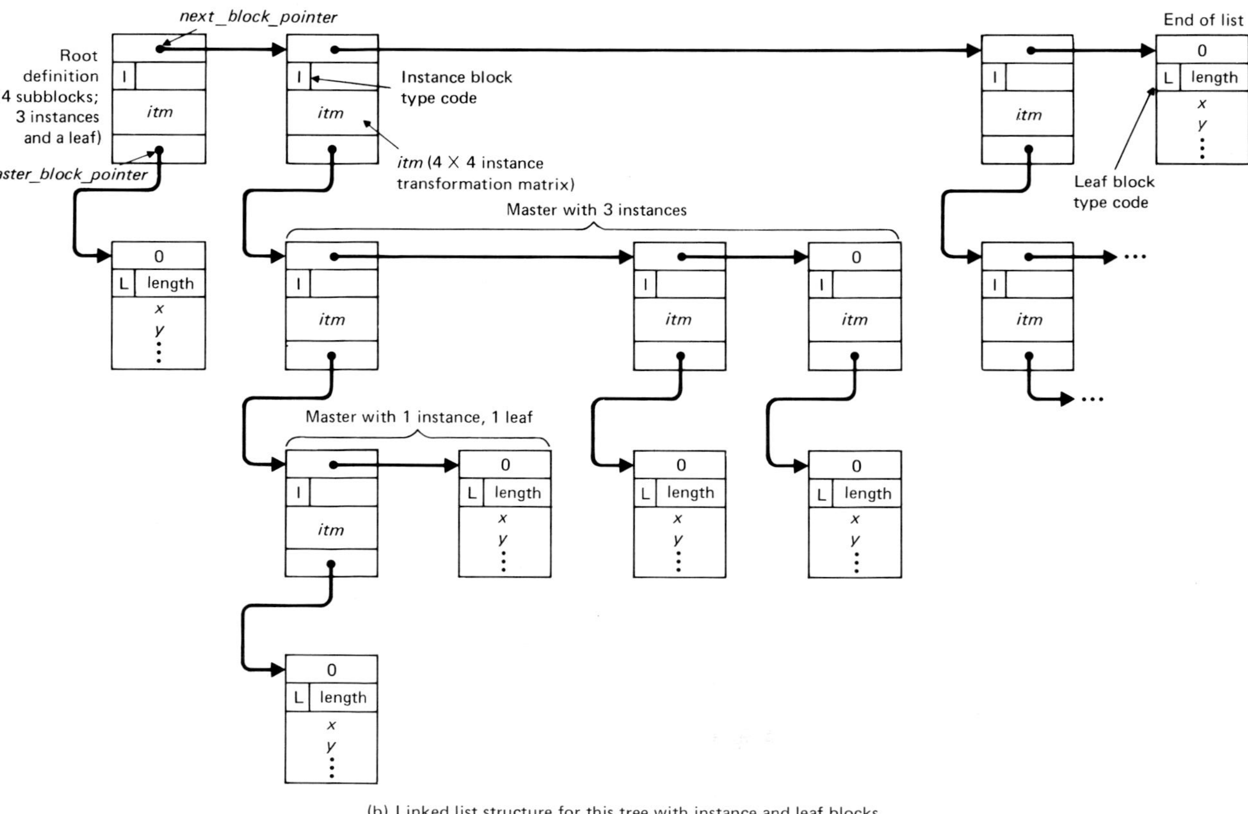

(b) Linked list structure for this tree with instance and leaf blocks

previous *LAYOUT* examples obviously won't do, since the tree structure is now dynamically alterable. Therefore, the *DISPLAY_D_STR* routine must do a general tree traversal through the data structure, using the *type* code, master block and linked list pointers, and the end-of-list flag to decide for each node when to go down (the node is an instance), when to go up (this is the last node so all descendant nodes have been processed), and when to process primitives with the CTM (the node is a leaf). In short, we again have the canonical prefix tree-traversal algorithm, but this time it must be explicitly coded in the data structure display algorithm rather than appear as a consequence of the order of access in the procedure calls, as in the previous algorithms of Example 9.2.

Another design issue concerns the structure of leaf objects. They could be homogeneous and contain only lines, points or text; alternatively, leaves could be heterogeneous, each with data for line, point, and/or text primitives. Leaves would need either appropriate block or primitive type codes, respectively, which would be checked by the tree-traverser code processing a leaf to produce the right kind of output primitives.

Example 9.4(a) gives an iterative algorithm which explicitly pushes and pops the environment as the algorithm descends or ascends in the tree. Example 9.4(b) is a simpler recursive algorithm which uses less code because it does not do explicit environment saving and restoring. It does, however, demand a compiler which can generate recursive code, and such code may have considerable run-time overhead.

Note that premultiplication of the CTM by the new *itm* allows the *itm* to affect the lower-level primitives first. In other words, as we saw in Example 9.2, both the iterative and recursive algorithms traverse the tree top-down starting with the root; they premultiply the CTM by each new *itm* found as they move down the tree. The resulting CTM maps primitives to the coordinate system of the root object in the order in which they were specified in the bottom-up construction process. For a three-level *LAYOUT* case, for example, desk coordinates X_{desk} would become

$$X_{\text{room}} = \{[(X_{\text{desk}} \cdot \text{ITM}_{\text{desk, desk\_chair}}) \cdot \text{ITM}_{\text{desk\_chair, cubicle}}] \cdot \text{ITM}_{\text{cubicle, room}}\}.$$

This shows the bottom-up instancing order for the desk with three types of parentheses: first from desk master coordinates to desk_chair module coordinates, then to cubicle coordinates, and finally to room (world) coordinates. Conversely,

$$X_{\text{room}} = \{X_{\text{desk}} \cdot [\text{ITM}_{\text{desk, desk\_chair}} \cdot (\text{ITM}_{\text{desk\_chair, cubicle}} \cdot \text{ITM}_{\text{cubicle, room}})]\}$$

shows top-down traversal order with $\text{ITM}_{\text{desk\_chair, cubicle}} \cdot \text{ITM}_{\text{cubicle, room}}$ being compounded first, then with the lower level's ITM, and this composite applied to master coordinates. Because of matrix associativity, both orders yield the same result. The choice of premultiplication for CTM functions now becomes clear: because the lower-level ITM is the most recently accessed as the tree is traversed top-down, it must premultiply the CTM because it must affect the coordinates first. In several packages [GINO76, VAND77], the application programmer can select either pre- or postmultiplication mode, typically using premultiplication for tree traversal and postmultiplication for geometric transformations within a node, mapping master-to-master coordinates. This topic is discussed in more detail in Section 9.9.

Example 9.4(a) Iterative tree-walker for general *n*-level data structure.

```
procedure TREE_WALK_2(p: pointer to root node; ctm: 3×3 matrix);
{this procedure traverses the 2D master/instance object hierarchy of Fig. 9.10(b) con-
  taining instance blocks and leaf blocks. The application program typically calls
  TREE_WALK_2 with the data structure pointer p obtained via user interaction and a
  CTM of identity or a geometric transformation of the root. Note that, as with routines
  above, no error-checking is done. Furthermore, this program is only pseudocode and
  not correct Pascal (see Exercise 9.19). The typed pointer p points at two different
  types of records, which is illegal in Pascal. A "variant record" would have to be used
  to hold either an instance or a leaf block, thereby allowing the single typed pointer.}
    p_stk:  stack of pointers;
  ctm_stk:  stack of matrices;
begin
  {initialize}
  EMPTY(p_stk);
  EMPTY(ctm_stk);
  TRANSLATE_CTM_ABS_2(0, 0);      {set translation, rotation, and scale pointers
                                    of CTM to identity transform}
  repeat
    begin
    {test for one of three conditions; note that p↑.typecode denotes the typecode field
      of the record pointed at by p}
    if p = nil    {end of list} then    {have finished processing subobjects of this}
      begin                             {node so pop back for more work}
        POP(ctm, ctm_stk);
        P_POP(p, p_stk);                {a separate POP for pointers}
        p := p ↑. next_block_pointer    {move to next block}
      end                               {on higher level, for next iteration}

    else if p↑.typecode = I then        {instance block—save and descend}
      begin
        P_PUSH(p, p_stk);               {a separate PUSH for pointers}
        PUSH(ctm, ctm_stk);
        SET_CTM_REL_2(p↑.itm);          {compose current level's itm with ctm}
        p := p ↑. master_block_pointer      {descend}
      end

    else if p ↑. typecode = L then      {leaf block—process primitives}
      begin                             {call appropriate primitive routines;
        .                                 coordinates transformed by ctm}
        .
        .
        p := p ↑. next_block_pointer    {move to next block on this
                                          level for next iteration}
      end
  until (p = nil) and (STACK_IS_EMPTY(stk))    {the final block on the root's
                                                  sublist has been processed}
end;    {TREE_WALK_2}
```

Example 9.4(b) Recursive tree walker.

```
procedure RECURSIVE_TREE_WALK_2(p:   pointer to root node;
                                ctm: 3 × 3 matrix);
{invoke with identity ctm or geometric transformation. Local values of ctm
  and p for each invocation are preserved by the recursion mechanism}
var pass_p: pointer temporary;
    pass_ctm: ctm temporary;
begin
  while p <> nil do
    begin
      {only two cases to process: recurse for an instance or
        process the primitives of a leaf}
      if p↑.typecode = I then                               {instance block}
        begin
          pass_p : = p↑.master_block_pointer;                {set up pointer}
          pass_ctm : = p↑.itm * ctm;                {and ctm for lower node}
          RECURSIVE_TREE_WALK_2(pass_p, pass_ctm)          {and process it}
        end

      else
        begin                                                   {leaf block}
          : call appropriate primitive routines
        end
        p := p ↑. next_block_pointer;  {processed this node, so advance}
    end    {while}
end;    {RECURSIVE_TREE_WALK_2}
```

In Examples 9.1–9.3 of *LAYOUT* variations, we had one- and two-level explicit procedure hierarchies driven by one- and two-level data structure hierarchies respectively. An interesting result of generalizing to n-level hierarchy is that in either n-level algorithm we have instead an n-level general data structure hierarchy and a *single* iterative or recursive data structure traversal procedure. This general procedure in effect compresses the explicit two-level procedure hierarchy. Conversely, the previous explicit procedure hierarchies may be viewed as having expanded, i.e., linearized, the recursive traversal for the specific cases of one- or two-level data structures.

Next, we summarize the various ways of representing the hierarchy we have encountered thus far and add some new representations as well.

9.6 HOW CAN HIERARCHY BE ENCODED?

Examples 9.2 and 9.3 showed that fixed hierarchies can be represented by a mixture of data structure and procedure hierarchy. By requiring n-level generality and run-time editing flexibility (not programmed here), we moved from a mixture of data and procedure hierarchy to a single procedure which was almost completely dominated by the general-purpose data structure of Fig. 9.10. This data structure requires a simple, nonspecialized, iterative or recursive tree traverser, which can be used for any data structure of the generic form of Fig. 9.10; as a "standard," application-independent module it can therefore be considered part of the modeling package rather than part of the application program. We now examine what other points on the data-procedure continuum are useful and under what circumstances.

9.6.1 Graphical Data Structures and Structured Display Files

First, what would be the ideal situation for maintaining and interpreting an object hierarchy for refresh systems? We would like the modeling system to create a single integrated representation containing both application data and the geometric object hierarchy. The graphics system would not need to compile the hierarchy to a simple segmented (linear) display file or raster bit map because the DPU could interpret it directly. In other words, the DPU would do model traversal, matrix composition, the entire viewing operation, and vector/character generation or scan conversion, all on the fly, for each refresh cycle. Then there is only a single shared representation into which the CPU writes and from which the DPU reads, once per frame, so that updates to this so-called *graphical data structure* are immediately visible. This strategy is ideal because:

1. It replaces picture compilation done by the graphics system software with hardware interpretation;
2. It makes updates immediately visible (as soon as a lowest-level master is changed, all its instances are changed automatically on the next refresh cycle); and
3. It obviates multiple representations of the same (hierarchical) information found for each instance in the linear display file or raster bit map; this avoids redundant storage, transforming from one form to another and maintaining these representations "in sync" as updating takes place on the model or on the screen.

Unfortunately, this solution has rarely been feasible because it requires general-purpose, powerful DPU hardware that can interpret complex modeling data structures containing both geometric data for display and other application data to be used by the CPU for analysis. What is an even more demanding requirement on refresh DPUs is that they must do the traversal and processing exceedingly quickly so as to avoid flicker. Even for DPUs with subhundred-nanosecond internal-cycle times, one can compute an upper bound on the number of instance blocks that can be traversed, matrices composed, transformations done to master coordinates, and primitives clipped, projected, and generated (or scan-converted), before flicker results—today's equipment certainly cannot handle any more than several hundred instances containing collectively fewer than a hundred thousand short (< 0.5 inch) vectors. The limits for on-the-fly scan-conversion are even much smaller if there is no double-buffered bit map.

Naturally, compromises are made to approach the ideal. First, because of the attractiveness of a single hierarchical representation for both CPU and DPU, software-assisted interpreters have been built, starting with Sketchpad, to provide smooth dynamics for modest (16-bit) integer hierarchies [SUTH63, CHRI67, NINK68, ADAG67]. More practically, we can eliminate flicker by using storage displays such as DVSTs. The amount of motion and update dynamics is now determined by the speed at which we can erase the old image and display the new. For a DVST the dynamics is then limited to that provided by buffered write-through mode. Alternatively, we can turn a refresh display into a storage display by converting the hierarchy to an intermediate nonhierarchical (i.e., postmodeling/viewing) representation at less than 30 Hz. A separate refresh processor then scans the simpler representation, either a vector linear display file (LDF) or a raster bit map, at refresh rates. In classic double-buffer mode the DPU independently traverses the graphical data structure as fast as possible (at least 10 Hz for smooth motion) to prepare the next buffer. The simple vector DPU which refreshes the LDF is called a *display controller* (DC) (see Fig. 9.11(a)). The architecture of this two-processor system which decouples the updating and refreshing tasks is discussed in the next chapter.

In the third case, it is not generally possible with current hardware to have the DPU itself traverse the application model directly if we need to store coordinates in conventional floating-point and/or store much application data in the model. Instead, a type of graphics package with facilities beyond those of SGP or even the Core can traverse the model to build an extract of it called the (hierarchically) *structured display file* (SDF). The SDF is a high-level display file suitable for a DPU (i.e., it contains only geometric information) which preserves the master/instance hierarchical structure and the individual instance transformations. This structure is also called an *untransformed* segmented display file because no modeling or viewing transformations have been applied in deriving it. Each master is considered as a high-level display file segment that is instance-transformed by a DPU-maintained CTM, clipped, and then mapped to the view surface. This last mapping is done either directly at 30–60 Hz or indirectly, again via a mapping to a device-dependent low-level segmented linear display file refreshed by a display controller (see Fig. 9.11(b)) or to a raster bit map. Architectures supporting SDFs or the SDF/LDF combination are discussed in the next chapter.

Strictly speaking, it is not proper to call the structured display file a form of segment *nesting,* since segments are not lexically nested, as in the block structure of procedural languages. Instead they are linked, subroutine-like, via DPU data types equivalent to CPU subroutine jumps with the addresses/names of lower-level segments and transformation "parameters". In some systems these names are actual addresses, while in others they are indices in a global segment directory which facilitates relocating of segments for dynamic creation and deletion of segments. This DPU data type is, of course, equivalent to a data structure instance block. Not surprisingly, then, structured display files look very much like the application data structure of Fig. 9.10 which is also a geometrically (display-) oriented data structure possibly containing nongeometric data as well.

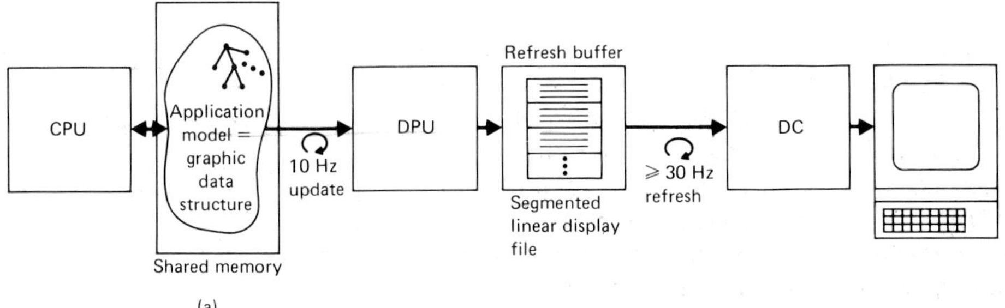

Fig. 9.11(a) The DPU traverses the hierarchical data structure at update rate (≥ 10 Hz), while the display controller traverses the segmented linear display file (LDF) at refresh rate (≥ 30 Hz).

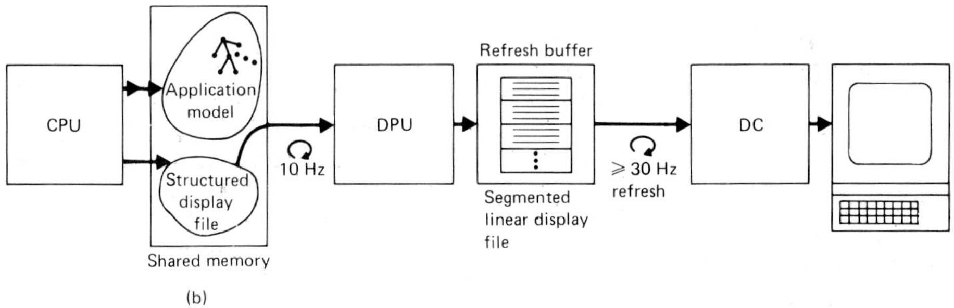

Fig. 9.11(b) The CPU extracts the structured display file (SDF) from the model on demand, while the DPU traverses the SDF at update rate (≥ 10 Hz) and the display controller traverses the LDF at refresh rate (≥ 30 Hz).

Structured display files are often confused with *display* (DPU) *subroutines,* an even simpler form of DPU hierarchy. Here we note only that the former contain primitives which are previewing, while the latter contain clipped primitives which are postviewing. DPU subroutines therefore cannot be used in general for representing modeling hierarchy. In the next chapter we elaborate on this distinction.

9.6.2 Procedure Hierarchy and Display Procedures

Our ideal graphics data structure has the advantage of instant updating, a single representation of the hierarchy, and no software for picture compilation. It is less than ideal, however, in that it must conform to instruction and data formats allowed by the DPU. The introduction of the structured display file allows an arbitrary application model but at the cost of introducing the separate SDF representation which must be compiled from the model. Naturally we would like a method that has the advantage of making pictures directly from the model without intermediate representation(s) but is not tied to a specific DPU-dependent representation.

Consider for a moment the flexibility of procedure hierarchy for defining objects. Inside the procedure one can have an arbitrary flow of control and data structure references. In fact, one extreme that is essentially a "pure" procedure, i.e., data-structure-free, is to define all objects with immediate (compile-time-bound) data for primitives and calls to lower-level procedures. The CPU could dynamically (30-60 Hz) trace out the procedure hierarchy via a call to the root object, use inline calls to the CTM modeling package to produce world coordinates, and use inline calls to the graphics package with CTM-transformed coordinates to produce an image (as in Examples 9.3 and 9.5).

Example 9.5 "Pure" procedure hierarchy with immediate values shown as symbolic constants (each procedure contains primitives and calls to subprocedures).

```
procedure ROOT_OBJECT;
  var stk : stack to save ctms;
begin
  .
  .                                   {arbitrary (nondrawing) code}
  .
  set up viewing specification;
  {next, set up for first instancing}
  PUSH(ctm, stk);
  TRANSLATE_CTM_REL_2(x1, y1);
  ROTATE_CTM_REL_2(theta1);
  SCALE_CTM_REL_2(sx1, sy1);
  SUB_OBJECT_1;                       {call first master}
  POP(ctm, stk);
  .
  .
  .
  {set up for second instancing}
  PUSH(ctm, stk);
  TRANSLATE_CTM_REL_2(x2, y2);
  ROTATE_CTM_REL_2(theta2);
  SCALE_CTM_REL_2(sx2, sy2);
  SUB_OBJECT_2;                       {call second master}
  POP(ctm, stk);
  .
  .
  LINE_ABS_2(xa1, ya1);               {some primitives}
  .
  .
  .
  LINE_REL_2(xn, yn);
  .
  .
  .
end;                                  {ROOT_OBJECT}
```

```
procedure SUB_OBJECT_1;
begin                                  {this is a leaf object}
  MOVE_ABS_2(xb1, yb1);
  LINE_REL_2(xb2, yb2);
  .
  .
  .
  MOVE_ABS_2(...);
  .
  .
  .
  LINE_REL_2(...);
end;                                   {SUB_OBJECT_1}

procedure SUB_OBJECT_2;
begin                                  {this contains calls to lower-level objects}
  MOVE_ABS_2(xc1, yc1);
  LINE_REL_2(xc2, yc2);
  .
  .
  .
  {now set up for a lower-level object; sequence identical to what's in root}
  PUSH(ctm, stk);
  TRANSLATE_CTM_REL_2(xd, yd);
  ROTATE_CTM_REL_2(thetad);
  SCALE_CTM_REL_2(sxd, syd);
  SUB_OBJECT_14;                       {call master}
  POP(ctm, stk);
  .
  .
  .
  LINE_REL_2(...);
end;     {SUB_OBJECT_2}
  .
  .
  .
```

The software "interpretation" of this procedure hierarchy is analogous to the software interpretation of the data structure hierarchy mentioned in the previous section, but is naturally at the opposite end of the data-procedure modeling spectrum. Note that now there is no explicit software module to traverse the hierarchy; the CPU traces out the procedure hierarchy in following the dynamic sequence of calls.

Since there is no general data structure hierarchy, there can be no dynamic creation of new objects—a new procedure cannot be dynamically created. Of course, at run time one can alter the definition of a particular object by using flow of control to include fewer or more primitives or calls to lower-level object procedures, and one can change the values of addressed data. As with data structure hierarchy, the root object's appearance is changed automatically the next time the procedure hierarchy is traced after any lower-level object is changed.

However, we have the same problem with this procedure hierarchy as with direct data structure interpretation: if the DPU is refreshed directly from the output produced by the CPU tracing the procedure hierarchy, the CPU may fall behind the DPU's refresh rate for more than modest-sized procedure hierarchies. Then we may again compile a segmented linear display file (or bit map) to separate update/model traversal from refreshing and to allow selective modification of pieces of the model and their corresponding segments without full reinterpretation.

Note that the *LAYOUT* Examples 9.1-9.3 lie somewhere in between the "pure" procedure with immediate (or addressed) data of Example 9.5 and "pure" data structure with its explicit tree-traversal procedure of Example 9.4.

Display procedures are a particular form of procedure hierarchy which provide an extension of both the syntax and the semantics of normal procedure calls [NEWM79]. They include the CTM manipulations and instance transformations surrounding the subprocedure invocation which thus far have been specified explicitly. The standard sequence (Examples 9.3, 9.5) of

> *PUSH;*
> instance transformations;
> object procedure call;
> *POP;*

is embodied in a convenient and natural shorthand for static hierarchies:

> *CHAIR_PROCEDURE* **scale** *sx, sy* **rotation** *theta* **at** *x,y*

If the language and compiler can't be easily extended with this new construct (the common case, of course), this extension can be approximated with a special procedure call such as

> *DISPLAY(CHAIR_PROCEDURE, sx, sy, theta, x, y)*;

The disadvantages of display procedures are that they not only share the weakness of restricted run-time updatability of procedure hierarchy in general, but also allow at most the three instance transformations to be specified, which must be performed in the order specified. At the cost of specifying *PUSH/POP* and the CTM manipulations explicitly, ordinary procedure invocations allow arbitrary combinations of instance transformations. Nonetheless, if display procedures could be efficiently interpreted [NEWM73a], they would allow both a convenient, high-level syntax suitable for most occasions and a reasonable degree of dynamic manipulation via editing the source text of the object-defining procedures rather than of data structures.

Such source text editing is akin to editing APL programs to achieve desired effects, and requires that the user have knowledge of the graphics programs. It is therefore still not as convenient or as general as *general* data structure routines which are driven by user interaction, not by his editing code. Display procedures could well become a viable option, however, when customized hardware suitable for high-speed interpretation of such a language is developed.

9.6.3 Symbol Systems

Some graphics packages contain or interface to a simple modeling package which supports not only the CTM and instance transformations, but also a special form of one- or multilevel objects used strictly for drawing purposes. As discussed in Section 9.2, such objects are naturally called *symbols,* because they are directly analogous to the symbol-shaped cut-outs on plastic templates and, unlike most objects, have no associated application data. As a simple example, *LAYOUT* could have been implemented with a symbol package because it uses no application data. (Note that the *INSERT_SEGMENT* facility of the Core derived GKS package [ISO81] inserts arbitrary NDC segments in the current open segment, and is therefore not a one-level (world coordinate) symbol facility.)

Table 9.2 shows a syntactic comparison between procedures, segments, and symbols. When the definition of a symbol

```
CREATE_SYMBOL;
.
.
.
< primitives >
.
.
.
CLOSE_SYMBOL;
```

is encountered at *symbol definition* time, it is compiled to an internal device-independent data structure storing master/world coordinates *before* the viewing operation has been applied, rather than to a displayable DPU segment *after* application of the viewing operation. The symbol can be subsequently invoked at *symbol use* time with an *INSERT* to be displayed inside the currently open DPU segment. When a symbol is invoked, the symbol system treats it as a user-defined primitive, retrieves its component coordinates from the data structure, and passes them to be individually processed through the viewing operation. This makes the symbol inclusion processed somewhat similar to the *INCLUDE_FILE* (*file_name*) facility for combining code segments at compile time, or to a macroassembly expansion.

TABLE 9.2. COMPARISON OF *N*-LEVEL SYMBOL HIERARCHY WITH PROCEDURES AND SEGMENTS

Functions	Procedure	(One-level) segment	One-level symbol	*n*-level symbol
Open	**procedure** *NAME*(...)	*CREATE_SEGMENT*(*id*)	*CREATE_SYMBOL*(*id*)	same as one-level
Close	**end**{*NAME*}	*CLOSE_SEGMENT*	*CLOSE_SYMBOL*	same as one-level
Invoke/call lower-level node	*NAME*(...)	—	—	*INSERT_SYMBOL*(*id*) *REFER_SYMBOL*(*id*)
Delete	—	*DELETE_SEGMENT*(*id*)	DELETE_SYMBOL	same as one-level
Display on screen	*NAME*(...)	*SET_VISIBILITY*(*id*, *on*)	in open DPU segment: *INSERT_SYMBOL*(*id*) or *INSERT_SYMBOL* (*id*, *sx*, *sy*, *theta*, *x*, *y*)	same as one-level

There are several advantages to calling a symbol over just calling an ordinary procedure in which the equivalent symbol is defined, as in *LAYOUT*. First, the symbol definition is compiled to primitives at the time when the application program is run (symbol-definition time), and thereafter all inclusions of the symbol use the compiled data structure. Using this data structure is, in general, more efficient than incurring the overhead of running through all the calls to the successive SGP output primitive procedures in an ordinary symbol-defining procedure each time that procedure is called. A more significant advantage occurs if symbols can be stored between user sessions. Then symbols used in common across a number of applications can be stored in public or private *libraries;* they can be retrieved simply by a compound name such as *library_name.symbol_name.* A third potential advantage is for the restricted but not unusual 2D application where no clipping is involved and where (integer) device coordinates are used as world coordinates. In this case, an "intelligent" graphics terminal, i.e., one with local memory and processing power connected over a low- or medium-bandwidth communications link to the host (Chapter 10), could store symbol definitions locally. By sending only the symbol's name for local expansion rather than all its component primitives individually, host/terminal traffic is compressed considerably.

CTM manipulations can be set up before a symbol is inserted. Alternatively, with the parameter-list syntax for *INSERT* shown in Table 9.2, instance transformation parameters could be included directly with the *INSERT* call, in a convenient way reminiscent of display procedure invocation.

For *n*-level symbol systems, hierarchy can be induced in two distinct ways. As in GPGS [CARU75, VAND77], *INSERT* can be used inside another symbol definition as well as inside a DPU segment. This causes the previously compiled data structure entries for the lower-level symbol to be included at the point of invocation in the higher-level symbol definition, at that symbol's definition time. This is again analogous to *INCLUDE_FILE* or macroexpansion inclusion. Alternatively, the *REFER* facility can cause just a pointer to the lower-level symbol to be compiled at symbol definition time. Then the invocation via *REFER* causes the body of the lower-level symbol to be accessed only at the time its higher-level caller is *INSERT*ed into a DPU segment. *INSERT* and *REFER* therefore differ simply in terms of when the instanced symbol is actually expanded, with *REFER* naturally more economical for storing symbol hierarchy in the library. As with instances and copies in object hierarchies, use of *REFER*ed symbols allow change of the master symbol to propagate at hierarchy traversal time while use of *INSERT*ed symbols does not, since the latter have lost their identity in the *INSERT* process.

Instance transformations may be set not only for symbol inclusion in a DPU segment, but also prior to either *INSERT* or *REFER* calls in a symbol definition (Fig. 9.12). This causes the lower-level symbol to be instanced by the CTM, either at the time of inclusion in the *INSERT*ing symbol in the case of *INSERT* (at the *INSERT*ing symbol's definition time) or only at the time the *REFER*ring symbol is included in an open DPU segment in the case of *REFER* (at its symbol use time). In

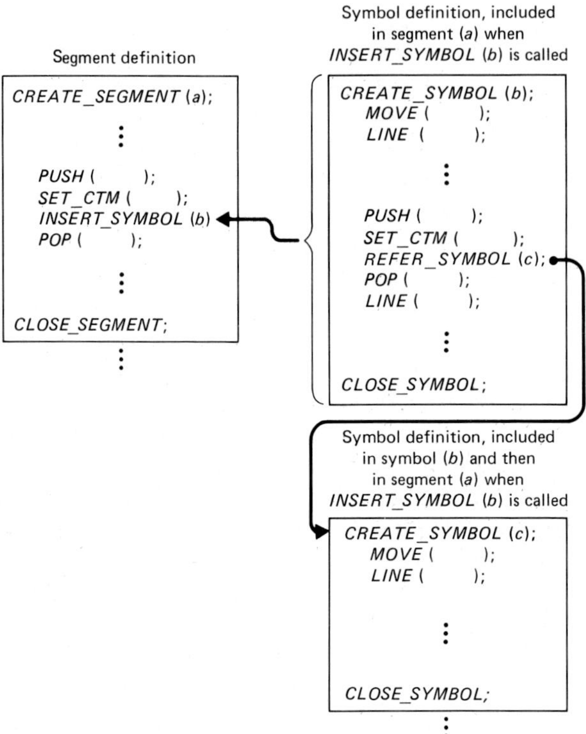

Fig. 9.12 Two-level symbol hierarchy.

the latter case, the entire symbol hierarchy formed by the root symbol and its *REFER*s to lower-level symbols, with associated composite instance transformation matrices, is traversed by the symbol package with a conventional tree traversal algorithm using a stack (such as that of Example 9.4). The resulting linearized world is processed by the graphics package through the viewing operation as if it had originally been specified inline in the segment itself, as for any other modeling system.

The distinction between ordinary symbol-defining procedures and symbols ("symbol procedures") can be difficult to grasp. Syntactically, they are nearly identical. The salient difference, as stated above, is that the symbol procedures are compiled at symbol definition time to an internal data structure subsequently accessible to the graphics package, while ordinary procedures result in compiled code with calls to output primitive procedures in the graphics package. These primitive procedures must be called and executed repeatedly for each primitive in each symbol-defining procedure invocation. Furthermore, it is impossible to delete a normal procedure at run time except by having flow of control branching around it, while a symbol (procedure) can be deleted simply with the *DELETE* command. (Any subsequent higher-level invocation of the deleted symbol, of course, generates an error.)

With symbols as a simple form of hierarchical model, as with procedure or data structure hierarchy, no change is seen in the picture displayed until the changed hierarchy is retraversed and recompiled to a new display file bit map. Furthermore, segments may be used in conjunction with symbols to allow selective modification, as usual. Finally, conventional procedures can include an arbitrary amount of data and processing not related to display, while symbol procedures are specialized for display. Symbol procedures, from that point of view, are the closest in spirit to display procedures.

Symbols are advantageous essentially only for drawing applications consisting of making and viewing pictures, since otherwise they duplicate geometric information from the more general application model containing both application data and geometric data. They should be viewed only as a simple way of having a package build and maintain (hierarchical) templates for standard drawing components. Even for drawing applications it is often necessary to do nontrivial editing, in which case editing an application-specific data structure is far easier than providing editing facilities in the symbol package beyond defining and deleting symbols. For example, it is difficult to specify device-independent mechanisms for inquiring about attributes or coordinate values of primitives and for subsequently editing them or the primitives themselves within the symbol. The ANSI X3H31 task group at this writing is considering these difficult issues as part of a study on how to change the Core to accommodate "structures" [ANSI81]. Structures are meant to replace segments and represent all primitives in modeling coordinates. Thus they are effectively symbols, as defined here, and the goal is to have them map naturally to the types of structured display files supported by the advanced architectures discussed in Chapter 10. In the same way that the Core can be viewed as creating a device-independent linear display file, the structure package can be viewed as creating a device-independent structured display file which is compiled to the SDF for a particular DPU.

The issue of structure inclusion is still a controversial one in graphics standardization. Some feel that the rapidly increasing number of displays with SDF architecture calls for modeling support in the graphics package to take advantage of this capability. Others believe that the original Core stress on the separation of modeling and viewing should remain, and that the application-dependent nature of modeling makes it difficult to go beyond standardizing on a rudimentary symbol package. In conclusion, symbol systems do not obviate the general need for the application model, and therefore have somewhat restricted utility.

9.6.4 Structure Editing and Segment/Group Pseudo-Hierarchy

We have seen so far that, for purposes of rough comparison, procedure hierarchy is syntactically convenient while data structure hierarchy allows greater run-time editing flexibility. Let us now summarize the forms of run-time editing allowed by the various forms of models. Procedures allow run-time editing of addressed data to change values of primitive coordinates and modeling transformations. Even structure can be affected by altering flow of control to include or exclude calls on primitives or subobjects, or to create or delete segments. The graphical data structure and structured display file techniques for modeling object hierarchy allow not only these forms of editing but also the run-time addition of arbitrary new objects. Any modeling technique can be used in conjunction with the segmented linear display file to allow relatively quick selective modification of model and picture.

In addition to editing by segment, many graphics packages allow finer control by defining the *group* as a collection of primitives within a segment named by a *pick_id.* A sequence of calls such as

```
CREATE_GROUP(pick_id);
.
.
.
⟨primitives⟩
.
.
.
CLOSE_GROUP;
```

would establish groups within a

```
CREATE_SEGMENT(id);
.
.
.
CLOSE_SEGMENT;
```

segment definition. For example, each point in a set of data points on a curve can be picked by the user if it is in its own named group. In even more sophisticated packages, primitives can be deleted from or added to the segment. Group overhead tends to be less than segment overhead because fewer operations and no attributes but *pick_id* are allowed. If some segment editing is allowed via a call such as

DELETE_GROUP(segment_id, pick-id)

somewhat more overhead is required in the segment to keep track of where groups start and end relative to the segment start (see Exercise 9.9). In a sense, group structure creates a very limited form of a two-level structured display file, without instance transformations and attributes for groups. Groups are in essence not full (sub)segments, but one-time local blocks which can be cheaply implemented on most DPUs.

9.6.5 Relational Databases as Application Data Structures

Having decided on a data structure hierarchy of the type shown in Fig. 9.10, one can implement a linked-list structure for both graphical and nongraphical data by using arrays and then do one's own storage management, or one can use the operating system's storage manager to build and modify the list structure. An alternative to either of these implementations is to use a database management system, such as a relational database system [DATE81], to store all of the graphical and nongraphical information, including the hierarchy, and then to construct the traverser by using normal database queries. The advantage of this strategy is that the application programmer need not write procedures to build and access linked-list modeling systems tailored to his application. Instead, the programmer can build on top of a general-purpose facility simply by defining tables of relations. Queries can then be formatted to retrieve specific n-tuples (or "associations"), which is similar to linked-list pointer chasing, or to enumerate all of the associations in a relation, which is similar to looping through an array or linked list.

Figure 9.13 is a symbolic representation of some sample relations for the simple two-level *LAYOUT* example. Needless to say, these relations are isomorphic to the structures of Figs. 9.8, 9.9, and 9.10(b), since they must contain the same information. (This is easily seen by looking at each n-tuple row as an instance block.) The difference is that creation, modification, and readout/query facilities already exist (courtesy of the relational database package). Naturally, some efficiency is lost by using such a general-purpose package, but for all but the most dynamic applications, this will probably be acceptable. Note that we haven't stored the address of relations in the relation itself—the system is responsible for mapping the symbolic name of a specific relation to its actual location. Thus names inside an association should in effect be viewed as indirect pointers, i.e., references to other relations.

In a specific implementation of this technique [WELL76], arbitrary relations may be declared by the programmer; in addition, however, a number of domain identifiers (column labels) have been predefined to have standard semantic interpretations. These include references to lower-level relations, instance transformation parameters which, when accessed, cause automatic CTM manipulations, and many other useful features. This scheme greatly simplifies the work of the model traverser and yet preserves full generality in that the programmer is free to establish arbitrary relations with domains in arbitrary order.

In another recent implementation [GARR80b], the application relations have no predefined domains. Rather, *output* or *graphical* relations, containing for example, lines and character strings, and *input* relations, containing reports of user actions, are predefined. The application program interaction dialogue procedure consists of *assertions* (i.e., declarations rather than procedures) defining dependencies of the *application relations* on the input relations. These dependencies map user actions into changes to the application relations. The application program procedures to display the application relations (i.e., the model) are another set of assertions defining dependencies of the graphical relations on the application relations.

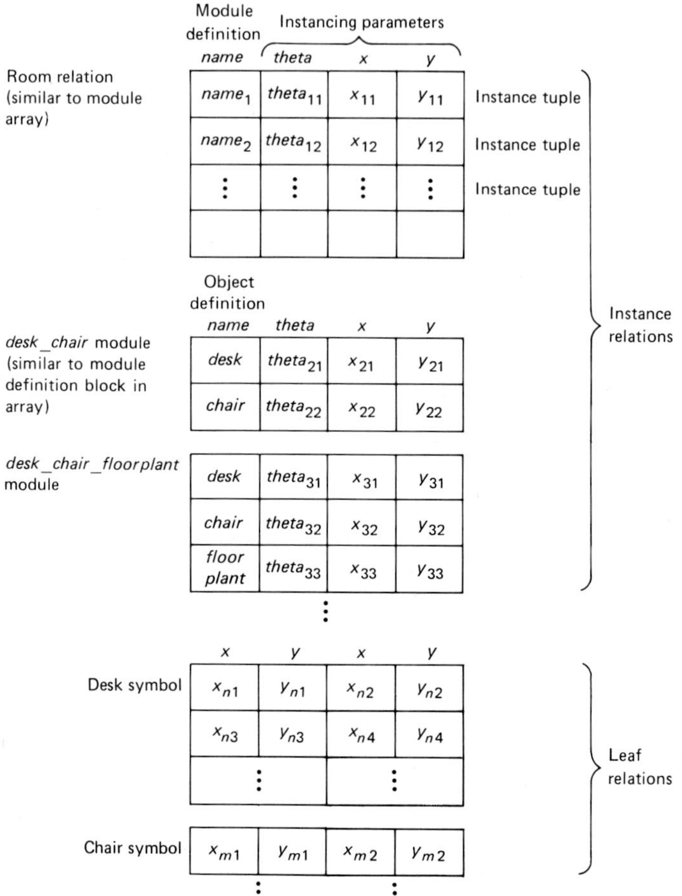

Fig. 9.13 Hierarchy implemented with a simple (relational) database.

Changes to the graphical relations are shown on the display device. Thus a user action changes the input relations, which causes changes to the application relations, which causes changes to the graphics relations, which causes changes to the image, all based on assertions about the relations. Only analysis programs are coded in a traditional procedural language.

Figure 9.14 compares the structure of a database-oriented system (9.14(c)) to the conventional application (9.14(a)) and modeling (9.14(b)) systems structures. Note that a modeling facility, whether implemented by the application program, a modeling package, or a relational database package, is more than a structured display file. The structured display file does preserve modeling hierarchy, but the modeling facility is used not only for display but for analysis of the modeled world as well. That is, one can put data into the model as well as take it out, whereas the structured display file is only meant to be read by the DPU for display purposes.

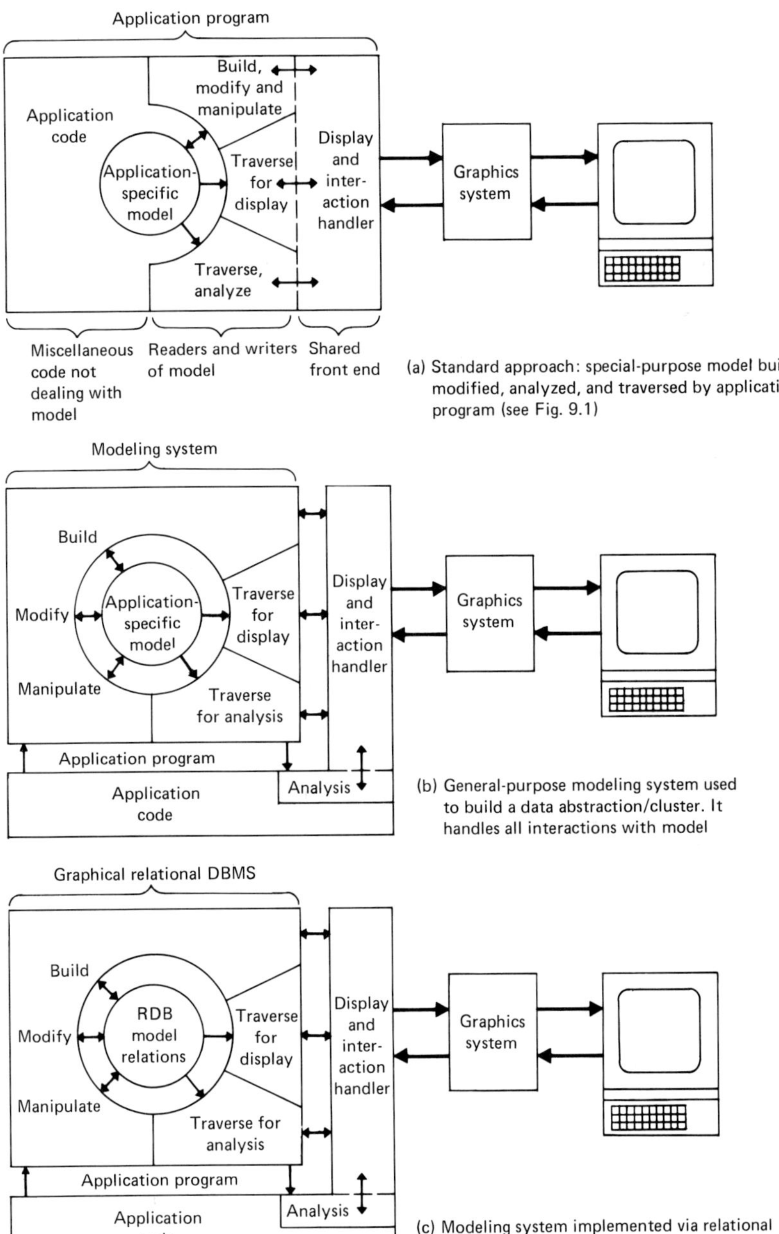

(a) Standard approach: special-purpose model built, modified, analyzed, and traversed by application program (see Fig. 9.1)

(b) General-purpose modeling system used to build a data abstraction/cluster. It handles all interactions with model

(c) Modeling system implemented via relational database management system

Fig. 9.14 Three ways of modeling.

9.6.6 Summary

Hierarchy can be found anywhere in the total system, and indeed in many places simultaneously. We have seen it first and foremost in the application *model,* in terms of a combination of data and procedure hierarchy. A reduced, graphics-only version of an untransformed, previewing hierarchy can be made either for software interpretation with a *symbol system* or for DPU interpretation with a *structured display file.* Either of these facilities can be used to generate a display directly or indirectly via the conventional (refreshed) segmented linear display file or raster bit map. In general, for any of these schemes a sequence of representations, each more DPU-specific than the previous one, of the object hierarchy and its picture is compiled, interpreted, and stored in various software and hardware subsystems in the object-to-picture transformation pipeline. Each representation is specialized for some particular purpose and each has advantages and disadvantages for a particular class of operations. As we generate more discrete representations, we generally gain efficiency and speed due to functional specialization, but at the cost of producing each representation while keeping all of them synchronized for updating. Our ideal in which the DPU is able to make pictures directly from an all-inclusive model (the *graphical data structure*) is thus approached only in rather special cases.

Next we discuss a few more issues generic to hierarchies. Then we turn to a closer inspection of the modeling/viewing interface and discuss particularly our desire to compose as many separate transformations as possible before applying them to endpoints, and the interaction between transforming and clipping.

9.7 MULTILEVEL CORRELATION

If one has an *n*-level hierarchical model and only a linearly segmented display file, how can one correlate a pick to the right place in the hierarchical model? First, if a "pure" data structure or procedure is interpreted on the fly, then the traversal can be stopped the moment a primitive is generated whose light falls within the field of view of a light pen. Alternatively, each primitive's x, y values can be clipped, as they are generated, against a small rectangular window (the *pick window*) surrounding a locator stylus used for pick simulation. The first primitive to satisfy the test causes object identification; a more expensive but more accurate algorithm is to find not the first but the closest primitive/object by maintaining a running minimum distance as the entire hierarchy is traversed, as in Section 5.3.2. As mentioned in Section 5.2.2, imprecise interrupts may occur with pen detects on fast vector displays because of the lack of synchronization inherent in the pipelined processing of the traversal/viewing operation and the low-level display generation process. It may be necessary to slow the pipeline down during correlation to effect synchronization.

Second, if there is a compiled segmented linear display file, we can get back only the segment name in many simple graphics packages, such as SGP, using the techniques of Section 4.3.4. The Core system allows one additional level of naming for group-like collections of primitives inside a segment via the *pick_id* attribute. This provides a two-level naming structure within a one-level editing structure. Each data point in a segment can then be uniquely picked, but cannot be moved or deleted without redrawing the entire segment.

GPGS allows an arbitrary block-structured naming convention for nested blocks of primitives inside segments [CARU75]. This permits one to use data structure pointers as block *pick_id*s by having all primitives that are generated from a given subobject share the subobject's unique data structure identifier/name. GPGS then provides the entire sequence of object names from the root to the picked node by returning the nested sequence of block *pick_id*s. An application programmer could get a limited but practical version of such hierarchical naming, using the Core, by assuming only a few levels of hierarchy and a modest number of objects per level, each named with a small integer identifier. Segment names would correspond to the highest level in the tree (the root's subobjects), while each *pick_id* would be composed by concatenating the bits of each subobject identifier. A *segment_id* with a 16-bit *pick_id,* which uses 8 bits each for two levels, could thus map a three-level hierarchy with each segment containing up to 256 subobjects, each of up to 256 subobjects. This is, in fact, a very large hierarchy.

For light-pen picking with buffer addresses and a linear display file using linked-list allocation, a multilevel correlation table could be set up to generalize the one-level table of Section 4.3.4 (Fig. 4.19). Fig. 9.15 shows a (nonclipped) circuit modeled as a two-level hierarchy consisting of two filters F_1 and F_2 and a diode D. Assume that the display code generated is stored in three segments, one for each of the root's subobjects. The table of buffer addresses and lengths of Fig. 9.15(c) is used to store the address ranges of blocks of primitives corresponding to each object in the buffer, as done in Fig. 4.19. Since code for blocks typically is nested in the buffer (R_1 in F_1 in CKT), the search which compares the buffer address returned by the correlation hardware against start addresses in the correlation table should not stop at the first object "in range." Instead, it should pick the subobject with the smallest range whose start address is closest to the picked element, since it represents the lowest-level (leaf) node. Thus the DPU counter address shown is resolved to the resistor R_2, not to F_2 or even CKT. The parental pointer is used to back-chain from any leaf node up through the modeling hierarchy, stopping where the user wishes. For example, picking a line in the resistor of F_2 could cause successive highlighting of only the resistor at level 2, of F_2 at level 1, or the entire picture at level 0, thus allowing the user to specify the proper object for the next operation (see Exercise 9.20).

In the case that (x, y) comparison picking is used for a multilevel modeling hierarchy and a linear display file, other techniques are used. First, in a brute-force way, the on-the-fly traversal of a model or structured display file can be simulated. The hierarchy could be retraversed until a screen primitive is generated whose (x, y) values lie within a tolerance of the (x, y) value returned from the physical locator. Alternatively, each primitive can be tested against a pick window. Naturally, this is a slow process because each primitive is clipped and transformed, and is therefore not

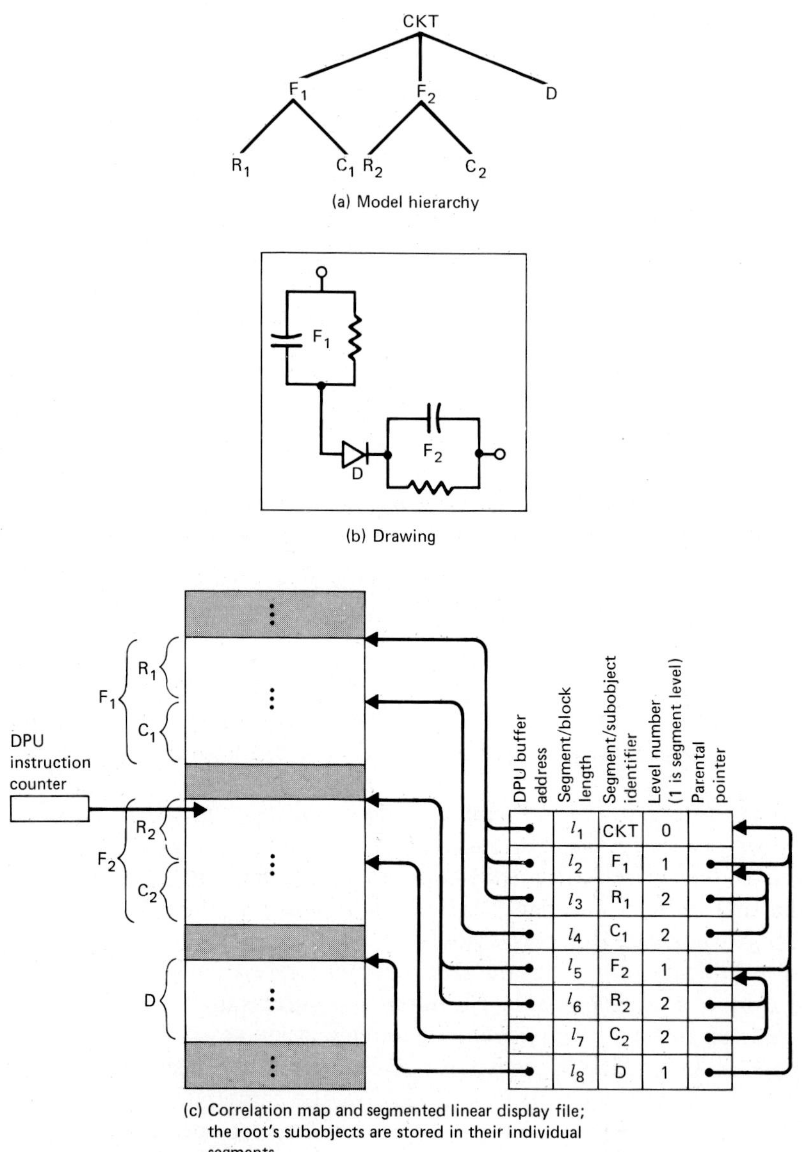

(a) Model hierarchy

(b) Drawing

(c) Correlation map and segmented linear display file; the root's subobjects are stored in their individual segments

Fig. 9.15 Hierarchical correlation map.

recommended unless there is hardware assistance (see Chapter 10). An improved method for 2D back-maps the locator (x, y) (or a pick window) into each object's master coordinates using the inverse of the (CTM · VT) composite matrix, so that the test can be done before transforming each primitive. A much better method that involves the use of extents is described in Section 9.12.2.

9.8 PASSING ATTRIBUTES

The issue of attributes is a complex one in computer graphics and one which at this writing is far from being clearly understood (or ripe for standardization). First of all, are attributes such as color, intensity, and line style part of the description of objects in the model, are they attributes of a particular visualization, or could they be both? No hard and fast rules exist; some objects, especially physical ones, have intrinsic color, while others, especially abstract ones, can be displayed in arbitrary user-specified colors (Chapter 17). Then the question arises of how attributes may be changed. Attributes such as segment visibility, detectability, e.g. for menu picking and feedback (see Exercise 2.18), and highlightability are clearly within the domain of graphical visualization and not in modeling, and should therefore be easily and dynamically changeable in the display file. The simple implementation techniques of Chapter 4 do indeed provide for such quick updating by changing a single word in the segment header. These are *dynamic segment* attributes because a single dynamic change affects each primitive in the segment.

Other attributes which are oriented toward modeling would require a change in the model, perhaps a retraversal and then a corresponding update of the display file. Should line style, color, and intensity, for example, be as easily changed in the modeling package as the SGP dynamic segment attributes within the graphics package? While this would be convenient from the application programmer's point of view, these attributes may not be as easily modified in the segments compiled for current DPUs—they may be encoded for each primitive rather than modally with a register whose contents can be easily updated for all following primitives. Attributes which are not easily modified for a segment because they are attached to each primitive's DPU code are called *static*. The graphics package does not permit the programmer to change static attributes of primitives after they have been generated. While a segment attribute could be static and a primitive attribute dynamic (via selective editing of its DPU code), there is a natural division into dynamic segment and static primitive attributes. In the Core, for example, the four dynamic attributes are segment attributes and all other attributes are static attributes,* on the assumption that most displays allow easy implementation of visibility, highlightability, detectability, and image transformation without having to alter each primitive in the segment. Only for DPUs without rotation and scale hardware would dynamic change in an image rotation or scale force SGP to recompile the entire segment. Conversely, graphics packages for such DPUs might support only image translation.

In the design of a package, then, we need to consider the following types of questions relating to attribute handling (see also [MICH78a] and [ANSI81]):

1. Which attributes are for modeling and which are for both modeling and viewing?
2. Which attributes are dynamically changeable (typically by altering only the segment header in the display file) and which are static and therefore can be changed only by the application programmer respecifying one or more segments for recompilation?

---

*The only static segment attribute is image transformation type, an efficiency mechanism.

3. What is the scope of application of an attribute? That is, which attributes apply to segments and which to primitives?
4. Can attributes be both primitive and segment attributes? If so, and if their values differ for a given primitive, which has precedence?
5. Similarly, how are attributes of higher- and lower-level objects reconciled, compounded, etc?
6. How are attributes best specified by the programmer and how and when are they bound to the capabilities of a particular display device?

As an example, suppose we had a brown mahogany desk and a black leather chair forming a desk–chair module; what should the module's color be? Should one be able to specify independently a walnut or blond color for the module which would override the colors of the component objects? Or are higher- and lower-level colors composed, i.e., mixed? As an alternative strategy, if a lower-level object doesn't have a color, it could inherit the color of its caller, but if it has a color, that color could override the color of the caller. Composing intensities might consist of multiplying them, or one might choose the lower of the two intensities. Clearly, a general choice among these strategies is impossible since it will depend on the situation and the application.

The way in which these issues are resolved will be reflected in the hierarchy traversal; during traversal we will encounter not only instance transformation "parameters" to compose with the CTM, but also attribute "parameters" to replace, be replaced by or be composed with the lower-level ones. Thus, instance blocks might contain, in addition to the ITMs, the attributes to be applied to the lower-level objects. Additionally, there might be a first, special block in each linked sublist defining a subobject which would encode the attributes of that subobject, to be overridden by, override, or be composed with the caller's attributes.

The stack might be used to save not only the CTM (and the object pointer) but also attributes in effect at the current level which must be restored when the subobject has been processed (see Exercise 9.12). Since we are using a variety of data formats, we might push and pop pointers to data rather than the varying-length data itself; alternatively, we could have individual stacks which are specialized to the different data formats.

9.9 PRE- AND POSTMULTIPLICATION

In Sections 9.4 and 9.5 we noted that the relative CTM routines (i.e., *ROTATE_CTM_REL*, etc.) premultiply the CTM in order to allow easy composition of the instance transformation matrices during the prefix tree traversal. At the same time we noted that if we specify individual geometric transformations explicitly inside a procedure so as to place objects in their own coordinate system, we must specify them in the *reverse* order to that in which they are to be applied. This allows the last-specified matrix, which is premultiplied last, actually to be applied to the object's coordinates first. But it would be more natural, both for such placement transformations and for normalizing transformations in viewing, to postmultiply the CTM and specify the transformations in the order M_1, M_2, M_3, . . . , in which they are to be multiplied: $X' = X \cdot M_1 \cdot M_2 \cdot M_3 \ldots$. As mentioned in Section 9.5, a simple system variable can be used to switch between these two equally reasonable matrix multiplication orders depending on whether one is sequentially transforming an object or traversing a hierarchy of objects.

Any desired result can be achieved in either mode by explicitly specifying the transformations in the appropriate order. Specifying the sequence of matrices *A, B, C* in postmultiplication mode is the same as specifying *C, B, A* in premultiplication mode: $X' = X \cdot ABC$. For example, if only postmultiplication is available, the hierarchy traverser could save all ITMs encountered in a stack and read them out in inverse order to postmultiply the CTM. Clearly premultiplication is preferred here, however! In order to predict what the result of a given sequence will be, it is best to express the sequence in the canonical mathematical form and then apply the successive transformations to a simple object in its own coordinate system (Fig. 9.16). Since matrix multiplication is noncommutative, the same sequence in pre- and post-order will generally yield totally different results. In particular, note that in Fig. 9.16(b) differential scale after rotation induces shearing, while the inverse doesn't.

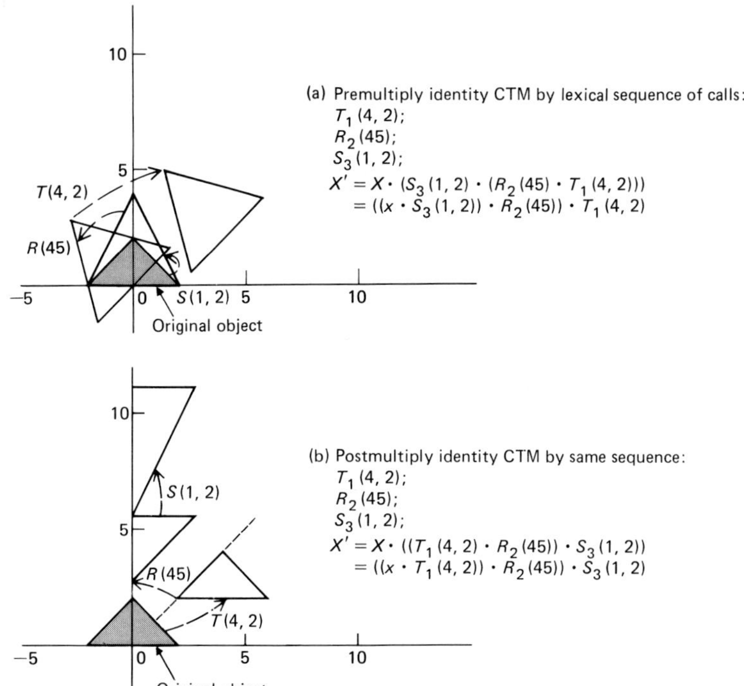

Fig. 9.16 Pictorial interpretation of pre- and postmultiplication to show that they yield different results for the same sequence of calls.

9.10 COMBINING MODEL TRAVERSAL WITH THE VIEWING OPERATION

In Chapter 4 we saw that the 2D viewing operation consisted of clipping in world coordinates followed by window-to-viewport mapping for upright windows (Fig. 9.17(a)), or window-to-viewport mapping followed by clipping for rotated windows in normalized device coordinates (Fig. 9.17(b)), or directly in physical device coordinates (Fig. 9.17(c)). The mathematics for the 2D window-to-viewport mapping is easily formulated as a matrix composition by using scale and translation transformations of Section 4.2.2, while the 3D case, which proved quite a bit more complex because of the projection step, was treated in Chapter 8. In essence, we saw that for 3D we don't have the flexibility of deciding where in the pipeline we can clip for maximum efficiency—for finite view volumes we must clip to the hither and yon planes lest we project (pieces of) invisible primitives on the projection plane which can't be removed by 2D windowing. Thus we get the intermixed sequence of transform, clip, and transform shown in Fig. 9.18; all normalizing transforms have been composed and the projection and window-to-viewport mapping can also be composed.

We now add two additional sets of transformations on either end of these pipelines and then ask how we can best compose the maximum number of matrices to avoid repetitive transforming of endpoints. On the input side we add the modeling (object placement and object instancing) transformations already composed by the model traverser in the CTM, and on the output side we add image transformations,

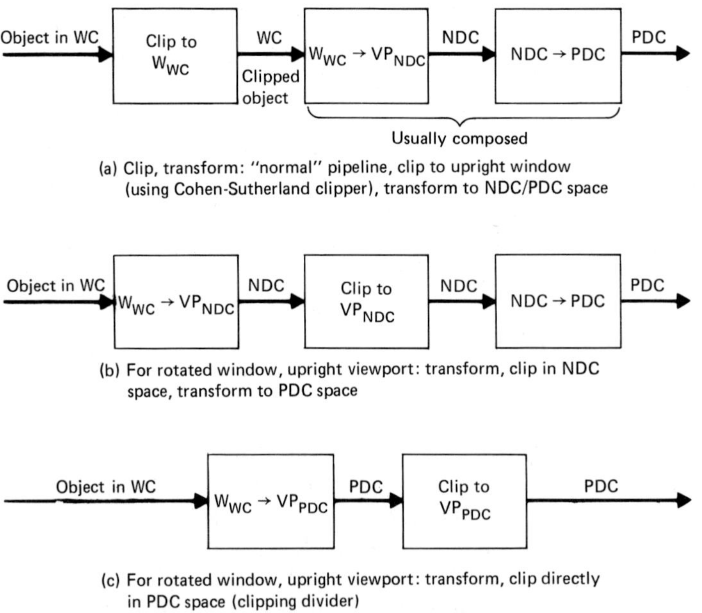

Fig. 9.17 2D viewing pipelines: object in WC→image in PDC.

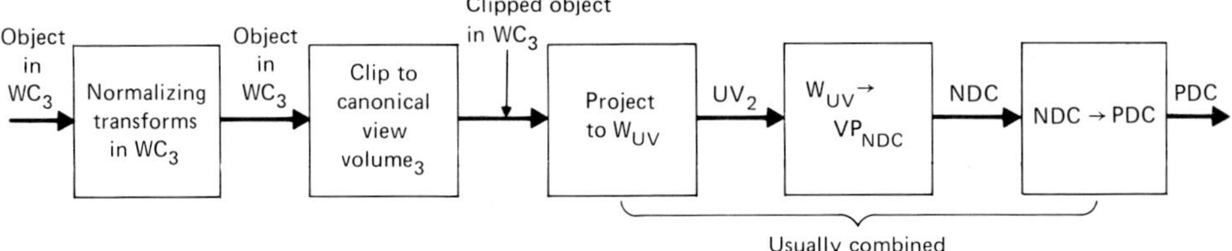

Fig. 9.18 3D viewing pipeline.

as discussed in Chapter 8. Fig. 9.19 shows the two complete 2D cases while Fig. 9.20 shows the 3D case. These figures show the maximum number of matrices that can be composed in each pipeline, in the style of Section 8.6. Note in Fig. 9.19(a) that mathematically we could compose the last three matrices, but because we often want to alter the image transformation dynamically, we either do that in NDC space or in PDC space, thereby composing only the last two steps.

Figs. 9.19(b) and 9.20 show the use of the "hook" mentioned in Section 9.4 for combining the CTM from the modeling package with preclipping transformations done in the graphics package. This simple mechanism can be used by the application or modeling program to pass the CTM to the graphics program so that it can process object master coordinates directly. Conversely, if the modeling system is an integrated part of an enhanced graphics package or if structured display files are used directly by a DPU, the traverser or DPU (respectively) can obtain the preclip composite normalizing/viewing transformation and compose the modeling CTM with it, as in Fig. 9.6. The tree-walking algorithms of Example 9.4 can therefore premultiply the viewing transformation by the root's placement or instancing transformations in the CTM and the body of the algorithm is unaltered: $X' = X \cdot CTM \cdot VT$.

Have we done the best we can in composing the matrices for separate steps? We could do better only if we managed to move clipping all the way to the end or all the way to the beginning of the pipeline, so that all transformations could be composed and we would have either the simplest clip-transform or transform-clip sequences. Of these two, clearly the clip-transform sequence is to be preferred because it eliminates invisible primitives as early as possible rather than unnecessarily transforming them and then discarding them.

9.11 CLIPPING IN MASTER COORDINATES

Next we examine the relationship in 2D between the three viewing parameters, the window, the viewport, and the window-to-viewport mapping. In Fig. 9.21 we see that, in the language of mathematical functions, the viewport is the image of the window under the window-to-viewport mapping. Conversely, the window is the viewport's pre-image under the mapping. In fact, we need to specify only two out of these three viewing parameters in order to derive the third uniquely. Typically, of course, this means that the programmer specifies the window and viewport and the package calculates the window-to-viewport mapping.

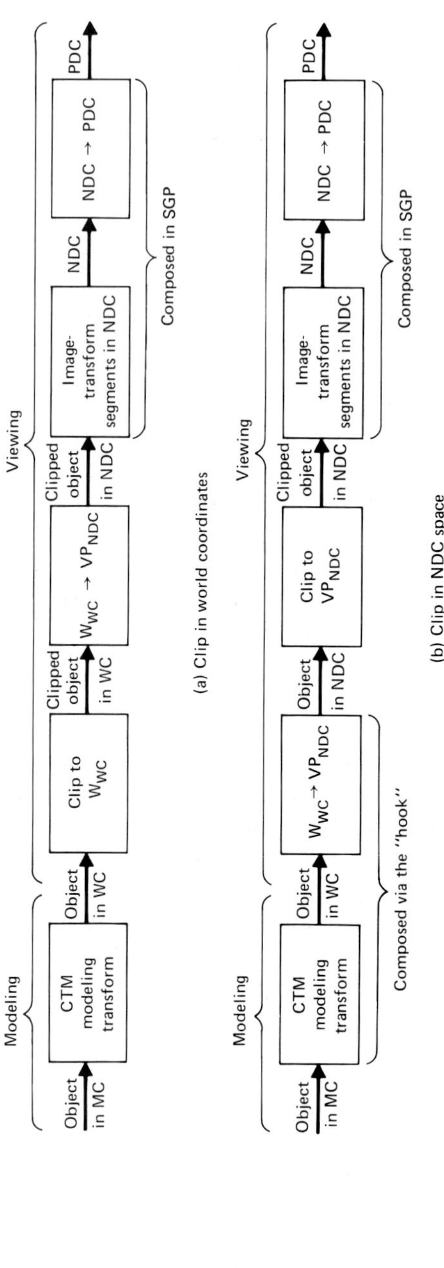

Fig. 9.19 Full 2D modeling/viewing pipeline: object in Master Coordinates (MC)→image in PDC.

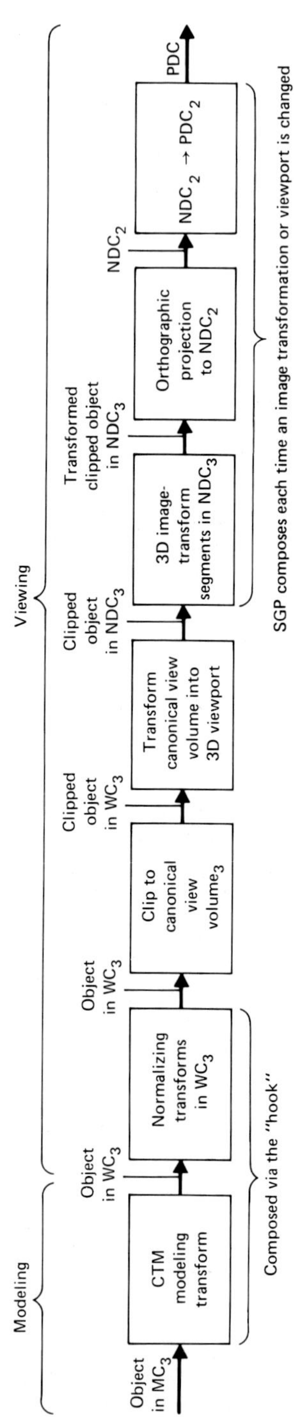

Fig. 9.20 Full 3D modeling/viewing pipeline: object in MC→image in PDC.

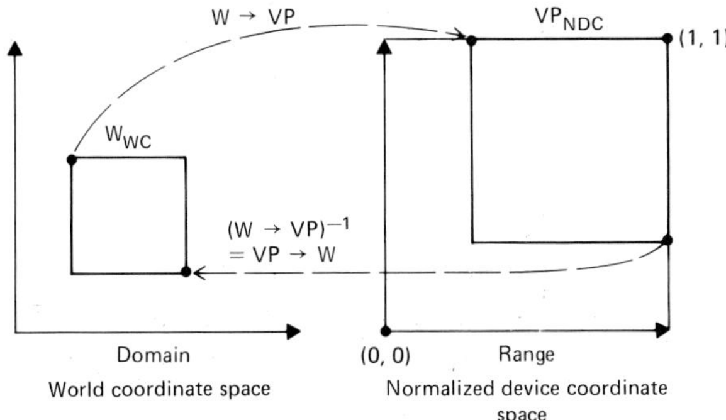

Fig. 9.21 The viewport is the image of the window-to-viewport mapping and the window is the image of the viewport-to-window mapping.

In Section 4.2.1 we established that one can clip before (in world coordinates) or after the mapping (in device coordinates). What would happen if we altered the pipeline of Fig. 9.19(b) to clip in master coordinates, before the CTM instance transformations are composed with the viewing transformations? This question is exactly analogous to the question of the relationship between window, viewport, and the window-to-viewport mapping. We are dealing here with a CTM transformation which also maps from one space to another with an associated clipping region, i.e., from master coordinate space to world coordinate space; in the latter, the clipping region (the window) is defined explicitly. As before, given two out of the three parameters, we can compute the third. Thus we can transform and then clip in world coordinates or equally well clip to the pre-image of the window and then transform. This pre-image, called a *clipbox,* can be computed as the image of the inverse of the composite CTM applied to the window (Fig. 9.22). It is also the pre-image of the composite of the CTM and the window-to-viewport mapping applied to the viewport.

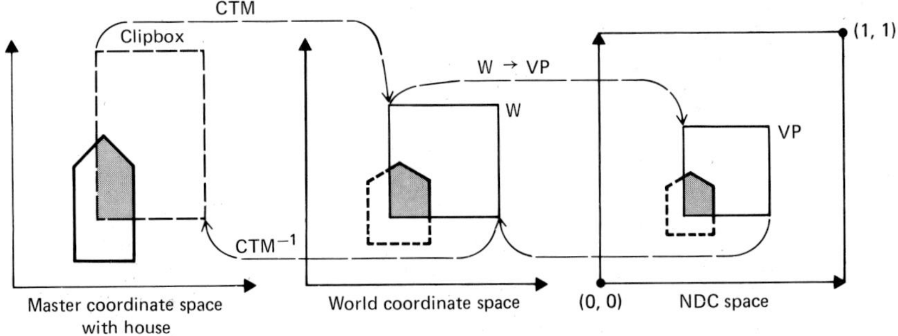

Fig. 9.22 The equivalence of clipping in object's master coordinate space to clipbox $CTM^{-1}(W)$, clipping in world coordinate space to window, and clipping in NDC space to viewport.

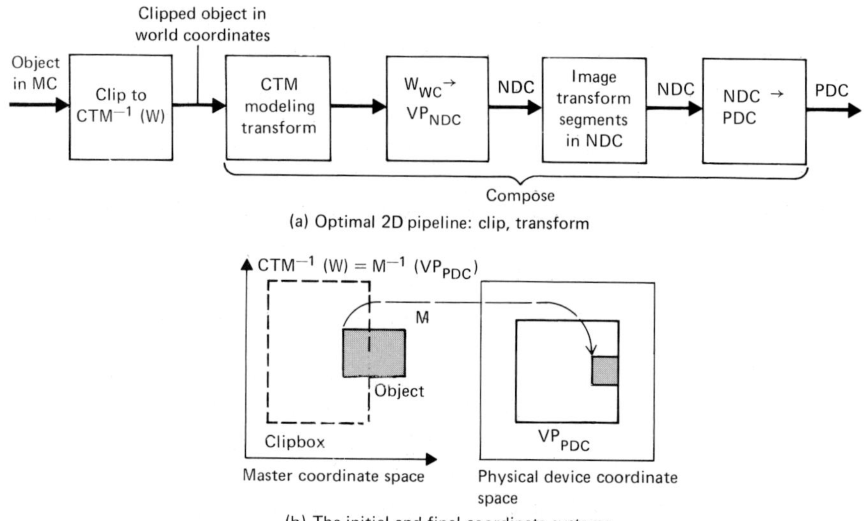

(a) Optimal 2D pipeline: clip, transform

(b) The initial and final coordinate systems

Fig. 9.23 Clip, transform visible 2D primitives only.

We now have three equivalent places to clip. The efficient pipeline of Fig. 9.23(a) results if we clip to the clipbox and then transform only the visible primitives with the single composite matrix M which results from multiplying the CTM, the window-to-viewport mapping, the image transformations (if any), and the NDC-to-PDC mapping (Fig. 9.23(b)). It is interesting to note that a proper understanding of hierarchy and transformations has allowed us to treat each object only once for clipping and once for transforming, all the way from master coordinates to the physical device.* In other words, with this approach we need not concern ourselves with all the successive individual modeling and viewing transformations which affected the object in its construction and viewing processes.

There is only one problem with this elegant solution: what happens if the CTM contains a rotation instance transformation or if the window is not upright (Fig. 9.24)? In either of these cases, the $CTM^{-1}(W)$ will produce a nonupright clipbox and we won't be able to use the Cohen–Sutherland clipper of Chapter 4. Instead, we will be forced to use the far more complex and expensive Sutherland–Hodgman polygon clipper of Chapter 11. If rotation (or shear for packages supporting it) is present, it is therefore far more efficient to transform all primitives at this node and then clip them to an upright window or an upright viewport than to clip invisible primitives first. A good compromise strategy, for the case of upright windows but the potential of rotation/shear instance transformations, is to check the instance transformations

*Again, for dynamic image transformations in software, it is more efficient to compose the CTM and the W→VP mapping and then dynamically alter the composite of the image transformation and the NDC→PDC mapping.

when traversing the hierarchy during compounding. If a rotation or shear is included at a given level, one then clips all objects below this node in world or device coordinates, and clips the others in their own master coordinates (Fig. 9.24). This algorithm, sometimes called *adaptive clipping* [NEWM79], is shown in Example 9.6 as a refinement of the iterative tree traverser of Example 9.4(a).

Example 9.6 A clipper which adapts to the presence of rotation and shear in the instance transformation.

```
procedure CLIPFIRST(p: pointer to master's root node);
  {This adaptive clipping procedure traverses a 2D master/instance object hierarchy. It
    clips an object in its master coordinates if the instance transformations do not in-
    clude rotation or shear, and in device coordinates if it does. It obtains the composite
    viewing transformation from a global array vtm in the graphics package, via the
    hook. As in Example 9.4(a), this is pseudocode, not legal Pascal.}

var    p_stk: stack of pointers;
     ctm_stk: stack of CTMs;
     clip_stk: stack of clipbox coordinates;
        vport: rectangle;
     clip_box: rectangle;
begin
  {initialize}
  EMPTY(stk);
  ctm := vtm;                              {initialize CTM to composite of
                                             all viewing transformations}
  clip_box := vport*INVERSE(ctm);          {the default, for no rotation/shear}
  repeat
    if p = nil {end of list} then          {have finished processing subobjects of
                                             this node so pop back for more work}
          begin
            C_POP(clip_box, clip_stk)      {a separate POP for clipbox coordinates}
            POP(ctm, ctm_stk);
            P_POP(p, p_stk);
            p := p↑. next_block_pointer    {move to next block on higher
                                             level for next iteration}
          end
    else if p↑.typecode = I then           {instance block - save state and descend}
          begin
            P_PUSH(p, p_stk);
            PUSH(ctm, ctm_stk);
            C_PUSH(clip_box, clip_stk);    {a separate PUSH for clipbox}
            SET_CTM_REL_2 (p↑.itm);        {compose CTM with this level's ITM}
            if new ctm does not include rotation then
              clip_box := vport * INVERSE(ctm)    {to clip in master coordinates}
            else clip_box := vport;               {to clip in device coordinates}
            p := p↑.master_block_pointer          {descend}
          end
```

(continued)

```
    else if (p↑.typecode = L) and (ctm includes rotation) then   {leaf node—
                                                                   rotation}
          begin  {transform, then clip}
              transform each primitive with CTM, then clip it against
              clip_box = vport and display visible portion;
              p := p↑.next_block_pointer;     {move to next block on this level for
                                                new iteration}
          end
    else if (p↑.typecode = L) and (ctm does not include rotation) then
          begin  {leaf node—no rotation, so clip, then transform}
            clip each primitive against clip_box, then transform and display visible
              portion;
            p := p↑.next_block_pointer          {move to next block on this level}
          end
  until (p = nil) and (STACK_IS_EMPTY(stk))      {last node in root's sublist}
end;    {CLIPFIRST}
```

Unfortunately, this solution, satisfactory for 2D, does not generally apply to 3D because the normalizing transformations and perspective generally introduce rotations and distortions due to shear. Only in the unusual case of a non-oblique parallel projection along the principal axes can we avoid rotation, let alone the shear of the normalizing and perspective transformations. If we used the inverse transformation to map the view volume to master coordinates, we would get the intractable skewed view volume which the normalizing transformations were designed to eliminate in the first place! The best we can do for 3D, therefore, is the transform–clip–transform sequence of Fig. 9.20.

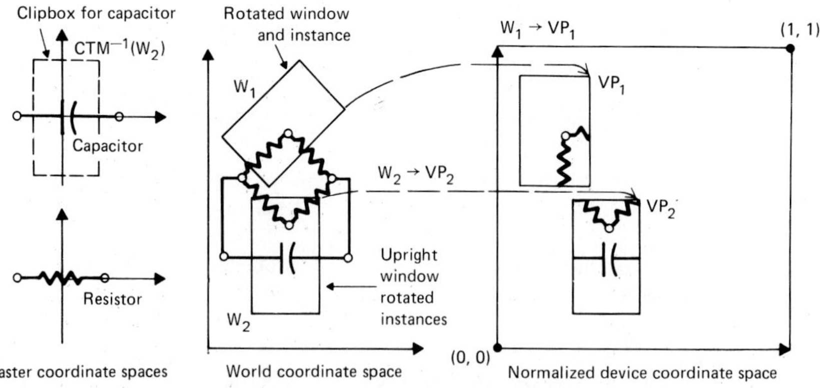

Fig. 9.24 Adaptive clipping: clip in master coordinate space (capacitor) unless there is rotation (resistor). Note that even though the clipboxes corresponding to W_1 would be upright in this special case, the presence of rotations still implies clipping to VP_1 for both resistor instances. Also, the clipboxes for W_2 or the resistor are rotated and again imply clipping to VP_2.

9.12 EXTENTS

The previous strategies for 2D and 3D do the best possible job of minimizing the number of individual transformations applied to coordinates and the number of coordinates to which they need be applied. In many cases, however, they still do far more work than is strictly necessary because they do not take advantage of the (hierarchical) structure of the objects in the way our experienced eyes would. Specifically, objects in a hierarchy tend to occupy only a finite subspace of the world, and one should be able to tell quickly whether that subspace intersects with the window before one starts clipping individual primitives. In other words, we want to take advantage of the geometric "locality" of objects, called *spatial coherence,* to obtain quick and trivial accept and reject tests for entire objects similar to the tests for clipping individual primitives.

In Chapters 4 and 5 we introduced the *screen extent* as an upright bounding rectangle for a segment's image, to be used in a quick and dirty comparison for a pick correlation. We now define another version of an *extent,* namely a 2D upright rectangle or 3D parallelepiped which bounds the object in its master coordinate space.* We simply test the extent (typically chosen to be as small as possible) for overlap with the clipbox (in 2D); conversely, for either 2D or 3D we can transform the extent with the CTM into NDC or PDC space (thereby avoiding taking the inverse of the CTM) and then test the transformed extent against the window or viewport, respectively. We can distinguish three cases for 2D clipping in device coordinates, as shown in Fig. 9.25.

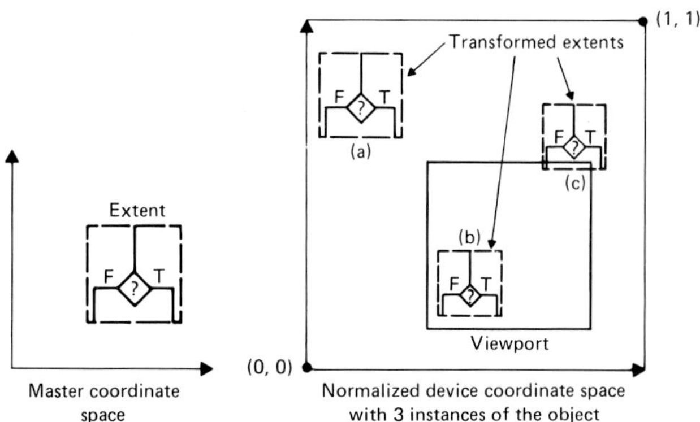

Fig. 9.25 Extents.

*The term *boxing* has been used [NEWM79] to denote the use of a bounding box (i.e., an extent) with display procedures.

Instance (a) can be trivially rejected because its transformed (screen) extent lies outside the viewport, so the master object's primitives need be neither transformed nor clipped. Similarly, instance (b) can be trivially accepted, and the master's primitives need only be transformed. Finally, instance (c) can be neither trivially accepted nor rejected, and the master's primitives require transforming and clipping.

Figure 9.26 shows that one can easily test where the transformed extent lies with respect to the viewport. Outcodes are used to check whether the main diagonal lies outside the viewport in a half space (a), inside the viewport (b), or neither (c, d). Note that we can test either the extent in master coordinates against the clipbox or the transformed extent in device coordinates against the viewport. The choice of where to test the extent does not mandate where the clipping is done, so that the adaptive strategy of suiting the clip/transform order to the particular case is still appropriate; we simply integrate extent testing with the basic algorithm of Example 9.6 (see Exercises 9.15 and 9.18).

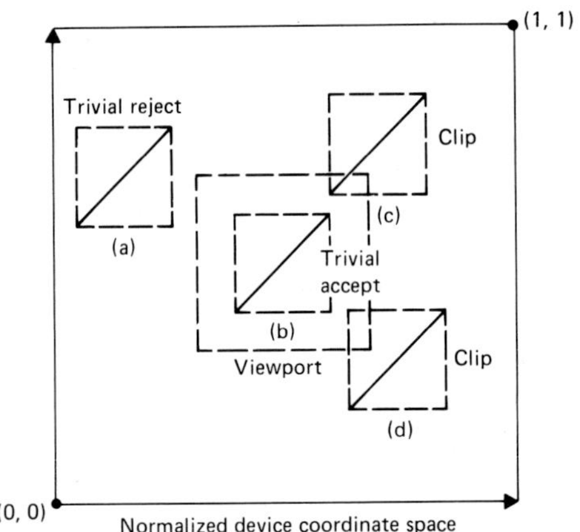

Fig. 9.26 Diagonal clip test for overlap.

9.12.1 Instance Transformations with Rotation or Shear

In order to process extents, we must first handle the case of CTMs which involve rotation or shear of the master. As shown in Fig. 9.27, the transformed extent is rotated, which necessitates polygon clipping with either the rotated extent or a rotated clipbox. By surrounding the transformed extent with its own upright extent (see Exercises 9.16 and 9.17) and testing the upright extent against the viewport, we sacrifice some precision of the test in return for speed. Unnecessary clipping may result, as shown in Fig. 9.28: in (a), an upright extent surrounds a rotated extent which lies completely outside the viewport, and in (b) a rotated extent and its upright extent both intersect the viewport when the object contained could be trivially accepted (visually, if not algorithmically).

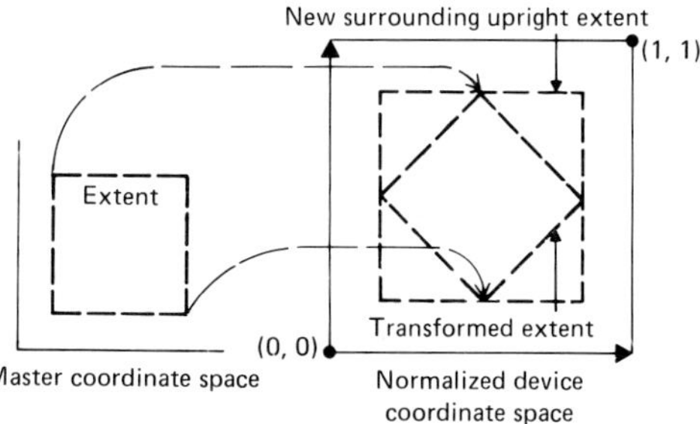

Fig. 9.27 Surrounding upright extent.

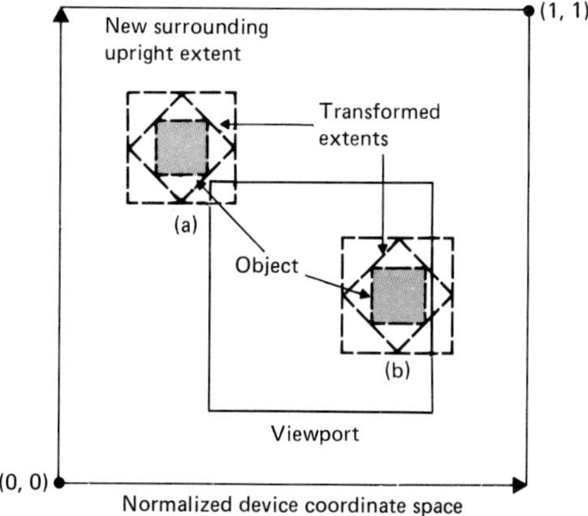

Fig. 9.28 Needlessly processed instances.

9.12.2 Clipping and Correlation for Hierarchy

In practice, the extra work of using extents and doing occasional unneeded clipping is more than worthwhile because of the savings achieved by a fast trivial accept/reject mechanism for entire objects. This is especially true for hierarchies, in which we can trivially accept or reject an entire subtree subtended by a node by computing its extent as the extent surrounding the extents of all its components. If we must clip, we clip the node's leaf primitives and then test each of the extents of its instances for selective clipping of daughter nodes. This technique means that when the instance transformations or coordinate values of a subobject are changed, the extents of all objects in the path from the object to the root must be updated. For a static procedure hierarchy with coordinates and instance transforms defined by immediate (constant) data, this poses no problem. However, in dynamic hierarchies where the application program can alter such values in real time, much update propagation may be necessary. For structured display files with extents interpreted on the fly by the DPU, it might be faster to test individual extents of component objects and not the aggregate extent, in order to avoid the update propagation. This trade-off is a function of tree depth.

Another use of extents is to speed up the pick correlation process of Section 9.7. Instead of transforming and clipping each primitive in a hierarchy to test its screen representation (if any) against an (x, y) value returned by the locator, we can again apply the inverse of the (CTM · VT) matrix to the point (x, y) in NDC space but now test this back-mapped point against the extent of each object in its master coordinate space instead of against each primitive in each object. Since extents yield a fairly crude approximation, a variety of rules may be used to get reasonable disambiguation of entities "near" the point. Thus, unlike the brute-force test where we may be satisfied with the first primitive which lies within a tolerance of the back-mapped (x, y) locator value, we should not be satisfied with the first leaf or subobject whose extent encloses the mapped point. If on a given level two subobject extents and three leaf extents enclose the point, for example, we may choose to calculate exact (floating-point) distances of only the primitives from the point, to pick the closest. For even better resolution at the cost of considerably more computation, the algorithm could recurse to the two subobjects (and their subobjects, etc.) to pick the closest among all five candidates. Note that this last technique is the generalization to hierarchy of the basic technique for extent picking described in Section 5.3.2. Furthermore, while it is primarily a 2D technique, it can be made to apply to 3D if either a 3D locator is available or reasonable assumptions can be made about a constant z value.

9.12.3 Extent Testing

The second extent implementation question is how to compute and test extents in the first place. There are essentially four possibilities.

In the simplest case, the programmer describes objects (and symbols) to the graphics package without knowing anything about their extents. For segments, the graphics package can store successive transformed but unclipped NDC primitives in a temporary buffer prior to linking them into the open segment, and maintain maximum and minimum x, y (and z) coordinates of these primitives on the fly. These extrema determine the upright extent of the transformed object. In the case of symbols, the symbol package can also record minima and maxima on the fly as it stores primitives in the symbol definition data structure. When the symbol is *INSERT*ed in the segment, the symbol system can pass the extent to the graphics package which transforms it and checks it against the viewport. In the case of a trivial reject, the symbol is ignored. If a trivial accept or clipping is indicated, the primitives are transformed (but again not yet clipped) and the min, max extent calculations of the segment are updated with the symbol's transformed extent.

Upon segment close, the extent is checked and the buffer is either freed (trivial reject), linked in as a segment (trivial accept), or clipped in (normalized) device coordinates and used to build a segment. At the cost of some temporary storage and needlessly transforming invisible primitives, this algorithm obviates initial clipping of all object and symbol primitives in master coordinates (as done in the "best" algorithm of the adaptive clipper), even if that clipping would have been mostly trivial accepts or rejects. Determining which strategy is better in what cases is left as a nontrivial exercise for the reader.

In the second case, we assume that the programmer knows the extent of the predefined objects at compile time. This knowledge can then be passed to the graphics system, so that it may determine the course of action to take.

Similarly, in the third case, the application program or modeling system can compute the extents at run time for dynamically defined objects and can then pass this knowledge to the graphics package. For example, the hierarchical data structure of Fig. 9.10 may be augmented with an extent block as the first block on the linked list for each node in the hierarchy (Fig. 9.29).

How is the extent information passed to the graphics package and what is the subsequent reaction to the outcome of the extent test? In order for the symbol system, the programmer, or the application program/modeling system to pass an extent to the graphics package, a new facility is needed. The *EXTENT_TEST_2* and *EXTENT_TEST_3* functions have as arguments the extrema of 2D or 3D extents respectively. They return one of three values (*accept, reject,* and *clip*) depending on the outcome of testing the passed extent (after transformation by the CTM, against the 2D viewport or 3D view volume). A three-way **case** can then deal with the outcome of the test. If *reject,* no primitives of this node need be passed to the graphics package—the symbol definition or the procedure defining the object in a procedure hierarchy is not invoked, nor is the node in a data structure hierarchy accessed. If *clip,* nothing special need be done and the object or symbol is treated as before. If *accept,* there is a choice, as follows.

In the simple case, clipping can be explicitly disabled in the package for this object or symbol via a new call, *CLIP(on/off)*. This facility is also useful in applications in which it is known beforehand that clipping need never be invoked because the entire world coordinate system will always be in view—as is the case, for example, when a 16-bit world coordinate system is chosen for a 16-bit DPU. Turning clipping off makes the viewing pipeline considerably more efficient and allows all separate modeling and viewing operations to be compressed to a single composite matrix multiplication!

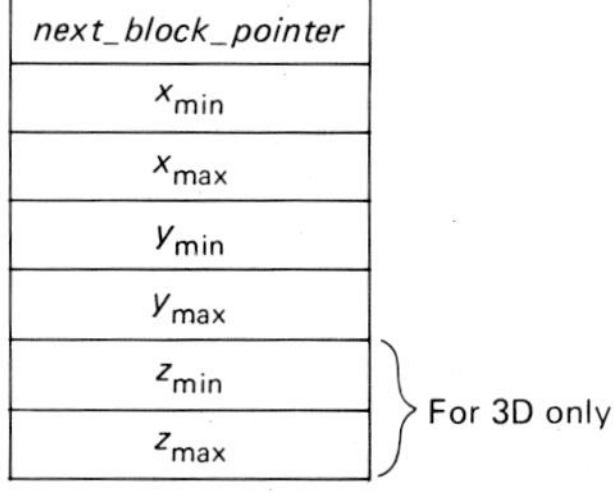

Fig. 9.29 Extent block.

In the more complex cases, one could argue that the programmer (or the modeling system) shouldn't have to turn clipping on and off explicitly and that the package should remember the extent and the results of the extent test so that it can distinguish between the trivial accept and clipping cases. That would be nice, but new problems arise: how long is an extent test operative, i.e., what is its scope? Objects and segments needn't be associated one to one, so that extent scope and segment scope are unrelated (they are "orthogonal"). That means that extents could remain in effect until reset by another extent, using modal scope, or they could be given block-structured scope with explicit *BEGIN_EXTENT, END_EXTENT* brackets. In either case, what would happen if a viewing change took place inside an extent scope? Should the package signal an error condition or automatically retest the last-stored extent against the new viewport or volume and continue processing normally? The package grows considerably more complex when we try to eliminate the need for explicit control of clipping! Programmer-controlled clipping appears the better choice.

The fourth way to test extents is at the other extreme and is unfortunately the most common one: the package has no extent facilities at all and they must be handled completely within the application program. The application program would then perform its own intersection test, providing it had either stored the viewing parameters or could request them from the package. In 2D this duplication of effort might be reasonable, but duplicating the much more complex 3D viewing/clipping pipeline in the application program makes no sense at all. Hence we conclude that it is desirable for applications which have logical grouping, i.e., those involving one or more levels of hierarchy, that the graphics package be able to test extents by using its clipping machinery and then give explicit control over the package's clipping to the application program, so it can deal with the outcome of the test.

9.12.4 Other Uses of Extents

Extents have been implemented in the firmware of the high-performance vector DPU of BUGS, the Brown University Graphics System [VAND74], not only to speed up clipping, but also to reject objects too small to be properly resolved on the screen, and to allow alternate representations of an object as a function of the size of its extent on the screen. The first feature, referred to as the *small-element discard,* is also described in [VECT78a] and serves three purposes. First, it is a means of uncluttering the screen by removing information too dense to be understood. Second, it obviates DPU processing of such objects and thereby conserves refresh buffer space and DPU/DC processing time. Third, it helps prevent the phosphor burnout caused by repeatedly overwriting a small area of the screen.

The second use of extents in BUGS is to allow it to present levels of detail, or alternatively to hide graphical information as it interprets a graphical data structure. For example, in a teaching application each object in the tree representing a microprocessor system whose internal workings are being simulated and animated has three alternate representations (see Fig. 1.4) [GURW81]. The CPU chip is a node in the hierarchy and is represented by a box with a label at the highest zooming level, a box with a few internal registers and I/O ports at the middle level, and a box with all programmer-accessible registers, flags, and ports at the lowest level (highest level of detail). Each of the three representations has the same extent in the object coordinate system but a different criterion of size stored in its graphical data structure. These sizes are adjacent, nonoverlapping subranges of the 0–1 NDC size range. The three alternate representations are invoked in turn with a conditional call that tests the size of the transformed extent against the stored range of each representation (actually, the size is represented by the length of the diagonal of the upright surrounding extent). If the extent size lies in the range of a representation, it is processed normally; otherwise the representation is discarded. In this manner, smooth, real-time panning and zooming not only produce images of objects which get smaller or larger with the degree of zoom, but also provide additional detail at two discrete zoom thresholds, when that level of detail can be conveniently visualized.

9.12.5 Extents as Assertions

The extent test lets the programmer call the graphics package to check on the intersection of the transformed extent with the viewport or view volume. It is therefore an assertion about the size of the associated object that may or may not be correct. What happens if the programmer makes a mistake? The problem will manifest itself in the form of improperly displayed pictures when information appears when it shouldn't or doesn't appear when it should. If the application programmer knows what to expect, he may get enough visual feedback to spot the error and fix it. A more foolproof method is to add an additional debugging feature to the graphics package that passes a code indicating whether any primitives were actually clipped which should have been trivially accepted or rejected. This can be accomplished by passing the supposed extent to the package, leaving clipping enabled, and passing all primitives of the object through the package; a flag that is accessible to the application program can then be set indicating whether any primitives were actually clipped and can be tested after each primitive call (or after an entire batch, for coarser but less expensive debugging). This debugging function is analogous to array subscript checking in that it need be done only once (at least for static data) and thereafter can be disabled for production run efficiency.

9.13 OBJECT WINDOWS AND INSTANCE RECTANGLES

In the previous sections we have shown that the modeling/viewing pipeline can be reduced to two basic operations: clipping (based on a variety of criteria) and coordinate transforming with a homogeneous transformation. Conceptually, if not in implementation, we transformed from local object master coordinates to the world coordinate system, clipped, and then transformed to physical device coordinates. Clipping to a clipbox in object master coordinates when possible was advocated on the grounds of efficiency, in order to avoid transforming invisible primitives; this strategy was shown to be the logical equivalent of instancing the object in its entirety and then clipping its primitives in the world coordinate system. Is there any point to instancing *pieces* of objects, that is, clipping to an *object window* in master coordinates, and then instance-transforming such a piece into an *instance rectangle* in a higher-level master (see Fig. 9.30)? Allowing clipping of objects at all levels is akin to building a collage of object parts, and still allows application of a final window or viewport clipping to the resulting whole. (This technique could certainly be useful for building 2D objects such as actual collages, but appears to have limited utility for 3D objects.) In the same way that a window maps to a viewport, and only two out of the three parameters (window, viewport, and window-to-viewport mapping) are needed to define the third, so too an object window maps to an instance rectangle via the instance transformation. An instance transformation could therefore be conveniently specified by the programmer or interactive user by specifying the object window and instance rectangle, i.e., specifying *what* is to be mapped *where.* This makes the instance transformation directly analogous to the window-to-viewport transformation.

As Mallgren and Shaw point out [MALL78], what is conceptually nice about allowing both clipping and transforming at all levels of a hierarchy is that it provides uniform treatment both of *clipping* at any level (it is the restriction or subsetting of the domain of a mapping) and of the instance and viewing transformations (as the actual *mappings*). The window-to-viewport mapping is simply the highest level of a so-called *graphical transformation* T that is the ordered pair $< G, R >$. Here G is

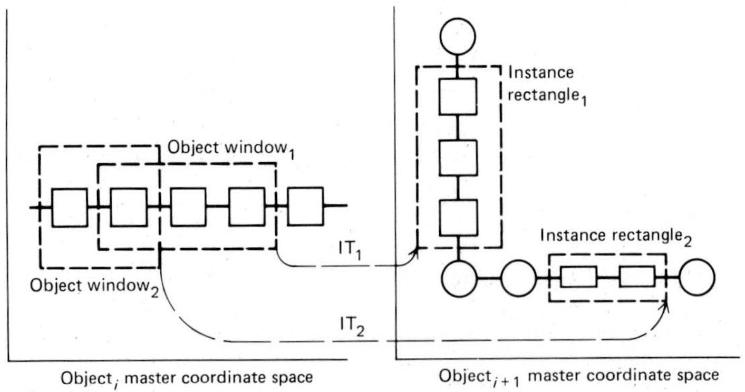

Fig. 9.30 Clipping in object coordinates: $IR_1 = OW_1 * IT_1$, $IR_2 = OW_2 * IT_2$.

the geometric mapping and R is the restriction of the domain. The complete window-to-viewport mapping, including clipping, is simply

$$< W \rightarrow VP, W > ,$$

where the first element is the mapping and the second is the window region. Similarly, the instancing of a clipped subobject$_i$ in higher level master subobject$_{i+1}$ is

$$< IT_{i,\, i+1}, OW_i > ,$$

where $IT_{i,\, i+1}$ is the instance transformation from level i to level $i + 1$, given that a leaf is at level 0, and OW_i is the *object window,* i.e., the domain restriction in the object$_i$ master coordinate system.

These graphical transformations have the fortuitous property that they may be composed in such a way that all geometric mappings in all regions are composed, resulting in a single composite G_{comp} transformation. The mathematics also shows that we may clip in master coordinates to a composite region R_{comp}, generalizing our previous results. In essence, this avoids the brute-force sequence of "clip to object window, transform clipped object, clip to object window at the next level, transform, clip", etc. The result is a composite graphical transformation

$$T_{comp} = < G_{comp}, R_{comp} >$$

Figure 9.31 shows how clipping regions are compounded. The composite region of a subobject is initialized to the object window in its master coordinate system. It is then transformed to the instancing subobject (i.e., into the instance rectangle) where it is intersected with its object window, forming, in general, a convex polygon. (In 3D, the composition yields convex polyhedra, which are even more difficult to visualize and work with.) This composite region is transformed by the instance transformation at the next level where it is again intersected (using a polygon clipper from Chapter 12) with the object window, etc. We can symbolize this at a high level as

$$R_i = (R_{i-1}) * (IT_{i-1,i}) \cap OW_i,$$

i.e., the region at level i is formed by instance transforming all points of the region at level $i-1$ and intersecting that transformed region with the object window at level i

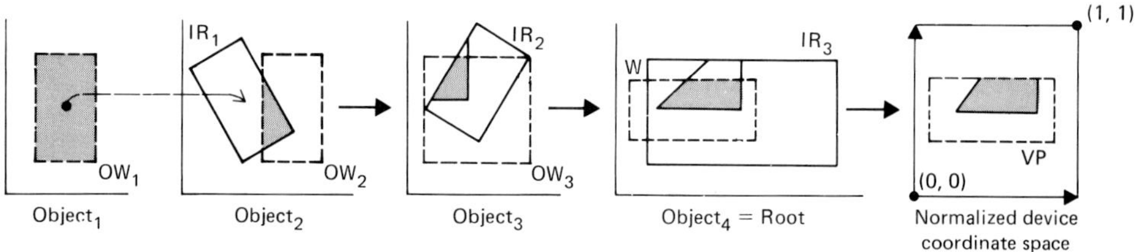

Fig. 9.31 Composite clip region (shaded) for Object$_1$ at successively higher levels.

When the final intersection against the viewport takes place, the transformed master object coordinates can then be clipped by using the same polygon clipper. The only way to avoid polygon clipping is to prevent rotation and shearing or to use the brute-force algorithm to clip against upright object windows, transform, clip, etc. (see Fig. 9.32). Another possible improvement is to clip in master coordinates to avoid transforming invisible primitives, by composing clipping regions from the viewport *down* to the object window in the object's master coordinate system. The composite region at level_i is then the image of the higher-level composite under the inverse of the instance transformation, intersected with the object window:

$$R_i = (R_{i+1} * \mathrm{IT}^{-1}_{i,\,i+1}) \cap \mathrm{OW}_i.$$

This strategy is clearly out of the question in 3D for all but nonoblique parallel projections.

Figure 9.33 shows a variety of simple cases of intersecting instance rectangle_{i-1} and object window_i. In general, if an intersection is ever empty, none of the object need be transformed and clipped, as was the case with extents. If the transformed composite region falls entirely within the object window, we cannot simply do a

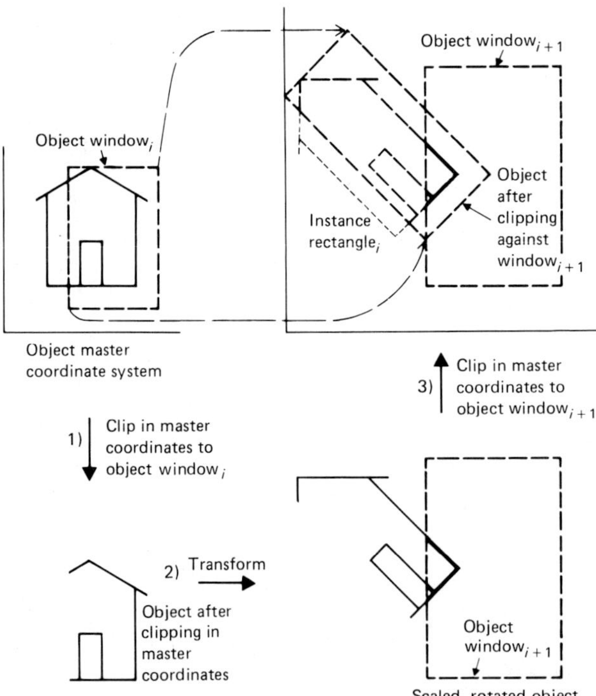

Fig. 9.32 Clip–rotate–clip sequence; the effect would be the same if the rotated object were clipped against the triangular region $\mathrm{IR}_i \cap \mathrm{OW}_{i+1}$.

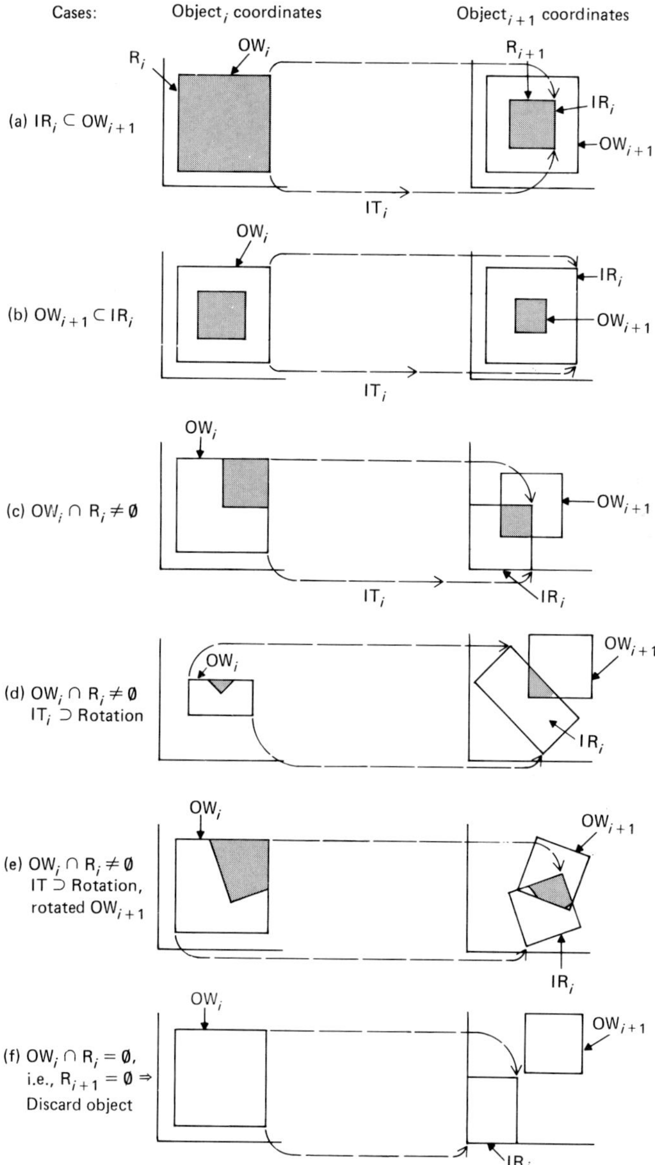

Fig. 9.33 Window compounding. From bottom up: new composite region equals intersection of old region transformed and OW_{i+1}, i.e., $R_{i+1} = (R_i \cdot IT) \cap OW_{i+1}$; from top down: new composite region equals intersection of old region and OW_i, i.e., $R_i = (R_{i+1} \cdot IT^{-1}) \cap OW_i$.

trivial accept, as with extents; we must transform and clip, since the new composite region is still a clipping region. Extents therefore are less powerful than object windows in that they allow clipping only at the root level, but they are far more practical because of their efficiency in clipping for trivial accepts. Extents, object windows, and adaptive clipping may all be combined to yield a complex but powerful and efficient traverser (Exercise 9.18).

An interesting variation on the notion of arbitrary clipping regions at any level in a hierarchy is that of *shielding,* also known as blanking. A shielded region is one in which no new information is allowed so as to preserve the appearance of what is already there. Thus an inverse clip is done—only primitives falling outside the region are allowed and those intersecting it are clipped at the edge, with the portion outside retained. Business graphics and page layout applications make use of this technique, for example, to prevent overwriting photographs or logos, or to create visually interesting effects. Usually the shielding occurs at the time window-to-viewport mapping is done, just before the device coordinate segment is created. A typical use of this feature is to superimpose a legend on a map or a plot. The map and legend viewports overlap but because the legend viewport is also defined as a shielded region, it will be protected. With bit map raster graphics shielding can be implemented with priorities (see Section 11.9).

Finally, the GKS *workstation* concept [ISO81] allows a second clipping/mapping operation to take place post-viewing, in NDC space. Essentially it may be thought of as taking a snapshot of the NDC "bulletin board" and then posting it via the workstation transformation on the physical display device. The two clipping regions in WC and NDC space may be composed to clip to the intersecting rectangle in NDC or PDC.

9.14 SUMMARY

In this chapter we have examined various means for representing logical subdivisions of objects into their components. Trade-offs between various model representations in the data structure procedure-hierarchy continuum were briefly examined, as were DPU hardware versus graphics package software solutions. As might be expected, practical systems contain a mix of hardware and software and have multiple hierarchical representations ranging from full application model to special-purpose symbol system to achieve optimal price/performance. Graphical data structures or (application-data-free) structured display files were shown to allow maximum flexibility for run-time dynamics, especially when combined with segmented linear display files for refreshing.

The concept of the current transformation matrix (CTM) and its use during top–down traversal of the hierarchy were found to lie at the heart of a modeling system. Given a general hierarchical data or (symbol) procedure structure, the traverser turned out to be a simple iterative or recursive tree traverser which compounded instance transformations in the CTM by using a stack. By examining various strategies for optimal ordering of clipping and geometric transforming operations, we then saw that many individual modeling and viewing operations could be collapsed into a single clipping operation and a single matrix transformation for 2D and a single clip and two transformations for 3D. Finally, extent definitions were used to speed up trivial accept and reject tests for entire objects, eliminating much unnecessary processing of subobjects: for trivial accept, clipping of subobjects and primitives could be avoided; for trivial reject, traversal, transformation and the entire viewing pipeline for object components could be eliminated.

EXERCISES

9.1 Investigate the use of modeling and simulation in an area of your choice and try to characterize the model in terms of its formal description (e.g., sets of simultaneous linear equations with adjustable coefficients, with input and output variables of your choice).

9.2 Construct the tree diagram for an object hierarchy in an area of your choice and then pseudocode the data structure (and associated procedures) defining the application model. Try to fit a complete application for processing this hierarchy to the conceptual model of Fig. 9.1 and describe any areas of mismatch.

9.3 Discuss how the associativity of matrix multiplication allows both bottom-up construction and top-down traversal for display purposes of master/instance object hierarchies. Show how instance transformations can be viewed as a change of coordinate systems. Give an example of the utility of allowing geometric master-to-master placement transformations at any level in the hierarchy, prior to instance transforming.

9.4 Implement a 2D or 3D CTM manipulation package to interface with SGP, including "the hook."

9.5 Implement the data structure traverser for the two-level linked-list structure of Fig. 9.9.

9.6 Read the original Sutherland paper on Sketchpad [SUTH63] and contrast the implementation with what has been presented in this chapter. How can his drawing constraint relations between primitives (e.g., lines parallel, of equal lengths, at specified angles, etc.) be added to our software? For example, should they be strictly in the domain of the application program (in the data structure) or should they be in SGP (as well)? Discuss the advantages of the various methods for encoding hierarchy in terms of the ease with which constraints are encoded and processed.

9.7 What sort of facilities should a general-purpose DPU have to process rather flexible graphical data structures?

9.8 Take an application area you are quite familiar with which involves more than a single level of hierarchy and discuss which type of encoding (display procedure, application program procedure, symbol, graphical data structure, structured display file, etc.) is most suitable in terms of the processing that is to be done. Take into account space–time trade-offs, flexibility, the need for rapid update response and binding time, etc. Pseudocode the application, remembering that one should design from the set of requirements derived from user-level interactions.

9.9 Design an extension to SGP which would permit segment editing of a) groups or even b) primitives for the DPU of Chapter 3. Consider both the calls and their implementation (at least at the pseudocode level).

9.10 Show how to implement GPGS-style block-structured *pick_id*'s in SGP.

9.11 If you have a relational database system available, write a simple application such as a program that allows the user to draw arbitrary combinations of triangles and squares, by using the database to hold the modeling information.

9.12 Show how to map attribute handling for the DPU of your choice in a consistent and useful manner to SGP facilities, not necessarily those of the Core.

9.13 Quantify the trade-offs in clipping in master coordinates, world coordinates, and screen coordinates for a flowchart drawing application. Make reasonable assumptions about the number of primitives, higher-level objects, etc., and obtain some running-time estimates for typical user situations.

9.14 Given a 2D application and upright windows and viewports, what is the optimal clipping strategy?

9.15 Write a simple algorithm for creating and clipping to upright extents.

9.16 Devise a clipping algorithm by using nonupright extents directly (a) in 2D, (b) in 3D.

9.17 Contrast the 3D algorithm for Exercise 9.16(b) with that required to implement the following upright surrounding extent algorithm (developed by J. Michener):

Let $A = (a_1, a_2, a_3)$ and $B = (b_1, b_2, b_3)$ denote any two opposite corners of an extent in an object's master coordinate system. Let

$$P = \begin{bmatrix} p_{11} & p_{12} & p_{13} \\ p_{21} & p_{22} & p_{23} \\ p_{31} & p_{32} & p_{33} \end{bmatrix}$$

be a rotation/shear/scale (linear) instance transformation which maps the master coordinate system to the world coordinate system (modulo translation).

$A \cdot P$ and $B \cdot P$ are two of the eight corners of the transformed local extent. The maximal and minimal x, y, and z coordinates among the right corners of the transformed local extent determine the upright surrounding extent. The following pseudocode algorithm determines *min* and *max* which are opposite corners of the upright surrounding extent:

```
min := max := A · P                    {plus any translation}
for i :=  1 to 3 by 1 do
  for j = 1 to 3 by 1 do
    begin
      temp = (B[i] − A[i]) · P[i,j];
      if temp > 0 then
        max[j] = max[j] + temp
      else min[j] = min[j] + temp
    end
```

The algorithm uses only nine comparisons and nine multiplications—the same number of multiplications as needed for B · P. The algorithm does not depend on $a_i < b_i$, so A and B can be any opposite corners. The algorithm is similar in spirit to the simplex method of linear programming—with six objective functions (min and max x, y, and z).

9.18 a) Write pseudocode for a general-purpose 2D hierarchy traverser that handles attributes and uses extents to do adaptive clipping.

b) Add an object window facility.

c) How does one test a CTM to see if it contains rotation or shear?

d) How could shielding be added?

9.19 Turn Example 9.4(a) into legal Pascal.

9.20 Implement the n-level correlation map discussed in Section 9.7. Can the parental pointers be eliminated by gathering "lineage" information during the correlation search?

9.21 To implement boxing in display procedures, one can either include an extent attribute in the declaration of a procedure or include an extent statement in the procedure body. In the latter case, it can have arguments which are functions of the parameters passed to the display procedure to determine its size, orientation, and location. Show how this facility might be compiled (say to symbolic Pascal code) which interfaces to a graphics package with an extent test mechanism.

9.22 Consider another useful trivial reject mechanism for correlation based on (x, y) locator comparison: divide the window into, say, a 4×4 matrix of sectors. For each leaf or subobject node, a record can then be kept of which sectors it passes through in a 16-bit *sectorcode* word which is an extension of the 4-bit outcode. Then one takes the sectorcode for the backmapped locator point in world coordinate space and **and**s it with the sectorcode words of each leaf and subobject for a quick trivial reject. Show how this algorithm can be usefully combined with extent testing. Should the sector test be done before or after the extent test?

9.23 Examine the tradeoffs in having symbol and "structure" systems versus just having a "synthetic camera" approach to graphics, leaving modeling to the application programmer. How can SDF architectures be best supported/taken advantage of? How should editing and attribute binding be handled in symbol/structure systems? The standard literature produced by ANSI and ISO committees provides much useful discussion on these complex issues.

10 Advanced Display Architecture

10.1 INTRODUCTION

In Chapter 3 we examined the system architecture of a simple DPU for refresh vector graphics that is typical of a large class of relatively inexpensive, straightforward displays. In Chapter 9 we took a brief look at a more sophisticated architecture capable of traversing - in real time - a modeling hierarchy containing a reasonably large number of vectors, while maintaining a flicker-free display. This was accomplished by separating hierarchy traversal from display refresh; refreshing is done either from a buffer containing a segmented linear display file holding the clipped, window-to-viewport mapped view of the model, or from an equivalent bit map representation of the image. This chapter examines other architectures of some typical refresh vector displays, while Chapter 12 treats those features unique to raster display architecture. However, many features of vector systems and the model we use below to describe vector systems apply to most raster systems as well, especially those which support a local display file and DPU in addition to the bit map refresh buffer. Therefore, unless otherwise noted, the discussion applies to both vector and raster systems.

10.2 BACKGROUND

The incremental growth of DPU features described in Chapter 3 mirrors an actual progression in DPU architecture design which is readily noticeable in the historical evolution of both commercial and experimental display systems. The user's tendency to want the increased functionality and/or power made available by spending "just a little more money" for increased hardware has been described in an engaging paper by Myer and Sutherland [MYER68]. They used the term *wheel of reincarna-*

tion to describe the process of adding successively more arithmetic and logic/decision-making capability via extra registers and instructions into the DPU until it becomes essentially a full-fledged CPU. This CPU-like DPU then acquires its own rudimentary DPU, starting the next incremental growth cycle. The authors characterized a number of then-popular display systems in terms of the number of times each design had gone around the wheel, and prescribed some guidelines for desirable stopping points.

The purpose of enriching the DPU is to enhance its performance—for example, increasing its ability to handle more complex display file structures and commands, to display larger numbers of output primitives without flicker, and especially to offload from the host CPU time-consuming tasks which bog down the CPU and prevent quick response to a user's request for a change to the model and/or its image. The wheel of reincarnation for display processor design is analogous to the trend to offload mainframes (and even minicomputers) by distributing "intelligence" to I/O controllers, thereby making the controllers more capable and independent of the mainframe. As an example, IBM I/O channels are in fact special-purpose programmed CPUs with easily as much power as the mainframe itself, and CDC's peripheral processing units are minicomputers. Similarly, microprocessors are often embedded in disk controllers to handle the many options and exceptions inherent in disk I/O. In the coming age of inexpensive logic and memory, the tendency to decentralize computing power and make intelligent microprocessor-based peripherals will accelerate. (The computer industry labels any device with a (micro) processor inside as intelligent, whether it appears so to the user or not.) Graphic system architecture is a prime candidate for such functional specialization, primarily because the performance gains are so noticeable to the user and also because the tasks to be done are well-defined and repetitive.

In an ideal world of zero-cost logic and memory, which tasks would we choose to implement with special-purpose hardware and which with software running on general-purpose hardware? Because interactive graphics is so performance-sensitive, we would choose to carry out both the output and the input transformations (from model to image and from user action to model modification) in hardware, provided we could exercise some choices about the structure of the model, the interaction dialogue, etc. In essence, we would want to implement the standard algorithms of the entire output and input pipelines in customizable hardware for maximum performance. Thus we would be able to combine flicker-free display with dynamic updating of an application model and its views. More specifically, we would combine the best features of a flicker-free storage display with dynamic, selective updating. Such updating would be accomplished, as in Chapter 9, by retraversing and reprocessing the model every time the user made a change in it or in the viewing specification. Ideally, the viewing operation (especially for raster displays) should allow not only the standard planar geometric projections discussed in Chapter 8 but also hidden line or surface elimination, lighting and shading calculations, and the other forms of processing used to produce realistic-looking images of the type to be discussed in Chapters 14–16.

At present, however, only very expensive computer-generated imagery systems for airplane and ship simulators come close to fulfilling this far-reaching desire, since the algorithms for producing realistic pictures are computationally extremely time-consuming. This is especially true for hidden-surface removal (Chapter 15) and shading/lighting models (Chapter 16). We will therefore restrict this chapter to a discussion of architectural features for doing model traversal and display of 2D and 3D "wire-frame" objects without hidden-surface elimination and other advanced realism effects, since hardware to handle modeling and viewing of wire-frame objects is within the current state of the art for the mass market.

By and large, the designs of commercially available products have been motivated primarily by a bottom-up concern with cost-effective hardware technology that meets performance constraints and not by a more general top-down, "software-first" strategy based on user requirements. A proper top-down strategy would not only include cost-effectiveness and performance, but would also take into account programmability and extensibility. The preoccupation with hardware is understandable in the light of the concern with performance, as measured only by the number of elements processed per refresh cycle for a flicker-free display. Another contributing factor is the lack of software standardization in the graphics field. As the first software standards like the Core System are promulgated (e.g., ISO's GKS [ISO81]), we hope to see greater standardization at the architecture level to support the Core and other high-level packages such as those for hierarchical modeling discussed in the previous chapter. Indeed, manufacturers are already supporting much of a Core-like package in firmware (microcode) or even in hardware so as to present a high-performance, high-level interface to a graphics program in the host. The host then is relieved from much processing, especially that of the output pipeline.

Commercial systems are thus the product of many hardware design compromises between speed, flexibility, and cost. These compromises depend upon a given manufacturer's design philosophy and intended marketplace; choices include vector refresh versus raster refresh versus storage tube systems, 2D only versus 2D and 3D, stand-alone versus satellite, and a primitive architecture focused on displaying the maximum number of simple DPU primitives versus a more complete architecture which includes support for modeling, viewing, clipping, and image transformations.

Because of the differing orientations and the lack of generally accepted and meaningful benchmarks, it has been very difficult to compare the relative performance of any two systems. Carlbom has developed performance modeling techniques for the quantitative analysis of the architectures of vector systems, as well as for benchmarking their performance as a function of an application-oriented instruction mix and their architectural characteristics [CARL80]. Her techniques can be carried over to raster graphics architecture with only minor changes. As with any computer performance evaluation, the application of this model requires a significant understanding of the internals of the architecture and the implementation details. Without going to that level of detail, we next describe some of today's most common architectures and some of their major qualitative differences in capability and performance.

We will use the approach of incrementally adding features to modify the simple DPU presented in Chapter 3 so that ultimately it evolves to the level of the system shown in Fig. 9.11 for doing model traversal and the entire viewing operation. (These increments do not reflect a strict historical progression.) We will also briefly discuss host-satellite configurations which include a division of labor between the time-shared host and the dedicated graphics satellite computer.

10.3 THE SIMPLE REFRESH DISPLAY

Many types of hardware enhancements to the primitive DPU of Chapter 3 are found in commercial systems today. The most important of these are additional primitives and attributes, a more comprehensive set of input devices and pick support, more flexibility in specifying coordinate values, and DPU subroutining.

10.3.1 Primitives

Among the additional primitives commonly found are the following:

- Analog or digital circle and circular arc generators or more general conic-section generators and parametric-curve generators (Chapter 13);
- Line primitives, such as *DRAW_FROM*(x, y) which draws from the specified point to the DPU's CP and leaves the beam at the CP, for efficient specification of lines sharing a common endpoint;
- 2D and 3D autoincrement vectors which advance one or two coordinates by fixed increments (either positive or negative) while altering the others by absolute or relative coordinate values. This facility is useful for plotting regular graphs and surfaces and saves the space otherwise used to specify the incremented coordinates;
- The polyline primitive to draw a sequence of connected line segments (*ABS_MOVE* followed by a sequence of *REL_DRAW*s or *ABS_DRAW*s, etc.); a polygon is a simple closed polyline, or a filled area in raster systems;
- Disconnected lines, equivalent to a sequence of *ABS_MOVE, REL_DRAW* pairs.

10.3.2 Attributes

Many different attributes (and their mode-setting registers and commands) exist currently. The most common of these include:

- Brightness or color—regulating the intensity of the beam(s);
- Line style—variations on dotting, dashing, and endpoints-only produced by blanking (turning off) and unblanking the beam as it is deflected in vector systems, or depositing an appropriate pattern of pixel values as the line is scan-converted in a raster system;

- Blinking or other highlighting features;
- Light pen detectability of vectors, characters and other primitives.

10.3.3 Data Addressing Modes

In contrast to the DPU of Chapter 3, many systems allow both immediate data and indirectly addressed data modes:

- Immediate coordinate values may be specified in various storage-efficient long and short ("packed") modes to accommodate long and short vectors, both absolute and relative.
- Similarly, coordinates in several long and short formats may be addressed through one (or more) levels of indirection. The advantages of addressed data are that different instructions can operate on the same coordinate data and that coordinate data can be changed easily by the application program. To see this, consider the line drawing of Fig. 10.1, and suppose that the application program which creates this drawing requires that the lines meet at point *A*, no matter where *A* is positioned (or repositioned). A DPU with only immediate operands (and no MOVE/DRAW_FROM primitive) will have two occurrences of point *A*'s coordinates: one for line *BA* and one for lines *DA* and *AC*. Repositioning *A* requires four changes in the DPU program, as shown in Fig. 10.2. With most graphics packages that do not allow segment editing, these changes can be made only by deleting and then recreating the segment containing this group of output primitives.

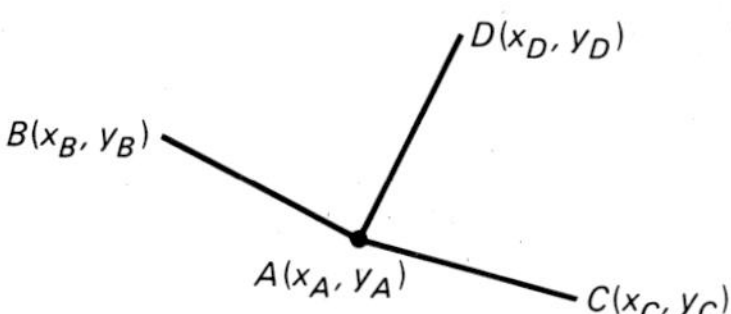

Fig. 10.1 Joined lines sharing common endpoint *A*.

Comments	Instruction	Data
Line *BA*:	LDXA	x_B
	LDYAM	y_B
	LDXA	x_A
	LDYAL	y_A
Line *DA*:	LDXA	x_D
	LDYAM	y_D
	LDXA	x_A
	LDYAL	y_A
Line *AC*:	LDXA	x_C
	LDYAL	y_C

(Bracketed: the two x_A, y_A pairs — Immediate data which must be changed if *A* is moved)

Fig. 10.2 DPU code using immediate data for coordinates.

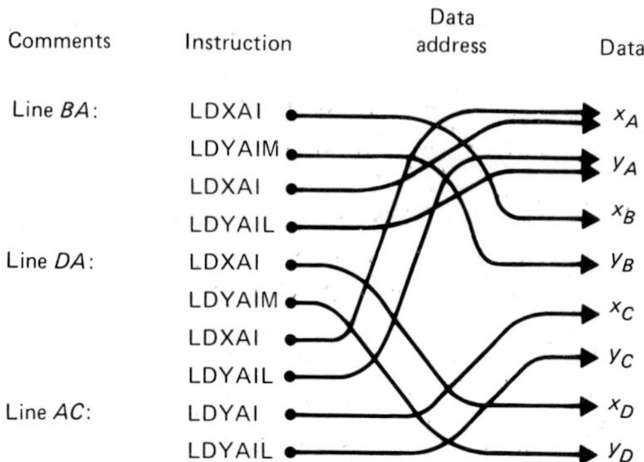

Fig. 10.3 DPU code with addressed data—addresses shown as pointers.

If, instead, the instructions contain addresses for coordinate operands, as in Fig. 10.3, the problem of updating the DPU program when A moves is much simpler, because only the referenced data values need be changed, not the DPU instructions themselves. If the DPU program is stored in a memory shared by the DPU and a host computer, this updating can be done very simply, because the addresses given for x_A and y_A can be the application data structure's memory locations for x_A and y_A. If the application program updates the data structure by performing an assignment into the variable whose address is in the line-drawing instruction, the DPU program is automatically updated, and the graphics package need not be invoked! The technique works equally well whether an endpoint is referenced once or many times. With multiple references, as in the example at hand, the constraint of matching endpoints is very nicely maintained automatically. The disadvantage of this scheme is the memory cost of the additional address references; immediate data is therefore preferred for images which needn't be frequently updated. ([CARL80] gives quantitative guidelines for the use of addressed data.) The graphics package must let the programmer indicate when an address is being passed and when immediate data is being passed.

To accomplish this communication, two concerns must be addressed. First, the DPU need not be traversing continually, as in the case of a storage display or the high-performance displays discussed below which have both a structured display file for modeling and a (segmented) linear display file for refreshing. In this case, the application program will also have to cause the DPU to traverse the DPU program (e.g., the SDF) in order to make the changes appear on the display. Second, the address linkage between variables in the application program and the DPU line-drawing instructions must be established by the assembler at assembly time, by the linkage editor before program execution begins, or by the graphics subroutine package at execution time.

■ In another variation on addressed data, some systems have registers which can be loaded with coordinate data either by input devices or under CPU program control; these registers can be specified in DPU instructions as sources of coordinate data operands for dynamic selective updating. For example, the dragging function can be easily implemented by having the absolute move at the start of a segment use the DPU's locator registers as the source of its operands. Variables accessible by the host CPU or input device registers that can be used directly by the DPU for coordinate values are sometimes called *dynamic variables.*

10.3.4 Text Facilities

Two typical extensions of the rather crude facilities of the DPU discussed in Chapter 3 are:

- Characters in more than one size, orientation (e.g., horizontal or vertical), style (e.g., italics produced by shearing the character), or spacing. Note in Fig. 10.4 the difference between character orientation and character-string orientation.

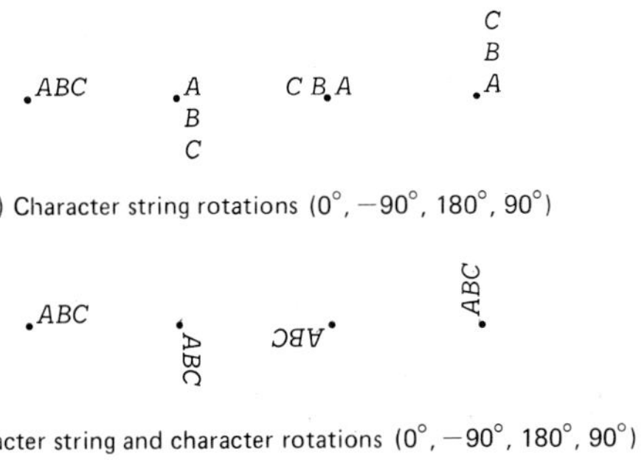

(a) Character string rotations (0°, −90°, 180°, 90°)

(b) Character string and character rotations (0°, −90°, 180°, 90°)

Fig. 10.4 Character versus character-string orientation (the CP is shown by a dot).

- "User-programmable fonts" in which special characters or entire fonts (character sets) can be specified as patterns to be loaded (or "burned") in the memory used by the character generator. Even simple application-specific symbols such as standard shapes used for circuit layout, flowcharting, or command and control applications may be economically generated in this way.

10.3.5 DPU Subroutine Capability

The DPU (display) subroutine facility is directly analogous to a CPU subroutine jump/return mechanism and is typically implemented by using a pushdown stack to save the return addresses. In more sophisticated displays, the DPU can save some or all of its state information, such as DPU registers and DPU attribute and mode flags. Each DPU subroutine describes an image and may be thought of as a segment; as the term is used in SGP, the Core System and this book, segments can contain output primitives only, but it is convenient to extend the notion so that segments may contain calls to lower-level segments as well as output primitives. Display systems with DPU subroutining thus make available a facility for segment/image hierarchy in which one can very efficiently display a diagram consisting of multiple copies of standard components: the calling segment contains an absolute move followed by a jump to the image subroutine composed of relative draws for each repeated image (Fig. 10.5). (If image transformations are available, we need not use this "relocatable" subroutine trick.)

We refer to DPU subroutining as *image hierarchy*. The temptation is strong to think of it as an object hierarchy since images can call images as deeply as the push-down stack will allow; this is inaccurate, however, because DPU subroutining takes place in image space, i.e., device coordinate space, *after* any modeling transforms and the entire viewing operation, including clipping, have been applied by the graphics package. Also, objects need not map one-to-one to segments (or images), depending on how segments and the viewing operation are specified, and therefore any object hierarchy need not map to a corresponding image hierarchy.

One can use DPU subroutining as a rudimentary modeling system to create an object hierarchy *only* if one is willing to treat the DPU's coordinate system as the world coordinate system, have translation as the only instance transformation, and disallow clipping to a window. Then the entire image space "world" is in view, but wraparound may occur if a subroutined image is translated to the edge of the screen. Many simple applications can be implemented with these restrictions; however, when they are too confining and a software package supporting general modeling hierarchy is needed, the subroutine facility cannot, unfortunately, be utilized *at all.*

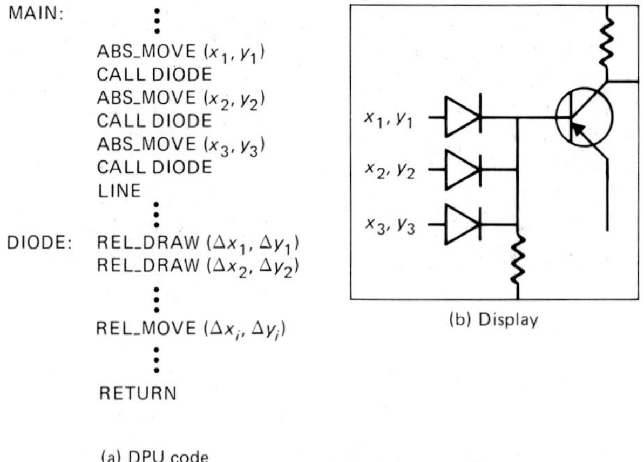

Fig. 10.5 Partially completed circuit showing three uses of the diode incremental subroutine. The resistors would be drawn in the same way.

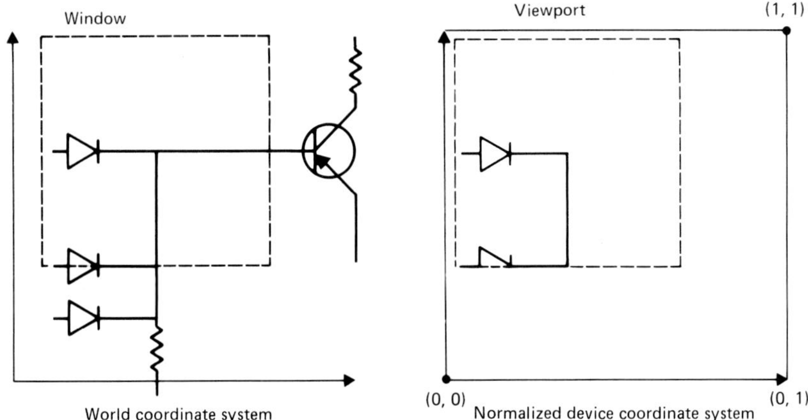

Fig. 10.6 A window on a modeling hierarchy mapping two instances of the same diode master to two distinct DPU code segments representing them (four lines for the one wholly included, three for the one partially included).

This disappointing result is due to the fact that general instance transformations followed by clipping may result in the compilation of different DPU code for each instance of an object master (Fig. 10.6). This prevents the "obvious" mapping of an object master to a DPU image "master." Only if hardware support for world coordinate transformations (which take place before the viewing operation) is available can we make use of DPU subroutining for modeling—in effect, we have then built up the DPU to a structured display file level (Section 10.5). Note also that if the DPU does not have facilities for saving and restoring attributes and modes, there is no clean mechanism for passing and resetting attributes in the image hierarchy equivalent to that advocated for the modeling hierarchy of Chapter 9.

Finally, inexpensive displays can make good use of DPU subroutining for software character generation. High-quality stroke or bit map definitions of characters in any desired font can be stored as display subroutines and invoked via a fast subroutine jump which stores only the return address.

10.3.6 Pick Correlation Hardware for Vector Displays

Correlation software was discussed in Sections 4.3.4 and 9.7. A name register supports a single level of naming, when there are no display subroutines. Inside a diode segment we would then find DPU code such as

```
DIODE: LOAD NAME_REG(segment_name)
       REL_DRAW( , )
       REL_DRAW( , )
           .
           .
           .
```

When the DPU halts, the pick software obtains the segment name simply by reading the name register. If n-level display subroutines are supported, the name register is easily generalized by using a separate pushdown stack for image names or by stacking names along with the return addresses (and segment attributes and other state information). The correlation mechanism can then return the sequence of names to the application program which can, for example, highlight the successive segments/objects in the tree to allow the user to identify the object actually intended to be picked. In this manner it is possible, if desired, to progress up the hierarchy from a leaf node to the root. If there is no separate name stack, this correlation logic is a bit more complex because the names must be distinguished from the other information on the stack. Name stacking implements the block-structured naming conventions mentioned for modeling hierarchies in Section 9.7.

Correlation in raster displays is typically based on (x, y) comparison of physical locator values.

10.4 VECTOR TRANSFORMATIONS AND CLIPPING IN IMAGE SPACE

The next set of additions to the DPU to be discussed are typically used to provide some type of support for general transformations and clipping in 2D device coordinate (image) space. As with DPU subroutining, these operations take place after the software viewing operation which includes world coordinate space clipping. Simple software packages may provide only such raw image space coordinates and operations, leaving the task of implementing modeling and viewing capabilities to the programmer. Image operations on raster bit maps are rather different from those for vector displays since they operate on individual pixels—these are discussed in Chapters 11 and 12.

10.4.1 Image Transformations

Image transformations operate on transformed, clipped device coordinate image space, and are not to be confused with world coordinate instance transformations applied before viewing in a structured display file DPU (Section 10.5). Originally provided via analog circuits, they are now implemented in less expensive, more reliable digital logic. Integer addition and multiplication are used to transform twenty thousand or more endpoints per refresh cycle. The usual transformations are translation (which affects absolute as well as relative coordinates and obviates the need for the ABS_MOVE, REL_DRAW trick for placing instances via DPU subroutines), scaling, and rotation. Rotation is a bit more complex than translation and scaling in that it involves more coordinate transformation arithmetic. Transformations are typically specified via transformation registers which can be written (and read out) by the DPU. The transformation register values are calculated by the graphics package and stored in the segment headers as the operands of load-register instructions. These cause the DPU to load the transformation registers when a segment is entered. The DPU executes these load instructions each time it refreshes a segment. More sophisticated DPUs may have additional facilities for saving, composing, and restoring image transformation values and for making them available to the graphics package for storage in the application data structure. By using a display subroutining facility, the DPU then traverses an image hierarchy and composes the image transformation stored in each called segment's header with the equivalent of a CTM stored in the set of transformation registers. After the third-dimension (z) value has been determined, it may be used for a form of depth cueing by interpreting the z signal as intensity modulation—the larger the value of z, the dimmer the beam (see Chapter 14).

10.4.2 Scissoring and Quadrant Selection

Several ways of dealing with wraparound, varying in expense and power, have been made available in display systems in the past. The first scheme is relatively simple and is known as *scissoring, blanking,* or *clamping.* Instead of using X,Y beam coordinate registers with the same number of bits as are needed for the resolution of the monitor (typically 10 or 12 bits), additional high-order bits are provided. This allows additions of coordinates of relative vectors to carry into the 13th or higher bit without causing digital overflow, while absolute commands still affect only the low-order 10 or 12 bits. The vector generator driven from these registers may then produce beam position voltages from such extended coordinates which correspond to positions outside the visible screen area. However, the voltages passed to the X and Y deflection amplifiers (or those passed from the deflection amplifiers to the CRT monitor coils) are *clamped* at the window edge by analog *clamping circuits* (also called *clipping circuits*) which prevent the voltages from exceeding the thresholds which correspond to the screen edges (Fig. 10.7(a)). At the same time, the beam is turned off (blanked) until it returns from the window edge (Fig. 10.7(b)).

The effect is equivalent to that of a screen embedded in a larger space, as if the blanked beam were able to travel outside the screen area and return. As long as incrementing the registers will not cause overflow, the beam will return properly and the image will be correct, i.e., as if clipped, as in Fig. 10.7(b). If the registers do overflow, wraparound occurs in the containing space and, when the beam returns to the viewing area, in the viewing area as well (Fig. 10.7(c)).

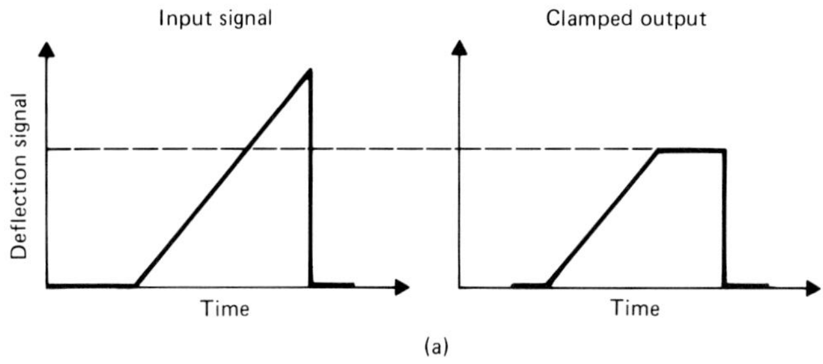

Fig. 10.7(a) Voltage clamping (clipping).

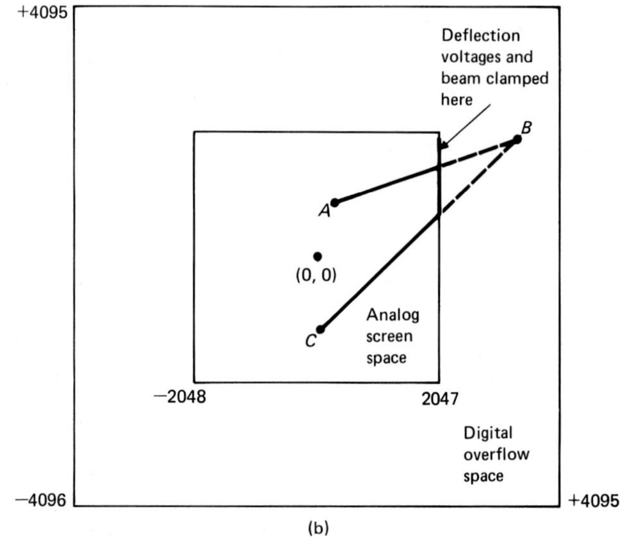

Fig. 10.7(b) Clamping handling overflow of screen space.

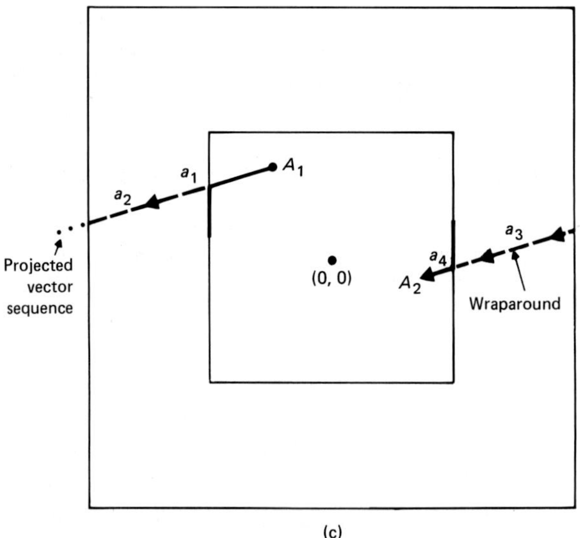

Fig. 10.7(c) Wraparound in overflow space producing undesirable results in screen space.

This technique has several shortcomings. It requires the vector generator to produce signals lying outside the range corresponding to the screen region, and this is time-consuming. It also requires expensive analog circuitry to deflect vectors linearly and repeatably over the wider range. In effect, the time spent on processing invisible lines is not spent productively, and this reduces the number of visible lines which can be drawn without flicker.

In a second scheme, called quadrant selection, the programmer sets up registers to select any 12 contiguous bits from the X and Y registers to define the location of the screen in a 16-bit coordinate space. This is more general than the previous technique of just restricting the screen to the center of a 1- or 2-bit larger coordinate system. In effect, the programmer now thinks of image space as a $2^{16} \times 2^{16}$ plane from which a $2^n \times 2^n$ square can be selected for display. For example, selecting the high-order 12 bits drops the four low-order bits' worth of resolution to give an overview of the entire coordinate plane on the screen, scaled down by a factor of 16. Conversely, the 16-bit coordinate values can be treated as consisting of two components: the 12 lower-order bits that specify coordinates in a screen-sized square and the four higher-order bits that specify the location of that square on an image plane consisting of a grid of 16 × 16 squares, each of screen size. Thus the 16-bit coordinates (1011*xxxxxxxxxxxx*, 0011*yyyyyyyyyyyy*) in the square whose origin is at point (1011, 0011) in the grid, map on the screen to (*xxxxxxxxxxxx*, *yyyyyyyyyyyy*). Picking 12 bits in the middle yields lower resolution (due to dropping the low-order bits) for a larger square located at the point specified by the dropped upper bits.

A crude combination of panning and scaling is thus implemented in this second scheme, but in a 2D image space, and with panning and scaling not independent of each other. Furthermore, neither of these schemes totally prevents wraparound, allows the window to be of arbitrary size or location in the larger coordinate system, or supports viewporting—the pseudo-clipping effects are achieved by simple digital field selection and/or analog manipulation rather than by algorithmic clipping as part of a general viewing operation applied to 2D or 3D world coordinates. These schemes are therefore rather limited in their usefulness and are becoming obsolete.

10.5 HIGH-PERFORMANCE DISPLAYS WITH MODELING TRANSFORMATIONS AND VIEWING OPERATION

10.5.1 Adding Transformations

Thus far, the additions to the Chapter 3 DPU provide powerful output generation features, but we are still restricted to an integer or fractional image coordinate system (typically ranging from 10 to 16 bits for coordinate representation, to be plotted on a screen with resolution from 10 to 12 bits), rudimentary clipping, and no general window-to-viewport mapping. Significant software may be required to compensate for missing features, and some hardware features (for example, display subroutining or image space clipping) may not even be usable by general-purpose modeling/viewing software.

The next major improvement therefore is to implement DPU support for a full modeling/viewing pipeline. These advanced architectures were mentioned briefly in Section 9.6. The first step in this process is to add a structured display file capability for traversing an object hierarchy and composing instance transformations. Next we add a full viewing operation with 2D and 3D world coordinate space clipping, perspective and parallel projection for 3D, and window-to-viewport mapping. The transformation hardware is then used both for modeling and for viewing transformations, in the manner of Section 9.10. (Most systems support only modeling/viewing transformations or the simpler image transformations, not both.)

The 4×4 digital *matrix transformation processor* [SUTH68] and the *clipping divider* using the Cohen–Sutherland midpoint clipper described in Section 4.2.1 [SPRO68] were first implemented in 1968. Shortly thereafter this experimental hardware appeared commercially and became less costly and therefore more common with time. While the early units were hard-wired [EVAN71], later units were microprogrammed to reduce cost and increase flexibility [VAND74, VECT78a, VECT78b, EVAN77a, EVAN77b]. Unfortunately, all these systems were based on integer arithmetic, with the world coordinate system restricted to 16-bit integers for the software to take advantage of the hardware.* One would prefer to use a floating-point coordinate system, but the need for speed has prohibited such time-consuming operations until very recently, when hardware performance improvements and creative architecture design made it possible. Announced in mid-1981, the very high performance PS300 system [EVAN81] described below has a floating-point modeling/viewing pipeline. Also, Clark's VLSI Geometry Processor design [CLAR80] holds promise of an inexpensive solution to the problem of implementing a fast floating-point transformation and clipping pipeline. It also clips polygons by using the algorithm developed in Chapter 11.

Another limitation of most current modeling/viewing graphics architectures is that they treat text in a different pipeline from lines—a separate character generator may perform translation, scale, and perhaps even rotation, but only in image coordinates, not in the world coordinate system subject to the full viewing operation. For example, proper perspective images of a truck with letters on its side that is moving across the screen must be obtained by processing the lettering as collections of world coordinate lines/strokes, not as characters displayed by the character generator. The PS300 character generator passes component strokes into the full pipeline in just this way, for maximum flexibility while retaining high speed. In the Core, a distinction is made between the text that can be readily supported by most character generators, which is typically used for putting up menus and prompts on a 2D plane, and text composed of 2D or 3D software characters. The first type is specified with *string-*

*In FGP34 software for the VG34000 there is an initial software clip to a 2D square or 3D cube still in floating-point world coordinates, followed by a mapping to the maximum square or cube in the 16-bit integer coordinate system which the hardware supports and in which the modeling transformation and viewing operation take place [VECT78a].

precision or *character-precision* attributes to produce low- and medium-quality text, respectively; the second is specified as *stroke-precision* text. (The terminology refers to the smallest unit whose position and size can be accurately specified—the smaller the unit, the higher the quality of the text.) Some rudimentary software packages allow the text to be plotted only in physical device coordinates; SGP as a Core subset also is primitive in that it supports only low-quality text, clipped on an all-or-nothing text string basis.

10.5.2 Adding a Display Controller

In the architectures described thus far, the DPU traverses a graphic data structure or structured display file with nested objects (or the more primitive image space DPU subroutine hierarchy) during each refresh cycle, continually reinterpreting the hierarchy. The advantage of this strategy is twofold. First, pick correlation is relatively simple, in that the DPU can be stopped at the point in the hierarchy at which a picked primitive is located. (Actually, a correlation mechanism using buffer addresses (Section 9.7) may require a bit of software to find the exact primitive from the address held by the DPU's instruction counter when it is halted, since the proper address is one or more locations before that in the instruction counter. This happens because most high-performance systems gain speed by overlapping tasks through *hardware pipelining* of separate units. These carry out the separate processes of obtaining world coordinate values (possibly through one or more levels of indirectness), doing the multiplication of the transformation matrix and the vector endpoint, clipping, window-to-viewport mapping and primitive generation. This pipelining typically causes the DPU to be ahead of the vector or character generator.) The second advantage is that selective updating of the hierarchy by the host CPU causes an immediate update on the screen during the next traversal. The real disadvantage of refreshing directly from a structured display file is that the DPU spends a lot of its time in each refresh cycle state-saving and restoring, fetching, decoding, and matrix multiplying in addition to decoding and generating primitives for the vector generator; this preparation of DPU code often causes the vector generator to wait for the DPU (for all but long vectors, in most 1981 systems), and this in turn limits the amount of information which can be displayed without flicker.

The solution proposed in Section 9.6 which became increasingly common in the seventies was to interpose a refresh buffer between the powerful, CPU-like DPU and a much simpler DPU called the *display controller* (DC) in Fig. 9.11. (This evolution is a perfect example of the "wheel of reincarnation.") The DPU cycles through the structured display file to compile a new linear display file from the object hierarchy; meanwhile, the previously-created display file is refreshed by the display controller in a classical double-buffer fashion. The linear display file buffer may allow segmentation for modular updating, just as in the simple DPU of Chapter 3. As an alternative (or even in addition) to the linear display file buffer we can implement a raster bit map/frame buffer, to gain most of the same advantages if scan conversion can be done quickly enough (Section 10.8 below).

As we noted in Section 9.6, this two-processor architecture decouples the update and hierarchy traversal process from the refresh process and lets each run at its own speed. Dynamics requires at least 10 Hz and refreshing at least 30 Hz. By freeing the DPU from refreshing and letting an independent processor traverse a far simpler representation, much larger hierarchies can be displayed flicker-free. Indeed, for nondynamic graphics, the DPU can then be considered a fast "hardware compiler" of arbitrarily large structured display files!

Another advantage of this scheme is the ability to amortize the cost of the complex and expensive DPU by time-sharing it among multiple displays, each refreshed from its own linear display file buffer (or bit map). Occasionally further multiplexing can be added by sharing a single display controller refreshing a segmented linear display file among multiple screens, but this quickly leads to flicker problems (see [FOLE71] for a technique to analyze the flicker-free display capacity of such configurations).

The cost of the two-processor DPU/DC scheme is an intermediate representation (the linear display file or bit map), extra hardware, somewhat slower updating for dynamics (noticeable if it drops below 10 Hz but in that case the single-DPU system would have bad flicker), and more complex correlation for vector systems with a light pen pick. Correlation requires that the linear buffer address obtained from the display controller during a pick be mapped into the corresponding object hierarchy address. Since the two processors are not synchronized, one way to accomplish this is to have the DPU run through the hierarchy again until the counter storing the load address for the refresh buffer is incremented to the buffer address that was returned by the display controller. This complex scheme leads to slow response to a pick. Furthermore, if the CPU alters the structured display file while the time-consuming correlation process is taking place, anomalies may occur—the user may point to the representation of some object whose structured display file definition has already been altered.

As hardware prices continue to drop, we may expect many manufacturers to adopt this architecture for their commercial display systems because it provides the best combination of dynamic updating and flicker-free presentations. They can be expected to increase the number of bits in the integer world coordinate system of the structured display file, and then convert to floating-point when VLSI chips such as the Geometry Processor are readily and cheaply available.

10.6 FUNCTIONAL MODEL FOR HIGH-PERFORMANCE ARCHITECTURES*

10.6.1 The Output Pipeline

The functional model illustrated in Fig. 10.8 was developed as a basis for performance modeling and quantitative comparison of the architecture of modern high-performance vector systems discussed above. The model characterizes systems at a

*The material in this section is largely based on [CARL80].

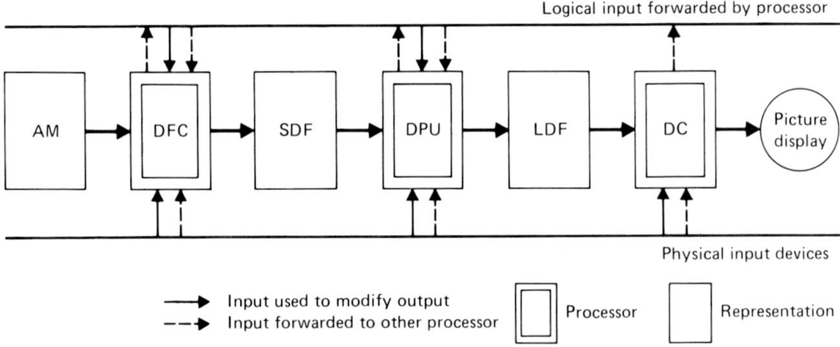

Fig. 10.8 Functional model (from [CARL80]): AM—application model, DFC—display file compiler, SDF—structured display file, DPU—display processing unit, LDF—linear (segmented) display file, DC—display controller.

level of abstraction sufficiently high to hide unimportant implementation details. Unlike other models in the literature, it is capable of describing not only a wide range of equipment, including most raster systems, but also input handling. An alternate conceptual model related to this one but not dealing with performance measurement is proposed in [KILG81].

The functional model consists of a pipeline of logical processors operating on representations of objects. A logical processor in the functional model corresponds to one or more physical processors, and two logical processors in the model may share a physical processor. Similarly, representations may reside in one memory or in different memories.

The *output* pipeline consists of the four representations of objects discussed in Chapter 9:

- The AM (the application model), which contains a description of both graphical and nongraphical properties of a (hierarchical) object in a format determined by the application program and/or modeling package;
- The SDF (the structured display file), which contains a (hierarchical) description of the graphical representation of the object, typically (in 1981) in integer world coordinates or in integer coordinates mapped by software from floating-point world coordinates;
- The LDF (the (segmented) linear display file), which contains graphical primitives and mode settings describing the object produced after modeling and viewing;
- The display screen, which shows the image of the object.

The pipeline also contains three logical processors, each mapping one representation to the next:

- The DFC (the display file compiler), which is the part of the application program containing the model traverser and calls to the graphics package to map the AM to the SDF;
- The DPU (the display processing unit), which maps the SDF to the LDF;
- The DC (the display controller), which maps the LDF to the image on the display screen.

The *input* portion of the functional model is described by the data flow from the input devices into the different processors in the pipeline. The mapping from one object representation to another is always subject to modification by input.

The input data is categorized for each processor with respect to two aspects of its processing:

- How it enters the processor—the input either enters directly from an input device or is forwarded by another processor;
- How it is processed by the processor—the input is either forwarded to another processor or is used by the processor to modify its output, or both.

Each type of input is described in more detail below.

As with the output portion of the functional model, it is the *logical* operation of the input portion that is emphasized. Although an input device may be *physically* connected to several processors over a bus, on the level of abstraction of the functional model it is *logically* connected only to the processor that actually processes its input data. Logical input devices can, of course, modify the processing in several processors in the pipeline. The change in one representation is reflected in all following representations in the pipeline and thereby changes the processors' behavior.

Each *representation* contains a complete description of what is displayed. The successive representations differ only in the level of abstraction/detail of object description (pre- or postclipping, and in 3D pre- or 2D post-projection) and in the degree of machine dependence: representations become successively more low-level and more machine-dependent, i.e., less abstract. Each processor operates on a representation and may also receive input from input devices either directly or through another processor, as discussed below.

As a more precise conceptualization of the familiar output pipeline from application model through image on the screen, the functional model is capable of abstracting a wide number of different architectures. Specific systems may not explicitly store all representations (or include their corresponding processors), but they all do in fact generate the equivalent data, if only in a transient way. For example, the unbuffered, high-performance systems do not have an explicit LDF, but the DPU must generate low-level primitives of the type stored in a linear buffer to be supplied to the vector generator. The output of the DPU is simply executed immediately rather than being placed into the refresh buffer for subsequent execution.

Conceptually, input modeling does not appear as straightforward as output modeling since there is no pipeline. (In actuality, the output model is far more complex, however, because of the pipelining and complexity of individual steps.)

10.6.2 Input

Note that one physical input device may correspond to two logical input devices, each with a different function. The two logical input devices can be connected either to the same processors or to two different ones. For example, a user may control the movement of a locator cursor with a tablet and also cause the application program to read the (x, y) coordinates of the tablet/cursor when some specific event occurs. In the present model, this is done with two separate logical devices:*

- The DC reads the tablet coordinates and updates the cursor position. The tablet input goes to the DFC.
- The DFC reads the tablet coordinates. Logically, the tablet input is to the DFC. Depending on physical connections, the DFC may access the input device directly or obtain the input data from a lower-level processor.

Some input details of the functional model are illustrated in Fig. 10.9.

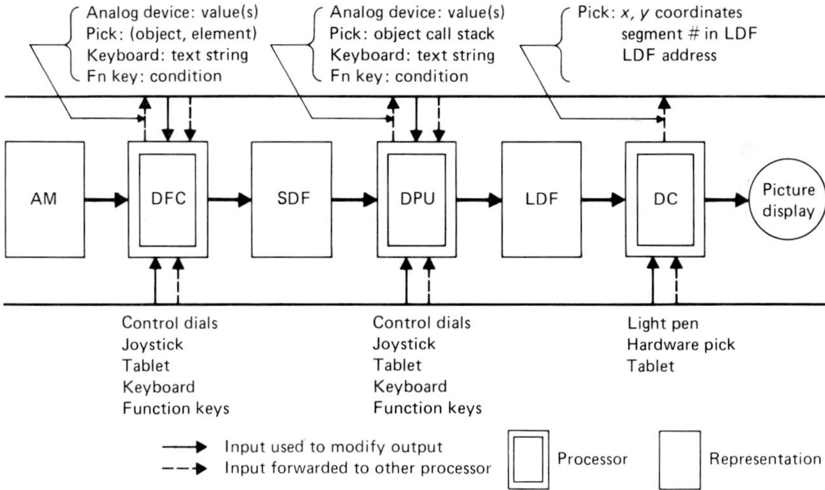

Fig. 10.9 Functional model—input and output (from [CARL80]).

---

*The term *logical device* is used here in a slightly different sense from that used in our discussion of SGP/Core logical devices. This is because this functional model describes hardware architecture, not software facilities.

As was discussed in the previous subsection, input is categorized at each processor by two aspects of its processing: how it enters the processor and how it is processed by that processor. Some input data is collected by a processor only for transfer to a higher-level processor, possibly after some transformation of the data. Other input data is used by a processor to modify the way in which it maps one representation into another. The first type of input is illustrated by dashed lines in Fig. 10.9, the second type by solid lines.

All three processors can receive input data, and the data may be processed before it is passed on to a higher-level processor. For example, characters may be formatted into a text string, control dial values may be filtered, and light-pen pick data may be used to identify the item in the next higher-level data structure that corresponds to the primitive identified on the screen by the light pen. The input data varies among processors only in the types of changes it may make to the output of the processor. Thus, input into the DFC causes changes in terms of application objects, while input into the DC causes changes in terms of individual character string or line primitives, as discussed below.

In principle, almost all physical devices can be connected to each processor. Two exceptions are the light pen and the physical locator-based pick using analog comparison: they can be connected only to the DC. Because of the overlapped processing in the pipeline, only the DC can identify the primitive that was picked using a light-pen device. Similarly, since the hardware pick uses the analog output of the DC as the input for the comparator, only the DC can identify what primitive was indicated by the cursor. In practice only a few input devices are connected directly to the DC. Input into the DFC can cause the most general type of changes, i.e., changes in terms of application objects. These changes range from modification of individual items in the SDF to modification of the structure of the SDF. The DFC can receive input directly from all physical devices (except the light pen and the hardware pick) and can receive input forwarded from lower-level processors.

The input into the DPU is more restricted than the input into the DFC in the type of changes it may cause. The processing of individual items, such as coordinate data, transformation data, and flags in the SDF, can be modified and, as a result of a change to a transformation, an entire instance of an object can be affected. Also, flags may be used to select one or another part of the SDF to be compiled to the LDF.

The input capabilities of the DPU vary a great deal from one system to another. In some cases all devices except the light pen and the hardware pick may be processed. In other systems the DPU may maintain only a cursor and a text buffer, and in still others the DPU may handle no input at all.

The input into the DC affects the mapping of the LDF to the image on the display screen. The input to the DC can cause only very restricted types of changes to the image: only individual coordinate positions and attributes can be modified. For example, primitives can be highlighted upon a pick, a cursor position can be updated, or a light pen tracking cross position can be updated. The only devices generally attached to the DC are the light pen and the locator device.

In the following section, the output and the input processing in two commercial high-performance vector graphics systems popular in the late seventies are described in some detail. We will see that systems which appear to have rather different architectures can nonetheless be mapped onto the same functional model and that the use of this model therefore greatly facilitates a structured comparison.

10.6.3 Two Case Studies

This section describes the high-level architectures of the Evans & Sutherland Multipicture System 2, or MPS [EVAN77a, EVAN77b], and the Vector General 3400, or VG3400 [VECT78a, VECT78b]. The hardware components of the systems are discussed and the relationships between the architectures and the functional models are illustrated. Figures 10.10 and 10.11 show the architecture of the E&S MPS and its structure on the level of abstraction of the functional model, while Figs. 10.12 and 10.13 show the corresponding diagrams for the VG3400. Note that we generally use vendors' names for components in referring to hardware units, while the names defined above are still used for the logical processors and representations used in the functional model.

Evans & Sutherland Multipicture System 2. The MPS consists of seven components:

- Picture controller interface
- Picture system data bus
- Picture system memory
- Picture processor
- Picture generator
- Picture display
- Interactive devices

The picture system data bus, picture processor, picture system memory, and picture generator are collectively called the *central graphics processor*. Each central graphics processor can support up to four picture stations (each of which consists of a set of interactive devices and a picture display). The central graphics processor is connected through the picture controller interface to the *picture controller,* which is considered part of the total display system. It is a general-purpose computer, either a DEC PDP-11 or a VAX 11/780. Each picture controller can support up to four central graphics processors. In our discussion below we will consider the simple case where the picture controller supports a single central graphics processor, which in turn supports a single picture station. The picture controller contains the application program, the AM, and the DFC. The E&S-supplied software includes a set of FORTRAN-callable subroutines that are used by the DFC to build the SDF from the object representation in the AM and to modify the SDF according to input data.

AM, DFC

Picture controller
DEC PDP-11 or VAX

Picture
controller
interface

Picture system data bus

MAP input
controller

MAP output
formatter

MAP matrix
arithmetic
processor

256 k
16-bit
words

Refresh
controller

Line
generator

Character
generator

Picture processor
DPU

Picture system
memory
SDF, LDF

Picture generator
DC

Central graphics processor

Picture
display

Light pen

Picture system
interactive
devices

Picture stations

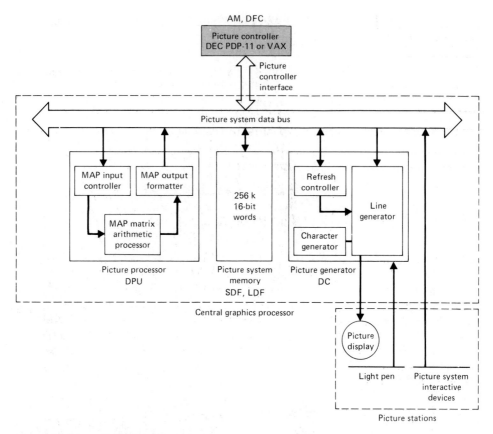

Fig. 10.10 E&S PS2 structural model (Evans and Sutherland Computer Corporation, PS2 Reference Manual).

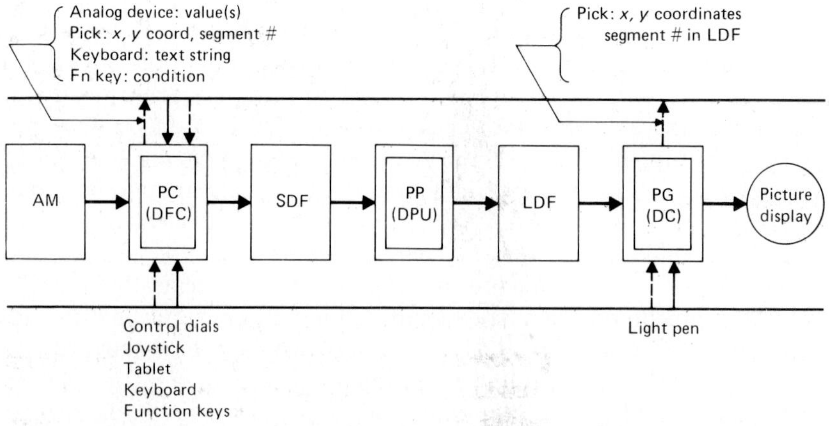

Fig. 10.11 Functional model of the E&S PS2 (from [CARL80]).

The *picture controller interface* handles communication between the picture controller and the MPS over three I/O paths:

- The direct I/O path for single words of data or control information;
- The direct memory access path for data block transfers;
- The interrupt path, to transmit interrupts to the picture controller from the input devices and from other units such as the picture generator.

The synchronous *picture system data bus* enables the picture controller to access all the components of the MPS. The *picture system memory* stores both the SDF and the LDF. The SDF contains primitives, attributes, object calls, and viewing and modeling transformations. The *picture processor,* as the DPU, compiles the SDF in the picture memory to a LDF. The picture processor composes transformations, applies the transformations to the primitives, and clips the portions of the transformed object that are outside the window. The clipped object is projected onto the projection plane, and the resulting projection is mapped to the viewport.

The LDF contains primitives and mode settings. The LDF may be single-buffered, double-buffered, or segmented. When the LDF is in double-buffer mode, the DC continually reads one half of the buffer while the DPU updates the other; in segmented-buffer mode, the LDF is divided into several segments and each of these can be individually updated.

The *picture generator, line generator,* and *character generator* function together as the DC. The picture generator controls the processing of the LDF; the line generator converts the data in the LDF to analog signals that position the electron beam and control the intensity in the display monitor; the character generator interprets the full ASCII character set. New fonts can also be defined by the programmer. Individual characters in a text string are not subject to the modeling/viewing transformations; only the starting point of a text string is transformed.

The MPS supports seven *input devices* (collectively considered as part of the display station), all of which are interfaced directly to the picture system data bus. The input devices are:

- Data tablet
- Control dials
- Function switches
- Alphanumeric keyboard
- Light pen
- Joystick
- Lighted function buttons

With the exception of the light pen, all these devices can be accessed directly by application program, and other input data is used as input by the DFC.

The picture processor cannot accept any input data at all, and the picture generator has access only to the light pen.

Vector General 3400. The VG3400 consists of eight components:

- Host computer interface
- GP bus
- Graphics processor
- Refresh buffer
- MD bus
- Display control unit
- Monitor
- Peripheral devices

These components are connected to a *host computer* which, as for the MPS, is considered part of the total display system. Again, as in the MPS, this is a general-purpose computer such as the DEC PDP-11 or VAX 11/780. The host computer contains the application program, the AM, the DFC and (unlike the MPS) the SDF. The VG-supplied software includes a set of FORTRAN-callable subroutines that are used by the DFC to build the SDF from the object representation in the AM and to modify the SDF according to the input data.

As in the MPS, the SDF contains primitives, attributes, object calls, and modeling and viewing transformations. Unlike the MPS, it may also contain general-purpose instructions, such as arithmetic, boolean, and control instructions.

The host computer interfaces with the VG3400 through the *host computer interface*. The interface unit handles communication between the host computer and the VG3400 over the same three I/O paths as the MPS:

- Programmed I/O path (PIO)
- Direct memory access path (DMA)
- Interrupt path

The interface unit, the graphics processor, the refresh buffer, and the input devices (except the light pen and the hardware pick) are connected to an asynchronous bus, the *GP bus*.

The *graphics processor* is the DPU. It compiles an SDF in the host computer memory to an LDF that is stored in the refresh buffer. The graphics processor is a general-purpose processor; in addition to traversing a hierarchy and transforming and clipping primitives, it also executes general-purpose arithmetic, logic, and flow of control instructions.

The LDF resides in the *refresh buffer* and contains primitives and attribute settings. The LDF cannot be segmented; instead, the VG3400 provides an edit-aid feature which allows the user to make tentative deletions, insertions, and modifications to the LDF. The edit-aid feature can, for example, be used as a buffer in which a part of the object may be modified while the remainder is unchanged.

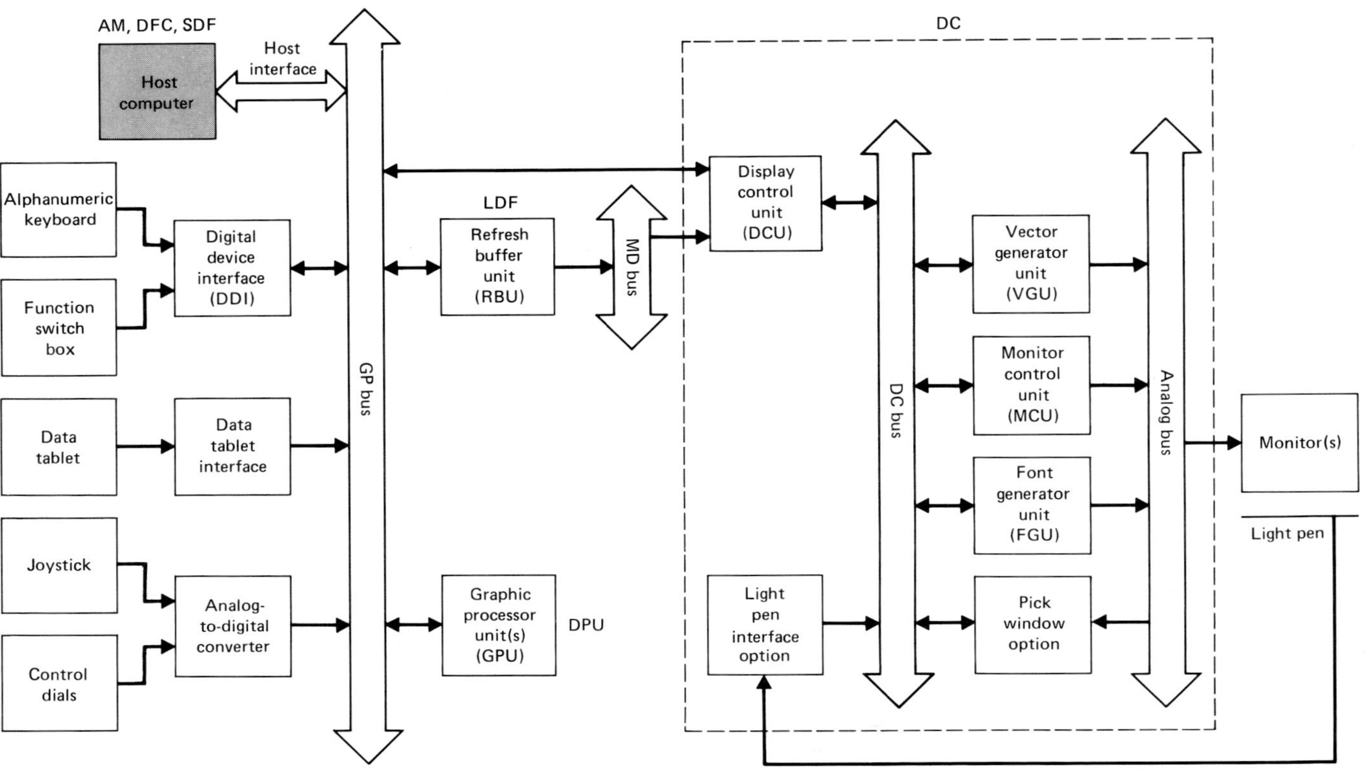

Fig. 10.12 VG3400 structural model (Vector General, Inc., VG3400 Programming Concepts Manual).

The *display control unit* and the VGU, MCU, and FGU function as the DC. The display control unit uses the *MD bus* to access the LDF. The VGU converts the data in the LDF to analog signals that position the electron beam and control the intensity in the display monitor. The FGU can interpret the full ASCII character set, and contains a transformation matrix which is loaded with the current transformation matrix. Characters are thus subject to the modeling/viewing transformation (with the exception that perspective foreshortening is not applied to individual characters in a text string). As with the MPS, multiple DC's can be connected via their own refresh buffers.

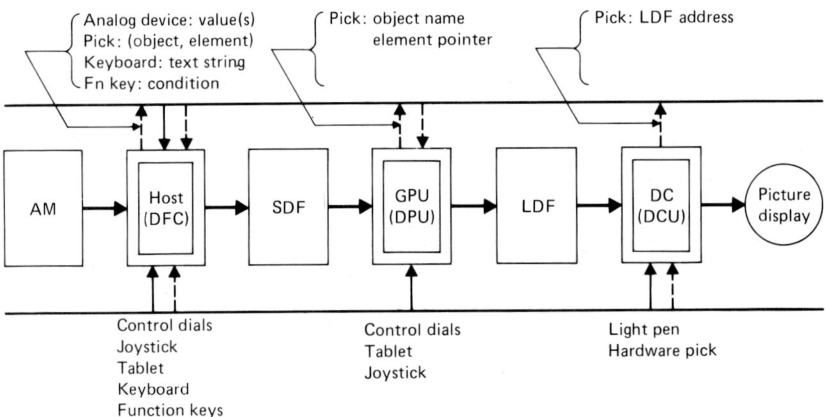

Fig. 10.13 Functional model VG3400 (from [CARL80]).

The VG3400 supports seven *input devices:*

- Data tablet
- Control dials
- Function keys
- Alphanumeric keyboard
- Light pen
- Joystick
- Hardware pick

All the devices are interfaced directly to the GP bus (except the light pen and the hardware pick, which are interfaced to the DC). The input devices connected to the GP bus can be accessed by the DFC in the host. Some input data is passed to the application program and other input data is used as input to the DFC.

The device registers storing the digitized values of sampled devices, i.e., the control dials, joystick, and data tablet, can be accessed directly by the graphics processor. Individual coordinates and transformation data can be updated according to the values of these analog devices each time the SDF is compiled—these are the dynamic variables of Section 10.3.3 on data addressing modes.

Only the light pen and the hardware pick are attached directly to the DC. Both devices can modify the output to the LDF in that both may highlight a picked item. The data of the light pen and the hardware pick can also be forwarded to a higher-level processor. The element in the AM corresponding to the item picked on the display screen is found through a two-step process: first the word in the LDF is used to find the corresponding word in the SDF and then the object call stack at the time of execution of this word is passed to the DFC, which in turn establishes the desired (object, element) pair.

A functional comparison of the E&S MPS and the VG3400. The MPS and the VG3400 are similar in that both implement the SDF and the LDF as actual data structures. However, the object representations and the processors differ a great deal in complexity and philosophy. The MPS picture processor (which functions as the DPU) is a special-purpose processor whereas the VG3400 graphics processor unit is a general-purpose processor. As a result of the differences in object representations, input processing in the two systems also differs a great deal. Some examples of the differences between these two systems are next discussed briefly (see [CARL80] for a more detailed and quantitative comparison).

a) Address modes—the MPS allows only immediate data; the VG3400 allows both immediate data and referenced data. For generality, the VG3400's referenced data may access any location in the host, the general-purpose registers in the graphics processor, and the analog input device registers, to create powerful dynamic variables which can be easily updated by the DPU or the application program. If the SDF contains references to locations in the host computer, these locations are considered in the functional model as part of both the SDF and the AM. Because the SDF is in the host memory, the application program can modify the data in the AM, and thereby the contents of the SDF as well, in the manner discussed for addressed data in Section 10.3. If some of the immediate data in the MPS is to be modified, (part of) the AM must contain pointers to these data items. The actual coordinate data is located in the SDF and another copy may be located in the AM. Because the SDF in the MPS has only immediate data and is not stored in host memory, it is much more difficult to update it than in the VG3400—architectural decisions do have impact on software.

b) Object calls—in the VG3400 the objects are referenced through a directory for easy relocatability in memory management; in the MPS object references are direct pointers. The MPS stack cannot contain the names of the calling objects; as a result, the name of a picked object must be determined either by using a correlation table or by placing each instance of an object in a separate segment in the LDF.

c) General-purpose instructions—the VG3400 allows arithmetic, boolean, and control instructions; the MPS allows no general-purpose instructions.

d) Transformations—in the MPS all transformations are represented as general 4×4 homogeneous matrices; in the VG3400 the rotation, scaling, and translation parameters are stored individually and a transformation matrix is composed each time the SDF is compiled. The VG3400 does not support shearing transformations and allows only uniform scaling.

e) Text—in the VG3400 the modeling/viewing transformations apply to text, with the restriction that perspective transformations do not apply to individual characters. In the MPS only the starting point of a text string is subject to transformation.

f) Interaction—in the VG3400 the SDF and its compilation to the LDF may be modified by input from the analog devices by the use of indirectly addressed data. The MPS does not allow any input from analog devices into the DPU; all input goes to the DFC. Any modifications made to the SDF in the MPS on the basis of input from analog devices are the result of modifications by the DFC using pointers, stored in the AM, to locations in the SDF.

g) Segmentation—in the MPS the LDF can be segmented so that pieces of an object may be modified without the DPU regenerating the entire LDF. This is possible on the VG3400 only in a very limited fashion, by means of the edit-aid feature.

In [CARL80], the author shows with benchmarks that in many contexts the general-purpose nature and flexibility of the VG3400 causes a significant decrease in performance relative to the MPS. Thus graphics systems designers must consider very carefully the flexibility/performance trade-offs for systems in which response to user interaction, dynamic object/image changes, and number of flicker-free primitives are of paramount importance.

10.7 THE EVANS & SUTHERLAND PS300—ANOTHER TURN ON THE WHEEL

The power of the structured display file approach to highly dynamic vector graphics is well illustrated by the E&S PS300 [EVAN81], announced in mid-1981 (Fig. 10.14). This exceptional graphics system has gone around the wheel of reincarnation sufficiently far to add a powerful microprocessor, the M68000, as a Graphics Control Processor (GCP) dedicated to handling graphics tasks. It currently communicates at relatively low speed (via a 9600-baud RS232C interface) with the host computer on which the application model is stored, and handles input device interaction for modifying the SDF and/or the viewing specification. Thus there is a clear division of labor between the application handling host and the object hierarchy/graphics handling satellite; they communicate only via a human-readable character string command language. The objective of this design is to make a self-sufficient "viewing engine" which needs no intervention from the host computer, unlike the MPS and VG3400 which relied on the host for a variety of tasks, including compilation and updating of the SDF.

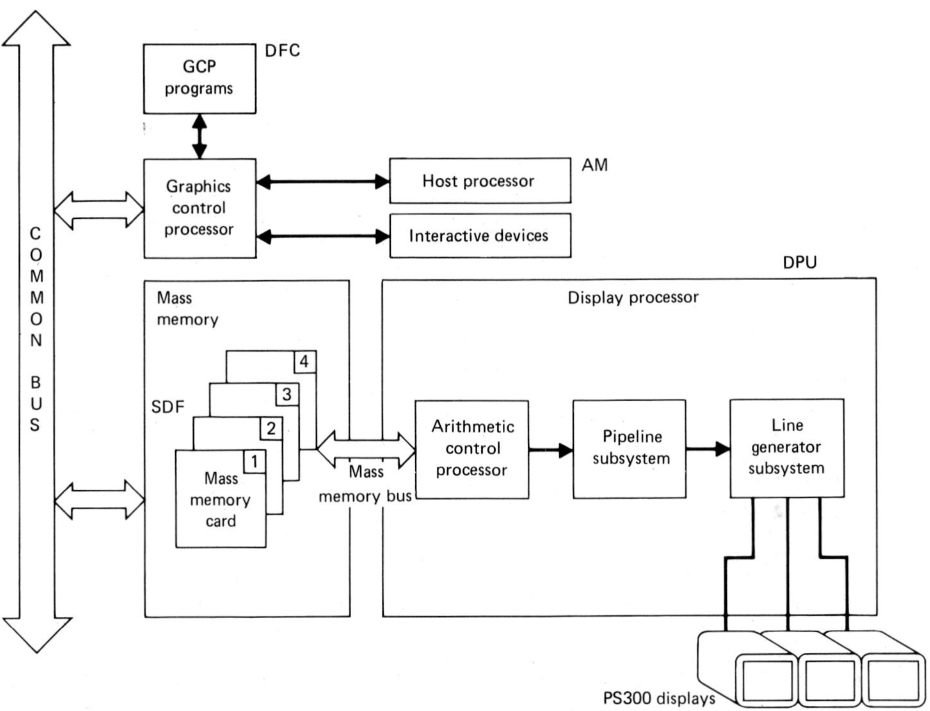

Fig. 10.14 PS300 functional block diagram: AM—application model; DFC—display file compiler.

The M68000, in one 16-Mbyte logical address space, accesses both private memory (currently 128 kbyte) storing GCP programs and the mass memory storing the SDF (upgradable in 1-Mbyte increments). Graphics control programs are specified in a special-purpose language as combinations of n-input, m-output black-box procedures connected in what is called a *function network*. Such an interconnection of black boxes resembles a data flow architecture: a procedure is activated only when all its input parameters have data items in their corresponding input queues. These data items can come from other procedures, input devices, and the application program, and typically are geometric data such as scalars, vectors, matrices, character strings, and Pascal-like records of these primitives. All input devices (initially keyboard, function keys, data tablet, and control dials) are serviced by the GCP. Function networks typically wait on such user input and then selectively update *copies* of subobjects and matrices in the SDF. When the update of the copies is finished, pointers to old and new data structures are swapped. Thus a small, localized amount of double-buffering provides very simple and fast incremental updating.

The SDF is specified by the host as a sequence of commands (similar to those for building symbol hierarchies in the previous chapter) to be executed by the GCP. The PS300 is the first system to support an SDF with floating-point modeling coordinates, albeit of a somewhat specialized form to gain efficiency. Each component of point (x, y, z) is represented by a 16-bit fraction; all three share the same 8-bit exponent. Viewing and modeling matrix components have 32-bit fractions and 8-bit exponents each, and numerical computations use 24-bit fractions and 8-bit exponents. In this scheme, sections of large objects (e.g., the tail section of a 747 airplane) can be defined as reasonably compact subobjects in their own local coordinate systems with limited precision. Subobjects can subsequently be assembled with modeling transformations which have maximum precision.

The SDF contains a symbol/object hierarchy whose root has an associated Core-style perspective or parallel viewing specification. The Display Processor/DPU traverses the SDF nominally at 30–60 Hz, doing all hierarchy traversal, matrix composition, viewing and vector generation on the fly, without compiling a separate LDF. As remarked in Section 9.6.1, for a sufficiently fast DPU this is the ideal case because it provides both immediate updating on each frame and simplicity by avoiding dual representations and their synchronization. Pick correlation within a hierarchy yields the object name hierarchy and the index of the vector in the vector list within the lowest-level object.

The DPU is in fact a pipeline of three separate processors composed of bit slices. The processing in the pipeline is overlapped to gain considerable speed. The first processor (arithmetic control processor) handles SDF traversal and matrix–matrix and matrix–vector multiplication for modeling transformations which are composed with the normalizing transformations of the viewing operation, as in Section 9.10. It also does clipping to a normalized 3D view volume using line equations. The second processor (the pipeline subsystem) does projection and window-to-viewport mapping. The third is a digital vector generator that uses an incremental algorithm. Another unusually powerful feature of the system is that characters are decomposed into strokes which are passed through the entire vector pipeline to provide realistic 3D text transformations.

Performance measurement on the PS300 is even trickier than on its simpler predecessors. The number of flicker-free vectors is a function of many parameters, such as the length and angle of vectors, 2D versus 3D, number of nodes in the hierarchy, and ratio of trivially accepted/rejected to clipped vectors. For the simple case of a modest 2D hierarchy of about 60 nodes and a viewing transformation without any clipping, more than 95 000 small (not exceeding 0.1 inch) vectors can be handled at 30 Hz. At the other extreme of a sizeable (i.e., several hundred nodes) 3D hierarchy with a full perspective viewing transformation including clipping, at least 20 000 vectors can be handled under the following typical conditions: about half of the vectors are short (not exceeding 0.1 inch) and about half are medium sized (not exceeding 2 inches); furthermore, some 85% of the vectors are trivially rejected or accepted and only 15% actually need be clipped. Note that this heavy processing load involves handling at least 20 000 3D vectors in a 1/30 of a second; thus one vector every 1.5 microseconds is the throughput of the full 3D floating-point pipeline under these conditions! This number compares very favorably with the number of short 16-bit integer vectors processed under simpler conditions by prior systems. The pipeline is designed so that hierarchy traversal and its associated processing do not add significant overhead to the viewing operation and vector generation stages.

The VG33000 takes a basically similar approach, having both a M68000 and a floating-point object hierarchy. It also allows local object updating, interaction handling, etc., but with less powerful viewing hardware and therefore both lower performance and lower cost.

Four questions remain at the time of writing:

1. Will 9600-baud communication suffice for a use profile which includes considerable interaction with application data and/or frequent changes of display models? Certainly browsing through a pictorial database cannot be done at this rate.

2. Will programmers be satisfied not to have general-purpose access to the M68000 via a standard high-level language? Such access would make the PS300 an independent (satellite) computer system rather than an intelligent peripheral.

3. Even if refreshing 50 000–100 000 short vectors provides an order of magnitude increase in the complexity of object hierarchies that can now be interpreted on the fly, wouldn't the increased complexity of an LDF and its DC be worth it for traversing even more complex hierarchies? For example, shading of polygons can be done nicely by filling in the polygon with adjacent parallel vectors—this technique uses many vectors!

4. Does the pipeline allow an easy replacement of the vector generation stage by a scan conversion unit which doesn't materially slow down the pipeline for creating a double-buffered bit map, in the style of the Megatek system discussed next?

10.8 EXTENSIONS FOR RASTER GRAPHICS—MEGATEK 7200

The functional model of Section 10.6 is readily extended to raster graphics by including scan-conversion capabilities in either the DPU or the display controller to make an image-creation system. In addition, we include a buffer which holds the scan-converted image (the *bit map* or BM) and an image display system (IDS) for reading the bit map and doing any color-table mapping before generating display monitor signals. Figure 10.15 shows this version of the functional model. It parallels the earlier model directly: the BM replaces the LDF, and the IDS replaces the DC. In fact, the IDS is often called a DC, although it is generally far simpler, since it deals primarily with strings of pixels rather than with output primitive instructions to be decoded. In both models, the image representation for refresh is tailored to optimize

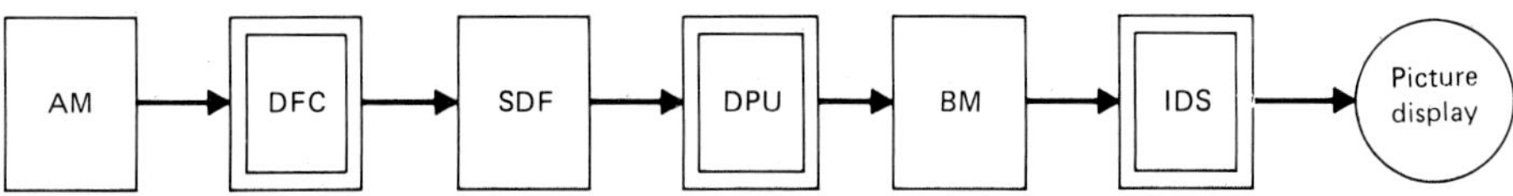

Fig. 10.15 Functional model of a high-performance raster system: BM—bit map; IDS—image display system.

the scan method (random or raster). An alternative implementation, which combines vector and raster graphics architectures and also the MPS and VG3400 technique of driving multiple display controllers with a single DPU, is the 1981 Megatek 7200 implementation.

The Megatek 7200 provides an unusual facility for high-performance dynamics in both vector and raster mode. It is one of the first systems in a moderate price range to provide real-time raster scan conversion. Non-hierarchical pictures containing up to 50000 short connected vectors can be scan-converted at 10 Hz, averaging 160 nanoseconds per pixel. Note that describing the capabilities of a raster system by the number of vectors it can display relates to the 7200's method of using vectors in the raster display: unlike the generally similar Sanders Graphic 8 system [SAND80], which provides for arbitrary polygon-area fill, Megatek creates solid areas by scan-converting adjacent parallel vectors which fill the area. An optional polygon fill processor can be used to generate the vectors. The advantage of this "vectorized raster," or "rasterized vector" system is that it provides flicker-free display of arbitrary numbers of dynamically modified vectors, and thereby gives the appearance of a dynamic raster display.

The components of the 7200 "Graphics Engine," illustrated in Fig. 10.16, are:

- *Host interface.* This unit provides an interface to the host computer. It also contains logic to control activity on both the graphics data bus and the graphics peripheral bus.

- *Vector memory.* This buffer stores the structured display file only, although in principle it could hold a linear display file as well.

- *Graphics processor.* The graphics processor contains logic to traverse the structured display file and to pass information either to the optional hardware clip, rotate, scale, and translate module, or directly to the vector generator. It also contains facilities for hardware image translation and hardware character generation.

- *Hardware clip, rotate, scale, and translate module* (HCRST). This optional processor can be considered part of the 7200's DPU. It performs a limited set of image transformations and image clipping. It does not allow the full generality of a user-loadable 4×4 homogeneous coordinate transformation matrix or matrix composition. Also, it does not allow perspective projections or an intensity depth cueing facility. Megatek thus has made a design decision to stress speed and low cost over functionality. This trade-off, while limiting the user's viewing options (or forcing the transformation to take place in the host), does provide very impressive results in the amount of vector data available for scan conversion in real time.

- *Graphics data bus.* This is a 32-bit wide, bi-directional bus over which all image data passes, two 12-bit coordinates at a time. In addition to coordinate data, the data bus also handles display-related peripheral communications.

- *Graphics peripheral bus.* This is a bus over which host-directed interaction information from the user is sent.

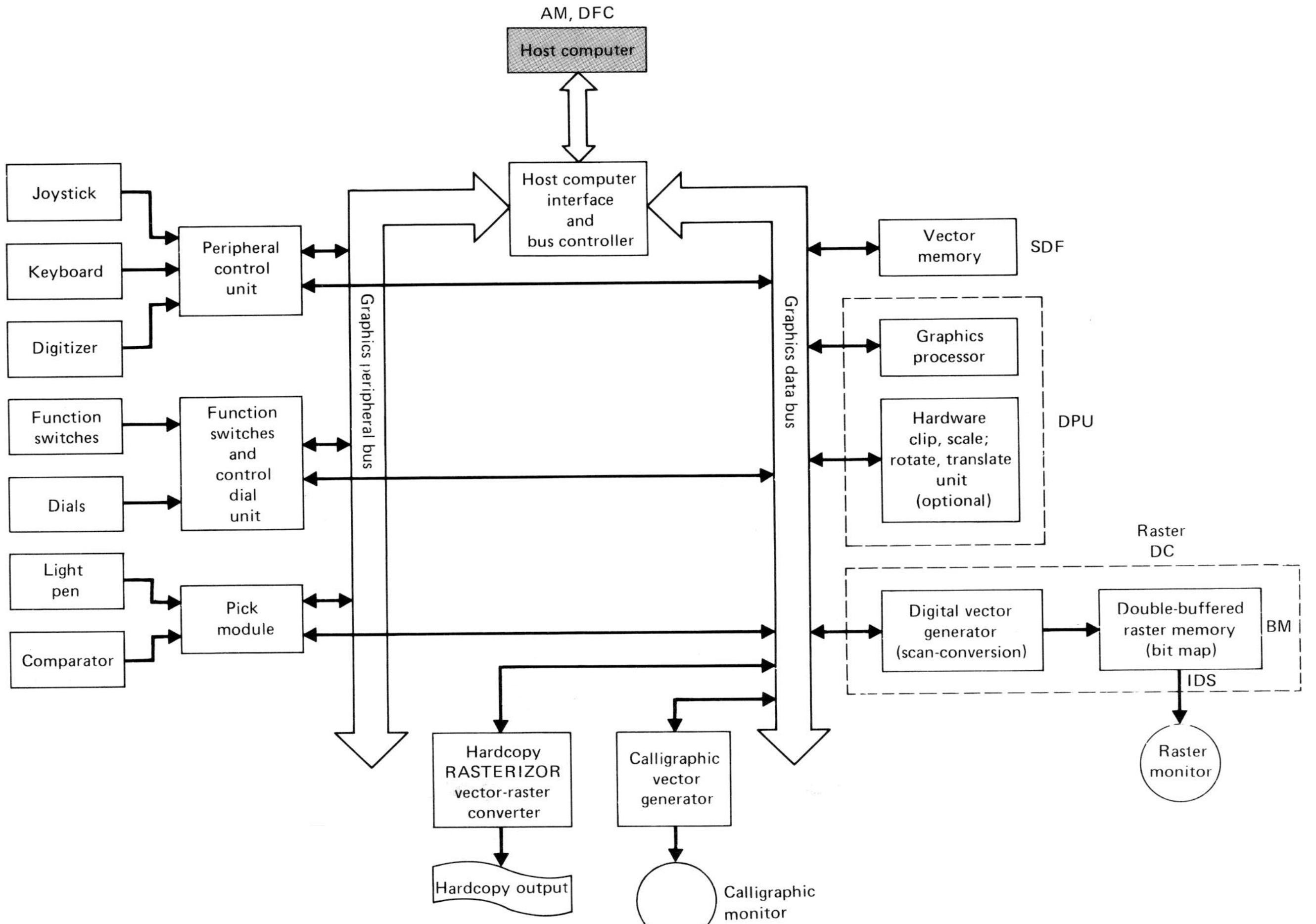

Fig. 10.16 MEGATEK 7200 "graphics engine."

- *Input devices.* The 7200 supports a joystick, trackball, digitizer (typically a tablet), a keyboard, function switches and control dials, and a pick device (typically a locator with a hardware comparator). The joystick, keyboard, and digitizer are interfaced through a separate peripheral control unit.

- *Output devices.* The 7200 supports three types of devices: a raster display, a vector display, and a hard-copy device. The *raster display* is interfaced through a *digital vector generator* (DVG). The DVG performs the vector scan conversion on the LDF passed to it by the DPU, using Bresenham's algorithm (see Chapter 11). The converted LDF is stored in double-buffered raster memory, from which it is displayed on the color raster monitor. One can chose 512 by 512 resolution of four-bit pixels or 1024 by 1024 resolution but half the update rate. The vector display (called calligraphic monitor) is driven directly from the *calligraphic vector generator* (CVG), optimized for short vectors. The hard-copy device (typically either an electrostatic or impact dot matrix plotter) is driven by the "RASTERIZOR" unit, which does a high-resolution vector-to-raster conversion.

The 7200, like the PS300, is connected as an intelligent peripheral via a simple, microprocessor-based serial (or parallel) communications interface to a host (e.g. PDP-11, VAX-11/780 or DG NOVA). The DFC runs on the host to map the application model to a structured display file. This type of interface provides flexibility at relatively lower cost than that of the somewhat older and more complex hardwired interfaces of the MPS and the 3400, and we therefore expect this interface method to become rather commonplace in the early 1980s. Again as in the PS300, the host graphics package transmits high-level commands to the 7200 which create the structured display file; included are commands to create and delete segment, create output primitive in current segment, set up and get input from interaction devices. One can think of this style of host-peripheral transmission as sending an encoded structured display file and editing commands which operate on it. Alternatively, in less sophisticated displays, the host could send commands to form the clipped, segmented linear display file, possibly using display subroutines for symbols entirely within the window. This type of transmission sends only viewable information and is therefore more compact, if less powerful, than sending a full untransformed, unclipped object hierarchy in the SDF.

10.9 MULTIPROCESSOR AND HOST-SATELLITE GRAPHICS

The interface microprocessor of an intelligent peripheral such as the Megatek 7200, if not constantly involved in communication and bus control, could be used for other, application-independent output and input functions. This would be the case if all of the hardware units on the bus participated in distributed bus arbitration and if the bandwidth of the host connection were low. Among such output functions would be object and/or segment creation and modification functions and local generation of primitives from high-level specifications sent by the host, for example for graphing grids, arbitrary conics and application-dependent symbols (via a downloaded symbol library). Input functions could include many of the interaction techniques described in Chapter 5 such as echoing, rubberbanding, dragging (and possibly other image transformations), gridded and constrained drawing, sketching (i.e. freehand drawing) and hierarchical correlation for object updating if a structured display file is supported. In effect, the PS300 is designed for this kind of host-independent processing.

The purpose of this local processing is to minimize both the load on the host computer and the communication traffic. Both reasons are most valid in the case of a time-shared host communicating with display peripherals over relatively low-bandwidth communication lines (e.g., 1200 baud to 19.6 kbaud). Network graphics used, for example, in graphical teleconferencing [OBRI79] is a similar case, as is the Canadian Telidon system shown in Color Plate 10 [BROW79]. In the latter system the microprocessor in the box attached to a home TV is capable of generating (scan-converting) characters, lines, arcs, and polygons as well as handling phone-line communication; it is a combination interface/DPU. Handling low-level interaction locally also provides instant feedback to simple user input which would be nearly impossible otherwise. Finally, in the case of (large) time-shared mainframes, any off-loading typically also implies cost reduction since use of a built-in processor already purchased adds no incremental cost.

A graphics system which has a (micro)processor in the host interface used for high-level DPU code generation and interaction handling may be viewed not merely as an intelligent peripheral but as a satellite computer system capable of nontrivial local work. Since its functionality is limited and cannot be changed by the application programmer, it is a *fixed-function satellite* computer system. If there is enough capacity in the processor, however, we need not be satisfied with treating the satellite simply as a "black-box" peripheral; we can make it possible for the application programmer to write arbitrary application code for the satellite to turn the graphics peripheral into a general-purpose *programmable satellite.* This host-satellite configuration predates the Alto/Ethernet environment of Xerox PARC by some five years; both configurations are a natural outgrowth of the incremental-growth process of the wheel of reincarnation. Thus a PDP-11-based E&S MPS or VG3400 may be used either in self-sufficient, stand-alone mode or in satellite mode to a larger mainframe. The PS300 is halfway in between fixed-function and programmable satellite since one can write specialized "function network" programs for the M68000 but doesn't have a general-purpose programming language. Also, the intelligence of the 7200 Host Interface can be increased to programmable satellite status by another turn on the wheel with the addition of an 8086 microprocessor. It will allow local event handling, multitasking and running of user programs.

Continuing on the wheel, modern display satellites have frequently become multiple-processor systems in their own right. For example, the high-performance Brown University (vector) Graphics System, BUGS [VAND74], is a fully programmable, shared-memory multiprocessor which runs stand-alone or as a satellite attached to the IBM 370 time-shared mainframe (Fig. 10.17). BUGS consists of two

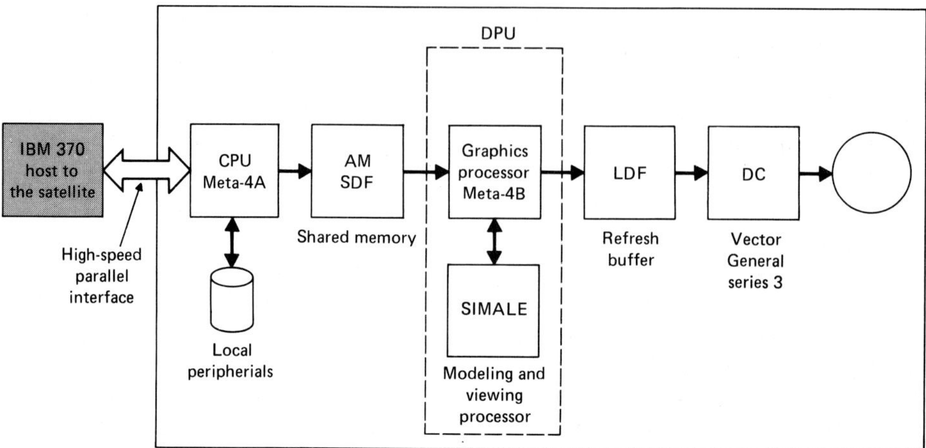

Fig. 10.17 BUGS (Brown University Graphics System) as a high-performance multiprocessor intelligent satellite.

identical 90-nanosecond microprogrammed minicomputers (DSC Meta-4s) which act as CPU and graphics processor, sharing a common 64-kbyte memory holding application software and a structured display file. The Meta-4A CPU and Meta-4B graphics processor both emulate 16-bit IBM 370-like target machines with general-purpose instruction sets, while the Meta-4B also has SDF traversal and other graphics instructions. In addition, it has a peripheral (the SIMALE) which is a 38-nanosecond microprogrammed computer with four-way parallel integer arithmetic and a limited but general-purpose instruction set interpreted out of a dynamically-paged control store. As a superset of the clipping divider, this machine handles 2D, 3D, and 4D instance transformations, extent testing (Section 9.12), clipping, projection, and character-by-character text handling for medium-quality text, and generates a double-buffered linear display file. The Meta-4B graphics processor and SIMALE together comprise the DPU. BUGS was the first display system to go around the wheel of incarnation several times and to make such extensive use of microprogramming for speed, flexibility, and ease of implementation.

Since the late 1960s, considerable research and experimentation has been devoted to automatic means of solving the key problem of host/satellite computation: how to partition the application programs to produce an "optimal" division of labor between host and satellite. The idea is to offload programs from the host to the satellite in such a way as to provide maximum response to user interaction and minimal load on the host.

This partitioning problem actually arises only when the intelligent satellite is not powerful enough in processor speed or memory or lacks hardware such as a floating-point processor. This is still often the case today, but will be decreasingly so in the future as the processor in the satellite acquires the requisite power through peripherals and adequate speed, memory, and instruction repertoire. It is interesting to note that the PS300 is restricted by design not to become a self-sufficient display-oriented computer system (like the Alto personal computer and especially its commercial successors described in Chapter 12), despite the fact that the M68000 is certainly powerful enough to allow it. For now at least, it is strictly a specialized viewing engine, with a predefined division of labor.

In effect, host-satellite cooperation and division of labor is an elementary form of distributed processing, with relatively tight coupling between modules on host and satellite. Mathematical models [STON78] have shown that the common-sense rules of thumb previously verified experimentally are valid most of the time: if possible, put interaction and display-building modules on the graphics satellite, and only very large-scale (floating-point) computation and archival database manipulations on the more powerful host. The code which affects the application model in response to user input should also run locally, if there is room.

The ICOPS system implemented on BUGS [VAND74] allows dynamic (run-time) migration of modules as load on the host varies, with the model calculating the optimal division of labor as a function of the host's availability—the more the host is loaded, the less powerful it appears to be relative to the satellite and the more attractive it is to run modules on the satellite. Stone's model also predicts breakpoints for load on the host at which entire tightly coupled clusters migrate to the satellite as the load on the host increases.

In addition to optimal partitioning problems, the other major problem for host-satellite graphics has been the design of conventions and software which allow the programmer to write application programs as if for a "virtual uniprocessor." This means that the programmer can write the code in a high-level language without considering the eventual division of labor or partitioning prescribed by the model, the low-level communications protocols, or the dissimilar computers and operating systems of host and satellite. Experimental systems which implement such a uniprocessor model have been created by using compilers which generate code for migratable modules for both computers. These have been described in [HAML75] and [VAND74] for PL/I and ALGOL-W, respectively. In both these approaches, the program is segmented at the procedure level and parameters are passed either in the normal way if caller and callee are co-located on the same processor, or transparently via a run-time monitor by using the communications link if they are not. While these experimental systems have demonstrated the feasibility of the basic mechanisms, unfortunately the algorithms have not been applied commercially. This is probably because it is easier to avoid the division-of-labor problem (by having the graphics system be either entirely stand-alone or just a peripheral) and simply to provide customers with a low-level communication package with which they can do their own implementation.

10.10 SUMMARY

This chapter has described some modern functional capabilities and architectures of vector systems, with reference to raster systems to show that they too can be modeled by the simple functional (pipeline) model. Distributed intelligence, typically via multiple processors, will continue to make display systems more powerful and more self-sufficient, as they make their turns on the wheel of reincarnation. Manufacturers will continue to sell both stand-alone systems containing their own hosts (perhaps linkable in turn as satellites to large main-frame hosts) and intelligent peripherals which can be attached to the minicomputer or main-frame host of the customer's choice, typically via easy-to-implement communications interfaces.

VLSI will create dramatic price/performance improvements in DPU architectures, providing, for example, both floating-point world coordinate systems for our SDFs and their modeling–viewing transformations, and affordable real-time scan conversion of vectors, characters, and polygons to implement dynamic raster graphics of the type now done only for million-dollar flight simulators. Finally, as memory prices drop and logic becomes sufficiently fast, high-resolution solid-area raster graphics will largely take the place of vector graphics because of the former's greater versatility and expressiveness. Raster systems now compete with storage tube devices in that they provide not only flicker-free display but also dynamics and selective updating, and with far greater brightness, gray scale and especially color. Similarly, dynamic scan conversion of vector data results in a flicker-free refreshed pseudovector display, with (vector-filled) solid area as an extra feature. The only disadvantage of raster graphics is the discrete nature of the pixel representation, leading to "jaggies" and other display defects discussed in the following chapter. In time, these effects may be minimized by increasing spatial resolution and by using intensity resolution in dynamic antialiasing techniques; these subjects are also discussed in the next chapter.

EXERCISES

10.1 It is common to compare vector DPU architecture to CPU architecture; for example, the X–Y beam position registers may be viewed as accumulators which can be loaded absolutely or incrementally, instructions have data operands which are typically specified with immediate values but may be referenced through one or more levels of addressing, and flow of control may be very similar, especially if there is subroutining. There are some differences, nonetheless. For example, discuss instruction formats of a vector display and instruction mixes; consider mode setting versus an opcode/operand(s) format, etc.

10.2 What is the ideal architecture to support SGP? (First define what could be meant by "ideal.") Conversely, what sort of graphics/modeling package would best support a graphics data structure architecture?

10.3 Investigate the syntax and semantics of the Core CTM *hook* first mentioned in Section 9.4, Fig. 9.6. How would you implement it on a high-performance vector display such as the E&S PS300?

10.4 Analyze a modern vector-refresh system to determine which of its features support which portions of a modeling package and which a graphics/viewing package (for a 3D pipeline). Pay attention to coordinate spaces, limitations on transformations, status saving, attributes, nonuniform treatment of text and other primitives, etc.

10.5 In the architecture of Exercise 4, how many processors and intermediate representations are there? What is the low-level architecture which is visible and potentially controllable by programming at the device-dependent assembly language level? How much of that functionality would be hidden/inaccessible by the use of SGP? What, then, would be the cost/benefit trade-off between the two levels of support?

10.6 Image space transformations can be viewed as "the poor man's modeling transformations." Under what conditions are they so usable? What might they be used for even if full modeling/viewing transformations are available?

10.7 Could you see any advantage to having workstation-style image-space clipping for vectors analogous to image-space transformations? How about for raster systems?

10.8 How is performance of a refresh vector system best characterized? Where would you add more processing power and/or memory in an existing high-performance system such as the E&S PS300 if cost were no object, to allow even greater pipelining/parallelism? What use could be made of multiple pipelines and/or special-purpose processing engines?

10.9 What are the trade-offs in having the CPU and DPU sharing memory? Again, in an ideal system, what would you choose to do and why?

10.10 Discuss how hardware attributes (such as color) may be reflected to either or both modeling and graphics packages.

10.11 Chapter 9 makes no mention of the problem of application data structures/models which are partially stored in secondary storage, except for symbol libraries. Discuss the problems of hardware traversal of models too large to fit entirely in DPU primary memory, exploiting whatever analogies with ordinary CPU data structure problems seem appropriate. (In 1981 this was still a problem for most architectures; it will be far less so as memory becomes truly "zero-cost.")

11 Raster Algorithms and Software

11.1 INTRODUCTION

We now turn our attention away from classical vector graphics and toward the new and rapidly expanding area of raster graphics. The growth of raster graphics has been driven by the microelectronics revolution, which allows processors and large amounts of random-access memory to be manufactured on small silicon chips. The processor and a few memory chips are used for the image creation system, which scan-converts output primitives such as lines, characters, polygons, etc. Many more memory chips are used for the refresh buffer, from which the image is displayed, one scan line at a time. Chapter 1 gave some background on the growth of raster graphics, while Chapter 3 outlined the basic structure of a typical raster display. In the first part of this chapter we present some of the many scan-conversion algorithms, and in the second part we discuss capabilities which are useful in a raster graphics subroutine package. The next chapter is a detailed discussion of raster graphics hardware.

The scan-conversion algorithms used in a raster display will be invoked quite often—typically hundreds or even thousands of times each time an image is created or modified. Hence, they must not only create visually satisfactory images, but must also execute as rapidly as possible. Indeed, speed versus image quality is the basic trade-off in selecting scan-conversion algorithms: some are fast and give jagged edges, while others are slower but give smoother edges. However, whichever way the trade-off is resolved, faster is better. Thus, the algorithms use incremental methods which minimize the number of calculations (especially multiplies and divides) performed during each iteration. Speed can be increased even further by using multiple processors, all simultaneously scan-converting output primitives into a multiported refresh buffer.

11.2 SCAN-CONVERTING LINES

The basic task of a scan-conversion algorithm for lines is to compute the coordinates of the pixels which lie near the line on a two-dimensional raster grid. In discussing this task we assume that the starting and ending points for the line have integer coordinates (the generalization is left as an exercise). The basic strategy used by the line scan-conversion algorithm in Chapter 3 is to increment x, calculate $y = mx + b$, and intensify the pixel at $(x, ROUND(y))$. This calculation of m times x takes time, however, and slows the scan-conversion process. Furthermore, floating-point (or binary-fraction) data representation must be used to ensure sufficient accuracy.

11.2.1 The Basic Incremental Algorithm

We can eliminate the multiplication by noting that if $\Delta x = 1$, then $m = \Delta y/\Delta x$ reduces to $m = \Delta y$, that is, a unit change in x changes y by m, which is the slope of the line. Thus for all points (x_i, y_i) on the line we know that if $x_{i+1} = x_i + 1$, then $y_{i+1} = y_i + m$, that is, the next values of x and y are defined in terms of their previous values, as shown in Fig. 11.1. If $m > 1$, then a step in x will create a step in y that is greater than 1. Thus we must reverse the roles of x and y, by assigning a unit step to y and incrementing x by $\Delta x = \Delta y/m = 1/m$. This is what is meant by an *incremental algorithm:* at each step we make incremental calculations based on the preceding step. The procedure *LINE* to implement the technique, limited to the case of $-1 < m < 1$, appears below. The procedure *WRITE_PIXEL,* used by *LINE,* places a value into the refresh buffer pixel whose coordinates are given as the first two arguments.

```
procedure LINE(                         {assumes slope between +1 and -1}
   x1, y1,                              {start point}
   x2, y2,                              {end point}
   value : integer);                    {value to place in pixels near line}
   var dy, dx, x, y, m: real;
begin
   if x1 <> x2
      then begin
         dy := y2 - y1;
         dx := x2 - x1;
         m := dy/dx;
         y := y1;
         for x := x1 to x2 do
            begin
               WRITE_PIXEL(x, ROUND(y), value);     {sets pixel to value}
               y := y + m                    {step y by slope m}
            end
      end
      {if "line" really a point, plot it; else, error}
      else if y1 = y2 then WRITE_PIXEL(x1, y1)
                      else ERROR
end    {LINE}
```

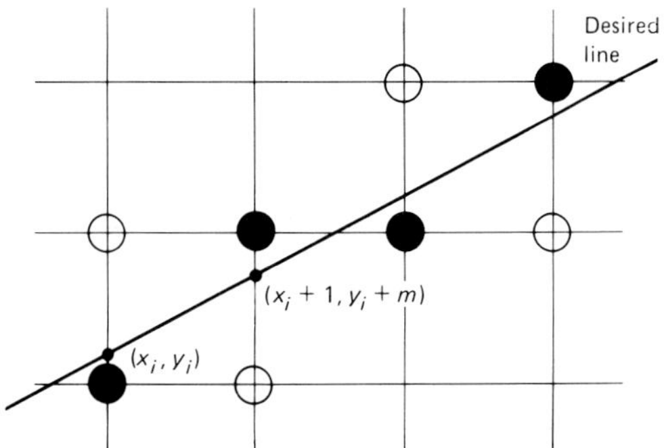

Fig. 11.1 Incremental calculation of y by rounding y to selected pixel (designated by black circle).

11.2.2 Bresenham's Line Algorithm

The difficulties with *LINE* are that rounding y to an integer takes time, and the variables y and m must be real or fractional binary rather than integer, because the slope is a fraction. *Bresenham's algorithm* [BRES65] is attractive because it uses only integer arithmetic. No real variables are used, and hence rounding is not needed. We assume, for simplicity, that the slope of the line is between 0 and 1. The algorithm uses a decision variable d_i which at each step is proportional to the difference between s and t shown in Fig. 11.2. The figure depicts the ith step, at which the pixel p_{i-1} has been determined to be closest to the actual line being drawn, and we now want to decide whether the next pixel to be set should be T_i or S_i. If $s < t$, then S_i is closer to the desired line and should be set; else T_i is closer and should be set. Said differently, we choose S_i if $s - t < 0$, otherwise we choose T_i.

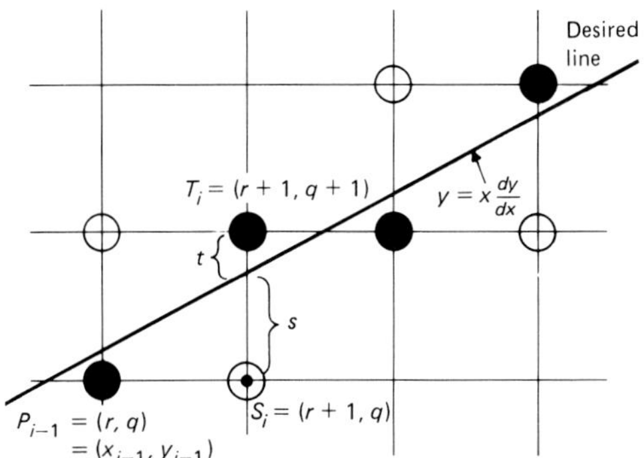

Fig. 11.2 Geometry for Bresenham's algorithm. Black circles are pixels selected by Bresenham's algorithm.

The line being drawn is from $(x1, y1)$ to $(x2, y2)$. Assuming that the first point is nearer the origin, we translate both points by $T(-x1, \ -y1)$, so it becomes the line from (0, 0) to (dx, dy), where $dx = x2 - x1$ and $dy = y2 - y1$. The equation of the line is now $y = (dy/dx)x$. Referring to Fig. 11.2, we represent the coordinates (after the translation) of P_{i-1} as (r, q). Then $S_i = (r + 1, q)$ and $T_i = (r + 1, q + 1)$.

From the examination of Fig. 11.2 we can write

$$s = \frac{dy}{dx}(r + 1) - q, \qquad t = q + 1 - \frac{dy}{dx}(r + 1).$$

Therefore

$$s - t = 2\frac{dy}{dx}(r + 1) - 2q - 1. \tag{11.1}$$

When $s - t < 0$, we choose S_i. Manipulating (11.1), we have

$$dx(s - t) = 2(r \cdot dy - q \cdot dx) + 2dy - dx.$$

Now dx is positive, so we can use $dx(s - t) < 0$ as the test for choosing S_i. We define this as d_i; then

$$d_i = 2(r \cdot dy - q \cdot dx) + 2dy - dx.$$

With $r = x_{i-1}$ and $q = y_{i-1}$, this is

$$d_i = 2x_{i-1}dy - 2y_{i-1}dx + 2dy - dx. \tag{11.2}$$

Adding 1 to each index gives:

$$d_{i+1} = 2x_i \cdot dy - 2y_i \cdot dx + 2dy - dx.$$

Subtracting d_i from d_{i+1}, we get

$$d_{i+1} - d_i = 2dy(x_i - x_{i-1}) - 2dx(y_i - y_{i-1}).$$

We know that $x_i - x_{i-1} = 1$. Rewriting this, we get

$$d_{i+1} = d_i + 2dy - 2dx(y_i - y_{i-1}).$$

If $d_i \geq 0$, then T_i is selected, so $y_i = y_{i-1} + 1$ and

$$d_{i+1} = d_i + 2(dy - dx). \tag{11.3}$$

If $d_i < 0$, then S_i is selected, so $y_i = y_{i-1}$ and

$$d_{i+1} = d_i + 2dy. \tag{11.4}$$

Hence we have an iterative way to calculate d_{i+1} from the previous d_i and to make the selection between S_i and T_i. The initial starting value d_1 is found by evaluating (11.2) for $i = 1$, knowing that $(x_0, y_0) = (0, 0)$. Then

$$d_1 = 2dy - dx. \tag{11.5}$$

The arithmetic needed to evaluate (11.3), (11.4), and (11.5) is minimal: it involves addition, subtraction and left shift (to multiply by 2). This is important, because time-consuming multiplication is avoided. Further, the actual inner loop is quite simple, as seen in the following Bresenham's algorithm (note that this version works only for lines with slope between 0 and 1; generalizing the algorithm is left as an exercise for the reader):

```
procedure BRESENHAM(x1, y1, x2, y2, value: integer);
  var dx, dy, incr1, incr2, d, x, y, xend: integer;
begin
  dx := ABS(x2 - x1);
  dy :=  ABS(y2 - y1);
  d:= 2 * dy - dx;                  {initial value for d from (11.5)}
  incr1 := 2 * dy;                  {constant used for increment if d < 0}
  incr2 : = 2 * (dy - dx);          {constant used for increment if d ≥ 0}
  if x1 > x2
    then begin                      {start at point with smaller x}
      x := x2;
      y := y2;
      xend := x1
      end
    else begin
      x := x1;
      y := y1;
      xend := x2
      end
  WRITE_PIXEL(x, y, value);         {first point on line}
  while x < xend do begin
    x := x + 1;
    if d < 0
      then d := d + incr1           {choose Si—no change in y}
      else begin                    {choose Ti—y is incremented}
        y := y + 1;
        d := d + incr2
        end
      WRITE_PIXEL(x, y, value)      {the selected point near the line}
  end    {while}
end    {BRESENHAM}
```

For a line from point (5, 8) to point (9, 11), the successive values of d are 2, 0, −2, 4, and 2. Figure 11.3 shows which pixels are set and the ideal path of the line.

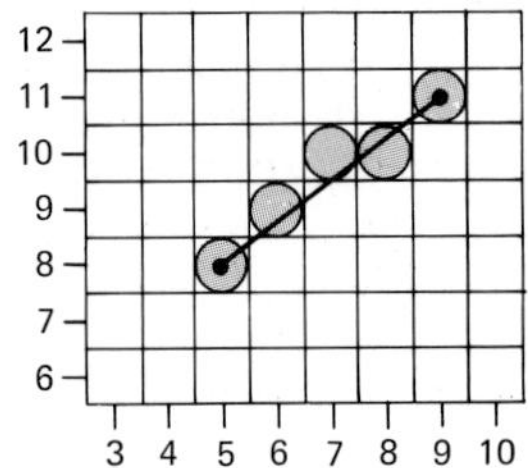

Fig. 11.3 Line from point (5, 8) to point (9, 11) drawn with Bresenham's algorithm.

The line appears jagged, in part because of the enlarged scale of the drawing and in part due to the approximations involved in attempting to draw a line on a discrete grid of points.

11.2.3 Antialiasing Lines

A more pleasing line can be drawn by applying what have come to be known as *antialiasing* and *dejagging* techniques. These techniques, which have their roots in sampling theory, were first applied to graphics by Catmull [CATM74, CATM78a], Crow [CROW77b], and Shoup [SHOU73]. The essential idea is that a pixel, which has a nonzero area on the screen, should be used to represent the nonzero area of the world which is mapped onto the pixel, as depicted in Fig. 11.4. A necessary corollary is that visible lines and characters in the real world have nonzero width; they are no longer mathematical entities made up of line segments of zero width.

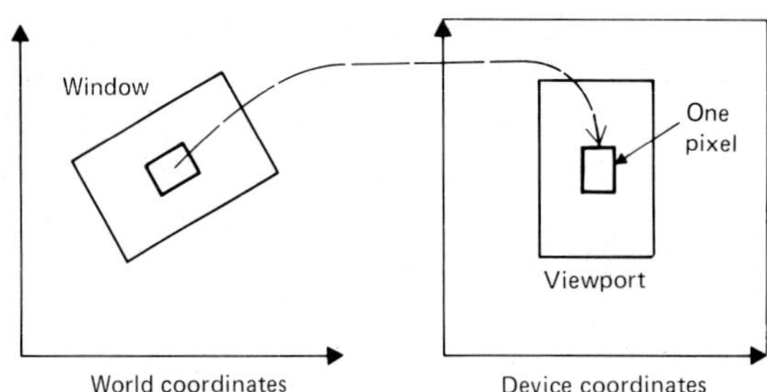

Fig. 11.4 Rectangular area in world coordinates maps into the area covered by one pixel on the screen.

How can we apply this notion? Figure 11.5 shows a line of nonzero width superposed on a raster. The raster grid has been shifted in x and y by half a unit, because we want to focus on the area covered by the pixels which are now positioned in the *center* of each grid box, not on the grid intersections. Thus, a pixel is represented by a square area within the grid. (This is, in itself, an idealization: the intensity distribution of an intensified pixel is approximately normal, and the tails of the distribution overlap into adjacent pixels.)

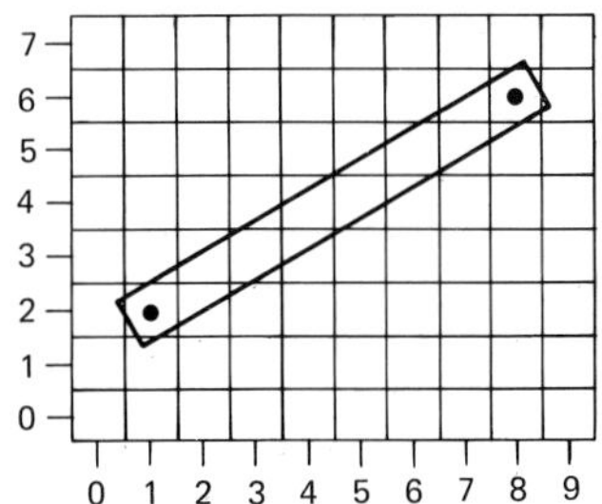

Fig. 11.5 Line of nonzero width from point (1, 2) to point (8, 6).

Each pixel overlapped by the line must have an intensity proportional to the area of the pixel covered by the line. Thus for a white line on a black background, pixel (2,2) would be about 50% white while pixel (3,2) would be about 10% white. Pixels such as (2,4) would be completely black. (For lines of less than maximum intensity, these percentages would be scaled down accordingly.) Figure 11.6 shows lines drawn with and without this type of antialiasing. Note that the smoothing of the lines is achieved at the expense of a slight blurring of the line edges.

Computing the fraction of each pixel overlapped by the rectangular area of the line can be quite time-consuming. Crow [CROW78b], and Barres and Fuchs [BARR79] have developed relatively efficient ways to organize the computations, but the latter's algorithm requires that all line segments be specified before any pixels are generated. Speed will increase in the future (Piller [PILL80] and Gupta et al [GUPT81b] have developed hardware-implemented parallel processing approaches) but, if speed is most important, alternatives are either to live with jagged lines or to use a larger refresh buffer with a high-resolution CRT. Doubling the refresh buffer in both x and y from the typical 512 to 1024 quadruples the number of pixels, doubles the time to scan-convert a line into the buffer, and does not completely remove jagged edges. However, scan-converting a line at doubled resolution is typically faster than antialiasing the line at the original resolution.

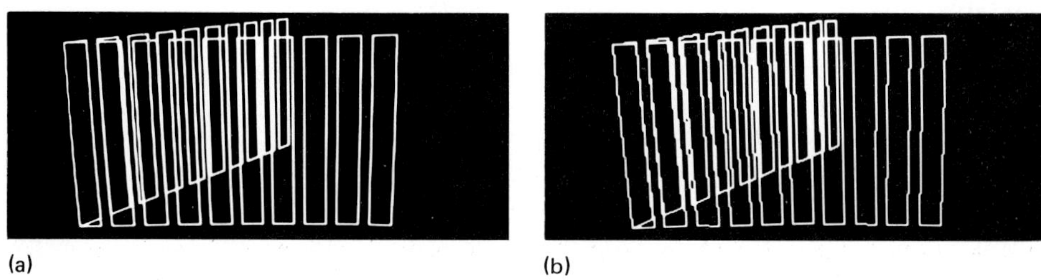

Fig. 11.6 Lines displayed (a) with and (b) without antialiasing (courtesy Jose Barros and Henry Fuchs).

11.2.4 Constant-Intensity Lines

Antialiasing solves another problem encountered with the more straightforward approaches. Consider the two scan-converted lines shown in Fig. 11.7. The diagonal line has a slope of 1, and hence is $\sqrt{2}$ times longer than the horizontal line. Yet each line has the same number of pixels (10) set on. If the intensity of each pixel is *I,* then the intensity per unit length of line *A* is *I,* while for line *B,* it is only $I/\sqrt{2}$, which can be easily detected by a viewer. A simple way to correct this particular problem is to compensate the intensity used to display a line to account for the line's slope. Antialiasing, however, achieves this same objective because the area covered by the line determines how much intensity is distributed along its length. If we consider the lines in Fig. 11.7 as rectangles of height *w,* then line *A* would cover $10w$ units of area and line *B* would cover $10\sqrt{2}w$ units, and intensity per unit length will be constant.

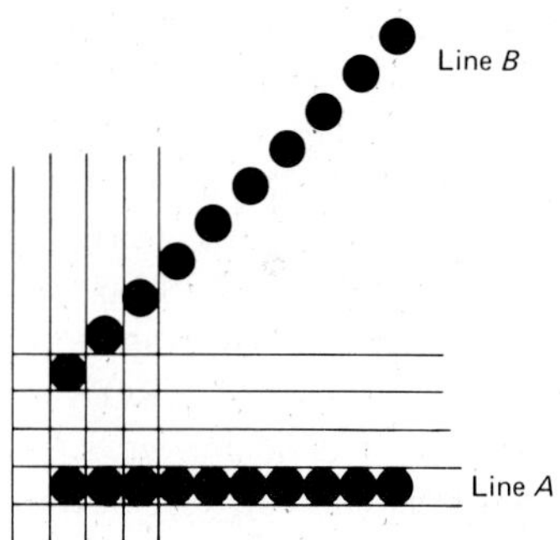

Fig. 11.7 The unequal-intensity problem.

11.2.5 Efficiency in Writing the Refresh Buffer

There is one final issue to discuss in line scan-conversion. Thus far we have not examined the procedure *WRITE_PIXEL(x, y, value*), which places *value* into the pixel located at (x, y). Some refresh buffers are actually organized to use x and y directly as a compound address, but suppose that we have a system which expects an ordinary single address. How is this address related to x and y? (Note that this problem is analogous to determining the address at which the element of a 2D array is stored.) If the refresh buffer runs from (0,0) to (x_{max}, y_{max}) and is stored in row order starting at *base,* then

$$address(x, y) = base + y(x_{max} + 1) + x. \tag{11.6}$$

If the coordinate system of the buffer is addressed from x_{min} to x_{max} and from y_{min} to y_{max}, then

$$address(x, y) = base + (y - y_{min})(x_{max} - x_{min} + 1) + (x - x_{min}). \tag{11.7}$$

By algebraic manipulation and precomputation of resulting constants, the arithmetic involved here can be reduced to a multiply and two adds.

Multiplications are avoided in the main body of Bresenham's algorithm, but if *WRITE_PIXEL* is invoked on each iteration and must perform this address calculation, then we still have one multiply per iteration. This can be avoided by recognizing that

$$address(x + 1, y) = address(x, y) + 1 \tag{11.8}$$

and

$$address(x, y + 1) = address(x, y) + (x_{max} - x_{min} + 1). \tag{11.9}$$

These recurrence relations can be used to modify the algorithm to avoid the address-calculation multiplication. Use of *WRITE_PIXEL* is replaced by incrementing logic plus a procedure *PIXEL_AT_ADDR(address, value)* which places *value* into *address*. Making the actual program changes is left as an exercise to the reader.

11.3 SCAN-CONVERTING CHARACTERS

The common technique of displaying characters with a dot matrix was discussed in Chapter 3. The same basic technique is used for raster displays: the dot pattern for a character is loaded into the refresh buffer at the desired position. The smallest grid on which characters can be defined with reasonable legibility is 5×7; for upper- and lower-case character definitions, a 5×9 matrix is necessary. Higher quality characters require a larger matrix.

11.3.1 Proportional Spacing and Descenders

We can very easily create a raster character generator which provides two features of conventional typeset print lacking in many display systems: proportional spacing and descenders. Proportional spacing is the variation of the spacing between the centers of characters that takes into account the difference in width between, for instance, an "i" and a "w"; with proportional spacing not all characters occupy the same number of horizontal raster units. Descenders (the part of a character descending below the base line, as in the lower-case characters "g", "j", "p", "q", and "y") are displayed by shifting their defining matrixes downwards with respect to other characters, as in Fig. 11.8.

Associated with each character code is a matrix of bits defining the character; in the matrix a **true** means that the pixel corresponding to the matrix coordinates is part of the character and therefore is set to a color different from the background. Proportional spacing and descenders are provided by associating with each character's dot matrix definition a width and a boolean which, if **true,** means that the character has a descender. The following Pascal code shows how characters might be defined and displayed.

```
type char_def =
  record
    char_array: array[0..6, 0..8] of boolean;
         width: integer;                {width of character - 1}
       descend: boolean                 {true for descender}
  end;
  char_set = array[32..127] of char_def; {printable ASCII characters}
procedure CHARACTER(
  definition: char_def;                 {definition of character to display}
        x, y: integer;                  {lower-left corner of nondescender
                                          characters}
       value: integer);                 {value to place in refresh buffer}
  var y_offset, i, j: integer;
begin
  if definition.descend then y_offset := -3
                        else y_offset := 0;
  for i := 0 to definition.width do
    for j := 0 to 8 do
      if definition.char_array[i, j]
        then WRITE_PIXEL(x + i, y + j + y_offset, value)
end    {CHARACTER}
```

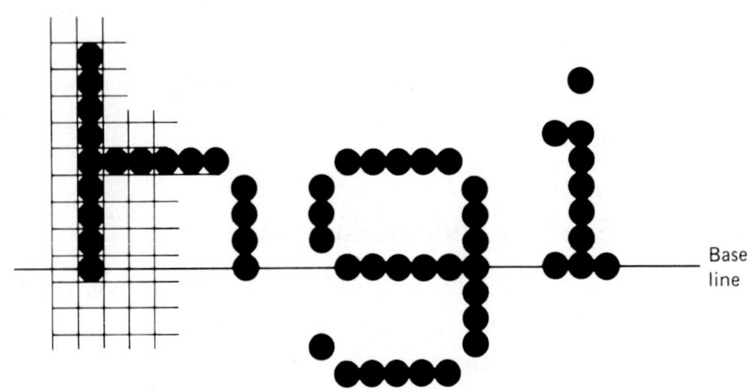

Fig. 11.8 Characters with ascender (h), descender (g), and a narrow character (i).

11.3.2 Antialiasing Characters

The *CHARACTER* procedure assumes that all pixels in a character are displayed with the same intensity value. But we saw in the earlier discussion of antialiasing that to produce nonjagged diagonal lines, we need to vary the intensity in proportion to the area of a pixel covered by the object being displayed. If we think of a character as an object overlaying the pixels, as with the block "M" in Fig. 11.9, we can calculate the intensity value of each pixel. This has been done in the figure by assuming available intensity values of 0 to 3.

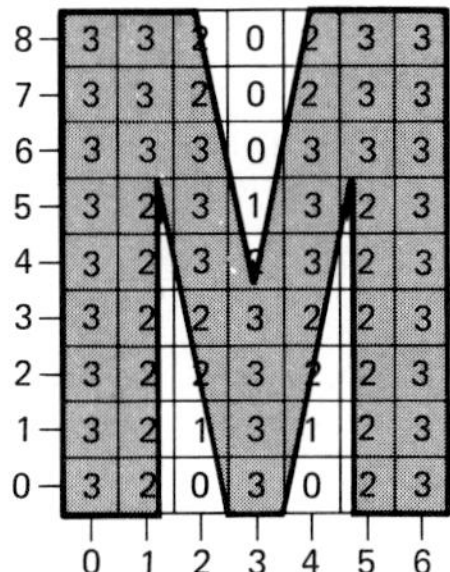

Fig. 11.9 A block "M" and its definition to four intensity levels.

The procedure *CHARACTER* can be modified to place different intensity values into the refresh buffer by changing the array of booleans to an array of integers (containing pixel values). Then the body of the iteration becomes:

```
if definition.char_array[i, j] > 0
  then WRITE_PIXEL(x + i, y + j + y_offset, definition.char_array[i, j])
```

The last parameter to the *CHARACTER* procedure, *value,* is no longer used: the value is implicit in the character definition. Futher modifications, given as exercises, are to treat the values in *definition.char_array* as fractional quantities to be used in scaling the intensity passed as the parameter *value,* and to replace *WRITE_PIXEL* with *PIXEL_AT_ADDR*.

11.4 SCAN-CONVERTING CIRCLES

There are several very easy but inefficient ways to scan-convert a circle. Consider, for simplicity, the circle centered at the origin, for which

$$x^2 + y^2 = R^2.$$

Solving for y, we get

$$y = \pm\sqrt{R^2 - x^2}. \tag{11.10}$$

To draw a quarter circle, we can increment x from 0 to R in unit steps, solving for $+y$ at each step (the other quarters are drawn by symmetry). This works, but is inefficient because of the multiply and square-root operations. Furthermore, there will be large gaps in the circle for values of x close to R because the slope of the circle becomes infinite as x approaches R (see Fig. 11.10). A similar inefficient method, which does avoid the large gaps, is to plot $R \cos\theta$ or $R \sin\theta$ by stepping θ from 0 to 90°.

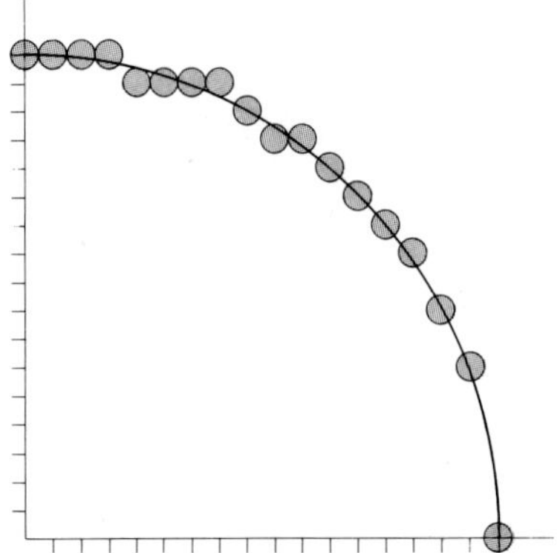

Fig. 11.10 A quarter-circle generated with unit steps in x and with y calculated and then rounded.

11.4.1 Eight-Way Symmetry

This process can be improved somewhat by taking greater advantage of the symmetry in a circle. Consider first a circle at the origin. If the point (x, y) is on the circle, then we can trivially compute seven other points on the circle, as shown in Fig. 11.11. Therefore if we use Eq. (11.10) or some other more efficient mechanism to compute y for values of x between 0 and $R/\sqrt{2}$ (the point at which $x = y$), seven additional points on the circle are also available; this range of x corresponds to the 45° segment of the circle in the figure. For a circle centered at the origin, the points can be displayed with procedure *CIRCLE_POINTS* (the procedure is easily generalized to the case of circles with arbitrary origins):

```
procedure CIRCLE_POINTS(x, y, value: integer);
begin
   WRITE_PIXEL(x, y, value);
   WRITE_PIXEL(y, x, value);
   WRITE_PIXEL(y, -x, value);
   WRITE_PIXEL(x, -y, value);
   WRITE_PIXEL( -x, -y, value);
   WRITE_PIXEL( -y, -x, value);
   WRITE_PIXEL( -y, x, value);
   WRITE_PIXEL( -x, y, value)
end    {CIRCLE_POINTS}
```

11.4.2 Bresenham's Circle Algorithm

Bresenham [BRES77] has developed an incremental circle generator which is more efficient than either of the above methods. Conceived for use with pen plotters, the algorithm generates all points on a circle centered at the origin by incrementing

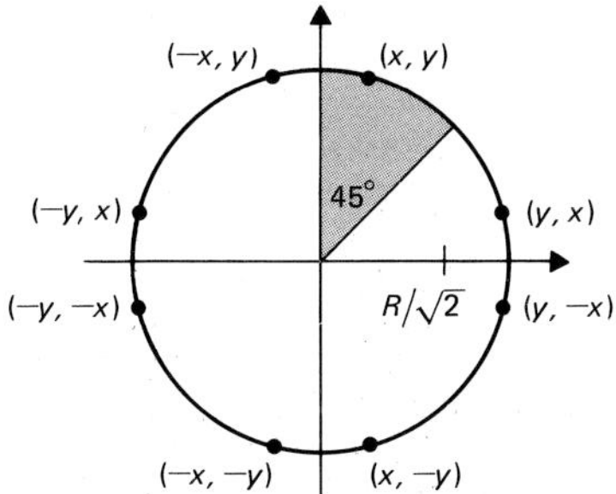

Fig. 11.11 Eight symmetrical points on a circle.

360° around the circle. We present an adaptation of the algorithm which increments through only 45° of a circle, from $x = 0$ to $x = R/\sqrt{2}$, and uses the *CIRCLE_POINTS* procedure to display points on the entire circle.

At each step, the algorithm selects the point $P_i\,(x_i, y_i)$ which is closest to the true circle and which therefore makes the error term

$$D(P_i) = (x_i^2 + y_i^2) - R^2$$

closest to zero; that is, $|D(P_i)|$ is minimized at each step. As with Bresenham's line-drawing algorithm, the fundamental strategy is to select the nearest point by using decision variables whose values can be incrementally calculated with only a few adds, subtracts, and shifts. The signs of the variables are used to make the decisions.

What decisions are to be made? Consider Fig. 11.12 which shows a small part of the pixel grid and the various possible ways (A to G) that the true circle might cut through the grid.* Assume that the point P_{i-1} has been determined to be the closest to the circle for $x = x_{i-1}$. Now for $x = x_{i-1} + 1$ we must determine whether T_i or S_i is closer to the circle.

Let us define

$$D(S_i) = [(x_{i-1} + 1)^2 + (y_{i-1})^2] - R^2, \tag{11.11}$$

$$D(T_i) = [(x_{i-1} + 1)^2 + (y_{i-1} - 1)^2] - R^2. \tag{11.12}$$

These are the differences between the squared distances from the origin (the center of the circle) to S_i (or to T_i) and to the actual circle. If $|D(S_i)| \geq |D(T_i)|$, then T_i is closer (or equidistant) to the actual circle than is S_i. Conversely, if $|D(S_i)| < |D(T_i)|$, then S_i is closer to the actual circle than is T_i.

*Bresenham's original circle algorithm was not limited to the 45° segment being examined here and therefore considers cases F and G, for which the point directly below P_{i-1} might be selected.

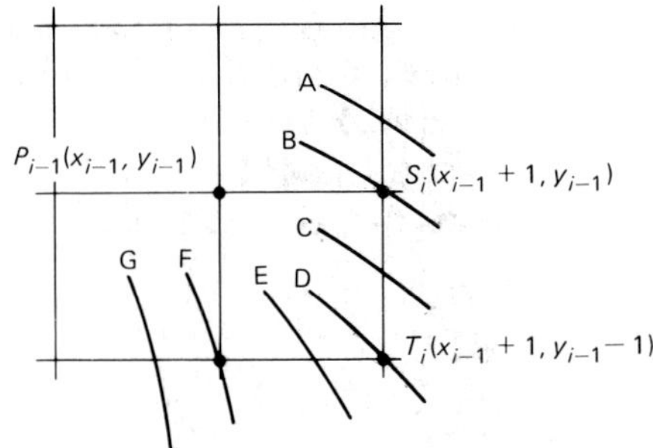

Fig. 11.12 Decision points for Bresenham's circle generator.

Now if we define

$$\mathbf{d}_i = |D(S_i)| - |D(T_i)|,$$

then the point T_i is selected when $\mathbf{d}_i \geq 0$; otherwise the point S_i is selected.

In case C, we have $D(S_i) > 0$, because S_i lies outside the circle, and $D(T_i) < 0$, because T_i lies inside the circle. This means we can base decisions on d_i instead of $\mathbf{d}_i$, where

$$d_i = D(S_i) + D(T_i). \tag{11.13}$$

Now if $d_i \geq 0$, then T_i is selected; otherwise, $d_i < 0$, so S_i is selected.

Consider now cases A and B and the corresponding value of d_i from (11.13). It is clear that $D(T_i) < 0$, because T_i is inside of the true circle. Similarly, $D(S_i) \leq 0$ (the equality occurs in case B; the inequality in case A). Therefore, $d_i < 0$ for cases A and B. The same selection rules applied to the preceding discussion of case C will therefore properly lead to the choice of S_i, using (11.13).

Finally, consider cases D and E. First, $D(S_i) > 0$, because S_i is outside the true circle. Similarly, $D(T_i) \geq 0$ (the equality is for case D; the inequality for case E). Therefore, $d_i \geq 0$ for cases *D* and *E*, so the decision rules developed above for case C apply here also: if $d_i \geq 0$, choose T_i. We can always use d_i instead of $\mathbf{d}_i$.

We are not finished yet: calculating the decision variable (11.13) as it is currently expressed requires several multiplications. However, a series of algebraic manipulations shows that

$$d_1 = 3 - 2R.$$

If S_i is chosen (because $d_i < 0$), then

$$d_{i+1} = d_i + 4x_{i-1} + 6;$$

if T_i is chosen (because $d_i \geq 0$), then

$$d_{i+1} = d_i + 4(x_{i-1} - y_{i-1}) + 10.$$

These specific algebraic results and consequent algorithm were derived by J. Michener by applying Bresenham's methodology. Expression (11.13) for d_i is expanded by using (11.11) and (11.12). By substituting $i - 1$ for i, an expression for d_{i-1} is found; then the difference $d_i - d_{i-1}$ is formed and evaluated for each of the two possible moves. The following procedure is based on these results:*

```
procedure MICH_CIRCLE(radius, value: integer);
  {assumes center of circle is at origin}
  var x, y, d: integer;
begin
  x := 0;
  y := radius;
  d := 3 - 2 * radius;
  while x < y do begin
    CIRCLE_POINTS (x, y, value);
    if d < 0
      then d := d + 4 * x + 6              {select S}
      else begin                           {select T— decrement y}
        d := d + 4 * (x - y) + 10;
        y: = y - 1
      end
    x := x + 1
  end     {while}
  if x = y then CIRCLE_POINTS (x,y,value);
end     {MICH_CIRCLE}
```

If *CIRCLE_POINTS* is called when either $x = y$ or $r = 1$, then each of four pixels is set twice. On a raster display, this is no problem. If the algorithm were used with a film recorder, however, double exposure of these points to the light source would cause their intensity to be greater than that of the other points. Figure 11.13 shows one octant of a circle of radius 17 generated with the algorithm (compare the results to Fig. 11.10).

Other techniques have been developed for drawing circles [BADL77, DORO79, HORN76, SUEN79] and for more general curves than circles. Jordan, Lennon, and Holm [JORD73b] developed a general and efficient method for most curves which can be expressed as $f(x, y) = 0$ and have continuous derivatives. The method was later shown to have a few limitations [BELS76, RAMO76]. Special cases of such curves include conic sections (particularly the circle) and straight lines. While the algorithm can be simplified in these special cases, there is still slightly more work per iteration involved than for Bresenham's line and circle algorithms. This is important because of the stringent speed requirements for our scan-conversion algorithms. On the other hand, the algorithm of Pitteway [PITT67], while more complicated to derive, requires even less work per iteration than does Bresenham's general formulation for 360° circles, and equivalent work for the 45° formulation given here.

---

*Another similar approach, developed by J. Bresenham, is described in Exercise 11.29.

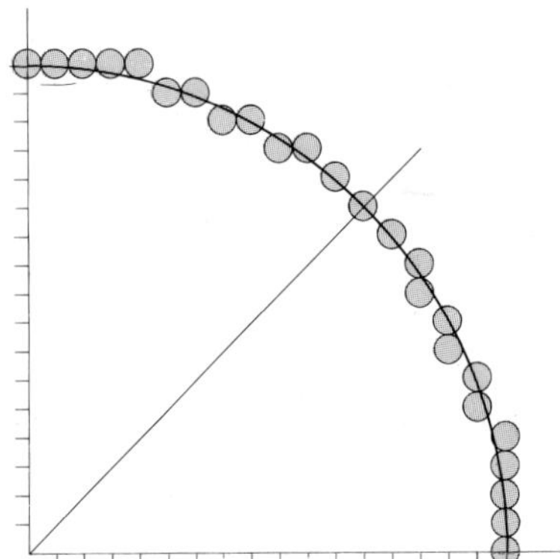

Fig. 11.13 Octant of circle generated with Bresenham's algorithm; second octant generated by symmetry.

11.5 REGION FILLING

A region is a group of adjacent, connected pixels. Regions can be created and defined either by assigning a specific value to all the pixels contained in the region or by assigning a specific value to the pixels bordering on the region. Figures 11.14 and 11.15 are examples of such regions: Fig. 11.14 shows regions with all black pixels; Fig. 11.15 shows regions surrounded by a border of black pixels. All but one of these four regions has some interior holes, and all the regions are nonconvex. Another way to define regions in terms of polygons is discussed in the following sections.

In many interactive raster applications, especially in animation and graphic arts, the user interactively defines regions of adjacent pixels which are to be filled with a given pixel value, denoted here as *new_value*. A variation is to fill the region with a pattern of different pixel values rather than with a single value. Painted scenes (see Color Plate 8) can be created by using this variation. The user outlines an area by interactive sketching, then chooses a color and points at any interior point of the region. In response, the computer fills the region. The same sequence of actions can be employed to produce a bar chart in which the bars are of different colors.

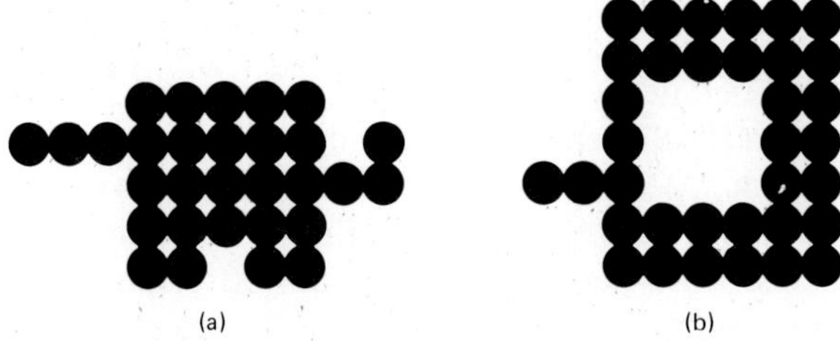

Fig. 11.14 Interior-defined 4-connected regions occupied by black pixels.

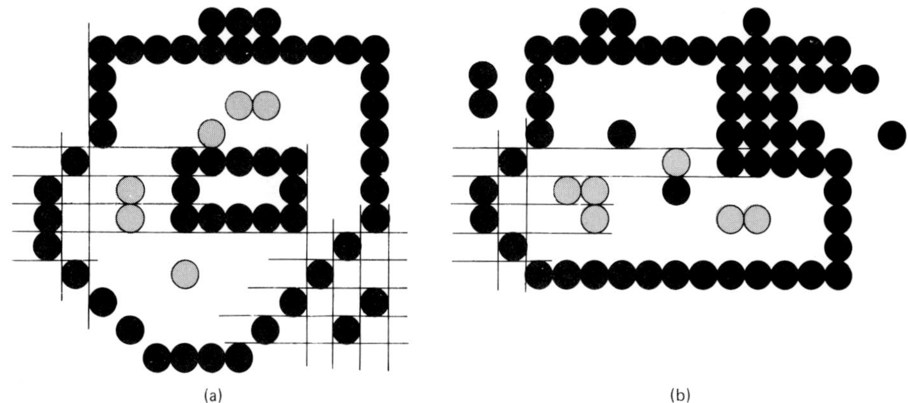

Fig. 11.15 Boundary-defined 4-connected regions surrounded by boundary of black pixels. Note that pixels outside the boundary can also have the value of boundary pixels.

11.5.1 Types of Regions

Regions defined by interior values are called interior-defined: all pixels in the region have value *old_value,* and no pixels on the boundary of the region have a value of *old_value.* Algorithms which operate on such regions to set all their pixels to *new_value* are called *flood-fill algorithms.*

Regions defined by a boundary are called *boundary-defined:* pixels on the boundary have value *boundary_value,* while pixels in the region have some value other than *new_value.* Algorithms which operate on such regions to set all their values to *new_value* are called *boundary-fill algorithms.*

Before considering the algorithms, we need to define more precisely the notion of a connected region of adjacent pixels. This is important because there are two sorts of regions of interest to us: *4-connected* and *8-connected.* Algorithms for 8-connected regions will work on 4-connected regions, but the converse is not true. All pixels in a 4-connected region can be reached one from the other by a sequence of any of the four one-pixel moves: up, down, left, right. Figure 11.14 shows two interior-defined 4-connected regions in black. Notice that, as in (b), holes within a region are permissible. Figure 11.15 shows two boundary-defined 4-connected regions with black boundaries and white and gray interiors. In this case the pixels inside the region can have any value but that of the black pixels. In Fig. 11.15(a), the inner rectangular area defines one region, the area outside the rectangle and inside the outer boundary defines a second region, and the inner rectangle forms a hole in the outer region. In Fig. 11.15(b), the inner black pixels again form holes in the region.

All pixels in an 8-connected region can be reached from all others by a sequence of any of the eight one-pixel vertical, horizontal, or diagonal moves. Figure 11.16

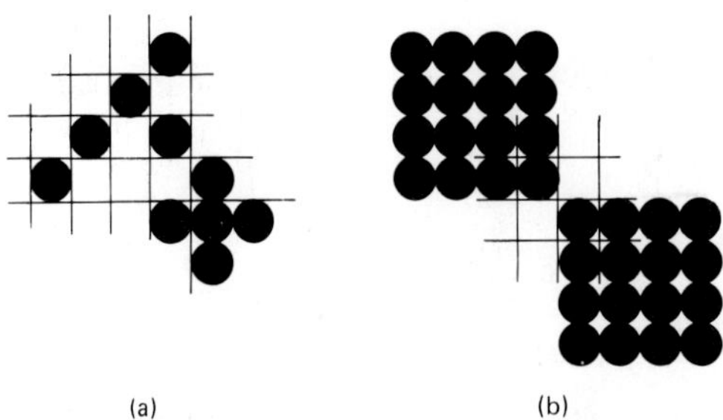

Fig. 11.16 Interior-defined 8-connected regions occupied by black pixels.

shows interior-defined 8-connected regions with black pixels. Figure 11.17 shows boundary-defined 8-connected regions surrounded by black boundaries. It is interesting to note that the boundary of an 8-connected region is 4-connected, while the boundary of a 4-connected region is 8-connected.

An algorithm which fills 8-connected regions must of course "jump" the diagonal connections between pixels, perhaps giving unexpected results. For instance, if we were to apply an 8-connected fill algorithm to the upper-left square of Fig. 11.16(b), the lower-right square would also be filled, even if we intended otherwise. However, the use of a 4-connected fill algorithm on the upper-left square would not cause the filling to spread to the lower-right square.

11.5.2 The Simple Recursive Algorithm

A very simple algorithm to set the pixels of a 4-connected interior-defined region is:

```
procedure FLOOD_FILL_4(
  x, y,                        {starting point in 4-connected interior-defined
                                 region}
  old_value,                   {value in interior-defined region}
  new_value: integer);         {replacement value for old_value}
                               {old_value must not equal new_value}

begin
  if READ_PIXEL(x, y) = old_value
    then begin
      WRITE_PIXEL(x, y, new_value); {change value}
      {attempt to propagate in each of four directions}
      FLOOD_FILL_4(x, y - 1, old_value, new_value);
      FLOOD_FILL_4(x, y + 1, old_value, new_value);
      FLOOD_FILL_4(x - 1, y, old_value, new_value);
      FLOOD_FILL_4(x + 1, y, old_value, new_value)
    end
end     {FLOOD_FILL_4}
```

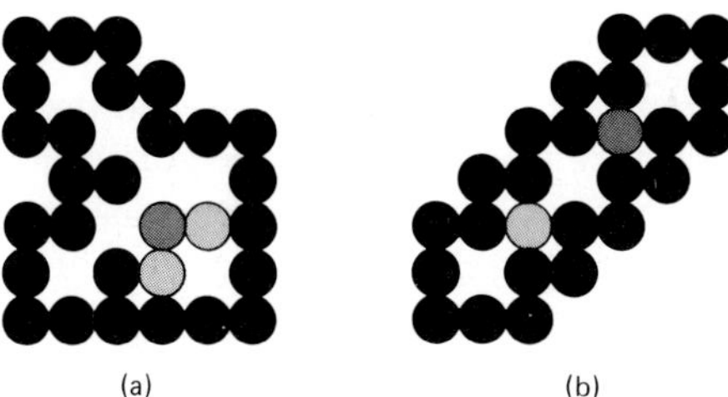

(a) (b)

Fig. 11.17 Boundary defined 8-connected regions surrounded by boundary of black pixels.

The basic strategy the algorithm uses is to first determine whether the pixel at (x,y) is in part of the region which has not yet been visited and therefore still has value *old_value.* If so, the value is changed and the four neighboring pixels are then examined. This algorithm can be adapted to flood-fill an interior-defined 8-connected region by propagating in eight rather than in four directions.

Similarly, a simple algorithm to set the pixels of a boundary-defined 4-connected region is:

```
procedure BOUNDARY_FILL_4(
  x, y,                        {starting point in boundary-defined 4-con-
                                 nected region}
  boundary_value,              {value on boundary}
  new_value: integer);         {replacement value}
  {it is permissible to have new_value = boundary_value; otherwise no pixels in region
    may be initially set to new_value}
begin
  if READ_PIXEL(x, y)< >boundary_value      {boundary not reached and}
  and READ_PIXEL(x, y)< >new_value          {previously filled pixel not reached}
    then begin
      WRITE_PIXEL(x, y, new_value);         {change value}
      {attempt to propagate in 4 directions}
      four calls to BOUNDARY_FILL_4
    end
end    {BOUNDARY_FILL_4}
```

The basic strategy is clearly the same as for *FLOOD_FILL_4,* except that the test for whether the pixel at (x,y) is in part of the region which has not yet been visited is in two parts: a comparison with *boundary_value* to find out if the pixel is part of the region, and a comparison with *new_value* to find if the pixel has yet been visited. This test accounts for the restriction that no pixels in the region may initially be set to *new_value* (unless *new_value* = *boundary_value,* in which case the pixels already set to *new_value* are on the boundary of the region rather than being part of the region). Again, this procedure can be made into *BOUNDARY_FILL_8* by propagating in eight rather than four directions.

11.5.3 Decreasing the Recursion Depth

These procedures are simple, but highly recursive, and the many levels of recursion take time and may cause stack overflow when memory space is limited. Much more efficient approaches to region filling have been developed [LIEB78, SMIT79, PAVL81]. They require considerably more logic, but the depth of the stack is no problem except for degenerate cases. The basic algorithm works with *runs,* which are horizontal groups of adjacent pixels within the region. Runs are bounded at both ends by pixels with value of *boundary_value* and contain no pixels of value *new_value.* Runs are filled in iteratively by a loop. A run is identified by its rightmost pixel; at least one run from each unfilled part of the region is kept on the stack.

The algorithm proceeds as follows: the contiguous horizontal run of pixels containing the starting point is filled in. Then the row above the just-filled run is examined from right to left to find the rightmost pixel of each run, and these pixel addresses are stacked. The same is done for the row below the just-filled run. When a run has been processed in this manner, the pixel address at the top of the stack is used as a new starting point. When the stack is empty, the algorithm terminates. Figure 11.18, adapted from Smith [SMIT79], shows how a typical algorithm works. In Fig. 11.18(a), the run which contains the starting point has been filled in, and the addresses of numbered pixels have been saved on a stack. The numbers indicate order on the stack: 1 is at the bottom and is processed last. The figure shows only part of the region-filling process: the reader is encouraged to complete the process, step by step, for the rest of the region.

11.6 POLYGON CLIPPING

One of the advantages of raster graphics is that filled regions can be displayed. In the preceding section we saw how to fill regions which are defined by pixel values in the refresh buffer. In many applications, however, the regions to be filled are defined by polygons whose vertices are stored in the application data structure. To be displayed, the polygons must first be passed through the viewing transformation and clipping process and be converted into device coordinates, after which they can be filled. In this section we discuss the clipping process; in the next section, the polygon-filling process.

An algorithm which clips a polygon and creates new polygon(s) must deal with many different cases, such as those shown in Fig. 11.19. Case (a) is particularly difficult: the concave polygon clips into two separate polygons. The clipping job seems rather overwhelming. Each edge of the polygon must be tested against each edge of the window: new edges must be added, and existing edges must be discarded, retained, or divided. Sometimes several polygons result from clipping a single polygon. We need an organized way to go about dealing with all these cases.

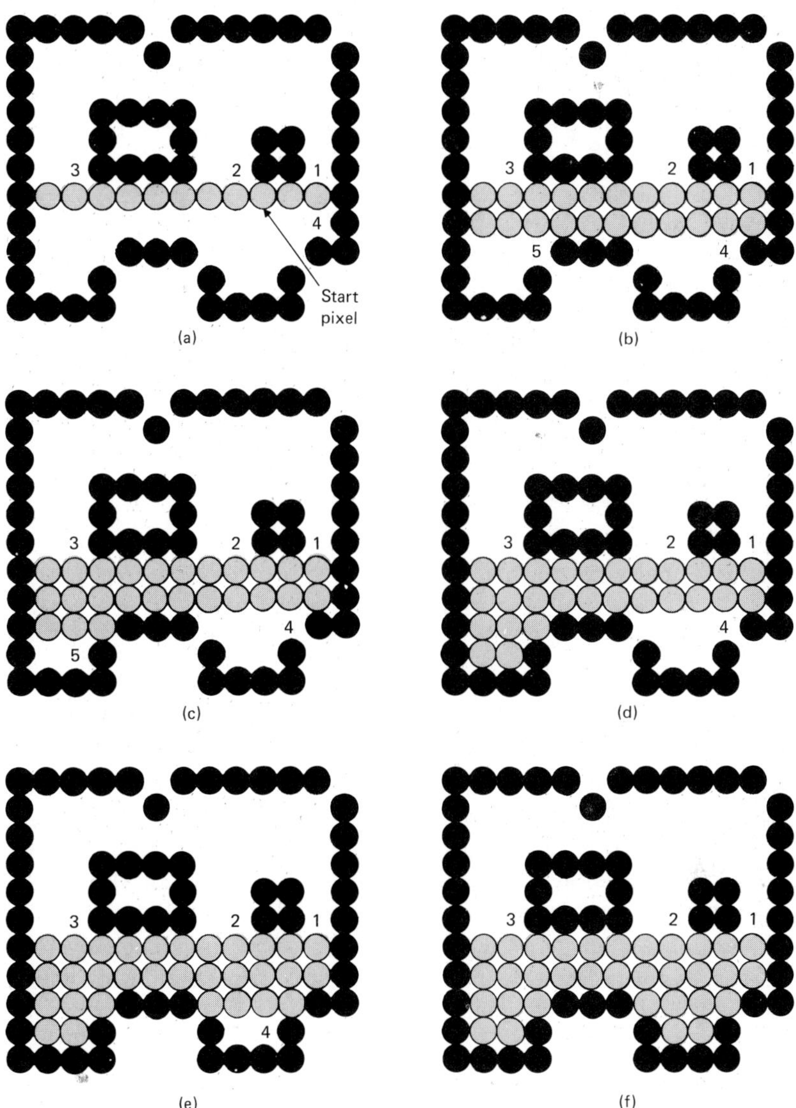

Fig. 11.18 Filling of boundary-defined regions; numbered pixels are stacked.

11.6.1 The Sutherland–Hodgman Algorithm

Sutherland and Hodgman's [SUTH74b] polygon clipping algorithm uses a divide-and-conquer strategy by solving a series of simple and identical problems which, when combined, solve the overall problem. The simple problem is to clip a polygon

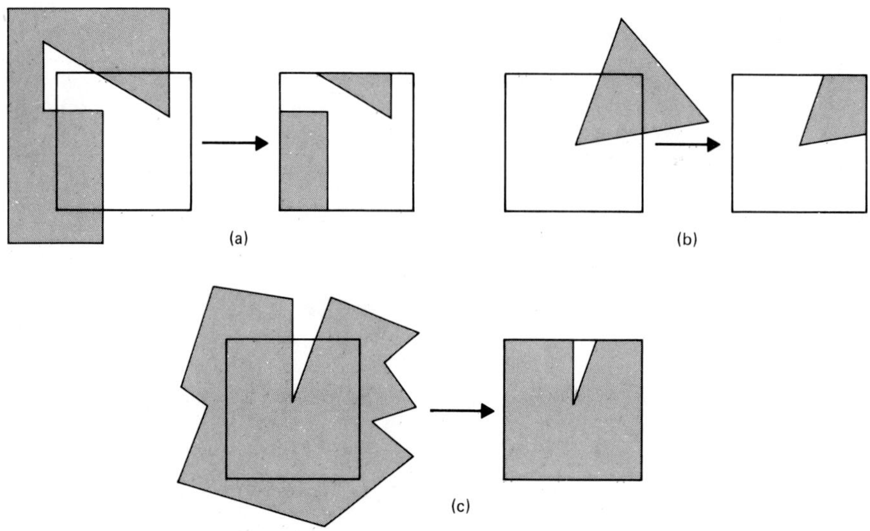

Fig. 11.19 Examples of polygon clipping.

against a single clip boundary. Successive clips against four clip boundaries, each defined by one edge of the window as in Fig. 11.20, clip a polygon against a rectangular window.

The actual algorithm is in fact more general: a polygon (convex or concave) can be clipped against any convex clipping polygon, and in 3D, polygons can be clipped against convex polyhedron volumes defined by planes. The algorithm accepts a series of polygon vertices $v_1, v_2, \ldots, v_n$. The polygon edges are from v_i to v_{i+1} and from v_n to v_1. The algorithm clips against an edge and outputs another series of vertices defining the clipped polygon.

The algorithm, called here *S_H_CLIP,* "marches" around the polygon from v_n to v_1 and then on around to v_n, at each step examining the relationship between successive vertices and the clip boundary. Either zero, one, or two vertices are added to the output list of vertices which define the clipped polygon. There are four possible cases to be analyzed, as shown in Fig. 11.21.

Let us consider the polygon edge from vertex s to vertex p in Fig. 11.21. In case 1, when the polygon edge is completely inside the clip boundary, vertex p is added to the output list. In case 2, the intersection point i is output as a vertex because the edge intersects the boundary; the start point was already output for case 1. In case 3, both vertices are outside the boundary, and there is no output, while in case 4, the intersection point i and p are both added to the output list.

Procedure *S_H_CLIP* given below accepts an array *in_v* of vertices and creates another array *out_v* of vertices. To keep the code simple, we do not show error

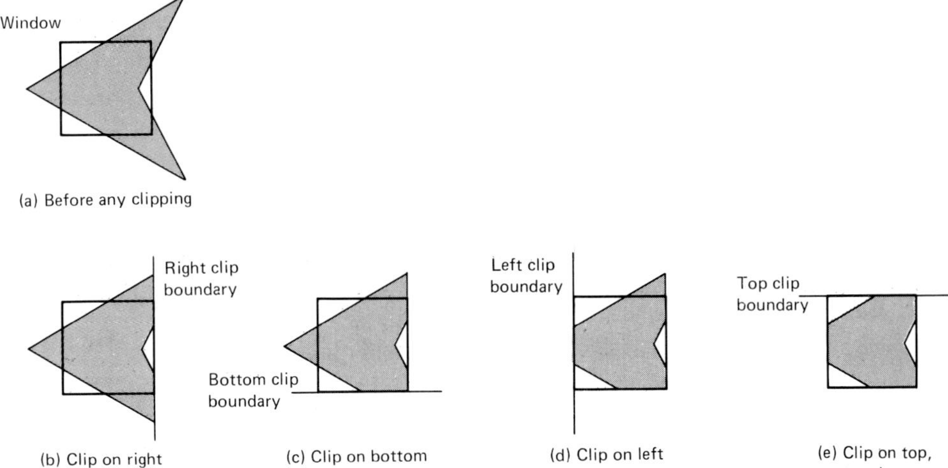

Fig. 11.20 Polygon clipping, edge by edge.

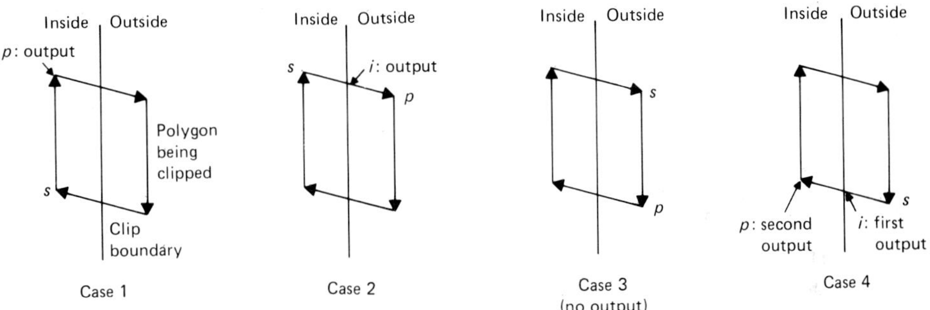

Fig. 11.21 Four cases of polygon clipping.

checking on array bounds and use the procedure *OUTPUT(out_v)* to place a vertex into *out_v*. The function *INTERSECT(s, p, clip_boundary)* calculates the intersection of the polygon edge from vertex *s* to vertex *p* with *clip_boundary*, which is defined by two points on the boundary. The function *INSIDE* returns **true** if the vertex is on the inside of the clip boundary, where "inside" is defined as being to the right of the clip boundary when one looks from the first point to the second point of the clip boundary definition (see Fig. 11.22). The test is based on the cross product of the vector from P_1 to P_2, with the vector from P_1 to the point being tested. If the cross product is along the positive z-axis, the point is to the left and thus outside; if it is along the negative z-axis, the point is inside. The cross product of two vectors $v = (v_x, v_y)$ and $w = (w_x, w_y)$ in the xy-plane (as these are) is just a vector of magnitude $v_x w_y - v_y w_x$ along the z-axis. If this quantity is negative, the tested point is inside. In the case at hand, we let $v = \overline{P_1P_2}$ and $w = \overline{P_1P_4}$ or $\overline{P_1P_3}$.

```
type  vertex = array [1..2] of real;
    boundary = array [1..2] of vertex;
vertex_array = array [1..max] of vertex;
                {max is a declared constant}
procedure S_H_CLIP(
              in_v : vertex_array,         {input vertex array}
             out_v : vertex_array,         {output vertex array}
         in_length : integer,              {actual length of in_v}
        out_length : integer,              {actual length of out_v}
     clip_boundary : boundary);            {edge against which to clip}
         var i, p, s : vertex,
                   j : integer;
begin
  out_length := 0;                         {used by OUTPUT}
  s := in_v [in_length];                   {start with the last vertex in in_v}
  for j := 1 to in_length do begin
    p := in_v [j];
    {now s and p correspond to the vertices in Fig. 11.21}
    if INSIDE(p, clip_boundary)
      then                                 {cases 1 and 4}
        if INSIDE(s, clip_boundary)
          then OUTPUT(p)                   {case 1}
          else begin                       {case 4}
            i := INTERSECT(s, p, clip_edge);
            OUTPUT(i);
            OUTPUT(p)
          end
      else                                 {cases 2 and 3}
        if INSIDE(s, clip_boundary)
          then begin                       {case 2}
            i := INTERSECT(s, p, clip_edge);
            OUTPUT(i)
          end;                             {no action for case 3}
        s := p                             {advance to next pair of vertices}
  end    {for loop}
end    {S_H_CLIP}
```

Sutherland and Hodgman show how to structure the algorithm so that it is reentrant [SUTH74b]. As soon as a vertex is output, the clipper calls itself with the vertex, and clipping is performed against the next clip boundary, so that no intermediate storage is necessary for the partially clipped polygon. In essence, the polygon is passed through a "pipeline" of clippers, and each step can be implemented as special-purpose hardware, with no intervening buffer space.

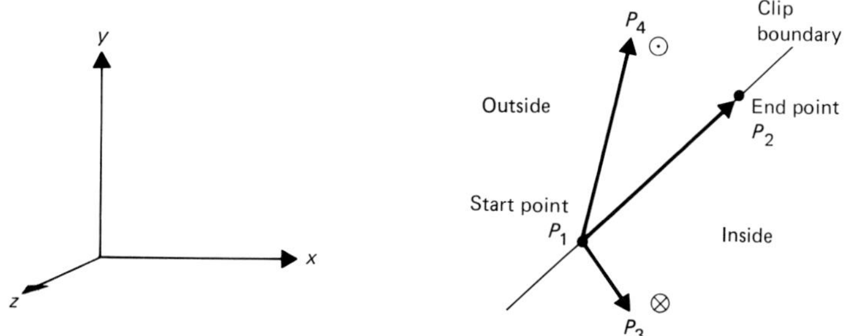

Fig. 11.22 Clip boundary defined by directed line segment from P_1 to P_2. Point P_3 is inside ($\overline{P_1P_2} \times \overline{P_1P_3}$ has negative z in right-hand coordinate system), while point P_4 is outside ($\overline{P_1P_2} \times \overline{P_1P_4}$ has positive z).

11.6.2 The Weiler–Atherton Algorithm

There is a problem with the clipped polygon of Fig. 11.19(a) because it has extraneous edges along the window boundary. Figure 11.23 shows the same situation. The extra edges can be eliminated by additional processing steps. Alternatively, the more general (and more complex) Weiler-Atherton algorithm can be used [WEIL77]. It clips one concave polygon against another concave polygon and even allows both polygons to have interior holes. Both the Sutherland-Hodgman and Weiler-Atherton algorithms can be structured to output the polygon(s) both inside and outside the clip polygon.

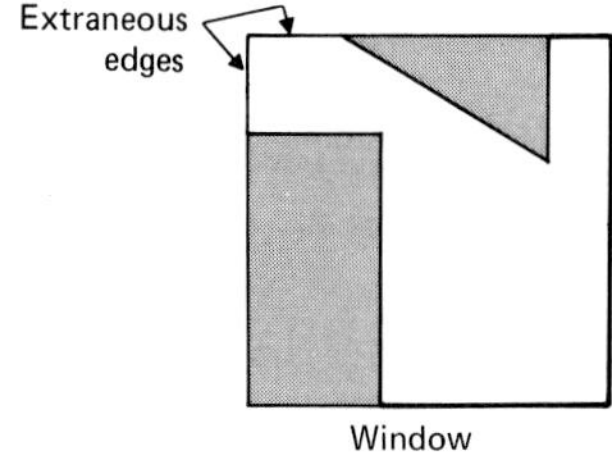

Fig. 11.23 Clipped polygon (with eight edges) created by the Sutherland–Hodgman algorithm. The Weiler–Atherton algorithm outputs two separate polygons.

The Weiler-Atherton algorithm clips a *subject polygon* against a *clip polygon* by tracing around the border of the subject polygon in the clockwise direction until an intersection with the clip polygon is encountered. If the edge enters the clip polygon, the algorithm then proceeds along the subject polygon edge. If the edge leaves the clip polygon, the algorithm makes a right turn and follows the clip polygon. In either case, the intersection is remembered and used to ensure that all paths are traced exactly once. Figure 11.24 shows the sequence of steps which this algorithm follows in the clipping situation originally depicted in Fig. 11.19(a).

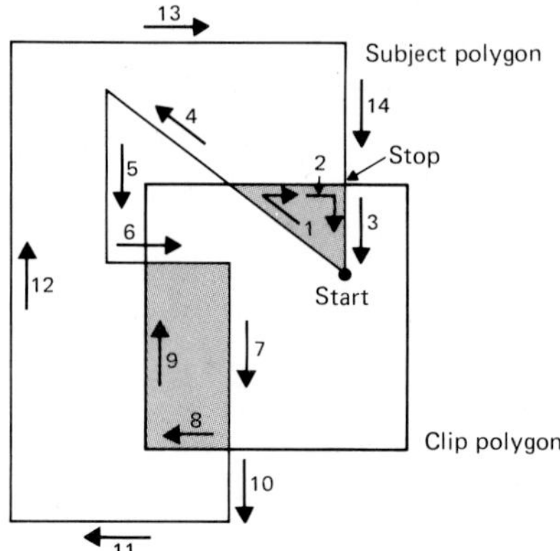

Fig. 11.24 Weiler–Atherton clipping: any start point may be used; two polygons (shaded regions) result.

11.7 SCAN-CONVERTING POLYGONS

After a polygon has been clipped and mapped into the raster device coordinate system, we are ready to scan-convert it into a refresh buffer, so that its edges and interior are set to the desired values. The basic strategy we will develop is to create and fill in the polygon one scan line (row of pixels) at a time. The algorithm which does this is called the *scan-line algorithm.*

11.7.1 Region Filling and Polygon Filling

There is an important difference between region filling and polygon scan-conversion. In region filling, the region is defined by pixel values in the refresh buffer. In polygon scan-conversion, the region is defined by the polygon vertices and absolutely no assumptions are made about what initial values are in the refresh buffer. Only in special cases can region filling be used to implement polygon scan-conversion. To do so, the entire refresh buffer must be initialized to *old_value.* We would then scan-convert the polygon edges to a value of *boundary_value,* find some point (x, y) interior to the polygon, and call

BOUNDARY_FILL_4(x, y, *boundary_value*, *new_value*),

Alternatively, we could scan-convert the edges by using some reserved pixel value for polygon edges. After the region is filled by *BOUNDARY_FILL_4,* the edges would again be scan-converted, but this time to a nonreserved value. Neither of these solutions is attractive, however, since the necessary initial conditions can almost never be assumed, the use of a special pixel value for edges limits flexibility, and the refresh buffer may be difficult or slow to access or may not exist at all.

11.7.2 Using the Vertex List and Scan-Line Coherence

The scan-conversion algorithm described next avoids all these complications because it operates not on the refresh buffer but on the polygon vertex list. Figure 11.25, which illustrates the basic polygon scan-conversion process, shows a polygon and one scan line passing through it. We must determine which pixels on the scan line are within the polygon, and set the corresponding pixels (in this case, 2 through 4 and 9 through 13) to their appropriate values. By repeating this for each scan line which intersects the polygon, we scan-convert the entire polygon.

A simple way to decide which pixels on the scan line are in the polygon is to test each individual pixel, one after the other. This is rather inefficient, because in general a sequence of adjacent pixels will be in the polygon. This observation is based on the notion of *spatial coherence:* very often the polygon being operated on does not change as we move from pixel to pixel or from scan line to scan line. We take advantage of this coherence by looking for only those pixels at which changes occur. In the case at hand, we have *scan-line coherence:* later we will use edge coherence.

In scan line 8 of Fig. 11.25 there are two runs of pixels within the polygon. The runs can be filled in by a three-step process:

1. Find the intersections of the scan line with all edges of the polygon,
2. Sort the intersections by increasing x-coordinate, and
3. Fill in all pixels between pairs of intersections.

In Fig. 11.25, the sorted list of x-coordinates is (2, 4, 9, 13). We therefore fill in pixels in the intervals from 2 to 4, and from 9 to 13.

The first step of this process is based on simple calculations, by intersecting each scan line with each polygon edge which crosses the scan line. Horizontal edges cannot intersect scan lines and are not used at all. The second two steps of the process, sorting and filling, are seemingly simple to perform.

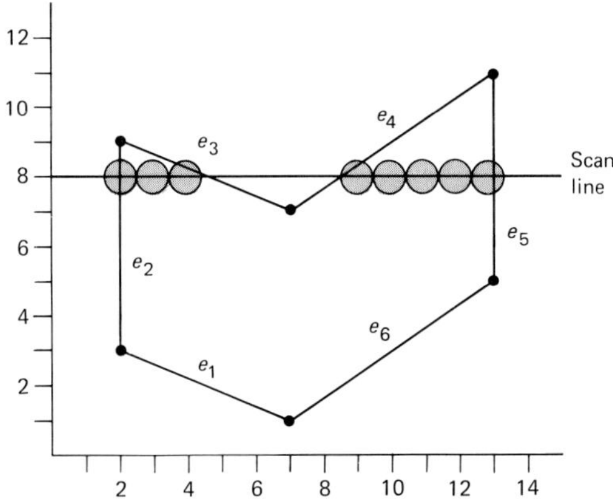

Fig. 11.25 Polygon and scan-line.

11.7.3 Vertex Intersections: A Special Case

There is a potential problem with the sorting and filling process, however. If the number of intersections on the sorted list is odd, the filling step will not work properly. This can happen when a scan line intersects a vertex and thus introduces two intersections to the intersection list. Consider, for example, the scan line for $y = 3$ in Fig. 11.25. Its intersections with polygon edges are at 2, 2, and 10. Thus the sequence from 2 to 2 (i.e., the pixel at $x = 2, y = 3$) would be filled, the sequence from 3 to 9 would not be filled, and the sequence from 10 to the right edge of the buffer would be filled, when the single sequence from 2 to 10 should really be filled.

The solution which might first come to mind is to count just one intersection for scan lines passing through a vertex. But this does not give the proper results for the vertices at scan lines 1, 7, 9, or 11. The proper solution is to count two intersections at vertices which represent local minima or maxima, but to count just one intersection at the other vertices. A local minimum occurs at a vertex when the y-coordinates of the preceding and succeeding vertices are greater than that of the vertex being examined. A local maximum is similarly defined. The vertices at scan lines 1 and 7 are local minima, while those at scan lines 9 and 11 are local maxima. They all contribute two intersections to their respective scan lines, while the vertices at scan lines 3 and 5 contribute just one intersection. An easy way to make sure that such intermediate vertices are intersected just once is to shorten one of the incident edges, as shown in Fig. 11.26, prior to calculating intersections. This shortening would be done only if the vertex lies on a scan line, which would always be true if the vertex coordinates are integers but would seldom be true if the vertex coordinates are specified to a higher resolution than that of the raster grid itself.

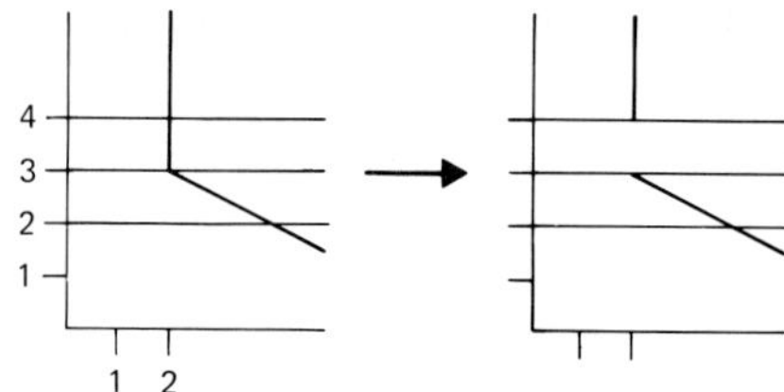

Fig. 11.26 Shortening of polygon edge.

11.7.4 Edge Coherence and the Scan-Line Algorithm

Step 1 in our procedure, i.e., calculating intersections, can be slow. Each polygon edge must be tested for intersection with each scan line. Very often just a few of the edges will be of interest. Furthermore, we notice that many of those edges intersected by scan line i will be also intersected by scan line $i + 1$. This *edge coherence* (analogous to the scan-line coherence discussed earlier) occurs along an edge for as many scan lines as intersect the edge. As we move from one scan line to the next, we can compute the new x-intersection of the edge based on the old x-intersection, just as with scan-converting lines:

$$x_{i+1} = x_i + \frac{1}{m}, \tag{11.14}$$

where m is the slope of the edge. The slope m is of course just $\Delta y/\Delta x$, and we have $\Delta y = 1$, so $1/m$ is just Δx.

We can exploit this edge coherence and at the same time avoid unnecessary comparisons of scan lines and edges by scan-converting the polygon scan line by scan line, bottom to top (or top to bottom), using the *scan-line algorithm*. For each scan line we work only with the set of edges it intersects, defined by the *active-edge table* (AET). As we move to the next scan line, new x-intersections are calculated using Eq. (11.14), any new edges intersected by this next scan line are added to the AET, and edges in the AET not intersected by this next scan line are deleted. The lines in the AET are kept sorted on their x-intersection value, so that the sequences of pixels to be filled are easily determined.

To make the addition of edges to the AET efficient, we create an *edge table* (ET) containing all edges sorted by their smaller y-coordinate. The ET is typically built by using a bucket sort with as many buckets as there are scan lines. Within each bucket, edges are kept in order of increasing x-coordinate of the lower endpoint by means of an insertion sort. Each entry in the ET contains the larger y-coordinate of the edge (y_{max}), the x-coordinate of the bottom endpoint (x_{min}), and the x increment used in stepping from one scan line to the next ($1/m$). Fig. 11.27 shows how the six edges from Fig. 11.25 would be sorted, under the assumption that the appropriate edges have been shortened by one scan line each to assure that double intersections are avoided. Figure 11.28 shows the AET at scan lines 9 and 10 for the polygon of Fig. 11.25.

Once the ET has been formed, the processing steps for the scan-line algorithm are:

1. Set y to the smallest y-coordinate which has an entry in the ET, i.e., to the first nonempty bucket.
2. Initialize the AET to be empty.
3. Repeat until the AET and ET are empty:

   3.1 Move information from ET bucket y into the AET, maintaining AET sort order on x.

   3.2 Fill in desired pixel values on scan line y by using pairs of x-coordinates from the AET.

   3.3 Remove from the AET those entries for which $y = y_{max}$.

   3.4 For each entry remaining in AET, replace x by $x + 1/m$. This places the next scan-line intersection into each entry in the AET.

   3.5 Because the previous step may have caused the AET to become out of order on x, re-sort the AET.

   3.6 Increment y by 1, to the coordinate of the next scan line.

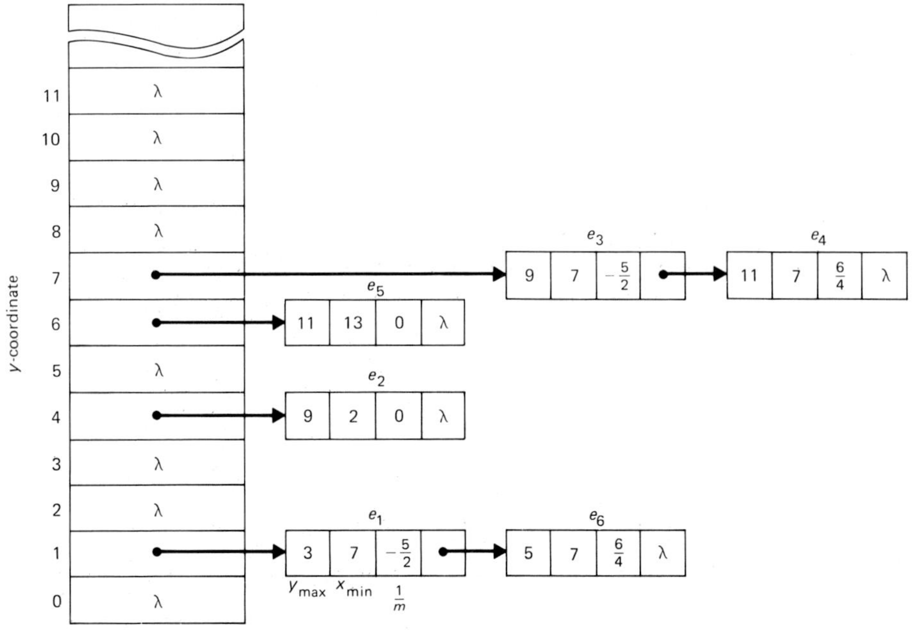

Fig. 11.27 Bucket-sorted edge table for Fig. 11.25, with edges e_2 and e_5 shortened.

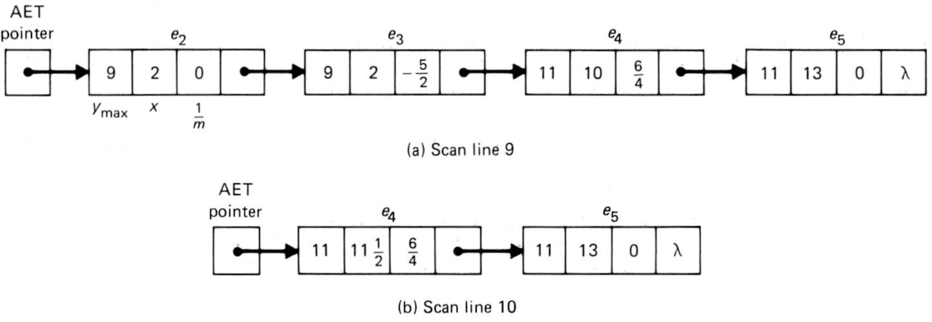

Fig. 11.28 Active-edge table.

This algorithm uses both edge coherence and scan-line coherence, along with sorting, to scan-convert a polygon efficiently. In Chapter 15 we will see how the algorithm can be extended to hidden-surface removal.

11.7.5 Antialiasing Polygons

In our discussion of scan-conversion we have thus far neglected the question of jagged polygon edges and the use of antialiasing techniques to smooth them. To deal with this, we use the notion (illustrated in Fig. 11.4) of considering the entire area which maps onto a pixel when deciding what value to display at the pixel.

Pitteway and Watkinson have developed an efficient extension of Bresenham's line algorithm to estimate the area of each pixel on each side of a polygon edge. [PITT80]. For simplicity, assume the line is $y = mx$, where $0 \le m \le 1$. Consider the quantity $mx - y$ evaluated at the point midway between T_i and S_i of Fig. 11.2. The coordinates of this point are $(x_{i-1} + 1, y_{i-1} + 0.5)$. If the quantity is negative, S_i is selected; otherwise T_i is selected. If we define $d = (mx - y) + (1 - m)$, then d is in the range of 0 to 1, and the test is against $1 - m$ rather than zero as in the original algorithm. The variable d serves to estimate the pixel coverage at each step: the closer d is to 1, the more of the pixel is covered and the greater the corresponding intensity. The basic structure of the algorithm for the line $y = mx$, with m between 0 and 1, is:

```
x := 0;
y := 0;
a := 1 - m;
d = 0.5;
WRITE_PIXEL(x, y, d)
repeat
  if d < a
  then d := d + m        {horizontal move}
  else begin             {diagonal move}
    d := d - a;
    y := y + 1
  end
  x := x + 1
  WRITE_PIXEL(x, y, d)
until x = x_end
```

Figure 11.29 shows the line $y = (5/7)x$ from (0, 0) to (7, 5). The shaded pixels represent those generated by Bresenham's basic algorithm, and across the top of the figure are the values of d applied to each of these pixels. The values of d can be used to interpolate between the pixel values on each side of the edge, in order to determine the appropriate pixel values.

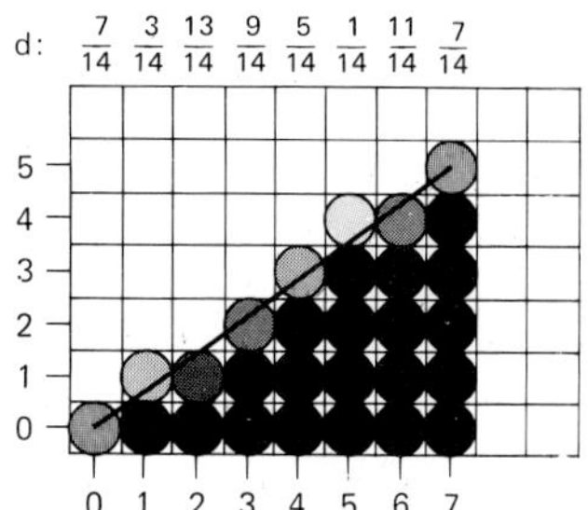

Fig. 11.29 Edge shading.

This approach is fast and efficient so long as just one edge of the polygon passes through the area covered by a pixel. At polygon vertices and for very narrow polygons, situations such as in Fig. 11.30 suggest that more detailed calculations must be performed. This figure also suggests that polygon vertices need not be restricted to be integer coordinates of the pixel centers. Crow has shown that when a sufficient number of intensity levels is used to display long thin polygons, the eye can distinguish such subpixel-level detail [CROW78b]. Many levels of intensity can, within limits, thus be used to create additional spatial resolution at the expense of intensity resolution. This is the converse of techniques (to be discussed in Chapter 17) by which intensity resolution is gained at the expense of spatial resolution.

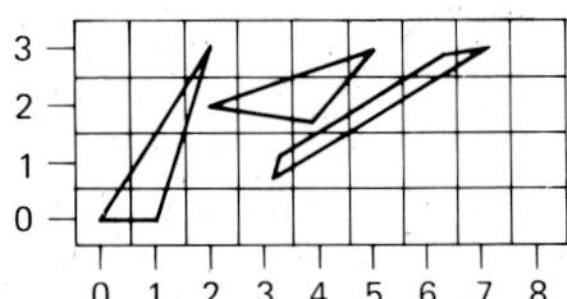

Fig. 11.30 Small polygons for which simple antialiasing is ineffective.

These area-overlap calculations need not have any more precision than will be usable with the display: if a pixel can take on any of eight values, then accuracy of one part in eight is sufficient. In any case, additional accuracy becomes useless at some point between one part in 32 and one part in 64 because the eye is unable to perceive the differences. If only low accuracy is needed, scan-conversion can be done by using standard techniques on an imaginary grid two or three times finer than that of the actual display device[CROW81]. The number of subpixels turned on within a grid is counted and used as the value for the actual display (Fig. 11.31). For better antialiasing, the area of a pixel can be thought of as a window, and all nearby polygons are clipped against the window to determine the area of the window (i.e., pixel) covered by each polygon, as described by Catmull [CATM78a].

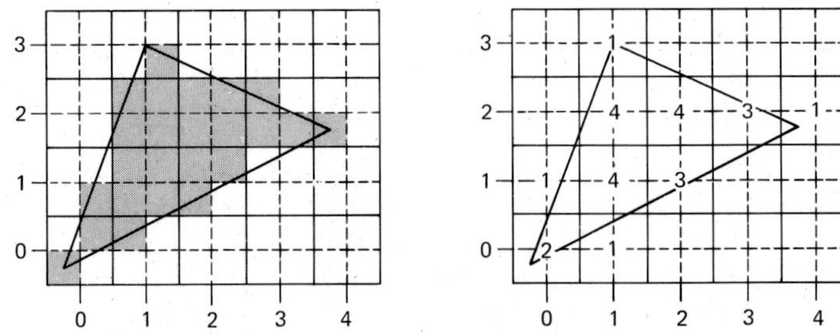

Fig. 11.31 Pixel values on right grid are count of number of subpixels set on left grid.

The techniques described here for scan-converting polygons can be extended to areas bounded by combinations of lines and curves. The notion of scan-line coherence extends naturally to curved edges and is particularly simple if the curve is monotonic. If not, the curve is subdivided into monotonic segments, and each curve segment is then treated similarly to an edge in the ET and AET, with difference equations used to calculate successive scan line intersections.

11.8 UNSEGMENTED GRAPHICS SUBROUTINE PACKAGE WITH TEMPORAL PRIORITY

We have described a number of algorithms for scan-converting output primitives into a refresh buffer. How can these algorithms be combined with other useful functions to form an integrated raster graphics subroutine package?

The first step is to consider the simple case in which, so far as the graphics package is concerned, the refresh buffer itself contains the sole definition of an image. In some ways this is like a storage tube display—the difference is that the computer can read the contents of the refresh buffer but cannot read those of a storage tube. While there is neither a segmented display file nor a pseudodisplay file in the sense of the graphics package SGP discussed in Chapters 2 and 4, there typically is an application data structure.

As output primitives are scan-converted into the refresh buffer, the more recently displayed ones may overlap and thus replace (parts of) existing primitives; thus there is a temporal (time-based) priority among output primitives. Temporal priority among output primitives is the only possible priority so long as the graphics package does not explicitly keep a record of output primitives. Notice, though, that on a film recorder the effects would be different: the colors from overlapping primitives would mix together. Hence temporal priority is intertwined with the existence of a refresh buffer.

As a starting point for developing the raster graphics subroutine package, we will use all of the SGP capabilities except segments and the logical pick device, which cannot be used without the naming capabilities provided by segments.

11.8.1 Operations on the Refresh Buffer

The two most fundamental primitive operations which we add to SGP for raster graphics are functions to read and modify specific pixels of the refresh buffer. We can use the procedures introduced earlier in this chapter

READ_PIXEL(x, y, value) and *WRITE_PIXEL(x, y, value)*

to obtain and to modify the value at (x, y), respectively.

The way in which parameter *value* modifies a pixel being written into by *WRITE_PIXEL* is controlled modally by another procedure:

RASTER_OP(op).

The parameter *op* is used to specify how *value* affects the current pixel value at (x, y). If $op = replace$, the old value (the value in the refresh buffer) is replaced by *value* (this is the default for *op*). If $op = or$, then *value* and the old value are combined with the logical **or** operation; if $op = and$, logical **and** is used; if $op = xor$, **exclusive or** is used. In this last case, an inversion of all the bits of the old value results if *value* has all its bits set to **true.** In general, each of the 16 boolean functions of two variables could be provided. Non-boolean operations, such as pixel value addition or subtraction, could also be provided this way. A number of commercial raster systems support all of these operations. The usefulness of some of these operations is illustrated in the next chapter.

Very often one needs to move a block of pixels into the refresh buffer, out of the buffer, or within the buffer. This would be done to display or save an image stored as a pixel array, or to reposition a part of the image such as a block of text. These operations can be done with the functions:

READ_BLOCK(to_array, xmin, xmax, ymin, ymax)
WRITE_BLOCK(from_array, xmin, xmax, ymin, ymax)
COPY_BLOCK(from_xmin, from_xmax, from_ymin, from_ymax, to_xmin, to_ymin)

The arrays *to_array* and *from_array* are presumed to contain

$$(xmax - xmin + 1)\ (ymax - ymin + 1)$$

pixel values stored in row-major order. In the *COPY_BLOCK* procedure, only the lower-left corner of the destination area need be given, because the size of the area being moved is given implicitly as part of the source specification. The setting of *op* given by *RASTER_OP* affects the results of all these move operations.

The *COPY_BLOCK* procedure can be called with overlapping source and destination areas in the refresh buffer, as shown in Fig. 11.32. The procedure copies in such a way that no pixel in the overlapping area is written into before it is read. *COPY_BLOCK* does not change the source area of the refresh buffer, except where such an overlap occurs.

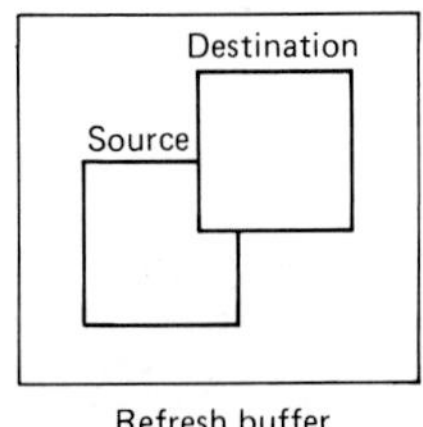

Fig. 11.32 Movement of block of pixels from source area to destination area.

These three block-oriented operations can be integrated into a single copy procedure which copies from an arbitrary source (array in memory or refresh buffer) to an arbitrary destination (array in memory or refresh buffer). This is especially desirable if, as discussed in the next chapter, the refresh buffer is part of the associated computer's address space, because then all three copies can be implemented with identical code. The Bit-Blt operation of the Alto system (Section 12.6) is a hardware implementation of the copy operation.

The flood-fill and boundary-fill procedures from Section 11.4 can also be added to our raster graphics subroutine package. They are especially useful for interactive painting applications.

11.8.2 Output Primitives

The operations mentioned thus far manipulate only pixels or arrays of pixels and are device-dependent in that they assume a certain size refresh buffer. A raster subroutine package should also have SGP's device-independent output primitives, with extensions to account for at least some of the additional facilities possible with raster graphics: filling bounded areas, many colors, and changing the appearance of all pixels of a given value by modifying the look-up table. We do not describe how to access other capabilities of raster systems such as the general image display system capabilities described in Chapter 12.

Among the output primitives will be the familiar line and text string and the *current position* (CP). Naturally, the windows, viewports, and even 3D output primitives from SGP can be used. Bounded areas require a new construct, the polygon, which might be specified with:

```
BEGIN_POLYGON;
  MOVE( , );
  LINE( , );
  LINE( , );
  LINE( , );
  LINE( , );
     .
     .
     .
  LINE( , );
END_POLYGON
```

The bracketed *MOVE* and *LINE* calls define a sequence of lines which is automatically closed by *END_POLYGON* to form a polygon. Several existing packages use this approach. However, with this strategy the same output primitives are used for drawing lines and defining polygons. Program debugging is made more difficult, since the meaning of an isolated call to *LINE* depends on whether a *BEGIN_POLYGON* is currently active. Furthermore, many subroutine calls are needed to define a polygon.

The first objection can be removed by introducing a *VERTEX* output primitive to be used in place of *LINE* within the *BEGIN_POLYGON . . . END_POLYGON* pairs:

```
BEGIN_POLYGON;
  VERTEX( , );
  VERTEX( , );
     .
     .
     .
  VERTEX( , );
END_POLYGON
```

Even with *VERTEX,* the need for multiple subroutine calls for every polygon remains. It is preferable to use a procedure of the form:

POLYGON_ABS_2(x_array, y_array, n)

The *n* vertices are stored in the two arrays. The polygon is automatically closed by an edge from the *n*th to the first vertex, and the current position is set to the first vertex. Similar procedures for circles and other bounded areas can easily be defined.

11.8.3 The Burden of Temporal Priority

Whatever the output primitive, be it a line, text, or region, it is scan-converted and displayed as soon as it is specified to SGP, independently of the primitive's spatial relationship to other primitives. The value of *op* always determines how the pixel values are modified. The immediate display of output primitives defines a temporal priority relationship among the primitives, be they 2D or 3D. No hidden-surface removal is performed on the primitives. It is the use of temporal priority which eliminates the need for a pseudo display file and makes implementation of this graphics package quite straightforward. In the next section we consider alternatives to temporal priority.

While temporal priority is simple, its use can place a heavy burden on the application programmer. For instance, if the programmer wants to move part of the refresh buffer and have the viewer see what was previously displayed there, the application program must keep track of and redisplay the previously displayed information. This is a common operation, found in text-processing and office automation and used extensively with personal computers such as the Alto system (mentioned in Chapters 1 and 11) for an interactive programming environment in which programs, menus, and the results of program executions are displayed in various overlapping areas on the screen [KAY77b, TEIT77, BYTE81].

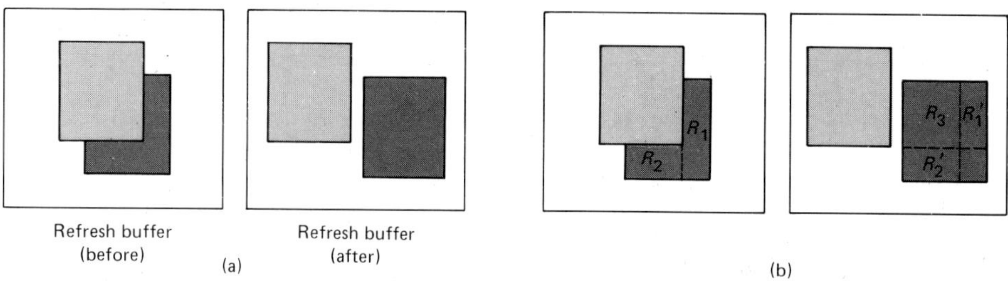

Fig. 11.33 Moving one region of the refresh buffer from behind another.

To illustrate the problem further, consider Fig. 11.33 (modified from [SPRO79]). Part (a) shows the desired operation. There are three possible solutions to the problem. One is to set regions R_1 and R_2 to the background color and then redraw the region (in its new position) from the application data structure—a slow process. Another possibility is to copy R_1 to R_1' and R_2 to R_2'; region R_3 is then set to the background color and redrawn from the application data structure with an appropriate window and viewport. The third possibility is to store the entire obscured region before it is obscured; it thus can be restored whenever needed.

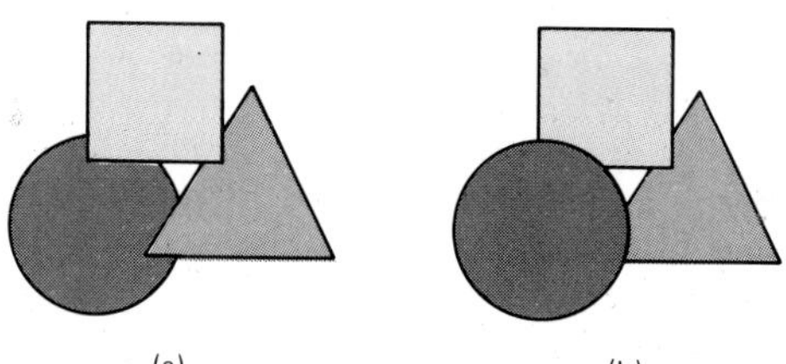

Figure 11.34 Two orders of overlapping.

As another example, consider Fig. 11.34(a), which depicts three overlapping filled areas. If the visibility priority relations among the areas change to that of Fig. 11.34(b), the areas would have to be redisplayed by the application program in the order of triangle first, square next, and circle last.

11.8.4 Attributes of Output Primitives

Attributes of output primitives especially important in raster graphics have to do with color (or intensity) and the filling of polygons. Because raster systems often have video look-up tables, it is unwise to treat color as a static primitive attribute. Instead, the color index, which points into the look-up table, should be used as the static attribute. This permits the dynamic change of the association of a color index with a color by changing the look-up table. The procedure

SET_CURRENT_INDEX(index)

establishes *index* as the value to be placed into pixels falling on lines and characters and within polygons. For systems with no look-up table, the association of *index* to color or intensity is fixed; with a look-up table, the procedure

REDEFINE_INDEX(index, red, green, blue)

establishes a new association which applies essentially instantaneously* to all pixels with a value of *index*.

The other attribute specific to raster graphics determines whether and how polygons are filled in. There are at least three possibilities, which can be specified with

SET_CURRENT_POLYGON_TYPE(type)

The polygon may be filled with a single value (given as the current index), so that it has a constant-colored interior. Alternatively, the polygon may be filled with a repeating pattern of pixel values. In this case the polygon vertex coordinates are transformed to device coordinates, and the resulting boundary is filled with the pattern, beginning at some reference point, as shown in Fig. 11.35. As a special case, the pattern array may be large enough to fill the polygon without being repeated at all. The pattern itself is specified by

SET_PATTERN(pattern_array, x_size, y_size)

and the reference point, in normalized device coordinates, by

SET_REF_POINT(x, y)

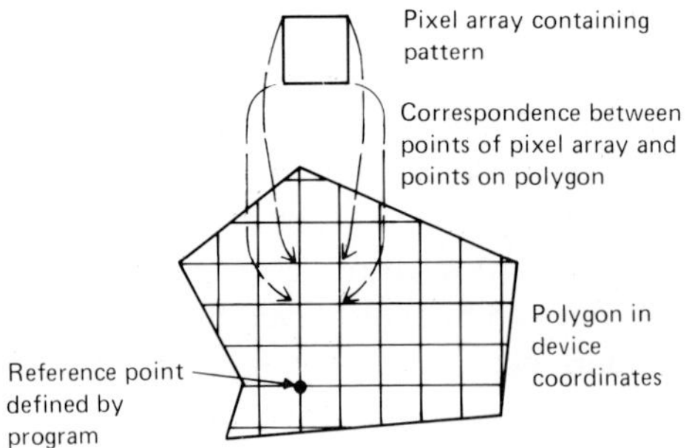

Fig. 11.35 Replication of pixel array to fill polygon.

---

*Some raster systems provide no means to control *when* the look-up table is modified: if the change occurs in the middle of a raster scan, a transient visual effect may appear. If many entries are changed in sequence, the effect can be even more visible, because it lasts longer. The ideal raster system double-buffers its look-up table, swapping one table for the other only during the beam fly-back period at the end of a scan. Many graphics packages include a subroutine that allows multiple look-up table entries to be changed with a single call.

The final possibility is for the polygon to be filled in world coordinates with an intensity or color pattern before the polygon is projected. Each of the square areas of the polygon covered by a color element from the pattern array is projected onto the device raster grid, and the appropriate pixel values, perhaps computed by considering the fractional area of each device raster covered by different parts of the pattern, are then displayed. This technique could be used, for example, to place a texture pattern onto the walls of a building. The texture would then map onto the screen just as it would be seen by a camera.

Figure 11.36 diagrams a simple case of polygon filling in world coordinates, in which a rotated rectangular polygon is more densely covered by pixel values than is the coarser raster display grid. The value to display in each pixel of the raster display grid is determined from a weighted average of the values in the pattern covering the rectangle. Figure 11.37 shows a more difficult case. A rectangular polygon, covered with a pattern array, is projected in perspective onto the raster display grid. The shaded pixel area on the raster display grid is covered by irregular portions of four different areas from the projected patterns, and its color should take into account the colors of the four areas. Both this and the previous case are best processed by making use of the antialiasing notions discussed earlier in this chapter. Recent papers by Weiman [WEIM80] and Catmull and Smith [CATM80] describe the

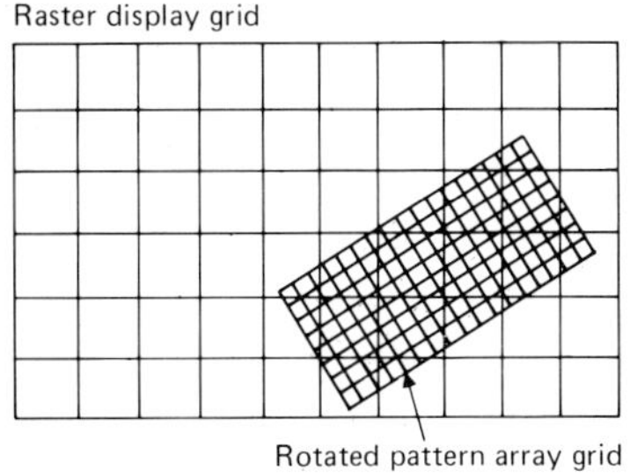

Fig. 11.36 High-resolution pattern array rotated and superimposed on a lower-resolution display grid.

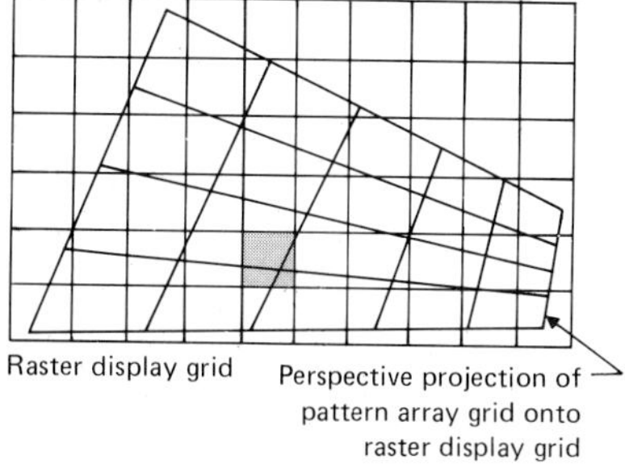

Fig. 11.37 Pattern array grid that has undergone a perspective projection onto the raster display grid.

mathematics of the process. Color Plates 13 and F–J (rear end papers) are actual examples of this technique.

Other attributes of output primitives, such as line style and character font, are completely unaffected by the vector/raster distinction. With the exception of picking, which, as remarked earlier, cannot work without segments, all of the SGP input capabilities can be used. Thus the functions described here, plus the 2D/3D viewing functions and most of the input functions from earlier chapters, combine to create a raster graphics subroutine package based on temporal priority.

11.9 SEGMENTED GRAPHICS SUBROUTINE PACKAGE WITH PRIORITY

The use of temporal priority places on the application programmer the heavy burden of creating output primitives in a certain sequence to ensure the desired visual results. This burden can be taken on by the graphics package, though at the expense of more complexity in the package and perhaps longer response time when the image is modified.

11.9.1 Explicit Priority

The simplest form of nontemporal priority (with respect to visibility) is *explicit priority,* in which the priority of groups of output primitives is declared explicitly. This strategy requires that we use the segmentation capability (originally introduced in Chapter 2) so that priority can be explicitly specified as a segment attribute, with lower numbers corresponding to higher priority. It also means that the graphics package must maintain a pseudo display file.

The code sequence

```
CREATE_SEGMENT(5);
  SET_PRIORITY(5, 3);      {segment 5 has priority 3}
  TRIANGLE;
CLOSE_SEGMENT;
CREATE_SEGMENT(31);
  SET_PRIORITY(31, 2);     {segment 31 has priority 2}
  SQUARE;
CLOSE_SEGMENT;
CREATE_SEGMENT(17);
  SET_PRIORITY(17, 5);     {segment 17 has priority 5}
  CIRCLE;
CLOSE_SEGMENT;
UPDATE
```

will produce Fig. 11.34(a). The *UPDATE* procedure call at the end of the sequence causes the graphics package to draw all the existing segments in accordance with their priorities; in the meantime, output primitives are just accumulated in the pseudo display file. Priorities are relative, so not all priorities in the sequence 0, . . . , *N* need be used.

The procedures *SQUARE, TRIANGLE,* and *CIRCLE* are presumed to exist. *TRIANGLE* here shows the general form:

```
procedure TRIANGLE;
begin
  SET_CURRENT_POLYGON_TYPE(solid_filled);
  SET_CURRENT_INDEX(6);
  REDEFINE_INDEX(6, 0.8, 0.8, 0.8);
  {equal values of R, G and B => intensity of 0.8}
  {following output primitives will have intensity of 0.8 until index 6 is redefined}
  {each procedure should use a different index}
  BEGIN_POLYGON;
    VERTEX(5.0, 5.0);
    VERTEX(15.0, 5.0);
    VERTEX(10.0, 15.0);
  END_POLYGON
end    {TRIANGLE}
```

It we allow segment priority to be a dynamic attribute, then a call to:

```
SET_PRIORITY(17,1);
UPDATE
```

(if executed after the above code sequence) would produce Fig. 11.34(b).

A simple way to implement explicit priorities is to sort the segments by priority each time *UPDATE* is invoked. The segments can then be displayed (scan-converted) in the order of highest numerical priority first, lowest numerical priority last. This is one of several ways to perform what is in fact hidden-surface removal (other methods are discussed in Chapter 15).

Efficiency is an important concern in designing a segmented graphics package for raster systems. Each time *UPDATE* is called, a considerable amount of processing is required, causing response time problems. The ultimate solution is faster processors and/or parallel processors to do the hidden-surface removal and scan-conversion [FUCH77c, KAPL79, PARK80]; there are, however, other nearer-term partial solutions. Fast but inaccurate deletions can be performed by scan-converting the deleted segment into the refresh buffer, placing the background color into all pixels. This will change some pixel values incorrectly. Figure 11.38 shows the effect of deleting the circle from Fig. 11.34(a). To deal with such problems, an operating system process, executing at low priority, can then redisplay the remaining segments correctly, in this case giving the proper results shown in Fig. 11.40. (See [BAUD80].)

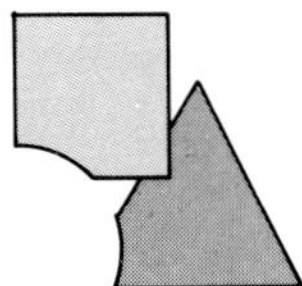

Fig. 11.38 Deletion of circle by setting pixels to background color.

Another method which improves efficiency is to use the screen extents introduced in Chapter 4. The screen extent of the segment being deleted is first set to the background color. Then only those portions of the remaining segments which lie within the screen extent of the deleted segment are redisplayed. To do this, the segments are clipped against the screen extent, and whatever survives the clipping process is redisplayed. While the clipping takes time, savings can still be realized by reducing the amount of information to be redisplayed. Figure 11.39 shows the first step; Fig. 11.40, the second.

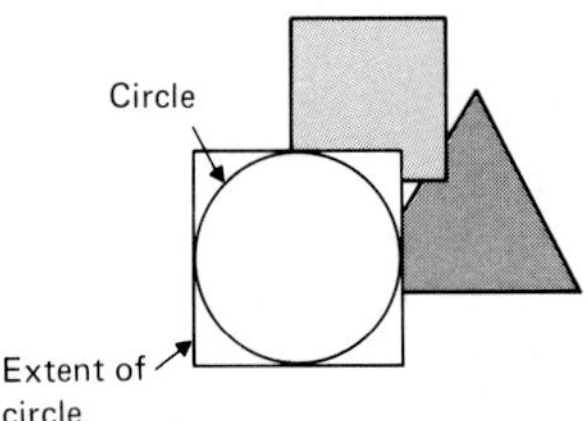

Fig. 11.39 Circle extent reset to background.

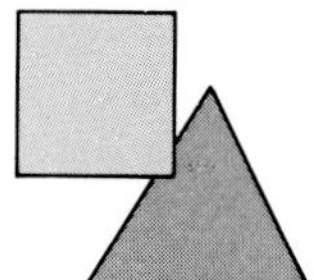

Fig. 11.40 Areas within circle extent have been redisplayed.

Yet another way to improve response time is to have two display modes, *fast* and *priority*. In fast-display mode, polygon outlines are displayed but not filled; thus they can be displayed as they are created. Only in priority-display mode are the priorities used and the polygons filled in. The interactive user would be given a way to select between the two modes; for fast interaction, the fast-display mode would be chosen, while to view the full effect of an image, the priority-display mode would be chosen.

11.9.2 Geometrical Priority

The richer but computationally more complex form of nontemporal priority is *geometrical priority,* better known as hidden-surface removal. We use the *x, y,* and *z*-coordinates of output primitives and the viewing specification (view plane normal, view up, etc., as discussed in Chapter 8) to determine which (parts of) output primitives are visible. Algorithms for hidden-surface removal are described in Chapter 15. Hidden-surface removal does not require use of segments, because the priorities are implicit in the geometry. This is of course no reason to exclude segments, which are just as useful for interaction when geometrical priority is involved as they are with temporal or explicit priority.

However, there is a difficulty with geometrical priority. Very often a display must include several views of the same object, taken from different orientations and perhaps with different types of projections. A typical display might show front, top, and side orthographic projections plus a cabinet oblique projection, each in a separate viewport. However, if one viewport partially overlaps another viewport, geometrical priority by itself is not sufficient because it determines visibility for the output primitives in a single viewport, but not between viewports. Thus, we need some way to control priorities between viewports. One way to do this is to assign each viewport an explicit priority; however, to change viewport priorities, the viewports would have to be named, and this introduces more concepts to the graphics package.

We solve the overlapping viewport problem by using the existing concepts of 3D normalized device coordinate (NDC) space and 3D viewports. A view volume in world coordinates is transformed into each 3D viewport, as in Fig. 11.41. Hidden-surface removal is performed on all the contents of 3D NDC space whenever *UPDATE* is called, with the viewing direction being a parallel projection onto the front face of NDC space. Therefore hidden-surface removal is performed both within and between viewport contents.

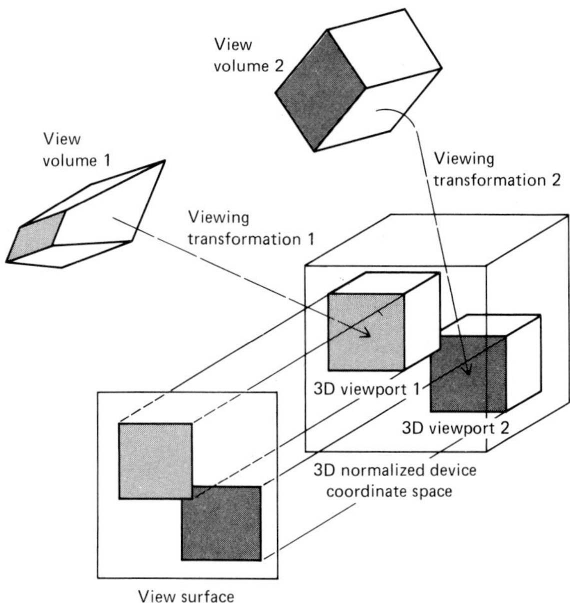

Fig. 11.41 Creation of a display from two view volumes. The view surface displays a parallel projection of the contents of 3D NDC space.

In some cases, such as displaying an airport runway and surrounding buildings, a single 3D viewport would be used, of size equal to the unit cube. In other cases, if front, top, side, and isometric projections of the same object are displayed simultaneously, several nonintersecting viewports would be used (Fig. 11.42). In still other cases, as when displaying an object with a superposed cutout showing enlarged detail of a particular area, overlapping (as seen from the view surface) viewports would be used (Fig. 11.43). Algorithms for hidden-surface removal can exploit the fact that all output primitives are contained within 3D viewports to avoid unnecessary comparisons between output primitives which are in different 3D viewports.

Geometrical priority with 3D viewports accommodates temporal priority and explicit priority as special cases. Consider first temporal priority. The default viewport (which is 2D) is on the front face of 3D NDC space. In this case, output primitives, after being transformed into NDC space, have no depth, and thus the hidden-

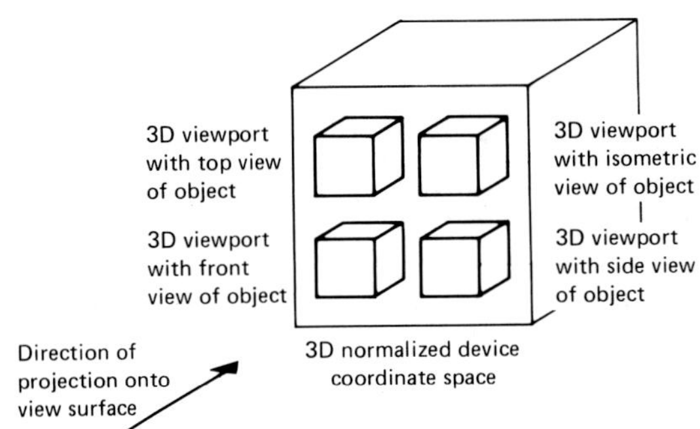

Fig. 11.42 Arrangement of four 3D viewports so that the resulting display will have four separate views on view surface.

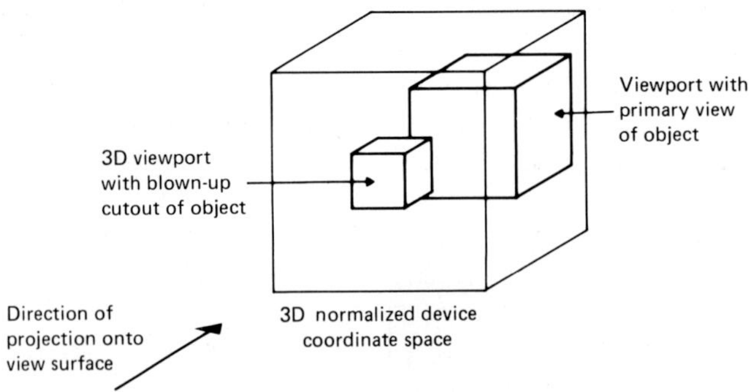

Fig. 11.43 Arrangement of two 3D viewports so that the resulting display will have the forward 3D viewport superimposed in front of the rearward 3D viewport.

surface algorithms have no basis for deciding which output primitives are visible. It is in just this case that temporal priority is used. The temporal priority is applied to the projections of the output primitives onto the projection plane, and hence can be used either with 2D or 3D world coordinate output primitives that fall on the front of NDC space.

Consider next the case of explicit priority, in which each segment has an explicit priority for visibility. To provide explicit priorities (from 0 to N) in a geometrical-priority system, a segment with priority P is placed in a viewport on the $z = P/N$ plane of 3D NDC space, with corner points $(x_{min}, y_{min}, P/N)$ and $(x_{max}, y_{max}, P/N)$, as in Fig. 11.44. Once all the segments are defined, hidden-surface removal is performed: the segments (and hence the planes) can be defined in arbitrary order.

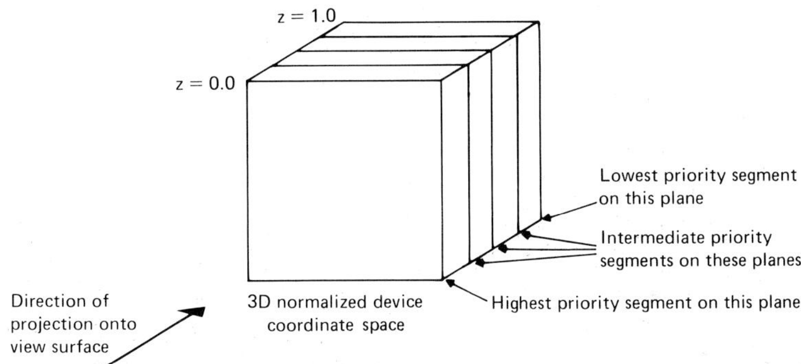

Fig. 11.44 Use of viewports on parallel planes in 3D NDC space to implement explicit (2½D) depth priority.

Segment priorities can be made dynamic simply by applying an image transformation to the segment: a translation along the z-axis of NDC space is used to reposition a segment's image onto a different plane of constant z.

In this and the preceding section we have shown how graphics packages can be structured to accommodate some of the unique capabilities of raster displays while at the same time drawing heavily upon concepts developed for vector displays. In fact, the polygons and other filled areas, color attribute, and the three types of priority have been successfully defined and integrated into the Core System [FOLE79a, FOLE79b, FOLE81b, GSPC79, WENN80]. An implementation of a Core-like system with hidden-surface removal is described in [LAIB80]. Thus, vector and raster displays can be used side by side, driven by the same application program. Of course, the operations performed directly on the refresh buffer, such as copying a block of pixels, will not make sense on a vector display. Rather, one seeks a sensible level of compatibility which reflects the capabilities of each technology.

EXERCISES

11.1 Generalize the procedure *BRESENHAM* to draw lines of any slope.

11.2 Derive a formula for the intensity of pixels on a line of slope m which keeps constant the intensity per unit length of line.

11.3 Code Bresenham's line-drawing algorithm for a micro- or minicomputer. Calculate the time needed by the algorithm for initialization and for each iteration.

11.4 Using Eqs. (11.8) and (11.9), rewrite Bresenham's algorithm to avoid calling *WRITE_PIXEL* (and thus to avoid its address calculation multiplication) by calling *PIXEL_AT_ADDR,* as discussed at the end of Section 11.1.

11.5 Determine whether Bresenham's line algorithm can take advantage of symmetry by using the decision variable d to draw simultaneously from both ends of the line toward the center. Does your procedure consistently accommodate the equal-error or arbitrary-choice case which arises when dx and dy have a largest common factor c and dx/c is even while dy/c is odd ($0 < dy < dx$) as in the line between (0, 0) and (24, 9)? Does it deal with the subset case in which dx is an integer multiple of $2dy$ such as for the line between (0, 0) and (16, 4)? (Contributed by J. Bresenham.)

11.6 The line scan-conversion algorithms in Section 11.1 assume that the endpoints have integer coordinates. Develop algorithms in which this assumption is not necessary.

11.7 What is the visual effect of applying procedure *LINE* in Section 11.1 to lines with slopes greater than 1 or less than -1?

11.8 Demonstrate that Bresenham's line algorithm properly forces an appropriate sign for a correct move in the degenerate situations in which the current selected point is (x,y) and the true line intersection for the next abscissa $x + 1$ falls not between ordinate value y and $y + 1$ but

a) between y and $y - 1$, as from the point (2, 1) for the line from (0, 0) to (7, 2);

b) between $y + 1$ and $y + 2$, as from the point (2,1) for the line from (0, 0) to (7, 5).

(Contributed by J. Bresenham.)

11.9 Modify the procedure *CHARACTER,* as suggested at the end of Section 11.2, to use *PIXEL_AT_ADDR* rather than *WRITE_PIXEL.*

11.10 Write a *TEXT* subroutine to display a text string at an (x, y) position assuming that the arrays of character descriptions are indexed by character codes.

11.11 Using *MICH_CIRCLE* as a starting point, write a procedure to draw a circle with the pixels on its border set to *b_value* and pixels on its interior set to *i_value.*

11.12 Derive the expressions for the decision variable used in *MICH_CIRCLE.*

11.13 Implement the circle-drawing algorithms of Bresenham, Pitteway [PITT67], and Jordan et al. [JORD73b]. Calculate the initialization time and the time per iteration.

11.14 Generalize *CIRCLE_POINTS* and *MICH_CIRCLE* to work with circles positioned at an arbitrary integer center point.

11.15 Develop a circle scan-converter which does antialiasing.

11.16 Complete the steps for the region fill shown in Fig. 11.18. Notice the effect when the filling "curls around" the interior holes in the region.

11.17 Implement the region fill strategy described at the end of Section 11.4. If necessary, refer to [SMIT79] for details.

11.18 Design a flood fill algorithm which allows the new interior value *new_value* to have the same value as *boundary_value.*

11.19 Design a polygon scan-conversion algorithm which sets boundary pixels to one value and interior pixels to a second value. The resulting boundary will in general be 8-connected.

11.20 Consider a convex polygon with n vertices being clipped against a rectangular window. What is the maximum number of vertices in the resulting clipped polygon? The minimum number? Consider the same problem for a concave (nonconvex) polygon. How many polygons might result? If a single polygon results, what is the largest number of vertices it might have?

11.21 Integrate the Pitteway–Watkinson [PITT80] algorithm into a polygon scan-converter.

11.22 Explain why the Sutherland–Hodgman algorithm can use only convex clipping regions.

11.23 Some refresh buffers are mapped onto sequential memory locations such that location (0, 0) of the buffer is at *base* and location (x_{max}, y_{max}) is at $base - (x_{max} + 1) * (y_{max} + 1)$; that is, the buffer is allocated to memory in descending rather than in ascending order. Rewrite Eqs. (11.6) through (11.9) to account for this.

11.24 Program the *COPY_BLOCK* procedure of Section 11.7, assuming the existence of *READ_PIXEL* and *WRITE_PIXEL.*

11.25 Write a modified *COPY_BLOCK* procedure which places a pixel value *replace_value* into all parts of the source area which are not overlapped by the destination area.

11.26 Show how *WRITE_BLOCK* can be used as part of a character string display procedure.

11.27 Write a procedure:

PATTERN_FILL(pattern_array, x_size, y_size, x_min, x_max, y_min, y_max)

to fill the designated rectangular area with the pattern array of pixel values whose size is *x_size* by *y_size.* If *pattern_array* is smaller than the area, repeat the pattern as often as necessary to fill the area exactly. The value in the lower-left corner of *pattern_array* should occur at (*x_min*, *y_min*).

11.28 Extend *PATTERN_FILL* to *POLY_FILL(pattern_array, x_size, y_size, x_ref, y_ref, n, x_array, y_array).*

11.29 Rewrite *MICH_CIRCLE* for the case of an integer-radius, 45° segment by using an integer decision variable e, where

$$d_i = 2e_i + 1 \qquad \text{and} \qquad e_0 = 1 - R.$$

Observe that when $D(T) \geq 0$, then $D(S) > 0$, and hence

$$D(T_i) + D(S_i) = d_i > 0,$$

so that a test of d_i or $0.5d_i$ would force a proper T selection when $D(T) \geq 0$. Introducing auxiliary variables

$$u_i = 1 + 2x_i, \qquad u_0 = 1,$$
$$v_i = 1 + 2x - 2y, \qquad v_0 = 1 - 2R,$$

we note that for the integer-center point, integer-radius case, d_i cannot be zero and hence e_i cannot be -0.5. This allows us to employ a decision rule:

If $e_i < 0$, then move axially (i.e., $x_{i+1} = x_i + 1$ and $y_{i+1} = y_i$) and update

$$u_{i+1} = u_i + 2, \qquad v_{i+1} = v_i + 2, \qquad e_{i+1} = e_i + u_{i+1}.$$

If $e_i \geq 0$, then move diagonally (i.e., $x_{i+1} = x_i + 1$ and $y_{i+1} = y_i - 1$) and update

$$u_i + 1 = u_i + 2, \qquad v_i + 1 = v_i + 4, \qquad e_{i+1} = e_i + v_{i+1}.$$

The revised approach reduces the work per iteration to that of Pitteway's circle algorithm and, as a consequence of the integer-radius, integer-center-point constraint, selects the same path. (Contributed by J. Bresenham).

11.30 Analyze the behavior of the Pitteway–Watkinson algorithm (Section 11.7.5) when d is represented with limited precision. What cumulative errors can occur?

11.31 Show how the polygon scan-conversion algorithm can be modified to sort monotonic-increasing sequences of edges rather than single edges during the initial bucket sort to build the ET. This reduces the number of entries in the ET and decreases the number of times that the AET has new entries added from the ET, and hence decreases the number of times the AET must be resorted on x. Note that each entry in the ET and AET is now a sequence of edges rather than just one edge, so the algorithms must be slightly modified.

11.32 Implement the Sutherland–Hodgman or Weiler-Atherton algorithm for 3D clipping.

11.33 Extend the Sutherland–Hodgman algorithm to eliminate the overlapping polygon edges illustrated in Figure 11.23.

11.34 Extend either of the polygon clippers to return the polygon(s) both inside and outside the clipping region.

12 Raster Display Architecture

12.1 INTRODUCTION

The organization of raster graphics hardware was introduced in Chapter 3 in our general discussion of graphics hardware. In Chapter 11 raster graphics software was discussed; we now return to raster hardware for a more thorough discussion. In Section 12.2 we present a simple raster display system organization, shown in Fig. 12.1, and its instruction set. In Section 12.3 we show how to program the raster display, using as examples short sequences of display instructions which achieve various visual effects. In Section 12.4, which concentrates on the image display system and its video look-up table, we emphasize various creative uses for the look-up table. In the final sections we consider other raster architectures in which the refresh buffer is organized and integrated into the overall system in different ways.

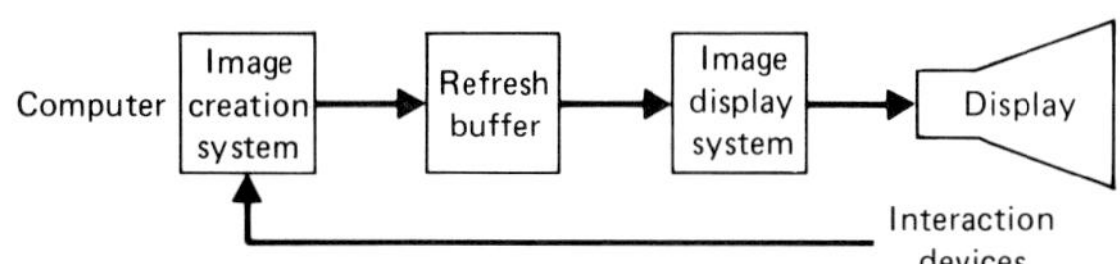

Fig. 12.1 Basic architecture of a complete raster display system.

12.2 A SIMPLE RASTER DISPLAY SYSTEM

A raster display consists of an image creation system, an image storage system (refresh buffer, bit map, frame buffer), and an image display system. The system whose characteristics vary most widely between manufacturers is the image creation system, which scan-converts output primitives into the refresh buffer. The instruction set design and processing speed of the image creation system establish most of the characteristics of a raster display. Furthermore, this system is particularly malleable because it is typically implemented with a microprocessor. The display instruction set is simply interpreted by a microprocessor program.

In this section we assume that the refresh buffer is 512×512, with three bits per pixel and origin at the lower-left corner. Other refresh buffer sizes (and origins) are also used—a 480 scan-line by 640 pixel buffer matches the aspect ratio of most TV monitors, and thus makes efficient use of the display area without resorting to nonuniform scaling in x and y to map the refresh buffer to the screen. The origin is sometimes in the upper-left corner to match the start of the raster scan. There is no advantage in this arrangement, however. We will also assume in this section that the eight-entry video look-up table in the image display system has six bits per entry: two for red, two for green, and two for blue.

In the following description of the instructions accepted by the image creation system, mnemonic names are used because we are not concerned with the details of op-code and data field arrangement within an instruction. Unless otherwise noted, all data is immediate: addresses are generally not used in the instructions. The display has a number of registers, which are introduced as needed in specific instructions. The instructions are:

1. MOVE X, Y—The X and Y registers, which define the current position (CP), are set to the position (X, Y). Since the refresh buffer is 512×512, the X and Y registers each require nine bits.

2. MOVER DX, DY—Values DX and DY are added to the X and Y registers, thereby making a relative change to the CP.

3. LINE X, Y—A line from CP to (X, Y) is scan-converted into the refresh buffer. Pixels on the scan-converted line are set to the current contents of a three-bit color register. The CP becomes (X, Y).

4. LINER DX, DY—A line from CP to CP + (DX, DY) is scan-converted. The current position is changed in x by DX, and in y by DY. Note that there is no explicit point command; rather, points are created with the sequence of commands:

```
MOVE X, Y
LINER 0, 0
```

5. TEXT N, STRING—The N characters whose codes are contained in STRING are displayed, starting at the CP. Characters are defined on a 7×9 pixel grid, with two extra raster units of vertical and horizontal spacing to separate lines and characters. If the right edge of the refresh buffer is encountered, a carriage return and line feed are injected. If the bottom of the refresh buffer is encountered, the CP is

reset to the top left corner of the buffer. The contents of the color register are used in scan-converting characters into the refresh buffer. The CP is updated to the location at which character N + 1 would be displayed if it existed.

6. RECT X,Y—A filled rectangle with one corner at the CP and the other corner at (X, Y) is placed in the refresh buffer. The CP is updated. All pixels on the boundaries and within the rectangle are set to the contents of the color register. The CP is set to (X, Y). The entire refresh buffer can be set to the contents of the color register with:

```
MOVE 0, 0
RECT 511, 511
```

7. RECTR DX, DY—A filled rectangle with one corner at CP and the other corner at CP + (DX, DY) is placed in the refresh buffer. The CP is updated.

8. BFILL I—The boundary-defined 4-connected region bordered by pixels of value I and containing the CP as an interior point is filled with the pixel value in the color register. Pixels with the value I are not changed. Note that if the region is not closed then the entire refresh buffer, except for pixels with value I, is filled. Figure 12.2 shows several examples of how the fill command works. BFILL does not affect the CP.

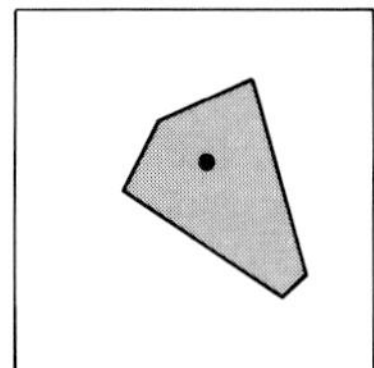
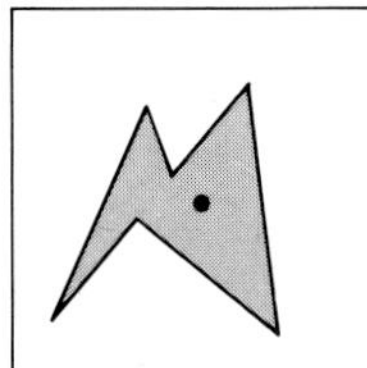
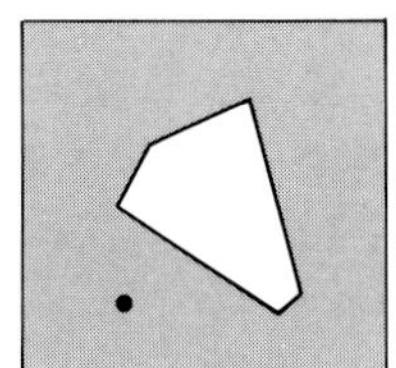
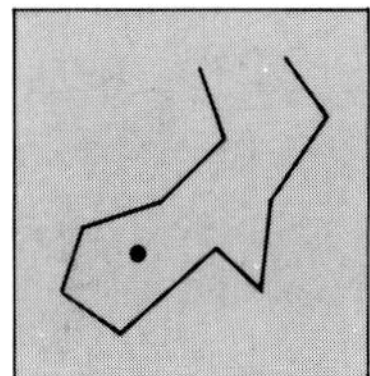

Fig. 12.2 Examples of regions defined by pixel value I (dark line) filled with contents of color register (shaded). The dot represents CP.

9. FFILL I—The interior-defined 4-connected region defined by pixels of value I and containing the CP as an interior point is filled with the pixel value in the color register. FFILL does not affect the CP.

10. COLOR I—The 3-bit value I is loaded into the 3-bit color register. This value is then placed into the refresh buffer by the line, text, rectangle, and fill commands.

11. TABLE I, V—Entry I of the video look-up table is loaded with value V. The range of I is 0 to 7, the range of V is 0 to 63.

12. WBLOCK X, Y, VALUES—A rectangular area of the refresh buffer is loaded from the list VALUES, which follows the instruction. The area of the image storage loaded is the rectangle defined by the CP and (X, Y). The current position becomes (X, Y). The list VALUES is stored in row-major order (a row at a time, left to right, top to bottom). The length of VALUES must be the same as the number of pixels in the rectangle.

13. WBLOCKR DX, DY, VALUES—A relative write block command. The area of the refresh buffer loaded is the rectangle defined by the CP and CP + (X, Y). The CP is updated by DX and DY.

14. RBLOCK X, Y, ADDR—A rectangular area of the refresh buffer is read into CPU memory starting at the address in ADDR, in row-major order. Pixel values in the refresh buffer are not changed.

15. RBLOCKR DX, DY, ADDR—A relative read block command.

16. CBLOCK XMIN, XMAX, YMIN, YMAX, XTO, YTO—A rectangular block of pixel values (XMIN, XMAX, YMIN, YMAX) is copied *within* the refresh buffer. The lower left corner of the block is copied to (XTO, YTO). Thus pixels in the block defined by XTO, XTO + (XMAX − XMIN), YTO, YTO + (YMAX − YMIN) will be changed. If the source and destination blocks partially overlap one another, the copy is done so no information from the source block is lost. The CP is not used to help define either of the blocks because the command is fundamentally different from previous commands: output primitives are neither inserted into nor read from the image storage.

17. RDLOCATOR ADDR—Read the locator position, returning the coordinates to the address given by ADDR. A locator connected to the image creation system is read and its coordinates, which range from 0 to 511 in X and Y, are provided by the image creation system in response to this command.

18. FEEDBACK SWITCH—Turn locator feedback on or off, depending on the value of SWITCH. The locator feedback is a small cursor which the image display superposes on (mixes with) the image from the refresh buffer.

19. WMODE MODE—The write mode for loading values into the refresh buffer is set to one of two modes: *replace* or *exclusive-or*. In *replace* mode, new values placed into pixels of the refresh buffer replace the old values. (For simplicity, the preceding descriptions of commands have been written as though *replace* were the only write mode.) In *exclusive-or* mode, new values placed into pixels of image storage undergo an exclusive-or operation with the current value of the pixel, and the result of this operation is placed into the pixel.

The write mode applies to all commands which change pixel values: LINE, LINER, TEXT, RECT, RECTR, FFILL, BFILL, WBLOCK, WBLOCKR, and CBLOCK. The utility of the exclusive-or mode will be illustrated in the next section.

For the moment, we simply note that if a pixel value A undergoes two successive exclusive-or operations with some other value B, then the result is the original pixel value. This is shown formally by the following Boolean expressions:

$$(A \oplus B) \oplus B = A \oplus (B \oplus B) = A \oplus 0 = A.$$

by associativity

Figure 12.3 summarizes the commands accepted by our simple raster display. Note that the set of commands defining an image need not be executed at the rate of thirty times per second: the image display system takes care of the refresh process. Efficiency of command encoding and formatting is thus not so critical, so we are not concerned with these details. The next question is how the commands are actually presented to the image creation system for execution.

1.	MOVE	X, Y
2.	MOVER	DX, DY
3.	LINE	X, Y
4.	LINER	DX, DY
5.	TEXT	N, STRING
6.	RECT	X, Y
7.	RECTR	DX, DY
8.	BFILL	I
9.	FFILL	I
10.	COLOR	I
11.	TABLE	I, V
12.	WBLOCK	X, Y, VALUES
13.	WBLOCKR	DX, DY, VALUES
14.	RBLOCK	X, Y, ADDR
15.	RBLOCKR	DX, DY, ADDR
16.	CBLOCK	XMIN, XMAX, YMIN, YMAX, XTO, YTO
17.	RDLOCATOR	ADDR
18.	FEEDBACK	SWITCH
19.	WMODE	MODE

Fig. 12.3 Raster display commands.

Raster display systems which follow the generic form we have described (image creation system, image storage system, image display system) receive the commands through an interface to a general-purpose computer. The interface may be a direct-memory access port or a communications line. In either case, the graphics application program and graphics subroutine package execute on the computer, create one or more commands for the display, and send the commands to the display for actual execution. Note that several of the commands (RBLOCK, RBLOCKR, RDLOCATOR) result in the return of information to the computer.

The overall speed with which all or part of the image storage can be changed is dependent upon how fast:

- The application program operates,
- The computer prepares instructions to the display,
- The instructions are conveyed to the display, and
- The image creation system executes instructions.

These processes can of course be partially overlapped, because they may be performed with different processors. It is the last process which is often the bottleneck, because the scan conversion algorithms typically require many iterations. Usually, the faster this process, the faster the overall system response time to user commands. As has been stressed many times, response time is critical to user satisfaction; while most raster displays are still too slow, like all hardware, they are becoming faster every year. The fastest commercial system available in 1981 [MEGA81] that uses special-purpose hardware can scan-convert a line at the rate of six pixels per microsecond, i.e., less than 100 microseconds for a full-screen line of 512 pixels.

Some contemporary raster displays have additional instructions. For example, the WMODE instruction might permit logical or arithmetic operations other than the *exclusive-or* and *replace,* as discussed with *RASTER_OP* in Section 11.8.1.

Some systems have a set of *clip registers* (called *window registers* by some vendors). The registers define a rectangular region of the refresh buffer and hence of the screen. Output primitives are clipped at the edge of the viewport, and RBLOCK and WBLOCK operations apply only to the interior of the viewport. The viewport may also be used as the source or destination for CBLOCK (copy block), reducing the number of explicit operands needed in the instruction itself. (CBLOCK is sometimes called a "bit-mover" instruction.)

The Bit-Blt (bit-boundary block transfer) instruction, first developed on the Alto, combines many of the above ideas into a powerful bit-moving instruction [KAY77a, INGA81]. (Bit-Blt is described as *RasterOp* in [NEWM79].) The operation provides a powerful capability for bitwise operations on rectangular areas of one-bit per pixel refresh buffers. For efficiency, Bit-Blt is best implemented in hardware or firmware.

The instruction copies a source array into a destination array, where the two are combined by any of the 16 logical functions of two variables or by arithmetic operations such as addition and subtraction. The use of the *exclusive-or* is illustrated in Section 12.3.2. The *and* uses its source as a mask to selectively clear parts of the destination, while the *or* selectively sets parts of the destination. Thus the *or* can be used to "paint" shapes into the refresh buffer, perhaps under control of a mouse or tablet. Another use of *or* is to place text characters defined by bit arrays into the refresh buffer without changing the background pixels around those that form the character itself. This is essential if character boxes overlap, as in kerning of italic characters. For multi-bit per pixel systems, the bit array is used as a selective write mask, as in Section 11.3.

Some versions of Bit-Blt also use a 16×16 pixel halftone array which functions as an additional mask [INGA81]. The halftone array can be used in place of the source or can be *and*ed with the source prior to combination with the destination. A halftone array with alternating pixels on and off, when combined with a source, will create a stippled or textured effect in the destination. If the halftone array is smaller than the source array, the halftone array is replicated as necessary to match the size of the source. This same version of Bit-Blt also allows a clipping region to be associated with the destination. This can be used, for instance, to provide clipping of characters defined by bit arrays much more easily than by performing the clipping as part of the viewing transformation processing. This speed is crucial, especially for smooth scrolling of text by units of less than one character height.

The RBLOCK and WBLOCK instructions in our simple raster display may have modifier bits to control the sequence in which pixels are read from or written into the refresh buffer. Any of eight sequences are possible, formed from the various combinations of column-major or row-major, top-to-bottom or bottom-to-top, and left-to-right or right-to-left orderings. This allows, for instance, an image to be inverted by reading it from the buffer top-to-bottom and writing it back bottom-to-top. Many systems also have a *mask register* to specify which bits of a pixel may be modified whenever the refresh buffer is written into. The register is normally loaded with all bits on; however, to allow only bit 2 of each pixel to be modified, the register would be loaded with 100_2. Then subsequent execution of commands which write into the refresh buffer affects only bit 2 of each pixel. This is useful for placing different images in different planes of the refresh buffer, as discussed further in Section 12.4.1. A read mask register is useful also for selectively accessing pixel values during reads, copies, flood fills, etc., and when double buffering between two images, each on its own (set of) plane(s).

There are typically additional output primitives beyond those discussed here, such as conic sections, graph grids, and even simple pie or bar charts. These are useful for applications written for a specific display, but may be hard to integrate into a general-purpose device-independent graphics package because of clipping and viewing transformation complications.

The microcoded interpreter for the display instructions is typically stored in ROM. However, some systems allow RAM to be substituted and provide a mechanism for loading code to interpret additional instructions or to modify the existing code. This provides a useful extensibility capability.

Other normally found input devices include the alphanumeric keyboard, often with a bank of programmable function keys. Characters typed are echoed at a position defined by a loadable register. Some raster displays even have a light pen, which returns the (x, y) device coordinate location of the detected pixel. All these devices have associated registers which can be read to obtain status and input information, and other registers which can be written into to enable/disable, etc.

12.3 PROGRAMMING THE RASTER DISPLAY

We now consider several simple examples to show how the commands for our raster display might be used. The examples assume that the video look-up table has been loaded in the following way:

Entry number	Contents (binary)	Color specified
0	000000	black
1	000011	100% blue
2	001100	100% green
3	110000	100% red
4	111111	white
5	001001	67% green, 33% blue
6	010010	67% blue, 33% red
7	100100	67% red, 33% green

12.3.1 Simple Diagrams

A white line on a black background is drawn with:

```
WMODE   REPLACE    Replacement mode
COLOR   0          Pixel value of 0 is black
MOVE    0, 0
RECT    511, 511   Makes entire image black
COLOR   4          Pixel value of 4 is white
MOVE    100, 100
LINER   300, 300   Draws line from (100, 100) to (400, 400)
```

The block diagram shown in Fig. 12.4 is created by the following commands:

```
WMODE   REPLACE        Replacement mode
COLOR   4              Pixel value of 4 is white
MOVE    0, 0
RECT    511, 511       White background on entire image
COLOR   0              Pixel value 0 is black
MOVE    50, 200        Set up for rectangle on left
RECTR   150, 80        Black rectangle 150×80
MOVE    200, 240       Set up for line
LINER   100, 0         Draw line
MOVE    300, 200       Set up for rectangle on right
RECTR   150, 80        Black rectangle 150×80
COLOR   4              Pixel value 4 is white
MOVE    70, 250
TEXT    5, "IMAGE"
MOVE    70, 220
TEXT    6, "BUFFER"
MOVE    320, 250
TEXT    5, "IMAGE"
MOVE    320, 220
TEXT    7, "DISPLAY"
```

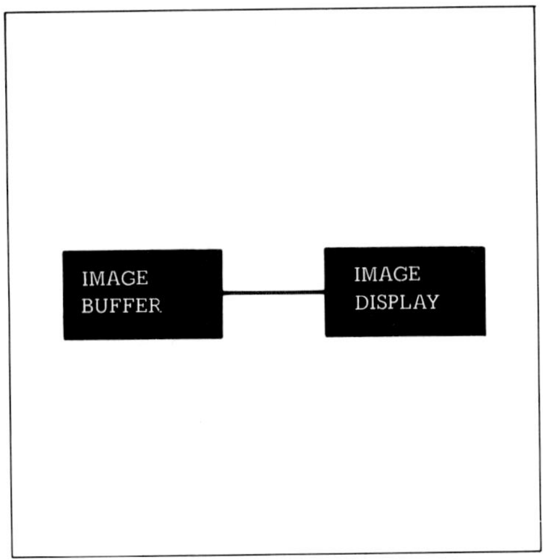

Fig. 12.4 Image created by program in text.

12.3.2 Rubber-band Line Drawing

Our next example shows how to use the write mode to do rubber-band line drawing, as described in Chapter 5. This technique is easily generalized to dragging of objects. Three different sequences of display commands are shown: the first initializes the process by drawing a line, in exclusive-or mode, from the starting to the ending position of the rubber-band line. In the example, an instruction line such as

```
MOVE    XSTART, YSTART
```

is interpreted to mean that the values of variables XSTART and YSTART have been incorporated into the MOVE command as immediate data. The initialization code is:

```
INIT:   WMODE   XOR               Set exclusive-or mode
        COLOR   7                 Binary 111 will be used to exclusive-
                                  or, thus inverting all bits
        MOVE    XSTART, YSTART
        LINE    XEND, YEND        Draw line
```

The line which is drawn is not of a single color. Rather, the color at each pixel is determined by using as an index into the look-up table the exclusive-or of the pixel value (represented in binary) with 111. For example, if the pixel value were originally 100 (color white), the new value would be 011 (color red). If entries 3 and 4 of the look-up table had the same color specification, then the pixel's color would be unchanged.

The second sequence of display instructions is executed 20 to 30 times a second to obtain the real-time dynamics of rubber-banding. Its execution could be triggered by a real-time clock or by an interrupt from the display to the computer after each raster scan cycle has been completed. The code at ERASE uses another exclusive-or with 111 to reset all pixels on the current rubber-band line to their previous values. Then the application program reads the locator, and the code at DRAW draws a line to the new position:

```
ERASE:   MOVE        XSTART,  YSTART    Go over current
         LINE        XEND,    YEND      rubber-band line
         RDLOCATOR   XEND     YEND      Read locator into XEND,
                                        YEND

DRAW:    MOVE        XSTART,  YSTART    Draw a new
         LINE        XEND,    YEND      rubber-band line
```

The final code sequence, sent by the computer to the display when the user has indicated (perhaps using a PFK) that the line is in its final position, draws the line in the desired color, assumed here to be green:

```
FINI:    WMODE       REPLACE            Reset replace mode
         COLOR       2                  Pixel value 2 into
         MOVE        XSTART,  YSTART    color register
         LINE        XEND,    YEND      Line is now green
```

The overall program schema within which these three code segments would be used is:

```
Initialize rubber-band line drawing
  send code sequence INIT to display
repeat
  Send code sequence ERASE to display
  Send code sequence DRAW to display
until user action
send code sequence FINI to display
```

When scan-converting the same line twice to reset on the second scan-conversion those pixels set on the first scan-conversion, it is important that the start and end points of the line be specified in the same order, since some line scan-conversion algorithms may not visit the same pixels if the endpoint order is reversed.

12.4 THE IMAGE DISPLAY SYSTEM

The image display system reads the refresh buffer a row at a time to drive the raster scan. Many raster displays (as well as commercial TV) use an *interlaced* scan: all odd-numbered scan lines are displayed in 1/60 of a second, and all even-numbered scan lines are displayed in the next 1/60 of a second, for an overall frame time of

1/30 second. This interlacing helps to avoid flicker because adjacent scan lines are displayed 1/60 second apart, even though each scan line is only displayed each 1/30 second. Flicker will occur for horizontal lines one pixel wide since they are refreshed only at 30 Hz. The trend, however, is toward faster refresh rates: many modern systems, especially those with less than 1280×1024 resolution, double the rates, halving the frame time to 1/60 second. This removes all vestiges of flicker, but at the cost of more (and/or faster) refresh buffer accesses per second and significantly higher-bandwidth deflection amplifiers. An alternative is of course phosphors with a longer decay time, but then afterimages become a concern.

The image display system's video look-up table is useful for more than just assigning colors or intensities to pixel values. To simplify the present examples of these other uses, we now assume a monochromatic display with three bits per pixel and with three bits in each look-up table entry. In addition to the two following examples, Chapter 17 discusses the use of the look-up table for gamma correction. Further examples are given in [SLOA79].

12.4.1 Multiple Images in Refresh Buffer

We usually think of a $512 \times 512 \times 3$ bit refresh buffer as containing a single image with three bits per pixel. However, we can also think of it as containing two images, one with two bits per pixel, the other with one bit per pixel. Yet another possibility is that there be three separate images, each with one bit per pixel. The look-up table is then used to select or combine the separate images to form a single composite image displayed on the view surface. For instance, to display only image 2, defined by the high-order bit of each pixel value, we would load the table as shown in Fig. 12.5. To display image 0, which is the image defined by the low-order bit of each pixel, the table would be loaded with a 7 in those locations for which the low-order bit is 1 and with a 0 for the other locations: 0, 7, 0, 7, 0, 7, 0, 7.

Entry number (decimal)	Entry number (binary)			Contents of look-up table (decimal)
0	0	0	0	0
1	0	0	1	0
2	0	1	0	0
3	0	1	1	0
4	1	0	0	7
5	1	0	1	7
6	1	1	0	7
7	1	1	1	7
	Image 2	Image 1	Image 0	0 = black 7 = white

Fig. 12.5 Look-up table to display image defined by high-order bits of each pixel.

Entry number (decimal)	Entry number (binary)			Contents of look-up table (decimal)
0	0	0	0	0
1	0	0	1	2
2	0	1	0	2
3	0	1	1	4
4	1	0	0	2
5	1	0	1	4
6	1	1	0	4
7	1	1	1	6
	Image 2	Image 1	Image 0	

Fig. 12.6 Look-up table to display sum of three images.

If the displayed image is to be the sum of the three images and each image which is "on" at a pixel is to contribute two units of intensity, then we would load the table as shown in Fig. 12.6. If one of the three pixel bits is on, a 2 is placed in the table; if two of three, a 4; and if three of three, a 6.

As a final example, think of each image as being defined on parallel planes, as in Fig. 12.7. The plane of image 2 is closest to the viewer; the plane of image 0, furthest away. Image 2 therefore obscures both images 0 and 1, while image 1 obscures only image 0. This priority can be reflected in the look-up table, as shown in Fig. 12.8. In this case, image 2 is displayed at intensity 7, image 1 at intensity 5, and image 0 at intensity 3, so that "closer" images appear brighter than those further away. Where no image is defined, intensity 0 is displayed.

This technique can be used to implement dynamic segment priorities if there are no more segments than there are planes (this is true only in special cases). "Window managers," such as described in [TEIT77], provide a specialized form of explicit priority among windows whose viewports overlap on the screen. They are easily implemented with this method.

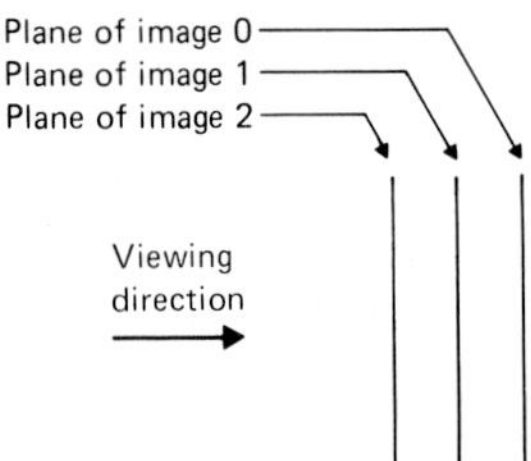

Fig. 12.7 Relation of images to viewing direction.

Entry number (decimal)	Entry number (binary)			Contents of look-up table (decimal)	
0	0	0	0	0	no image present
1	0	0	1	3	image 0 visible
2	0	1	0	5	image 1 visible
3	0	1	1	5	image 1 visible
4	1	0	0	7	image 2 visible
5	1	0	1	7	image 2 visible
6	1	1	0	7	image 2 visible
7	1	1	1	7	image 2 visible
	Image 2	Image 1	Image 0		

Fig. 12.8 Look-up table to prioritize three images.

Yet another possibility is to use the look-up table to store a weighted sum (interpolation) of the intensities of two images, creating a "double exposure" effect. If the weight applied to one image is decreased over time as the other weight is increased, a "fade-out" and "fade-in" effect results. If colored images are used, the details of what colors are displayed during the fade sequence will depend upon the color space in which the weighted sum is calculated (see Chapter 17).

12.4.2 Animation

Another use of the look-up table, simple animation of repetitive actions, is described in [SHOU79]. The limitations on scan-conversion rates still preclude reloading the refresh buffer each 1/30 of a second, except in special cases of very simple figures or with expensive equipment. However, the look-up table can easily be reloaded at the end of a raster display cycle, while the CRT beam is returning to the upper left of the screen. If the appropriate images have been loaded into the refresh buffer, a look-up table change can step the displayed image through an animation sequence.

Suppose we want to display a bouncing ball. Figure 12.9 shows how the refresh buffer could be loaded; the numbers indicate the pixel values placed in each region of the buffer. Figure 12.10 shows how the look-up table would be loaded at each step to display a complete bounce sequence, from peak to peak. The idea is always to display all but one of the balls at the background color 0. By cycling the contents of the look-up table, motion effects can result.

For more complicated cyclic animation, such as rotating a complex wire-frame object, it may be impossible to keep the separate images from overlapping in the refresh buffer. This will cause some of the images to have "holes" in them when displayed. A few such holes are not especially distracting, especially if realism is not an objective. In the limit as more holes appear, the animation loses its effectiveness.

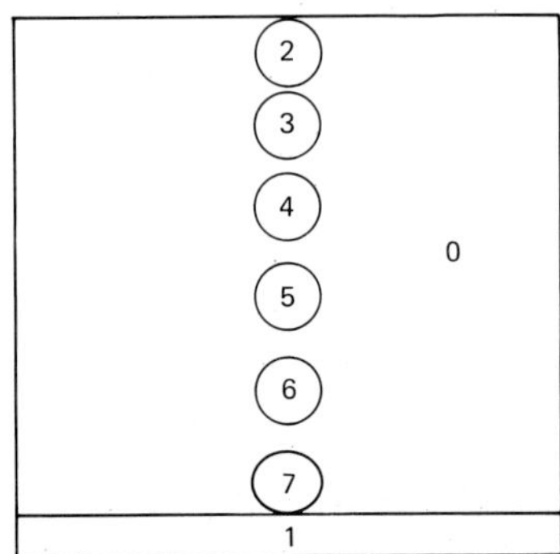

Fig. 12.9 Contents of refresh buffer for bouncing-ball animation.

Entry number	Colors loaded in table at each step in animation										
	1	2	3	4	5	6	7	8	9	10	11
0	white	white	white	white	white	white	white	white	white	white	white
1	black	black	black	black	black	black	black	black	black	black	black
2	red										red
3		red								red	
4			red						red		
5				red				red			
6					red		red				
7						red					

Fig. 12.10 Look-up table to bounce red ball on black surface against white background. Unspecified entries are white.

12.4.3 Refresh Buffer Transformation

In some image display systems the refresh buffer is decoupled from the view surface; that is, the direct, fixed correspondence between positions in the refresh buffer and positions on the view surface (i.e., CRT) is removed. What then defines the relation between the buffer and the display? It is the *image transformation,* which is essentially the same transformation as described in Chapter 8.

The refresh buffer contains an image which has been clipped and transformed (and perhaps projected) from world coordinates into device coordinates. The image transformation transforms from the refresh buffer to the view surface. In general, the transformation might include a translation, scaling, rotation, and an additional window operation. Only translation and integer scalings are available commercially, but prototype rotation and continuous zoom systems have been developed [WEIM80].

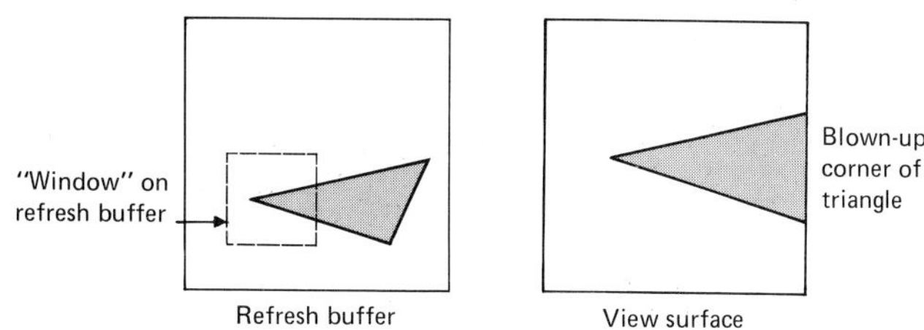

Fig. 12.11 Portion of refresh buffer blown-up on view surface.

Figure 12.11 shows the type of transformation found on some raster displays. Part of the refresh buffer, defined by a window, is blown up to fill the entire view surface. The ratio between the size of the window and the view surface is constrained to be an integer (3, in Fig. 12.11). Pixels in the refresh buffer outside the window are not used, and none of the pixel values are modified: the transformations are repeated (30 times a second) by the image display system.

The image transformation can be changed many times a second—up to 30, the refresh rate—to give the real-time dynamics effect of panning over and/or zooming into an image. Another animation effect is possible through "partitioning" the refresh buffer into 4, 8, or 16 areas, each containing a different image. The image transformation is changed periodically to display first one area, then the next, etc.

The scaling needed to enlarge an image is trivially accomplished by repeating pixel values from within the window as the image is displayed. For a scale factor of 2, each pixel value is used four times, twice on each of two successive scan lines. Figure 12.12 shows the effect of scaling up a letter and adjoining line by a factor of 2. Unless the image storage has higher resolution than the image display, zooming in does not reveal more detail about the image: it is merely enlarged, having a more jagged appearance. Thus this animation effect loses spatial resolution but maintains a full range of colors, while the animation described in the previous section maintains spatial resolution but decreases the number of colors available in any one frame.

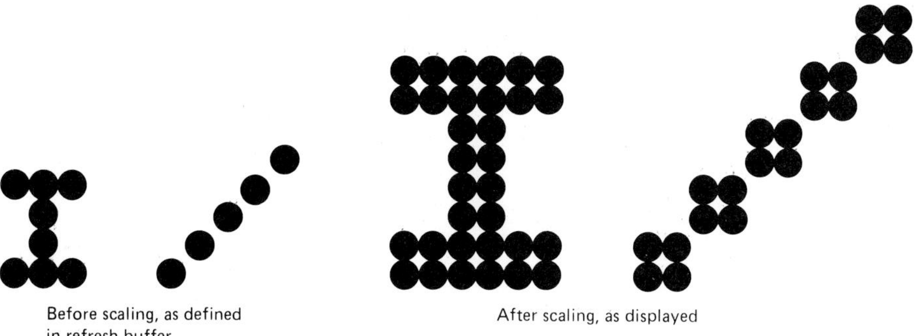

Fig. 12.12 Effect of scaling up by 2.

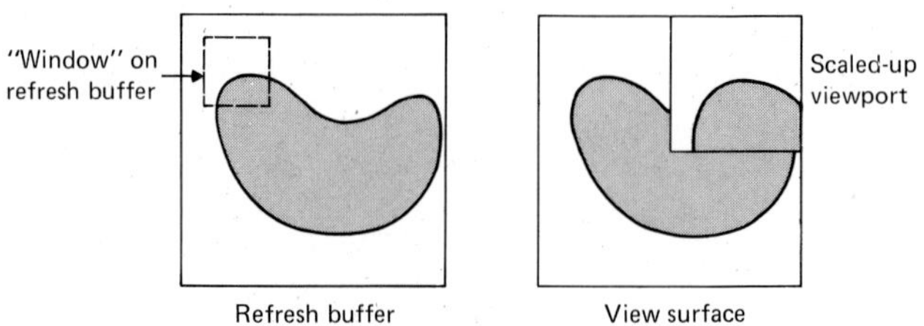

Fig. 12.13

In a more general application of image transformations, the scaled image covers only the part of the view surface defined by a viewport, as in Fig. 12.13. Now we must define to the system what is to appear on the view surface outside of the viewport. One possibility is to display some constant color or intensity; another, shown here, is to display the refresh buffer using the identity image transformation. The hardware implementation for this is simple. Registers containing the viewport boundary coordinates are compared to the X, Y registers defining the raster scan's current position. If the beam is in the viewport, pixels are fetched from within the window area of the refresh buffer and replicated as required. Otherwise, pixels are fetched from the position in the refresh buffer with the same (x, y) coordinates as the beam.

Single VLSI chips to implement many of these image display system functions are being produced, so it is likely that the capabilities will become quite common. The work station concept found in the graphics subroutine package GKS provides a convenient way to make these capabilities available to the application programmer [ENCA80].

12.4.4 Video Mixing

Another important function the image display system can perform is video mixing. Two images, one defined in the refresh buffer and the other defined by an analog video signal coming from a TV camera, VTR, video disk, or even another graphics system, may be merged to form a composite image. Examples of this technique are seen regularly on commercial television. Figure 12.14 shows the overall system organization.

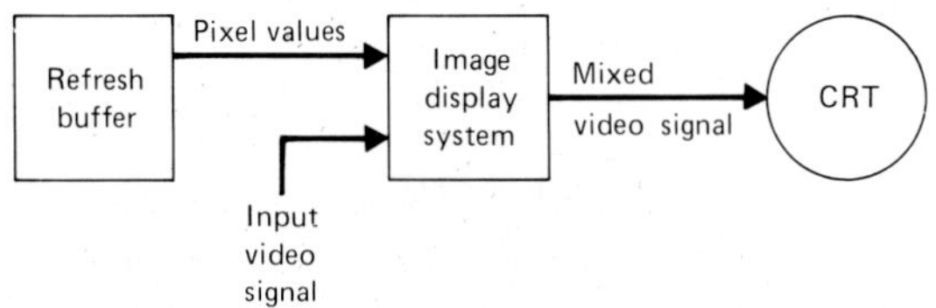

Fig. 12.14 Video mixing with refresh-buffer image.

The key question in video mixing is to determine, for each pixel, whether the pixel value from the refresh buffer (look-up table, if one exists) or that from the analog video signal is to be used to control the CRT beam. This decision is typically made on the basis of a *mixing register*. If the value of a pixel from the refresh buffer equals that in the mixing register, the video signal is displayed; otherwise, the refresh buffer pixel value is displayed. The mixing register is normally set to the background value in the refresh buffer, although interesting effects can be achieved by using other pixel values instead.

This mixing is currently practical only with 480 scan-line systems, because this is approximately the number of visible scan lines in NTSC TV signals which are broadcast and recorded. (NTSC is an encoding of the YIQ color representation described in Chapter 17.) Most raster systems have an optional NTSC output signal for recording or for driving standard TV sets. Unfortunately, the bandwidth of the NTSC signal does not match that of a 512 pixel per scan-line image, so sharp color transitions are usually blurred, causing a loss of detail.

Another form of mixing done by the image display system is superposition of the cursor symbol on the displayed image. Some systems have several different cursor symbols; the most flexible systems allow a user-defined cursor symbol, for example, 32×32 pixels in size. This allows small symbols to be dynamically translated to their desired position by using a tablet or other locator without affecting the contents of the refresh buffer.

12.5 ALTERNATIVE RASTER DISPLAY ARCHITECTURES

We have considered the refresh buffer, the image creation system, and the associated computer as three separate subsystems. This is indeed the way in which most commercial raster systems have traditionally been organized. Several important variations on this design exist, however, and will be discussed here.

All the variations are based on recognizing that a raster system requires three memory areas, for:

1. Application program and data,
2. Image creation (scan-conversion) programs and data, and
3. Refresh buffer.

There are also two active processes:

1. The application program process,
2. The image creation process.

The memory areas are traditionally three separate address spaces, and the processes execute on two separate processors. In the following two alternative designs, the numbers of processors and address spaces are reduced, potentially but not necessarily to one each.

12.5.1 Single-Processor System

The image creation system is almost invariably implemented as a microprocessor. Why not use it to execute the application program also? If this is done, a single-CPU system emerges, as in Fig. 12.15. This makes the overall system less expensive, because there is now only a single processor. On the other hand, the system is also slower, since when a scan-conversion algorithm is being executed, the application program is idled, and vice versa.

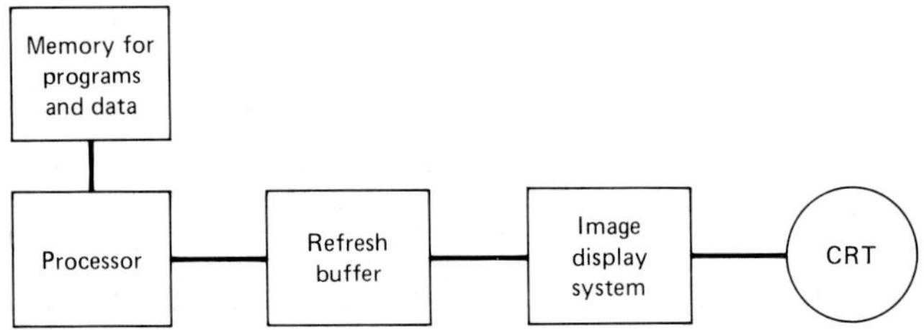

Fig. 12.15 Single-processor raster display.

This situation is quite similar to that in satellite graphics, discussed briefly in Chapter 10. Many raster systems can be thought of as fixed-function satellite graphics systems: the image creation system performs a fixed set of graphics-oriented functions. By adding application programming, we have a programmable satellite. In the limit, such a system can become independent of the host computer. Satellite graphics evolved in just the reverse way, starting with a single computer and display and then evolving into a two-computer satellite environment to off-load the central computer.

Many single-processor raster displays are organized so the graphics functions can be invoked in any of three ways:

- By subroutine call from an application program executing on the single processor,
- By keyboard type-in, directly from a user, and
- By communications link input from some other computer.

The single-processor system can thus be used flexibly in many different ways.

12.5.2 Single Address-Space System

Another architectural variation concerns the relation of the refresh buffer to the memory of the image creation system. The buffer and the memory are usually in separate address spaces, because a million-pixel image storage requires 20-bit addresses, while typical computers used in the image creation system have at most

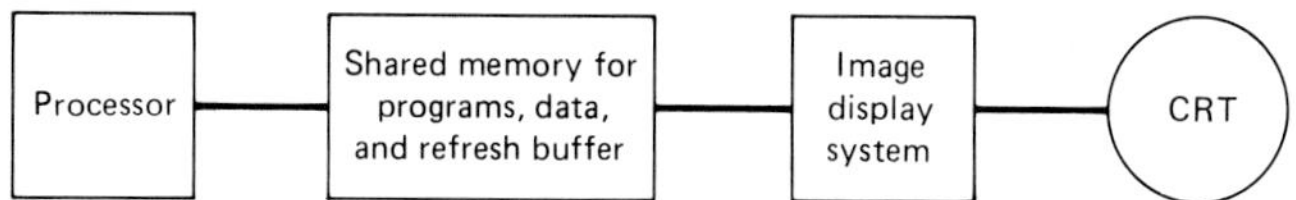

Fig. 12.16 Single address-space system.

16-bit addresses. A single address-space system (Fig. 12.16), implemented by using either memory-mapping, a computer with a large address space, or a low-resolution display, can simplify programming of the image creation system. Most home computers have this architecture, as do the powerful Alto and PERQ (discussed in Chapter 1 and in Section 12.6) and the system described in [BECH80].

Programming such systems is especially simple if addressing modes are provided for treating the refresh buffer as a 2D address space rather than as a conventional linear (1D) address space. Another useful feature is to permit the image to be refreshed starting at any address. This allows a new image to be built up in one part of memory while another image is displayed. Parts of a displayed image can be changed quickly, just by memory-to-memory moves of pixel values.

This simple architecture must be carefully implemented, lest memory accesses by the image display slow down the processor to execute instructions at a small fraction of its capacity. By accessing memory at the approximately 100 nanoseconds per pixel rate of a 512×512 resolution system (see p. 131), the image display could lock out the processor except during beam retrace. To avoid this, the memory must be interleaved, with more than one pixel fetched during each access cycle. Typical systems fetch 8, 16, or even 32 pixels in one access cycle.

12.5.3 Refresh Buffer Organizations

The final architectural alternatives we will consider are those involved in the organization of the refresh buffer. We have so far assumed the existence of one memory location for each and every pixel, and have further assumed that pixels which are adjacent on a row (or alternatively, on a column) occupy sequentially adjacent locations in the refresh buffer. Neither of these assumptions need be true.

One can easily imagine a scheme in which individual scan lines are physically contiguous in memory, but with the scan lines themselves forming a linked list. A scan line would then consist of storage for the pixels on the line, plus an additional location containing an address pointing to the next scan line. The image display system would use the address to locate the next scan line during the time the beam retraces from the right to the left edge of the CRT. Alternatively, a physically contiguous vector of addresses, called the *scan line directory* in Fig. 12.17, could be used to point to each scan line.

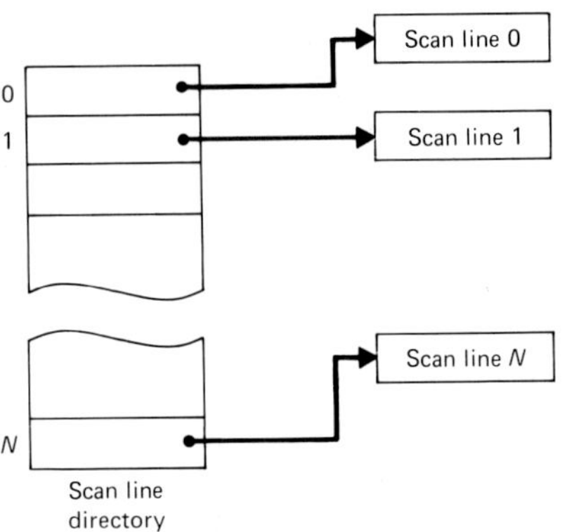

Fig. 12.17 Noncontiguous image storage.

Such arrangements facilitate rapid changes to parts of the image. Even more flexibility is possible if the scan line table's address is given in a register rather than being fixed. Another possibility, described in [NEGR77], is to include a repetition count with each scan line address. The count controls how often each pixel value from a scan line is replicated. A low-resolution image can be displayed by making N successive entries in the scan line directory point to the same scan line, with each entry specifying N as the repetition count. Using this method, a constant-color image can be defined as a single scan line of one pixel.

The *run-length coding* technique, long used for facsimile and photo transmission, eliminates repetitive specification of sequences of equal pixel values. Each scan line is broken up into a series of runs of equal-valued pixels. Figure 12.18 shows a scan line with just three runs of D_i pixels, each with intensity I_i. Each run can be encoded as the tuple (D_i, I_i). Each I_i can be an intensity or an R_i, G_i, B_i color triple; it can also be an index into the image display system's video look-up table. D_i and I_i are usually stored as one byte each.

A variation on run-length coding is to allow a linear intensity change in a run; this would facilitate Gouraud shading, discussed in Chapter 16. To do this, each run is coded as a length D_i, initial intensity I_i, and change in intensity per pixel dI_i. If $dI_i = 0$, the run is displayed at constant intensity. With this coding method, a video look-up table would not normally be used. If one were used, it would need to be carefully loaded so that all the index values for each run, defined by

$$I_i + k \cdot dI_i, \qquad k = 0, 1, 2, \ldots, D_i,$$

would produce reasonable sequences of intensities or colors.

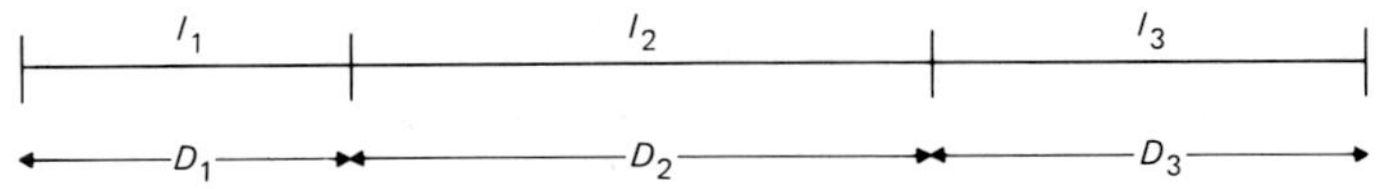

Fig. 12.18 Run-length coding.

Run-length coding can substantially reduce the amount of memory needed to store images. Its advantage is maximized, of course, for images made up of a few long runs. With two bytes per run, many very realistic computer-generated images can be stored in about 10% of the space needed with a traditional byte-per-pixel refresh buffer.

This tenfold data compaction is especially important for transmission of images and for video animation, since 30 frame per second animation at a resolution of $512 \times 512 \times 8$ bits requires processing of 7.5 million bytes of information per second. Such information quantities and rates are very expensive to provide, while operating at 10% of these values is quite practical. A small contemporary 64 Mbyte disk can store over a minute of 15 frames per second animation for frames with an average of 20,000 runs, each encoded in 16 bits [IKON81]. To store the equivalent on encoded frames for a 512×512 display would take 256 Kbytes $\times$ 15 fps $\times$ 60 sec = 230.4 Mbytes, and would require a transfer rate of 15×256 Kbyte/sec or 3.75 Mbyte/sec. The second figure is well beyond the capacity of most mini- and micro-computer disk controllers, I/O interfaces, and busses.

Why then is run-length coding not universally used? Because it has several disadvantages to weigh against its advantages. First, there is a rapid increase in image storage size as the average run length decreases. As runs approach a length of 1, the image storage approaches twice that required with a traditional system. Furthermore, the image display system, already made more complicated by run-length coding, usually cannot actually display long sequences of very short runs: there simply is not enough time (in the approximately 100 nanoseconds per pixel available on a 512×512 display) to fetch and decode many successive runs which are each one pixel long.

Even with those many images for which run-length coding is quite satisfactory, there is another disadvantage: changing an image is difficult. Consider Fig. 12.19(a), which shows a long run of intensity I_i. The run can be coded as (D_i, I_i). Part (b) of the same figure shows the results after adding a segment of intensity I_2. Now the coding is $(D_a, I_1,)$, (D_b, I_2), (D_c, I_1). The runs are normally stored sequentially in the refresh buffer, so that adding the two new runs implies shifting the storage locations of all succeeding runs.

A generalization of run-length coding from 1D to 2D is described in [HART78] and [THAC81]. Areas of constant intensity are represented with very few bytes, while areas where the image varies are represented by one bit per pixel.

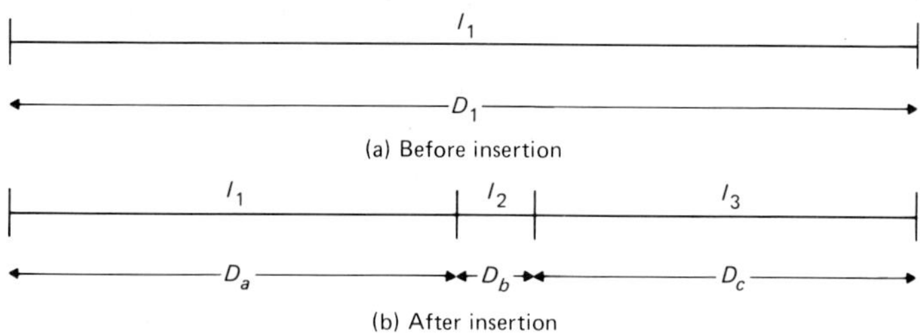

Fig. 12.19 Modifying a run-length coded image.

Cell encoding is another way to avoid the use of one physical memory location per pixel. The image is divided into rectangular cells, typically ranging from 6 × 8 to 10 × 14 pixels in size. Each cell is then encoded in the refresh buffer by some number of bytes which is less than would be required by a normal refresh buffer. In the coding method used with the Tektronix 4025 and 4027 displays, a cell whose pixels have the same value is represented by one or two bytes. Cells in which the pixels have different values are fully represented at the pixel level by dynamically allocating, whenever required, memory to store a cell of 8 × 14 pixels.

With this type of cell coding, there is no fixed and unchanging relationship between pixels and memory locations. Another type of cell encoding assigns a set of fixed memory locations to each cell, which typically contains either a character or some limited graphics. Figure 12.20 shows such an encoding with two bytes per cell; the cells are 6×8 pixels. The type bit indicates how to interpret byte 0. In one case, the byte is a character code: the character is displayed in the foreground color (one of eight) given in byte 1, and the remaining pixels appear in the background color. In the other case, byte 0 is interpreted as 8 separate bits. Each bit determines the color (foreground or background) of one subcell of 2×3 pixels within the 6×8 cell, as in Figure 12.21. Unfortunately, this coding scheme does not allow each individual pixel to be separately set to any one of the eight available colors. This technique is a compromise between the size of the refresh buffer and image complexity. Run-length coding and other cell codings (see, for example, [JORD74]) are other such compromises.

From a larger perspective, recognize that the refresh buffer exists to hold the image in a form which the image display can scan through at least 30 times per sec-

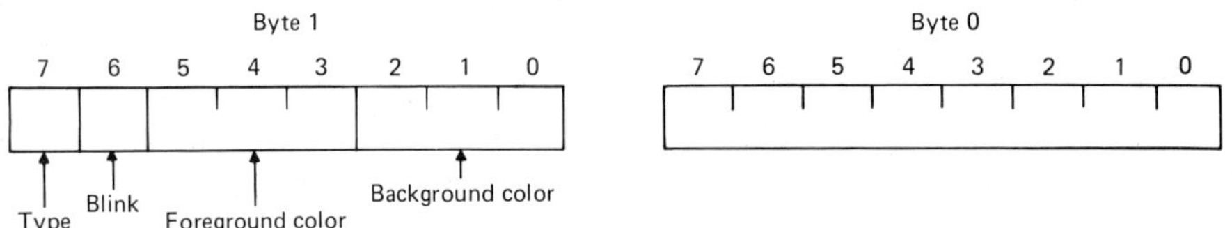

Fig. 12.20 Cell coding.

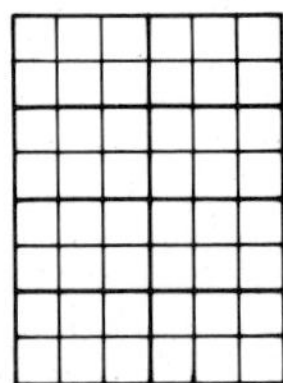

Fig. 12.21 A cell of a cell-coded display with eight subcells of six pixels each.

ond. Now suppose that the image creation system were fast enough to create a new image from input commands (MOVE, LINE, TEXT, etc.) 30 times per second, from top to bottom, producing each scan line in the time taken to draw a raster scan line on the display. Then the refresh buffer is unnecessary, and *on-the-fly* scan conversion is being done. This method has been used not only for 2D scan conversion but also for 3D hidden surface removal. Such on-the-fly systems are still prohibitively expensive, however, except for systems of very limited capability. It is reasonable to expect the VLSI revolution to impact this area: research is already underway on techniques for using multiple special-purpose microprocessors for on-the-fly scan conversion.

12.6 RASTER ARCHITECTURE FOR PERSONAL COMPUTERS

In Chapter 1 we described briefly what might be called the *Xerox PARC model* of computing. It is a local network of hundreds of personal minicomputers (such as Altos, Dolphins, and Dorados) and several shared-access computers, called *file servers* and *printer servers,* which handle large-scale file storage and various types of printers, respectively. This configuration was first designed in 1973 at PARC as an experimental vehicle to test the idea that computing services traditionally provided by time-sharing systems could instead be provided by relatively small dedicated computers with occasional access to larger machines for database access, large-scale computation, and other peripherals such as printers. In fact, the services provided go considerably beyond those available on most time-sharing systems in terms of the local computing power available on a dedicated basis, and especially in terms of the quality of the user interface provided by the high-bandwidth, high-resolution black-and-white raster display (808 × 608 pixels). All user interactions with the dedicated computer take place at high speed and with output of text and graphics of considerably higher quality than that of conventional alphanumeric and even many graphics terminals. The user–computer dialogues created in this extraordinarily rich environment have set a new standard which we expect to be widely emulated by similar designs in the 1980s [PERQ80, NEWE79, WARD79, APOL81, GUPT81b]. Indeed, we feel that the PARC model is likely to become the preferred means for most computer users, both for programmers and for end users, such as those in office environments, where personal computer workstations will be used by both professional and support staff.

The architecture of the Alto itself is based on a versatile 170-nanosecond cycle time, microprogrammable 32-bit host [THAC81]. This host multiplexes 16 fixed tasks in a simple priority scheme. One task is the emulation of a relatively simple target architecture which supports 16-bit instructions while other microprogram tasks help hardware I/O controllers control the local peripherals. These peripherals include a 2.5 megabyte cartridge disk, the raster display, a keyboard and mouse, and the connection to the Ethernet local network [METC76].

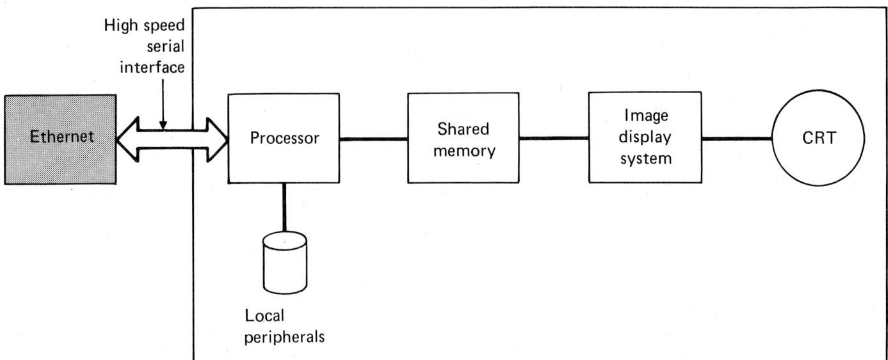

Fig. 12.22 The Alto personal computer (highly schematic) and its connection through the Ethernet local network.

Figure 12.22 shows a simplified abstraction of the Alto (here the target processor and display system are shown as separate units, though in fact they are largely microprograms sharing the same host). The memory "shared" by the processor and display system contains the refresh bit map which, for the maximal 808×608 display, consumes approximately half of a standard 128 kilobyte memory. The bit map does not record blank areas of the screen—control blocks are used to chain together partial bit maps for only those rectangular blocks on the screen in which information actually exists. Therefore many images do not require nearly as much memory or as many processor/memory cycles as a fully expanded bit map representation would require. Characters and symbols are generated by copying their bit map representations, and windows are quickly moved on the screen, both using fast Bit-Blt raster-op microcode for block operations.

As mentioned above, commercial versions of powerful personal computers as nodes in a local network with file and printer servers based on the Alto model are now being sold by various vendors. These are typically based on bus-oriented architectures that use a standard microprocessor such as the Motorola 68000 as the CPU, and additional microprocessors to manage the display and other peripherals. In some systems, the display is refreshed out of shared memory, in others out of private memory, which is typically within the (virtual) address space of the CPU. Both these solutions allow the type of fast updating popularized by the Alto. Optional "engines" based on fast bit slice or discrete logic may be used to perform block copy and scan conversion by means of the algorithms of Chapter 11. Regardless of the particular implementation, the basic notion of high-bandwidth graphical I/O as the standard user interface remains at the core of the archtecture. In addition, these powerful personal computers typically provide some form of memory management such as paged and/or segmented virtual memory, a local disk, keyboard, locator device, high resolution black-and-white monitor, and a network interface. Large members of future commercial families may in fact rival the large mainframes of the late 1970s and early 1980s in terms of speed (nearly a million fixed point operations per second) and amount of local memory (1–4 megabyte). For instance, the Star, a descendent of the Alto introduced in 1981, has 384 kilobytes of main memory, a much faster processor than the Alto, and a display resolution of 809 lines of 1024 pixels each.

It is the tight integration between CPU and display system (the single address space system of Section 12.5.2) found in these computers that accounts for their responsiveness. The shared memory architecture eliminates I/O delays which would be incurred in formatting and sending display commands to a separate image creation system. Instead, the CPU directly modifies a representation of the image (the bit map or an encoded form thereof), and the results are immediately visible. Consequently this is becoming the architecture of choice for many graphics applications and for graphical interfaces to programming environments. Color capability, with look-up table manipulations, will be an increasingly common option.

EXERCISES

12.1 Design a program, showing detailed display instruction sequences, to allow a user to sketch in one color a free-hand closed contour which is then filled in with some other color. Have the user specify an interior point of the contour with the locator.

12.2 Sketch out a program, showing detailed display instruction sequences, to drag some object (a house, for instance) on the screen until the user indicates completion of the drag.

12.3 Show how to load the look-up table for a monochromatic display (Section 12.3), so that the displayed image is the difference of the images in planes 2 and 0. Offset the intensity scale so that a difference of zero is displayed as intensity level three, allowing "negative" intensity differences to be shown.

12.4 Make a block diagram (similar to Fig. 3.36) of the image display system, showing the additional registers and comparisons needed to display an image like that of Fig. 12.13.

12.5 Write a procedure to run-length code an image stored in a 2D array of pixels, and another procedure to decode it.

12.6 Write a procedure to scan-convert a line into a run-length coded refresh buffer.

12.7 Write a procedure to scan-convert a rectangle into a run-length coded refresh buffer. Repeat for a polygon and for a character.

12.8 Modify BRESENHAM in Chapter 11 to scan-convert a zero-length line as a single pixel. (The current algorithm does nothing to zero-length lines.)

12.9 Experiment with your raster display to determine whether its line scan-conversion algorithm affects the same pixels independently of which end of a line is the start point and which is the end point.

12.10 Design the register level logic for an image display system to display a refresh buffer organized as in Fig. 12.17. Repeat for run-length coded images.

12.11 Write a set of subroutines to simulate the raster system described in Section 12.2. Use a line printer or raster display for output.

13
Representation of 3D Shapes

13.1 INTRODUCTION

Many applications of computer graphics involve the representation of 3D shapes: design of airplanes, reconstruction of solids from cross-sectional CAT scans, robotic assembly, and many more. The need to represent 3D shapes arises in two types of situations. First, we may want to represent an existing object: a face, a clay model of a car, or a mountain. In general, of course, an existing object cannot be precisely matched by its representation. In the worst case, an infinity of (x, y, z) triples are needed, one for each point on the object's surface. In the best case, the object can be exactly defined by combinations of mathematical surfaces, such as planes, spheres, etc. In the typical case, we pick out a set of points on the object and require either that the representation be *exact* only at those points, or that the distances between the points and the representation be small. Representations of existing surfaces thus must satisfy such requirements.

The second case in which 3D representations are needed is in computer-aided design. Here we have no pre-existing model of the object of interest: the user, perhaps working from a rough sketch, interactively "sculpts" a 3D shape. In this case, the representation used should allow the interactive user to manipulate the surface easily, so that it can be molded into the desired form.

We already know how to display 3D objects once they are reduced to a series of lines in world coordinates and how to traverse a hierarchical data structure whose lowest-level parts are lines. Although representing a 3D object as a collection of lines allows us to create a line display of the object, it does not allow us to remove hidden surfaces from the display, calculate the weight or volume of the object or create assembly instructions for a robot. The collection of lines is inadequate because lines alone do not define surfaces, and it is surfaces that are needed to perform hidden-

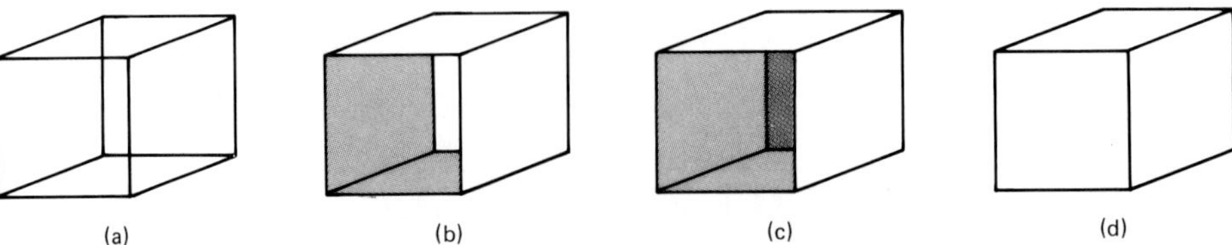

Fig. 13.1 (a) A collection of 12 lines; (b) the same 12 lines defining a four-sided object open at both ends; (c) the same 12 lines defining an open box; (d) the same 12 lines defining a cube.

surface calculations, volume calculations, etc. Figure 13.1 shows that a collection of lines can represent several different 3D shapes. Thus we conclude that a higher-level output primitive, a surface, is needed to represent 3D shapes.

This chapter introduces the general area of *geometric modeling,* also called *shape modeling.* This area is quite broad (see [BARN75] for a collection of papers on the subject, and [FAUX79] for a text). We will focus on two commonly used 3D representations of 3D surfaces: polygon meshes and parametric bicubic patches. A *polygon mesh* is a set of connected polygonally bounded planar surfaces. The exterior of most buildings can be easily and naturally represented by a polygon mesh, as can many desks and cabinets. Polygon meshes are also used to represent objects with curved surfaces, as shown in Fig. 13.2. The disadvantage of this technique, however, is that the representation is only approximate. Figure 13.3 shows a cross section of a curved object and of the polygon mesh used to represent it. The obvious errors in the representation can be made arbitrarily small by using more and more polygons to create a better piecewise-linear approximation, but this increases both space requirements and the execution time of algorithms which process the representation.

Parametric bicubic patches define the coordinates of points on a curved surface by using three equations, one for each of x, y, and z. Each equation has two variables (parameters) and terms for all powers of the parameters up to their cube (hence the terms *bi* and *cubic*). The boundaries of the patch are parametric cubic curves. Many fewer bicubic patches than polygonal patches are needed to represent a curved surface to a given accuracy. On the other hand, the algorithms for working with bicubics are more complex than those for working with polygons. We begin this chapter by discussing polygon meshes, then move on to bicubic surfaces.

In the two previously mentioned methods, a 3D solid is modeled as a closed surface. *Solid modeling,* on the other hand, deals directly with solid objects, using as primitives solids such as cubes, cones, spheres, and cylinders which are added and subtracted to form various shapes. The roller-bearing in Color Plate 14 is defined in this way. (See [BRAI75, VOEL77, VOEL78, and REQU80] to learn more about solid modeling, which is not discussed in this text.)

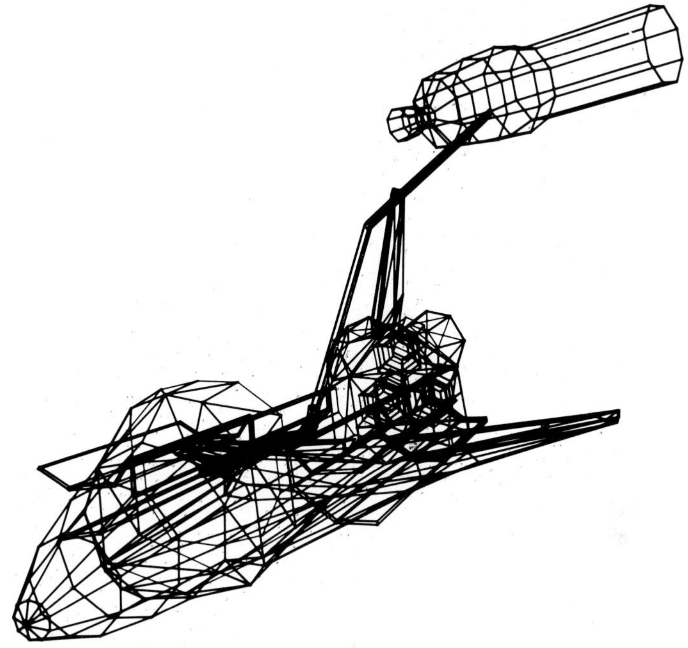

Fig. 13.2 3D object represented by polygons (courtesy Evans & Sutherland).

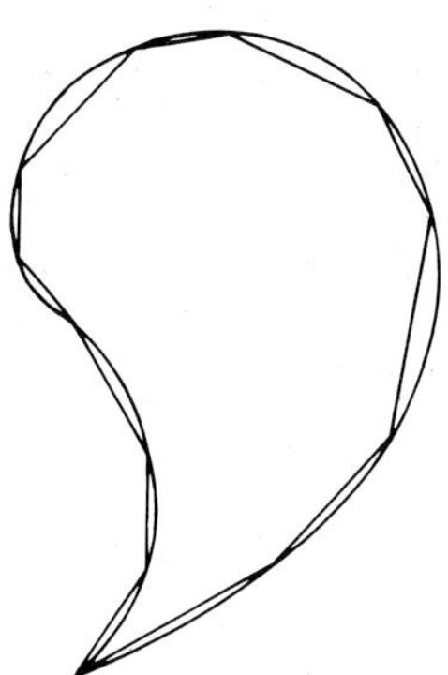

Fig. 13.3 Cross section of curved object and polygon approximation.

13.2 POLYGON MESHES

A polygon mesh is a collection of *vertices, edges,* and *polygons.* Vertices are connected by edges, while polygons can be thought of as sequences of edges or of vertices. A mesh can be represented in several different ways. Each representation has its advantages and disadvantages: the task of the application programmer is to choose the representation best suited to the application at hand. Of course, several representations might well be used in a given application: one for external storage, another for internal use, and yet another for communicating with the user.

Various criteria can be applied to evaluate the several representations, such as:

- Amount of storage space needed;
- Ease of identifying edges incident on a vertex;
- Ease of identifying polygons sharing an edge;
- Ease of identifying the two vertices of an edge;
- Ease of identifying all edges of a polygon;
- Ease of displaying a polygon mesh;
- Ease of identifying errors in representation (e.g., a missing edge, vertex, or polygon).

These criteria will be mentioned as we discuss the following representations. In general, the more explicitly the relations between polygons, vertices, and edges are represented, the faster the operations will be and the more space the representation will require. We now describe three polygon mesh representations.

13.2.1 Explicit Polygons

Each polygon is represented by a list of vertex coordinates:

$$P = ((x_1, y_1, z_1), (x_2, y_2, z_2), \ldots, (x_n, y_n, z_n)).$$

The vertices are stored in the order in which they would be encountered by traveling around the polygon. There are edges between successive vertices in the list, and between the last and first vertices. For a single polygon this is very space-efficient, but for a polygon mesh, much space is lost by duplicating the coordinates of shared vertices. Even worse, there is no explicit representation of shared edges and vertices. For instance, finding all polygons which share a vertex requires comparing the coordinate triples of one polygon with the coordinate triples of all other polygons (see Fig. 13.4). The most efficient way to do this would be to sort all N coordinate triples, but this is at best an $N \cdot \log_2 N$ process, and even then, there is the danger that the same vertex might, due to computational round-off, have slightly different coordinate values in each polygon, so that a correct match might never be made.

This polygon mesh is displayed by displaying the edges of each polygon; however, this means that shared edges are drawn twice, once for each polygon. On the other hand, displaying a *single* polygon is quite trivial.

13.2.2 Polygons Defined by Pointers into a Vertex List

With this representation, each vertex in the polygon mesh is stored just once, in the vertex list $V = (x_1, y_1, z_1), \ldots, (x_n, y_n, z_n))$. A polygon is defined by a list of pointers (or indexes) into the vertex list. A polygon made up of vertices 3, 5, 7, and 10 in the vertex list would be represented as $P = (3, 5, 7, 10)$.

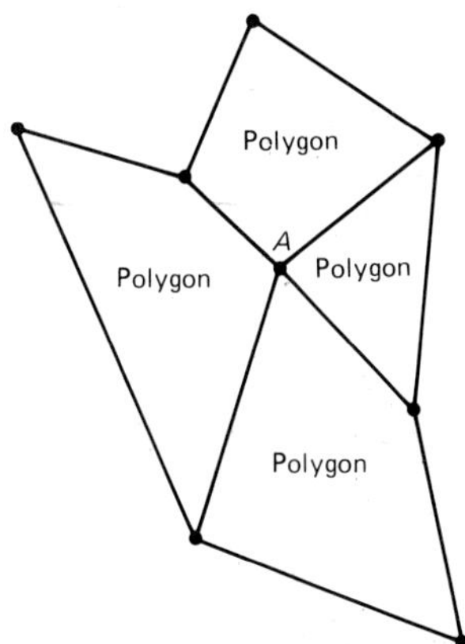

Fig. 13.4 Shared vertex *A*.

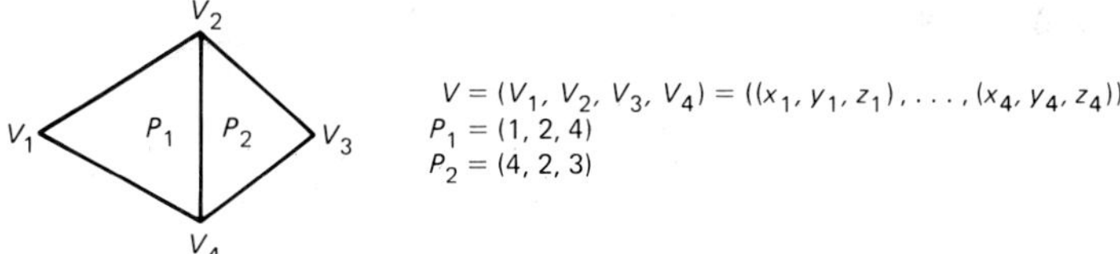

Fig. 13.5 Polygon defined by indexes into a vertex list.

Figure 13.5 shows an example of this representation, which has several advantages over the explicit polygon representation. Since each vertex is stored just once, considerable space is saved. Furthermore, the coordinates of a vertex can be easily changed. On the other hand, it is still hard to find polygons which share an edge, and shared polygon edges are still drawn twice when all polygon outlines are displayed. These two problems can be eliminated by representing edges explicitly, as in the next method.

13.2.3 Explicit Edges

In this representation we again have the vertex list V, but now represent a polygon not as a list of pointers to the vertex list but rather as a list of pointers to an edge list in which each edge occurs just once. Each edge in the edge list points to the two vertices in the vertex list defining the edge and also to the one or two polygons to which the edge belongs. Hence we describe a polygon as $P = (E_1, \ldots, E_n)$, and an edge as $E = (V_1, V_2, P_1, P_2)$. When an edge belongs to only one polygon, either P_1 or P_2 is null. Figure 13.6 shows an example of this representation.

With the explicit edge representation, the polygon mesh is displayed by displaying all edges rather than by displaying all polygons, and thus multiple display of shared edges is avoided. On the other hand, a single polygon is also easily displayed.

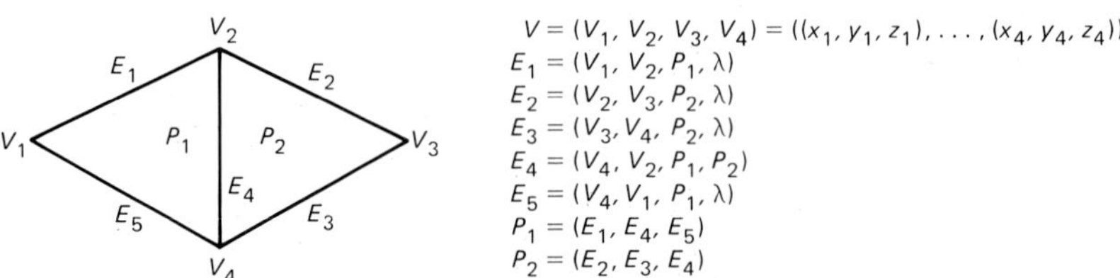

V_2
E_1
E_2
V_1
P_1
P_2
V_3
E_4
E_5
E_3
V_4
$V = (V_1, V_2, V_3, V_4) = ((x_1, y_1, z_1), \ldots, (x_4, y_4, z_4))$
$E_1 = (V_1, V_2, P_1, \lambda)$
$E_2 = (V_2, V_3, P_2, \lambda)$
$E_3 = (V_3, V_4, P_2, \lambda)$
$E_4 = (V_4, V_2, P_1, P_2)$
$E_5 = (V_4, V_1, P_1, \lambda)$
$P_1 = (E_1, E_4, E_5)$
$P_2 = (E_2, E_3, E_4)$

Fig. 13.6 Polygon mesh representation (λ represents null).

In some applications of polygon meshes edges are shared by more than two polygons. Consider, for instance, a mapping application in which political subdivisions (counties, states, etc.) are represented by polygons. An edge (or series of edges) representing part of the boundary between two states is also a boundary of a county in each state, and perhaps of a city as well. Thus an edge could belong to as many as six polygons. If townships, precincts, and school districts are also considered, the number goes up accordingly. Similarly, in some 3D applications, such as the description of a honeycomb-like sheet metal structure, edges are shared by at least three polygons. For such applications the edge descriptions can be extended to include an arbitrary number of polygons: $E = (V_1, V_2, P_1, P_2, \ldots, P_n)$.

In none of these representations is it easy to determine which edges are incident to a vertex: all edges must be searched. Of course, additional information can be explicitly represented to permit determining such relationships. For instance, a representation used by Baumgart [BAUM75] expands the edge description to include pointers to the two adjoining edges of each polygon, while the vertex description includes a pointer to an (arbitrary) edge incident on the vertex, and thus more polygon and vertex information is available.

13.3 CONSISTENCY OF POLYGON MESH REPRESENTATIONS

How do we know whether a polygon mesh representation is consistent, i.e., that all polygons are closed, all edges are used at least once but not more than some (application-defined) maximum, and each vertex is referenced by at least two edges? In some applications, we would also expect the mesh to be connected (any vertex can be reached from any other vertex by moving along edges), or planar (the binary relation on vertices defined by edges can be represented by a planar graph), or to have no holes (there exists just one boundary—a connected sequence of edges each of which is used by one polygon). Consistency is a reasonable concern because the meshes are often generated interactively, sometimes by operators digitizing drawings, so errors are inevitable.

Of the three representations, the explicit edge scheme is the easiest to check for consistency, because it contains the most information. For example, to make sure that all edges are part of at least one but no more than some maximum number of polygons, we can do the following:

```
for each edge j in set of edges do
  use_count_j := 0
for each polygon P_i in set of polygons do
  for each edge j of polygon P_i do
    use_count_j := use_count_j + 1
for each edge j in set of edges do
    begin
      if use_count_j = 0 then ERROR
      if use_count_j > maximum then ERROR
    end
```

This is by no means a complete consistency check. For example, an edge used twice in the same polygon goes undetected. A similar procedure can be used to make sure that each vertex is part of at least one polygon; this will be true if at least two different edges of the same polygon refer to the vertex. Also, it is an error for the two vertices of an edge to be the same, unless the degenerate case of edges with zero length is allowed.

We can determine whether each polygon in a mesh has at least one shared edge, in which case no polygon stands alone. Note that this is *not* the same as each vertex being reachable from any other vertex. The algorithm is:

```
for each polygon P_i in set of polygons do
  begin
    shared_edge := false
    repeat for each edge E_j of polygon P_i
      if E_j is shared then shared_edge := true
    until shared_edge
    if not shared_edge then ERROR
  end
```

More detailed testing is also possible; one can check, for instance, that each polygon referred to by an edge E_i refers in turn back to the edge E_i. This ensures that all references from polygons to edges are complete. Similarly, we can check that each edge referred to by a polygon P_i refers back to polygon P_i, which ensures that the references from edges to polygons are complete.

A polygon mesh may define a *polyhedron* (a volume completely enclosed by polygons). A pyramid and cube are examples of polyhedra. For a polyhedron, each edge of the polygon mesh must have two adjoining polygons. An edge with just one adjoining polygon is next to a hole in the polyhedron—to see this, consider the difference between a covered and uncovered shoe box. If more than two polygons adjoin, the polyhedron has extra internal or external polygons.

13.4 PLANE EQUATIONS

When working with polygons or polygon meshes, we frequently need to know the equation of the plane in which the polygon lies. In some cases, of course, the equation is known implicitly through the interactive construction methods used to define the polygon. But if not, we can use the coordinates of three vertices to find the plane. To do this, recall the plane equation

$$Ax + By + Cz + D = 0. \tag{13.1}$$

Given three points, we have

$$\begin{aligned} Ax_1 + By_1 + Cz_1 + D = 0, \\ Ax_2 + By_2 + Cz_2 + D = 0, \\ Ax_3 + By_3 + Cz_3 + D = 0. \end{aligned} \tag{13.2}$$

If the three points are not collinear, the equations can be solved for $A, B, C,$ and D by arbitrarily assigning a value to one of the coefficients and then solving the resulting set of three equations in three unknowns. For instance, we could set $D = 1$, and then solve. Unfortunately, problems arise if D is really 0.

A more robust approach is to recognize that if the points P_1, P_2, P_3, and (x, y, z) are on the plane, then

$$\begin{aligned} Ax + By + Cz + D = 0, \\ Ax_1 + By_1 + Cz_1 + D = 0, \\ Ax_2 + By_2 + Cz_2 + D = 0, \\ Ax_3 + By_3 + Cz_3 + D = 0, \end{aligned} \tag{13.3}$$

If there is a solution to this set of homogeneous equations, the determinant of its coefficients must be zero:

$$\begin{vmatrix} x & y & z & 1 \\ x_1 & y_1 & z_1 & 1 \\ x_2 & y_2 & z_2 & 1 \\ x_3 & y_3 & z_3 & 1 \end{vmatrix} = 0. \tag{13.4}$$

Expanding by cofactors about the first row, we have:

$$x \begin{vmatrix} y_1 & z_1 & 1 \\ y_2 & z_2 & 1 \\ y_3 & z_3 & 1 \end{vmatrix} - y \begin{vmatrix} x_1 & z_1 & 1 \\ x_2 & z_2 & 1 \\ x_3 & z_3 & 1 \end{vmatrix} + z \begin{vmatrix} x_1 & y_1 & 1 \\ x_2 & y_2 & 1 \\ x_3 & y_3 & 1 \end{vmatrix} - \begin{vmatrix} x_1 & y_1 & z_1 \\ x_2 & y_2 & z_2 \\ x_3 & y_3 & z_3 \end{vmatrix} = 0. \tag{13.5}$$

The determinants, including their signs, are the coefficients A, B, C, and D. The determinants can be expanded to find expressions for the coefficients. For example,

$$A = y_1(z_2 - z_3) + y_2(z_3 - z_1) + y_3(z_1 - z_2). \tag{13.6}$$

Whichever method is used, the three points cannot be collinear: three points on a line do not define a plane. Collinearity is easy to determine, as it occurs if all four cofactors in (13.5) are zero.

In some cases the vector normal to the plane may already be known. The *x, y,* and *z* components of the normal vector are *A, B,* and *C* of the plane Eq. (13.1). Then to find *D,* some point on the plane is substituted into the plane equation, which is then solved for *D*.

If the vertices may be nonplanar (perhaps because of the method by which the polygons were generated), then another technique, suggested by M. Newell and reported in [SUTH74c], is better. It can be shown that the coefficients *A, B,* and *C* are proportional to the areas of the projections of the polygon onto the *yz, xz,* and *xy* planes, respectively. For example, if the polygon is parallel to the *xy* plane, then $A = B = 0$, as expected: the projections of the polygon onto the *yz* and *xz* planes have zero area. This method is better because the areas of the projections are a function of the coordinates of all the vertices and so are not sensitive to the choice of a few vertices which might happen not to be coplanar with most or all of the other vertices.

For instance, the area *C* of the polygon projected onto the *xy* plane is just

$$C = \frac{1}{2} \sum_{i=1}^{n} (y_i + y_{i \oplus 1})(x_{i \oplus 1} - x_i), \tag{13.7}$$

where the operator $\oplus$ is normal addition except that $n \oplus 1 = 1$.

Equation (13.7) gives the sum of the areas of all the trapezoids formed by successive edges of the polygons. Some of the trapezoids have negative areas, so the areas between the axis and the polygon are subtracted from the sum. Figure 13.7 shows the areas and calculation for a triangle in the *xy* plane.

Once we determine the plane equation by using all the vertices, we can estimate how nonplanar the polygon is by calculating the distance from the plane to each vertex. This distance, for the vertex at (x, y, z), is:

$$d = \frac{Ax + By + Cz + D}{(A^2 + B^2 + C^2)^{1/2}}. \tag{13.8}$$

This distance may be either positive or negative, depending on which side of the plane the point is located. If the vertex is on the plane, then $d = 0$.

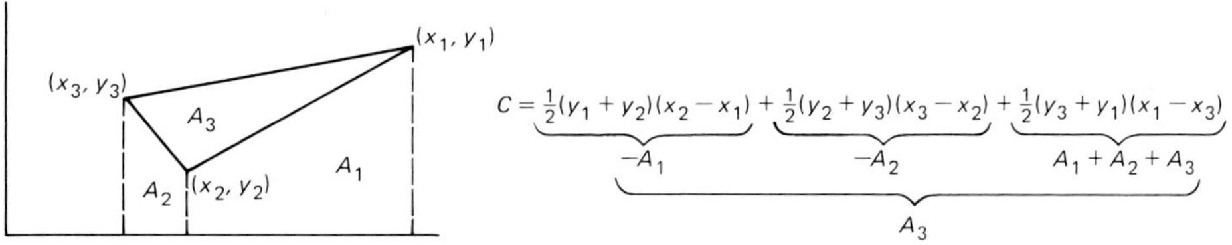

Fig. 13.7 Calculating the area *C* of a triangle by using Eq. (13.7).

13.5 PARAMETRIC CUBIC CURVES

We move now, in two steps, toward representing curved surfaces. The first step, taken in this section, is representing a 3D curve. In the next section, we generalize the mathematical development from 3D curves to 3D curved surfaces.

There are two basic ways to represent curves: as functions of the variables $x,y,$ and z, or as functions of a parameter such as t. In the first case, we deal with functions of the form

$$x = x, \qquad y = f(x), \qquad z = g(x) \tag{13.9}$$

to define points (x,y,z) on a curve. This representation, however, leads to many difficulties: an infinite slope may be required at some point on a curve, but infinity is difficult to represent. A curve segment is bounded by a starting and ending point, but testing whether a point is on the bounded segment is hard, especially if the curve loops; plotting the curve as a smooth line requires (as we saw in Chapter 11) that the slope of the curve be considered.

The parametric representation of 3D curves substantially reduces these difficulties, since it allows closed and multiple-valued functions to be easily defined and replaces the use of slopes (which may be infinite) with that of tangent vectors (which need never be infinite).

A parametric cubic curve is one for which x, y, and z are each represented as a third-order (that is, cubic) polynomial of some parameter t. Because we deal with finite segments of a curve, we limit the range of the parameter, without loss of generality, to $0 \le t \le 1$. Hence,

$$\begin{aligned} x(t) &= a_x t^3 + b_x t^2 + c_x t + d_x, \\ y(t) &= a_y t^3 + b_y t^2 + c_y t + d_y, \qquad 0 \le t \le 1, \\ z(t) &= a_z t^3 + b_z t^2 + c_z t + d_z. \end{aligned} \tag{13.10}$$

The derivatives of $x(t)$, $y(t)$, and $z(t)$ with respect to the parameter t are all of the same form. For $x(t)$, the form is

$$\frac{dx}{dt} = 3a_x t^2 + 2b_x t + c_x. \tag{13.11}$$

The three derivatives form the *tangent vector*. The slopes of the curve are ratios of the tangent vector components:

$$\frac{dy}{dx} = \frac{dy/dt}{dx/dt}, \qquad \frac{dx}{dz} = \frac{dx/dt}{dz/dt}, \qquad \text{etc.} \tag{13.12}$$

The slopes are actually independent of the length of the tangent vector. If we multiply the derivatives by k, we have

$$k\frac{dx}{dt}, \qquad k\frac{dy}{dt}, \qquad k\frac{dz}{dt}. \tag{13.13}$$

Then:

$$\frac{k\,dy/dt}{k\,dx/dt} = \frac{dy/dt}{dx/dt} = \frac{dy}{dx}. \tag{13.14}$$

Henceforth we will work explicitly with derivations only for $x(t)$, to find convenient ways to define a_x, b_x, c_x, and d_x. The derivations and resulting formulas for $y(t)$ and $z(t)$ are exactly analogous and are not given.

Why do we consider cubic curves? Because no lower-order representation of curve segments can provide continuity of position and slope at the point where curve segments meet and at the same time ensure that the ends of the curve segment pass through specified points. Recognize that our ultimate objective is to represent a curve by a series of curve segments like the two segments in Fig. 13.8. At the join-point, the curve segments and their tangent vectors are equal. This continuity is important: imagine a representation of the cross-section of an airplane which introduced slope or position discontinuities.

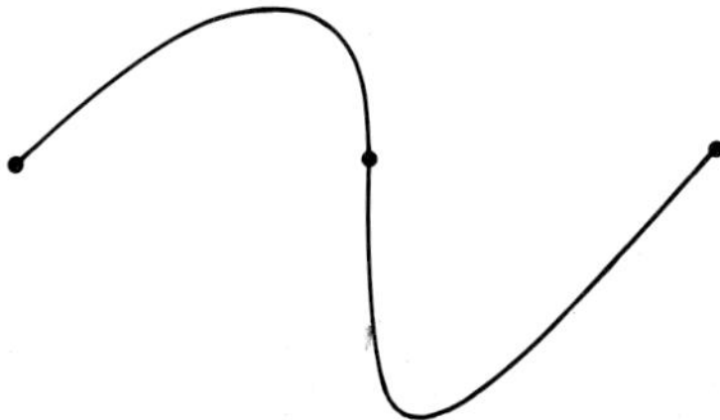

Fig. 13.8 Two curve segments joined together.

In the remainder of this chapter we use the general notation $C^{(i)}$ to describe continuity: curves are said to be $C^{(0)}$ continuous if they have no discontinuities and to be $C^{(1)}$ continuous if in addition their tangents are continuous. In general, $C^{(i)}$ continuity means that the function and its first i derivatives are continuous.

The parametric cubic, with its four coefficients, is the lowest-order parametric curve that can be forced to meet four conditions (position and tangent vector at each end of the segment) by appropriate selection of its coefficients. Higher-order parametrics can also be used, but tend to have undesirable wiggles or oscillations. The cubic is also the lowest-order parametric which can describe a nonplanar curve [PETE74], a necessity for describing 3D curves.

We will consider in detail just three of the many ways to define a cubic parametric curve: the *Hermite* (which defines the positions and tangents at the curve's endpoints, as just discussed), the *Bezier* (which defines the positions of the curve's endpoints and uses two other points, generally not on the curve, to define indirectly the tangents at the curve's endpoints), and the *B-spline* (which approximates the endpoints rather than matching them, allowing both the first and second derivatives to be continuous at the segment's endpoints). We will see that each of these three forms has certain advantages and disadvantages.

13.5.1 Hermite Form

Let us see how the Hermite form of a cubic is determined from endpoints and endpoint tangents. We are given the points P_1 and P_4 and the tangent vectors R_1 and R_4. (We index the points as 1 and 4 rather than 1 and 2 for consistency with the notations to be used for Bezier and B-spline curves.) We want to find a_x, b_x, c_x, and d_x from (13.10), subject to the conditions:

$$x(0) = P_{1_x}, \qquad x(1) = P_{4_x}, \qquad x'(0) = R_{1_x}, \qquad x'(1) = R_{4_x}. \tag{13.15}$$

We use the subscript x to refer to the x-component of the points and tangent vectors.

Rewriting $x(t)$, we have

$$x(t) = [t^3 \quad t^2 \quad t \quad 1] \begin{bmatrix} a \\ b \\ c \\ d \end{bmatrix}_x \tag{13.16}$$

$$= [t^3 \quad t^2 \quad t \quad 1] C_x \tag{13.17}$$

$$= TC_x. \tag{13.18}$$

Here T is the row vector of powers of t, while C_x is the column vector of coefficients of $x(t)$.

Now we express the conditions (13.15) by using Eq. (13.17):

$$\begin{aligned} x(0) &= P_{1_x} = [0 \quad 0 \quad 0 \quad 1]\ C_x, \\ x(1) &= P_{4_x} = [1 \quad 1 \quad 1 \quad 1]\ C_x. \end{aligned} \tag{13.19}$$

To continue with the tangent vector conditions, we first differentiate (13.17) with respect to t, obtaining

$$x'(t) = [3t^2 \quad 2t \quad 1 \quad 0]\ C_x. \tag{13.20}$$

Then

$$x'(0) = R_{1_x} = [0 \quad 0 \quad 1 \quad 0]\ C_x, \tag{13.21}$$

$$x'(1) = R_{4_x} = [3 \quad 2 \quad 1 \quad 0]\ C_x. \tag{13.22}$$

The four conditions in (13.19), (13.21), and (13.22) can be gathered together into a single matrix equation:

$$\begin{bmatrix} P_1 \\ P_4 \\ R_1 \\ R_4 \end{bmatrix}_x = \begin{bmatrix} 0 & 0 & 0 & 1 \\ 1 & 1 & 1 & 1 \\ 0 & 0 & 1 & 0 \\ 3 & 2 & 1 & 0 \end{bmatrix} C_x. \tag{13.23}$$

Inverting the 4×4 matrix achieves our objective of solving for C_x, giving

$$C_x = \begin{bmatrix} 2 & -2 & 1 & 1 \\ -3 & 3 & -2 & -1 \\ 0 & 0 & 1 & 0 \\ 1 & 0 & 0 & 0 \end{bmatrix} \begin{bmatrix} P_1 \\ P_4 \\ R_1 \\ R_4 \end{bmatrix}_x = M_h\, G_{h_x}. \tag{13.24}$$

Here M_h is the *Hermite matrix* and G_h is the *Hermite geometry vector.* Applying this result to (13.18), we obtain

$$x(t) = TM_hG_{h_x}. \tag{13.25}$$

By symmetry,

$$y(t) = TM_hG_{h_y}, \tag{13.26}$$

$$z(t) = TM_hG_{h_z}. \tag{13.27}$$

The equations for $x(t)$, $y(t)$, and $z(t)$ are frequently written in the literature as

$$P(t) = TM_hG_h. \tag{13.28}$$

Given a P_1, P_4, R_1 and R_4, we can evaluate $x(t)$, $y(t)$, and $z(t)$ for $0 \leq t \leq 1$ and find all points on the cubic curve from P_1 to P_4 with starting tangent vector R_1 and ending tangent vector R_4.

If we take the product TM_h, we have:

$$TM_h = [(2t^3 - 3t^2 + 1) \quad (-2t^3 + 3t^2) \quad (t^3 - 2t^2 + t) \quad (t^3 - t^2)]. \tag{13.29}$$

Postmultiplying this by G_{h_x} yields:

$$\begin{aligned} x(t) = TM_hG_{h_x} &= P_{1_x}(2t^3 - 3t^2 + 1) + P_{4_x}(-2t^3 + 3t^2) \\ &+ R_{1_x}(t^3 - 2t^2 + t) + R_{4_x}(t^3 - t^2). \end{aligned} \tag{13.30}$$

The four functions of t in the product TM_h are often called *blending functions,* since the first two functions blend P_1 and P_4, while the other two blend R_1 and R_4, producing the "blended" sum $x(t)$.

Figure 13.9 shows a series of Hermite curves. The only difference in their geometry matrices is the length of the tangent vector, as indicated in the figure. The longer the vector, the stronger the curve is "pulled" in the direction of the vector before it begins to move toward the opposite endpoint. In all cases, the tangents to the curves at the endpoints have the same direction. Fig. 13.10 shows another series of Hermite curves, this time with constant tangent vector length but with changing tangent direction.

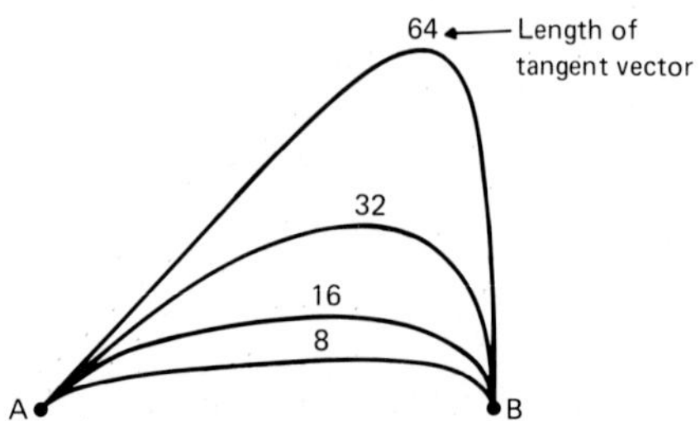

Fig. 13.9 Family of Hermite parametric cubic curves. Tangent-vector directions are fixed: 45° at *A*, − 90° at *B*. The magnitude of the vector varies and is given with each curve.

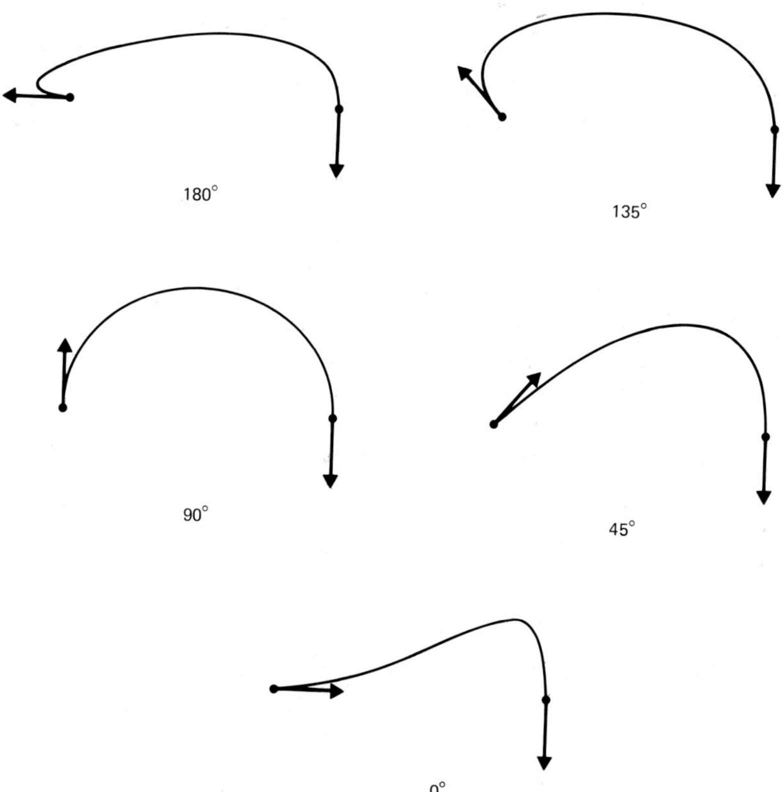

Fig. 13.10 Family of Hermite parametric cubics. The tangent-vector direction at right is fixed at − 90°; at left it varies and is shown with each curve. The magnitude of all tangent vectors is fixed.

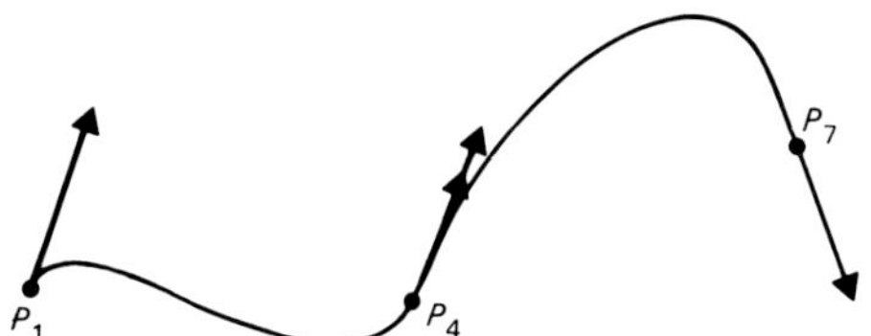

Fig. 13.11 Two Hermite cubics joined at P_4. Tangent vectors at P_4 have same directions but different magnitudes.

Figure 13.11 shows two Hermite curves sharing a common endpoint. The geometry vectors which provide $C^{(1)}$ continuity at P are:

$$\begin{bmatrix} P_1 \\ P_4 \\ R_1 \\ R_4 \end{bmatrix} \quad \text{and} \quad \begin{bmatrix} P_4 \\ P_7 \\ kR_4 \\ R_7 \end{bmatrix}. \tag{13.31}$$

13.5.2 Bezier Form

The form for defining a cubic developed by Bezier is very similar to the Hermite form but differs in the definition of the endpoint tangent vectors [BEZI72, BEZI74]. For the Bezier form, four points are used, as in Fig. 13.12. The tangent vectors of the endpoints are determined from the line segments P_1P_2 and P_3P_4. Specifically, the tangent vectors R_1 and R_4 of the Hermite form are defined to have the relation to the four Bezier points P_1, P_2, P_3 and P_4:

$$R_1 = 3(P_2 - P_1) = P'(0), \qquad R_4 = 3(P_4 - P_3) = P'(1).$$

Therefore the relation between the Hermite geometry matrix G_h and the Bezier geometry matrix G_b is

$$G_h = \begin{bmatrix} P_1 \\ P_4 \\ R_1 \\ R_4 \end{bmatrix} = \begin{bmatrix} 1 & 0 & 0 & 0 \\ 0 & 0 & 0 & 1 \\ -3 & 3 & 0 & 0 \\ 0 & 0 & -3 & 3 \end{bmatrix} \begin{bmatrix} P_1 \\ P_2 \\ P_3 \\ P_4 \end{bmatrix} = M_{hb}G_b. \tag{13.32}$$

Substituting in (13.25), we have:

$$x(t) = TM_hG_{h_x} = TM_hM_{hb}G_{b_x}.$$

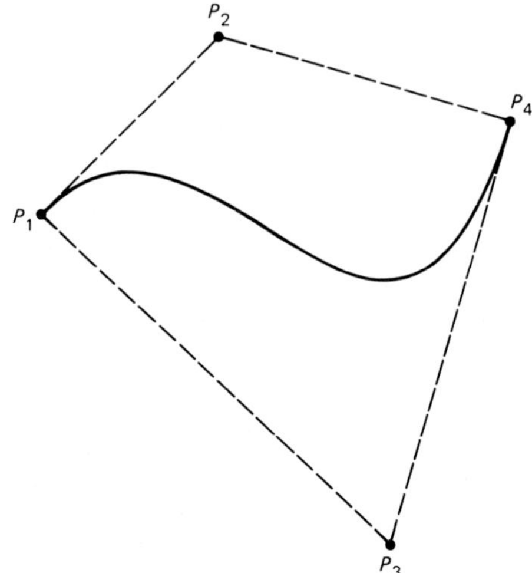

Fig. 13.12 Bezier curve and its four control points. Dashed line shows convex hull of the control points.

Defining the product $M_h M_{hb}$ as M_b, we have $x(t) = TM_b G_{b_x}$, which is now the Bezier form. The matrix M_b obtained from the product $M_h M_{hb}$ is

$$M_b = \begin{bmatrix} -1 & 3 & -3 & 1 \\ 3 & -6 & 3 & 0 \\ -3 & 3 & 0 & 0 \\ 1 & 0 & 0 & 0 \end{bmatrix}. \qquad (13.33)$$

Figure 13.13 shows two Bezier curves with a common endpoint. The $C^{(1)}$ continuity at the common endpoint is guaranteed when $\overline{P_3P_4} = k\overline{P_4P_5}$.

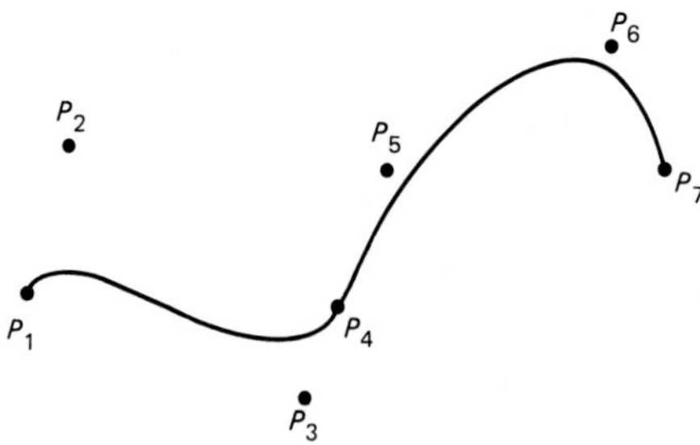

Fig. 13.13 Two Bezier cubics joined at P_4. Points P_3, P_4, and P_5 are collinear. Curves are the same as in Fig. 13.11.

Two characteristics of the Bezier form tend to make it more widely used in graphics than the Hermite form. First, the geometry matrix (of four points) has intuitive appeal for an interactive user since, by moving the points with a locator device, one can easily mold the curve to a desired shape. With the Hermite form, tangent vectors must be directly specified; this is a more difficult job to do interactively, and the concept is unfamiliar to some users. On the other hand, forcing a curve to match a known tangent vector is easier with the Hermite form. Second, the four control points define a convex polygon (the *convex hull*) which bounds the Bezier curve (see Fig. 13.12). Intuitively, the convex hull of points in a plane is the area defined by a rubber band stretched around all the points, or in 3D, by a balloon tightly stretched around all the points. The convex hull is useful in clipping a curve against a window or view volume. It is treated like the extent used in Chapter 9: rather than clip the curve immediately, we first test the convex hull, and only if it intersects the window or view volume need we then examine the curve itself.

We can better understand the convex hull property of the Bezier form by taking the product TM_bG_b:

$$(1 - t)^3P_1 + 3t(t - 1)^2P_2 + 3t^2(1 - t)P_3 + t^3P_4. \tag{13.34}$$

Examining the polynomial coefficients of the four points, we see that each ranges in value between 0 and 1 and that their sum is 1 for $0 \le t \le 1$. Thus, this expression is just a weighted average of the four control points. It can be shown that the weighted average of n points falls within the convex hull of the n points: this can be seen intuitively by considering $n = 2$ and $n = 3$, and then generalizing.

13.5.3 B-Spline Form

The B-spline cubic representation does not in general pass through *any* control points, but is continuous and also has continuity of tangent vector and of curvature (that is, its first and second derivatives are continuous at the endpoints) while the Hermite and Bezier forms have only first-derivative continuity at endpoints (but do pass through control points). Thus, we can say that the B-spline form is "smoother" than the other forms. This terminology traces back to the long flexible strips of metal, called splines, used by draftsmen to lay out the surfaces of airplanes and ships. The metal splines, unless severely stressed, also have second-order continuity. The B-spline formulation is

$$x(t) = TM_sG_{s_x}, \tag{13.35}$$

where

$$M_s = \frac{1}{6}\begin{bmatrix} -1 & 3 & -3 & 1 \\ 3 & -6 & 3 & 0 \\ -3 & 0 & 3 & 0 \\ 1 & 4 & 1 & 0 \end{bmatrix}. \tag{13.36}$$

To approximate the control points $P_1, P_2, \ldots, P_n$ by a series of B-splines, we use a different geometry matrix between each *pair* of adjacent points. The approximation from near P_i to near P_{i+1} uses

$$G_s^i = \begin{bmatrix} P_{i-1} \\ P_i \\ P_{i+1} \\ P_{i+2} \end{bmatrix}, \qquad 2 \le i \le n-2. \tag{13.37}$$

We now show the first- and second-derivative continuity at point P_{i+1}. Evaluating (13.35) with $G_{s_x} = G_{s_x}^i$ and $t = 1$, we have

$$x^i(1) = \frac{x_i + 4x_{i+1} + x_{i+2}}{6}. \tag{13.38}$$

Similarly, differentiating (13.35) and evaluating at $t = 1$, we get

$$\left.\frac{dx^i}{dt}\right|_{t=1} = \frac{-x_i + x_{i+2}}{2}. \tag{13.39}$$

Differentiating and evaluating again, we get

$$\left.\frac{d^2x^i}{dt^2}\right|_{t=1} = x_i - 2x_{i+1} + x_{i+2}. \tag{13.40}$$

Now repeating the process for $G_{s_x} = G_{s_x}^{i+1}$ and evaluating at $t = 0$, we have

$$x^{i+1}(0) = \frac{x_i + 4x_{i+1} + x_{i+2}}{6}, \tag{13.41}$$

$$\left.\frac{dx^{i+1}}{dt}\right|_{t=0} = \frac{-x_i + x_{i+2}}{2}, \tag{13.42}$$

$$\left.\frac{d^2x^{i+1}}{dt^2}\right|_{t=0} = x_i - 2x_{i+1} + x_{i+2}. \tag{13.43}$$

The expressions for the x-coordinates of the two curve segments and for their first two derivatives are identical where they meet, at $x^i(1) = x^{i+1}(0)$.

We also see from these expressions that the join points and their derivatives are weighted sums of the three immediately adjacent points. Figure 13.14 shows a B-spline approximation to several points. Because points 5, 6, and 7 have the same x value, the curve passes through the x-coordinate of point 6, as required by Eq. (13.38).

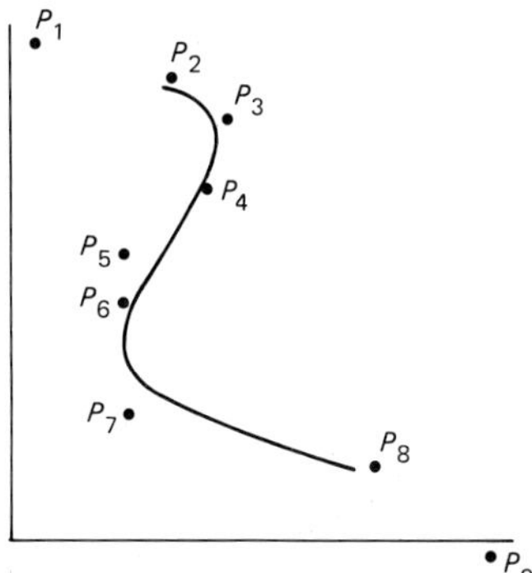

Fig. 13.14 B-spline cubic through nine points. Points P_5, P_6, and P_7 have the same x-coordinate, so the curve goes through x-coordinate of P_6.

The convex hull property of Bezier curves holds for B-spline curves as well: the convex hull for the curve from near P_i to near P_{i+1} is that of the four control points used to generate the curve: $P_{i-1}, P_i, P_{i+1}, P_{i+2}$.

13.5.4 Comparison of the Hermite, Bezier, and B-Spline Forms

Each of these three representations is useful in different circumstances. The Hermite form is good for approximating existing surfaces when a combination of point matching and tangent vector matching is needed, while the B-spline form is good for approximating points and providing $C^{(2)}$ continuity.

Both Bezier and B-spline forms are suited for interactive manipulation, because their geometry vectors contain only points. Both forms have the convex hull property, which is useful when displaying the curve. Note, though, that a curve originally defined in one form can be converted into another form by calculating one form's geometry vector in terms of the other's. Therefore, the Hermite form, which does not have the convex hull property, can be converted to the Bezier form, which does.

13.6 PARAMETRIC CUBIC SURFACES

We are now ready to generalize from cubic curves to bicubic surfaces defined by cubic equations of two parameters, s and t. Varying both parameters from 0 to 1 defines all points on a surface patch. If one parameter is assigned a constant value and the other parameter is varied from 0 to 1, the result is a cubic curve. As with curves, we will work only with the parametric equation for x, denoted by $x(s, t)$.

The form of $x(s, t)$ is:

$$\begin{aligned} x(s, t) = {} & a_{11}s^3t^3 + a_{12}s^3t^2 + a_{13}s^3t + a_{14}s^3 \\ & + a_{21}s^2t^3 + a_{22}s^2t^2 + a_{23}s^2t + a_{24}s^2 \\ & + a_{31}st^3 + a_{32}st^2 + a_{33}st + a_{34}s \\ & + a_{41}t^3 + a_{42}t^2 + a_{43}t + a_{44}. \end{aligned} \tag{13.44}$$

This is more conveniently written as

$$x(s,t) = SC_xT^T, \tag{13.45}$$

where $S = [s^3 \quad s^2 \quad s \quad 1]$, $T = [t^3 \quad t^2 \quad t \quad 1]$, and T^T is the transpose of T. This is called the *algebraic* form of representation, because C_x gives the coefficients of the bicubic polynomial. There is also a C_y and C_z which give the coefficients of $y(s, t)$ and $z(s, t)$.

13.6.1 Hermite Form

We want some approach analogous to that of the preceding section which allows the use of control points and tangent vectors to define the bicubic coefficients. Consider Eq. (13.25) for the cubic curve, with t replaced by s:

$$x(s) = SM_hG_{h_x}. \tag{13.46}$$

Let us rewrite (13.46) so that the Hermite geometry matrix is not a constant but rather a function of t:

$$x(s,t) = SM_hG_{h_x}(t) = SM_h \begin{bmatrix} P_1(t) \\ P_4(t) \\ R_1(t) \\ R_4(t) \end{bmatrix}_x . \tag{13.47}$$

The functions $P_{1_x}(t)$ and $P_{4_x}(t)$ define the x-components of the starting and ending points for the curve in the parameter s. For any specific value of t, two specific endpoints are defined. Similarly, $R_{1_x}(t)$ and $R_{4_x}(t)$ define the tangent vectors at the endpoints of the cubic in s. Figure 13.15 shows a $P_1(t)$ and $P_4(t)$, and the cubic in s defined for $t = 0$, 0.2, 0.4, 0.6, 0.8, and 1.0. We can think of the surface patch as an interpolation between $P_1(t)$ and $P_4(t)$: the initial tangent vector for the interpolation is $R_1(t)$ and the final tangent vector is $R_4(t)$. In the special case that the interpolants are straight lines, a *ruled surface* is produced. If the curves $P_1(t)$ and $P_4(t)$ are also coplanar, the ruled surface is planar and the surface patch is a four-sided polygon.

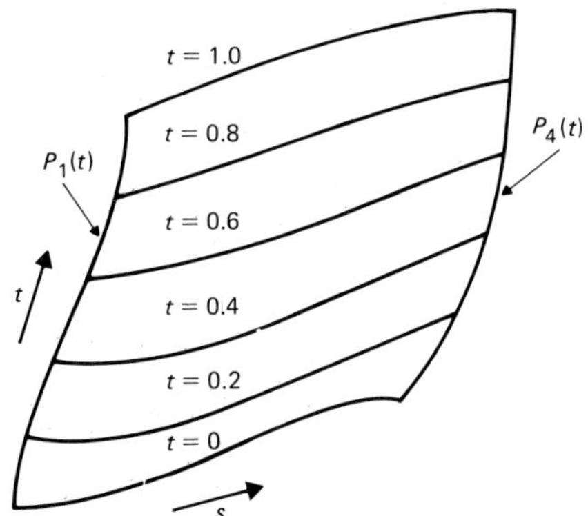

Fig. 13.15 Lines of constant parameter value on bicubic surface: $P_1(t)$ is at $s = 0$, $P_4(t)$ is at $s = 1$.

Now let $P_1(t)$, $P_4(t)$, $R_1(t)$, and $R_4(t)$ each be cubics represented in Hermite form, so that:

$$P_{1_x}(t) = TM_h \begin{bmatrix} q_{11} \\ q_{12} \\ q_{13} \\ q_{14} \end{bmatrix}_x, \tag{13.48}$$

$$P_{4_x}(t) = TM_h \begin{bmatrix} q_{21} \\ q_{22} \\ q_{23} \\ q_{24} \end{bmatrix}_x, \tag{13.49}$$

$$R_{1_x}(t) = TM_h \begin{bmatrix} q_{31} \\ q_{32} \\ q_{33} \\ q_{34} \end{bmatrix}_x, \tag{13.50}$$

$$R_{4_x}(t) = TM_h \begin{bmatrix} q_{41} \\ q_{42} \\ q_{43} \\ q_{44} \end{bmatrix}_x. \tag{13.51}$$

The four cubics can be expressed in a row vector as

$$[P_1(t) \quad P_4(t) \quad R_1(t) \quad R_4(t)]_x = TM_h \begin{bmatrix} q_{11} & q_{21} & q_{31} & q_{41} \\ q_{12} & q_{22} & q_{32} & q_{42} \\ q_{13} & q_{23} & q_{33} & q_{43} \\ q_{14} & q_{24} & q_{34} & q_{44} \end{bmatrix}_x . \tag{13.52}$$

Transposing both sides of the equation by using the identity $(ABC)^T = C^T B^T A^T$ gives:

$$\begin{bmatrix} P_1(t) \\ P_4(t) \\ R_1(t) \\ R_4(t) \end{bmatrix}_x = \begin{bmatrix} q_{11} & q_{12} & q_{13} & q_{14} \\ q_{21} & q_{22} & q_{23} & q_{24} \\ q_{31} & q_{32} & q_{33} & q_{34} \\ q_{41} & q_{42} & q_{43} & q_{44} \end{bmatrix}_x M_h^T T^T = Q_x M_h^T T^T. \tag{13.53}$$

We now substitute (13.53) into (13.47):

$$x(s, t) = SM_h Q_x M_h^T T^T. \tag{13.54}$$

Similarly,

$$y(s, t) = SM_h Q_y M_h^T T^T, \tag{13.55}$$

$$z(s, t) = SM_h Q_z M_h^T T^T. \tag{13.56}$$

How are Q_x, Q_y, and Q_z defined in terms of points and slopes? Examination of Eqs. (13.47) and (13.48) shows that q_{11} is $x(0,0)$ because it is the starting point for $P_{1_x}(t)$, which is in turn the starting point for $x(s,0)$. Similarly, q_{12} is $x(0, 1)$ because it is the ending point of $P_{1_x}(t)$, which is in turn the starting point for $x(s, 1)$. We also see that q_{13} is

$$\frac{dx}{dt}(0, 0),$$

because it is the starting tangent vector for $P_{1_x}(t)$, and q_{33} is

$$\frac{d^2x}{ds\,dt}(0, 0),$$

as it is the starting tangent vector of $R_{1_x}(t)$, which is in turn the starting slope of $x(s, 0)$.

Using these interpretations, we can write

$$Q_x = \left[\begin{array}{cc|cc} x_{00} & x_{01} & \dfrac{dx}{dt_{00}} & \dfrac{dx}{dt_{01}} \\ x_{10} & x_{11} & \dfrac{dx}{dt_{10}} & \dfrac{dx}{dt_{11}} \\ \hline \dfrac{dx}{ds_{00}} & \dfrac{dx}{ds_{01}} & \dfrac{d^2x}{ds\,dt_{00}} & \dfrac{d^2x}{ds\,dt_{01}} \\ \dfrac{dx}{ds_{10}} & \dfrac{dx}{ds_{11}} & \dfrac{d^2x}{ds\,dt_{10}} & \dfrac{d^2x}{ds\,dt_{11}} \end{array}\right]. \tag{13.57}$$

The upper left 2×2 partition contains the four corners of the surface patch, the upper right and lower left partitions specify the slopes along each parametric direction at the corners, while the lower right partition gives the partial derivatives at the corners with respect to both parameters. These partials are often called the *twists,* because the greater they are, the greater the twist (like a corkscrew) at the corner of the surface patch. Figure 13.16 shows a patch whose corners are labeled to indicate these parameters. Note that the Hermite form of bicubic surface patches is one form of the *Coons' patch* [COON67], so named because it was worked on extensively by the late Steven Coons [HERZ80], an early pioneer in the application of computer graphics to computer-aided design. They are also called Ferguson surfaces, after another early developer of surface representations [FERG64, FAUX79].

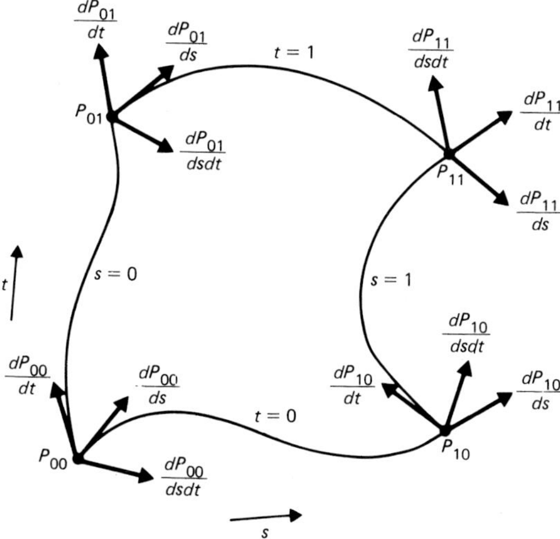

Fig. 13.6 Parameters for Hermite surface. Each vector is a three-tuple, the x-component of which is given by Eq. (13.57).

Just as the Hermite cubic permits $C^{(1)}$ continuity from one curve segment to the next, so too the Hermite bicubic permits $C^{(1)}$ continuity from one patch to the next. The necessary conditions are that the curves along the common edge be the same on each patch, and that the tangent vectors across the edge be in the same direction (they may have different magnitudes). If the common edge has a fixed value of parameter s (i.e., t varies from 0 to 1), then there must be correspondence between rows of the patch's matrices. Recall from Eqs. (13.48) through (13.51) that the first row of Q defines the $s = 0$ edge of the patch, the second row defines the $s = 1$ edge, the third row defines the tangent vector along the $s = 0$ edge, and the fourth row defines the tangent vector along the $s = 1$ edge. We show below the required correspondences between matrices for patches 1 and 2, so that the $s = 1$ edge of patch 1 and the $s = 0$ edge of patch 2 have $C^{(0)}$ and $C^{(1)}$ continuity; empty cells of each matrix are unconstrained, and can have arbitrary values.

Patch 1 matrix

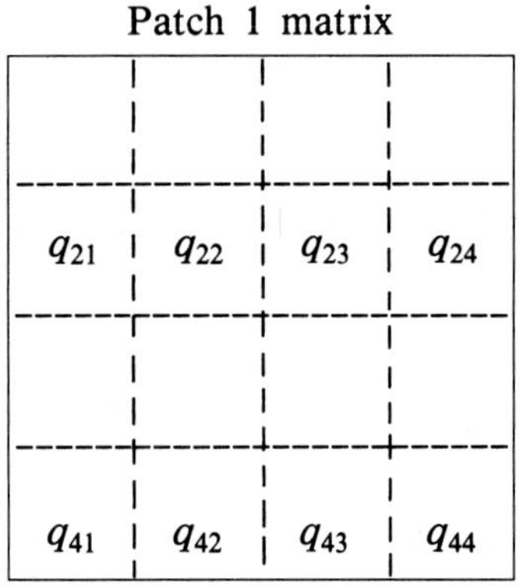

Patch 2 matrix

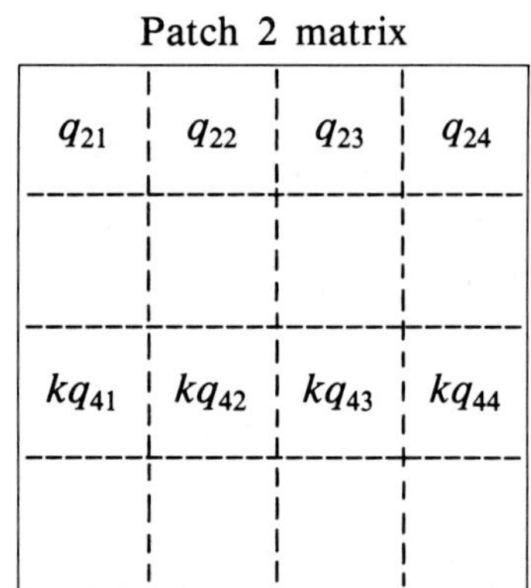

If the common edge were for a fixed value of parameter t, then columns rather than rows would be constrained:

Patch 1 matrix

	q_{12}		q_{14}
	q_{22}		q_{24}
	q_{32}		q_{34}
	q_{42}		q_{44}

Patch 2 matrix

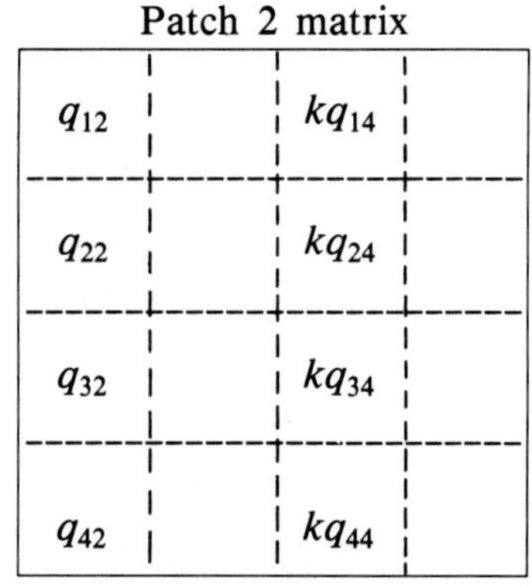

Figure 13.17 shows two patches that share a common edge.

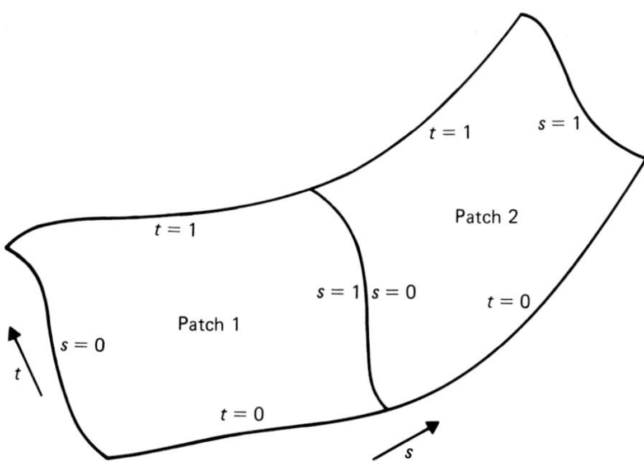

Fig. 13.17 Two joined patches.

13.6.2 Bezier Form

The equations for bicubic Bezier patches are derived in exactly the same way as for Hermite bicubic patches. The results are:

$$
\begin{aligned}
x(s, t) &= SM_bP_xM_b^TT^T, \\
y(s, t) &= SM_bP_yM_b^TT^T, \\
z(s, t) &= SM_bP_zM_b^TT^T,
\end{aligned}
\tag{13.58}
$$

The geometry matrix P consists of 16 control points, as shown in Fig. 13.18. Bezier surfaces are attractive in interactive design for the same reasons that Bezier curves are attractive: the control points can be easily manipulated to change the shape of the surface patch. The convex hull property of Bezier curves also holds for Bezier surfaces.

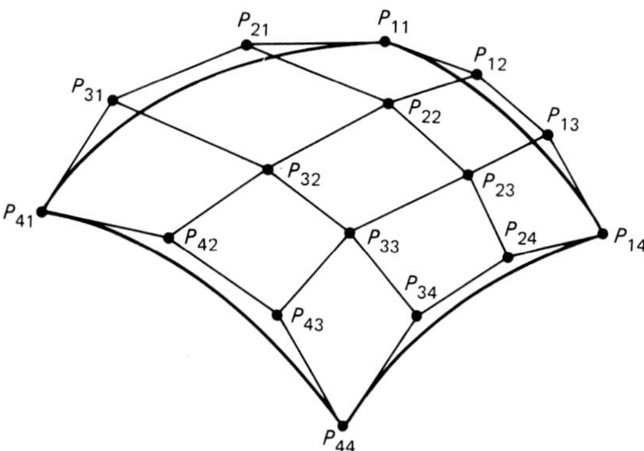

Fig. 13.18 Sixteen control points for Bezier bicubic patch.

Continuity across patch edges is obtained by making the four control points on the edges equal. Continuity of tangent vector, and hence $C^{(1)}$ continuity, is obtained by additionally making the two sets of four control points on either side of the edge collinear with the points on the edge. Thus in Fig. 13.19 the following sets of control points are collinear: (P_{13}, P_{14}, P_{15}), (P_{23}, P_{24}, P_{25}), (P_{33}, P_{34}, P_{35}), and (P_{43}, P_{44}, P_{45}). In addition, the ratios of the lengths of the collinear line segments must be constant.

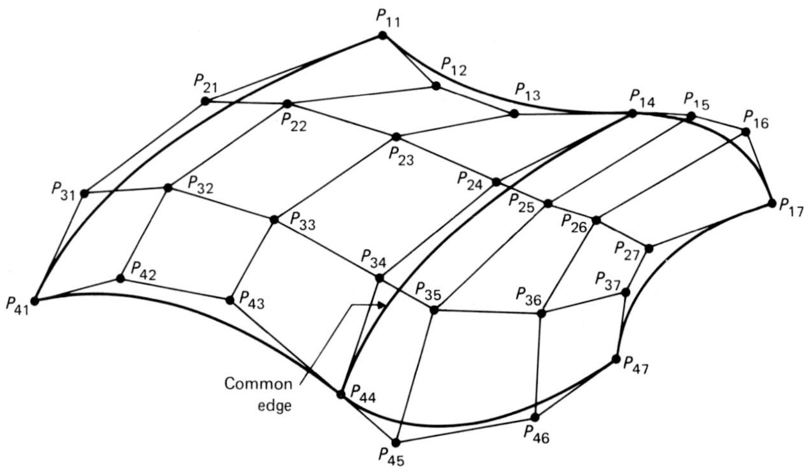

Fig. 13.19 Two Bezier surface patches joined along edge defined by P_{14}, P_{24}, P_{34}, and P_{44}.

13.6.3 B-spline Form

B-spline patches are analogous to the preceding cases:

$$\begin{aligned} x(s, t) &= SM_sP_xM_s^TT^T, \\ y(s, t) &= SM_sP_yM_s^TT^T, \\ z(s, t) &= SM_sP_zM_s^TT^T. \end{aligned} \qquad (13.59)$$

As with B-spline curves, $C^{(2)}$ continuity is obtained. The matrix of 16 control points defines the patch, and in general the points are not on the patch.

13.7 TRANSFORMING CURVES AND PATCHES

To transform a 3D curve or patch, we could calculate points on the curve or patch and then transform the points, one by one. Fortunately, there is a better way: we can instead transform the geometry matrix of points (or of points and tangent vectors) defining the curve or surface and then use this transformed matrix to generate points on the transformed curve or surface. This approach can be used with all of the curve and patch representations.

To transform a geometry matrix, each point or tangent vector is written as a four-element row vector: points are written by adding a 1 as the fourth component, and tangent vectors by adding a 0 as the fourth component. Recall from our introduction to transformations that the fourth component of the row vector is multiplied by the translation component of the 4×4 transformation matrix. Because the tangent vector specifies a direction rather than a position, addition of the 0 means that the vector is not translated but is still rotated and scaled.

The rewritten geometry matrix is now transformed by the 4×4 transformation matrix. Thus a bicubic surface can be transformed by transforming the 16 elements of its geometry matrix rather than by transforming the infinite number of points on the curve's surface.

13.8 CALCULATION OF POINTS ON A BICUBIC SURFACE

We often want to display objects made up of bicubic patches by drawing a number of the curves on the patches which are defined by constant s and constant t, to produce pictures such as Figs. 13.20 (a single patch) and 13.21 (multiple patches). The basic idea is to draw piecewise linear approximations to the parametric curves on the surface of the patch. A simple way to do this is:

```
for each patch do
  begin
    {draw curves of constant s}
    for s := 0 to 1 by epsilon do
      begin                       {trace out a curve of constant s, by varying t}
        MOVE_ABS_3(X(s, 0), Y(s, 0), Z(s, 0));
        for t:= epsilon to 1 by epsilon do
          LINE_ABS_3(X(s, t), Y(s, t), Z(s, t))
      end
    {draw curves of constant t}
    for t := 0 to 1 by epsilon do
      begin                       {trace out a curve of constant t, by varying s}
        MOVE_ABS_3(X(0, t), Y(0, t), Z(0, t));
        for s := epsilon to 1 by epsilon do
          LINE_ABS_3(X(s, t), Y(s, t), Z(s, t))
      end
  end
{X, Y, Z are procedures to evaluate bicubics for x, y, and z, respectively}
```

This method has the unfortunate characteristic that the surface equations are evaluated about $2/\epsilon^2$ times. For $\epsilon = 0.1$, this is 200; for $\epsilon = 0.01$, this is 20000. Each evaluation takes many multiplications and additions.

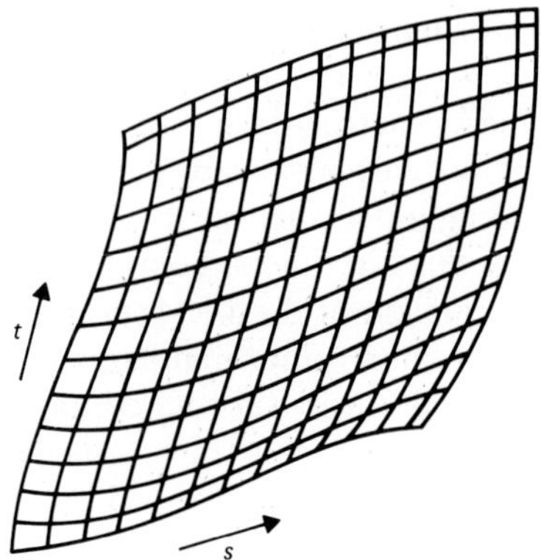

Fig. 13.20 Single surface patch depicted by curves of constant s and constant t.

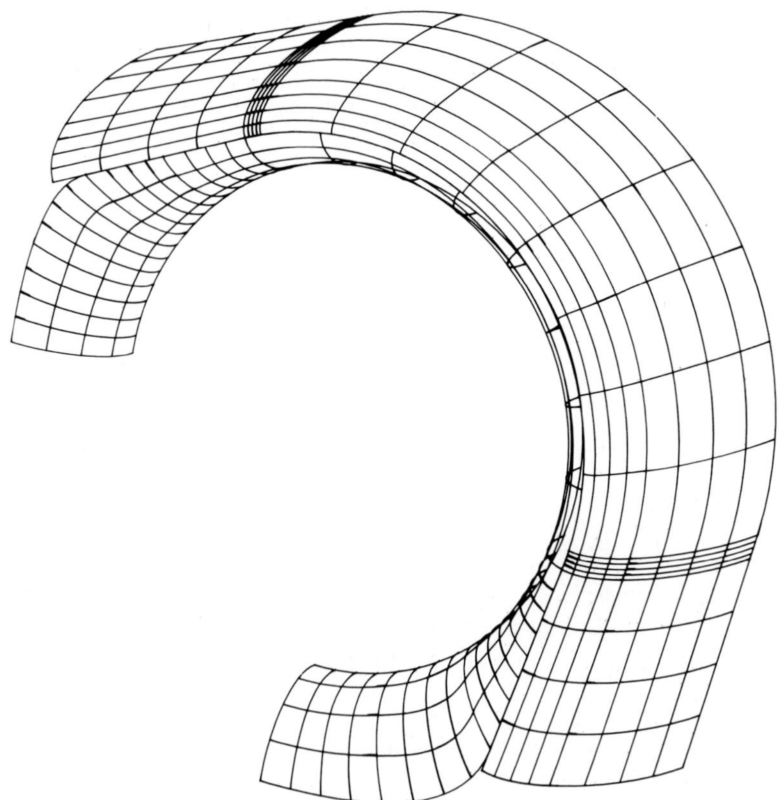

Fig. 13.21 Jet-engine intake specified by series of 3D surface patches (courtesy McDonnell Douglas Corporation, CADD system).

Horner's rule for factoring polynomials can be used to reduce the number of multiplications each time a parametric bicubic is evaluated. For a cubic polynomial, the rule is

$$f(t) = [(at + b)t + c]t + d. \tag{13.60}$$

The rule can clearly be extended to bicubics, but even so, much work is still needed.

A much more efficient way of repeatedly evaluating the bicubic is by using *forward differences.* The forward difference of a function $f(t)$ is

$$\Delta f(t) = f(t + \delta) - f(t), \qquad \delta > 0. \tag{13.61}$$

We can rewrite this as

$$f(t + \delta) = f(t) + \Delta f(t). \tag{13.62}$$

This means we can determine $f(t + \delta)$ if we know $f(t)$ and $\Delta f(t)$. Rewriting (13.62) in iterative terms, we see that this is

$$f_{n+1} = f_n + \Delta f_n, \tag{13.63}$$

where we evaluate f in constant steps of size δ, so n and t are related by $t = \delta \cdot n$, and $f_n = f(t_n)$.

For a third-order polynomial,

$$f(t) = at^3 + bt^2 + ct + d, \tag{13.64}$$

so the forward difference is

$$\begin{aligned} \Delta f(t) &= a(t + \delta)^3 + b(t + \delta)^2 + c(t + \delta) + d - (at^3 + bt^2 + ct + d) \\ &= 3at^2\delta + t(3a\delta^2 + 2b\delta) + a\delta^3 + b\delta^2 + c\delta. \end{aligned} \tag{13.65}$$

Thus $\Delta f(t)$ is a second-order polynomial. This is unfortunate, since evaluating (13.63) still involves evaluating a second-order polynomial, plus an addition. Let us in turn apply forward differences to $\Delta f(t)$ to see if its evaluation can be simplified.

Considering $\Delta f(t)$ as a function in its own right, we write:

$$\Delta^2 f(t) = \Delta(\Delta f(t)) = \Delta f(t + \delta) - \Delta f(t). \tag{13.66}$$

Applying this to (13.65) gives

$$\Delta^2 f(t) = 6a\delta^2 t + 6a\delta^3 + 2b\delta^2. \tag{13.67}$$

This is now a first-order equation in t. Rewriting (13.66) and using the index n, we obtain

$$\Delta^2 f_n = \Delta f_{n+1} - \Delta f_n \tag{13.68}$$

or

$$\Delta f_{n+1} = \Delta f_n + \Delta^2 f_n. \tag{13.69}$$

Replacing n by $(n - 1)$ yields

$$\Delta f_n = \Delta f_{n-1} + \Delta^2 f_{n-1}. \tag{13.70}$$

Now to evaluate Δf_n for use in (13.63), we simply need to evaluate $\Delta^2 f_{n-1}$ and add it to Δf_{n-1}. Because $\Delta^2 f_{n-1}$ is linear in t, this is less work than evaluating Δf_n directly from the second-order polynomial (13.65).

We repeat the process once more, to avoid evaluating (13.67):

$$\Delta^3 f(t) = \Delta(\Delta^2 f(t)) = \Delta^2 f(t + \delta) - \Delta^2 f(t). \tag{13.71}$$

Applying this definition to (13.67) gives

$$\Delta^3 f(t) = 6a\delta^3. \tag{13.72}$$

This third difference is a constant, so its evaluation is trivial. Now we rewrite (13.71) using index n to obtain:

$$\Delta^3 f_n = \Delta^2 f_{n+1} - \Delta^2 f_n, \tag{13.73}$$

or

$$\Delta^2 f_{n+1} = \Delta^2 f_n + \Delta^3 f_n = \Delta^2 f_n + \Delta^3 f_0. \tag{13.74}$$

Replacing n by $(n - 2)$, we get

$$\Delta^2 f_{n-1} = \Delta^2 f_{n-2} + \Delta^3 f_{n-2} = \Delta^2 f_{n-2} + 6a\delta^3. \tag{13.75}$$

This can now be used in (13.70) to obtain Δf_n, which is then used in (13.63) to find f_{n+1}.

To use the forward differences in an algorithm which iterates on n from $n = 0$ to $n\delta = 1$, we compute the function and the first, second, and third forward differences at $t = 0$ (or $n = 0$) by using (13.64), (13.65), (13.67), and (13.72):

$$\begin{aligned} f_0 &= d, & \Delta f_0 &= a\delta^3 + b\delta^2 + c\delta, \\ \Delta^2 f_0 &= 6a\delta^3 + 2b\delta^2, & \Delta^3 f_0 &= 6a\delta^3. \end{aligned} \tag{13.76}$$

These initial calculations can be done by direct evaluation of the four equations. It is useful to note, though, that

$$\begin{bmatrix} f_0 \\ \Delta f_0 \\ \Delta^2 f_0 \\ \Delta^3 f_0 \end{bmatrix} = \begin{bmatrix} 0 & 0 & 0 & 1 \\ \delta^3 & \delta^2 & \delta & 0 \\ 6\delta^3 & 2\delta^2 & 0 & 0 \\ 6\delta^3 & 0 & 0 & 0 \end{bmatrix} \begin{bmatrix} a \\ b \\ c \\ d \end{bmatrix}, \tag{13.77}$$

or, rewriting (13.77),

$$D_0 = E(\delta)\, A. \tag{13.78}$$

We now repeat the following steps $1/\delta$ times, with n initially 0:

$$f_{n+1} = f_n + \Delta f_n, \tag{13.79}$$

$$\Delta f_{n+1} = \Delta f_n + \Delta^2 f_n, \tag{13.80}$$

$$\Delta^2 f_{n+1} = \Delta^2 f_n + \Delta^3 f_0. \tag{13.81}$$

Note that if the calculations are performed in the order shown, no storage for intermediate results is needed. For cubic curves there are of course three functions, $x(t)$, $y(t)$, and $z(t)$, each of which is treated this way.

To extend forward differences to surfaces, we work with

$$x(s, t) = SC_xT^T. \tag{13.82}$$

By analogy with the initialization for curves for which

$$D_0 = E(\delta)A, \tag{13.83}$$

we calculate for surfaces:

$$D_{00} = E(\epsilon)C_xE(\delta)^T, \tag{13.84}$$

where ϵ is the step size in parameter s and δ is the step size in parameter t. The matrix D_{00} is 4×4, and the first row contains the values f_0, Δf_0, $\Delta^2 f_0$, and $\Delta^3 f_0$ needed to compute $x(0,t)$, while the first column contains the corresponding values to compute $x(s,0)$.

After computing $x(0,t)$ for all steps in t, how can we proceed to compute $x(\epsilon,t)$? The iteration is very similar to that for curves, but is performed on all rows of D_{00}:

$$\begin{aligned} \text{Row } 1 &= \text{Row } 1 + \text{Row } 2, \\ \text{Row } 2 &= \text{Row } 2 + \text{Row } 3, \\ \text{Row } 3 &= \text{Row } 3 + \text{Row } 4. \end{aligned} \tag{13.85}$$

Now row 1 is used for $x(\epsilon, t)$. The steps of (13.85) are repeated, and row 1 now defines $x(2\epsilon, t)$, etc.

To work with $x(s, 0)$, $x(s, \epsilon)$, . . . $x(s, 1)$, the first column is used to compute values, and *column* is substituted for *row* in (13.85). Alternatively, D_{00}^T can be used in place of D_{00}, so that rows are always used.

EXERCISES

13.1 For each polygonal representation, calculate how much space would be required in 3D to represent (a) a triangle; (b) a cube; (c) a mesh of 10 × 10 square polygons. Assume pointers and indexes take the same amount of space as an x, y, or z value.

13.2 Write a procedure to check the explicit edge representation of a polygon mesh (Section 13.2.3) to make sure that each vertex is part of at least one polygon and that no edge has the same vertex at each end (which would imply an edge length of zero).

13.3 Write a procedure to test the explicit edge representation of a polygon mesh (Section 13.2.3) to ensure that each polygon is closed. If a polygon is not closed, report the number of breaks in it.

13.4 Evaluate Eq. (13.30) and its derivative at $t = 0$ and $t = 1$ to see that the constraints of the geometry vector are indeed satisfied.

13.5 Consider the two Hermite curve segments with geometry vectors as in Eq. (13.11). Show that at P_4, the segments are continuous, the first derivative is continuous, and the second derivative is *not* continuous.

13.6 Prove that for two joined Bezier curves to have first-order continuity, it is necessary to have $\overline{P_3P_4} = k\overline{P_4P_5}$, as asserted in Section 13.5.2.

13.7 A cubic polynomial is to pass through each of four points, at parameter values of 0, 1/3, 2/3, and 1. Find the matrix M such that $x(t) = TMP_x$. This is called *Lagrange interpolation.*

13.8 Prove by induction on n that the weighted average of n points lies in the convex hull of the n points.

13.9 Write a program to plot Bezier curves, given the geometry matrix G_b.

13.10 Write a program to plot a B-spline, given n points p_1 , . . . , p_n.

13.11 Show that the four functions of t which form the B-spline blending functions (found from the product TM_s) sum to 1 and are in the range of 0 to 1 for values of t between 0 and 1.

13.12 Show that Eq. (13.44) reduces to a cubic curve if t (or s) is assigned a value.

13.13 Prove that a bicubic surface can be transformed by transforming the geometry matrix of points and/or tangent vectors which defines the surface.

13.14 Determine how many multiplications and additions are needed to evaluate the point $(x(s, t), y(s, t), z(s, t))$, given the algebraic matrices M_x, M_y, and M_z.

13.15 Using Horner's rule, how many multiplications and additions are needed to evaluate a bicubic surface point?

13.16 Prove that a parametric cubic curve can be nonplanar.

13.17 Four Coons' patches share a common corner point, and each pair of patches has a common edge with $C^{(1)}$ continuity. What conditions must the four matrices satisfy?

13.18 Modify the program in Section 13.8 to display a patch with step size E_t on parameter t and step size E_s on parameter s, with n_t lines of constant t and n_s lines of constant s.

13.19 Define a data structure (using, for instance, Pascal records) to define a collection of Bezier patches and their relationships to up to four other patches. The relationships are:

a) common edge shared with $C^{(0)}$ continuity, and

b) common edge shared with $C^{(1)}$ continuity.

Now write a procedure which allows any point P_{ij} of a patch's 4×4 geometry matrix to be set to a new value, with *all* changes to neighboring patches' matrices made automatically. In some cases a new value for a control point may cause other control points for the same patch to change also, in order to maintain a constant ratio between tangent vector lengths.

13.20 What shape of curve results if $P_1 = P_4$ and $R_1 = R_4$ for the Hermite representation?

13.21 Can a doughnut-shaped (toroidal) surface be created with a Hermite surface patch? Explain your answer.

14
The Quest for Visual Realism

14.1 INTRODUCTION

In this chapter we discuss an important application of computer graphics: creating realistic images of 3D objects. Two very effective approaches which help produce realism are removal of hidden surfaces and shading of visible surfaces. Computer graphics techniques for this are introduced in the present chapter and discussed in detail in Chapters 15 and 16. Color, also important in producing realistic images, is discussed in Chapter 17, the final chapter of this text.

The quest for realistic computer graphics presentations has been underway since the mid-sixties and has produced some very impressive pictures, as exemplified by many of the Color Plates in this text. The objective of the quest has been to produce computer-generated images which are so realistic that the observer believes the image to be that of a real object rather than of a synthetic object existing only in the computer's memory. This is an important goal in fields such as simulation, design, and entertainment.

Simulation systems present images which are not only realistic, but also change dynamically. For example, a flight simulator shows the view that would be seen from the cockpit of a moving plane. To produce the effect of motion, a new, slightly different image is generated and displayed about 30 times a second. Simulators have been used to train not only airplane pilots, but also the Apollo spacecraft and Columbia space shuttle pilots. Color Plates 16, B, and C show pictures generated by simulators.

Designers of such 3D objects as automobiles, airplanes, and buildings want to see how a preliminary design will look. The creation of realistic computer-generated images is in many instances an easier, less expensive, and more effective way of seeing preliminary results than building models and prototypes; it also allows more alternative designs to be considered. Because the design work proper is also often computerized, a digital description of the 3D object is already available to use as the basis for creating the images.

The world of entertainment is beginning to use computer-generated imagery both in the traditional area of animated cartoons and, more recently, in the creation of realistic and surrealistic images for logos, ads, and science fiction movies. Computer-generated cartoons can mimic traditional animation, but they can also transcend the limits of manual techniques by introducing more complicated motions and richer or more realistic images. Color Plates 2, 21, and the plates on the endpapers are examples of such images.

The fundamental difficulty in achieving total visual realism is the complexity of real images. Observe the richness of your environment. There are many surface textures, subtle color gradations, shadows, reflections, and slight irregularities (scuffs on the floor, chips in the paint, marks on the wall). These all combine in our mind to create a ''real'' visual experience. Techniques have been developed to simulate some of these visual effects with a computer. In many cases, the computational costs in performing the simulations can be high: the creation of pictures such as those in Color Plates 2 and 20 takes many minutes of processing time on a powerful contemporary computer.

A subgoal in the quest for realism has been to provide sufficient information on a display to allow the viewer to understand the 3D spatial relationships among several objects. This can be achieved at a significantly lower cost than complete realism and is a common requirement in computer-aided design and many other application areas. Of course, highly realistic images also convey 3D spatial relationships, but they usually convey much more as well. Figure 14.1, a simple line drawing, suffices to persuade us that one building is partially behind the other. There is no need for the building surfaces to be filled in with shingles and bricks, nor for shadows cast by the buildings to appear.

The fundamental difficulty in depicting spatial relationships is that all practical display devices have been 2D. Therefore 3D objects must be projected into two dimensions, with the considerable attendant loss of information which can sometimes create ambiguities in the image. The techniques discussed in this chapter can

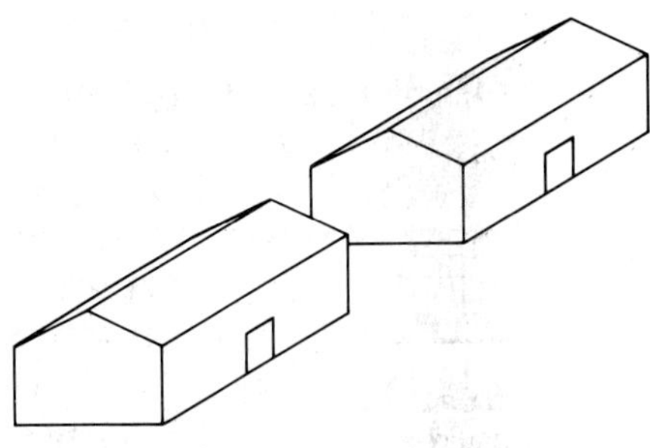

Figure 14.1

be used to add back information of the type normally found in a visual environment, so that human depth perception mechanisms will properly resolve the remaining ambiguities.

Consider Fig. 14.2(a), a 2D projection of a cube. The ambiguity lies in not knowing whether the cube in (a) represents the cube in (b) or in (c) of Fig. 14.2. As Necker observed in 1832, the mind can imagine that either (b) or (c) is the correct interpretation. Indeed, one can easily cause a reversal between the two alternatives, because there simply is not enough information for an unambiguous interpretation.

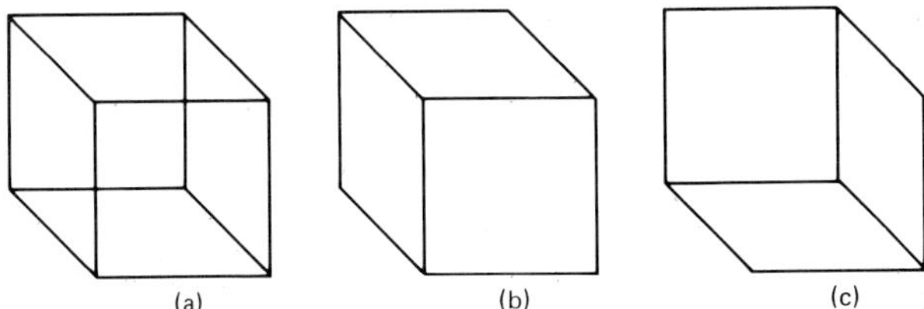

Fig. 14.2 The Necker cube illusion. Is the cube in (a) oriented like the cube in (b) or in (c)?

The more the viewers know about the object being displayed, the more readily they can form what Gregory calls an *object hypothesis* [GREG70]. Figure 14.3 shows a stairway—but is it a view we see by looking down a stairway or by looking up from underneath the stairway? We are likely to choose the former interpretation, probably because we more frequently see stairways under our feet than over our head, and therefore we "know" more about stairways as viewed from above. With a small stretch of the imagination, one can visualize the alternative interpretation of the figure. However, with a blink of the eye, a reversal occurs for most viewers and the stairway again appears to be viewed from above.

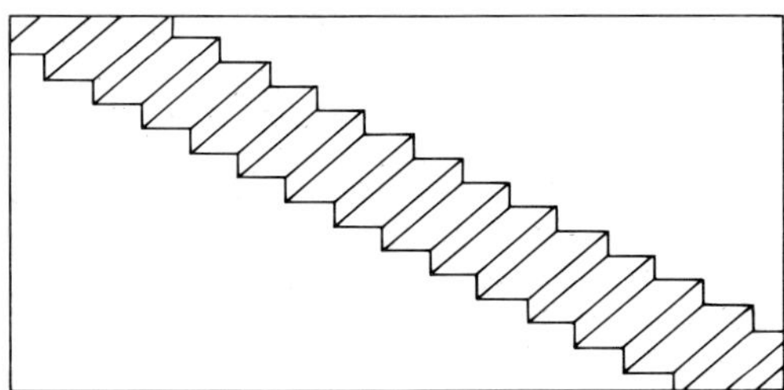

Fig. 14.3 The Schröder stairway illusion. Is the stairway being viewed from above or from below?

14.2 TECHNIQUES FOR DISPLAYING DEPTH RELATIONSHIPS

In this section we continue to focus on the subgoal of realism, that of showing 3D depth relationships on a 2D surface. This goal is served by the planar geometric projections described in Chapter 8. The pros and cons of the many different projections are discussed in [CARL78]. Both parallel and perspective projections, which are the two classes of projections, convey depth information.

14.2.1 Parallel Projections

The easiest projection, the parallel orthographic, simply discards depth information. To compensate for this, top, front, and side views are shown together, as for the block letter "L" in Fig. 14.4. It is not difficult to understand this particular drawing; however, drawings of complicated manufactured parts may require many hours of study to be understood. Training and experience sharpen one's interpretive powers; familiarity with the types of objects being represented hastens the formulation of a correct object hypothesis.

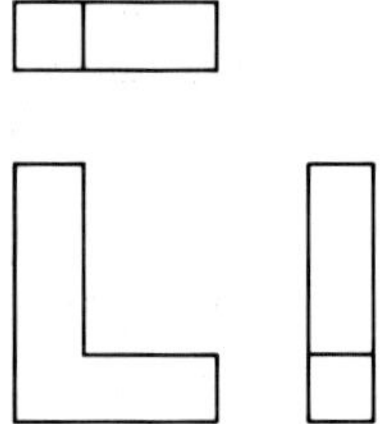

Fig. 14.4 Front, top, and side orthographic projections of block letter "L".

14.2.2 Perspective Projections

The perspective projection, unlike the parallel projection, does not completely discard depth information. Rather, the size of objects is scaled inversely as their distance from the viewer. A perspective projection of a cube shown in Fig. 14.5 reflects this scaling. But there is still ambiguity: the projection could just as well be a

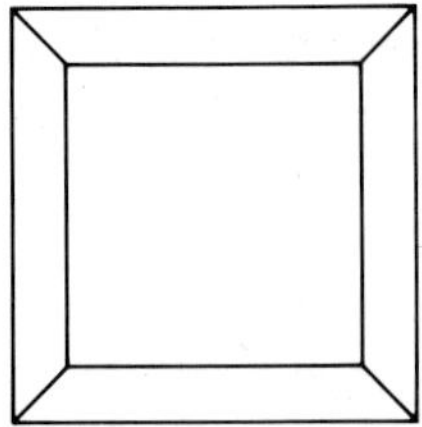

Fig. 14.5 Perspective projection of a cube.

picture frame, or the parallel projection of a truncated pyramid or the perspective projection of a rectangular parallelepiped with two equal faces. If one's object hypothesis is that of a truncated pyramid, then the smaller square represents the face closer to the viewer; if the hypothesis is that of a cube or rectangular parallelepiped, then the smaller square represents the face further from the viewer.

Our interpretation of perspective projections is often based on the assumption that a smaller object is further away. In Fig. 14.6 we would probably assume that the larger house is nearer to the viewer. However, the house which appears larger (a mansion, perhaps) may actually be more distant than the one which appears smaller (a cottage, perhaps), at least so long as there are no other cues, such as trees and windows. Potmesil has recently modeled camera optics, producing images whose focus *and* size vary with distance [POTM81].

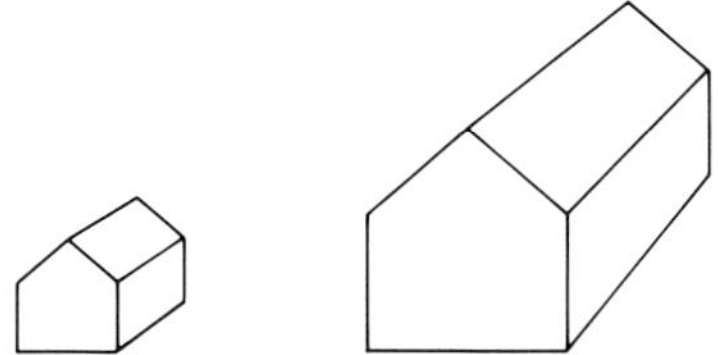

Fig. 14.6 Perspective projection of two houses.

When the viewer knows that the projected objects have many parallel lines, perspective does convey depth, because the parallel lines seem to converge at their vanishing points. This convergence may actually be a stronger depth cue than the decreasing size effect. Wright found that perspective projections of stick-figure molecule representations were less convincing than parallel projections, explaining this by the lack of converging parallel lines in molecular structures [WRIG72].

14.2.3 Intensity Depth Cueing

The depth (distance) of an object can be represented by varying degrees of intensity: objects intended to appear closer to the viewer are displayed at higher intensity (see Fig. 14.7). To implement intensity depth cueing, the depth (z-coordinate) information must be available to the DPU. In vector displays, the vector generator uses the starting and ending z-coordinates to interpolate intensity. In raster displays, the line scan-conversion algorithm performs the same function. The eye's intensity resolution is lower than its spatial resolution, so that intensity cueing cannot be used to depict small differences in distance from the viewer. It is quite effective, however, for depicting large differences.

Depth cueing has some parallels in real vision: only in song can one "see forever" on a clear day. Distant objects appear dimmer than closer objects, especially on a hazy day. In large part, though, the viewer's response to depth cueing in graphics seems learned rather than intuitive.

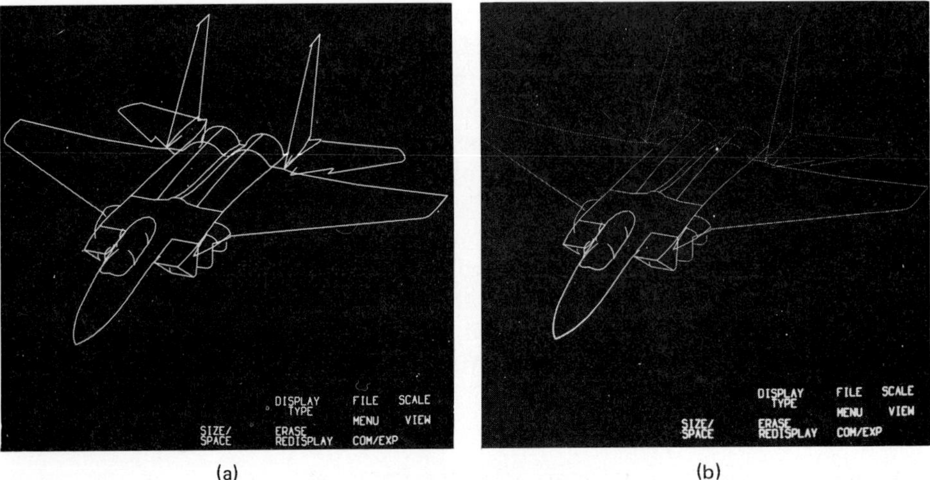

(a) (b)

Fig. 14.7 An image of an airplane (a) without and (b) with intensity depth cueing (courtesy of McDonnell Douglas Corporation, CADD system).

14.2.4 Depth Clipping

Further depth information can be provided by depth clipping (called *z-axis cut-off* in some hardware implementations). The back clipping plane is placed to cut through the object being displayed. Partially clipped lines, etc., are then known by the viewer to be cut by the clipping plane. By varying the back plane dynamically, more depth information can be made available to the viewer. Figure 14.8 shows the airplane of Fig. 14.7 with a back clipping plane which removes the tail and part of one wing.

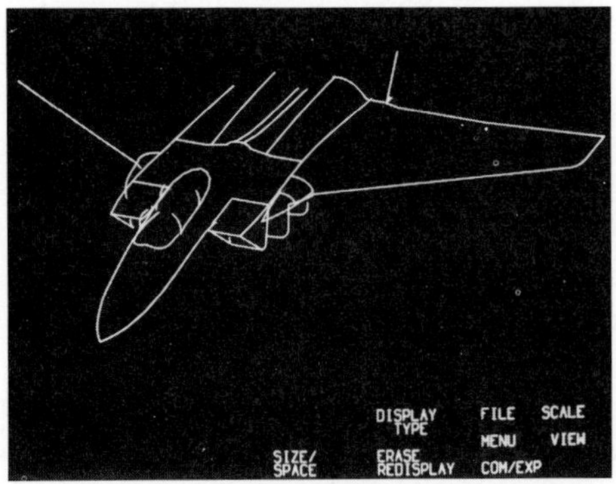

Fig. 14.8 Depth clipping (courtesy of McDonnell Douglas Corporation, CADD system).

14.2.5 Dynamic Projections

If a series of projections of the same object is rapidly displayed, each from a slightly different viewpoint around the object, then the object appears to rotate. By integrating the information in each view, the viewer creates the object hypothesis. A projection of a rotating cube, for instance, provides two types of information. There is the series of different projections, which are themselves useful. Second, there is the motion effect, in which the maximum angular velocity of points near the center of rotation is lower than that of points distant from the center of rotation.

This technique is very effective, but its use requires special-purpose transformation hardware for all but simple objects. It is interesting to note that one cannot infer the sense of rotation from orthographic projections of a rotating object: there are insufficient visual cues. By using intensity depth cueing *and* dynamic rotation, however, the sense of rotation can be deduced.

14.2.6 Hidden-Edge and Hidden-Surface Removal

Hidden-edge removal is applied when objects are displayed as lines which represent edges of the surfaces making up the object, as in Color Plate 14(a). Hidden-surface removal is used when objects are displayed as filled-in surfaces, as in Color Plate 14(b). In the former case, *edges* obscured by visible surfaces are removed and not displayed, while in the latter case *surfaces* obscured by visible surfaces are removed and not displayed.

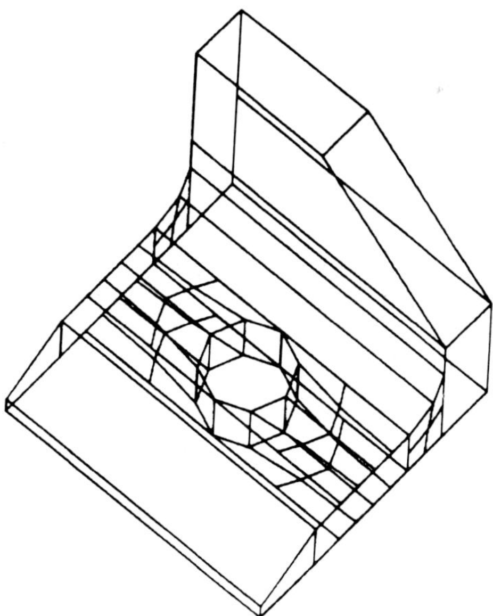

Fig. 14.9 Line drawing of bracket (courtesy The Boeing Company).

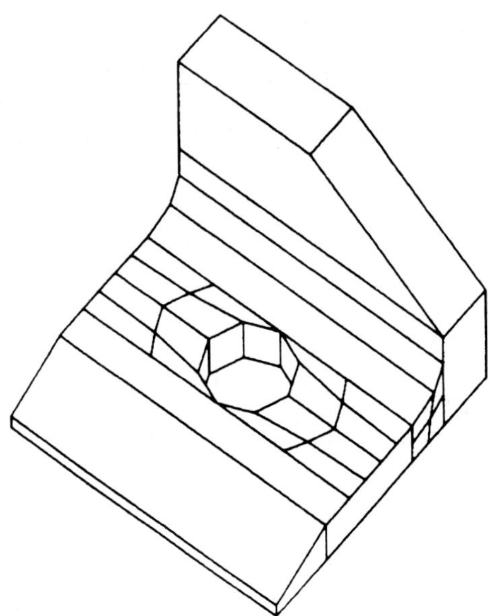

Fig. 14.10 View of bracket with hidden edges removed (courtesy The Boeing Company).

Figures 14.1, 14.2, 14.9, 14.10 and Color Plate 14(a) show the usefulness of hidden-edge removal. Showing hidden edges as dashed lines is also helpful and conveys even more information. Since hidden-edge removal algorithms are time-consuming and conflict with response time requirements in interactive graphics, they are typically executed as an option which the user soon learns to invoke sparingly, only when really needed.

With hidden-surface removal we move beyond showing depth relationships into the domain of realism. Because both hidden-edge-removed and hidden-surface-removed views conceal *all* the internal structure of objects, they are not necessarily the most effective way to show depth relations. The hidden-edge-removed view of Color Plate 14(a) and the hidden-surface-removed view of Color Plate 14(b), while realistic, convey less depth information than do the exploded and cutaway views in Color Plates 14(c) and 14(d). On the other hand, the hidden-surface-removed view in Fig. 14.11 conveys a better sense of the bracket's appearance than do Figs. 14.9 and 14.10.

14.3 STEREOPSIS

All the techniques discussed above present the same image to both eyes of the viewer. Now conduct an experiment: look at your desk or table top first with one eye, then with the other. The two views are slightly different, because our eyes are separated one from the other by a few inches (see Fig. 14.12). The *binocular disparity* caused by this provides a very powerful depth cue called *stereopsis.* Our brain fuses the two separate images into one which is interpreted as three-dimensional.

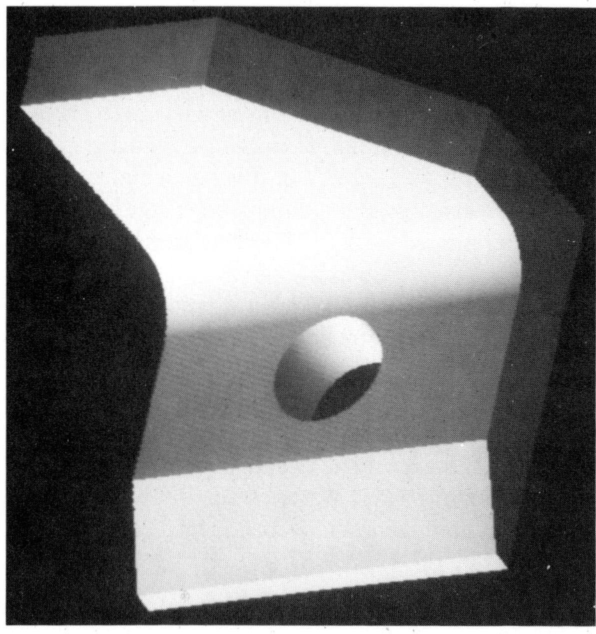

Fig. 14.11 View of bracket with hidden surfaces removed (courtesy Boeing Corporation).

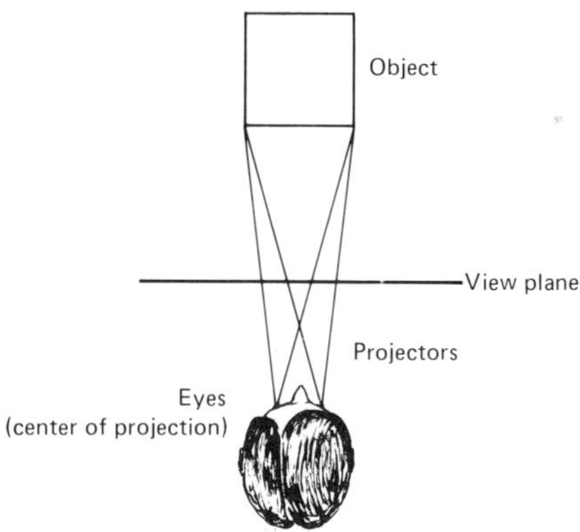

Fig. 14.12 Binocular disparity.

The two separate images are called *stereo pairs;* they were used in the stereopticons popular in our great-grandparents' days and are used today in the common childrens' toy, the View-Master^{TM}. Color Plate 15 shows a stereo pair of a space-filled molecule representation. The two images can be fused into one 3D image by viewing the pair in such a way that each eye sees only one image; this can be achieved by placing a stiff piece of paper between the two images perpendicular to the page.

To achieve the highly realistic effects which can be produced by stereopsis, the interactive system designer must present views to each eye which differ from each other in the appropriate way. There are many ways to do this. First, we can use two separate CRTs with an optical system of prisms and lenses to bring the images to the eyes. In one example of this technique, two small CRTs are mounted on a helmet worn by the user (Fig. 14.13) [SUTH68]. In this particular case, the helmet's position and orientation are sensed by the computer driving the CRTs, and the viewer wearing the helmet is presented with a visual environment which changes as he moves.

A second method uses a single CRT and a system of shutters over the eyes. Alternating refresh cycles display left- and right-eye views in synchronism with the opening and closing of the shutters, which are typically a series of opaque and clear openings on a rotating cylinder or disk held in front of the eyes. User mobility is somewhat limited with this apparatus, but several viewers are easily accommodated. In another arrangement, the user wears a pair of glasses with lenses made of lead lanthanum zirconate titanate (PLZT) wafers (Fig. 14.14): an electrical field causes the material to switch, in about one millisecond, from clear to opaque or back to clear, creating a shutter [ROES76, ROES79].

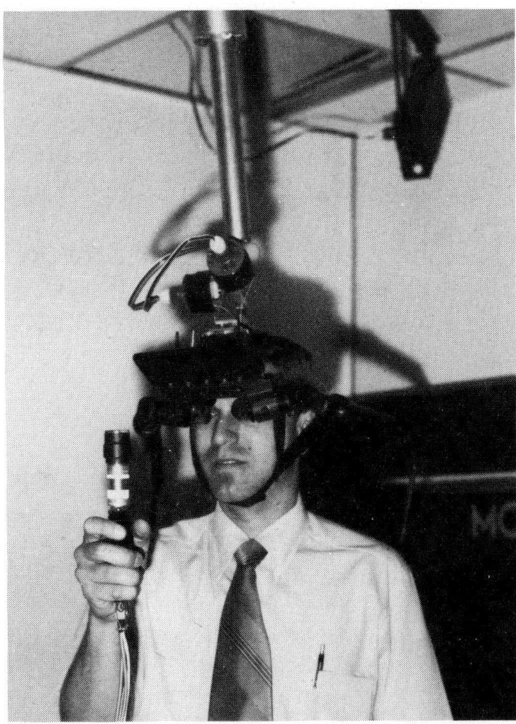

Fig. 14.13 Head-mounted displays (courtesy University of Utah).

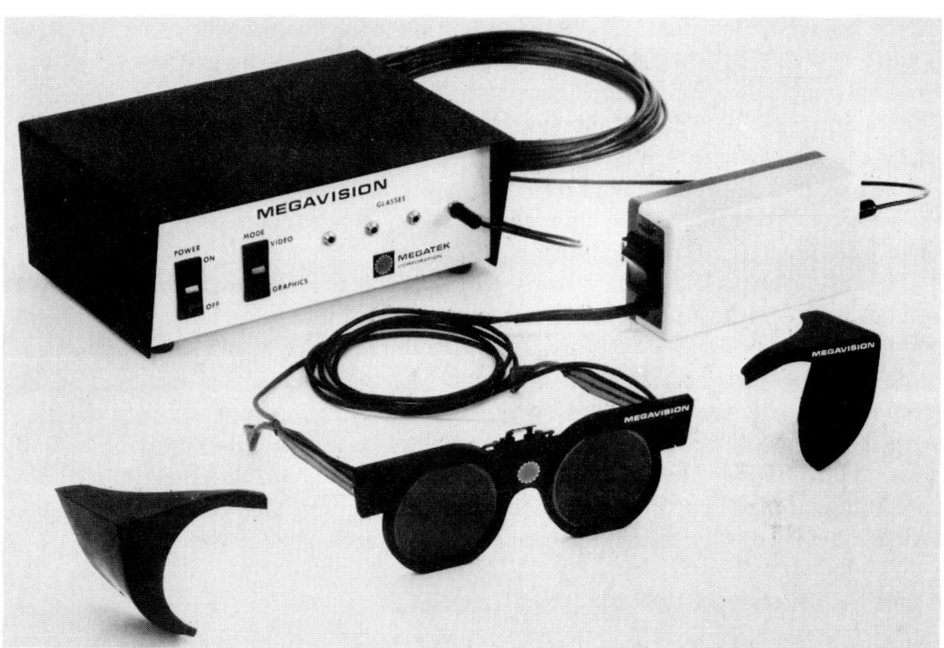

Fig. 14.14 Stereo viewing glasses (courtesy Megatek, Inc.).

These two methods are relatively expensive, but do provide a full-screen view to each eye. The third method is simpler and less expensive, but uses the two halves of a single CRT for the two views. A system of filters, either colored or polarized, is used so each eye sees only the appropriate view. Figure 14.15 shows the basic idea, in which a half-silvered mirror transmits some light from the lower half of the screen and also reflects some light from the upper half of the screen. The user can move about freely and still see the stereo effect. This type of system, first developed by Ortony [ORTO71], has been further refined by Feldmann for displaying large mole-

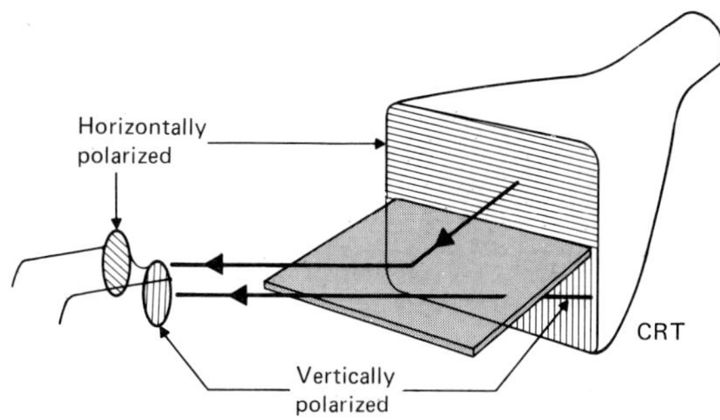

Fig. 14.15 Stereo viewing by means of half-silvered mirror and polarizing filters. Colored filters can be used instead.

cules. Readers interested in further understanding of stereopsis are referred to [JULE71] and [JULE74]. Lipscomb gives a comprehensive discussion of methods for displaying stereo pairs and other depth cues [LIPS79].

All these techniques, including the use of stereo pairs, "trick" the viewers into imagining that they are seeing a 3D scene. None of the techniques really recreate a 3D environment, although the head-mounted display does provide a single user with the parallax effect, that is, the apparent change in view as the head moves, which is the crucial missing link in all the other techniques.

Traub [TRAU67] and then Rawson [RAWS69] devised a system to display a true 3D image. A flexible mylar mirror is made to vibrate so as to change its focal length. The reflection of a CRT image is viewed in the mirror. The CRT is synchronized with the mirror's vibrations in such a way that objects are displayed at the moment when the focal length of the mirror places the object at the right depth.

Another method for true 3D, not yet usable in real time, is the computation and creation on a film negative of a hologram. The difficulties with this method are both computation time and the real-time control of the transmittance of the film through which coherent light is passed to recreate a 3D image.

14.4 APPROACHES TO VISUAL REALISM

So far we have focused primarily on techniques for line drawings, but some of these methods are applicable also to the more realistic shaded images shown in various Color Plates. The first step toward achieving the realism seen in these figures is hidden-surface removal. The value of hidden-surface removal becomes apparent when comparing the space shuttles shown in Fig. 13.2 and Color Plate 16 and when comparing the different presentations of the car shown in Fig. 16.8.

Objects whose hidden surfaces are to be removed must be modelled either as solids or as collections of surfaces, as discussed in Chapter 13. When viewed from a given location, some of the surfaces will be obscured by others, some will be partially obscured, and some will be completely visible. Algorithms for hidden-surface removal are discussed in the next chapter.

The next step toward achieving realism is the shading of the visible surfaces. The appearance of a surface depends on the types of light sources illuminating the object, the properties (color, texture, reflectance) of the surface, and the position and orientation of the surface with respect to the light sources and other surfaces. The light source can be a *point source,* like the sun or an incandescent bulb, or a *distributed source,* like a bank of fluorescent lights; in many real visual environments there is also a considerable amount of ambient light impinging from all directions.

The easiest light source to model is *ambient light,* because it produces a constant illumination on all surfaces, regardless of their orientation. Unfortunately, ambient light by itself produces very unrealistic images since few real environments are illuminated solely by ambient light. Under ambient light alone, two adjacent faces of a cube would be shaded the same, and their common edge would not be distinguishable.

A more complex (to model) but more realistic light source is the point source, for which the illumination of a surface depends on its orientation: if it is normal to the incident light rays, the surface is brightly illuminated. The more oblique the surface is to the light rays, the less the illumination. This variation in illumination is, of course, a powerful cue to the 3D structure of an object.

Further realism can be introduced by reproducing the *shadows* cast by objects illuminated by a point source. Color Plate 17 shows a scene with different numbers of light sources, some of which produce shadows. Color Plate 20 shows more shadows. The shadows enhance realism and provide additional depth cues: if object *A* casts a shadow on surface *B*, then *A* is between *B* and the light source. Figure 14.16 illustrates a cube, a viewpoint, a backdrop, and several light sources in positions *L*1, *L*2, and *L*3. Only *L*2 casts a shadow onto the part of the backdrop invisible from the viewpoint because the shadow is obscured by the cube. A light source at the viewpoint or anywhere on the straight line through *L*2 and beyond to infinity would also produce a shadow invisible from the viewpoint. Light sources *L*1 and *L*3 cast shadows which are visible to the viewer.

Another way to enhance realism is to reproduce *surface properties.* Some surfaces are dull and disperse reflected light in many directions, while others are shiny and reflect light only in certain directions. Surfaces can also be translucent, i.e., transmitting (and refracting) some light, while also reflecting some light. Color Plates 13 and 20, among others, illustrate the reproduction of these phenomena by means of computer graphics.

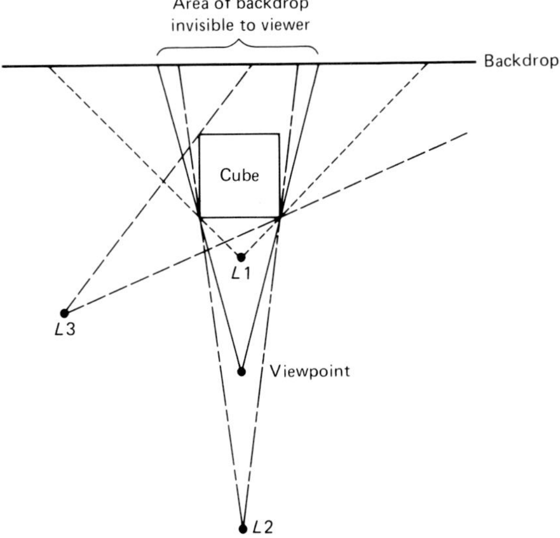

Fig. 14.16 Shadows cast by three light sources.

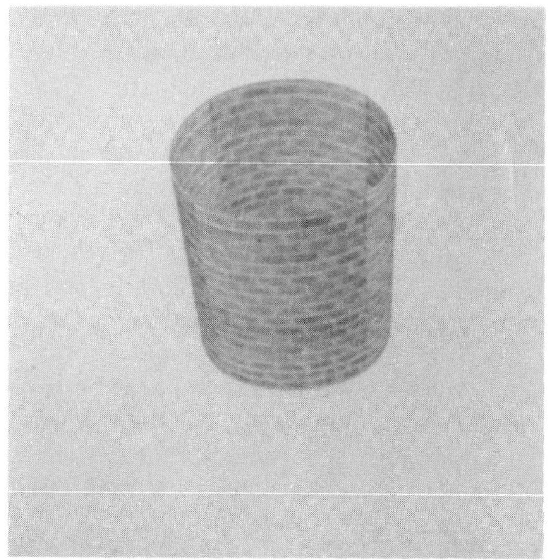

Fig. 14.17 Brick-texture pattern mapped onto a bicubic surface (courtesy E. Catmull).

Another property of surfaces is their *texture:* few surfaces are perfectly smooth, yet this is how they are modeled by polygons and bicubic parametrics. Color Plates 18 and 19 show how realism can be enhanced by texturing surfaces. Similarly, few surfaces have a perfectly constant color: more typically, they are patterned. Thus we can further enhance realism by including surface patterns (such as the bricks in Fig. 14.17) in the shading process.

Methods for modeling the light sources and surface properties introduced here are discussed in more detail in Chapter 16.

15
Algorithms for Removing Hidden Edges and Surfaces

15.1 INTRODUCTION

Given a 3D object and a viewing specification defining the type of projection, the projection plane, etc., we wish to determine which edges and surfaces of the object are visible from the center of projection (for perspective projections) or along the direction of projection (for parallel projections), so that we can display only the visible edges and surfaces. While the statement of this fundamental idea is simple, its implementation requires a large amount of computer time, which has encouraged the development of numerous carefully structured algorithms.

The need for this care can be easily seen from the analysis of two fundamental approaches to the problem. One approach is to think of the object as a collection of n polygonal faces and to decide which face is visible at each resolution point on the display device. Doing this for one resolution point requires the examination of all n faces to determine which is closest to the viewer. For N resolution points, the effort is proportional to nN, where N is usually between 250 000 and 4 000 000.

The second approach is to compare each of the n faces to the remaining $n - 1$ faces in order to eliminate faces or portions of faces that are not visible. The computational effort here is proportional to n^2. While one might therefore believe that this second approach would be superior for even the largest realistic values of $n = 100{,}000$ to $n = 200{,}000$, its individual steps are more time-consuming, so it is slower, even for smaller n.

In the excellent survey paper by Sutherland, Sproull, and Schumacker [SUTH74c] these approaches are called *image space* algorithms and *object space* algorithms, respectively. The authors discuss and categorize ten algorithms developed through 1972. Later in this chapter we describe four of those algorithms as well as additional algorithms developed since 1972.

It is important to organize hidden-surface algorithms to make each step as efficient as possible. The next two sections of this chapter describe some general ways to do so, and later sections describe specific algorithms for removing the hidden surfaces from the display of 3D objects defined with polygonal faces. Some of these algorithms can also be adapted for use as hidden-edge removal algorithms. Algorithms for displaying objects defined by curved-surface patches are briefly described as well. The class of specialized algorithms to display single-valued functions of two variables is not described: see [BUTL79, WRIG73].

15.2 SIMPLIFYING DEPTH COMPARISONS: THE PERSPECTIVE TRANSFORMATION

Hidden-surface removal must clearly be done in a 3D space prior to the projection into 2D which destroys the depth information needed for depth comparisons. The basic depth comparison can be typically reduced to the following question: given $P_1 = (x_1, y_1, z_1)$ and $P_2 = (x_2, y_2, z_2)$, does either point obscure the other? This question is the same as: are P_1 and P_2 on the same projector (see Fig. 15.1)? If the answer is YES, a comparison of z_1 and z_2 tells us which point is closer to the viewer. If the answer is NO, then neither point can obscure the other.

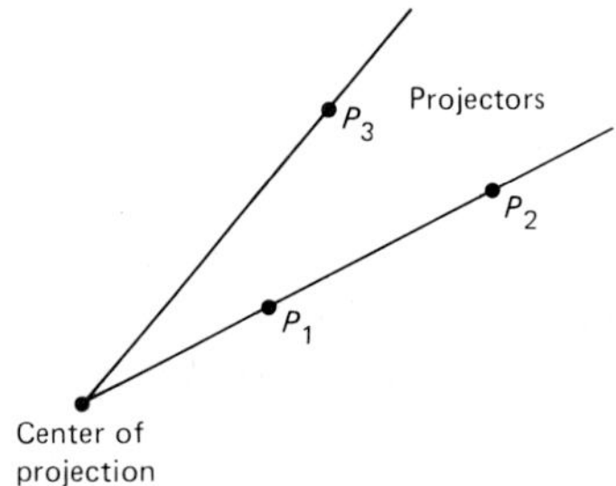

Fig. 15.1 If two points are on the same projector (here, P_1 and P_2), then one obscures the other; otherwise, they do not (like P_1 and P_3 or P_2 and P_3).

Depth comparisons are typically done after the normalizing transformation (Chapter 8) has been applied, so that parallel-projection projectors are parallel to the z-axis and perspective-projection projectors emanate from the origin. Therefore, for a parallel projection, the points are on the same projector if $x_1 = x_2$ and $y_1 = y_2$. For a perspective projection, we must unfortunately perform four divisions in order to determine if $x_1/z_1 = x_2/z_2$ and $y_1/z_1 = y_2/z_2$, in which case the points are on the same projector. Moreover, if P_1 is later compared against some P_3, two of the divisions must be repeated.

Unnecessary divisions can be avoided by transforming a 3D object so that the parallel projection of the transformed object is the same as the perspective projection of the untransformed object. Then, the test for one point obscuring another is the same as for parallel projections. The transformation distorts the objects and moves the center of projection to infinity on the negative z-axis, making the projectors parallel (see Fig. 8.40). Figure 15.2 shows the effect of this transformation. The essence of such a transformation is that it preserves relative depth, straight lines, and planes and at the same time performs the perspective foreshortening. As discussed in Chapter 8, the division which accomplishes the foreshortening is done just once per point, rather than each time two points are compared. The matrix

$$M = \begin{bmatrix} 1 & 0 & 0 & 0 \\ 0 & 1 & 0 & 0 \\ 0 & 0 & \dfrac{1}{1 - z_{v.min}} & 1 \\ 0 & 0 & \dfrac{-z_{v.min}}{1 - z_{v.min}} & 0 \end{bmatrix}. \qquad (15.1)$$

transforms the normalized perspective view volume into the rectangular parallelepiped bounded by:

$$-1 \leq x \leq 1, \qquad -1 \leq y \leq 1, \qquad 0 \leq z \leq 1. \qquad (15.2)$$

Clipping, however, cannot be done against the rectangular parallelepiped defined by Eqs. (15.2) for the reason discussed in Chapter 8: the division by z, required by M to create the parallelepiped, destroys information needed to deter-

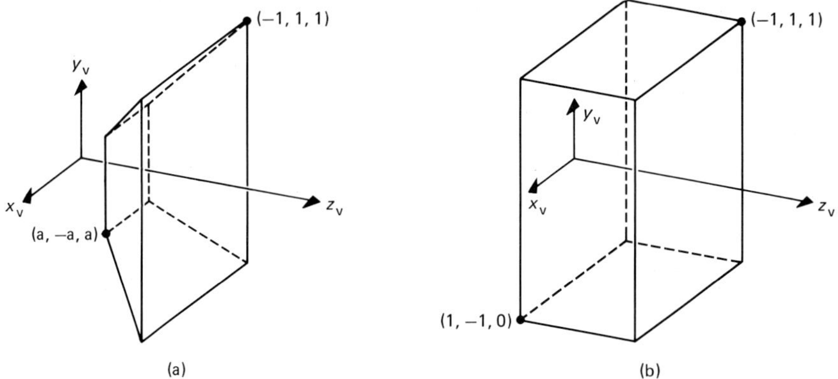

Fig. 15.2 The normalized perspective view volume (a) before and (b) after transformation by M.

mine whether a point has a positive or negative z-coordinate. Clipping can be done against the normalized truncated pyramid view volume prior to application of M, but then the clipped results would have to be multiplied by M. A more attractive alternative is to incorporate M into the perspective normalizing transformation N_{per} from Chapter 8, so that just a single matrix multiplication is needed and then clip in homogeneous coordinates prior to the division. If we call the results of that multiplication (X, Y, Z, W), then the clipping limits become:

$$-W \leq X \leq W, \qquad -W \leq Y \leq W, \qquad 0 \leq Z \leq W. \tag{15.3}$$

These limits are derived from Eqs. (15.2) by replacing x, y and z by X/W, Y/W, and Z/W, respectively, to reflect the fact that the x, y, and z of (15.2) result from division by W. After the clipping, we divide by W to obtain (x_p, y_p, z_p). (See [BLIN78a] for a discussion of clipping if the sign of W differs for the endpoints of a line.)

At this point, we can proceed with hidden-surface elimination unfettered by the complications suggested by Fig. 15.1. Of course, when a parallel projection is specified, the perspective transformation M is unnecessary, because the normalizing transformation N_{par} for parallel projections makes the projectors parallel to the z_v-axis.

15.3 AVOIDING DEPTH COMPARISONS: EXTENTS

Screen extents, introduced in Chapter 4 as a way to avoid unnecessary clipping, are used by several algorithms in order to avoid unnecessary comparisons between objects. Figure 15.3 shows two 3D polygons, their projections, and the extents surrounding the projections. In this case the extents do not overlap, so the edges of one polygon need not be tested for overlap against the edges of the other polygon.

The polygons are assumed to have been transformed by the matrix M of Section 15.2. Therefore, projection onto the xy-plane is done trivially by setting $z = 0$ for each vertex. Were M not used, the projection would include division by z.

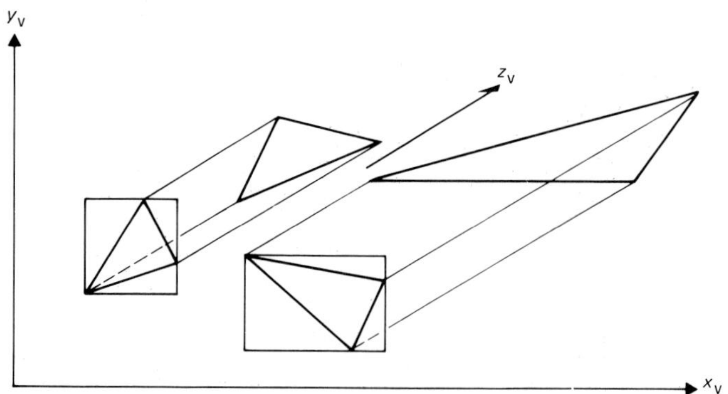

Fig. 15.3 Two polygons, their projection onto the xy-plane, and the extents surrounding the projections.

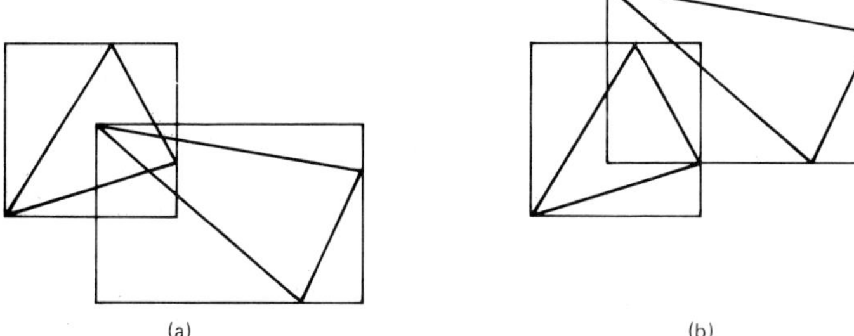

Fig. 15.4 Extents bounding polygons: (a) extents and polygons overlap; (b) extents overlap, while polygons do not.

If the extents overlap, one of two cases occurs, as shown in Fig. 15.4: either the polygons' projections also overlap, as in case (a), or they do not, as in case (b). In both cases more comparisons are performed to determine details of the overlap. In case (b), the comparisons will establish that the two polygons really do not overlap: in a sense, the overlap of the extents signalled a "false alarm."

Extents can be used as in Chapter 9, to surround the polygons themselves rather than their projections: in this case the extents become solids. Alternatively, extents can be used to bound a single dimension, in order to determine, say, whether or not two polygons overlap in z. Figure 15.5 shows the use of extents in such a case; here an extent is the infinite area bounded by the minimum and maximum z-values for each polygon. There is no overlap in z if

$$z_{\max 1} \le z_{\min 2} \quad \text{or} \quad z_{\max 2} \le z_{\min 1}. \tag{15.4}$$

In all these cases, the most complicated part of the job is finding the extent itself. This can be done by iterating through the list of vertex coordinates and recording the largest and smallest values for each coordinate.

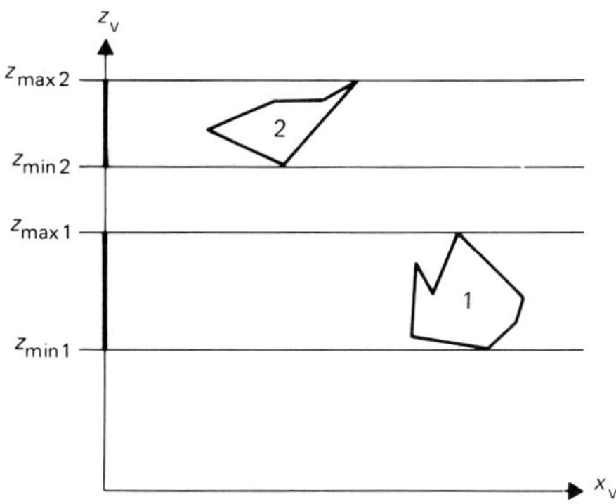

Fig. 15.5 One-dimensional extents of two polygons; extents do not overlap.

15.4 THE DEPTH-SORT ALGORITHM

This algorithm, developed by Newell, Newell, and Sancha [NEWE72], takes a straightforward approach:

1. Sort all polygons according to the largest z-coordinate of each;
2. Resolve any ambiguities this may cause when the polygons' z-extents overlap;
3. Scan-convert each polygon in descending order of largest z-coordinate.

The basic idea is to sort the polygons by their distance from the viewpoint and to place them into the refresh buffer in order of decreasing distance. Because the nearest polygons are scan-converted last, they obscure polygons which are further away by writing over them in the refresh buffer. As each polygon is scan-converted, its pixel values are computed by using one of the intensity or color shading rules in the next chapter. The algorithm is a hybrid between an image and an object space algorithm: some steps are performed in object space; others, in image space.

This algorithm can easily work with the explicit priority discussed in Section 11.9. The priority takes the place of the maximum z-value, and there can be no depth ambiguities because each priority is thought of as corresponding to a different plane of constant z.

Figure 15.6 shows some of the types of ambiguities which may need to be resolved as part of step 2. How are the ambiguities resolved? Let the polygon at the end of the sorted list of polygons be called P. Before this polygon is scan-converted into the refresh buffer, it must be tested against each polygon Q whose z-extent overlaps the z-extent of P. The test is a sequence of up to five steps which are performed in order of increasing complexity. As soon as one succeeds, P is scan-converted. The five checks are:

1. The polygons' x-extents do not overlap, so the polygons do not overlap.
2. The polygons' y-extents do not overlap, so the polygons do not overlap. (Note that tests 1 and 2 together treat extents as first introduced in the previous section.)

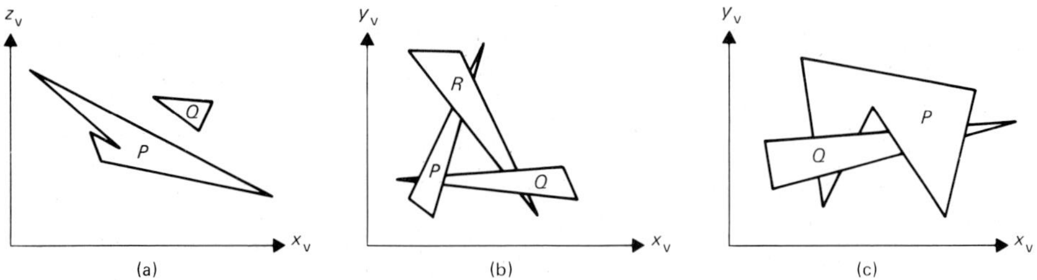

Fig. 15.6 Some cases in which z-extents of polygons overlap.

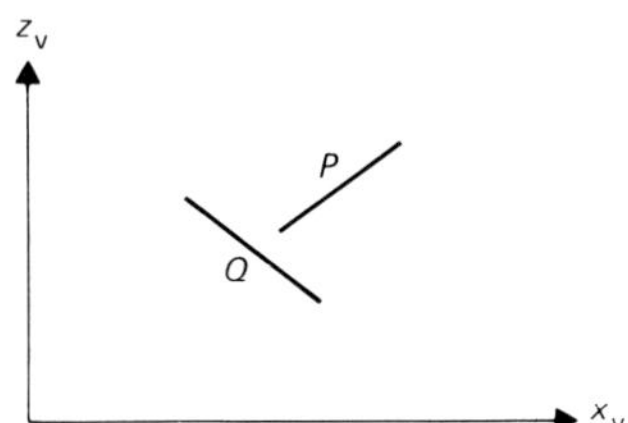

Fig. 15.7 Test 3 is true.

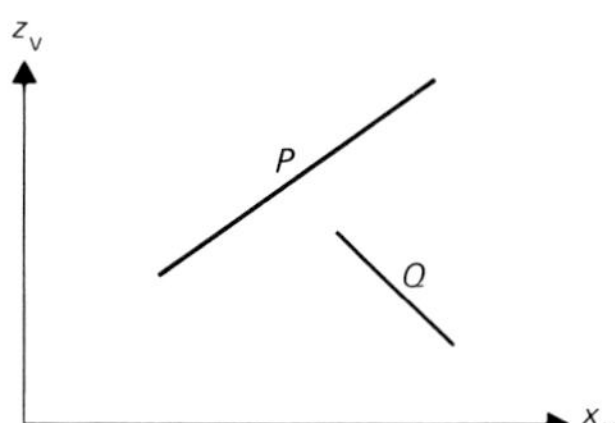

Fig. 15.8 Test 3 is false, but test 4 is true.

3. P is wholly on that side of the plane of Q which is further from the viewpoint (this is not the case in part (a) of Fig. 15.6, but is true for Fig. 15.7).
4. Q is wholly on that side of the plane of P which is nearer the viewpoint (this is not the case in part (a) of Fig. 15.6, but is true for Fig. 15.8).
5. The projections of the polygons onto the xy (screen) plane do not overlap (this is determined by comparing the edges of one polygon to the edges of the other).

Exercise 15.7 suggests a way to implement tests 3 and 4.

If all five tests fail, we assume for the moment that P actually obscures Q, and thus swap P and Q in the list, marking Q as having been moved into its new position at the end of the list. For case (a) of Fig. 15.6, this is correct: we would now compare Q against P, discovering on the basis of test 3 (with P and Q exchanged) that Q should be scan-converted first. In cases (b) and (c) of Fig. 15.6, however, Q would sooner or later be swapped again, since there is no plane which separates the polygons, and the algorithm would loop forever.

To avoid looping, we make the restriction that a polygon which is moved to the end of the list (and hence is marked) cannot be moved again. Instead, either polygon P or Q is divided by the plane of the other (see Section 11.6 on polygon clipping, treating the clip edge as a clip plane). The original polygon is discarded, its pieces are added into the list in order, and the algorithm proceeds as before.

With this algorithm, polygons toward the rear of the object are displayed first but may then be obscured. This can help the observer understand the depth relationships in the object, but this also means that some polygons are unnecessarily scan-converted. The algorithm is not well-suited for use with raster-scan film recorders, because the film, once exposed to a polygon, cannot be "unexposed" if a second polygon is later superimposed on top of the first.

Hidden-edge removal is also possible with the depth-sort algorithm. The refresh buffer is initialized to some value V_0. When a polygon is scan-converted, its edges are set to a different value V_1 and its interior pixels are all set to V_0. If the polygon overlaps one which was earlier scan-converted, setting the interior of the new polygon to V_0 will obliterate edges of the previous polygon. A similar method can be used with the other algorithms discussed in this chapter.

The previously mentioned algorithms for displaying single-valued functions of two variables work similarly to the depth sort algorithm, except the processing goes from the front (smallest z) to the back. An explicit sort is unnecessary, because the function is single-valued. As a new face on the surface representing the function is displayed, only that part of the face outside the perimeter of previously-displayed faces is displayed, and the perimeter is enlarged appropriately. The new algorithm by Sechrest and Greenberg works from bottom-to-top rather than from front-to-back [SECH81].

15.5 THE *z*-BUFFER ALGORITHM

Another algorithm, even simpler than the preceding one, is the z-buffer or depth-buffer image space algorithm. It requires that we have available not only a refresh buffer in which intensity values are stored, but also a *z-buffer* in which z-values can be stored for each pixel. The z-buffer is initialized to the largest representable z value, while the refresh buffer is initialized to the background pixel value. Then each polygon is scan-converted into the refresh buffer, but without the initial sorting required of the depth-sort algorithm. During the scan-conversion, the following steps are performed for each point (x, y) inside a polygon:

1. Calculate the polygon depth $z(x, y)$ at (x, y);
2. If $z(x, y)$ is less than the z-buffer value at (x, y), then
   a) Place $z(x, y)$ into the z-buffer at (x, y) and
   b) Place pixel value of polygon at $z(x, y)$ into the refresh buffer at (x, y).

When the condition in step 2 is true, the polygon point is closer to the viewer than the point whose intensity is currently in the refresh buffer at (x, y), and therefore new depths and intensities are recorded.

The entire process is nothing more than a search over each set of pairs $\{z_i(x, y), V_i(x, y)\}$ for fixed x and y, to find the smallest z_i. The corresponding pixel value V_i is placed in the refresh buffer. The z-buffer records the smallest z encountered for each (x, y) as the search progresses. The objects appear on the screen in the order in which the polygons are processed, not necessarily either front-to-back or back-to-front.

This algorithm has the disadvantage of requiring a large amount of space for the z-buffer, but is simple to implement. The performance of the algorithm tends to be constant because, on the average, the number of pixels covered by each polygon decreases as the number of polygons in the view volume increases. Therefore the average size of each set of pairs being searched tends to be fixed (see Section 15.8).

A given polygon is presumably scan-converted one scan line at a time. The calculation of z for each point on a scan line can be simplified by taking advantage of the fact that a polygon is flat. Normally, to calculate z, we would solve the plane equation

$$Ax + By + Cz + D = 0 \tag{15.5}$$

for the variable z:

$$z = \frac{-D - Ax - By}{C}. \tag{15.6}$$

Now, if at (x, y) Eq. (15.6) evaluates to z_1, then at $(x + \Delta x, y)$, the value of z is:

$$z_1 - \frac{A}{C}(\Delta x). \tag{15.7}$$

The quotient A/C is constant and $\Delta x = 1$, so only one subtraction is needed to calculate the depth at $(x + 1, y)$, given the depth at (x,y).

15.6 SCAN-LINE ALGORITHMS

These algorithms, developed by Wylie, Romney, Evans, and Erdahl [WYLI67], Bouknight [BOUK70a, BOUK70b], and Watkins [WATK70], operate in image space to create an image one scan line at a time. We present here the basic approach used by all three of the algorithms along with some of the embellishments of each individual algorithm.

The approach is an extension of the polygon scan-conversion algorithm described in Section 11.7 and thus uses *scan-line coherence* and *edge coherence*. The difference is that we deal not with just one polygon but with all the polygons which define an object. The first step is to create an *edge table* (ET) for all nonhorizontal edges of all polygons. Entries in the ET, which are sorted into buckets based on each edge's smaller y-coordinate and within buckets based on x and then on inverse slope, contain:

1. The x-coordinate of the end with the smaller y-coordinate;
2. The y-coordinate of the edge's other end;
3. The x-increment Δx, used in stepping from one scan line to the next (Δx is the inverse slope of the edge);
4. The polygon identification indicating to which polygon the edge belongs.

Also required is a *polygon table* (PT) which contains at least the following information for each polygon:

1. The coefficients of the plane equation;
2. Shading or color information for the polygon;
3. An in/out boolean flag, initialized to *false* and used during scan line-processing.

Figure 15.9 shows the projection of two triangles onto the *xy*-plane; hidden edges are shown as dashed lines. The sorted ET for this figure contains entries for *AB, AC, FD, FE, CB,* and *DE*. The PT has entries for *ABC* and *DEF*.

The *active-edge table* (AET) used in Section 11.7 is again developed, and it is always kept in order of increasing *x*. By the time the algorithm has progressed upwards to the scan line $y = \alpha$, the AET contains *AB* and *AC*, in that order. The edges are processed from left to right. To process *AB*, we first invert the in/out flag of polygon *ABC*. In this case the flag becomes *true;* thus the scan is now "in" the polygon, so the polygon must be considered. Now because the scan is "in" only one polygon, the polygon must be visible, so the shading for *ABC* is applied to the *span* from edge *AB* to the next edge in the AET, edge *AC*. At this edge the flag for *ABC* is inverted to *false*, so that the scan is now not "in" any polygons. Furthermore, because *AC* is the last edge in the AET, the scan-line processing is completed. The AET is updated from the ET, is again ordered on *x*, and the next scan-line is processed.

When the scan-line $y = \beta$ is encountered, the ordered AET is *AB, AC, FD,* and *FE*. Processing proceeds much as before. There are two polygons on the scan-line, but the scan is "in" only one polygon at a time.

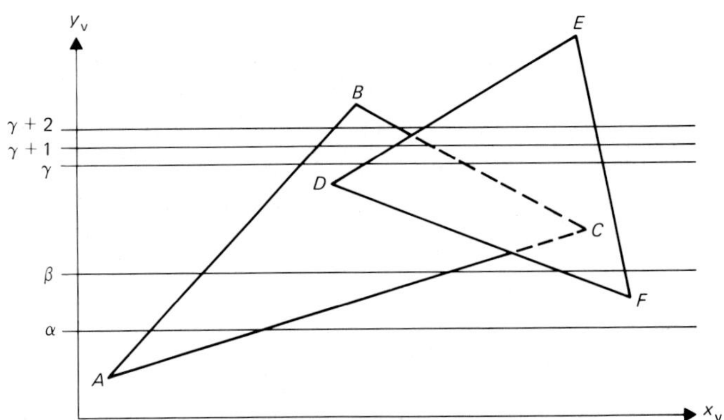

Fig. 15.9 Two polygons.

For scan-line $y = \gamma$, things are more interesting. Entering *ABC* causes its flag to become *true.* The shading rule for *ABC* is used for the span up to the next edge, *DE.* At this point the flag for *DEF* also becomes *true,* so the scan is "in" two polygons (it is useful to keep an explicit list of polygons whose in/out flag is *true* and also a count of how many polygons are on the list). We obviously must now decide whether *ABC* or *DEF* is closer to the viewer. This is determined by evaluating the plane equations of both polygons for z, at $y = \gamma$ and with x equal to the intersection of $y = \gamma$ with edge *DE.* This value of x is in the AET entry for *DE.* In our example, *DEF* has a smaller z and thus is visible. Therefore the shading for *DEF* is used for the span to edge *BC,* at which point *ABC*'s flag becomes *false* and the scan is again "in" only one polygon *DEF* whose shading rule continues in use to edge *FE.* Figure 15.10 shows the relationship of the two triangles and the $y = \gamma$ plane; the two thick lines are the intersections of the triangle with the plane.

Suppose there was a large polygon *GHIJ* behind both *ABC* and *DEF,* as in Fig. 15.11. Then, when the $y = \gamma$ scan comes to edge *CB,* the scan is still "in" polygons *DEF* and *GHIJ,* so depth calculations are again performed. However, these calculations can be avoided if we assume that none of the polygons *penetrates* one another (a reasonable assumption when real objects are being modeled). This assumption means that when the scan leaves *ABC,* the depth relationship between *DEF* and *GHIJ* cannot change and that we continue to be "in" *DEF.* Therefore depth computations are unnecessary when the scan leaves an obscured polygon and are required only when leaving an obscuring polygon.

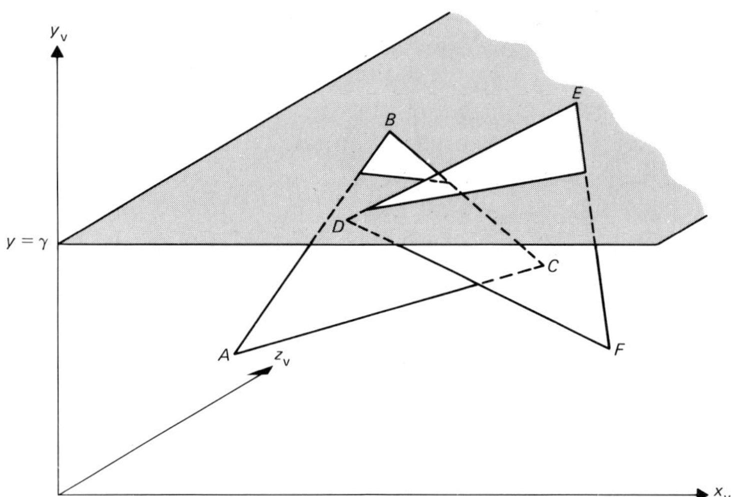

Fig. 15.10 Intersections of triangles *ABC* and *DEF* with plane $y = \gamma$.

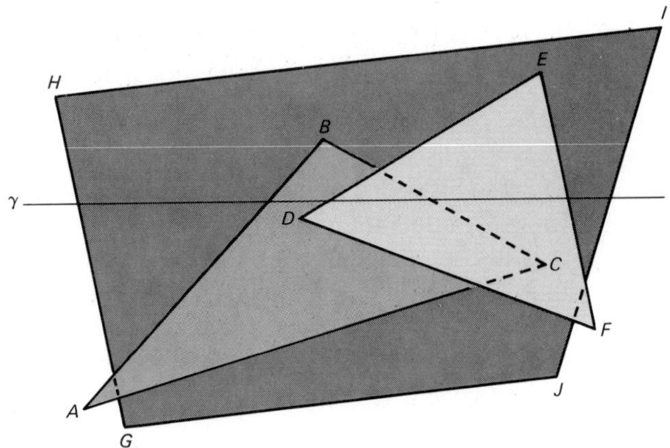

Fig. 15.11 Three nonpenetrating polygons.

Figure 15.12 shows penetrating polygons. To use this algorithm properly, we break up *KLM* into *KLL'M'* and *L'MM'*, introducing the *false edge M'L'*. Alternatively, the algorithm can be modified to find the point of penetration on a scan-line as the scan line is processed.

Another algorithm modification is to use *depth coherence*. If the same edges are in the AET on one scan line as in the immediately preceding scan line and if they are in the same order, then no changes in depth relationships have occurred and no new depth computations are needed. The record of visible spans on the previous scan line (*AB* to *DE* and *DE* to *EF* in Fig. 15.9) then defines the spans on the next scan line. Such is the case for scan lines $y = \gamma$ and $y = \gamma + 1$ in Fig. 15.9, for both of which the spans from *AB* to *DE* and from *DE* to *FE* are visible.

In Fig. 15.9, the depth coherence is lost in going from $y = \gamma + 1$ to $y = \gamma + 2$ because edges *DE* and *CB* change order in the AET (a situation which the algorithm

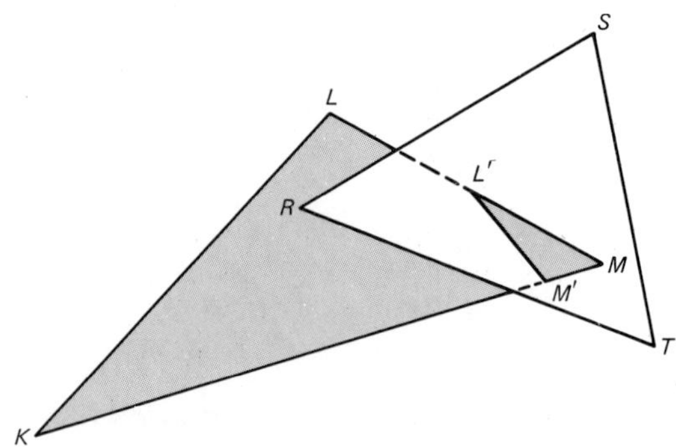

Fig. 15.12 Polygon *KLM* pierces polygon *RST* at the line *L'M'*.

must accommodate). The visible spans therefore change and in this case become *AB* to *CB* and *DE* to *FE*. Hamlin and Gear [HAML77] show how depth coherence can sometimes be maintained even when edges do change order in the AET.

We have not yet discussed how the background is treated. The simplest way is for the refresh buffer to be initialized to some appropriate pixel value, so the algorithm need only process scan lines that intersect edges. Another way is to include in the object definition a large square polygon that is further away from the viewpoint than any others, is parallel to the projection plane, and has the desired shading. A final alternative is to modify the algorithm to explicitly place the background pixel value into the refresh buffer whenever the scan is not "in" any polygon.

15.7 AREA-SUBDIVISION ALGORITHMS

The area-subdivision algorithms all follow the "divide and conquer" strategy seen earlier in the line and polygon clipping algorithms, and thus are a departure from the strategies used by the previous algorithms. An area of the projection plane image is examined. If it is "easy" to decide which polygon or polygons are visible in the area, the appropriate polygons are displayed. Otherwise the area is subdivided into smaller areas and the decision logic is recursively applied to each of the smaller areas. As the areas become smaller, fewer and fewer polygons will overlap each area, and ultimately a decision will be possible. This is clearly an image space approach. It exploits *area coherence,* the tendency for at least small areas of an image to be contained in at most a single polygon.

At each stage in the recursive subdivision process, the projection of each polygon has one of four relationships to the area of interest (see Fig. 15.13):

a) *Surrounding polygons* completely contain the (shaded) area of interest;
b) *Intersecting polygons* intersect the area;
c) *Contained polygons* are completely inside the area;
d) *Disjoint polygons* are completely outside the area.

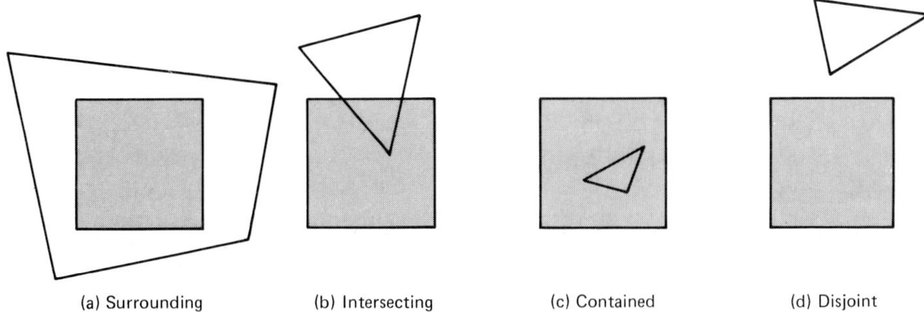

Fig. 15.13 Four relations of polygons to an area element.

Disjoint polygons clearly have no influence on the area. The part of an intersecting polygon that is outside the area is also irrelevant, while the part of an intersecting polygon that is interior to the area is the same as a contained polygon and can be treated as such.

There are four cases in which a decision about an area can be made easily so it need not be further divided to be conquered. They are:

1. All of the polygons are disjoint from the area, so the background pixel value can be displayed in the area.
2. There is either only one intersecting or only one contained polygon. The area is first filled with the background pixel value and then the polygon is scan-converted. (On many displays it is more convenient to initially set the entire refresh buffer to the background.) If the polygon is intersecting, only the contained part is scan-converted.
3. There is a single surrounding polygon, but no intersecting or contained polygons. The area is filled with the pixel value of the surrounding polygon.
4. More than one polygon is intersecting, contained in, or surrounding the area, and at least one of them is a surrounding polygon. In this case we use a simple test to determine whether one of the surrounding polygons is in front of all the other polygons: the z-coordinates of the planes of all surrounding, intersecting, and contained polygons are computed at the four corners of the area; if there is a surrounding polygon whose four such z-coordinates are smaller (closer to the viewpoint) than any of the other z-coordinates, then the entire area can be filled with the pixel value of this surrounding polygon.

Cases 1, 2, and 3 are simple to detect. Case 4 is further illustrated in Fig. 15.14. In (a), the four intersections of the surrounding polygon are all closer to the viewpoint (which is at infinity on the $-z_v$-axis) than any of the other intersections. Thus, the entire area is filled with the surrounding polygon's value. In (b), no decision can be made, even though the surrounding polygon seems to be in front of the intersecting polygon, because on the left the plane of the intersecting polygon is in front of the plane of the surrounding polygon. Note that the Newell, Newell, and Sancha algorithm would accept this case without further subdivision if the intersecting polygon is wholly on the side of the surrounding polygon which is further from the viewpoint. The present algorithm, however, always subdivides the area to simplify the problem.

After subdivision, only contained and intersecting polygons need to be reexamined: surrounding and disjoint polygons of the original area remain surrounding and disjoint polygons of each subdivided area. Subdivision normally ends when the resolution of the display device has been reached: on a 512 × 512 raster display, at most nine subdivisions would be made. If after this maximum number of subdivisions none of cases 1 to 4 has occurred, then the depth of all relevant polygons is

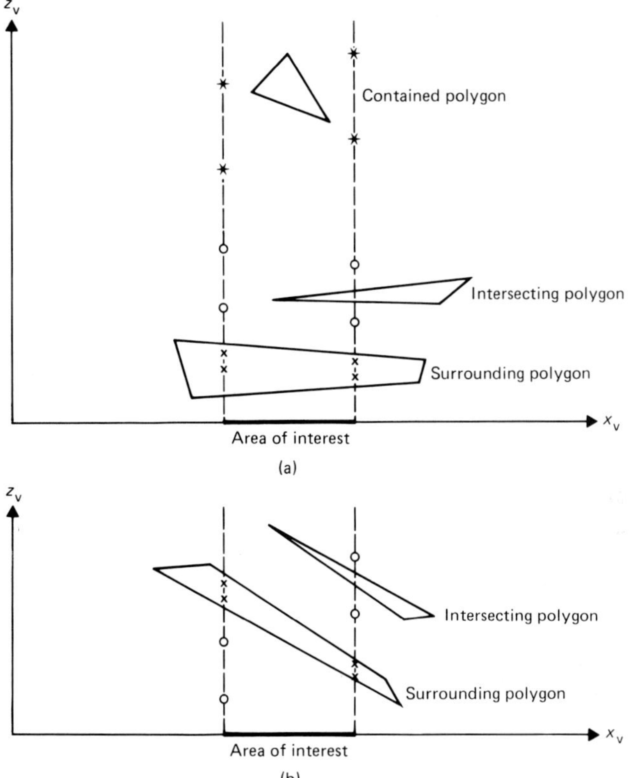

Fig. 15.14 Two examples for case 4 in recursive subdivision. Legend: ×—intersection of surrounding polygon plane; ∘—intersection of intersecting polygon plane; ∗—intersection of contained polygon plane.

computed at the center of this pixel-sized indivisible area. The polygon with the smallest z-coordinate defines the shading of the area. Alternatively, for antialiasing, several further levels of subdivision could be used to determine the composite pixel value which blends together all polygons visible in the area (see Section 11.7.5).

The original subdivision algorithm developed by Warnock [WARN69] subdivided an area into four square areas. Figure 15.15 shows a simple scene and the subdivisions necessary for its display. The numbers in each subdivided area correspond to the four stopping rules listed above. Unnumbered areas are those in which none of the four cases is true. In this example, subdivision is limited to a depth of five for purposes of illustration.

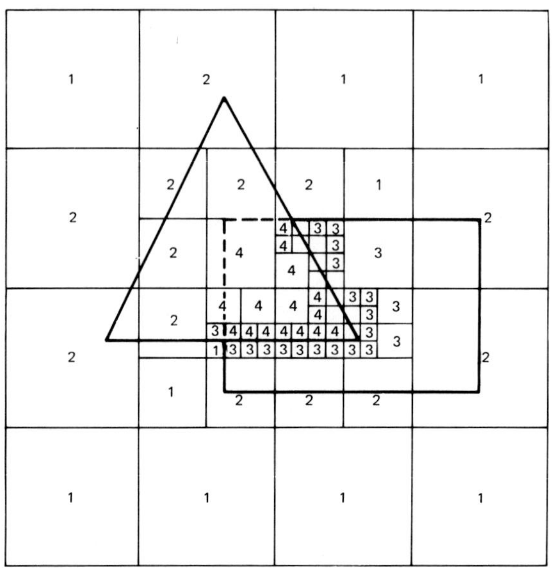

Fig. 15.15 Area subdivision into squares.

A common variation of the equal-area subdivision is to divide about the vertex of a polygon (if there is a vertex in the area) in an attempt to avoid unnecessary subdivisions. This strategy can obviously work, as shown in Fig. 15.16.

Another strategy, developed by Weiler and Atherton [WEIL77], subdivides the screen area along polygon boundaries rather than along rectangle boundaries. The first step, not mandatory but useful to improve efficiency, is to sort polygons on some value of z, such as the minimum z-coordinate of a polygon's vertices. The polygon at the head of the sorted list is used for the initial subdivision, which is performed by using the algorithm briefly described in Section 11.6.2. For the example in Figs. 15.15 and 15.16, the triangle would be used. The resulting subdivision of the rectangle into two polygons is shown in Fig. 15.17. Now, considering the triangle as our area of interest and using our earlier terminology, we classify the triangle as a surrounding polygon, the smaller part (A) of the rectangle as a contained polygon, and the larger part (B) of the rectangle as a disjoint polygon. Case 4 is then found to be true, because the surrounding polygon (the triangle) is well forward of the contained polygon. Therefore, the shading rule for the triangle is applied to the triangular area C. The larger part (B) of the rectangle has only itself as a surrounding polygon, with the two other polygons A and C being disjoint. This is a case 3 situation, so the shading rule for the rectangle is applied to area B.

The power of the Weiler–Atherton subdivision algorithm is that it can greatly reduce the number of subdivision steps from that required by the two other methods. On the other hand, each subdivision takes more work than in the other methods.

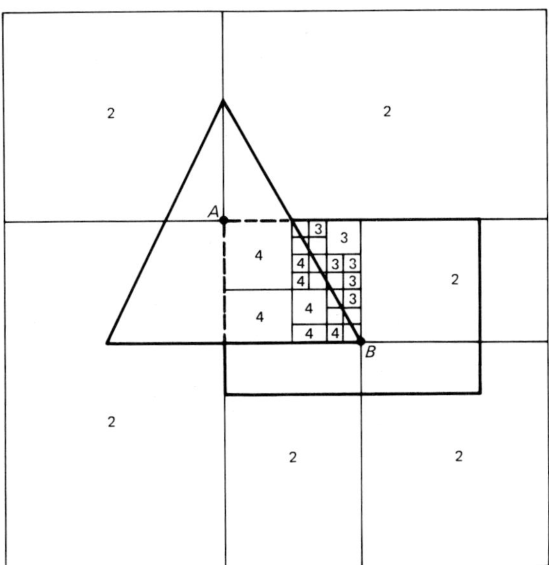

Fig. 15.16 Area subdivision about circled polygon vertices. First subdivision is at vertex *A*; second, at vertex *B*.

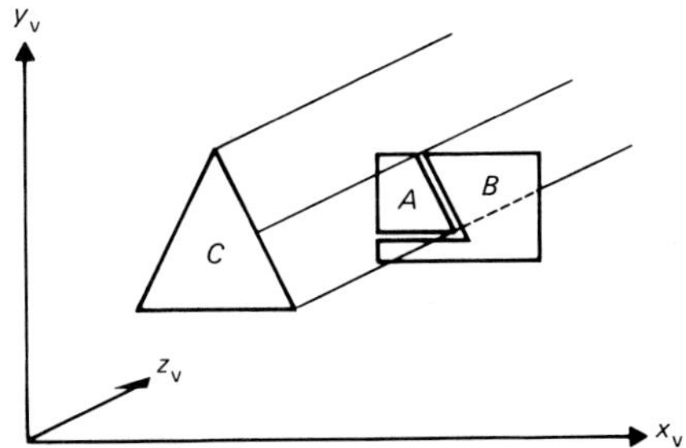

Fig. 15.17 Subdivision of simple scene about triangular polygon.

15.8 ALGORITHM EFFICIENCY

Sutherland, Sproull, and Schumacker [SUTH74c] point out that hidden-surface removal can be considered as a large sorting process. This is not surprising, because we have seen many instances of sorting and searching in the algorithms. A major factor in these algorithm's execution efficiency is use of an efficient sorting algorithm. Equally important is avoiding any more sorting than is absolutely necessary, a goal typically achieved by using coherence. For example, the scan-line algorithm uses scan-line coherence to eliminate the need to do a complete sort on x for each scan line. A new algorithm by Hubschman and Zucker uses frame-to-frame coherence to avoid unnecessary comparisons when working with animation sequences [HUBS81].

The depth-sort algorithm sorts on z and then on x and y (by use of extents); it is thus called a zxy algorithm. The scan-line algorithm sorts on y (by use of a bucket sort) and then on x (initially with an insertion sort, then with a bubble sort as each scan line is processed), and finally searches in z for the polygon nearest the viewpoint; it is thus called an yxz algorithm. The area subdivision does a parallel sort on x and y and then searches in z, and hence is an $(xy)z$ algorithm. The z-buffer algorithm does no explicit sorting and searches only in z; it is called an (xyz) algorithm.

Sancha has convincingly argued that the order of sorting is unimportant: there is no intrinsic benefit in first sorting on y in preference to x or z, etc. [SUTH74c]. This is because the *average* object is equally complex in all three dimensions. This is not to say, however, that all algorithms are equally efficient: they differ in how effectively coherence is used to avoid sorting and in the use of space–time trade-offs. The results reported in [SUTH74c, Table VII], which compare the estimated performance of the four basic algorithms we have presented, are summarized in Table 15.1. It is suggested in [SUTH74c] that because these are only estimates, small differences should be ignored, but that ". . . we feel free to make order of magnitude comparisons between the various algorithms to learn something about the effectiveness of the various methods."

The depth-sort algorithm is efficient for small numbers of polygons because the simple overlap tests almost always suffice to decide if a polygon can be scan-converted. With more polygons, the more complex tests are more frequently needed, and polygon subdivision is more likely to be required. The z-buffer algorithm has constant performance because, as the number of polygons in a scene increases, the number of pixels covered by a single polygon decreases. On the other hand, its memory needs are high. The individual tests and calculations involved in area subdivision are relatively complex, so it is generally slower than the other methods.

TABLE 15.1 RELATIVE ESTIMATED PERFORMANCE OF FOUR HIDDEN-SURFACE REMOVAL ALGORITHMS

	Number of polygonal faces in scene		
Algorithm	100	2500	60000
Depth sort	1*	10	507
z-buffer	54	54	54
Scan line	5	21	100
Warnock area subdivision	11	64	307

*Entries normalized so this case is unity.

15.9 ALGORITHMS FOR CURVED SURFACES

All of the algorithms thus far described are for objects defined by planar polygonal faces. Objects defined by curved surfaces must first be approximated by many small facets before any of the algorithms can be used. While this can be done, it is often preferable to deal directly with curved surfaces.

Quadratic surfaces are in general non-planar, and have the analytical form:

$$a_1x^2 + a_2y^2 + a_3z^2 + a_4xy + a_5yz + a_6zx + a_7x + a_8y + a_9z + a_{10} = 0. \quad (15.8)$$

If a_1 through a_6 are all zero, the surface degenerates to a plane. Familiar objects composed of quadratic surfaces include the sphere (one surface), the capped cylinder (three surfaces), the capped cone (two surfaces), and the ellipsoid (one surface). The Mathematical Applications Group, Inc. (MAGI) has developed a complete set of programs for defining and displaying objects made up of quadratic surfaces [MATH68]. The object in Color Plate 14 is so defined.

Several algorithms have been developed by Weiss [WEIS66], Woon [WOON71], Mahl [MAHL72], and Levin [LEVI76] for removing the hidden surfaces of objects defined by quadratic surfaces. They all find the intersections of two quadratic surfaces, yielding a fourth-order equation in x, y, and z. The roots of the equation must be found numerically. Levin reduces this to a second-order problem by parameterizing the intersection curves.

Spheres, being a special case of quadratic surfaces, are easier to work with, and are of particular interest because molecules are typically displayed as collections of colored spheres (see Color Plate 15). A number of molecule-display algorithms have been developed [KNOW77, MAX79, PORT78, PORT79, STAU78].

Even more flexibility can be had with the parametric bicubic surfaces of Chapter 13 because they are more general and allow tangent continuity at patch boundaries. Catmull [CATM75] developed the first algorithm for display of such surfaces. A patch is subdivided (in s and t) until its projection onto the display is about the size of a pixel. A z-buffer algorithm is used to determine whether the small area is visible (with respect to all previously processed patches). If so, a shade for the small area is calculated and placed in the refresh buffer. Catmull's approach, though slow, is effective and has been influential in setting directions for the work of others, as typified in [BLIN76b] and [WILL78].

Since then, two different algorithms have been developed by Blinn and Whitted [BLIN80]. They are both scan-line algorithms. Blinn deals directly with the parametric representation. For the scan-line $y = \alpha$, he finds all s and t values that satisfy the equation

$$y(s, t) - \alpha = 0. \quad (15.9)$$

These values of s and t are then used to evaluate $x(s,t)$ and $z(s,t)$. Unfortunately, Eq. (15.9) does not have a closed-form solution and its roots are therefore found numerically using Newton's method. There are also special cases in which the roots cannot be found, causing the algorithm to fail. Similarly, Whitted uses numerical methods plus some approximations to the curve in the xz plane defined by the intersection of the $y = \alpha$ plane with the bicubic surface patch.

The most fruitful approach to date is based on the adaptive subdivision of each bicubic patch until each subdivided patch is within some given tolerance of being flat. The tolerance depends upon the resolution of the display device and the orientation of the area being subdivided with respect to the projection plane, so unnecessary subdivisions are eliminated. Once sufficiently subdivided, the small polygonal areas defined by the four corners of each patch are processed by a scan-line algorithm, allowing polygonal and bicubic surfaces to be readily intermixed.

Algorithms that use this basic idea have been developed by Carpenter and Lane [BLIN80, LANE79] and Clark. They differ in the choice of basis functions used to derive the subdivision difference equations for the surface patches and in the test for "flatness." The Carpenter and Lane algorithm does the subdivisions only as required when the scan line being processed begins to intersect a patch, rather than in an advance preprocessing step as Clark's algorithm does. This saves large amounts of memory, but on the other hand, Clark's method may require fewer subdivisions and is guaranteed not to introduce tears into the bicubic surface patch at the subdivisions.

Whitted [WHIT80], expanding on work by Appel [APPE68] and MAGI [MATH68], has developed an elegant and simple (though slow) algorithm that can process polygonal, bicubic, quadratic, and other patches. At the same time, it does shading calculations and can also deal with transparent and translucent surfaces. It will be described in the next chapter, which deals with shading.

EXERCISES

15.1 Prove that the transformation M in Section 15.2 preserves (a) straight lines, (b) planes, and (c) depth relationships.

15.2 Given a plane $Ax + By + Cz + D = 0$, apply M from Section 15.2 and find the new coefficients of the plane equation.

15.3 Which of the hidden-surface algorithms can be readily adapted to perform anti-aliasing at polygon edges?

15.4 How can the scan-line algorithm be extended to deal with polygons with shared edges? Should shared edges be represented once, as a shared edge, or twice, once for each polygon it borders, with no record being kept of the fact that it is a shared edge? When the depth of two polygons is evaluated at their common shared edge, the depths will of course be equal. Which polygon should be declared visible, given that the scan is entering both?

15.5 The area-subdivision algorithm generates a quad tree (tree with nodes of out-degree four). Show the quad trees corresponding to Figs. 15.15 and 15.16. Label all nodes on the first tree to indicate how the square (S) and triangle (T) relate to the node, as (a) disjoint, (b) contained, (c) intersecting, and (d) surrounding.

15.6 For each of the four hidden-surface algorithms we have discussed, explain how piercing polygons would be handled. Are they a special case which must be explicitly treated or do they "fall out" as part of the basic algorithm?

15.7 Consider tests 3 and 4 of the depth-sort algorithm. How might they be implemented efficiently? Consider examining the sign of the equation of the plane of polygon P for each vertex of polygon Q, and vice versa. How does one know to which side of the plane a positive value of the equation corresponds?

15.8 How could the algorithms described here be modified to display hidden edges as dotted lines?

15.9 A *polyhedron,* discussed briefly in Chapter 13 on object representations, is a closed volume bounded by polygons. A *convex* polyhedron has interior angles less than 180°, and thus from any viewpoint each polygonal surface of the polyhedron is either completely visible or completely hidden. Find a simple test to determine the visibility of the polygons of a convex polyhedron which involves the direction of projection and the normals to the polygons. *Note:* For the test to be valid, the normal used for each polygon must consistently be inward (pointing into the polyhedron) or outward. The test can be applied to eliminate some faces from further consideration by the actual hidden-surface algorithm.

15.10 Consider the appropriateness of adapting each of the four hidden-surface algorithms to hidden-edge algorithms to use with a vector output device, without use of an intermediate representation in raster form. Which algorithms could be adapted? How? Which algorithms could not be adapted? Why not?

15.11 How can these algorithms be adapted to work with polygons containing holes?

16 Shading Models

16.1 INTRODUCTION

The second step in creating an image, after hidden surfaces have been removed, is to shade the visible surfaces, taking into account the light sources, surface characteristics, and the positions and orientations of the surfaces and sources. The basic concepts used in this chapter were introduced in Section 14.4, so we begin at once, working first with very simple shading models and moving toward the more complex.

16.2 DIFFUSE REFLECTION AND AMBIENT LIGHT

Dull matte surfaces exhibit *diffuse reflection,* scattering light equally in all directions, so that the surfaces appear to have the same brightness from *all* viewing angles. For such surfaces, Lambert's cosine law relates the amount of reflected light to the cosine of the angle θ between the direction $\bar{L}$ to the point light source of intensity I_p and the normal $\bar{N}$ to the surface, shown in Fig. 16.1. That is, the amount of reflected light seen by the viewer is independent of the viewer's position. The diffuse illumination is:

$$I_d = I_p k_d \cos\theta. \tag{16.1}$$

The diffuse-reflection coefficient k_d is a constant between 0 and 1 and varies from one material to another. Assuming that the vectors $\bar{L}$ and $\bar{N}$ have been normalized, we can rewrite Eq. (16.1) by using the dot product:

$$I_d = I_p k_d(\bar{L} \cdot \bar{N}). \tag{16.2}$$

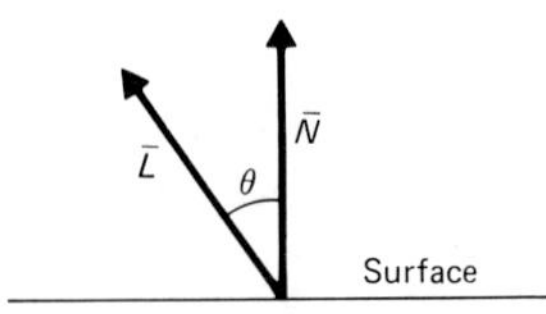

Fig. 16.1 Incident light and surface normal.

Objects illuminated with only a point light source look harsh. The effect is similar to that seen when pointing a flashlight at an object in an otherwise black room. This is because, unlike in most real visual environments, there is no ambient light. This is a light of uniform brightness caused by the multiple reflections of light from the many surfaces present in most real environments. An object shielded from the rays coming directly from a point light source is still visible due to ambient light.

The shading rule:

$$I = I_a k_a + I_p k_d(\bar{L} \cdot \bar{N}) \tag{16.3}$$

includes the term I_a to account for ambient light, while k_a indicates how much of the ambient light is reflected from the object's surfaces.

The point source of light is most conveniently assumed to be coincident with the viewer's eye, so no shadows can be cast. This also means that light rays striking a surface will all be parallel (after the application of matrix M of (15.1) for perspective projections). But now if two surfaces of the same color are parallel and one overlaps the other in the image, their surface normals are the same, so the shading on the surfaces will be equal and the surfaces will be indistinguishable. This can be corrected by recognizing that light energy falls off as the inverse square of the distance the light travels from the source to the surface and back to the eye at the viewpoint. Calling this distance R, we have:

$$I = I_a k_a + I_p k_d(\bar{L} \cdot \bar{N})/R^2. \tag{16.4}$$

In practice, however, this does not work well either. With the light at infinity for a parallel projection, the distance R is also infinite. Even for a perspective projection, $1/R^2$ can have a wide range of values, because the viewpoint is often relatively close to the object. This gives considerably different shades to surfaces that have the same angle θ between $\bar{N}$ and $\bar{L}$. More realistic effects are actually achieved by replacing the R^2 with $r + k$, where k is a constant and r is the distance from the perspective viewpoint to the surface:

$$I = I_a k_a + I_p k_d(\bar{L} \cdot \bar{N})/(r + k). \tag{16.5}$$

Figure 16.8 uses this shading rule.

Diffuse reflection of light from colored surfaces is treated by writing separate equations for cyan, magenta, and yellow light, with the triple (k_{dc}, k_{dm}, k_{dy}) defining the reflection constants for each color. The subtractive primaries are used here because the reflection of light is a subtractive process, as we shall see in the next chapter. For a yellow surface, for example, we would have $k_{dy} = 1.0$, $k_{dm} = 0.0$, and $k_{dc} = 0.0$. That is, all yellow light is reflected, while all the magenta and cyan light is absorbed. If the illuminating light is colored, its three subtractive primary components are reflected in proportion to k_{dc}, k_{dm}, and k_{dy}, respectively, and the ambient light is the same color as the point source. Therefore, for the cyan component,

$$I_c = I_{ac}k_{ac} + I_{pc}k_{dc}(\bar{L} \cdot \bar{N})/(r + k), \tag{16.6}$$

with similar equations for I_m and I_y, the magenta and yellow components.

16.3 SPECULAR REFLECTION

Specular reflection is observed on any shiny surface. Illuminate an apple with a bright light: the *highlight* is caused by specular reflection, while the light reflected from the rest of the apple is caused by diffuse reflection. Also note that at the highlight, the apple appears to be not red, but rather white, which is the color of the incident light.

Now move your head and notice how the highlight also moves. This is because shiny surfaces reflect light unequally in different directions: on a perfectly shiny surface (such as a perfect mirror), light is reflected *only* in the direction for which the angles of incidence and reflection are equal. This means that the viewer can see specularly reflected light only when the angle α in Fig. 16.2 is zero. For nonperfect reflectors, such as the apple, the intensity of the reflected light falls off sharply as α increases. The shading model developed by Phong Bui-Tuong [BUIT75] approximates this rapid fall-off by $\cos^n\alpha$. The value of n typically varies from 1 to 200, depending on the surface. For a perfect reflector, n would be infinite. This $\cos^n\alpha$ model for specular reflection is a reasonable approximation but is based on an empirical observation, not on a fundamental model of the specular reflection process.

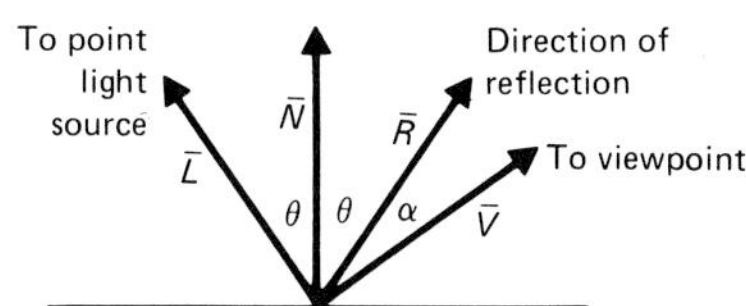

Fig. 16.2 Specular reflection.

For real materials, the amount of incident light which is specularly reflected depends on the angle of incidence θ. If we write the fraction of specularly reflected light as $W(\theta)$, then:

$$I = I_a k_a + \frac{I_p}{r + k} [k_d \cos\theta + W(\theta) \cos^n\alpha]. \tag{16.7}$$

If $\bar{R}$ and $\bar{V}$, the vectors in the direction of reflection and the viewpoint, are normalized, then $\cos\alpha = \bar{R} \cdot \bar{V}$. Very often, $W(\theta)$ is set to a constant k_s, which is selected experimentally to produce aesthetically pleasing results. Then Eq. (16.7) can be rewritten as:

$$I = I_a k_a + \frac{I_p}{r + k} [k_d(\bar{L} \cdot \bar{N}) + k_s(\bar{R} \cdot \bar{V})^n]. \tag{16.8}$$

When dealing with color, the cyan equation is

$$I_c = I_{ac} k_{ac} + \frac{I_{pc}}{r + k}\left[k_{dc}\,(\bar{L} \cdot \bar{N}) + k_s(\bar{R} \cdot \bar{V})^n \right], \tag{16.9}$$

with similar equations for magenta and yellow. Note that k_s is *not* dependent on the color of the surface.

If the light source is at infinity, $\bar{L} \cdot \bar{N}$ is constant for a given polygon, while $\bar{R} \cdot \bar{V}$ varies across the polygon. With bicubic surfaces, or for a light source which is not at infinity, both $\bar{L} \cdot \bar{N}$ and $\bar{R} \cdot \bar{V}$ vary across the surface. Calculating these dot products for each pixel on a scan line can be time consuming, so Phong developed an efficient method for their incremental evaluation along a scan line.

The Torrance–Sparrow model [TORR66, TORR67], developed by illumination engineers, is a theoretically-based model of a reflecting surface, in contrast to the empirically-derived Phong $\cos^n\alpha$ model. The surface is assumed to be a collection of microscopic facets, each a perfect reflector. The orientation of each facet is given by the Gaussian probability distribution function. The geometry of the facets and the direction of the light (assumed to be from an infinitely distant source, so all rays are parallel) determines the intensity and direction of specular reflection as a function of I_p, $\bar{N}$, $\bar{L}$, and $\bar{V}$. Experimental measurements show a very good correspondence between the actual reflection and the reflection predicted by this model.

Figure 16.3 illustrates a collection of facets, of which only those that reflect light toward the viewer are considered in the model. In this example, only facets *a, c,* and *e* are so oriented; they illustrate the three reflection situations that the model accounts for. All of facet *a* is exposed to the light, and all rays are reflected toward the viewer. Facet *c,* however, is partially shielded from the light as shown by the dotted line. Only the part of the facet that is exposed to the rays causes reflection toward the viewer. Facet *e* is fully exposed to the rays, but some of the reflected rays actually hit surface *f* and are reflected in some other direction, becoming part of the diffuse reflection.

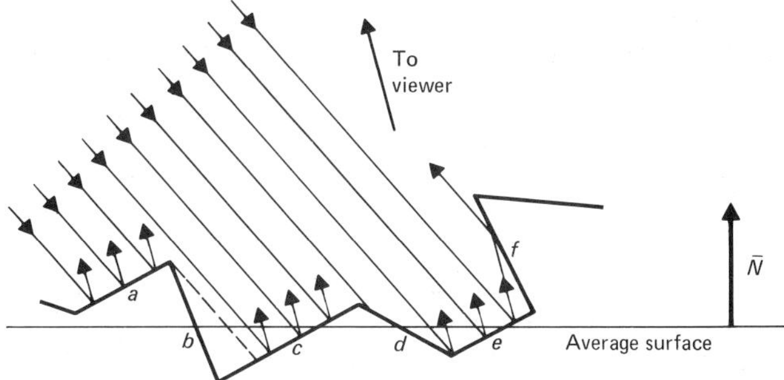

Fig. 16.3 Light rays reflecting from microfacets of surface.

Blinn adapted the Torrance-Sparrow model to computer graphics, giving the mathematical details and comparing it to the Phong model in [BLIN77a]. He created Figs. 16.4 and 16.5, which represent the reflected illumination from a surface for angles of incidence of 30° and 70°, respectively. In each figure the vertical arrow represents the surface normal; the incoming arrow, the direction of light rays; and the outgoing arrow, the direction of reflection for a perfect reflector. The rounded part of each figure is the diffuse reflection, while the bump is the specular reflection. For the 30° case the figures are nearly similar, but for 70°, the Torrance-Sparrow model has much higher specular reflectance, and the peak occurs at an angle greater than the angle of incidence. Figure 16.6, also by Blinn, shows the very real difference in the visual effect of the two models as a light source moves away from the viewpoint to the side and then to the rear of a metallic sphere.

As the quest for realism continues, even more sophisticated shading models are being developed: [COOK81] is an excellent example. In the next section we shall see how to apply any shading model to surfaces defined by polygon meshes.

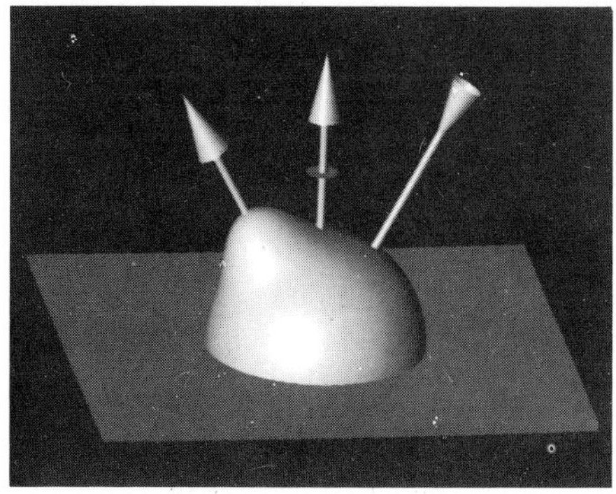

(a) Phong model

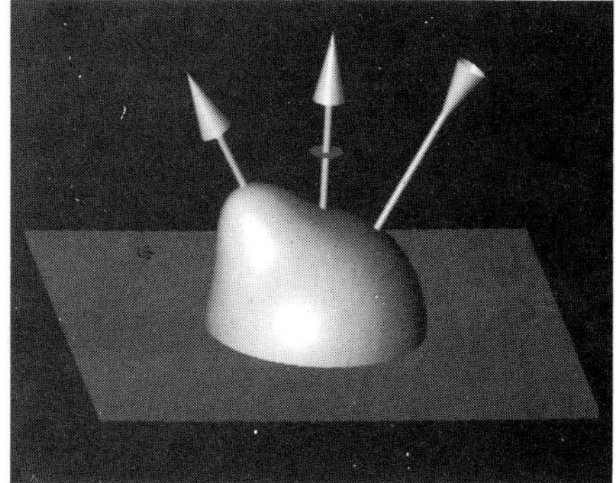

(b) Torrance-Sparrow model

Fig. 16.4 Comparison of Phong and Torrance–Sparrow models for a 30° angle of incident light (by J. Blinn [BLIN77a], courtesy University of Utah).

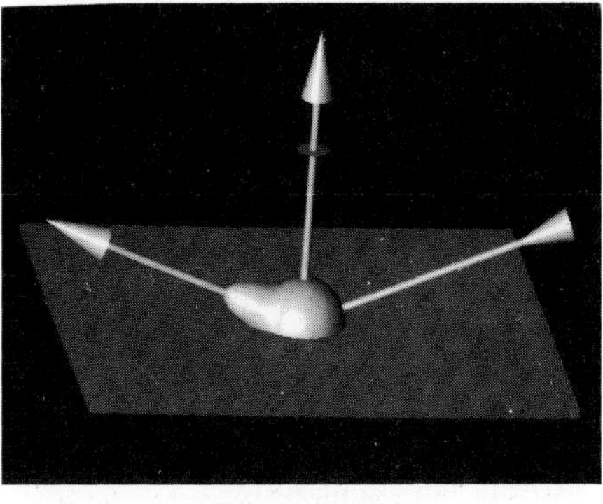

(a) Phong model

(b) Torrance-Sparrow model

Fig. 16.5 Comparison of Phong and Torrance–Sparrow models for a 70° angle of incident light (by J. Blinn [BLIN77a], courtesy University of Utah).

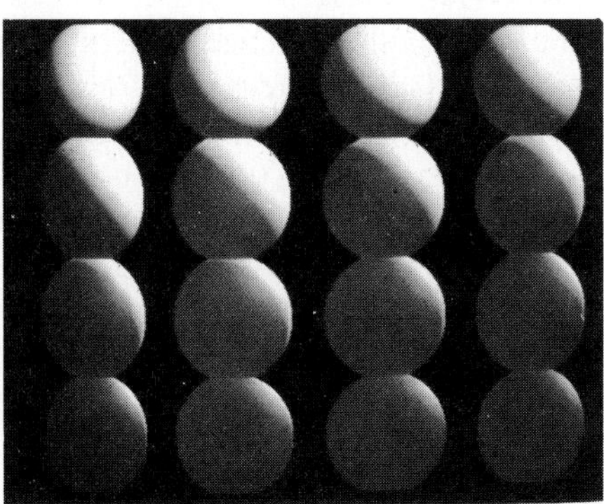

(a) Phong model

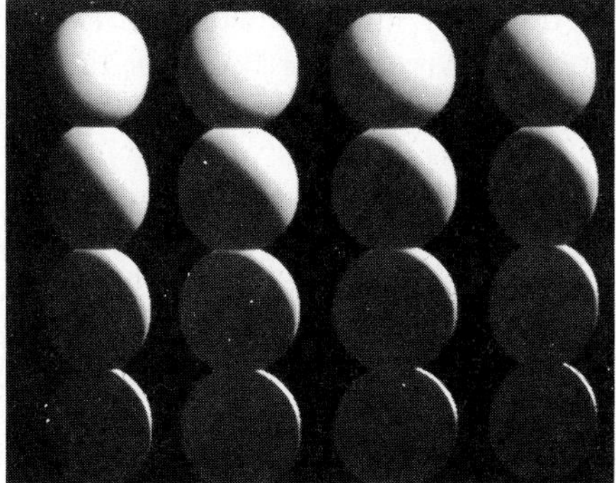

(b) Torrance-Sparrow model

Fig. 16.6 Comparison of the Phong and Torrance–Sparrow models for a metallic sphere illuminated by a light source from different directions. Differences are most apparent for back-lit cases (bottom rows) (by J. Blinn [BLIN77a], courtesy University of Utah).

16.4 POLYGON MESH SHADING

There are three basic ways to shade objects defined by polygon meshes. In order of increasing complexity, they are: constant shading, intensity interpolation shading, and normal-vector interpolation shading. In each case, any of the shading models from the previous two sections can be used. Recall that color shading just involves three equations rather than one.

Constant shading calculates a single intensity value for shading an entire polygon. Several assumptions are made:

1. The light source is at infinity, so $\overline{N} \cdot \overline{L}$ is constant across the polygonal face;
2. The viewer is at infinity, so $\overline{N} \cdot \overline{V}$ is constant across the polygon face;
3. The polygon represents the actual surface being modeled, and is not an approximation to a curved surface.

If either of the first two assumptions is unacceptable, then an average $\overline{L}$ and $\overline{V}$ might be used, perhaps calculated at the center of the polygon.

The final assumption is most often the one which is incorrect and has a much more substantial effect on the resulting image than the other two. The effect is that each visible polygonal facet of the approximated surface is distinguishable, because each is a slightly different intensity than its neighbors. The difference in shading on adjacent facets is accentuated by the Mach band effect, which was discovered in 1865 by E. Mach and is described in detail in [RATL65]. The effect is one of exaggeration of intensity change at any edge where there is a discontinuity in magnitude or slope of intensity. Figure 16.7 shows, for two separate cases, the actual and perceived changes in intensity along a surface. The effect is caused by *lateral inhibition* of the receptors in the eye, whose response to light is influenced by adjacent receptors in inverse relation to the distance to the adjacent receptor. Receptors immediately to the brighter side of an intensity change have more response than those further from the edge, because they receive less inhibition from their neighbors on the darker side. Similarly, receptors immediately to the darker side of an intensity change will have less response than those further into the darker area, because they receive more inhibition from their neighbors on the brighter side.

Figure 16.8(b) shows a car with constant shading. The Mach band effect is quite evident. Even though the polygonal patches are quite noticeable, the image is much more realistic than that in Fig. 16.8(a), which shows only the polygon edges.

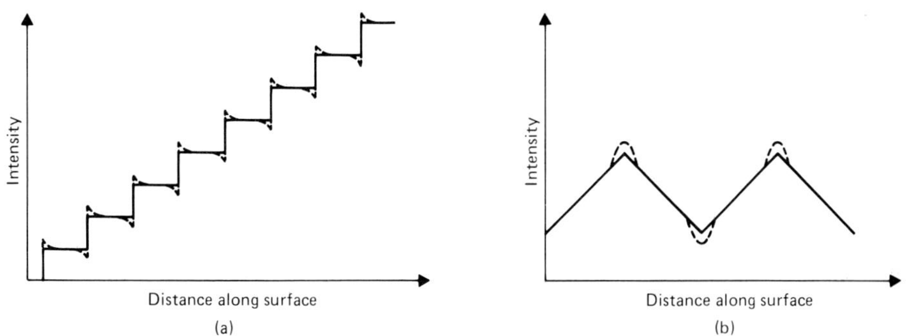

Fig. 16.7 Mach band effect—actual and perceived intensities: dashed lines—perceived intensity; solid lines—actual intensity.

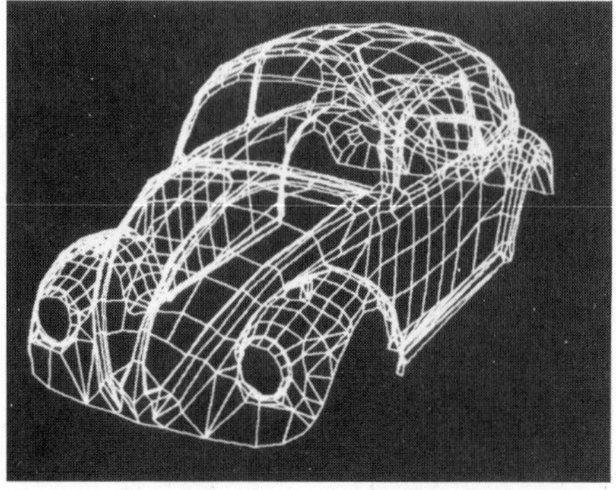

(a) Polygon outlines

(b) Constant shading

(c) Gouraud shading

Fig. 16.8 Car body displayed three ways (courtesy University of Utah).

Intensity interpolation shading, usually known from the name of its developer as *Gouraud* shading [GOUR71], eliminates intensity discontinuities. Figure 16.8(c) shows a Gouraud-shaded car. The intensity ridge running down the hood on the right side of the picture, close to the fender, is a Mach band caused by a rapid change in the slope of the intensity curve: Gouraud shading does not completely eliminate such intensity changes.

The Gouraud shading process consists of four steps. First, surface normals are calculated. Second, *vertex normals* are calculated by averaging the surface normals of all polygonal facets that share the vertex (Fig. 16.9). If an edge is meant to be visible (such as at the joint between a planes' wing and body), then two vertex normals, one for each side of the edge, are found by separately averaging the normals of polygons on each side of the edge. Third, *vertex intensities* are found by using the vertex normals with any desired shading model. Finally, each polygon is shaded by linear interpolation of vertex intensities along each edge and then between edges along each scan line (Fig. 16.10).

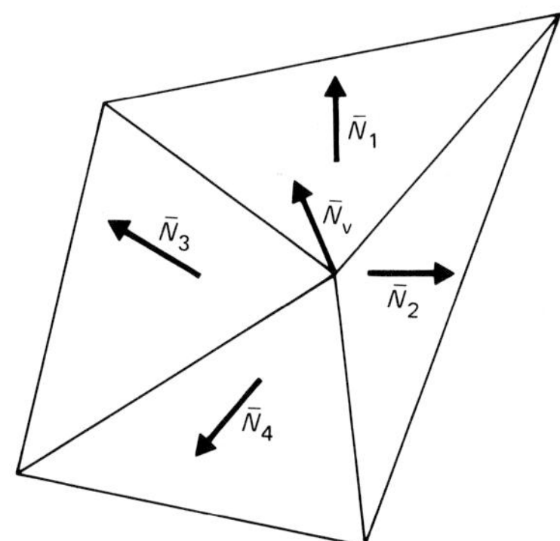

Fig. 16.9 Vertex normals: $\overline{N}_v = (\overline{N}_1 + \overline{N}_2 + \overline{N}_3 + \overline{N}_4)/4$.

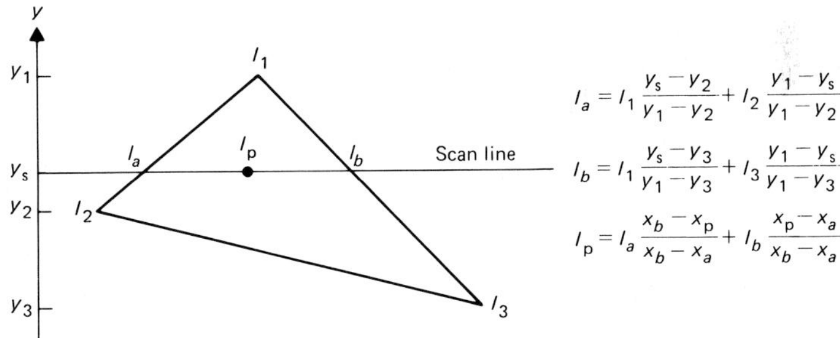

Fig. 16.10 Intensity interpolation along polygon edges: I_a is interpolated from I_1 and I_2; I_b from I_1 and I_3; I_p from I_a and I_b.

The interpolation along edges can easily be integrated with the scan-line hidden-surface algorithm. With each edge we store the starting intensity and the change of intensity for each unit change in y. Filling in a visible span of a scan line is done by interpolating the intensity values of the two edges that bound the span. For colored objects, each color component would be interpolated separately.

Normal-vector interpolation shading, developed by Phong Bui-Tuong [BUIT75], interpolates the surface normal vector $\overline{N}$ rather than intensity across a visible span of a polygon on a scan line, between starting and ending normals which are themselves interpolations along polygon edges from vertex normals computed just as with intensity interpolation shading. The interpolation along edges can again be made by means of incremental calculations, with all three components of the normal vector being incremented from scan line to scan line.

At each pixel along a scan line a new intensity calculation is performed by using any of the shading models. Substantial improvements over intensity interpolation occur when a specular-reflectance model is used, because highlights are more faithfully reproduced. But even without specular reflectance, the results of normal-vector interpolation are superior to intensity interpolation because an approximation to the normal is used at each point. This reduces Mach band problems, but greatly increases the cost of applying the shading model.

To shade bicubic surface patches, the surface normal is calculated for each pixel from the surface equations in Chapter 13. This is also an expensive process. Then any of the shading models can be used to calculate intensity. But before a shading model can be applied to planar or bicubic surfaces, we must know which, if any, light sources actually illuminate a point. This means that shadows must be considered.

16.5 SHADOWS

Shadow algorithms for point light sources are identical to hidden-surface algorithms! The hidden-surface algorithm determines which surfaces can be seen from the viewpoint, and the shadow algorithm determines which surfaces can be "seen" from the light source. The surfaces that are visible both from the viewpoint and from the light source are not in shadow. Those that are visible from the viewpoint but not from the light source are in shadow. This logic can easily be extended to multiple light sources. Note that with this simple approach, shadows from distributed light sources have not been modeled. If they were, both the umbra and penumbra of the shadow would have to be calculated.

Recognizing that shadow and hidden-surface algorithms are the same suggests that we in fact process the object description by using the same algorithm, once for the viewpoint, and once for each point light source. Then the results are combined to determine which parts are visible to the viewer and to one or more light sources, and then the scene is shaded. By organizing the computations properly, it is possible to perform the shadow calculation just once for a series of scenes of the same objects seen from many different viewpoints, so long as the light sources are fixed with respect to the objects. This is due to the fact that shadows are not dependent on the viewpoint.

Several ways to generate shadows, primarily for polygonal objects, are reviewed in [CROW77a]. In a variation of one of the approaches [ATHE78], any object polygon which is completely or partially visible from the light source has added to it a second coplanar polygon which is the visible (from the light source) part of the object polygon. The second polygon is calculated using the polygon clipper of Chapter 11. These *surface detail polygons* are not used for hidden-surface removal, but are used for shading. The part of a polygon that is visible from the viewpoint and is covered by one of these polygons is shaded to account both for the diffuse and specular reflection from the light source, as well as for ambient light. The part of a polygon that is visible from the viewpoint but is *not* covered by a surface detail polygon is therefore in shadow and is shaded only to account for ambient light. Color Plate 17 was generated this way. Figure 16.11 shows the detail polygons created on two surfaces of a cube when they are partially shadowed by a triangle. The detail polygons cover those parts of the cube which *are* visible from the light source.

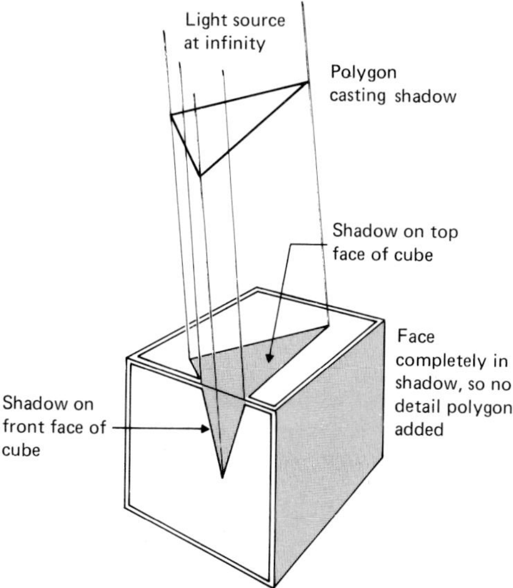

Fig. 16.11 Polygons added to cube to show parts illuminated by light source.

Another way to do shadowing, called *ray tracing,* deals with surfaces that transmit as well as reflect light and is discussed in the next section.

16.6 LIGHT-TRANSMITTING SURFACES

Just as surfaces can have specular and diffuse reflection, so too they can have specular and diffuse transmittance. Specular transmission of light occurs through *transparent* materials, such as glass or polished lucite. We can usually see clearly through transparent material, although in general the rays will have been refracted, that is, bent. Diffuse transmission occurs through translucent materials such as frosted glass. Rays passing through *translucent* materials are jumbled by surface or internal irregularities. Thus, an object seen through translucent material is very blurred.

Little work with diffuse transmission of light has been pursued, but specular transmission has been modeled in several ways. The simplest way is to ignore refraction, so that light rays are not bent as they pass through the surface. This means that whatever is visible on the line of sight passing through a transparent surface is also geometrically located on that line of sight. With refraction, the geometrical and optical lines of sight are different. In Fig. 16.12, if refraction is considered, object A is visible through the transparent object along the line of sight shown, while if refraction is ignored, object B is visible.

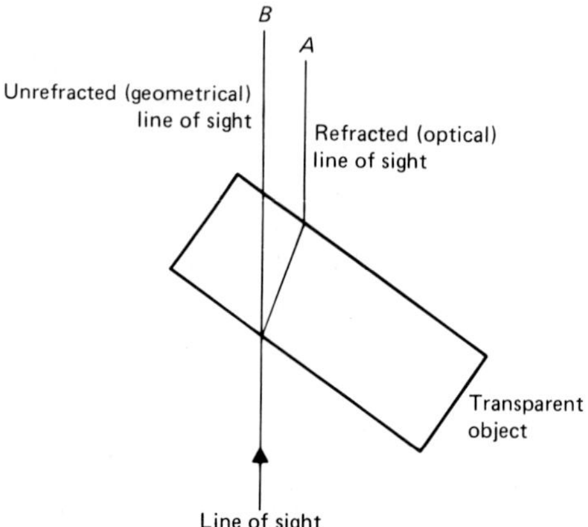

Fig. 16.12 Refraction.

Several hidden-surface algorithms can be adapted to model unrefracted transmission of light. Of the four algorithms discussed in the preceding chapter, only the *z*-buffer algorithm cannot be adapted because the surfaces are processed in arbitrary order. With the scan-line algorithm, when the forward polygon is transparent, we simply determine the nearest of the other polygons the scan is "in," as in Fig. 16.13. The shading calculation is then a weighted sum of the individual shades calculated for the two polygons:

$$I = kI_1 + (1 - k)I_2. \tag{16.10}$$

The parameter k measures the "transparency" of polygon 1: when k is 0, the polygon is perfectly transparent and contributes nothing to the intensity I. When k is selected as 1, polygon 1 is opaque, and transmits no light.

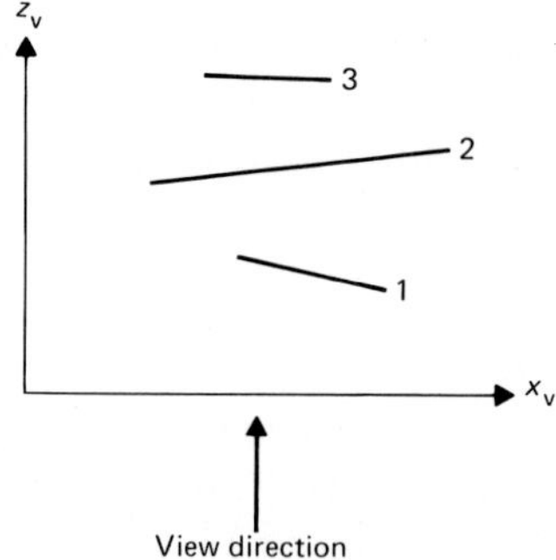

Fig. 16.13 Cross section of three polygons on plane of constant y_v. Polygon 2 can be seen through the transparent polygon 1.

Whitted [WHIT80] and Kay [KAY79] have implemented simple but powerful approaches based on earlier ray-tracing algorithms [APPE68, MATH68]. Just as Blinn successfully turned to a theoretical rather than an empirical specular-reflection model, so too Whitted and Kay turned to basic optics. Whitted's approach is more general (but computationally more expensive) than Kay's, and is briefly described here. The fundamental idea is to trace light rays and to determine which ones end up at the viewpoint. Unfortunately, an infinite number of rays emanate from each point light source, and most of them never reach the viewpoint. Thus, the tracing starts at the viewpoint and traces rays backwards through each pixel to their origin.

In general, a ray of light striking the surface of an object breaks into three parts: diffusely reflected light, specularly reflected light, and transmitted (and hence refracted) light. Similarly, a ray of light leaving the surface of an object is in general the sum of contributions from three sources. This means that each time a ray leaves an object, up to three new rays should be traced. Unfortunately, diffuse reflection generates an infinite number of rays, so only rays from specular reflection and refraction are traced; Eq. (16.3) is used to model ambient and diffuse light.

Figure 16.14 shows the tree grown in the process of tracing a particular ray backwards: S_i is the light ray that comes into surface i at such an angle that it is specularly reflected and leaves as part of the outgoing ray; similarly, T_i is the light ray incident on surface i such that it is transmitted and leaves as part of the outgoing ray. Each node of the tree corresponds to a surface. After the tree is completely grown, the intensities at each leaf node are computed and then used to compute the intensity at their parent nodes, until the root node is reached.

An infinite number of rays could be traced backwards, but only those rays that pass through the viewpoint (i.e., center of projection) and the *corners* of pixels are actually traced. This permits anti-aliasing to be performed, because the intensities can be averaged to calculate the intensity of the pixel. If the four rays through the corners of a pixel subtend a volume in space that contains a lot of fine detail, the pixel is subdivided and additional rays are traced, to help the anti-aliasing process.

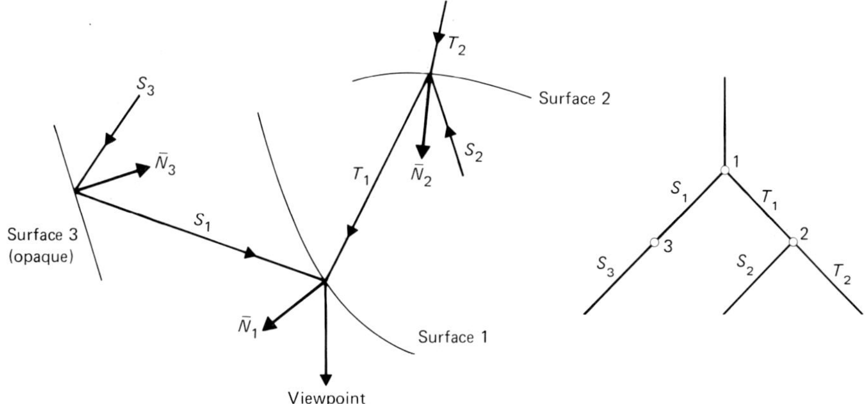

Fig. 16.14 Tree grown from tracing a single ray to viewer.

If the display device resolution is $N \times M$ pixels, then at least $(N + 1)(M + 1)$ rays are traced. Each ray must be tested for intersection with each object in the scene. The testing is expedited by the use of 3D extents around each object. Only if the ray pierces the extent is the object itself examined to find an intersection. If an intersection is found, the surface properties are examined to determine whether to split the ray. Each resulting ray is itself traced by growing the tree described previously. Even with the use of extents, however, ray tracing is a very slow process—slower than any of the others we have discussed. Color Plate 20 shows the results of this algorithm.

As ray tracing is developed further, speed increases will undoubtedly come from the application of coherence or other properties of the objects being displayed. Ray tracing also lends itself to parallel processing, because rays can be traced independently of one another; VLSI implementations may therefore be expected.

16.7 SURFACE DETAIL

All the shading algorithms we have described, when applied to either planar or bicubic surfaces, produce very smooth and uniform surfaces—in marked contrast to most of the surfaces we see and feel. There are two types of surface detail: color and texture. Color detail is applied to a smooth surface without appearing to change the geometry of the surface, while texture detail gives the appearance of a roughened surface.

Color detail at a gross level can be easily introduced with surface detail polygons, to show features (such as doors, windows, and lettering) on a base polygon (such as the side of a building). Surface detail polygons are coplanar with the base polygon and are flagged in the data structure so the hidden-surface removal algorithm can give them priority over the base polygon. The surface detail polygons that represent shadows are flagged separately (see Section 16.5).

As color detail becomes finer and more intricate, explicit modeling with polygons becomes less practical. An alternative—mapping a digitized photograph of detail onto a surface—was pioneered by Catmull [CATM74] and refined by Blinn and Newell [BLIN76b]. Other adaptations are described in [AOKI78, DUNG78]. The idea is that a pattern array that represents a digitized image is mapped onto either a planar or a curved surface, as described in Section 11.8.4. Values from the pattern array are used to scale the diffuse component of intensity.

One pixel on the screen may often be covered by a number of cells from the pattern array. To avoid aliasing problems, all relevant cells must be considered. This is done by determining the four points on the pattern array which map onto the four corners of the screen pixel. The points on the pattern array are connected to form a four-sided polygon, and the values of the contained cells are weighted by the fraction of each cell contained in the polygon and then summed. As shown in Fig. 16.15, the mapping is done in two steps: the fixed mapping of the pattern onto the object surface, and then the viewing transformation mapping of the object onto the screen. Figure 16.16 is an example of mapping a photograph onto a surface.

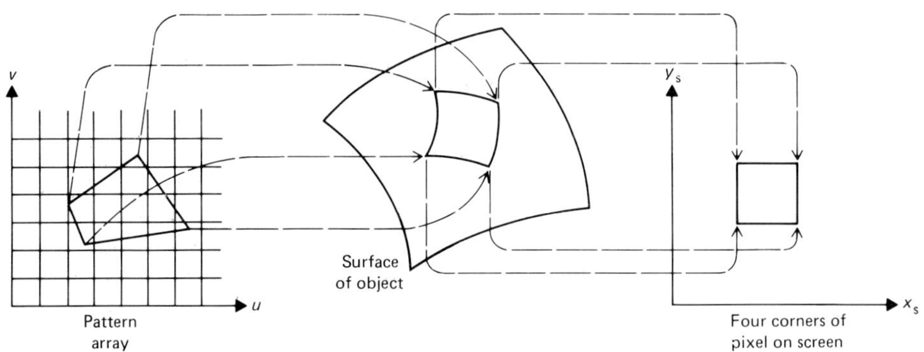

Fig. 16.15 Mapping from pixel array to object surface to screen. Averaged value of cells in pattern array is placed in pixel.

Fig. 16.16 Picture mapped onto bicubic surface (cylinder) (courtesy E. Catmull).

Mapping of pattern arrays affects a surface's coloration, but the surface continues to appear geometrically smooth. Two approaches are available for providing *texture detail* on surfaces. The first, developed by Blinn [BLIN78b], avoids explicit geometrical modeling of the texture while at the same time producing very satisfactory visual effects. Blinn recognized that modeling the actual geometry of the roughness was unnecessary, and instead suggested that the surface normal be perturbed before it is used in the shading model, just as slight roughness in a surface would perturb the surface normal. This method is not quite realistic because the texture does not affect the silhouette edges of textured objects, but this is generally acceptable. Color Plates 18 and 19 show a random texture applied to a doughnut and a regular texture applied to a strawberry.

The second method, recently applied independently by Carpenter as well as by Fournier and Fussell and described in [CARP82, MAND82], uses *fractal surfaces,* a class of irregular shapes that are probabilistically defined and accurately model natural shapes, such as terrains, coastlines, river networks, snowflakes, and tree branches (see Color Plates 21(a) and 21(b)). Color Plate 21(b), a very convincing image of a jagged mountain, was created by first approximating the mountain with a mesh of quadrilaterals (which need not be planar). Each was then recursively subdivided a number of times to create the rough, jagged terrain. A quadrilateral is subdivided as shown in Fig. 16.17: the four edges of the original (shaded) quadrilateral are subdivided by using a random function to calculate points P_1, P_2, P_3, and P_4. These points and the random function are used to find P_5, and then the four new quadilaterals are defined. Thus, many quadrilaterals are defined from the initial approximation. The final steps are to perform hidden-surface removal combined with application of an appropriate shading model.

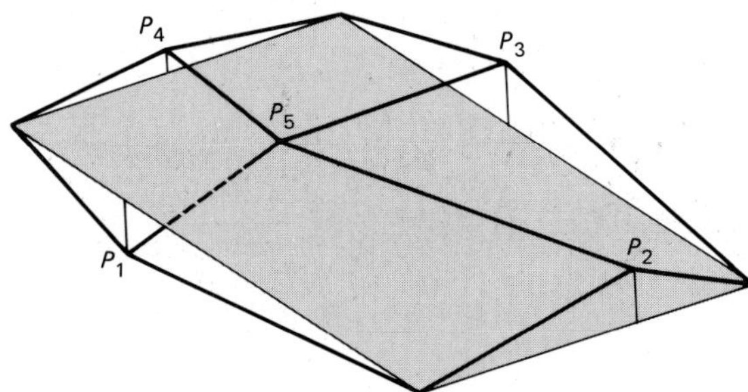

Fig. 16.17 Subdivision of a quadrilateral (shaded) into four smaller quadrilaterals. The five points are found by using a random function. Applied recursively, the process creates irregular surfaces.

EXERCISES

16.1 In Gouraud linear-interpolation shading, Mach bands can occur where there is a large change in slope of the intensity-versus-distance plot. Work out a method of using higher-order interpolation across a scan line to eliminate these discontinuities.

16.2 Investigate Torrance–Sparrow and Trowbridge–Reitz shading methods [BLIN77a, BLIN78c]. Can interpolation of the normal vector be used as in Phong shading?

16.3 Describe how the depth sort and the area-subdivision hidden-surface algorithms can be modified to accomodate nonrefracting transparent surfaces. Why is refraction difficult to integrate into these algorithms?

16.4 Why can the z-buffer algorithm not process transparent surfaces?

16.5 Design an algorithm to efficiently determine whether a line pierces a 3D solid rectangular extent defined by x_{min}, x_{max}, y_{min}, y_{max}, z_{min}, and z_{max}.

16.6 Another type of 3D extent is a sphere that completely contains an object. Develop an algorithm to determine efficiently whether a line pierces a sphere of radius r centered at point (x_0, y_0, z_0).

16.7 Compare the efficiencies of the algorithms developed in Exercises 16.5 and 16.6. Which one of these algorithms should be used in the ray-tracing algorithm?

17 Intensity and Color

17.1 INTRODUCTION

The growth of raster graphics has made the use of color and gray scale an integral part of contemporary computer graphics. Color is an immensely complex subject that deals with both physics and physiology. Many professional careers have been fruitfully devoted to developing theories, measurement techniques, and standards for color, and yet no one theory of human color perception is universally accepted. We cannot, in this brief chapter, even begin to survey the field of color. Instead, our objective is to introduce those color concepts that are most relevant to computer graphics. Readers desiring a deeper knowledge of the subject are referred to the vast literature on color, such as [HUNT75, JUDD75, and WASS78].

The color of an object depends not only on the object itself, but also on the light source illuminating the object and on the human visual system. Furthermore, some objects reflect light (wall, desk, paper) while other objects also transmit light (cellophane, glass). If red light is used to illuminate a surface that reflects only blue light, the surface will appear black. Similarly, a green light viewed through glass that transmits only red will also appear black. We will initially avoid many of these complications by concentrating on achromatic colors, i.e., colors described as black, dark gray, light gray, and white.

17.2 ACHROMATIC COLOR: INTENSITY

An observer of achromatic colors does not experience any of the color sensations we associate with red, blue, yellow, etc. Achromatic light is what we see on a black and white TV set. The only attribute of achromatic light is its intensity, or amount. It is useful to associate a scalar with the intensity, defining 0 as black and 1 as white. A value of 0.5 would be a medium gray.

A black and white TV can produce many different levels of gray at a single pixel position. Line printers, pen plotters, and electrostatic plotters produce only two levels: the white (or light gray) of the paper and the black (or dark gray) of the ink or toner deposited on the paper. Certain techniques (discussed below) allow such inherently *bi-level* devices to be used to produce additional intensity levels.

A natural concern and question is: "How many intensities are enough?" By "enough" we will mean the number needed to reproduce a continuous-tone black and white photo in such a way that the reproduction appears to be continuous. Figure 17.1 shows a continuous-tone photo, while the succeeding five figures show the same photo reproduced at 4, 8, 16, 32, and 64 levels. With four and eight levels, there is significant *contouring*: the transitions from one intensity level to the next are conspicuous. Contouring is barely detectable with 32 levels, and disappears with 64. We thus conclude that 64 intensity levels are generally sufficient for reproducing continuous-tone black and white images without contouring. When some computer-generated images are shown on a raster display with 128 intensity levels, however, contouring is still present, suggesting that 256 levels may sometimes be needed.

17.2.1 Selecting Intensities—Gamma Correction

Which 256 intensity levels should be used? We surely will not use 128 in the range of 0 to 0.1 and 128 more in the range of 0.9 to 1.0. The transition from 0.1 to 0.9 will certainly be visible, causing contouring. We might be inclined to distribute the levels evenly over the range of 0 to 1, but this ignores an important characteristic of the eye, which is sensitive to ratios of intensity levels rather than to their absolute values. That is, we perceive the intensities 0.10 and 0.11 to differ just as much as do the intensities 0.50 and 0.55. Therefore, the intensity levels should be spaced logarithmically rather than linearly. To have 256 intensities starting with the lowest attainable intensity I_0, and up to a maximum intensity of 1.0 (each r times higher than the preceding intensity, we derive the following relations:

$$I_0 = I_0, \quad I_1 = rI_0, \quad I_2 = rI_1 = r^2 I_0, \quad I_3 = rI_2 = r^3 I_0, \quad \ldots, \quad I_{255} = r^{255} I_0 = 1.$$

Therefore,

$$r = \left(\frac{1}{I_0}\right)^{1/255} \quad \text{and} \quad I_j = I_0^{(255-j)/255}, \quad 0 \le j \le 255. \tag{17.1}$$

Displaying the intensities defined by (17.1) on a CRT is a tricky process, and recording the intensities on film is even more difficult. This is because there are nonlinearities in the CRT and film. For instance, the intensity of light output by a phosphor is related to the number of electrons N in the beam by

$$I = kN^{\gamma} \tag{17.2}$$

for constants k and γ. The number of electrons N is proportional to the control grid voltage which is in turn proportional to the intensity value V specified for the pixel.

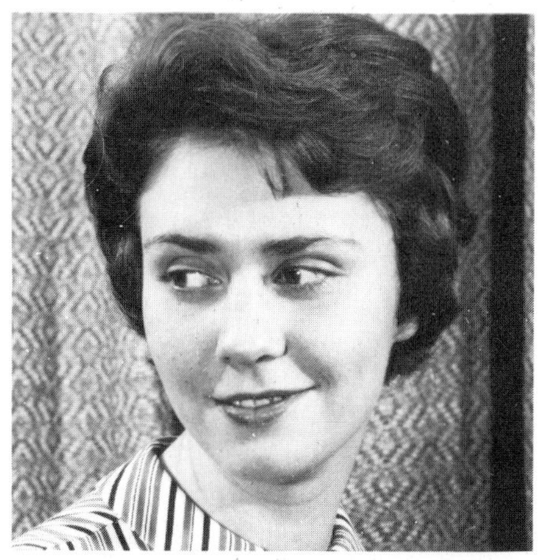

Fig. 17.1 Continuous-tone photo (courtesy J. Jarvis, Bell Laboratories).

Fig. 17.2 Photo reproduced with 4-level display (courtesy J. Jarvis, Bell Laboratories).

Fig. 17.3 Photo reproduced with 8-level display (courtesy J. Jarvis, Bell Laboratories).

Fig. 17.4 Photo reproduced with 16-level display. Some contouring remains on face; fine detail in hair begins to stand out (courtesy J. Jarvis, Bell Laboratories).

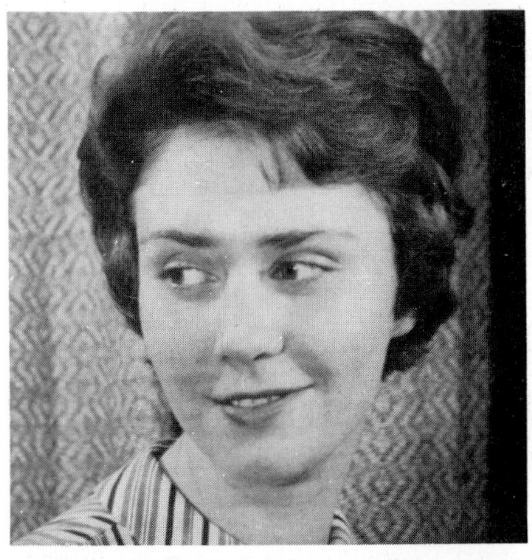

Fig. 17.5 Photo reproduced with 32-level display (courtesy J. Jarvis, Bell Laboratories).

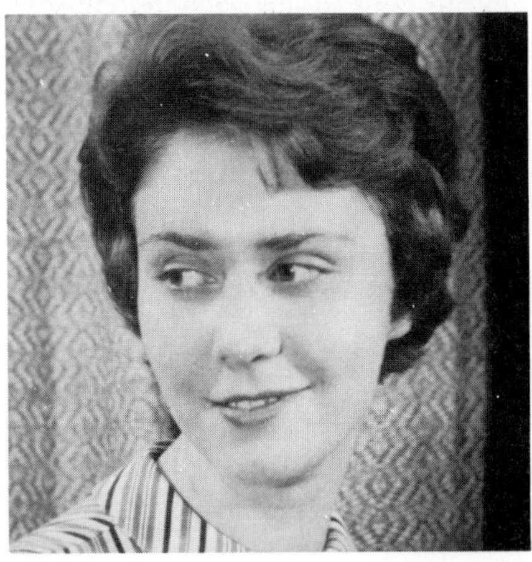

Fig. 17.6 Photo reproduced with 64-level display. Differences from previous figures are subtle (courtesy J. Jarvis, Bell Laboratories).

Therefore, for some other constant c,

$$I = cV^{\gamma}. \tag{17.3}$$

Rewriting (17.3), we have

$$V = \left(\frac{I}{c}\right)^{1/\gamma}. \tag{17.4}$$

Now, given a desired intensity I, we first determine the nearest I_j. This can be done by searching through a table of the available intensities as calculated from (17.1) or from its equivalent:

$$j = ROUND\left(\log_r \frac{I}{I_0}\right). \tag{17.5}$$

After j is found, we next calculate

$$I_j = r^j I_0. \tag{17.6}$$

The next step is to determine the pixel value V_j needed to create the intensity I_j, by using (17.4):

$$V_j = \left(\frac{I_j}{c}\right)^{1/\gamma}. \tag{17.7}$$

If the raster display has no look-up table, then V_j is placed in the appropriate pixels. If there is a look-up table, then j is placed in the pixels and V_j is placed in entry j of the table.

The values of c, γ, and I_0 depend on the CRT in use, so in practice the look-up table is loaded by an experimental method based on actual measurement of intensities, as described in [CATM79]. Use of the look-up table in this general manner is called *gamma-correction,* after the exponent in Eq. (17.2). Note that some raster displays include gamma correction, in which case I_j rather than V_j would be placed either in the refresh buffer or look-up table.

17.2.2. Halftone Approximation

Many displays and hard-copy devices are bi-level, i.e., produce just two intensity levels, and even 2 or 3 bit-per-pixel raster displays produce fewer intensity levels than we might desire. How can we expand the range of available intensities? The answer lies in the *spatial integration* our eyes perform. If we view a very small area (say a 0.02×0.02 inch square) from a normal viewing distance, the eye will integrate fine detail within the small area and record only the overall intensity of the area.

This phenomenon is used in printing black and white photos in newspapers, magazines, and books, in a technique called *halftoning*. Each small resolution unit is imprinted with a circle of black ink whose area is proportional to the blackness (1 − intensity) of the area in the original photo. Figure 17.7 shows a greatly enlarged part of a halftone pattern. Newspaper halftones use a resolution of 60 to 80 dots per inch, while magazine and book halftones use up to 150 dots per inch.

Fig. 17.7 Enlarged halftone pattern, Dot size varies inversely with intensity of original photo.

Graphics output devices can approximate the variable-area dots of halftone reproduction. For example, a 2×2 pixel area of a bi-level display can be used to produce five different intensity levels at the price of cutting the spatial resolution in half along each axis. The patterns shown in Fig. 17.8 can be used in the 2×2 areas. The idea is to fill the 2×2 area with a number of dots which is proportional to the desired intensity. Figure 17.9 shows a face defined on a 256×256 grid displayed on a 512×512 bi-level display by means of 2×2 patterns. In general, an $n \times n$ group of bi-level pixels can provide $n^2 + 1$ intensity levels. We are trading spatial resolution, which is being decreased, for intensity resolution, which is being increased. The use of a 3×3 pattern cuts spatial resolution by one-third on each axis, but provides 10 intensity levels. Of course, even larger patterns can be used, but the spatial versus intensity resolution trade-off is limited by our visual acuity (about one minute of arc in normal lighting).

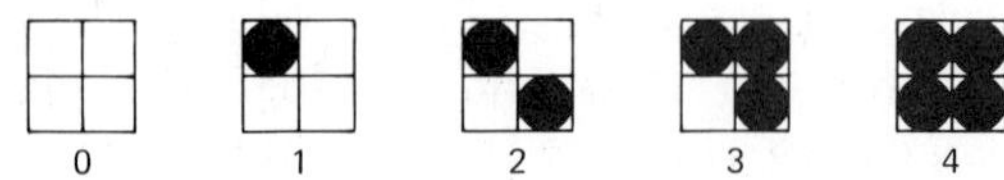

Fig. 17.8 Five intensity-level approximations by means of 2×2 patterns.

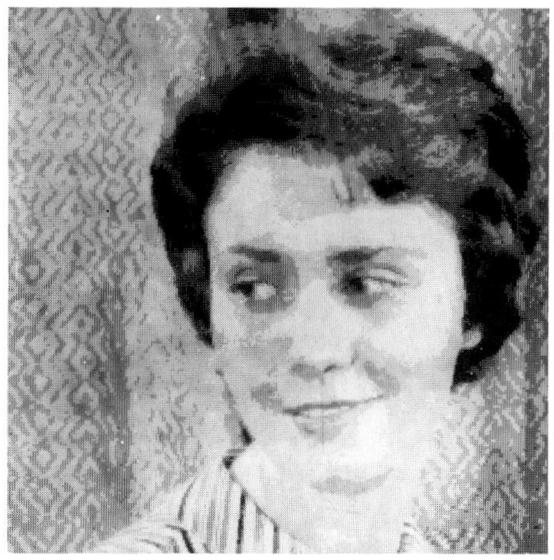

Fig. 17.9 Photo of 256 × 256 points displayed on 512 × 512 display by means of 2 × 2 patterns (courtesy J. Jarvis, Bell Laboratories).

One possible set of patterns for the 3 × 3 case is shown in Fig. 17.10. Note that these patterns can be represented by the matrix

$$\begin{bmatrix} 7 & 9 & 5 \\ 2 & 1 & 4 \\ 6 & 3 & 8 \end{bmatrix}.$$

To display a given intensity, all cells whose values are less than or equal to the intensity are set to on.

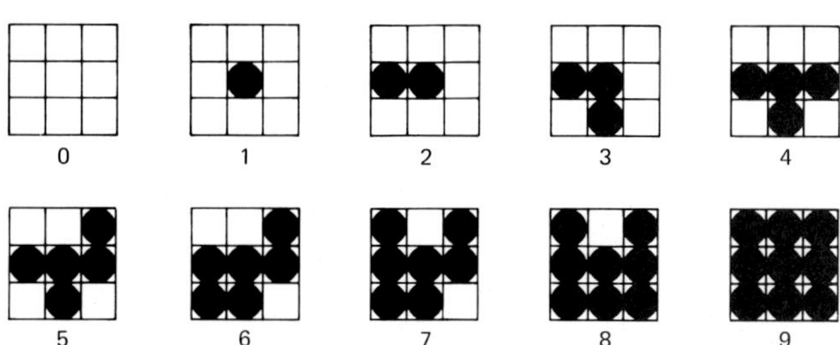

Fig. 17.10 Ten intensity-level approximations by means of 3 × 3 patterns.

The $n \times n$ pixel patterns used to approximate the halftones must be designed so that they are not conspicuous in an area of identical intensity values. For instance, if we used the pattern in Fig. 17.11 rather than the one in Fig. 17.10, then horizontal lines would be visible in any large area of the image that has intensity 3. Another consideration in choosing patterns is that they form a *growth sequence,* in which a pixel that is intensified for intensity level j is intensified for all levels $k > j$. This minimizes the differences in the patterns for successive intensity levels, thereby minimizing the contouring effects.

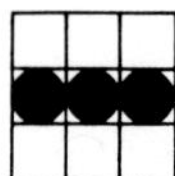

Fig. 17.11 A pattern that should not be used to approximate halftones.

Halftone approximation is not limited to bi-level displays. Suppose we have a display with two bits per pixel and hence four intensity levels. The halftone technique can be used to increase further the number of intensity levels. If we use a 2×2 pattern, we have a total of four pixels at our disposal, each of which can take on three values besides black, allowing us to display $4 \times 3 + 1 = 13$ intensities. One possible set of growth sequence patterns for this case is shown in Fig. 17.12. The intensities of the individual pixels sum to the intensity level represented by each pattern.

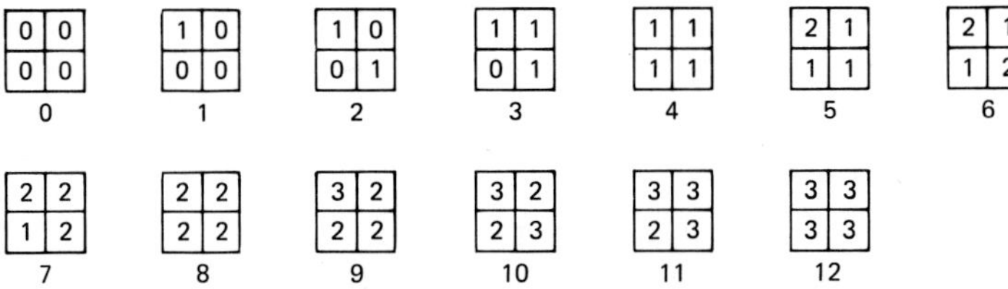

0	1	2	3	4	5	6
0 0	1 0	1 0	1 1	1 1	2 1	2 1
0 0	0 0	0 1	0 1	1 1	1 1	1 2

7	8	9	10	11	12
2 2	2 2	3 2	3 2	3 3	3 3
1 2	2 2	2 2	2 3	2 3	3 3

Fig. 17.12 Halftone patterns for intensity levels 0 to 12 based on 2×2 patterns of 4-level pixels.

These preceding techniques are appropriate if the resolution of the image to be displayed is lower than the resolution of the display device, allowing the use of multiple display pixels for one image pixel. What if the image and device resolutions are the same? The *ordered dither* technique can be used to display an $m \times m$ image with multiple levels of intensity on an $m \times m$ bi-level display.

In ordered dither, the decision to intensify or not to intensify the pixel at point (x, y) depends on the desired intensity $I(x, y)$ at that point and on an $n \times n$ dither matrix $D^{(n)}$. The dither matrix is indexed from 0 to $n - 1$ along its rows and columns. Each of the integers 0 to $n^2 - 1$ appears once in the matrix. For instance, when $n = 2$, we have

$$D^{(2)} = \begin{bmatrix} 0 & 2 \\ 3 & 1 \end{bmatrix}. \tag{17.8}$$

This is the same representation as used for growth sequences. To process the point at (x, y), we first compute

$$i = x \text{ modulo } n, \qquad j = y \text{ modulo } n.$$

Then if

$$I(x, y) > D_{ij}^{(n)}, \tag{17.9}$$

the point at (x, y) is intensified; otherwise it is not. Notice that large areas of fixed intensity are displayed exactly as by the previous methods, so the effect of ordered dither is apparent only in areas of changing intensity. Matrices for various values of n have been developed by Bayer [BAYE73] to minimize the amount of texture they introduce into displayed images.

The dither matrix used to display an image must be able to specify the number of intensity levels in the image. Recurrence relations have thus been developed [JUDI74] to compute $D^{(2n)}$ from $D^{(n)}$. Their application to $D^{(2)}$ produces:

$$D^{(4)} = \begin{bmatrix} 0 & 8 & 2 & 10 \\ 12 & 4 & 14 & 6 \\ 3 & 11 & 1 & 9 \\ 15 & 7 & 13 & 5 \end{bmatrix} \tag{17.10}$$

and

$$D^{(8)} = \begin{bmatrix} 0 & 32 & 8 & 40 & 2 & 34 & 10 & 42 \\ 48 & 16 & 56 & 24 & 50 & 18 & 58 & 26 \\ 12 & 44 & 4 & 36 & 14 & 46 & 6 & 38 \\ 60 & 28 & 52 & 20 & 62 & 30 & 54 & 22 \\ 3 & 35 & 11 & 43 & 1 & 33 & 9 & 41 \\ 51 & 19 & 59 & 27 & 49 & 17 & 57 & 25 \\ 15 & 47 & 7 & 39 & 13 & 45 & 5 & 37 \\ 63 & 31 & 55 & 23 & 61 & 29 & 53 & 21 \end{bmatrix}. \tag{17.11}$$

Figure 17.13 shows a face drawn on a 512×512 bi-level display by using $D^{(8)}$. Compare this bi-level result to the multilevel pictures shown earlier in this section. Further examples of pictures displayed by means of ordered dither are in [JARV76a, JARV76b], as are descriptions of still other ways to display continuous-tone images on bi-level displays.

Fig. 17.13 Photo reproduced with $D^{(8)}$ ordered dither on 512×512 display (courtesy J. Jarvis, Bell Laboratories).

17.3 CHROMATIC COLOR

The visual sensations caused by color are much richer than the sensations caused by achromatic light. Subjective discussions of color usually involve three dimensions, known as *hue, saturation,* and *brightness,* as a descriptive tool. Hue is the term we use to distinguish between colors such as red, green, yellow, etc. Saturation refers to purity, i.e., how little the color is diluted by white light, and distinguishes pink from red, sky blue from royal blue, etc. In other words, saturation determines how pastel or strong a color appears. Brightness embodies the achromatic notion of intensity, used in the preceding sections, as a factor independent of hue and saturation.

We are interested in specifying and measuring color. One way to do this is by visually comparing a sample of unknown color against a set of "standard" samples. The widely used Munsell color specification system includes sets of published standard colors [MUNS76] organized in a three-dimensional space of hue, value (brightness), and chroma (saturation). Each color has a name, and is an equal perceived "distance" in color space (as judged by many observers) from its neighbors. In [KELL76] there is an extensive discussion of standard samples, charts depicting the Munsell space, and tables of color names. The Ostwald [OSTW31] system is similar but somewhat less used. There is also the relatively new Coloroid system of Nemcsics [NEMC80].

Artists use another approach, specifying color as different *tints, shades,* and *tones* of strongly saturated, or pure, pigments. A tint results from adding white pigment to the pure pigment, thereby decreasing saturation. A shade comes from adding a black pigment to the pure pigment, resulting in decreased brightness. A tone is the consequence of adding both black and white pigments to a pure pigment.

All these steps produce different colors of the same hue, with varying saturation and brightness. Mixing just black and white pigments creates grays. Figure 17.14 shows the relationships of tints, shades, and tones. We could think of using the percentage of pigments which must be mixed to match a color as a measurement of a color.

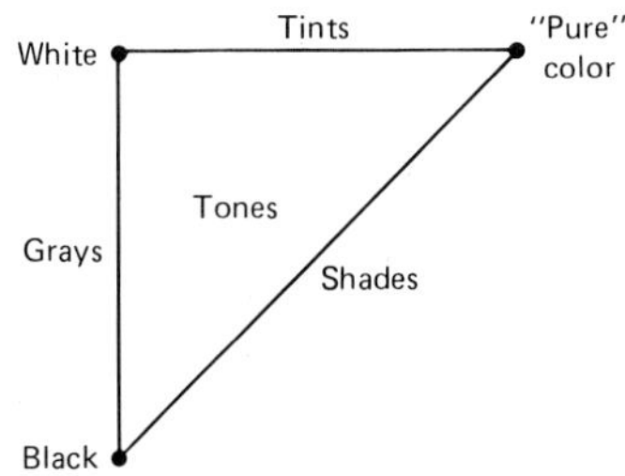

Fig. 17.14 Tints, tones, and shades.

17.3.1 Color in Physics and Physiology

Unfortunately, the Munsell and pigment mixing methods are subjective, i.e., depend on the observers' judgments as to color matches. What we really need is an objective way of specifying colors. For this we turn to physics, wherein visible light is treated as electromagnetic energy with a spectral energy distribution in the visible part of the spectrum, which ranges from violet through indigo, blue, green, yellow and orange, to red (remembered by the mnemonic VIB-GY-OR or, in reverse, Mr. ROY G. BIV). Figure 17.15 shows a typical spectral energy distribution of a light source, and represents an infinity of numbers, one for each wavelength in the visible spectrum (in reality, the distribution would be defined by a large number of sample points on the spectrum). Fortunately, we can represent the visual effect of any spectral distribution in a much more concise way, by the triple (dominant wavelength, purity, luminance). This implies that many different spectral energy distributions produce the same color: they "look" the same. This means that the relationship between spectral distributions and colors is many-to-one.

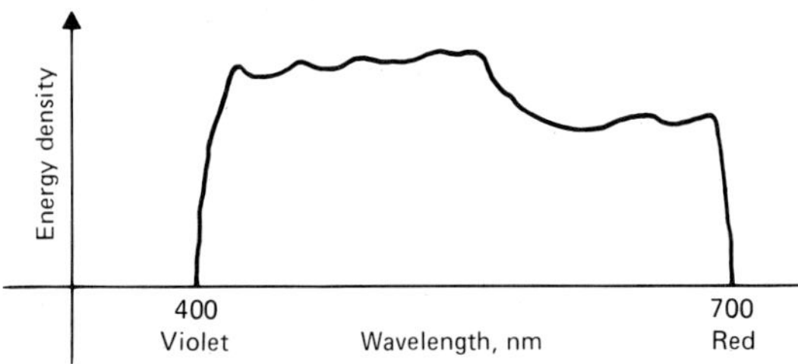

Fig. 17.15 Typical spectral energy distribution.

The components of the triple have the following interpretations: *dominant wavelength* is the wavelength of the color we "see" when viewing the light, and corresponds to the subjective notion of hue; *purity* corresponds to saturation of the color; and *luminance* is the amount of light. For achromatic light, luminance is the light's intensity. The purity of a colored light is the proportion of pure light of the dominant wavelength and white light needed to define the color. A completely pure color, which is thus 100% saturated, contains no white light. A half-and-half mixture would be 50% saturated. White light and hence all gray levels are 0% saturated, containing no color of any dominant wavelength.

Figure 17.16 shows one of the infinitely many spectral distributions which will produce a certain color of light. At the dominant wavelength there is a spike of energy of level e_2. White light, represented by the uniform distribution of energy at level e_1, is also present. Purity depends on the relation between e_1 and e_2. When $e_1 = e_2$, purity is 0%. When $e_1 = 0$, purity is 100%. Luminance, which can be thought of as the area under the curve (total energy), depends on both e_1 and e_2.

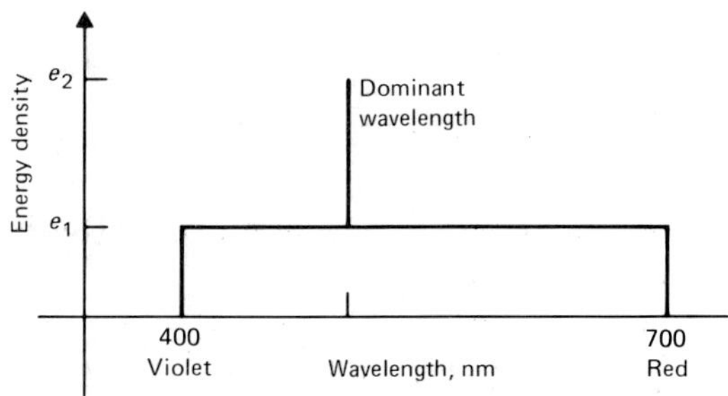

Fig. 17.16 Spectral energy distribution illustrating dominant wavelength, purity, and luminance.

Here then is a precise definition of color in terms of dominant wavelength, purity, and luminance. But how does this relate to the red, green, and blue phosphor dots on a color CRT and to the psychological-physiological *tri-stimulus theory* of color based on the hypothesis that there are three kinds of cones on the retina of the eye, each with peak sensitivities to light of either red, green, or blue hues? Experiments based on this hypothesis produce the response curves of Fig. 17.17. The curves show, for instance, that for 550 nanometer (nm) (formerly called millimicron) wavelength light, the blue receptors have a sensitivity of 0%; the green, about 55%; the red, about 45%. The curves also indicate that the blue receptors are far less sensitive than the red and green receptors. The sum of the three response curves, shown in Fig. 17.18, is known as the *luminosity curve*. It shows the eye's response to light of constant luminance as the dominant wavelength is varied: our peak sensitivity is to yellow-green light of wavelength around 550 nm.

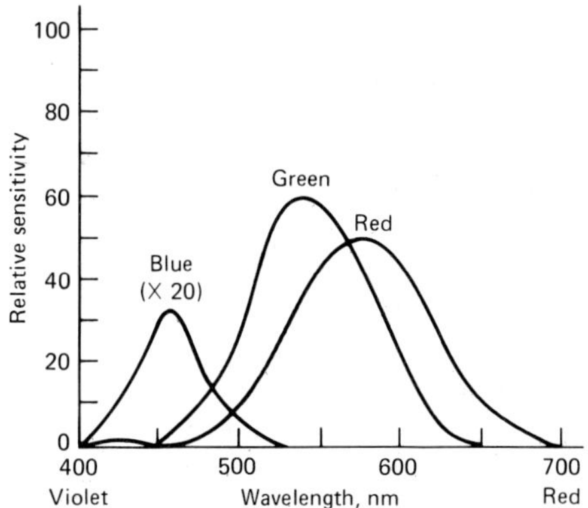

Fig. 17.17 Response characteristics of the eye.

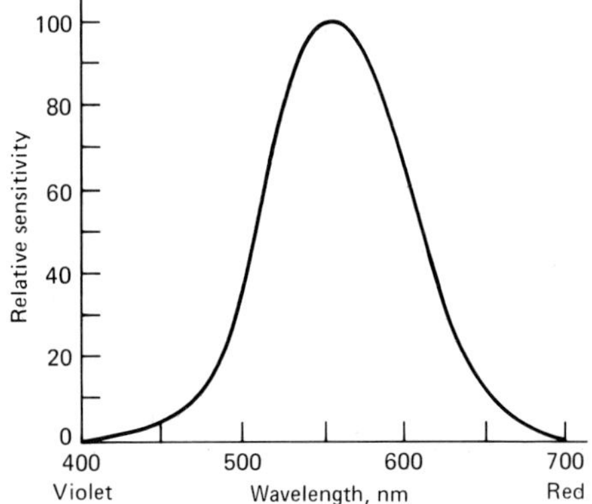

Fig. 17.18 Luminosity response of the eye.

The tri-stimulus approach is not the only theory used to explain color vision. Land's recent theories [LAND77], *opponent-color theory,* and *zone theory* are also used [WASS78]. The tri-stimulus theory, however, is attractive on an intuitive basis because it loosely corresponds to the notion that colors can be specified by weighted sums of red, green, and blue. This notion is in fact almost true: the three curves in Fig. 17.19 show the amounts of red (650 nm wavelength), green (530 nm), and blue (425 nm) light needed by an "average" observer to match a 100% pure light (a spectral color) of constant luminance, for all values of dominant wavelength in the visible spectrum.

Some colors actually cannot be matched, but it happens that by adding a primary to the color, it can then be matched by the other two primaries. A negative value in Fig. 17.19 indicates that the primary was added to the color being matched.

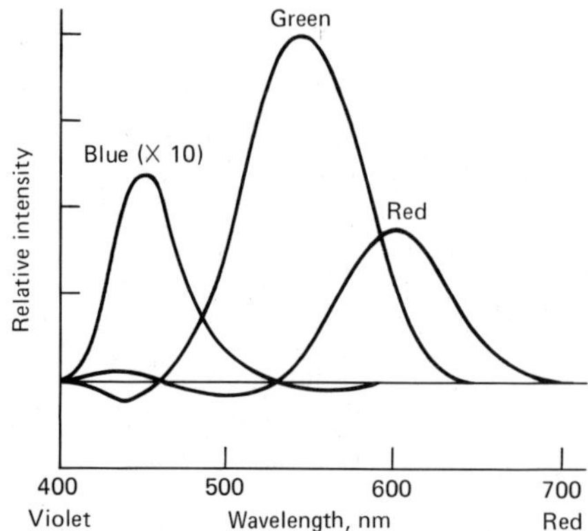

Fig. 17.19 Color matching coefficients. The blue primary has been scaled up by 10.

This does not mean that the notion of mixing red, green, and blue to obtain other colors is invalid; on the contrary, there is a huge gamut (range) of colors which can be matched by positive amounts of red, green, and blue. Otherwise color TV wouldn't work! It is important to notice that because the human eye is less sensitive to blue light than to green light, less blue light is required in the matching process.

The human eye can distinguish about 350,000 different colors. This figure is based on experiments in which many pairs of colors are judged side by side by many viewers. The viewer states whether the colors are the same or different. When the colors differ only in hue, then the wavelength between just noticeably different colors varies from greater than 10 nm at the extremes of the spectrum to about 1 nm for blue and yellow. Except at the spectrum extremes, most distinguishable colors are within 3 nm. Altogether about 128 hues are distinguishable. If colors differ only in saturation, we can distinguish from 16 (for yellow) to 23 (for red and violet).

17.3.2 The CIE Chromaticity Diagram

Matching and therefore defining a colored light with a mixture of three fixed primaries is a desirable approach, but the concept of negative weights suggested by Fig. 17.19 is unattractive. In 1931, the *Commission Internationale L'Eclairage* (CIE) defined three primary colors (X, Y, Z) that can be combined, with positive weights, to define all light sensations we experience with our eyes. The CIE primaries, which are by themselves not visible, form an international standard for specifying color. The primaries are defined as three spectral energy distributions: the Y primary was intentionally defined to have an energy distribution which exactly matches the luminosity curve of Fig. 17.18.

Let (X, Y, Z) be the weights applied to the CIE primaries to match a color. We can define chromaticity values (which depend only on dominant wavelength and saturation and are independent of the amount of luminous energy) by normalizing against luminance (which is the total amount of light) as follows:

$$x = \frac{X}{X + Y + Z}, \qquad y = \frac{Y}{X + Y + Z}, \qquad z = \frac{Z}{X + Y + Z}. \tag{17.12}$$

Notice that we have forced $x + y + z$ to equal 1.

By plotting x and y for all visible colors, we obtain the CIE chromaticity diagram shown in Fig. 17.20. The interior and boundary of the horseshoe-shaped region represent all visible chromaticities. (All perceivable colors with the same chromaticity but different luminances map into the same point within this region.) The 100% pure colors of the spectrum are on the curved part of the boundary. Their wavelengths are indicated in the figure. Standard white light, meant to approximate sunlight, is formally defined by a standard light source known as *illuminant C* which is marked by the center dot. It is near but not at the point where $x = y = z = \frac{1}{3}$. Illuminant C is precisely defined in colorimetry (the science of color measurement) as a black-body radiator at 6504° Kelvin.

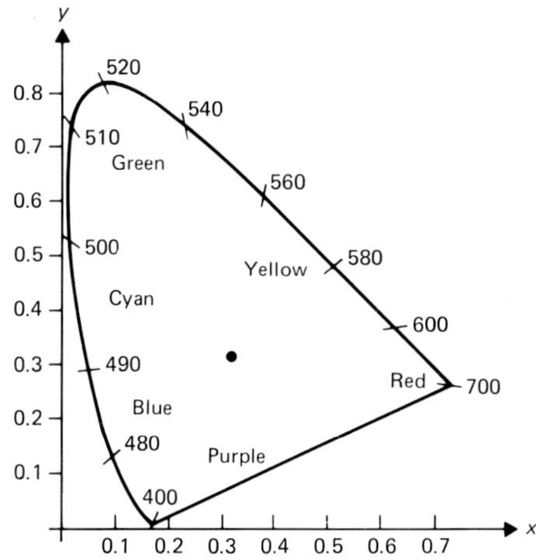

Fig. 17.20 The CIE chromaticity diagram, on the $X + Y + Z = 1$ plane. Wavelengths are in nanometers.

The CIE chromaticity diagram is useful in many ways. For one, it allows us to actually measure the dominant wavelength and purity of any color, by first matching the color by a mixture of the three CIE primaries. (There are instruments which can do this). Now suppose the matched color is at point A in Fig. 17.21. When two colors are added together, the new color lies somewhere on the straight line in the chromaticity diagram connecting the two colors being added. Therefore color A can be thought of as a mixture of "standard" white light (illuminant C) and the pure spectral light at point B. Thus B defines the dominant wavelength. The ratio of

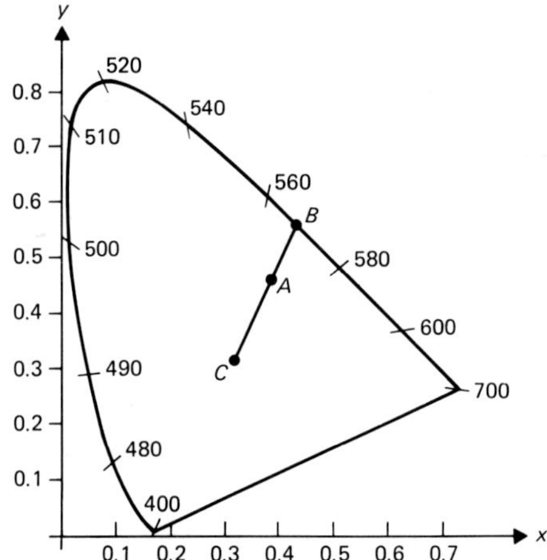

Fig. 17.21 Dominant wavelengths of color A is that of color B (about 565 nanometers).

length AC to length BC, expressed as a percentage, is the purity of A. The closer A is to C, the more white light A includes and the less pure it is. Because the diagram factors out luminance, color sensations which are luminance-related are excluded. Therefore brown, which is an orange-red chromaticity at very low luminance, is not shown.

Complementary colors are those that can be mixed to produce white light (such as D and E in Fig. 17.22). Here the weight w_D applied to chromaticity D in the mixture is the ratio of line length $\overline{CE}$ to line length $\overline{DE}$, and the weight w_E applied to chromaticity E is the ratio of line length $\overline{DC}$ to $\overline{DE}$: hence $C = w_D D + w_E E$. Representing a chromaticity by its (x, y) coordinates, we have

$$x_C = w_D x_D + w_E x_E \qquad \text{and} \qquad y_C = w_D y_D + w_E y_E.$$

Notice that $w_D = 1 - w_E$; this is just the parametric representation of a line used in Chapters 4 and 8, with $t = w_D$.

Some colors (such as E in Fig. 17.23) cannot be defined by a dominant wavelength and are thus called *non-spectral*. In these cases, the dominant wavelength is said to be the complement of that at point D and is designated by a "c" (in this case, about 560 nm c). The purity is still defined from the ratio of distances (in this case, CE and CF). The colors that must be expressed by using a complementary dominant wavelength are the purples and the magentas; they occur in the lower part of the CIE diagram.

Another use for the CIE chromaticity diagram is to define *color gamuts,* or color ranges. Any two colors (I and J in Fig. 17.24) can be added to produce any color on the connecting line by varying the relative luminances of the two colors be-

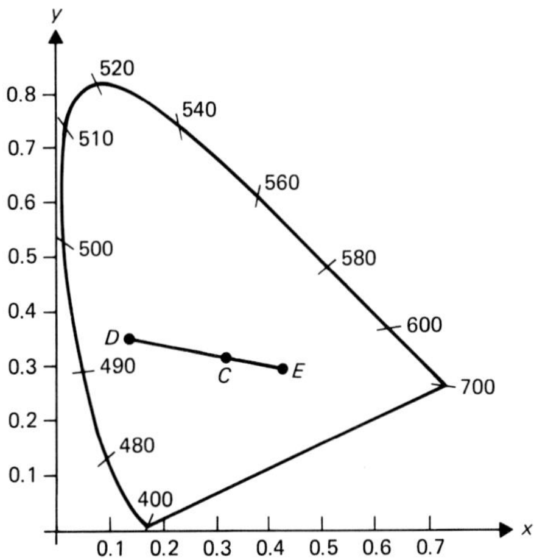

Fig. 17.22 Complementary colors.

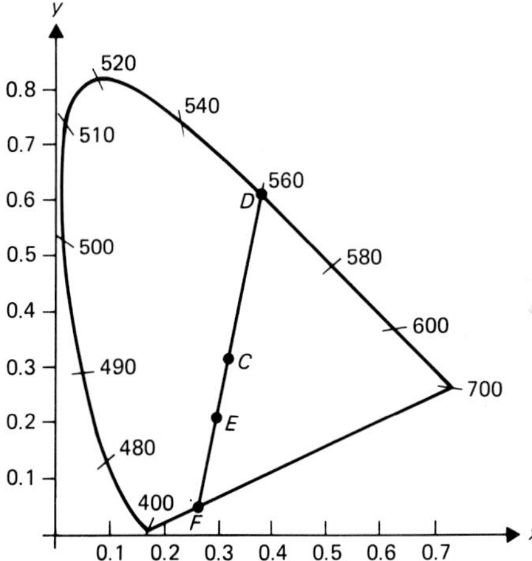

Fig. 17.23 The dominant wavelength of color *E* is defined as the complement of the dominant wavelength of color *D*.

ing added. A third color *K* (see Fig. 17.25) can be used with various mixtures of *I* and *J* to produce the gamut of all colors in triangle *IJK,* again by varying relative luminances. The shape of the diagram shows why visible red, green, and blue cannot be additively mixed to match all colors: no triangle whose vertices are within the visible area can completely cover the visible area. Any fully saturated color, because it contains no white light, can be specified as a mixture of just two primaries.

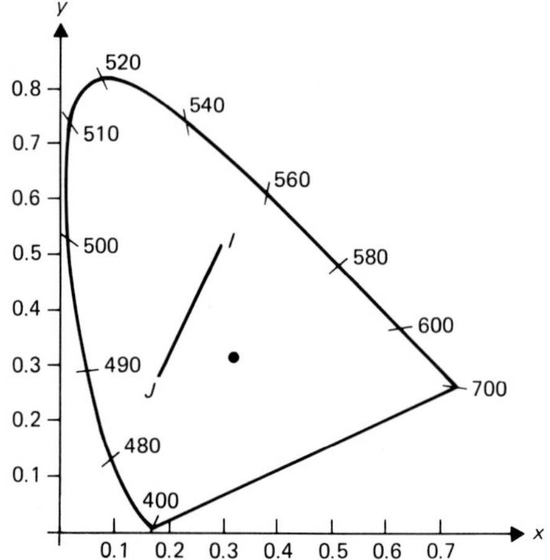

Fig. 17.24 Mixing two colors. All colors on connecting line can be created.

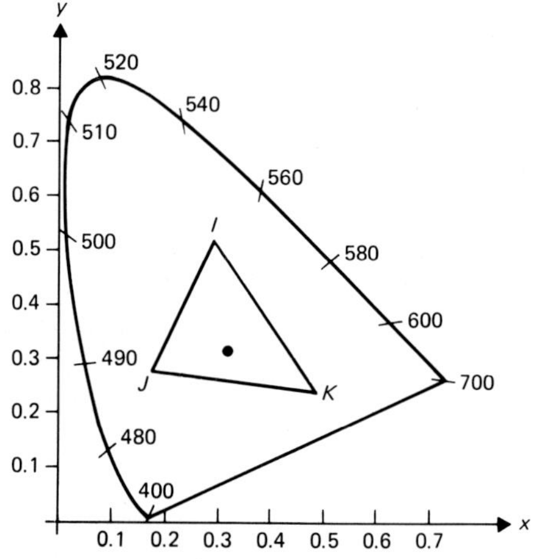

Fig. 17.25 Mixing three colors. All colors in triangle can be created.

Another use for the chromaticity diagram is to define and compare gamuts available from various color display and hardcopy devices. Color Plate 22 shows the gamuts for color TV, film, and print. The smallness of the print gamut with respect to the TV gamut suggests that if images originally created on a color TV must be faithfully reproduced by printing, a reduced gamut of colors should be used with the TV. Otherwise, accurate reproduction will not be possible. If, however, the goal is simply to make a pleasing rather than an exact reproduction, small differences in color gamuts are inconsequential.

17.4 COLOR MODELS FOR RASTER GRAPHICS

The purpose of a color model is to allow convenient specifications of colors within some color gamut. Our prime interest is the gamut for color TV, as defined by the RGB (red, green, blue) TV primaries in Color Plate 22. A secondary interest is the color gamut for hard-copy devices. A color model is a specification of a 3D color coordinate system and a 3D subspace in the coordinate system within which each displayable color is represented by a point. The color models discussed here are all based on the RGB primaries, although in general any three primaries could be used. The models specify only colors in the RGB gamut.

Three hardware-oriented models are the RGB, used with color TV monitors; YIQ, which is the broadcast TV color system; and CMY (cyan, magenta, yellow) for color printing devices. Unfortunately, none of these models are particularly easy for a programmer or application user to control, because they do not directly relate to our intuitive color notions of hue, saturation, and brightness. Therefore, another class of models has been developed with ease of use as a goal. Several such models exist; we shall discuss only two: the HSV and HLS models. These and other models are described in [GSPC79, JOBL78, MEYE80, and SMIT78].

17.4.1. The RGB Color Model

The red, green, and blue color model uses a cartesian coordinate system. The subspace of interest is the unit cube, shown in Fig. 17.26. The RGB primaries are additive, i.e., the individual contributions of each primary are added together to form a result. The main diagonal of the cube, with equal amounts of each primary, represents the gray levels. Color Plate 23 shows several views of RGB color space. The RGB model is of interest primarily because it is used in color TV monitors and in many raster displays. There is also a considerable body of knowledge concerning the eye's response and sensitivity to colors specified as (R,G,B) triples.

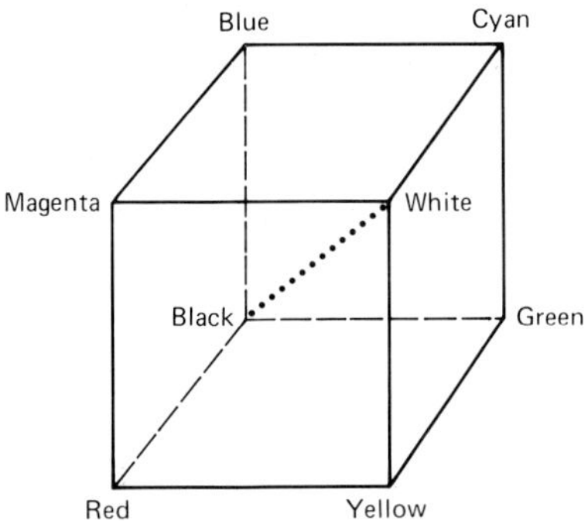

Fig. 17.26 RGB color cube. Grays are on the dotted main diagonal.

17.4.2 The CMY Color Model

Cyan, magenta, and yellow are the complements of red, green, and blue, respectively. They are called *subtractive primaries* because their effect is to subtract some color from white light. The subspace of the cartesian coordinate system for CMY is the same as for RGB, except that white (full light) is at the origin instead of black (no light). Colors are specified by what is removed or subtracted from white light, rather than by what is added to blackness.

A knowledge of CMY is important when dealing with hard-copy devices which deposit colored pigments onto paper, such as the Xerox copier and the Applicon ink jet plotter. When a surface is coated with cyan ink or paint, no red light is reflected from the surface. Cyan subtracts red from the reflected white light, which is itself the sum of red, green, and blue. Hence, in terms of the additive primaries, cyan is blue plus green. Similarly, magenta absorbs green so it is red plus blue, while yellow absorbs blue so it is red plus green. A surface coated with cyan and yellow absorbs red and blue, leaving only green to be reflected from illuminating white light. A cyan, yellow, and magenta surface absorbs red, green, and blue, and therefore is black. These relations, diagrammed in Fig. 17.27, can be seen in Color Plate 23 and are represented by the equations:

$$\begin{bmatrix} C \\ M \\ Y \end{bmatrix} = \begin{bmatrix} 1 \\ 1 \\ 1 \end{bmatrix} - \begin{bmatrix} R \\ G \\ B \end{bmatrix}. \qquad (17.13)$$

The unit column vector is the RGB representation for white and the CMY representation for black. Note that the Y in CMY is not the same as the Y in the CIE system.

The conversion from RGB to CMY is then

$$\begin{bmatrix} R \\ G \\ B \end{bmatrix} = \begin{bmatrix} 1 \\ 1 \\ 1 \end{bmatrix} - \begin{bmatrix} C \\ M \\ Y \end{bmatrix}. \qquad (17.14)$$

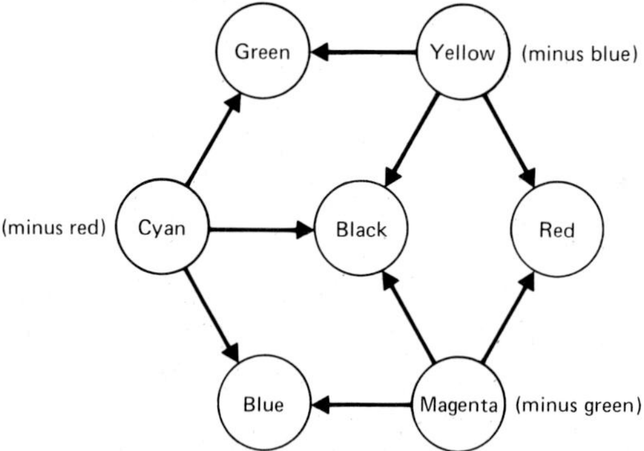

Fig. 17.27 Subtractive primaries (cyan, magenta, yellow) and their mixtures.

17.4.3 The YIQ Color Model

The YIQ model is important because it is used in commercial color TV broadcasting and is therefore closely related to color raster graphics. YIQ is a recoding of RGB for transmission efficiency and for downward compatibility with black and white TV. The Y in YIQ is in fact the same as the Y in the CIE's X, Y, and Z primaries: a primary whose spectral energy distribution matches the luminosity response curve. The Y component of a color TV signal is shown on black and white TV. The YIQ model is in a 3D cartesian coordinate system, with the subspace being the convex polyhedron that maps into the RGB cube. The RGB to YIQ conversion which performs the mapping is defined as:

$$\begin{bmatrix} Y \\ I \\ Q \end{bmatrix} = \begin{bmatrix} 0.30 & 0.59 & 0.11 \\ 0.60 & -0.28 & -0.32 \\ 0.21 & -0.52 & 0.31 \end{bmatrix} \cdot \begin{bmatrix} R \\ G \\ B \end{bmatrix}. \qquad (17.15)$$

The inverse of the matrix is used for the reverse conversion. Color Plate 24 shows planes of constant Y in the YIQ model. Further discussion of YIQ can be found in [SMIT78, PRIT77].

By specifying colors with the YIQ model, an important TV problem can be avoided: two colors that look quite different to our eyes may look exactly the same when transmitted or videotaped and then viewed on a black and white monitor. This can be avoided by guaranteeing that two colors that are meant to be distinguished one from the other (such as a filled area and its border) have different luminances (values of Y), so they are displayed at different intensities.

The YIQ model is designed to exploit a useful property of our visual system, which is more sensitive to changes in luminosity than to changes in hue or saturation. This suggests using more bits (or bandwidth) to represent Y than to represent I and Q, thus providing higher resolution in Y. Also, objects that cover a very small part of our field of view produce no color sensation, but are perceived only by their intensity. This suggests that less spatial resolution is needed for I and Q than for Y. The NTSC [PRIT77] encoding of YIQ into a broadcast signal uses both these properties to maximize the amount of information transmitted in a fixed bandwidth.

17.4.4 The HSV Color Model

The RGB, CMY, and YIQ models are hardware oriented. By contrast, Smith's HSV (hue, saturation, value) model [SMIT78] is user oriented, being based on the intuitive appeal of the artist's tint, shade, and tone. The subspace within which the model is defined is a hexcone, or six-sided cone, as in Fig. 17.28. The top of the hexcone corresponds to $V = 1$, which contains the maximum-value (intensity) colors. Note that complementary colors are 180° opposite one another as measured by H. This is the angle around the vertical axis, with red at 0°. The value of S is a ratio, ranging from 0 on the center line (V-axis) to 1 on the triangular sides of the hexcone. Saturation is measured relative to the gamut represented by the model, not relative to the CIE chart, and thus is not the same as purity.

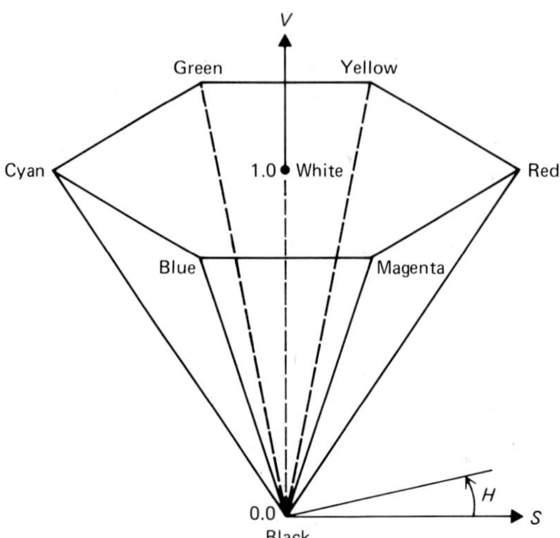

Fig. 17.28 Single hexcone HSV color model.

The hexcone is one unit high in V, with the apex at the origin. The point at the apex is black and has a coordinate of $V = 0$. Any value of S between 0 and 1 can be associated with the point $V = 0$. The point $S = 0$, $V = 1$ is white. Intermediate values of V for $S = 0$ (on the center-line) are the grays. When $S = 0$, the value of H is irrelevant and is called *undefined.* When S is not zero, H is relevant. For example, pure red is at $H = 0$, $S = 1$, $V = 1$. Indeed, any color with $V = 1$, $S = 1$ is akin to an artist's pure pigment used as the starting point in mixing colors. Adding white pigment corresponds to decreasing S (without changing V). Adding black pigment corresponds to decreasing V (without changing S). Tones are created by decreasing both S and V. Of course changing H corresponds to selecting the pure pigment with which to start. Thus H, S, and V each correspond one-to-one to concepts from the artists' color system.

The top of the HSV hexcone corresponds to the surface seen by looking along the principal diagonal of the RGB color cube from white toward black. Such a view is shown in Fig. 17.29 and in Color Plate 23(c). The RGB cube has subcubes, as illustrated in Fig. 17.30 on page 616. Each subcube, when viewed along its main diagonal, appears like the hexagon in Fig. 17.29, except smaller. Each plane of constant V in HSV space corresponds to such a view of a subcube in RGB space. The main diagonal of RGB space becomes the V axis of HSV space. Thus we see intuitively the correspondence between RGB and HSV. The following two algorithms define the correspondence precisely by providing conversions from one model to the other:

```
procedure RGB_TO_HSV(r, g, b: real; var h, s, v: real)
  {Given: r, g, b, each in [0, 1]}
  {Desired: h in [0, 360), s and v in [0, 1], except if s = 0,
    then h = undefined which is a defined constant whose value is outside the
    interval [0, 360]}
begin
  max := MAXIMUM(r, g, b);
  min := MINIMUM(r, g, b);
  v := max;                          {value}
  if max <>0
    then s := (max - min)/max        {saturation}
    else s := 0;
  if s = 0
    then h := undefined
    else                             {saturation not zero, so determine hue}
      begin
        rc := (max - r)/(max - min);       {rc measures "distance" of color
                                             from red}
        gc := (max - g)/(max - min);
        bc := (max - b)/(max - min);
        if      r = max then h := bc - gc  {resulting color between
                                             yellow and magenta}
        else if g = max then h := 2 + rc - bc {resulting color between cyan
                                             and yellow}
        else if b = max then h := 4 + gc - rc; {resulting color between
                                             magenta and cyan}
        h := h*60;                         {convert to degrees}
        if h < 0 then h := h + 360         {make nonnegative}
      end    {chromatic case}
end    {RGB_TO_HSV}
```

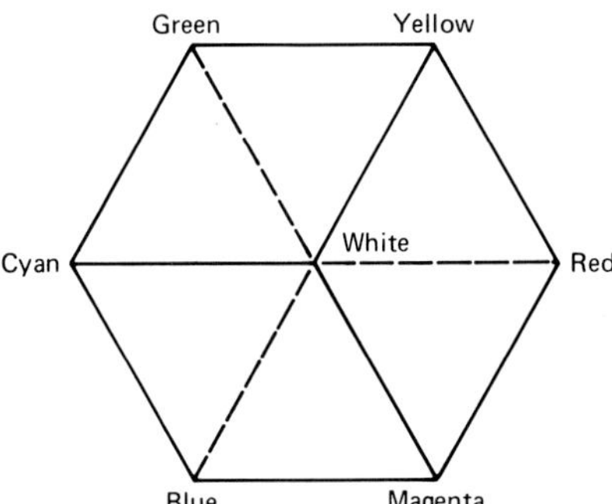

Fig. 17.29 RGB color cube viewed along principal diagonal. Visible edges of cube are solid, while the invisible ones are dashed.

```
procedure HSV_TO_RGB(var r, g, b: real; h, s, v: real);
  {Given: h in [0, 360] or undefined, s and v in [0, 1]}
  {Desired: r, g, b, each in [0, 1]}
begin
  if s = 0
    then                                  {achromatic color: there is no hue}
      if h = undefined
        then
          begin                           {this is the achromatic case}
            r := v;
            g := v;
            b := v
          end
        else ERROR                        {error if s = 0 and h has a value}
    else                                  {chromatic color: there is a hue}
      begin
        if h = 360 then h = 0;
        h := h/60;                        {h is now in [0, 6)}
        i := FLOOR(h);                    {largest integer <= h}
        f := h - i;                       {fractional part of h}
        p := v*(1 - s);
        q := v*(1 - (s*f));
        t := v*(1 - (s*(1 - f)));
        case i of
          0: (r, g, b) := (v, t, p);      {triplet assignment}
          1: (r, g, b) := (q, v, p);
          2: (r, g, b) := (p, v, t);
          3: (r, g, b) := (p, q, v);
          4: (r, g, b) := (t, p, v);
          5: (r, g, b) := (v, p, q);
        end     {case}
      end     {hue}
end     {HSV_TO_RGB}
```

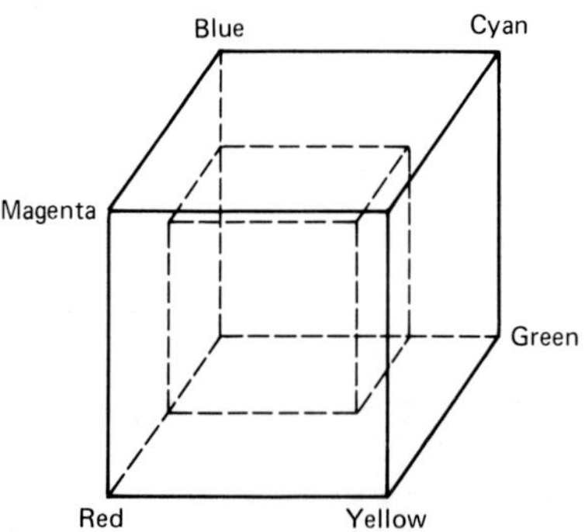

Fig. 17.30 RGB cube and a subcube.

17.4.5 The HLS Color Model

The HLS (hue, lightness, saturation) color model, used by Tektronix and based on the Ostwald [OSTW31] color system, forms the double hexcone subspace seen in Fig. 17.31. Hue is the angle around the vertical axis of the double hexcone, with red at 0°.* The colors occur around the perimeter in the same order they occur in the CIE diagram when its boundary is traversed counterclockwise: red, yellow, green, cyan, blue, and magenta. This is also the same order as in the HSV single hexcone model. In fact, one can think of HLS as a deformation of HSV, in which white is "pulled" upwards to form the upper hexcone from the $V = 1$ plane. As with the single hexcone model, the complement of any hue is located 180° further around the double hexcone, and saturation is measured radially from the vertical axis, from 0 on the axis to 1 on the surface. Lightness is 0 for black (at the lower tip of the double hexcone) to 1 for white (at the upper tip). Color Plate 25 shows an exploded view of the HLS model, in which the double hexcone has been topologically deformed into a double cone.

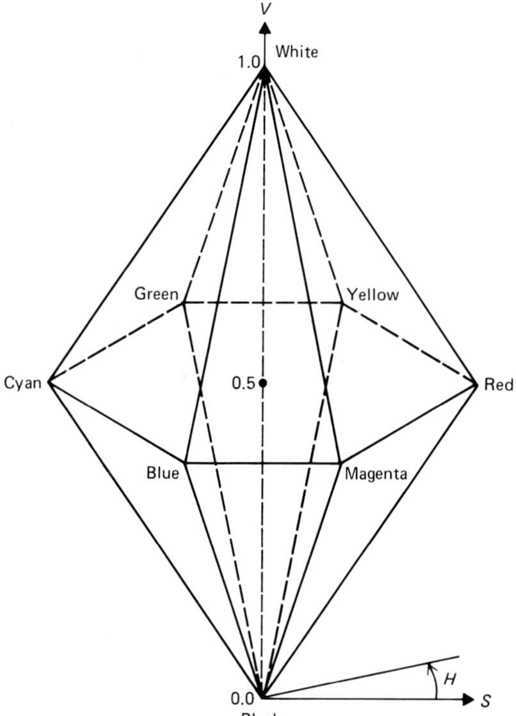

Fig. 17.31 Double hexcone HLS color model.

*For consistency with the HSV model, we have changed from the Tektronix convention of blue at 0° and depict the model as a double hexcone rather than as a double cone.

The HLS model, like the HSV model, is easy to use. The grays all have $S = 0$, but the maximally saturated hues are at $S = 1$, $L = 0.5$. If potentiometers are used to specify the color-model parameters, setting $L = 0.5$ to get the strongest possible colors is a disadvantage over the HSV model, in which $S = 1$ and $V = 1$ achieve the same effect. Notice, however, that neither the V in HSV nor the L in HLS corresponds to luminance in the YIQ model, so two different colors defined in either space can easily have the same luminance and be indistinguishable on black and white TV or videotape. Also note that, strictly speaking, "lightness" is a term normally used in discussing light reflection, and hence is used somewhat loosely here.

The following conversion procedures are modified from those given by Metrick [GSPC79] to leave H as *undefined* when $S = 0$ and to have $H = 0$ for red rather than for blue:

```
procedure RGB_TO_HLS(r, g, b: real; var h, l, s: real);
  {Given: r, g, b, each in [0, 1]}
  {Desired: h in [0, 360), l and s in [0, 1], except if s = 0,
    then h = undefined}
begin
  max := MAXIMUM(r, g, b);
  min := MINIMUM(r, g, b);
  l:= (max + min)/2;                    {lightness}
  {Calculate saturation}
  if max = min
    then                                {r = g = b: achromatic case}
      begin
        s := 0;
        h := undefined
      end     {achromatic case}
    else
      begin                             {chromatic case}
        if l<=0.5 then s := (max - min)/(max + min)
                  else s := (max - min)/(2 - max - min);
        {Calculate hue}
        rc := (max - r)/(max - min);
        gc := (max - g)/(max - min);
        bc := (max - b)/(max - min);

        if      r = max then h :=  bc - gc       {resulting color between
                                                   yellow and magenta}
        else if g = max then h :=  2 + rc - bc   {resulting color between
                                                   cyan and yellow}
        else if b = max then h := 4 + gc - rc;   {resulting color between
                                                   magenta and cyan}
        h := h*60;                               {convert to degrees}
        if h < 0.0 then h := h + 360             {make nonnegative}
      end     {chromatic case}
end     {RGB_TO_HLS}
```

```
procedure HLS_TO_RGB(var r, g, b: real; h, l, s: real);
  {given: h in [0, 360] or undefined, l and s in [0, 1]}
  {desired: r, g, b, each in [0, 1]}
function VALUE(n1, n2, hue)
  begin
    if hue > 360 then hue := hue - 360;
    if hue < 0        then hue       := hue + 360;
    if hue < 60       then VALUE := n1 + (n2 - n1)*hue/60;
    else if hue < 180 then VALUE := n2;
    else if hue < 240 then VALUE := n1 + (n2 - n1)*(240 - hue)/60;
    else                   VALUE := n1
  end    {VALUE};
begin
  if l<=0.5 then m2 :=  l*(1 + s)
            else m2  := l + s - l*s;
  m1 := 2*l - m2;
  if s = 0
    then                                {achromatic: there is no hue}
      if h = undefined
        then r := g := b := l           {this is the achromatic case}
        else ERROR                      {Error if s = 0 and h has a value}
    else                                {chromatic: there is a hue}
      begin
        r := VALUE(m1, m2, h + 120);
        g := VALUE(m1, m2, h);
        b := VALUE(m1, m2, h - 120)
      end
end    {HLS_TO_RGB}
```

17.4.6 Interpolating in Color Space

Color interpolation is necessary in at least three cases: Gouraud shading (Section 16.4), blending two images together as in a "fade-in", "fade-out" sequence, and combining the color of a partially transparent surface with that of another surface (Section 16.6). The results of the interpolation depend on the color model in which the colors are interpolated: hence care must be taken to select an appropriate model.

If the conversion from one color model to another transforms a straight line (representing the interpolation path) in one color model into a straight line in the other color model, the interpolation results in both models will be the same. This is the case for the RGB, CMY, and YIQ color models, all of which are related by simple affine transformations. However, a straight line in the RGB model does *not* in general transform into a straight line in either the HSV or HSL models. Consider, for example, the interpolation between red and green. In RGB, Red = (1, 0, 0) and Green = (0, 1, 0). Their interpolation (with both weights equal to 0.5 for convenience) is (0.5, 0.5, 0). Applying algorithm *RGB_TO_HSV* to this result, we have (60°, 1, 0.5). Now, representing red and green in HSV, we have (0°, 1, 1) and

(120°, 1, 1). But interpolating with equal weights in HSV we have (60°, 1, 1); thus the value differs by 0.5 from the same interpolation in RGB.

As a second example, consider interpolating red and cyan in both the RGB and HSV models. In RGB, we start with (1, 0, 0) and (0, 1, 1), respectively, and interpolate to (0.5, 0.5, 0.5) which in HSV is represented as (*undefined,* 0, 0.5). In HSV, red and cyan are (0°, 1, 1) and (180°, 1, 1). Interpolating, we have (90°, 1, 1): a new hue at maximum value and saturation has been introduced, whereas the "right" result from combining equal amounts of complementary colors is a gray value. Here again we have a case where interpolating and then transforming gives different results than transforming and then interpolating.

Which model should be used for interpolation? If the traditional results from additive colors are desired (note that interpolation is basically an additive process), then RGB is preferred to HSV or HLS. If, on the other hand, the objective is to interpolate between two colors of fixed hue (or saturation) and to maintain the fixed hue (saturation) for all interpolated colors, then HSV or HLS is preferable.

17.5 REPRODUCING COLOR HARD COPY

Color images are reproduced in print in a way similar to that used for monochrome images, but four sets of halftone dots are printed, one for each of the subtractive primaries, plus black. Black is used because in printing it is difficult to obtain a deep black by combining the three primaries. The dots are carefully positioned with repect to one another so as not to overlap. The orientation of each of the grids of dots is different, to avoid creating interference patterns. Color Plate 26 shows an enlarged halftone color pattern. Our eyes spatially integrate the light reflected from adjacent dots, so we see the color defined by the proportions of primaries in adjacent dots. This spatial integration of different colors is the same phenomenon we experience when viewing the triads of red, green, and blue dots on color TV.

We deduce, then, that color reproduction in print and on CRTs depends on the same spatial integration used in monochrome reproduction. The monochrome dithering techniques discussed in Section 17.2.2 can also be used with color to extend the number of available colors, again at the expense of resolution. Consider a color display with three bits per pixel—one each for red, green, and blue. We can use a 2×2 pixel pattern area to obtain 125 different colors, because each pattern can display five intensities for each of red, green, and blue, by using the halftone patterns in Fig. 17.8. This results in $5 \times 5 \times 5 = 125$ color combinations. Color Plate 27 shows 125 colors generated in exactly this way.

Not all color reproduction depends exclusively on spatial integration. For instance, the Xerox color copier and Applicon ink jet plotter actually mix subtractive pigments on the paper's surface to obtain a small set of different colors. In the case of the Xerox copier, the colored pigments are first deposited in three successive steps, then heated and melted together. The inks sprayed by the plotter mix before drying. Spatial integration may be used to further expand the color range.

17.6 COLOR HARMONY

Contemporary color display and hard-copy devices can produce a wide gamut of colors. Some color pairs harmonize well with one another, while other pairs clash with great dissonance. How can we select colors that harmonize? Many books have been written on color selection, including [BIRR61]; we state here a few of the simpler rules which will help produce color harmony.

The most fundamental rule is to use colors selected according to some method, typically by traversing a smooth path in a color model and/or by restricting the colors to planes (or hexcones) of constant value in a color model. This might mean using colors of the same hue, or two complementary colors and mixtures thereof, or colors of constant lightness or value. For instance, Color Plate 28 shows the use of colors chosen along a path in the RGB color model. Furthermore, colors are best spaced at equal *perceptual* distances in whatever subspace they are drawn from (this is not the same as being equally spaced increments of a coordinate in the subspace and can be difficult to implement). Note too that linear interpolation (as in Gouraud shading) between two colors produces different results in different color spaces (see Exercise 14).

A random selection of different hues and saturations will usually appear quite garish. Alvy Ray Smith described an experiment in which a 16×16 grid was filled with randomly generated colors. Not unexpectedly, the grid was unattractive. Sorting the 256 colors according to their H, S, and V and redisplaying them on the grid in their new order gave a remarkable improvement to the appearance of the grid.

More specific instances of these rules suggest that if a chart contains just a few colors, the complement of one of the colors should be used in the background. With an image containing many different colors, a neutral (gray) background should be used. If two adjoining colors are not particularly harmonious, a thin black border can be used to set them apart.

From a physiological viewpoint, the eye's low sensitivity to blue suggests that blue on a black background will be hard to distinguish. By inference, yellow (the complement of blue) on a white background (the complement of black) also will be relatively hard to distinguish (see Exercise 10). For the sake of those of us who are red–green color-blind (the most common form), it is also good to avoid reds and greens with low saturation and luminance.

17.7 USING COLOR IN INTERACTIVE GRAPHICS

There are two groups of people who must deal with color in interactive graphics systems: the programmer and the user. The programmer's job is to provide the user with an understandable color model or reasonable selection of colors. In simple applications, the programmer will assign colors when creating an image—the user will not be involved. This might be the case in command and control or data presentation applications. In other applications, the user will simply be presented with a fixed set of colors from which to select, typically in the form of a grid of color squares displayed across the bottom of the screen. A logical pick device is employed to select the desired color. Sometimes several sets of colors (usually called palettes) might be available, each one being a set of colors which have been chosen, by the rules of color harmony, as an attractive color scheme.

The most general application (with respect to color) allows the user to create a palette of colors, either by specification of points in some color space or constructively by blending a few base colors in various ways to create new hues and to make tints, tones, and shades of the hues. This would typically be done in painting and animation applications, where very fine control over color is necessary.

EXERCISES

17.1 Derive an equation for the number of intensities that can be represented by $m \times m$ pixel patterns, where each pixel has w bits.

17.2 Write the programs needed to gamma-correct a black and white display through a look-up table. Input parameters are γ, I_0, m, the number of intensities desired, and c, the constant in Eq. (17.3).

17.3 Write a general algorithm to display a pixel array on a bi-level output device. The inputs to the algorithm are: (a) an $m \times m$ array of pixel intensities, with w bits per pixel; and (b) an $n \times n$ growth sequence matrix. Assume that the output device has resolution of $m \cdot n \times m \cdot n$.

17.4 Repeat the previous problem by using ordered dither. Now the output device has resolution $m \times m$, the same as the input array of pixel intensities.

17.5 Write an algorithm to display a filled polygon on a bi-level device by using an $n \times n$ filling pattern.

17.6 If certain patterns are used to fill a polygon being displayed on an interlaced raster display, all of the "on bits" will fall either on the odd or the even scan lines, introducing a slight amount of flicker. Revise the algorithm from Exercise 5 to permute rows of the $n \times n$ pattern so that alternate replications of the pattern will alternate use of the odd and even scan lines. Figure 17.32 shows the results obtained by using intensity level one from Fig. 17.8, with and without this alternation.

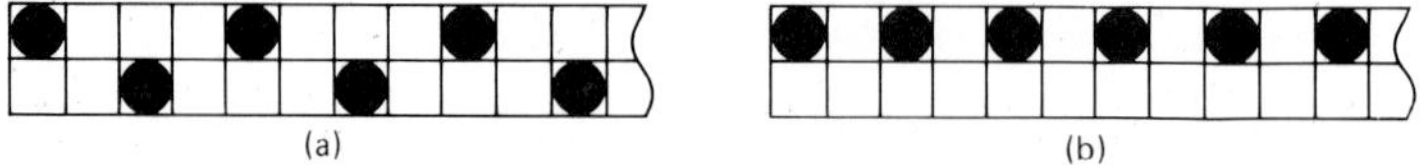

Fig. 17.32 Results obtained by using intensity level 1 from Fig. 17.8 in the following way: (a) with alternation (intensified pixels are on both scan lines), and (b) without alternation (all intensified pixels are on one scan line).

17.7 Plot the locus of points of the constant luminance values 0.25, 0.50, and 0.75, defined by $Y = 0.30R + 0.59G + 0.11B$, on the RGB cube, the HLS double cone, and the HSV hexcone.

17.8 Why are the opposite ends of the spectrum in the CIE diagram connected by a straight line?

17.9 For the YIQ, HSV, and HSL models, what combinations of R, G, and B define intensity?

17.10 Calculate the luminances of the additive and subtractive primaries in the YIQ model. Rank the colors by luminance. This gives their relative intensities, both on a black and white TV and as perceived by our eyes.

17.11 Discuss the design of a raster display which uses HSV or HLS as its color specification instead of RGB.

17.12 With which color models are the rules of color harmony most easily applied?

17.13 Calculate the x, y, and z coordinates of the RGB TV primaries from the CIE chromaticity diagram. Derive a transformation from the RGB to CIE color coordinates.

Bibliography

ADAG67 *Adage Software Reference Manual,* Adage Corporation, Boston, Mass., 1967.

AHUJ68a Ahuja, D. V. "An Algorithm for Generating Spline-like Curves," *IBM Systems Journal,* 7 (3/4), 1968, pp. 206–217.

AHUJ68b Ahuja, D. V. and S. A. Coons, "Geometry for Construction and Display," *IBM Systems Journal,* 7 (3/4), 1968, pp. 188–205.

AKIM70 Akima, H., "A New Method of Interpolation and Smooth Curve Fitting Based on Local Procedures," *Journal of the ACM,* 17 (4), October 1970, pp. 589–602.

AKIM74 Akima, H, "A Method of Bivariate Interpolation and Smooth Surface Fitting Based on Local Procedures," *Communications of the ACM,* 17 (1), January 1974, pp. 18–20.

AKIN68 Akin, R. H. and J. M. Hood, "Photometry," in H. R. Luxemberg and R. L. Kuehn (eds.), *Display Systems Engineering,* McGraw-Hill, New York, 1968.

ANDE71 Anderson, S. E., "Computer Animation: A Survey," *Journal of Micrographics,* 5 (a), September 1971, pp. 13–20.

ANSI81 American National Standards Institute, "ANSI X3H32 Proposal for Structure," Document X3H32/81-09R1, April 20, 1981; "ANSI X3H31 Attributes Proposal," Document X3H31/81-10R1, April 20, 1981; "ANSI X3H31 Status Report on the H31 Strawman Proposal on Input Functionality," Document X3H31/81-11R1, April 20, 1981.

AOKI78 Aoki, M. and M. Levine, "Computer Generating of Realistic Pictures," *Computers and Graphics,* 3 (1978), pp. 149–161.

APOL81 "Apollo Domain Architecture," Apollo Computer, North Billerica, MA, February 1981.

APPE67 Appel, A., "The Notion of Quantitative Invisibility and the Machine Rendering of Solids," *Proceedings of the ACM National Conference,* Thompson Books, Washington D.C., 1967, pp. 387.

APPE68 Appel, A., *Some Techniques for Shading Machine-Renderings of Solids,* SJCC 1968, Thompson Books, Washington, D.C., pp. 37–45.

ARMI70 Armit, A. P. and A. R. Forrest, "Interactive Surface Design." *Computer Graphics 1970,* Brunel University, April 1970.

ARMI71 Armit, A. P., "The Interactive Languages of Multipatch and Multiobject Design Systems," *Computer Aided Design,* 4 (1), Autumn 1971, pp. 10-15.

ARMS73 Armstrong, J. R., "Design of a Graphic Generator for Remote Terminal Application," *IEEE Transactions on Computers,* C-22 (5), May 1973, pp. 464-468.

ATHE78 Atherton, P., K. Weiler and D. Greenberg, "Polygon Shadow Generation," SIGGRAPH '78 proceedings, published as *Computer Graphics,* 12 (3), August 1978, pp. 275-281.

BADL77 Badler, N. I., "Disk Generators for a Raster Display Device," *Computer Graphics and Image Processing,* 6 (6), December 1977, pp. 589-593.

BAEC69 Baecker, R. M., "Picture-Driven Animation," SJCC 1969, AFIPS Press, Montvale, N.J., pp. 273-288.

BAEC76 Baecker, R. M., "A Conversational Extensible System for the Animation of Shaded Images," SIGGRAPH '76 proceedings, published as *Computer Graphics,* 10 (2), Summer 1976, pp. 32-39

BARN75 Barnhill, R. E. and R. F. Riesenfeld (eds.), *Computer Aided Geometric Design,* Academic Press, New York, 1975.

BARN78 Barnhill, R. E., J. H. Brown, and I. M. Klucewicz, "A New Twist in Computer Aided Geometric Design," *Computer Graphics and Image Processing,* 8 (1), August 1978, pp. 78-91.

BARR74 Barrett, R. C. and B. W. Jordan, Jr., "Scan-Conversion Algorithms for a Cell Organized Raster Display," *Communications of the ACM,* 17 (3), March 1974, pp. 157-163.

BARR79 Barros, J., and H. Fuchs, "Generating Smooth Line Drawings on Video Displays, SIGGRAPH '79 Proceedings, published as *Computer Graphics,* 13(2), August 1979, pp. 260-269.

BASK68 Baskin, H. B. and S. P. Morse, "A Multilevel Modeling Structure for Interactive Graphics Design," *IBM Systems Journal,* 7 (3/4), 1968, pp. 218-228.

BASK76 Baskett, F. and L. Shustek, "The Design of a Low-Cost Video Graphics Terminal," SIGGRAPH '76 proceedings, published as *Computer Graphics,* 10 (2), Summer 1976, pp. 235-240.

BATT71 Batter, J. J. and F. P. Brooks, Jr., *GROPE-1: A Computer Display to the Sense of Feel,* IFIP 1971, North-Holland, Amsterdam, pp. 759-763.

BAUD80 Baudelaire, P., and M. Stone, "Techniques for Interactive Raster Graphics," Proceedings 1980 SIGGRAPH Conference, published as *Computer Graphics,* 14(3), July 1980, pp. 314-320.

BAUM74 Baumgart, B. G., *Geometric Modeling for Computer Vision,* Stanford Univ. Computer Sci. Dept., AIM-249, STAN-CS-74-463, October 1974.

BAUM75 Baumgart, B. G., *A Polyhedron Representation for Computer Vision,* NCC 1975, pp. 589-596.

BAYE73 Bayer, B. E., "An Optimum Method for Two-Level Rendition of Continuous-Tone Pictures," *International Conference on Communications,* Conference Record, 1973, pp. (26-11)-(26-15).

BECH80 Bechtolsheim, A. and F. Baskett, "High-Performance Raster Graphics for Microcomputer Systems," Proceedings 1980 SIGGRAPH Conference, published as *Computer Graphics,* 14(3), July 1980, pp. 43–47.

BELS76 Belser, K., "Comment on an Improved Algorithm for the Generation of Nonparametric Curves," *IEEE Transactions on Computers,* C-25 (1), January 1976, p 103.

BERG78 Bergeron, R. D., P. Bono, and J. D. Foley, "Graphics Programming Using the Core System," *Computing Surveys,* 10(4), December 1978, pp. 389–443.

BERT79 Berthod, M. and J. Maroy, "Learning in Syntactic Recognition of Symbols Drawn on a Graphic Tablet," *Computer Graphics and Image Processing,* 9 (2), February 1979, pp. 166–182.

BEZI72 Bezier, P. *Numerical Control—Mathematics and Applications,* A. R. Forrest (trans.), Wiley, London, 1972.

BEZI74 Bezier, P., "Mathematical and Practical Possibilities of UNISURF," in R. E. Barnhill and R. F. Riesenfeld (eds.), *Computer Aided Geometric Design,* Academic, New York, 1974.

BIBB73 Bibberman, L. M., *Perception of Displayed Information,* Plenum, New York, 1973.

BIRR61 Birren, F., *Creative Color,* Van Nostrand Reinhold Co., New York, 1961.

BITZ66 Bitzer, D. L. and H. G. Slottow, *The Plasma Panel: A Digitally Addressable Display with Inherent Memory,* FJCC 1966, Spartan Books, Washington, D.C., pp. 541–547.

BLAT67 Blatt, H. *Conic Display Generator Using Multiplying Digital-Analog Converters,* FJCC 1967, Thompson Books, Washington, D.C., pp. 177–184.

BLIN76a Blinn, J. F. and A. C. Goodrich, "The Internal Design of the IG Routines: An Interactive Graphics System for a Large Time-sharing Environment," SIGGRAPH '76 proceedings, published as *Computer Graphics,* 10 (2), Summer 1976, pp. 229–234.

BLIN76b Blinn, J. F. and M. E. Newell, "Texture and Reflection in Computer Generated Images," *Communications of the ACM,* 19 (10), October 1976, pp. 542–547.

BLIN77a Blinn, J. F., "Models of Light Reflection for Computer Synthesized Pictures," SIGGRAPH '77 proceedings, published as *Computer Graphics,* 11 (2), Summer 1977, pp. 192–198.

BLIN77b Blinn, J. F., "A Homogeneous Formulation for Lines in 3-Space," SIGGRAPH '77 proceedings, published as *Computer Graphics,* 11 (2), Summer 1977, pp. 237–241.

BLIN78a Blinn, J. F. and M. E. Newell, "Clipping Using Homogeneous Coordinates," SIGGRAPH '78 proceedings, published as *Computer Graphics,* 12 (3), August 1978, pp. 245–251.

BLIN78b Blinn, J. F., "Simulation of Wrinkled Surfaces," SIGGRAPH '78 Proceedings, published as *Computer Graphics,* 12 (3), August 1978, pp. 286–292.

BLIN78c Blinn, J. F., *Computer Display of Curved Surfaces,* Ph.D. dissertation, Univ. of Utah, Dept. of Computer Science, December 1978.

BLIN80 Blinn, J. F., L. Carpenter, J. Lane, and T. Whitted, "Scan Line Methods for Displaying Parametrically Defined Surfaces," *Communications of the ACM,* 23 (1), January 1980, pp. 23–34.

BOEH71 Boehm, B. et al., "Interactive Problem-Solving—An Experimental Study of Lock-out Effects," *Proc. 1971 SJCC,* pp. 205–210.

BOLT79 Bolt, Richard A., *Spatial Data-Management,* report to DARPA, MIT Architecture Machine Group, Cambridge, Mass., 1979.

BOLT80 Bolt, R. A., " 'Put-That-There': Voice and Gesture at the Graphics Interface," SIGGRAPH '80 Proceedings, published as *Computer Graphics,* 14(3), July 1980, pp. 262–270.

BOND69 Bond, A. H., J. Rightnour and L. S. Coles, "An Interactive Display Monitor in a Batch-processing Environment with Remote Entry," *Communications of the ACM,* 12 (11), November 1969, pp. 595–603.

BOUK69 Bouknight, W. J., *An Improved Procedure for Generation of Half-tone Computer Graphics Representations,* Univ. Ill. Coord. Sci. Lab., R-432, September 1969.

BOUK70a Bouknight, W. J. and K. C. Kelly, *An Algorithm for Producing Half-tone Computer Graphics Presentations with Shadows and Movable Light Sources,* SJCC 1970, AFIPS Press, Montvale, N.J., pp. 1–10.

BOUK70b Bouknight, W. J., "A Procedure for Generation of Three-dimensional Half-toned Computer Graphics Representations," *Communications of the ACM,* 13 (9), September 1970, pp. 527–536.

BOWM68 Bowman, W. J., *Graphic Communication,* Wiley, New York, 1968.

BRAC70 Bracchi, G. and M. Somalvico, "An Interactive Software System for Computer Aided Design: An Application to Circuit Project," *Communications of the ACM,* 13 (9), September 1970, pp. 537–545.

BRAI75 Braid, I. C., "The Synthesis of Solids Bounded by Many Faces," *Communications of the ACM,* 18 (4), April 1975, pp. 209–216.

BREN70 Brenner, A. E. and P. de Bruyne, "A Sonic Pen: A Digital Stylus System," *IEEE Transactions on Computers,* EC-19 (6), June 1970, pp. 546–548.

BRES65 Bresenham, J. E., "Algorithm for Computer Control of Digital Plotter," *IBM Syst. J.,* 4 (1) 1965, pp. 25–30.

BRES77 Bresenham, J. E., "A Linear Algorithm for Incremental Digital Display of Circular Arcs," *Communications of the ACM,* 20 (2), February 1977, pp. 100–106.

BROW64 Brown, R., "On-Line Computer Recognition of Hand-Printed Characters," *IEEE Transactions on Computers,* EC-13 (12), December 1964, pp. 750–752.

BROW71 Brown, F. H. and M. T. Zayac, *A Multi-color Plasma Panel Display,* Owens-Illinois, 1971.

BROW79 Brown, H. G., C. D. O'Brien, W. Sawchuk and J. Storey, "TELIDON: A New Approach to Videotex System Design," *IEEE Transactions on Consumer Electronics,* Special Issue on TELETEXT and VIEWDATA, July 1979.

BUIT75 Bui-Tuong, Phong, "Illumination for Computer-Generated Pictures," *Communications of the ACM,* 18 (6), June 1975, pp. 311–317.

BURT76 Burtnyk, N. and M. Wein, "Interactive Skeleton Techniques for Enhancing Motion Dynamics in Key Frame Animation," *Communications of the ACM,* 19 (10), October 1976, pp. 564–569.

BURT72 Burton, R. P., *Real-time Measurement of Multiple Three-dimensional Positions,* Univ. Utah Computer Sci. Dept., UTEC-CSc-72-122, 1972, NTIS AD-262 028.

BURT74 Burton, R. P. and I. E. Sutherland, *Twinkle Box: A Three-dimensional Computer Input Device,* NCC 1974, AFIPS Press, pp. 513–520.

BURT77 Burton, W., " Representation of Many-sided Polygons and Polygonal Lines for Rapid Processing," *Communications of the ACM,* 20 (3), March 1977, pp. 166–171.

BUTL79 Butland, J., "Surface Drawing Made Simple," *Computer-Aided Design,* 11 (1), January 1979, pp. 19–22.

BYTE81 *BYTE,* Special Issue on Smalltalk, 6(8), August 1981.

CALI California Computer Products, Inc. *Calcomp Subroutine Reference Manual,* California Computer Products, Inc., Anaheim, California 92801.

CALV68 Calvert, T. W., *Projections of Multidimensional Data for Use in Man Computer Graphics,* FJCC 1968, Thompson Books, Washington, D.C., pp. 227–231.

CAPO76 Capowski, J. J., "Matrix Transform Processor for Evans and Sutherland LDS-2 Graphics System," *IEEE Transactions on Computers,* C-27 (7), July 1976, pp. 703–714.

CARD78 Card, S., W. K. English, and B. J. Burr, "Evaluation of Mouse, Rate-controlled Isometric Joystick, Step Keys, and Text Keys for Text Selection on a CRT," *Ergonomics,* 21 (8), August 1978, pp. 601–613.

CARD80 Card, S., T. Moran, and A. Newell, "The Keystroke-Level Model for User Performance Time with Interactive Systems," *Communications of the ACM,* 23(7), July 1980, pp. 396–410.

CARL78 Carlbom, I. and J. Paciorek, "Geometric Projection and Viewing Transformations," *Computing Surveys,* 1(4), 1978, pp. 465–502.

CARL80 Carlbom, Ingrid B., *System Architecture for High-Performance Vector Graphics,* Ph.D. thesis, Dept. of Computer Science, Brown University, Providence, R.I., 1980.

CARP82 Carpenter, L., A. Fournier, and D. Fussell, "Computer Rendering of Stochastic Models," *Communications of the ACM,* 25(7), June 1982, pp. 371–384.

CART75 Carterette, B. C. and M. P. Friedman (eds.), *Handbook of Perception,* Vol. V, *Seeing,* Academic Press, New York, 1975.

CARU75 Caruthers, L., and A. van Dam, *User's Tutorial for the General Purpose Graphics System,* Technical Report, Katholieke Universiteit, Nijmegen, The Netherlands, 1975.

CAST74 Castleman, P. A. et al., *The Implementation of the PROPHET System,* NCC 1974, AFIPS Press, p. 457–468.

CATM74 Catmull, E., *A Subdivision Algorithm for Computer Display of Curved Surfaces,* Univ. Utah Computer Sci. Dept., UTEC-CSc-74-133, December 1974.

CATM75 Catmull, E., "Computer Display of Curved Surfaces," *Proc. IEEE Conf. on Computer Graphics, Pattern Recognition and Data Structure,* May 1975, reprinted in *Tutorial and Selected Readings in Interactive Computer Graphics,* H. Freeman (ed.), IEEE, 1980, pp. 309–315.

CATM78a Catmull, E., "A Hidden-Surface Algorithm with Anti-Aliasing," SIGGRAPH '78 Proceedings, published as *Computer Graphics,* 12(13) August 1978, pp. 6–11.

CATM78b Catmull, E. and J. Clark, "Recursively Generated B-Spline Surfaces on Arbitrary Topological Meshes," *Computer Aided Design,* 10(6), November 1978.

CATM78c Catmull, E., "The Problems of Computer-Assisted Animation," SIGGRAPH '78 Proceedings, published as *Computer Graphics,* 12(3), August 1978, pp. 348–353.

CATM79 Catmull, E., "A Tutorial on Compensation Tables," SIGGRAPH '79 Proceedings, published as *Computer Graphics,* 13 (2), August 1979, pp. 1–7.

CATM80 Catmull, E. and A. R. Smith, "3-D Transformations of Images in Scanline Order," SIGGRAPH '80 Proceedings, published as *Computer Graphics,* 14(3), July 1980, pp. 279–285.

CHAS65 Chasen, S. H., *The Introduction of Man–Computer Graphics into the Aerospace Industry,* FJCC 1965, Spartan Books, Washington, D.C., pp. 883–892.

CHAS78 Chasen, S. H., *Geometric Principles and Procedures for Computer Graphics Applications,* Prentice-Hall, Englewood Cliffs, N.J., 1978.

CHEE73 Cheek, T. B., *A Graphic Display System Using Raster-Scan Monitors and Real-Time Scan Conversion,* 1973 SID Int. Symp. Dig. Tech. Papers, May 1973, pp. 56.

CHER76 Cheriton, D., *Man–Machine Interface Design for Timesharing Systems,* Proceedings ACM 1976 Conference, pp. 362–366.

CHRI75 Christ, Richard F., "Review and Analysis of Color Coding Research for Visual Displays," *Human Factors,* 17(6), June 1975, pp. 542–570.

CHRI67 Christensen, C. and E. N. Pinson, *Multi-function Graphics for a Large Computer System,* FJCC 1967, Thompson Books, Washington, D.C., pp. 697–712.

CITR68 Citron, J. and J. H. Whitney, *CAMP: Computer Assisted Movie Production,* FJCC 1968, Thompson Books, Washington, D.C., pp. 1299–1308.

CLAR76 Clark, J. H., "Designing Surfaces in 3-D," *Communications of the ACM,* 19(8), August 1976, pp. 454–460.

CLAR76a Clark, J. H., "Hierarchical Geometric Models for Visible Surface Algorithms," *Communications of the ACM,* 19(10), October 1976, pp. 547–554.

CLAR78b Clark, J. H., *Parametric Curves, Surfaces, and Volumes in Computer Graphics and Computer-aided Geometric Design,* NASA Ames Research Center, 1978.

CLAR8O Clark, J. H., "A VLSI Geometry Processor for Graphics," *IEEE Computer,* 12 (7), July 1980.

COHE69 Cohen, D. and T. M. P. Lee, *Fast Drawing of Curves for Computer Display,* SJCC 1969, AFIPS Press, Montvale, N.J., pp. 297–307.

COMB68 Comba, P. G., "A Procedure for Detecting Intersections of Three Dimensional Objects," *Journal of the ACM,* 15(3), July 1968, pp. 354.

COOK81 Cook, R. L. and K. Torrance, "A Reflectance Model for Computer Graphics," SIGGRAPH '81 Proceedings, published as *Computer Graphics* 15(3), August 1981, pp. 307–316.

COON66 Coons, S. A., "Computer Graphics and Innovative Engineering Design," *Datamation,* May 1966, pp 32.

COON67 Coons, S. A., *Surfaces for Computer Aided Design of Space Forms,* MIT Project Mac, TR-41, June 1967.

CORN70 Cornsweet, T. N., *Visual Perception,* Academic Press, New York, 1970.

CORN71 Cornwell, B., "Computer Generated Simulation Films," *Inf. Disp.,* 8(1), January 1971, pp. 21.

COTT72 Cotton, I., *Network Graphic Attention Handling,* Online 72 International Conference, Brunel University, Uxbridge, England, pp. 465-490.

CREA71 Creagh, L. T., A. R. Kmetz, and R. A. Reynolds, *Liquid Crystal Displays,* 1971 IEEE Int. Conv. Dig., pp. 630.

CROW77a Crow, F., "Shadow Algorithms for Computer Graphics," SIGGRAPH '77 Proceedings, published as *Computer Graphics,* 11(2), Summer 1977, pp. 242–247.

CROW77b Crow, F. C., "The Aliasing Problem in Computer-generated Shaded Images," *Communications of the ACM,* 20 (11), November 1977, pp. 799–805.

CROW78a Crow, F. C., "Shaded Computer Graphics in the Entertainment Industry," *Computer,* 11(3), March 1978, pp. 11–22.

CROW78b Crow, F., "The Use of Grayscale for Improved Raster Display of Vectors and Characters," SIGGRAPH '78 Proceedings, published as *Computer Graphics,* 12 (3), August 1978, pp. 1–5.

CROW81 Crow, F. "A Comparison of Antialiasing Techniques," *IEEE Computer Graphics and Applications,* 1(1), January 1981, pp. 40–49.

CSUR74 Csuri, C. A., *Real-Time Computer Animation,* IFIP 1974, North-Holland, Amsterdam, pp. 707–711.

DANI78 Danielsson, P. E., "Comments on a Circle Generator for Display Devices," *Computer Graphics and Image Processing,* 7(2), April 1978, pp. 300–301.

DATE81 Date, C., *An Introduction to Database Systems,* 3rd. ed., Addison-Wesley, Reading, Mass., 1981.

DAVI64 Davis, M. R. and T. O. Ellis, *The Rand Tablet: A Man-Machine Graphical Communication Device,* FJCC 1964, Spartan Books, Baltimore, Md., pp. 325–331

DAVI69 Davis, S., *Computer Data Displays,* Prentice-Hall, Englewood Cliffs, N.J., 1969.

DAVS62 Davson, H. (ed.), *The Eye,* Academic Press, New York, 1962.

DEFA76 DeFanti, T. A., *The Digital Component of the Circle Graphics Habitat,* NCC 1976, AFIPS Press, pp. 195–203.

DEFA80 DeFanti, T. A., ed., *SIGGRAPH Video Tape Review,* No. 1, 1980.

DENR75 Denert E., "GRAPHEX68: Graphical Language Features in Algol 68," *Computers and Graphics,* 1, 1975, pp. 195–202.

DENE74 Denes, P. R. and I. K. Gershkoff, "An Interactive System for Page Layout Design," *Proc. ACM Nat. Conf.,* 1974, p. 212.

DENE75 Denes, P. B., "A Scan-Type Graphics System for Interactive Computing," *Proc. IEEE Conf. on Computer Graphics, Pattern Recognition and Data Structure,* May 1975, pp. 21.

DERT66 Dertouzos, M. L. and H. L. Graham, *A Parametric Graphical Display Technique for Online Use,* FJCC 1966, Spartan Books, Washington, D.C., pp. 201-210.

DILL75 Dill, J. D. and J. J. Thomas, "On the Organization of a Remote Low Cost Intelligent Graphics Teminal," SIGGRAPH '75 Proceedings, published as *Computer Graphics,* 9(2), 1975, pp. 1-8.

DION78 Dionne, M. S. and A. K. Mackworth, "ANTICS: A System for Animating LISP Programs," *Computer Graphics and Image Processing,* 7(1), February 1978, pp. 105-119.

DONE78 Donelson, W. C., "Spatial Management of Information," Proceedings 1978 SIGGRAPH Conference, published as *Computer Graphics,* 12(3), August 1978, pp. 203-209.

DORO79 Doros, M., "Algorithms for Generation of Discrete Circles, Rings, and Disks," *Computer Graphics and Image Processing,* 10(4), August 1979, pp. 366-371.

DRUC68 Drucker, P. F., *The Age of Discontinuity: Guidelines to our Changing Society,* Harper & Row, New York, 1968.

DUBE78 Dube, R., G. J. Herron, F. F. Little, and R. F. Riesenfeld, "SURFED: An Interactive Editor for Free-Form Surfaces," *Computer Aided Design,* 10(2), March 1978, pp. 111-115.

DUDA68 Duda, R. D. and P. E. Hart, *Experiments in the Recognition of Hand-printed Text, II: Context Analysis,* FJCC 1968, Thompson Books, Washington, D.C., pp. 1139-1150.

DUNG78 Dungan, W., A. Stenger and G. Sutty, "Texture Tile Considerations for Raster Graphics," SIGGRAPH '78 Proceedings, published as *Computer Graphics,* 12(3), August 1978, pp. 130-134.

EAST68 Eastman Kodak, *Halftone Methods for the Graphics Arts,* Data Book Q-3, Eastman Kodak Company, Rochester, N.Y., 1968.

EAST75 Eastman, C., J. Lividini and D. Stoker, *A Database for Designing Large Physical Systems,* AFIPS Press, NCC 1975, pp. 603-611.

EAST77 Eastman, C. M. and M. Henrion, "GLIDE: A Language for Design Information Systems," SIGGRAPH '77 Proceedings, published as *Computer Graphics,* 11(2), 1977, pp. 24-33.

EMBL81 Embley, D. and G. Nagy, "Behavioral Aspects of Text Editors," *Computing Surveys,* 13(1), March 1981, pp. 33-70.

ENCA80 Encarnacao, J., *et. al.,* "The Workstation Concept of GKS and the Resulting Conceptual Differences to the GSPC Core System," SIGGRAPH '80 Proceedings, published as *Computer Graphics,* 14(3), July 1980, pp. 226-230.

ENGE75 Engel, S., and R. Granda, *Guidelines for Man/Display Interfaces,* Technical Report TR 00.2720, 1975, IBM, Poughkeepsie, NY.

ENGL68 Englebart, D. C. and W. K. English, *A Research Center for Augmenting Human Intellect,* FJCC 1968, Thompson Books, Washington, D.C., p. 395.

ENGL67 English, W. K., D. C. Englebart and M. L. Berman, "Display-selection Techniques for Text Manipulation," *IEEE Trans. on Human Factors in Electronics,* HFE-8(1), 1967, pp. 21–31.

ENTW77 Entwisle, J., "An Image-processing Approach to Computer Graphics," *Computers and Graphics,* 2(2), 1977, pp. 111–118.

ERDA Erdahl, A. C., *Displaying Computer-generated Half-tone Pictures in Real Time,* Univ. Utah Computer Sci. Dept., TR-14.

EVAN71 Evans & Sutherland Computer Corporation, *Line Drawing System Model 1: System Reference Manual,* Salt Lake City, Utah, 1971.

EVAN77a Evans & Sutherland Computer Corporation, *Picture System 2 User's Manual,* Evans & Sutherland Computer Corp., Salt Lake City, Utah, May 1977.

EVAN77b Evans & Sutherland Computer Corporation, *Picture System 2/PDP-11 Reference Manual,* E&S 901130-001-AL, Salt Lake City, Utah, 1977.

EVAN81 Evans & Sutherland Computer Corporation, *PS300 User's Manual,* Salt Lake City, Utah, 1981.

EVES65 Eves, H., *A Survey of Geometry,* Allyn and Bacon, Inc., Boston, 1965.

EWAL78 Ewald, R. H. and R. Fryer (eds.), "Final Report of the GSPC State-of-the Art Subcommittee," *Computer Graphics,* 12(1/2), June 1978.

FAIM69 Faiman, M. and J. Nievergelt (eds.), *Pertinent Concepts in Computer Graphics,* Proc. 2nd Univ. Ill. Conf. Computer Graphics, University of Illinois Press, Urbana, 1969.

FAUX79 Faux, I. D. and M. J. Pratt, *Computational Geometry for Design and Manufacture,* John Wiley, New York, 1979.

FEIN81 Feiner, S., S. Nagy, and A. van Dam, "An Integrated System for Creating and Presenting Complex Computer-Based Documents," Proceedings 1981 SIGGRAPH Conference, published as *Computer Graphics,* 15(3), August 1981, pp. 181–190.

FELD76 Feldmann, R. J., "The Design of Computing Systems for Molecular Modelling," *Ann. Rev. Biophys. Bioeng.,* 5, 1976, pp. 477–510.

FENG78 Feng, D. Y. and R. F. Riesenfeld, "A Symbolic System for Computer-aided Development of Surface Interpolants," *Software Pract. Exper.,* 8(4), July-August 1978, pp. 461–482.

FERG64 Ferguson, J., "Multivariate Curve Interpolation," *Journal of the ACM,* 11 (2), 1964, pp. 221–228.

FIEL77 Fields, A., R. Maisano and C. Marshall, *A Comparative Analysis of Methods for Tactical Data Inputting,* Army Research Institute, 1977.

FISH75 Fisher, M. A. and R. E. Nunley, "Raster Graphics for Spatial Applications," *Computer Graphics,* 9(2), Summer 1975, pp. 1–8.

FLOY75 Floyd, R. W. and L. Steinberg, "An Adaptive Algorithm for Spatial Gray Scale," *SID 1975 Int. Symp. Dig. Tech. Papers,* p. 36.

FOLE70 Foley, J. D., "Evaluation of Small Computers and Display Controls for

Computer Graphics," *Computer Group News,* 3(1), Jan./Feb. 1970, pp. 8-22.

FOLE71 Foley, J. D., "An Approach to the Optimum Design of Computer Graphics Systems," *Communications of the ACM,* 14(6), June 1971, pp. 380-390.

FOLE73 Foley, J. D., *Software for Satellite Graphics Systems,* Proc. of the ACM 1973 Annual Conference, pp. 76-80.

FOLE74 Foley, J. D. and V. L. Wallace, "The Art of Natural Graphic Man-Machine Conversation," *Proc. IEEE,* 62(4), April 1974, pp. 462-470.

FOLE76 Foley, J. D., "A Tutorial on Satellite Graphics Systems," *Computer,* 9 (8), August 1976, pp. 14-21.

FOLE79a Foley, J. D., *User's Manual: GWU Core System with Raster Extensions,* The George Washington University, Dept. of EE&CS, technical report GWU-EE/CS- 79-13, Washington, D.C., 1979.

FOLE79b Foley, J. D., J. Templeman, and D. Dastyar, "Some Raster Graphics Extensions to the Core System," SIGGRAPH '79 Proceedings, published as *Computer Graphics,* 13(2), August 1979, pp. 15-24.

FOLE80 Foley, J. D., "The Structure of Interactive Command Language," in R. A. Guedj, *et. al.,* eds., *Methodology of Interaction,* North-Holland, Amsterdam, 1980, pp. 227-234.

FOLE81a Foley, J. D., V. Wallace, and P. Chan, *The Human Factors of Interaction Techniques,* The George Washington University, Institute for Information Science and Technology Technical Report GWU-IIST-81-03, Washington, D.C., 1981. Also, University of Kansas, Department of Computer Science TR-81-3, Lawrence, Kansas, 1981.

FOLE81b Foley, J. D. and P.A. Wenner, "The George Washington University Core System Implementation," SIGGRAPH '81 Proceedings, published as *Computer Graphics,* 15(3), August 1981, pp. 123-131.

FORR72a Forrest, A. R., "Interactive Interpolation and Approximation by Bezier Polynomials," *Computer J.,* 15(1), January 1972, pp. 72.

FORR72b Forrest, A. R., "Mathematical Principles for Curve and Surface Representation," in *Curved Surfaces in Engineering,* I. J. Brown (ed.), IPC Science and Technology Press Ltd., Guildford, Surrey, England, 1972, pp. 5.

FORR72c Forrest, A. R., "On Coons and Other Methods for the Representation of Curved Surfaces," *Computer Graphics and Image Processing,* (1) 4, December 1972, pp. 341-354.

FORR74 Forrest, A. R., "A Computer Peripheral for Making Three-Dimensional Models," *Automatisme,* 16(6/7), June/July 1974, p. 347.

FREE67 Freeman, H. and P. P. Loutrel, "An Algorithm for the Solution of the Two-dimensional Hidden-Line Problem," *IEEE Transactions on Computers,* EC-16(6), December 1967, pp. 784-790.

FREE74 Freeman, H., "Computer Processing of Line-Drawing Images," *Computer Surveys,* 6(1), March 1974, pp. 57-93.

FREI79 Freiden, A., 'A CORE Viewing System for APL," *Computer Graphics,* 13(1), March 1979, pp. 55-77.

FRES76 "FRESS User's Manual," Text Systems, Inc., Barrington, R.I., 1976.

FRYE72 Fryer, R., "A Fortran Windowing Technique for Simulation and CAD," *Proceedings Vector General User's Group,* 1972, pp. 1–16.

FUCH77a Fuchs, H., J. Duran and B. Johnson, "A System for Automatic Acquisition of Three-Dimensional Data," *Proceedings of the 1977 NCC,* AFIPS Press, pp. 49–53.

FUCH77b Fuchs, H., Z. M. Kedem and S. P. Uselton, "Optimal Surface Reconstruction from Planar Contours," *Communications of the ACM,* 20(19), October 1977, pp. 693–702.

FUCH77c Fuchs, H., "Distributing a Visible Surface Algorithm over Multiple Processors," *Proceedings 1977 ACM National Conference,* pp. 449–450.

FUTR74 Futrelle, R. P., *GALATEA: Interactive Graphics for the Analysis of Moving Images,* IFIP, 1974, North-Holland, Amsterdam, pp. 712–716.

GALI69 Galimberti, R. and U. Montanari, "An Algorithm for Hidden-Line Elimination," *Communications of the ACM,* 12(4), April 1969, pp. 206–211.

GARR80a Garrett, M. "Logical Pick Device Simulation Algorithms for the Core System," *Computer Graphics,* 13(4), February 1980, pp. 303–313.

GARR80b Garrett, M. *A Unified Non-procedural Environment for Designing and Implementing Graphical Interfaces to Relational Data Base Management Systems,* Ph.D. dissertation, Dept of EE & CS Technical Report GWU-EE/CS-80-13, The George Washington University, Washington, D.C., 1980.

GELD53 Geldard, F. A., *The Human Senses,* John Wiley, 1953.

GENI Genisco Computers, Inc., *GCT-3011 Programmable Graphics Processor,* Genisco Computers, Inc., Irvine, Ca.

GEYE75 Geyer, K. E. and K. R. Wilson, "Computing with Feeling," *Proc. IEEE Conf. on Computer Graphics, Pattern Recognition and Data Structure,* May 1975, pp. 343–349.

GILO78 Giloi, W., *Interactive Computer Graphics—Data Structures, Algorithms, Languages,* Prentice-Hall, 1978.

GINO76 "Gino-F User Manual," Issue 2, Computer-Aided Design Centre, Cambridge, England, December 1976.

GOLD79 Goldberg, Adele and David Robson, *A Metaphor for User Interface Design,* Xerox Palo Alto Research Center, 1979.

GOOD75 Goodwin, N., "Cursor Positioning on an Electronic Display Using Lightpen, Lightgun or Keyboard for Three Basic Tasks," *Human Factors,* 17(3), June 1975, pp. 289–295.

GORD74a Gordon, W. J. and R. F. Riesenfeld, "Bernstein-Bezier Methods for the Computer-aided Design of Free-Form Curves and Surfaces," *Journal of the ACM,* 21(2), April 1974, pp. 393–410.

GORD74b Gordon, W. J. and R. F. Riesenfeld, "B-Spline Curves and Surfaces," in R. E. Barnhill and R.F. Riesenfeld (eds.), *Computer Aided Geometric Design,* Academic Press, New York, 1974.

GOUR71 Gouraud, H., "Continuous Shading of Curved Surfaces," *IEEE Transactions on Computers,* C-20(6), June 1971, pp. 623–628.

GRAY67 Gray, J. C., "Compound Data Structures for Computer Aided Design: A Survey," *Proc. ACM Nat. Conf.,* Thompson Books, Washington, D.C., 1967, pp. 355.

GREG70 Gregory, R. L., *The Intelligent Eye,* McGraw-Hill, London, 1970.

GRIF78a Griffiths, J. G., "A Surface Display Algorithm," *Computer Aided Design,* 10(1), January 1978, pp. 65–73.

GRIF78b Griffiths, J. G., "A Bibliography of Hidden-Line and Hidden-Surface Algorithms," *Computer Aided Design,* 10(3), May 1978, pp. 203–206.

GRON66 Groner, G. F., *Real-Time Recognition of Hand-Printed Text,* FJCC 1966, Spartan Books, Washington, D.C., pp. 591–602.

GRON71 Groner, G. F., R. L. Clark, R. A. Berman, and E. C. DeLand, *BIOMOD: An Interactive Graphics System for Modeling,* FJCC 1971, AFIPS Press, Montvale, N.J., pp. 369–378.

GROS76 Grossman, D. D., "Procedural Representation of Three-dimensional Objects," *IBM J. Res. Dev.,* 20(6), November 1976, pp. 582.

GSPC77 "Status Report of the Graphics Standards Planning Committee, *Computer Graphics,* 11, 1977.

GSPC79 "Status Report of the Graphics Standards Committee," *Computer Graphics* 13(3), August 1979.

GUED80 Guedj, R., et. al. (ed.), *Methodology of Interaction,* North-Holland, Amsterdam, 1980.

GUPT81a Gupta, S. and R. Sproull, "Filtering Edges for Gray-Scale Displays," SIGGRAPH '81 Proceedings, published as *Computer Graphics,* 15(3), August 1981, pp. 1–5.

GUPT81b Gupta, S., R. Sproull, and I. Sutherland, "A VLSI Architecture for Updating Raster-Scan Displays," SIGGRAPH '81 Proceedings, published as *Computer Graphics,* 15(3), August 1981, pp. 71–78.

GURW80 Gurwitz, R. F., et. al., "BUMPS: A Program for Animating Projections," SIGGRAPH '80 Proceedings, published as *Computer Graphics,* 14(3), July 1980, pp. 231–237.

GURW81 Gurwitz, R., R. Fleming and A. van Dam, "MIDAS: A Microprocessor Instructional Display and Animation System," *IEEE Transactions on Education,* February, 1981.

HAML75 Hamlin, G. and J. Foley, "Configurable Applications for Graphics Employing Satellites (CAGES)," SIGGRAPH '75 Proceedings, published as *Computer Graphics,* 9(2), Summer 1975, pp. 9–19.

HAML77 Hamlin, G. and C. Gear, "Raster-Scan Hidden Surface Algorithm Techniques," SIGGRAPH '77 Proceedings, published as *Computer Graphics,* 11(2), Summer 1977, pp. 206.

HANA80 Hanau, P. R., and D. R. Lenorovitz, "Prototyping and Simulation Tools for User/Computer Dialogue Design," SIGGRAPH '80 Proceedings, published as *Computer Graphics,* 14(2), July 1980, pp. 271–278.

HANS71 Hansen, W., "User Engineering Principles for Interactive Systems," *Proceedings 1971 Fall Joint Computer Conference,* pp. 523–532.

HART78 Hartke, D. H., W. M. Sterling, and J. E. Shemer, "Design of a Raster Display Processor for Office Applications," *IEEE Transactions on Computers,* C-27(4), April 1978, pp. 337–348.

HARV80 Harvard University Laboratory for Computer Graphics, Harvard Library of Computer Graphics Mapping Collection, Cambridge, MA. 1980.

HAYE81 Hayes, P., E. Ball, R. Reddy "Breaking the Man-Machine Communication Barrier," *Computer,* 14(3), March 1981, pp. 19–30.

HEIN75 Heindel, L. and J. Roberto, *LANG-PAK—An Interactive Language Design System,* Elsevier, New York, 1975.

HERO76 Herot, C. F., "Graphical Input Through Machine Recognition of Sketches," *Computer Graphics,* 10(2), Summer 1976, pp. 97–102.

HERO80 Herot, C. F., et. al. "A Prototype Spatial Data Base Management System," SIGGRAPH '80 Proceedings, published as *Computer Graphics,* 14(2), July 1980, pp. 63–70.

HERT74 Hertz, C. H. and A. Mansson, *Color Plotter for Computer Graphics Using Three Electrically Controlled Ink Jets,* IFIP 1974, North-Holland, Amsterdam, pp. 85–88.

HERZ80 Herzog, B., "In Memorium of Steven Anson Coons," *Computer Graphics,* 13 (4), February 1980, pp. 228–231.

HILE Hiler, H., *Color Harmony and Pigments,* Chicago, Favor, Ruhl, & Co.

HOEH71 Hoehn, H. J. and R. A. Martel, "A 60 Line per Inch Plasma Display Panel," *IEEE Transactions on Electronic Devices,* ED-18(9), September 1971, p. 659.

HORN76 Horn, B. K. P., "Circle Generator for Display Devices," *Computer Graphics and Image Processing,* 5, 1976, pp. 280–288.

HORN67 Hornbuckle, G. D., "The Computer Graphics/User Interface," *IEEE Trans.,* HFE-8(1), March 1967, pp. 17–20.

HOSA77 Hosaka, M. and F. Kimura, *An Interactive Geometrical Design System with Handwriting Input,* IFIP 1977, North-Holland, Amsterdam, p. 167.

HUBS81 Hubschman, H. and S. Zucker, "Frame-to-Frame Coherence and the Hidden Surface Computation: Constraints for a Convex World," SIGGRAPH '81 Proceedings, published as *Computer Graphics,* 15(3), August 1981, pp. 45–54.

HUNT75 Hunt, R. W. G., *The Reproduction of Color,* 3rd ed., Wiley, New York, 1975.

HURW67 Hurwitz, A., J. Citron, and J. Yeaton, *GRAF: Graphical Extensions to FORTRAN,* SJCC 1967, Thompson Books, Washington, D.C., pp. 553–557.

IBM International Business Machines Corp., *IBM 2250 Display Model 3,* Form No. A27-2721-0.

IEEE79 *IEEE Transactions on Consumer Electronics,* Special Issue on TELETEXT and VIEWDATA, July, 1979.

IKON81 Ikonas Graphics Systems, Inc., Raleigh, N. C.

INGA81 Ingalls, D., "The Smalltalk Graphics Kernel," special issue on Smalltalk, *BYTE,* 6(8), August 1981.

INTE Integrated Software Systems Corp., *DISSPLA Reference Manual,* Integrated Software Systems Corp., San Diego, Ca.

IRAN71 Irani, K. and V. Wallace, "On Network Linguistics and the Conversational Design of Queueing Networks," *Journal of the ACM,* 18, October 1971, pp. 616–629.

IRBY74 Irby, C. H., *Display Techniques for Interactive Text Manipulation,* NCC 1974, AFIPS Press, pp. 247–255.

ISO81 International Standards Organization, "Graphical Kernel System (GKS), Version 6.6," May 1981.

JACO48 Jacobson, E., *Basic Color—An Interpretation of the Oswald Color System,* Chicago, Paul Theobald, 1948.

JARV75 Jarvis, J. F., "Two Simple Windowing Algorithms," *Software—Practice and Experience,* 5, 1975, pp. 115–122.

JARV76a Jarvis, J. F., C. N. Judice, and W. H. Ninke, "A Survey of Techniques for the Image Display of Continuous Tone Pictures on Bilevel Displays," *Computer Graphics and Image Processing,* 5(1), March 1976, pp. 13–40.

JARV76b Jarvis, J. F. and C. S. Roberts, "A New Technique for Displaying Continuous Tone Images on a Bilevel Display," *IEEE Trans.,* COM-24(8), August 1976, pp. 891–898.

JARV77 Jarvis, J. F., "The Line Drawing Editor: Schematic Diagram Editing Using Pattern Recognition Techniques." *Computer Graphics and Image Processing,* 6(5), October 1977, pp. 452–484.

JENS74 Jensen, Kathleen and Niklaus Wirth, *Pascal User Manual and Report,* 2nd. ed. Springer-Verlag, New York, 1974.

JERN77 Jern, M., "Color Jet Plotter," *Computer Graphics,* 11(1), Spring 1977, pp. 18.

JOBL78 Joblove, G. H. and D. Greenberg, "Color Spaces for Computer Graphics," SIGGRAPH '78 Proceedings, published as *Computer Graphics,* 12(3), August 1978, pp. 20–27.

JOHN63 Johnson, C. I., *SKETCHPAD III: A Computer Program for Drawing in Three Dimensions,* SJCC 1963, Spartan Books, Balitmore, Md., pp. 347.

JOHN78 Johnson, S. and M. Lesk "Language Development Tools," *The Bell System Technical Journal,* 57(6,2) July-August 1978, pp. 2155–2176.

JORD73a Jordan, B. W., Jr. and R. C. Barrett, "A Scan Conversion Algorithm with Reduced Storage Requirements," *Communications of the ACM,* 16(11), November 1973, pp. 676–679.

JORD73b Jordan, B. W., W. J. Lennon, B. C. Holm, "An Improved Algorithm for the Generation of Non-parametric Curves," *IEEE Transactions on Computers,* C-22(12), December 1973, pp. 1052–1060.

JORD74 Jordan, B. W., Jr. and R. C. Barrett, "A Cell Organized Raster Display for Line Drawings," *Communications of the ACM,* 17(2), February 1974, pp. 70–77.

JUDD75 Judd, D. and G. Wyszecki, *Color in Business, Science, and Industry,* John Wiley and Sons, New York, 1975.

JUDI74 Judice, J. N., J. F. Jarvis, and W. Ninke, "Using Ordered Dither to Display Continuous Tone Pictures on an AC Plasma Panel," *Proc. SID,* Fourth Quarter 1974, pp. 161–169.

JULE71 Julesz, B., *Foundations of Cyclopean Perception.* Chicago, University of Chicago Press, 1971.

JULE74 Julesz, B., "Cooperative Phenomena in Binocular Depth Perception," *American Scientist,* 62, January–February 1974, pp. 32.

KAJI75 Kajiya, J. T., I. E. Sutherland, and E. C. Cheadle, "A Random-Access Video Frame Buffer," *Proc. IEEE Conf. on Computer Graphics, Pattern Recognition and Data Structure,* May 1975, pp. 1.

KAPL79 Kaplan, M. and D. Greenberg, "Parallel Processing Techniques for Hidden Surface Algorithms," SIGGRAPH '79 Proceedings, published as *Computer Graphics,* 13(2), August 1979, pp. 300–307.

KAPL80 Kaplan, G., "Words into Action," *IEEE Spectrum,* 17(6), June 1980, pp. 22–25.

KAY77a Kay, A. and A. Goldberg, "Personal Dynamic Media," *Computer,* 10(3), March 1977, pp. 31–42.

KAY77b Kay, Alan C., "Microelectronics and the Personal Computer", *Scientific American,* 237(3), September, 1977, pp. 230–244.

KAY79 Kay, D. and D. Greenberg, "Transparency for Computer Synthesized Images", SIGGRAPH '79 Proceedings, published as *Computer Graphics,* 13(2), August 1979, pp. 158–164.

KELL76 Kelly, K. and D. Judd, *COLOR—Universal Language and Dictionary of Names,* National Bureau of Standards Spec. Publ. 440, Government Printing Office Stock No. 003-003-01705-1, 1976.

KENN66 Kennedy, J. R., *A System for Time-Sharing Graphic Consoles,* FJCC 1966, Spartan Books, Washington, D.C., pp. 211–222.

KILG71 Kilgour, A. C., "The Evolution of a Graphic System for Linked Computers," *Software—Practice and Experience,* 1, 1971, pp. 259–268.

KILG81 Kilgour, A. C., "A Hierarchical Model of a Graphics System," *Computer Graphics,* 15(1), April 1981, pp. 35–47.

KLEM71 Klemmer, E. T., "Keyboard Entry," *Applied Ergonomics,* March 1971, pp. 2–6.

KNOT72 Knott, G. D. and D. K. Reece, "Modelab: A Civilized Curve-fitting System," *Proc. ONLINE 72,* Uxbridge, England, September 1972.

KNOW70 Knowlton, K. C., "EXPLOR: A Generator of Images from Explicit Patterns, Local Operations, and Randomness," *Proc. 1970 UAIDE Annual Meeting,* Stromberg Datagraphix, pp. 544.

KNOW72 Knowlton, K. C. and L. Harmon, "Computer-Produced Gray Scales," *Computer Graphics and Image Processing,* 1(1), April 1972, pp. 1.

KNOW75 Knowlton, K. C., "Virtual Pushbuttons as a Means of Person-Machine Interaction," *Proc. IEEE Conf. on Computer Graphics, Pattern Recognition, and Data Structure,* May 1975, pp. 350–351.

KNOW77 Knowlton, K. and Cherry, L., "ATOMS - A Three-D Opaque Molecule System for Color Pictures of Space-Filling or Ball-and-Stick Models," *Computers and Chemistry,* 1, 1977, pp. 161-166.

KNUT73 Knuth, D. E., *The Art of Computer Programming,* Volume 1: "Fundamental Algorithms", Addison-Wesley, Reading, Mass., 1973.

KRIL76 Kriloff, H., "Human Factor Considerations for Interactive Display Systems", in S. Treu, ed., *Proceedings ACM/SIGGRAPH Workshop on User-Oriented Design of Interactive Graphics Systems,* ACM 1976, pp. 45–52

KROE72 Kroemer, K. H. E., "Human Engineering the Keyboard," *Human Factors,* 14(1) February 1974, pp. 51-63.

KULS68 Kulsrud, H. E., "A General Purpose Graphic Language," *Communications of the ACM,* 11(4), April 1968, pp. 247–254.

LAFU76 Lafue, G., "Recognition of Three-dimensional Objects from Orthographic Views," SIGGRAPH '76 Proceedings, published as *Computer Graphics,* 10(2), Summer 1976, pp. 103–108.

LAIB80 Laib, G., R. Puk, and G. Stowell. "Integrating Solid Image Capability into a General Purpose Calligraphic Graphics Package," SIGGRAPH '80 Proceedings, published as *Computer Graphics,* 14 (3), July 1980, pp. 79–85.

LAMP78 Lampson, Butler W., "Bravo Manual," in *Alto User's Handbook,* Xerox Palo Alto Research Center, Palo Alto, CA, November 1978, pp. 31–62.

LAND69 Land, R. I. and I. E. Sutherland, "Real-Time, Color, Stereo, Computer Displays," *Applied Optics,* 8(3), 1969, pp. 721.

LAND77 Land, E. H., "The Retinex Theory of Color Vision," *Scientific American,* December 1977, pp. 108–128.

LANE79 Lane, J. and L. Carpenter, "A Generalized Scan Line Algorithm for the Computer Display of Parametrically Defined Surfaces," *Computer Graphics and Image Processing,* 11, 1979, pp. 290–297.

LAWS75 Laws, B. A., "A Gray-Scale Graphic Processor Using Run-Length Encoding," *Proc. IEEE Conf. on Computer Graphics, Pattern Recognition and Data Structure,* May 1975, pp. 7.

LECH69 Lechner, B. J., "Liquid Crystal Displays," in M. Faiman and J. Nievergelt (eds.), *Pertinent Concepts in Computer Graphics,* University of Illinois Press, Urbana, 1969.

LEE69 Lee, T. M. P., *A Class of Surfaces for Computer Display,* SJCC 1969, AFIPS Press, Montvale, N.J., pp. 309–319.

LEVI76 Levin, J., "A Parametric Algorithm for Drawing Pictures of Solid Objects Composed of Quadric Surface," *Communications of the ACM,* 19(10), October 1976, pp. 555–563.

LEVI80 Levin, J., "QUADRIL: A Computer Language for the Description of Quadric-Surface Bodies," SIGGRAPH '80 Proceedings, published as *Computer Graphics,* 14(3), July 1980, pp. 86–92.

LEVI78 Levine, K., "Core Standard Graphics Package for the VGI 3400," SIGGRAPH '78 Proceedings, published as *Computer Graphics,* 12(3), August 1978, pp. 298–300.

LEVI72 Levinson, J. Z., "Psychophysics and TV," in T. S. Huang and O. J. Tretiak (eds.), *Picture Bandwidth Compression,* Gordon and Breach Science Publishers, 1972.

LEVO77 Levoy, M., "A Color Animation System Based on the Multiplane Technique," SIGGRAPH '77 Proceedings, published as *Computer Graphics,* 11(2), Summer 1977, pp. 65–71.

LEWI68 Lewis, H. R., "SHAPESHIFTER: An Interactive Program for Experimenting with Complex-Plane Transformations," *Proc. ACM Nat. Conf.,* 1968, pp. 717.

LICK69 Licklider, J. C. R., *A Picture is Worth a Thousand Words—and It Costs . . .,* SJCC 1969, AFIPS Press, Montvale, N.J., pp. 617–621.

LIEB78 Lieberman, H., "How to Color in a Coloring Book", SIGGRAPH '78 Proceedings, published as *Computer Graphics,* 12(3), August 1978, pp. 111–116.

LIPS79 Lipscomb, J., *Three-dimensional Cues for a Molecular Computer Graphics System,* Ph.D. Dissertation, Dept. of Computer Science, Univ. of North Carolina, Chapel Hill, 1979.

LOUT70 Loutrel, P. P., "A Solution to the Hidden-Line Problem for Computer-drawn Polyhedra," *IEEE Transactions on Computers,* EC-19(3), March 1970, pp. 205–213.

LUXE68 Luxenberg, H. R. and R. L. Kuehn (eds.), *Display Systems Engineering,* McGraw-Hill, New York, 1968.

MACA68 Macaulay, M., *A Low Cost Computer Graphic Terminal,* FJCC 1968, Thompson Books, Washington, D.C., pp. 777–785.

MACC70 MacCallum, K. J., "Surfaces for Interactive Graphical Design," *Computer Journal,* 13(4), November 1970, pp. 352.

MAGN81 Magnenat-Thalmann, N. and D. Thalmann, "A Graphical Pascal Extension Based on Graphical Types," *Software-Practice and Experience,* 11, 1981, pp. 55–62.

MAHL72 Mahl, R., Visible Surface Algorithm for Quadric Patches, *IEEE Transactions on Computers,* C-21, Jan. 1972., pp. 1–4.

MALL78 Mallgren, A., and A. C. Shaw, "Graphical Transformations and Hierarchic Picture Structures," *Computer Graphics and Image Processing,* 8, October 1978, pp. 237–258.

MAND77 Mandelbrot, B. B., *Fractals: Form, Chance, and Dimension,* Freeman, San Francisco, 1977.

MAND82 Mandelbrot, B. B., *The Fractal Geometry of Nature,* Freeman, San Francisco, 1982.

MARC80 Marcus, A., "Computer-Assisted Chart Making from the Graphic Designer's Perspective," SIGGRAPH '80 Proceedings, published as *Computer Graphics,* 14(3), July 1980, pp. 247–257.

MART71 Martin, W. A., "Computer Input/Output of Mathematical Expressions," *2nd Symposium Symbolic Algebraic Manipulation,* ACM, March 1971, pp. 78.

MART73 Martin, J., *Design of Man-Computer Dialogues,* Prentice-Hall, Englewood Cliffs, N.J., 1973.

MARU72 Maruyama, K., "A Procedure to Determine Intersections Between Polyhedral Objects," *Int. J. Comp. Inf. Sci.,* 1(3), 1972, pp. 255–266.

MATH68 Mathematical Applications Group, Inc., "3-D Simulated Graphics," *Datamation,* February 1968.

MATS72 Matsushita, Y., "Hidden-Line Elimination for a Rotating Object," *Communications of the ACM,* 15(4), April 1972, pp. 245–252.

MAX75 Max, N. and W. Clifford, Jr., "Computer Animation of the Sphere Eversion," *Computer Graphics,* 9(1), Spring 1975, pp. 32–39.

MAX79 Max, N., "ATOMLLL: - ATOMS with Shading and Highlights," SIGGRAPH '79 Proceedings, published as *Computer Graphics 13*(2), August 1979, pp. 300–307.

MAXW46 Maxwell, E. A., *Methods of Plane Projective Geometry Based on the Use of General Homogenous Coordinates,* Cambridge Univ. Press, Cambridge, 1946.

MAXW51 Maxwell, E. A., *General Homogenous Coordinates in Space of Three Dimensions,* Cambridge Univ. Press, Cambridge, 1951.

MAZZ76 Mazziotta, J. C. and H. K. Huang, *THREAD (Three-dimensional Reconstruction and Display) with Biomedical Applications in Neuron Ultrastructure and Computerized Tomography,* NCC 1976, AFIPS Press, pp. 241–250.

MCCR75 McCracken, T. E., B. W. Sherman, and S. J. Dwyer III, "An Economical Tonal Display for Interactive Graphics and Image Analyst Data," *Computers and Graphics,* 1(1), 1975, pp. 79–94.

MCKE78 McKenzie, John, L. R. B. Elton, and R. Lewis, *Interactive Computer Graphics in Science Teaching,* Horwood, Chichester, 1978.

MCLA74 McLain, D. H., *Computer Construction of Surfaces through Arbitrary Points,* IFIP 1974, North-Holland, Amsterdam, pp. 717–721.

MCMA80 McManigal, D. and D. Stevenson, "Architecture of the IBM 3277 Graphics Attachment," *IBM Systems Journal,* 19(3), 1980, pp. 331–344.

MEGA81 Megatek Corporation, San Diego, CA, 1981.

MEHR72 Mehr, M. H. and E. Mehr, "Manual Digital Positioning in 2 Axes: A Comparison of Joystick and Track Ball Controls," *Proceedings 16th Annual Meeting,* Human Factors Society, 1972.

METC76 Metcalfe, R. M. and D. R. Boggs: "ETHERNET: Distributed Packet Switching for Local Computer Networks", *Communications of the ACM,* 19(7), July 1976, pp. 395–404.

METZ69 Metzger, R. A., *Computer Generated Graphic Segments in a Raster Display,* SJCC 1969, AFIPS Press, Montvale, N.J., pp. 161–172.

MEYE80 Meyer, G. W. and D. P. Greenberg, "Perceptual Color Spaces for Computer Graphics," SIGGRAPH '80 Proceedings, published as *Computer Graphics,* 14(3), July 1980, pp. 254–261.

MEYR81 Meyrowitz, N. and M. Moser, "BRUWIN: An Adaptable Design Strategy for Window Manager/Virtual Terminal Systems," *Proceedings of the 8th Annual Symposium on Operating Systems Principles (SIGOPS),* Pacific Grove, CA, December 1981.

MICH78a Michener, J. C. and J. D. Foley, "Some Major Issues in the Design of the Core Graphics System," *Computing Surveys,* 10(4), 1978, pp. 445–464.

MICH78b Michener, J. C. and A. van Dam, "A Functional Overview of the Core System with Glossary," *Computing Surveys,* 10(4), 1978, pp. 381–388.

MICH79 Michener, J. C., *Some Viewing Considerations for the 1979 GSPC Core System,* Intermetrics, 1979 (unpublished).

MICH80 Michener, J. C., and I. B. Carlbom, "Natural and Efficient Viewing Parameters," SIGGRAPH '80 Proceedings, published as *Computer Graphics,* 14(3), July 1980, pp. 238–245.

MILL68 Miller, R. B., *Response Time in Man-Computer Conversational Transactions,* 1968 FJCC, AFIPS Conf. Proc., Vol. 33, Montvale, N.J., AFIPS Press, 1968, pp. 267–277.

MILL71 Miller, S. W., "Display Requirements for Future Man-Machine Systems," *IEEE Trans.,* ED-18(9), September 1971, pp. 616.

MILL76 Miller, Lawrence H., *An Investigation of the Effects of Output Variability and Output Bandwidth on User Performance in an Interactive Computer System,* Report ISI/RR-76-50, Information Science Institute, University of Southern California, 1976.

MITC77 Mitchell, W. J., *Computer—Aided Architectural Design,* Petrocelli-Charter, New York, 1977.

MIYA75 Miyamoto, E. and T. O. Binford: "Display Generated by a Generalized Cone Representation," *Proc. IEEE Conf. on Computer Graphics, Pattern Recognition, and Data Structure,* May 1975, pp. 385–387.

MORA81 Moran, T., "The Command Language Grammar: A Representation for the User Interface of Interactive Computer Systems", *International Journal of Man-Machine Studies, 15,* 1981, pp. 3–50.

MORL76 Morland, D. V., "Computer Generated Stereograms," *Computer Graphics,* 10(2), Summer 1976, pp. 19–24.

MUNS76 Munsell Color Company, *Book of Color,* 2441 North Calvert Street, Baltimore, MD, 21218.

MUNS68 Munson, J. H., *Experiments in the Recognition of Hand-Printed Text, I: Character Recognition,* FJCC 1968, Thompson Books, Washington, D.C., pp. 1125–1138.

MYER68 Myer, T. H. and I. E. Sutherland: "On the Design of Display Processors," *Communications of the ACM,* 11(6), June 1968, pp. 410–414.

MYER75 Myers, A., *An Efficient Algorithm for Computer Generated Pictures,* Ohio State Univ. Computer Graphics Res. Group, 1975

NAGE79 Nagesh, A. R. and U. G. Gujar, *OSCUBA—A Buffered Core Graphics System,* School of Computer Science, University of New Brunswick, N.B., Canada, TR79-016, June 1979.

NAKE73 Nake, F. and A. Rosenfeld, eds., *Graphic Language,* North-Holland, 1972.

NEGR73 Negroponte, N., *Recent Advances in Sketch Recognition,* NCC 1973, AFIPS Press, pp. 663–675.

NEGR75 Negroponte, N. (ed.), *Computer Aids to Design and Architecture,* Petrocelli/Charter, New York, 1975.

NEGR77 Negroponte, N., "Raster-Scan Approaches to Computer Graphics," *Computers and Graphics,* 2(3), 1977, pp. 179.

NEMC80 Nemcsics, A., "The Coloroid Color System," *Color Research and Application,* 5(2), Summer 1980, pp. 113–120.

NEWE72 Newell, M. E., R. G. Newell, and T. L. Sancha, "A New Approach to the Shaded Picture Problem," *Proc. ACM Nat. Conf.,* 1972, pp. 443.

NEWE75 Newell, M. E., *The Utilization of Procedure Models in Digital Image Synthesis,* Univ. Utah Computer Sci. Dept., UTEC-CSc-76-218, Summer 1975, NTIS AD/A039 008/LL.

NEWE79 Newell, A., S. Fahlman, R. S. Sproull, *Proposal for a Joint Effort in Personal Scientific Computing,* Computer Science Department, Carnegie-Mellon University, August 1979.

NEWM68a Newman, W. M., "A Graphical Technique for Numerical Input," *Computer Journal,* 11(1), May 1968, pp. 63.

NEWM68b Newman, W. M., *A System for Interactive Graphical Programming,* SJCC 1968, Thompson Books, Washington, D.C., p. 47–54.

NEWM71 Newman, W. M., "Display Procedures," *Communications of the ACM,* 14(10), 1971, pp. 651–660.

NEWM73a Newman, W. M., *An Informal Graphics System Based on the Logo Language,* NCC 1973, AFIPS Press, pp. 651–655.

NEWM73b Newman, W. M. and R. F. Sproull, *Principles of Interactive Computer Graphics,* McGraw-Hill, New York, 1973.

NEWM74 Newman, W. M. and R. F. Sproull, "An Approach to Graphics System Design," *Proc. IEEE,* 62(4), April 1974, pp. 471–483.

NEWM76 Newman, W. M., "Trends in Graphic Display Design," *IEEE Transactions on Computers,* C-25(12), December 1976, pp. 1321–1325.

NEWM78 Newman, W. M. and A. van Dam, "A Brief History of Efforts towards Graphics Standardization," *Computing Surveys,* 10(4), 1978, pp. 365–380.

NEWM79 Newman, W. M. and R. F. Sproull, *Principles of Interactive Computer Graphics,* 2nd ed., McGraw-Hill, New York, 1979.

NG78 Ng, N. and T. Marsland, "Introducing Graphics Capabilities to Several High-Level Languages," *Software—Practice and Experience,* 8, 1978, pp. 629–639.

NINK65 Ninke, W. H., *Graphic 1: A Remote Graphical Display Console System,* FJCC 1965, Spartan Books, Washington, D.C., pp. 839.

NINK68 Ninke, W. H., *A Satellite Display Console System for a Multi-access Central Computer,* IFIP 1968, North-Holland, Amsterdam, pp. 962.

NOLL71 Noll, A. M., "Scanned-Display Computer Graphics," *Communications of the ACM,* 14(3), March 1971, pp. 143–150.

NOTL70 Notley, M. G., "A Graphical Picture Drawing Language," *Computer Bulletin,* 14(3), March 1970, pp. 68.

OBRI79 O'Brien, Michael T., *A Network Graphical Conferencing System,* RAND Corporation, Santa Monica, California, 1979 (N-1250-DARPA).

OPHI69 Ophir, D., B. Shepherd and R. J. Spinard, "Three-dimensional Computer Display," *Communications of the ACM,* 12(6), June 1969, pp. 309–318.

ORTO71 Ortony, A., "A System for Stereo Viewing," *Computer Journal,* 14(2), May 1971, pp. 140–144.

OSTW31 Ostwald, W., *Colour Science,* Winsor & Winsor, London, 1931.

PARE77 Parent, R. E., "A System for Sculpting 3-D Data," SIGGRAPH '77 Proceedings, published as *Computer Graphics,* 11(2), Summer 1977, pp. 138–147.

PARK72 Parke, F., "Computer Generated Animation of Faces," *Proceedings ACM National Conference 1972,* pp. 451.

PARK80 Parke, F., "Simulation and Expected Performance Analysis of Multiple Processor Z-Buffer Systems," SIGGRAPH '80 Proceedings, published as *Computer Graphics,* 14(3), July 1980, pp. 48–56.

PAVL79 Pavlidis, T., "Filling Algorithms for Raster Graphics," *Computer Graphics and Image Processing,* 10(2), June 1979, pp. 126–141.

PAVL81 Pavlidis, T., "Contour Filling in Raster Graphics," SIGGRAPH '81 Proceedings, published as *Computer Graphics,* 15(3), August 1981, pp. 29–36.

PEAR75 Pearson, D. E., *Transmission and Display of Pictorial Information,* Halstead Press (Wiley), New York, 1975.

PERQ80 PERQ, Three Rivers Computer Corporation, Pittsburgh, PA, 1980.

PETE74 Peters, G. J., *Interactive Computer Graphics Application of the Bi-Cubic Parametric Surface to Engineering Design Problems,* 1974 NCC, AFIPS Press, pp. 491–511.

PETT71 Petty, W. D. and H. G. Slottow, "Multiple States and Variable Intensity in the Plasma Display Panel," *IEEE Trans.,* ED-18(9), September 1971, pp. 654.

PFIS76 Pfister, G. F., "A High Level Language Extension for Creating and Controlling Dynamic Pictures," *Computer Graphics,* 10(1), Spring 1976, pp. 1–9.

PILL80 Piller, E., "Real-time Raster Scan Unit with Improved Picture Quality," *Computer Graphics,* 14(1 & 2), July 1980, pp. 35–38.

PITT67 Pitteway, M., "Algorithm for Drawing Ellipses or Hyperbolae with Digital Plotter," *Computer Journal,* 10(3), November 1967, pp. 282–289.

PITT80 Pitteway, M. and D. Watkinson "Bresenham's Algorithm with Grey Scale," *Communications of the ACM,* 23(11), November 1980, pp. 625–626.

PIZE75 Pizer, S., *Numerical Computing and Mathematical Analysis,* SRA, 1975.

POBG71 Pobgee, P. J. and J. R. Parks, *Applications of a Low Cost Graphical Input Tablet,* IFIP 1971, North-Holland, Amsterdam, pp. TA-4-169.

PORT78 Porter, T., "Spherical Shading," SIGGRAPH '78 Proceedings, published as *Computer Graphics,* 12(3), August 1978, pp. 282–285.

PORT79 Porter, T. "The Shaded Surface Display of Large Molecules," SIGGRAPH '79 Proceedings, published as *Computer Graphics,* 13(2), August 1979, pp. 234–236.

POTM81 Potmesil, M. and I. Chakravarty, "A Lens and Aperture Camera Model for Synthetic Image Generation," SIGGRAPH '81 Proceedings, published as *Computer Graphics,* 15(3), August 1981, pp. 297–305.

PREI78 Preiss, R. B., "Storage CRT Display Terminals: Evolution and Trends," *Computer,* 11(11), November 1978, pp. 20–28.

PRIN71 Prince, David, *Interactive Graphics for Computer Aided Design,* Addison-Wesley, 1971.

PRIT77 Pritchard, D. H., "U.S. Color Television Fundamentals - A Review," *IEEE Transactions on Consumer Electronics,* CE-23 (4), November 1977, pp. 467–478.

RAMO76 Ramot, J., "Nonparametric Curves," *IEEE Transactions on Computers,* C-25 (1), January 1976, pp. 103–104.

RATL65 Ratliff, F., *Mach Bands: Quantitative Studies on Neural Networks in the Retina,* Holden-Day, San Francisco, 1965.

RAWS69 Rawson, E. G., "Vibrating Varifocal Mirrors for 3-D Imaging," *IEEE Spectrum,* 6(9), September 1969, pp. 37.

REIS81 Reisner, P., "Formal Grammar and Human Factors Design of an Interactive Graphics System," *IEEE Trans. on Software Engineering,* SE-7(2), March 1981, pp. 229–240.

REQU80 Requicha, A., "Representations for Rigid Solids: Theory, Methods, and Systems," *Computing Surveys,* 12(4), December 1980, pp. 437–464.

RESC73 Resch, R. D., *The Topological Design of Sculptural and Architectural Systems,* NCC 1973, AFIPS Press, pp. 643–650.

RESC74 Resch, R. D., "Portfolio of Shaded Computer Images," *Proc. IEEE,* 62(4), April 1974, pp. 496–502.

RICH72 Richardus, P. and R. Adler, *Map Projections,* Elsiver North-Holland, New York, 1972.

RIES73 Riesenfeld, R. F., *Applications of B-spline Approximations to Geometric Problems of Computer-aided Design,* Univ. Utah Computer Sci. Dept., UTEC-CSc-73-126, March 1973.

RIES75a Riesenfeld, R. F., *Aspects of Modeling in Computer-aided Geometric Design,* NCC 1975, pp. 597.

RIES75b Riesenfeld, R. F., "Non-uniform B-spline Curves," *Proc. 2nd USA-Japan Computer Conf.,* 1975, pp. 551.

RIES75c Riesenfeld, R. F., "On Chaikin's Algorithm," *Computer Graphics and Image Processing,* 4(3), 1975, pp. 304–310.

ROBB70 Robbins, M. F. and J. D. Beyer, "An Interactive Computer System Using Graphical Flowchart Input," *Communications of the ACM,* 13(2), February 1970, p. 115–118.

ROBE63 Roberts, L. G., *Machine Perception of Three Dimensional Solids,* MIT Lincoln Lab, TR 315, May 1963. Also in J. T. Tippet, et al. (eds.), *Optical and Electro-Optical Information Processing,* MIT Press, Cambridge, Mass., 1964, pp. 159.

ROBE65 Roberts, L. G., *Homogeneous Matrix Representations and Manipulation of N-Dimensional Constructs,* Document MS 1405, Lincoln Laboratory, Massachusetts, 1965.

ROBE66 Roberts, L. G., *The Lincoln Wand,* FJCC 1966, Spartan Books, Washington D.C., pp. 223–228.

ROES76 Roese, J. A. and A. S. Khalafalla, "Stereoscopic Viewing with PLZT Ceramics," *Ferroelectrics,* 10(1/2/3/4), 1976, pp. 47–51.

ROES79 Roese, J. and L. McCleary "Stereoscopic Computer Graphics for Simulation and Modeling," SIGGRAPH '79 Proceedings, published as *Computer Graphics,* 13(2), August 1979, pp. 41–47.

ROET76 Roetling, P. G., "Halftone Method with Edge Enchancement and Moire Suppression," *J. Opt. Soc. Am.,* 66(10), October 1976, pp. 985–989.

ROGE76 Rogers, D. F. and J. A. Adams, *Mathematical Elements for Computer Graphics,* McGraw-Hill, New York, 1976.

ROMN68 Romney, G. W., G. S. Watkins, and D. C. Evans, *Real Time Display of Computer Generated Half-tone Perspective Pictures,* IFIP 1968, North-Holland, Amsterdam, pp. 973.

ROSE68 Rose, G. A., *Computer Graphics Communication Systems,* IFIP 1968, North-Holland, Amsterdam, pp. 211.

ROSE78 Rosenfeld, A., "Picture Processing: 1977," *Computer Graphics and Image Processing,* 7(2), April 1978, pp. 211–242.

ROSS63 Ross, D. T. and J. E. Rodriguez, *"Theoretical Foundations For The Computer-aided Design System,* SJCC 1963, Spartan Books, Baltimore, Md., pp. 305.

ROSS67 Ross, D. T., *The AED Approach to Generalized Computer-aided Design,* Proc. ACM Nat. Conf., Thompson Books, Washington, D.C., 1967, pp. 367.

ROUG69 Rougelot, R. S., "The General Electric Computer Color TV Display," in M. Faiman and J. Niervergelt, eds., *Pertinent Concepts in Computer Graphics,* University of Illinois Press, Urbana, 1969.

ROUG Rougelot, R. S. and R. A. Schumaker, *General-Electric Real-Time Display,* NASA Rep. NAS 9-3916.

RUBI76 Rubin, F., "Generation of Nonparametric Curves," *IEEE Transactions on Computers,* C-25(1), January 1976, p. 103.

SAND80 *The Graphic 8 System,* Sanders Corporation, Nashua, N.H., 1980.

SCAL76 Scala, J., *Teaching Art Through Computer Graphics,* NCC 1976, AFIPS Press, pp. 185–189.

SCHR76 Schrack, G., "Design, Implementation and Experiences with a Higher-Level Graphics Language for Interactive Computer-Aided Design Purposes," *Proc. ACM Symposium on Graphics Languages, Computer Graphics* 10(1), Spring 1976, pp. 10–17.

SCHW68 Schwartz, J. L. and E. F. Taylor, *Computer Displays in the Teaching of Physics,* FJCC 1968, Thompson Books, Washington, D.C., pp. 1285–1292.

SCIE70 Science Accessories Corporation, *Graf/Pen Sonic Digitizer,* Science Accessories Corp., Southport, Conn., 1970.

SECH81 Sechrest, S. and D. Greenberg, "A Visible Polygon Reconstruction Algorithm," SIGGRAPH '81 Proceedings, published as *Computer Graphics,* 15(3), August 1981, p. 17–27.

SECR68 Secrest, T. and J. Nievergelt (eds.), *Emerging Concepts in Computer Graphics,* 1967 Univ. Illinois Conf. Computer Graphics, Benjamin, New York, 1968.

SEYB81 Seybold, J. "The Xerox 'Professional Workstation' ", *The Seybold Report,* 10 (16), April 1981, pp. 3–18, Seybold Publications, Media, PA.

SHAM79 Shamos, M. I., *Computational Geometry,* Springer-Verlag, 1979.

SHAW70 Shaw, A. C., "Parsing of Graph-Representational Pictures," *Journal of the ACM,* 17(3), July 1970, pp. 453–481.

SHER79 Sherr, S., *Electronic Displays,* Wiley, New York, 1979.

SHNE79 Shneiderman, B., "Human Factors Experiments in Designing Interactive Systems," *Computer,* 12(12), December 1979, pp. 9–19.

SHOU73 Shoup, R. G., "Some Quantization Effects in Digitally Generated Pictures," *SID Int. Symp.,* 1973, pp. 58.

SHOU79 Shoup, R. "Color Table Animation," SIGGRAPH '79 Proceedings, published as *Computer Graphics,* 13(2), August 1979, pp. 8–13.

SIBE80 Sibert, J. L., "Continuous-color Choropleth Maps," *Geo-Processing,* 1, 1980, pp. 207–216.

SLOA79 Sloan, K. and C. Brown, "Color Map Techniques," *Computer Graphics and Image Processing,* 10(4), August 1979, pp. 297–317.

SLOT70 Slottow, H. G., "The Plasma Display Panel: Principles and Prospects," *1970 IEEE Conf. Displ. Devices,* pp. 57.

SLOT76 Slottow, H. G., "Plasma Displays," *IEEE Transactions on Electron Devices,* ED-23(7), July 1976.

SMIT70a Smith, L. B., "A Survey of Interactive Graphical Systems for Mathematics," *Computer Surveys,* 2(4), December 1970, pp. 261–297.

SMIT70b Smith, L. B., "Use of Interactive Graphics to Solve Numerical Problems," *Communications of the ACM,* 13(10), October 1970, pp. 625–634.

SMIT71 Smith, D. N., "GPL/I - A PL/I Extension for Computer Graphics," *Proc. SJCC 1971,* AFIPS Press, pp. 511–528.

SMIT78 Smith, A. R., "Color Gamut Transform Pairs," SIGGRAPH '78 Proceedings, published as *Computer Graphics,* 12(3), August 1978, pp. 12–19.

SMIT79 Smith, A. R., "Tint Fill", SIGGRAPH '79 Proceedings, published as *Computer Graphics,* 13(2), August 1979, pp. 276–283.

SNEE78 Sneeringer, J., "User-interface Design for Text Editing: A Case Study," *Software—Practice and Experience,* 8, 1978, pp. 543–557.

SPEE74 Speer, R., "Sources of Films in the U.S., Canada and Europe," *Computer Graphics,* 8(3), Fall 1974, pp. 64.

SPRO68 Sproull, R. F. and I. E. Sutherland, *A Clipping Divider,* FJCC 1968, Thompson Books, Washington, D.C., pp. 765–775.

SPRO73 Sproull, R. F., *Omnigraph: Simple Terminal-independent Graphics Software,* Xerox Palo Alto Research Center, CL-73-4, 1973.

SPRO74 Sproull, R. F. and E. L. Thomas, "A Network Graphics Protocol ," *Computer Graphics,* 8(3), Fall 1974, pp. 27.

SPRO75 Sproull, R. F. and W. M. Newman, "The Design of Gray-Scale Graphics Software," *Proc. IEEE Conf. on Computer Graphics, Pattern Recognition and Data Structure,* May 1975, pp. 18.

SPRO79 Sproull, R. F., "Raster Graphics for Interactive Programming Environments," SIGGRAPH '79 Proceedings, published as *Computer Graphics,* 13(2), August 1979, pp. 83–93.

STAC71 Stack, T. R. and S. T. Walker, *AIDS—Advanced Interactive Display System,* 1971 SJCC, AFIPS Press, pp. 113–121.

STAU78 Staudhammer, J., "On Display of Space Filling Atomic Models in Real-Time," SIGGRAPH '78 Proceedings, published as *Computer Graphics,* 12(3), August 1978, pp. 167–172.

STEP75 Stephenson, M. B. and H. N. Christiansen, "A Polyhedron Clipping and Capping Algorithm and a Display System for Three-dimensional Finite Element Models," *Computer Graphics,* 9(3), Fall 1975, pp. 1.

STON78 Stone, Harold, "Critical Load Factors in Two-Processor Distributed Systems," *IEEE Transactions on Software Engineering,* SE-4(3), May 1978, pp. 254–258.

SUEN79 Suenaga, Y., T. Kamae and T. Kobayashi, "A High-Speed Algorithm for the Generation of Straight Lines and Circular Arcs," *IEEE Transactions on Computers,* TC-28(10), October 1979, pp. 728–736.

SUTH63 Sutherland, I. E., *SKETCHPAD: A Man-Machine Graphical Communication System,* SJCC 1963, Spartan Books, Baltimore, Md. pp. 329.

SUTH66a Sutherland, I. E., "Computer Inputs and Outputs," *Scientific American,* September 1966.

SUTH66b Sutherland, I. E., "Ten Unsolved Problems in Computer Graphics," *Datamation,* 12(5), May 1966, pp. 22.

SUTH66c Sutherland, W. R., *On-line Graphical Specification of Computer Procedures,* MIT Lincoln Lab. Tech. Rep. 405, May 1966.

SUTH68 Sutherland, I. E., *A Head-mounted Three Dimensional Display,* FJCC 1968, Thompson Books, Washington, D.C., pp. 757–764.

SUTH69 Sutherland, W. R., J. W. Forgie, and M. V. Morello, *Graphics in Time-Sharing: A Summary of the TX-2 Experience,* SJCC 1969, AFIPS Press, N.J., pp. 629–636.

SUTH74a Sutherland, I. E., "Three-dimensional Data Input by Tablet," *Proc. IEEE,* 62(4), April 1974, pp. 453–461.

SUTH74b Sutherland, I. E. and G. W. Hodgman, "Reentrant Polygon Clipping," *Communications of the ACM,* 17(1), January 1974, pp. 32–42.

SUTH74c Sutherland, I. E., R. F. Sproull and R. A. Schumacker, "A Characterization of Ten Hidden-Surface Algorithms," *Computing Surveys,* 6(1), March 1974, pp. 1–55.

TALB71 Talbot, P. A., J. W. Carr, R. Coulter and R. C. Hwang, "Animator: An On-Line Two-dimensional Film Animation System," *Communications of the ACM,* 14(4), April 1971, pp. 251–259.

TANN78 Tannas, L., "Flat Panel Displays: A Critique," *IEEE Spectrum,* 15(7), July 1978.

TEIT64 Teitelman, W., *Real Time Recognition of Hand-drawn Characters,* FJCC 1964, Spartan Books, Baltimore, Md., pp. 559.

TEIT77 Teitelman, W., "A Display-Oriented Programmer's Assistant," *Proceedings 5th International Joint Conference on Artificial Intelligence,* 1977, pp. 905–915.

TEKT Tektronix, Inc., *4012 Graphic Computer Terminal,* Tektronix, Inc., Beaverton, Oregon.

TEMP81 Puk, R., *Template User's Manual,* Megatek Corporation, 1981.

THAC81 Thacker, C. P., E. M. McCreight, B. W. Mapson, R. F. Sproull, and D. R. Boggs, "Alto: A Personal Computer", in D. Siewiorek, G. Bell, and A. M. Newell, *Computer Structures: Readings and Examples,* 2nd ed., McGraw Hill 1981.

THAN76 Thanhouser, N., "Intermixing Refresh and Direct View Storage Graphics," SIGGRAPH '78 Proceedings, published as *Computer Graphics,* 10(2), Summer 1978, pp. 13–18.

THOR79 Thornton, R. W., "The Number Wheel: A Tablet Based Valuator for Three-dimensional Positioning," SIGGRAPH '79 Proceedings, published as *Computer Graphics,* 13(2), August 1979, pp. 102–107.

THRE78 Three Rivers Computing Corp., *Graphic Display Programmer's Guide,* Three Rivers Computing Corp., Pittsburgh, Pa., June 1978.

TILB76 Tilbrook, D., *A Newspaper Page Layout System,* M.Sc. Thesis, Department of Computer Science, University of Toronto, Canada, 1976. Demonstrated in SIGGRAPH Video Tape Review, 1, May 1980.

TIME73 Time, "News by Computer," *Time Magazine,* December 13, 1973, p. 64.

TORR66 Torrance, K. E. and E. M. Sparrow, "Polarization, Direction Distribution, and Off-Specular Peak Phenomena in Light Reflected from Roughened Surfaces," *J. Opt. Soc. Am.,* 56(7), July 1966, pp. 916–925.

TORR67 Torrance, K. E. and E. M. Sparrow, "Theory for Off-Specular Reflection from Roughened Surfaces," *J. Opt. Soc. Am.,* 57 (9), Sept. 1967, pp. 1105–1114.

TRAU67 Traub, A. T., "Stereoscopic Display Using Rapid Varifocal Mirror Oscillations," *Applied Optics,* 6, 1967, pp. 1085–1087.

TROW75 Trowbridge, T. S. and K. P. Reitz, "Average Irregularity Representation of Roughened Surfaces for Ray Reflection," *J. Opt. Soc. Am.,* 65 (5), May 1975, pp. 531–536.

VAND72a van Dam, A., "Microprogramming for Computer Graphics," *ACM SIC-MICRO Bulletin,* 1972.

VAND72b van Dam, A., "Some Implementation Issues Relating to Data Structures for Interactive Graphics," *International Journal of Computer and Information Sciences,* 1(4), 1972.

VAND74 van Dam, A., G. M. Stabler and R. J. Harrington, "Intelligent Satellites for Interactive Graphics," *Proceedings of the IEEE,* 62 (4), April 1974, pp. 483–492.

VAND77 van den Bos, J., L. C. Caruthers and A. van Dam, "GPGS: A Device-independent General Purpose Graphic System," SIGGRAPH '77 Proceedings, published as *Computer Graphics,* 11(2), Summer 1977, pp. 112–119.

VAND78 van den Bos, J. "Definition and Use of Higher-Level Graphics Input Tools," SIGGRAPH '78 Proceedings, published as *Computer Graphics,* 12(3), August 1978, pp. 38–42.

VECT78a Vector General, Inc., *Graphics Display System, Model 3404, System Reference Manual,* Pub. No. M110700REF, Woodland Hills, CA, 1978.

VECT78b Vector General Inc., *Series 3400 Technical Manual, Vol. I: Graphics Display System,* Pub. No. M110700, Woodland Hills, CA, 1978.

VERD71 Verdina, J., *Projective Geometry and Point Transformations,* Allyn and Bacon, Boston,1971.

VOEL77 Voelcker, H. B. and A. G. Requicha, "Geometric Modelling of Mechanical Parts and Processes," *Computer,* December 1977, pp. 48–57.

VOEL78 Voelcker, H. B. et al., "The PADL-1.0/2 System for Defining and Displaying Solid Objects," SIGGRAPH '78 Proceedings, published as *Computer Graphics,* 12(3), August 1978, pp. 257–263.

WALL76 Wallace, V. L., "The Semantics of Graphic Input Devices," Proc. SIGGRAPH/SIGPLAN Conf. on Graphics Languages, published as *Computer Graphics,* 10(1), April 1976, pp. 61–65.

WALT69 Walton, J. S. and W. M. Risen, Jr., "Computer Animation: On-line Dynamics Display in Real Time," *J. Chem. Educ.,* 1969, pp. 334.

WARD79 Ward, A. and C. Terman, *An Approach to Personal Computing,* Laboratory for Computer Science, M.I.T., Cambridge, MA, 1979.

WARN69 Warnock, J., *A Hidden-Surface Algorithm for Computer Generated Half-Tone Pictures,* Univ. Utah Computer Sci. Dept., TR 4-15, 1969, NTIS AD-753 671.

WARN80 Warnock, J., "The Display of Characters Using Grey Level Sample Arrays," SIGGRAPH '80 Proceedings, published as *Computer Graphics,* 14(3), July 1980, pp. 302–307.

WASS78 Wasserman, G., *Color Vision: An Historical Introduction,* John Wiley and Sons, New York, 1978.

WATK70 Watkins, G. S., *A Real-Time Visible Surface Algorithm,* Univ. Utah Computer Sci. Dept., UTEC-CSc-70-101, June 1970, NTIS AD-762 004.

WATS69 Watson, R. W., T. H. Myer, I. E. Sutherland, and M. K. Vosbury, *A Display Processor Design,* FJCC 1969, AFIPS Press, Montvale, N.J., pp. 209.

WEGN80 Wegner, P., *Programming with Ada: An Introduction by Means of Graduated Examples,* Prentice-Hall, Englewood Cliffs, 1980.

WEIL77 Weiler, K. and P. Atherton, "Hidden Surface Removal Using Polygon Area Sorting," SIGGRAPH '77 Proceedings, published as *Computer Graphics,* 11(2), Summer 1977, pp. 214.

WEIL80 Weiler, K., "Polygon Comparison Using a Graph Representation," SIGGRAPH '80 Proceedings, published as *Computer Graphics,* 14(3), July 1980, pp. 10–18.

WEIM80 Weiman, C., "Continuous Anti-Aliased Rotation and Zoom of Raster Images," SIGGRAPH '80 Proceedings, published as *Computer Graphics,* 14 (3), July 1980, pp. 286–293.

WEIN76 Wein, M. and N. Burtnyk, "Computer Animation," in J. Belzar, A.G. Holzman, and A. Kent (eds.) *Encyclopedia of Computer Science and Technology,* Vol. 5, Marcel Dekker, New York, 1976, pp. 397.

WEIN78 Wein, M., P. Tanner, G. Bechtold and N. Burtnyk, "Hidden Line Removal for Vector Graphics," SIGGRAPH '78 Proceedings, published as *Computer Graphics,* 12 (3), August 1978, pp. 173–180.

WEIN78 Weinberg, R., "Computer Graphics in Support of Space Shuttle Simulation," SIGGRAPH '78 Proceedings, published as *Computer Graphics,* 12 (3), August 1978, pp. 82–86.

WEIS66 Weiss, R. A., "Be Vision, a Package of IBM 7090 Fortran Programs to Draw Orthographic Views of Combinations of Planes and Quadric Surfaces," *Journal of the ACM,* 13(2), April 1966, pp. 194.

WELL76 Weller, D. and R. Williams, "Graphic and Relational Data Base Support for Problem Solving," SIGGRAPH '76 Proceedings, published as *Computer Graphics,* 10(2), Summer 1976, pp. 183–189.

WENN80 Wenner P. et al., *Design Document for The George Washington University Implementation of the 1979 GSPC Core System,* Institute for Information Science and Technology Technical report GWU-IIST-80-06, Washington, DC, 1980.

WENT65 Wentworth, J. W., *Color Television Engineering,* McGraw-Hill, New York, 1965.

WHIT80 Whitted, T., "An Improved Illumination Model for Shaded Display," *Communications of the ACM,* 23(6), June 1980, pp. 343–349.

WILL71 Williams, R., "A Survey of Data Structures for Computer Graphics Systems," *Computer Surveys,* 3(1), March 1971, pp. 1–17.

WILL72a Williams, R. and G. Krammer, "EX. GRAF: An Extensible Language Including Graphical Operations," *Computer Graphics and Image Processing,* 1, 1972, pp. 317–340.

WILL72b Williamson, H., "Hidden-Line Plotting Program," *Communications of the ACM,* 15(2), February 1972, pp. 100–103.

WILL74 Williams, R., "On the Application of Relational Data Structures in Computer Graphics," *Proc. 1974 IFIP Congress,* North-Holland Pub. Co., pp. 722-726.

WILL75 Williams, R. and G. M. Giddings, "A Picture-building System," *Proc. IEEE Conf. on Computer Graphics, Pattern Recognition, and Data Structure,* May 1975, pp. 304.

WILL78 Williams, L., "Casting Curved Shadows on Curved Surfaces," SIGGRAPH '78 Proceedings, published as *Computer Graphics,* 12(3), August 1978, pp. 270–274.

WIPK74 Wipke, W. T., S. R. Heller, R. J. Feldmann, and E. Hyde (eds.), *Computer Representation and Manipulation of Chemical Information,* Wiley, New York, 1974.

WISE69 Wiseman, N. E., H. U. Lemke, and J. O. Hiles, "PIXIE: A New Approach to Graphical Man-Machine Communication," Proc. 1969 CAD Conf., Southhampton, *IEE Conf. Pub.,* 51, pp. 463.

WOOD54 Woodson, W. E., *Human Engineering Guide,* Univ. of California Press, 1954.

WOOD71 Woodsford, P. A., "The Design and Implementation of the GINO 3D Graphics Software Package," *Software—Practice and Experience,* 1, 1971, pp. 335–335.

WOOD76 Woodsford, P. A., "The HRD-1 Laser Display System," SIGGRAPH '76 Proceedings, published as *Computer Graphics,* 10(2), July 1976, pp. 68–73.

WOON71 Woon, P. Y. and H. Freeman, "A Procedure for Generating Visible-Line Projections of Solids Bounded by Quadric Surfaces," *Proceedings 1971 IFIP Congress,* North-Holland Pub. Co., Amsterdam, 1971, pp. 1120-1125.

WRIG72 Wright, W. V., An Interactive Computer Graphic System for Molecular Studies, Ph.D. Dissertation, Dept. of Computer Sci., Univ. of N.C., Chapel Hill, N.C., 1972.

WRIG73 Wright, T. J., "A Two Space Solution to the Hidden Line Problem for Plotting Functions of Two Variables," *IEEE Transactions on Computers,* TC22 (1), January 1973, pp. 28–33.

WU77 Wu, S. C., J. F. Abel and D. P. Greenberg, "An Interactive Computer Graphics Approach to Surface Representation," *Communications of the ACM,* 20(19), October 1977, pp. 703-712.

WYLI67 Wylie, C., G. W. Romney, D. C. Evans, and A. C. Erdahl, *Halftone Perspective Drawings by Computer,* FJCC 1967, Thompson Books, Washington, D.C., pp. 49–58.

WYSZ67 Wyszecki, G. and W. S. Stiles, *Color Science,* Wiley, New York, 1967.

YAMA78 Yamaguchi, F., "A New Curve Fitting Method Using a CRT Computer Display," *Computer Graphics and Image Processing,* 7(3), June 1978, pp. 425–437.

YULE67 Yule, J. A., *Principles of Color Reproduction,* Wiley, New York, 1967.

Index

Plates E–J
Images of mandrill and its mapping onto various geometrical shapes (generated by Michael Potmesil, Image Processing Laboratory, Rensselaer Polytechnic Institute).

Plate E

Plate F

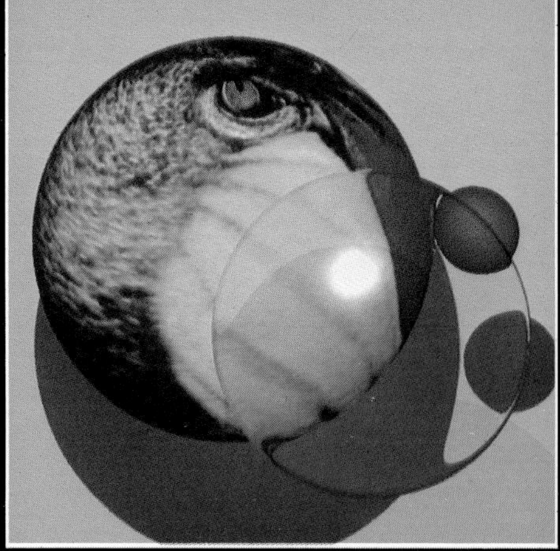

Plate G